THE
LAST
CRUSADERS

THE
LAST
CRUSADERS

East, West, and the Battle for the Center of the World

BARNABY ROGERSON

THE OVERLOOK PRESS
New York

First published in paperback in the United States in 2011 by
The Overlook Press, Peter Mayer Publishers, Inc.
141 Wooster Street
New York, NY 10012
www.overlookpress.com

For bulk and special sales, please contact sales@overlookny.com

Library of Congress Cataloging-in-Publication Data
Rogerson, Barnaby.
The last crusaders : the hundred-year battle for the center of the world /
Barnaby Rogerson. -- 1st ed.
p. cm.
Includes bibliographical references and index.
ISBN 978-1-59020-286-9 (hardcover)
1. Europe--History, Military--1492-1648. 2. Middle East--History,
Military. 3. Europe--Military relations--Middle East. 4. Middle
East--Military relations--Europe. 5. Christianity and other
religions--Islam--History. 6. Crusades. 7. Spain--History--House of
Austria, 1516-1700. 8. Turkey--History--Ottoman Empire, 1288-1918. 9. East
and West. 10. Balance of power--History. I. Title.
D214.R63 2010   956'.015--dc22
2009048627

Printed in the United States of America
1 3 5 7 9 8 6 4 2
ISBN 978-1-59020-440-5

For Dido, David and Shamos

Who shared the many landscapes of my childhood
but now have found their own

CONTENTS

Preface   xi
Acknowledgements   xv
Maps   xviii

Introduction   1

PART I: BIRTH OF NEW POWERS

1 THE CRUSADER PRINCE OF PORTUGAL
   Henry the Navigator, 1415–60   13

2 THE NAVIGATOR'S NEPHEW
   King Afonso the African, 1455–81, and King John II,
   1481–95   42

3 THE GREAT EAGLE
   Mehmet the Conqueror of Constantinople, 1450–80   63

4 RECONQUISTA
   The Crusade of Ferdinand of Aragon and Isabella
   of Castile against Muslim Granada, 1480–1510   114

5 BARBAROSSA
   The Emergence of the Muslim Corsairs, 1480–1510   148

6 THE JUST AND THE GRIM
   The Transformation of the Ottoman Empire under
   Sultans Bayezid II and Selim I, 1480–1520   165

PART II: STRUGGLE

7 CONQUEST OF COMMERCE
King Manuel, Hammer of Morocco, Lord of Guinea
and of the Conquest of the Navigation and Commerce of
Ethiopia, Arabia, Persia and India, 1499–1515   187

8 SHARIFS, SHEIKHS, SUFIS, SULTANS
AND SMUGGLERS
The Moroccan Struggle against the Portuguese
Crusade, 1515–50   205

9 THE RIVALS
The Division of Christendom between Charles V
and Francis I   230

10 THE OTTOMAN GOLDEN AGE
Suleyman the Magnificent and the Five Victories:
Belgrade, Rhodes, Mohacs, Tabriz and Baghdad, 1520–36   260

11 CORSAIR KINGDOMS
The Barbarossa Brothers, Uruj and Khizr, and
Condottiere Andrea Doria, 1512–34   273

12 EMPERORS AND SULTANS
Conquests, Crusades and Family Killings   289

PART III: DESTRUCTION

13 SKULL ISLANDS
The Battle of Djerba and the Siege of Malta,
1560–70   341

14 A BEARD FOR AN ARM
The Conquest of Cyprus and the Holy League's
Victory of Lepanto, 1570–4   367

15 THE LAST CRUSADE
The Battle of the Three Kings   399

Key characters   423

Comparative timelines   432

Family trees for the rulers of Morocco, Spain, Portugal
and the Ottoman Empire   446

Notes   450

Further reading   454

Index   460

PREFACE

I am British. A native islander who remains enraptured by the rocky shores and sandy beaches of my homeland, perched on the far edge of Europe, washed by storms, tides and surf incubated in the vast Atlantic Ocean. I am so much the native that I am genuinely thrilled by the idea of an outdoor picnic in virtually any season, especially if it involves a sturdy walk past some ancient stone circle or brooding hill-fort, ideally finished off by a bracing dip in any of our freezing seas.

But I am also a child of the Mediterranean, for my family was part of that diaspora of Britannia whose memories of home are as often centred around a military base in some far-distant land as around any village in Britain. Gibraltar, Malta, Cyprus, Suez, Aden, Trincomalee, Singapore and Hong Kong appear as often in the backdrop of a family photograph, or as place of birth in a passport, as anywhere within the British Isles. Generation after generation of the families that I am descended from, be they Scottish Covenanters from the Highlands, Catholic Irish, East Anglian Anglicans or Anglo-Irish, have sent their young men abroad. Not a few of them returned home broken by the experience, one or two came back enriched, but most of them only succeeding in filling some foreign field with their bones.

My first memories are as a water-baby, clutching on to my mother's back as we swam our way through what seemed like an endless summer of early childhood in the warm waters of the Mediterranean. The smell of jasmine and orange blossom, the sound of monastery bells, the scent of wild thyme and rosemary, the odour of hot sun on bare rocks and the whiff of carved limestone long sodden with the salt sea, still bring back those first memories. As a boy I grew up watching ancient harbours and exploring ruined fortresses, as well as looking out for the ship that

contained my father as the fleet swept in to fill the harbour of Malta or
Gibraltar with their disciplined menace. The neat lines of sailors in their
white summer uniforms cut an intriguing contrast with the grey guns
and the lines of jets marshalled on the flight decks of aircraft carriers.

My father told me stories about such fearsome corsair captains as
Dragut and Barbarossa before I could read, for we swam in the waters
and picnicked in the coves that they had once used. He was also, like his
naval father before him, a convinced partisan of Portugal and her
neglected history. The two of them would chatter away about their
affection for England's oldest ally, approvingly quoting the deeds of the
more bloodthirsty of the Portuguese admirals as role models for any
naval power. My father was also a Roman Catholic (something of a
rarity in the Royal Navy in his day) and liked to remind his Protestant
shipmates of the naval deeds of Catholic Christendom: how Don John
led the combined fleets of Catholic Christendom into the great naval
victory of Lepanto while the Protestants of England, France and
Holland skulked around the mudbanks of the North Sea. He was fond
of quoting from the verse of fellow British Roman Catholics such as
Chesterton, whose poem *Lepanto* never fails to evoke in me a thrill
tinctured with tragedy, despite its many glaring inaccuracies and prejudices. For this was the last time that medieval Christendom was united
under one flag, one military commander, one spiritual leader and one
language. The silken war banner of the commander of the Holy League
of Christendom was handed over to the son of a Holy Roman Emperor
by a saintly pope who blessed him in Latin. As Chesterton imagines it,
and as he dragged me as a child in his imaginative wake, here is
Lepanto:

> *White founts falling in the courts of the sun,*
> *And the Soldan of Byzantium is smiling as they run;*
> *There is laughter like the fountains in that face of all men feared,*
> *It stirs the forest darkness, the darkness of his beard,*
> *It curls the blood-red crescent, the crescent of his lips,*
> *For the inmost sea of all the earth is shaken with his ships.*
> *They have dared the white republics up the capes of Italy,*
> *They have dashed the Adriatic round the Lion of the Sea,*
> *And the Pope has cast his arms abroad for agony and loss,*
> *And called the kings of Christendom for swords about the Cross,*

The cold queen of England is looking in the glass:
The shadow of the Valois is yawning at the Mass:
From evening isles fantastical rings faint the Spanish gun,
And the Lord upon the Golden Horn is laughing in the sun.
Dim drums throbbing, in the hills half heard,
Where only on a nameless throne, a crownless prince has stirred,
Where, risen from a doubtful seat and half-attainted stall,
The last knight of Europe takes weapons from the wall,
The last and lingering troubadour to whom the bird has sung,
That once went singing southward when all the world was young,
In that enormous silence, tiny and unafraid,
Comes up along a winding road the noise of the Crusade.
Strong gongs groaning as the guns boom far,
Don John of Austria is going to the war,
Stiff flags straining in the night-blasts cold
In the gloom black-purple, in the glint old-gold,
Torchlight crimson on the copper kettledrums,
Then the tuckets, then the trumpets, then the cannon, and he comes
Sudden and still – hurrah!
Bolt from Iberia! Don John of Austria, is gone by Alcalar.

It is not just the smells and scents of the Mediterranean shore that
have worked themselves into my childhood memory, but the historical
fabric as well. After university I began writing guidebooks to the Islamic
countries of the Mediterranean (Morocco, Tunisia, Libya, Cyprus and
Turkey), which led to employment as a guide on lecture tours and then
as a travel journalist. There is hardly a city wall, a fortress, a harbour, a
castle, an empty battlefield, a ruined palace, a devastated city described
in this book which I have not explored over the last thirty years. So
although Britain is almost entirely absent from the story of *The Last
Crusaders*, I can yet write about this historical landscape with some of
the passion of a native.

ACKNOWLEDGEMENTS

The seed for this book was first planted by my childhood spent around the warm seas of the Mediterranean, filled with the scent of old stone, surf, rancid streets and scented courtyard gardens, but this intimacy with the past was nurtured by a succession of inspiring teachers. As a boy I was already travelling on the High Seas in the company of all those fine scholars with whom I shared an initial 'B'. Ernle Bradford and Fernand Braudel crisscross the Mediterranean with their works, the former with the scent of salt and sea air on his pages, the latter with the archival dust of true scholarship. E. V. Bovill first took me into Morocco and across the Sahara with the caravans, and told me about Dom Sebastian, while it was with Charles Boxer that I followed in the wake of the first Portuguese, Spanish and Dutch captains as they sailed across the Atlantic to create overseas empires. Boys seldom say thank you, but I think my history teachers must have been well aware of my high regard for them, which showed itself in the way I aped their mannerisms, such as the scruffy High Church Anglicanism of the Reverend Roger Horne at Cottesmore, the elegant tweed suits of Felipe Fernandez-Armesto and the Byronic limp of 'Stump' Davis at Charterhouse. Nor should I forget such inspiring tutors at St Andrews as Geoffrey 'Dutch Revolt' Parker and Alan Sykes.

Travel journalism has also been a kindly godmother to this book, allowing me to track down Portuguese, Ottoman and Spanish foot-marks on the far edges of this historical canvas – in the jungles of Venezuela, sub-Saharan Africa, the mountains of Ethiopia, the coast of Southern Arabia and India – as well as on such home territory as Malta, Tangier and Gibraltar. John Scott of Cornucopia, Tim Jepson at the *Telegraph*, Rahul Jacobs at the *Financial Times*, Sarah Spankie at *Condé*

Nast Traveller, Lucinda Bredin, Victoria Mather at *Vanity Fair*, Simon Calder at the *Independent*, Nick Smith at the *Geographical*, Catherine Fairweather at *Harper's Bazaar*, and Jonathan Lorie and Amy Sohanpaul at the *Traveller* have all unwittingly assisted this labour with their commissions while ignoring many of my more wilful suggestions. Travel maestros Tim Best, Nick Laing, Warwick Ball and Martin Randal have sent me off with luggage labels, introductions, tickets and ideas. Dozens of friends have also assisted me by allowing themselves to be led astray towards interesting ruins. Among the principal victims I must, as ever, thank my intrepid life-long travelling companions Mary Miers, Rose Baring, Mary North-Clow, James Graham-Stewart, Molly, Hannah and Kathy Rogerson, and Kate and Charlie Boxer.

There is also a tribe of nephews, nieces and god-children (both official and partially adopted) to whom I owe some explanation. For they have assisted in the construction of enormous sand castles on the beaches of the Uists in the Outer Hebrides, as well as in Norfolk and on the Burren shore, and helped create flint dams on Hampshire streams – so that I can revisit the drama of the great sixteenth-century sieges with the aid of stream and tide. If Jackson or Frank Boxer, Paddy or Rosie Fleming, Jack or Arri Fletcher, Lilith, Louis, Luke or Django Stapleton, Carlotta or Nicolas Rogerson, Aurea, Fred, Patrick or Flora Baring, Emma, Sophie or Edward Vaughan, Ossian or Finn O'Sullivan, Johnny or Felix Sattin, Issy, Bibbie, Harry or Anna Goodwin-Harris, Georgie Wilson, Tom or Hugh Fortescue, Olive, William, Anna or Alfie Baring ever get as far as reading about the siege of Malaga in this book (let alone the death of Dom Sebastian), they may at last understand what some of the over-excitable shouting has been about.

Rose Baring, my wife, business partner and moral compass, has read, reread, edited and discussed the developing manuscript, as has my agent and friend Michael Alcock. I have also been fortunate to have worked with an inspiring line-up of editors at Little, Brown, that started with Alan Samson and has gone on to include Catherine Hill, Steve Guise, Tim Whiting and Iain Hunt. Cumulatively their criticisms, questions, insightful suggestions and tactful editorial advice have now become an integral part of the book. The errors of emphasis and fact I claim as my own just as the consistently accurate spelling and much-improved grammar is all theirs.

The maps have once again been created by that cartographic crafts-man, Reginald Piggott, in the depths of Norfolk. I hope he is pleased to see his work under the same covers as the charts of Piri Reis, made specifically for the attention and tactical education of Sultan Suleyman the Magnificent.

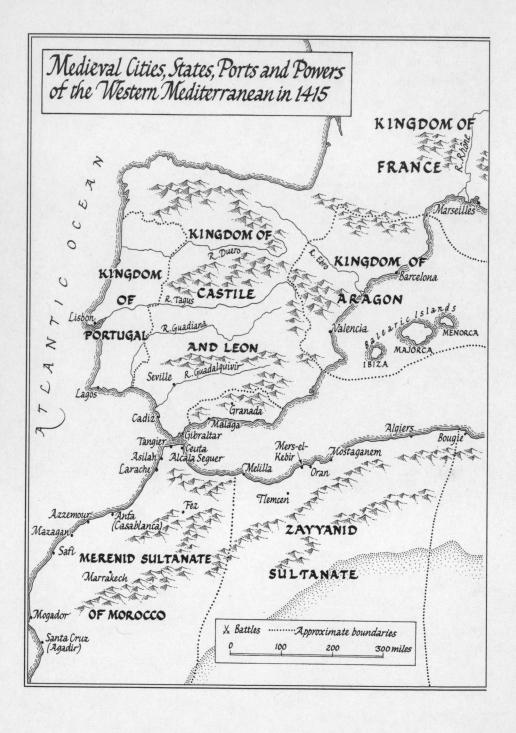

Medieval Cities, States, Ports and Powers of the Western Mediterranean in 1415

KINGDOM OF FRANCE

R. Rhône

ATLANTIC OCEAN

Marseilles

KINGDOM OF

R. Duero

KINGDOM OF CASTILE

R. Ebro

KINGDOM OF ARAGON

Barcelona

KINGDOM

OF

PORTUGAL

R. Tagus

R. Guadiana

AND LEON

Valencia

Balearic Islands

MENORCA

MAJORCA

IBIZA

Lisbon

Seville

R. Guadalquivir

Lagos

Cadiz

Granada

Malaga

Gibraltar

Algiers

Bougie

Tangier

Ceuta

Mers-el-Kebir

Mostaganem

Asilah

Alcala Seguer

Larache

Melilla

Oran

Tlemcen

Azzemour

Anfa (Casablanca)

Fez

ZAYYANID

Mazagan

Safi

MERENID SULTANATE

SULTANATE

Marrakech

Mogador

OF MOROCCO

Santa Cruz (Agadir)

X Battles ·········· Approximate boundaries

0   100   200   300 miles

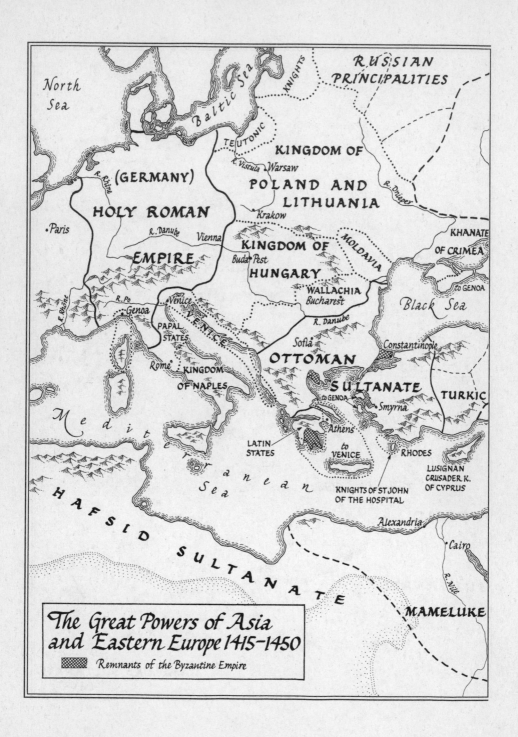

North Sea

Baltic Sea

RUSSIAN PRINCIPALITIES

KNIGHTS

TEUTONIC

R. Vistula   Warsaw

KINGDOM OF POLAND AND LITHUANIA

R. Dnieper

(GERMANY)

R. Rhine

HOLY ROMAN

Paris

R. Danube   Vienna

Krakow

KINGDOM OF HUNGARY

MOLDAVIA

KHANATE OF CRIMEA

EMPIRE

Buda Pest

WALLACHIA
Bucharest

to GENOA

R. Rhone

R. Po   Venice

Genoa

PAPAL STATES

VENICE

R. Danube

Black Sea

Sofia

OTTOMAN

Constantinople

Rome

KINGDOM OF NAPLES

SULTANATE

TURKIC

to GENOA

Smyrna

Mediterranean Sea

Athens

LATIN STATES

to VENICE

RHODES

LUSIGNAN CRUSADER K. OF CYPRUS

KNIGHTS OF ST JOHN OF THE HOSPITAL

HAFSID SULTANATE

Alexandria

Cairo

R. Nile

MAMELUKE

The Great Powers of Asia and Eastern Europe 1415–1450

Remnants of the Byzantine Empire

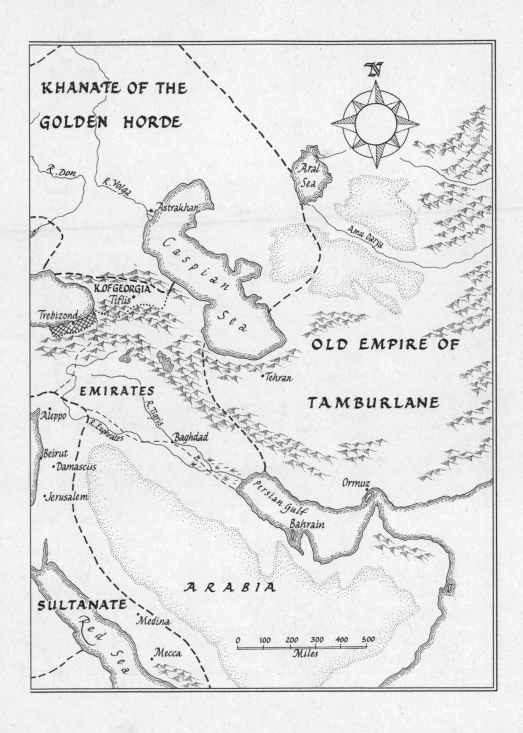

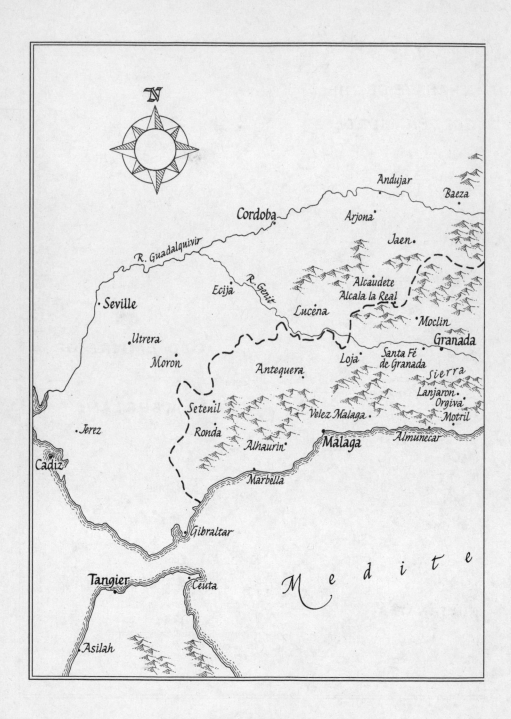

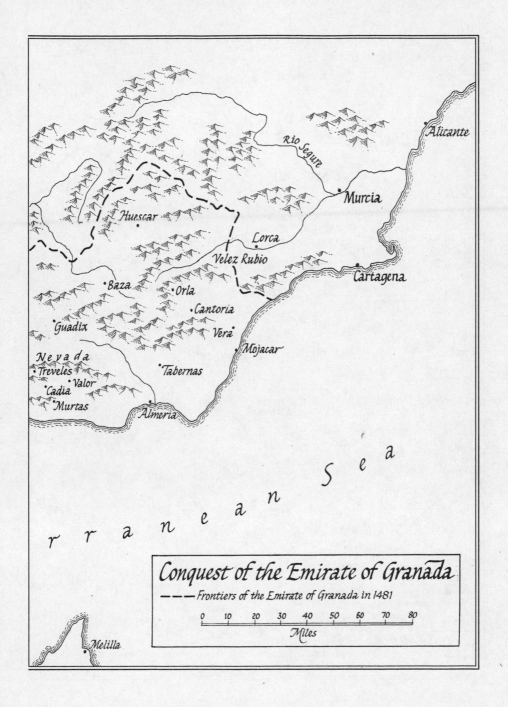

Alicante

Rio Segure

Murcia

Huescar

Lorca

Velez Rubio

Cartagena

Baza

Orla

Cantoria

Guadix

Vera

Mojacar

Nevada

Treveles

Valor

Tabernas

Cadia

Murtas

Almeria

r r a n e a n   S e a

Melilla

Conquest of the Emirate of Granada

— — — Frontiers of the Emirate of Granada in 1481

0   10   20   30   40   50   60   70   80

Miles

Expansion of the Ottoman Empire to 1326
Expansion to 1366
Expansion under Murat II to 1456
Expansion up to the death of Mehmet in 1486
Conquests of Selim the Grim up to 1520
Frontier at the end of Suleyman the Magnificent's
    reign in 1560

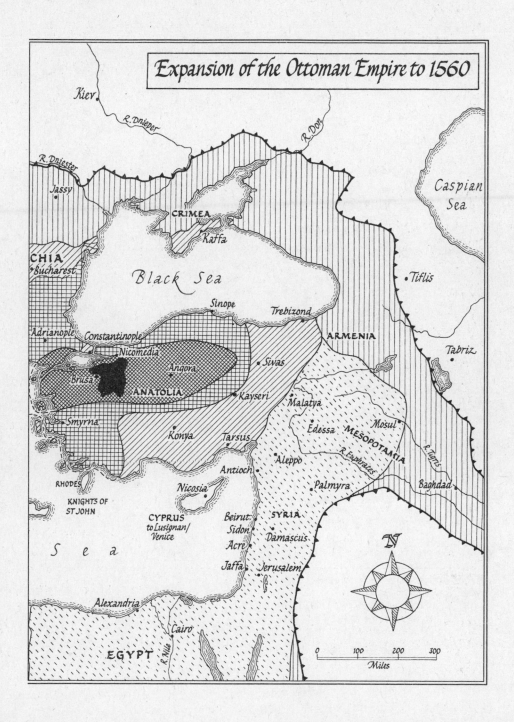

Expansion of the Ottoman Empire to 1560

Kiev

R. Dnieper

R. Dniester

R. Don

Jassy

CRIMEA

Kaffa

CHIA

Bucharest

Caspian Sea

Black Sea

Sinope

Trebizond

Tiflis

Adrianople

Constantinople

Nicomedia

Brusa

ANATOLIA

ARMENIA

Tabriz

Angora

Sivas

Smyrna

Kayseri

Malatya

Edessa

Mosul

MESOPOTAMIA

R. Tigris

Konya

Tarsus

Aleppo

R. Euphrates

Baghdad

RHODES

Antioch

Palmyra

KNIGHTS OF
ST JOHN

Nicosia

CYPRUS
to Lusignan/
Venice

Beirut
Sidon
Acre

SYRIA

Damascus

Sea

Jaffa

Jerusalem

N

Alexandria

Cairo

EGYPT

R. Nile

0   100   200   300
Miles

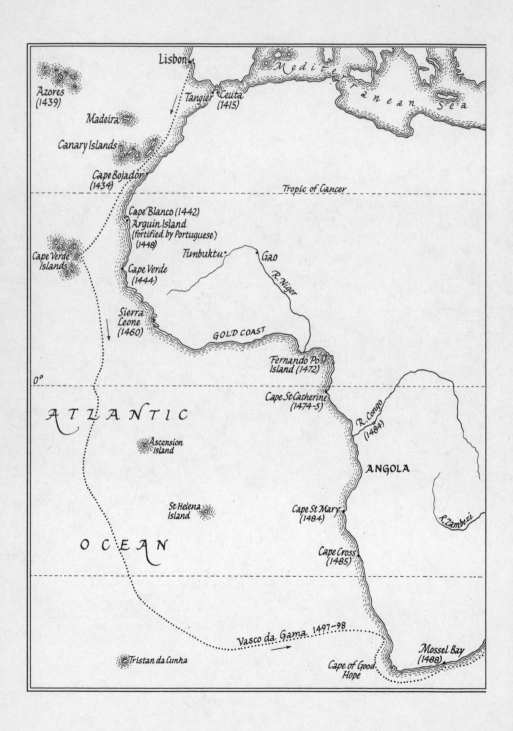

Lisbon

Medite r anean Sea

Azores
(1439)

Madeira

Tangier Ceuta
(1415)

Canary Islands

Cape Bojador
(1434)

Tropic of Cancer

Cape Blanco (1442)
Arguin Island
(fortified by Portuguese)
(1448)

Cape Verde
Islands

Timbuktu· Gao

Cape Verde
(1444)

R. Niger

Sierra
Leone
(1460)

GOLD COAST

Fernando Po
Island (1472)

0°

ATLANTIC

Cape St Catherine
(1474-5)

R. Congo
(1484)

Ascension
Island

ANGOLA

St Helena
Island

Cape St Mary
(1484)

R. Zambezi

OCEAN

Cape Cross
(1485)

Vasco da Gama 1497-98

Mossel Bay
(1488)

Tristan da Cunha

Cape of Good
Hope

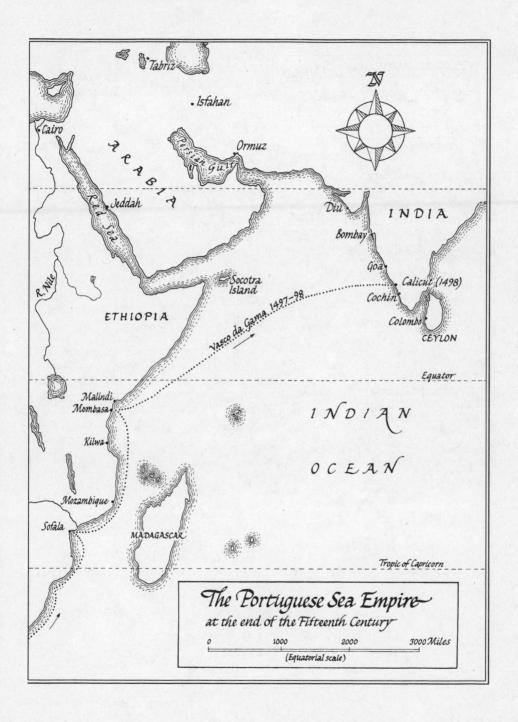

The Portuguese Sea Empire
at the end of the Fifteenth Century

0   1000   2000   3000 Miles

(Equatorial scale)

Principal Battles and Sieges of the Last Crusaders

0   100   200   300 Miles

Vienna

HUNGARY

Ottomans destroy
Hungarian Army
1526

(1526) ⚔ Mohács

R. Sava   R. Danube

✕ Belgrade
(Sieges of
1456, 1521)

WAL

BOSNIA

SERBIA

R. Po

Adriatic Sea

• Kosovo
✕ (1389)

PAPAL
STATES

CORSICA

Rome.

KINGDOM OF
NAPLES

ALBANIA

Sack of
Otranto
✕ (1480)

CORFU   ✕ (1538)
Preveze

Lepanto
✕ (1571)

SARDINIA

✕ (1535) Charles V
✕ (1573) Don John of Austria
✕ (1569, 1573) Uluch Ali

Palermo

SICILY

GREECE

Goletta

Tunis

TUNISIA

Sack of
Gozo   Siege of
(1551) ✕ ✕ MALTA
(1565)

Mahdia
(1550, 1554) ✕

Mediterr

✕ DJERBA

Ottoman naval victory (1560)
Siege of Fort (1560)

Tripoli
✕ Seized by Dragut
(1551)
(Held by Knights of
St John 1530–1551)

LIBYA

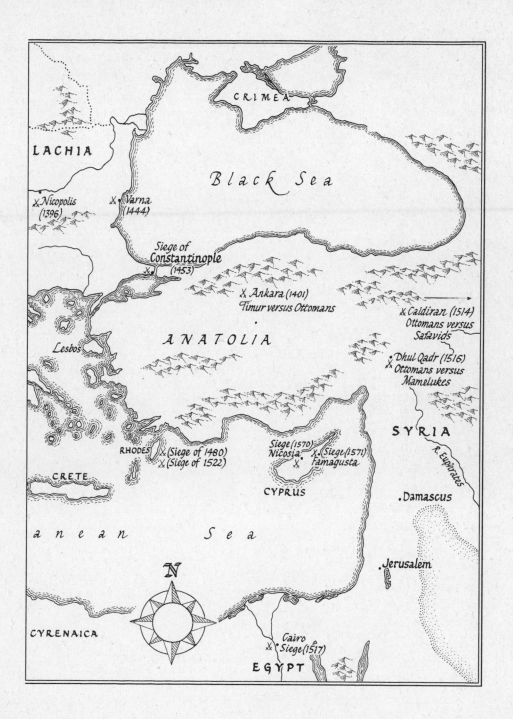

CRIMEA

LACHIA

Black Sea

X Nicopolis
(1396)

X Varna
(1444)

Siege of
Constantinople
(1453)

X Ankara (1401)
Timur versus Ottomans

X Caldiran (1514)
Ottomans versus
Safavids

ANATOLIA

Lesbos

Dhul Qadr (1516)
X Ottomans versus
Mamelukes

SYRIA

RHODES
X (Siege of 1480)
X (Siege of 1522)

Siege (1570)
Nicosia
X Siege (1571)
X Famagusta

CRETE

R. Euphrates

CYPRUS

Damascus

anean   Sea

Jerusalem

N

CYRENAICA

Cairo
X Siege (1517)

EGYPT

INTRODUCTION

The Last Crusaders is the product of a thirty-year quest, though what I hoped to discover at the beginning of this journey has long since been transmuted by the search. I set out to explain the last great tectonic shift in the balance of power in the Old World, when the eastern Mediterranean and the Middle East still dominated the global economy. This period of transformation began with the conquest of Byzantine Constantinople in 1453 by Mehmet the Conqueror, which was then counterbalanced by the conquest of the Moorish Emirate of Granada in 1490 by Ferdinand and Isabella. The brilliance of the two political masterminds who set these empires on their course of expansion, plotting, betraying, extorting and conquering their way to dominion and glory, has seldom been equalled. Certainly in terms of sheer villainy, energy, charisma and heroism, neither Mehmet the Conqueror nor Ferdinand of Aragon had any equal, then or since.

After these dramatic conquests both states also succeeded in expanding their power base, so that a generation later, around 1520, the Habsburg Empire of Spain in the West and the Ottoman Empire in the East had emerged as the two superpowers of the Mediterranean. As in the rivalry between Greece and Persia, or Carthage and Rome, they would gradually become embroiled in a furious fifty-year war for the mastery of the Inner Sea. The famous flashpoints of this contest, such as the siege of Malta and the battles of Preveza and Lepanto, would all be fought out in the central cockpit of the Mediterranean. After the battles for the possession of Cyprus and Tunisia in the 1570s, the exhausted armies, fleets and treasuries of both empires settled down to a truce. This ceasefire line was never to be effectively disputed again, so the boundaries drawn then have remained the national, cultural,

linguistic and religious frontiers to this day. Although they have
endured, they still remain politically pregnant. Many Greeks still make
an annual toast, 'Next year we shall return to Constantinople', just as
the families of exiled Moors are rumoured still to treasure the old keys
to their long-lost Andalusian mansions. Turkish Cypriots sigh for the
'fifty thousand martyrs' lost beneath the walls of Famagusta. And, while
on a recent visit to Malta, the standard of the Knights of St John once
more flew above the ramparts of Senglea and Birgu just as the minarets
of new mosques have returned again to the skyline of Granada.

I intended this history to follow the manner of Thucydides' assessment of Athens and Sparta: a sober analysis of the two powers, their
governance and capabilities, the unfolding conflict and then the resolution. However, the more I studied the more the intimate details of the
period took over. Instead of the orderly progression of historical inevi-
tability, the role of chance and the influence of personalities began to
dominate the record. Not to mention the caprice of the winds. It
became clear that it would be a complicated mission, because the tale
had dozens of different national variants, but this only added to the
challenge of the research.

The book would explain how a Portuguese Crusader, the Commander
of the last surviving priory of the Templar Order in Europe, would turn
himself into a Navigator Prince questing after Prester John. It would tell
the story of how Charles V had proved himself to be the very last
Emperor-knight of Christendom, fighting as a foot-soldier outside the
walls of both Tunis and Algiers. How he had been among the last to
wade through the Algerian surf back to the waiting ships of a Crusader
fleet, with 'stout Cortez' at his back (Hernan Cortes, the hero of the
conquest of Mexico) still begging his master to launch one last counter-
attack. It would explain the tactical brilliance of that *condottiere* of the
sea, the Genoese admiral Andrea Doria, who had switched sides with
remarkable effectiveness in the middle of a war. It would chronicle the
valiant defence by the Knights of St John of their island fortresses in
Rhodes and Malta. This order of fighting monks, recruited exclusively
from the nobility of Europe, were fully prepared to die in Christ's name,
though in their lives they followed little enough of his teachings. It
would recount the incredibly bloody and vicious but almost forgotten
sieges of Malaga, Goletta, Famagusta and Djerba, as well as the great
set-piece battles, such as Lepanto led by young Don John of Austria,

who was blessed by a saintly old Pope as commander of the massed galleys of the Holy League. Also I knew exactly where to conclude the story, with a tale that had haunted me since childhood: the Battle of the Three Kings. This is undoubtedly the very last, but also the most quixotic and magnificent conclusion to the five-hundred-year-old saga of the Crusades. Dom Sebastian, the boy-king of Portugal, backed by the resources of a worldwide mercantile empire, would throw down the gauntlet and pit the battle-hardened nobility of Portugal against the tribal cavalry of Morocco.

The Moroccan army was led that day by a Sharif-Sultan descended from the Prophet Muhammad, and it was his extraordinary personal adventures that added another element to the story of *The Last Crusaders*. While chronicling the various Crusader knights of Europe it would also be possible to interweave the story from the Muslim side – a mission that has never been attempted before.

Without losing a sense of balance, the book would explain some of the motivation behind the fearful destruction of the corsair pirate fleets, their favourite harbours and anchorages, as well as analyse the polyglot background of their great commanders such as Barbarossa, Dragut and Uluj Ali. It could also sketch out the personal motivations of five generations of Ottoman Sultans, and show the ways in which the dreams, slights, loves and aspirations of a Mehmet, a Bayezid, a Selim and a Suleyman affected grand strategy. In addition it would explain that, whatever Europeans might have been told in their history class about the Ottoman sieges of Vienna or the assaults on Venice, these Christian enemies on the far-western frontiers were not the principal concerns of the Ottoman Empire. The real challenge to their authority and their state came from within Islam, most especially from the charismatic leadership that emerged in this period from places like Iran and Morocco. Rulers such as Ismail (the first Shiite Shah of Iran) and Sharif Al-Qaim (who founded the Sharifian dynasty of Morocco) seemed to rise out of a political nowhere. They were descended from teachers of Sufi brotherhoods in obscure mountain regions, but their religious authority, wrapped in hidden expectations of the emergence of the Mahdi, 'the awaited one' who would appear at the end of the world, saw their influence rocket until each became unquestioned leader of hundreds of thousands of devoted warriors. This challenge to the spiritual authority of the Ottoman Sultans would only be resolved by a pitiless civil war, by massacre, by mass deportations, by an endless succession of frontier wars and assassinations.

My original conception of the two leading empires, Christendom and Islam, locked in an obsessive war of attrition had begun to weaken and dissolve at the edges. The conflict between the Habsburg Empire and the Ottoman Empire was certainly real, destructive and bloody – but it often took second place to obsessive rivalry with neighbours of their own faith. Just as the new Shiite Empire of Persia was always more of a threat to the Ottomans, so Charles V's enmity against King Francis of France was always a much greater source of obsessive passion than his crusades into North Africa. Nothing will quite equal the violence with which the red-hatted Kizilbas rebels were purged from within the territories of the Ottoman Empire, nor the slow, ruthless destruction of the Jews, converted Jews, Moors and Protestants in Habsburg Spain.

Similarly, the succession of crusading ventures launched by the kings of Portugal against neighbouring Morocco became ever more intriguing in the light of periods of truce, joint trading ventures and outright alliances against third parties. Corsair admirals like Barbarossa seemed to fit closer the pattern of endless enmity between the East and the West, but even they did not fit the mould of a holy warrior, for they could camp over the winter in Christian Toulon in conditions of perfect peace, undertake secret negotiations with the Holy Roman Emperor and join a French fleet in besieging an Italian port. Barbarossa and his successor captains also pursued political adventures of their own, against their theoretical Muslim liege lords, the various emirs and sultans along the North African shore. Rather than Muslim set against Christian in a chess-like conflict, it appeared more like a game of poker with a dozen players watching one another like hawks for the slightest weakness or advantage. Muslims would combine with Christians against other Muslim powers while the strong French alliance with the Ottoman Empire soon became a mainstay of diplomatic activity. Likewise, the leading Crusader monarch of his day would fake an international crusade in order to stab his Christian neighbour in the back while his guard was down.

Here are the sort of details that time and time again get whitewashed from the record of heroic national achievement. The story had also matured from a set of brightly-coloured heroes and villains into a set of characters of varying shades of grey that all leached towards a darker-hued evil. It became difficult to extract any sense of a religious morality from the actions of either the Muslim or Christian leadership. However, what they had in common was an ability to harness the religious passions of their people for their own ends. The most depraved, ruthless and emotionally isolated leaders survived, while the kind, the considerate, the quietists and the compassionate only succeeded in bringing ruin on themselves and their communities. Those who knew how to brew up hatred, greed and fear, and twist them to their own ends, were the ones who succeeded in achieving the most astonishing transformations. About this there can be no doubt. And, in some bizarre fulfilment of these monstrous crimes, the sovereign lords of the world empires, King Philip II and Suleyman the Magnificent, for reasons of state, transformed themselves into Saturn-like demons who destroyed the lives of their own sons.

The period covered in *The Last Crusaders*, between 1450 and 1590, changed the face of world history. The old patchwork of city-states, counties, duchies, emirates and sultanates were consumed by the creation of the first great nation states. This was the era when the complexities of ancient and medieval Persia were fused into the Shiite nation state of Iran, when multi-faith Anatolia was purged towards becoming Sunni Turkey, when the hotchpotch of Iberian kingdoms and their ancient communities of Jews and Muslims was tortured into becoming Catholic Spain. The modern borders of Algeria, Libya, Tunisia, Morocco, France, Spain, Portugal and Iran were defined by the needs of corsair captains and military garrisons. Perhaps most portentous of all for the future of our planet was the awful reality of Europeans' first contact with the wider world. The discovery of the routes to the coasts of North and South America, West Africa, East Africa, southern Arabia, India and the Far East led to their rapid and efficient exploitation. These routes were discovered not by scientific explorers and mystically inclined scholar-saints, but by men formed in the brutal experience of the Last Crusades; by men who had become long accustomed to use the banner of religion to enslave, steal, murder, pillage and burn their way towards ever greater power, wealth and glory. The story of the Last Crusaders is a vast, rich, complex and bloody tapestry that stretches from the shores of Venezuela to forts on the African coast and along the shores of Arabia and southern India.

I have resisted the temptation to be polemical or judgemental, let alone indulge in political comparisons with our own troubled times. The analogies are too apparent, too frequent and too poignant to require this. The essential structure of the book remains focused on the conflict between the two rival states, the Ottoman and Habsburg empires and their leadership, shadowed by the concerns of the other powers such as Persia, Portugal, Austria and Morocco. But a desire for a simple narrative has been replaced by the greater requirements of the truth as it revealed itself, and by the wish to give the communities despoiled by this period of history their brief testament to place beside the proud deeds of conquering princes.

We should all hear these stories at least once if we are to have any hope of understanding our modern age. For out of the conflicts of the Last Crusade emerged, almost by default, the very first of the European colonial empires. Portugal was propelled into becoming a world power, the first mercantile superstate (with bases in four continents) through waging her hundred-year Last Crusade against Morocco. It would be under the adapted banner of the Knights Templars that the first squadron of the Portuguese navy would conquer and kill its way along the coasts of India, East Africa and the East Indies. The commanders of this Portuguese conquest would win their entry into the chivalry of the Crusading Orders surrounded by dead Indians and Africans. In an exactly similar manner, the Spanish Crusade which conquered Muslim Granada in the fifteenth century would be the bloody role model for the creation of Spain's new empires in the Caribbean and South America. Whether one looks at the history of modern Cuba, Venezuela, Brazil, Bolivia, Mexico or even of that great republic that stands to their north, the violence and the emerging racism of this continuation of the Last Crusade of Christendom is a historical reality that lives on to this day.

So from the heartland of the familiar islands, beaches and cities of the central Mediterranean, the historical canvas of this book will now and then stretch to include the coasts of South America and China. This might seem ambitious, but it is the actions of some of the intriguing minor characters that take us on these journeys. No one can attempt to understand this pivotal age within the narrow frontiers of traditional, nation-based history. Hernan Cortes, having conquered Mexico in the name of the Emperor Charles V, would later stand at his shoulder, guarding him from the Arab cavalry that poured out of the walls of Algiers, and would beg him to once more return to the fray. How ironic that the man who with his own hands had imprisoned and murdered one Emperor – of Aztec Mexico – should act the supportive courtier to another. The Ottoman navy was led into battle by characters beyond the invention of any fiction. Barbarossa was Greek by blood but an Ottoman by birth and carved out an empire for himself in North Africa using exiles from Spain. One of his successors, the Ottoman admiral in chief, Uluj Ali, started life as a poor shepherd boy in the hills of southern Italy and only converted to Islam so that he could fight a man with a knife.

Looking back over the book, those heroes of thirty and twenty years ago have all been replaced. Gone are the gilded statues of brazen kings, in their place a mirage-like vision of bustling self-governing communities of merchants which will soon be utterly destroyed. It is instructive to imagine the shape and complexity of the ancient Moroccan city of Ceuta (the one surviving daughter of Carthage) before its sack by the Portuguese; of Byzantine Constantinople aglow with the renaissance in learning encouraged by the Palaeologue dynasty before the Ottoman soldiery breached its walls; of the garden city of Lusignan Nicosia, the Gothick finials of its many abbeys and churches scented by orange blossom and shaded by palms; of Nasrid Granada in its bustling heyday, filled with silk merchants, bookbinders and Moorish and Jewish traders up from Malaga, Tlemcen and Timbuktu; of the courtyard colleges of the Hafsid Sultans hidden among the alleys of Tunis, piled high with ancient volumes of learning that will be burned by Spanish troops or used as litter for their horses. For all these ancient cosmopolitan cityscapes were destroyed by the march of new national armies, bound to one Imperial paymaster and one presumed faith, by new techniques of warfare, the new mastery of the forge, the shipwright and the gunpowder mills. Later, after the slaughter of their inhabitants, the cities themselves will be quarried. Delicate traceries of Gothic trelliswork will be felled, arcaded courtyards will be smashed open, glazed tiles, arabesque columns, slim brick arches and frescoed vaults will be used as infill in the monstrously thick, ramped parapets required to withstand the new order of weaponry, just as the carved and cut marble of antiquity is smelted into lime mortar. But these conquerors will also build with a confidence, an elegance and a serenity that has not yet been equalled, so that the contradictions of this period, the beauty and the cruelty, the achievement and the destruction, have never dulled. It is one of the pleasures of history to know about these fascinating, violent, clever, cynical, creative and ambitious characters but never to have lived among them.

The Last Crusaders is divided into three parts, 'Birth of New Powers', 'Struggle' and 'Destruction', each of which chronicles a roughly forty-year period centred on the reign of one ruler. This allows for a specific national narrative. As a result, at the end of each part you are faced with a cumulative picture of the period viewed from four different perspectives: through the lenses of Portugal, Spain, Ottoman Turkey and the Corsairs of North Africa.

Before embarking on the story it is useful first to look over the far horizons, to scan the four quarters of the globe and remind ourselves of the fates of the various nations – in short, to examine the shape of the Old World in both 1360 and 1415. Our starting date of 1360 is based on a shared experience – which broke through all the barriers of creed, class, faith and tongue. The Black Death knew no frontiers. It united city and hamlet, nomad and peasant, Islam with Christianity, in shared suffering, as the bubonic plague rolled and billowed across the frontiers of the Old World, removing a third of the population by 1350. But once the plague pits had been sealed with lime, the political structures and military boundaries remained remarkably unchanged, even if social and economic realities had shifted. Our second date of 1415 is taken from the sack of the Moroccan city of Ceuta, the almost accidental start of Portugal's epic Crusade.

In 1360 in the far north-west corner of the great continent of Eurasia there is a broken archipelago of islands scattered before the Atlantic Ocean. The Kingdom of the Three Leopards, England, has started to internalise its undoubted energies in a vicious cycle of dynastic feuds that will collectively become known as the Wars of the Roses. Its monarchs will only be able to achieve brief periods of national unity by launching aggressive invasions of France. Yet the major beneficiary of this violent period is to be neither England nor France but the Duchy of Burgundy, which nearly succeeds in creating the separate Kingdom of Burgundy out of the dense swath of rich cities between the Rhine and the Seine.

Germany as defined by the wide frontiers of the Holy Roman Empire looks on the map as if it should be in a position to dominate commercially and politically the whole of Europe. This national frontier is, however, an imperial facade behind which exists a fractured mosaic of principalities, bishoprics, free cities, duchies and counties, all locked in ancient and vicious local rivalries. To the south of the Alps the Italian peninsula, with its rich density of cities separated by mountains and rivers, is even more politically dismembered than Germany. Yet the Italian city-states are old, rich, well armed and powerful enough to pursue their own murderous foreign policy agendas. Genoa is locked in perpetual rivalry with Venice. The large southern state of Naples (also known as the Kingdom of the Two Sicilies) occupies almost half the landmass of Italy and seems to offer the one instance of national unity. But it also stands as a perpetual warning, for over the centuries it has continually fallen into the hands of a succession of foreign dynasts, encouraging various French, German and Spanish monarchs to make use of Naples as a base for determined attempts to subdue all of Italy. At the centre of the Italian nation sit the Papal States, the source of at least half the machinations, disorder and instability that enliven Italian politics.

To the west of Italy lies the Iberian Peninsula. The region is still considered by the rest of Europe to be a borderland, a relict war zone, subdivided between a handful of heroic crusading kingships, such as Navarre, Castile, Leon, Aragon and Portugal. On the far-eastern frontier of Europe is a triangle of elective monarchies, Poland, Lithuania and Hungary, whose frontiers and fighters can defeat even the strength of the Holy Roman Empire of Germany. However, a powerful and deeply entrenched aristocracy is indifferent, if not hostile, to any central leadership and is brutally exploitative of both local towns and the peasantry.

To travel south or east of these Catholic kingdoms is to cross a cultural and linguistic frontier and enter the domain of Orthodoxy: the principalities, despotates and kingdoms of Wallachia, Moldovia, Serbia and Bulgaria. In the very far north stand a further half-dozen Orthodox principalities, such as the titular Grand Duchy of Vladimir, as well as those of Smolensk, Tver, Pskov and the northernmost republic of Novgorod. In the years after the Black Death they stood in a state of uneasy dependency on the Mongol Horde, the only undoubted world-class power of the period. Indeed none of these previous mentioned powers had the slightest chance of standing up to the vast cavalry armies of the Mongol Khans, the lineal heirs of Genghis Khan. The only thing that saved them was that they were on the poor north-western fringe of Eurasia and there were much richer pickings for the Mongols elsewhere.

The Khanate of the Golden Horde straddled over southern Russia and Caucasia, existing as the westernmost extension of an ethnic alli-ance with its Mongol-Turkic cousins who ruled as Khans over all of Central Asia, China and the Middle East. Scattered over the old domains of the Byzantine Anatolia, some two dozen Turkic Emirs ruled over the area we now know as Turkey. Whether they paid tribute or not, they all acknowledged the leadership of the great Mongol Khanates.

Only Egypt, of all the old lands of Islam, had been able successfully to resist the Mongols. To the west of Egypt, along the North African shore, there was no serious rival to the old Almohad Caliphate (that had ruled over all North Africa and southern Spain in its fundamentalist heyday), which had broken up into four rival states: the Nasrids of Granada, the Merenids of Morocco, the Zayyanids of western Algeria and the Hafsids of Tunisia, who bickered among one another for dom-inance.

Two generations later, in 1415, surprisingly little has changed. In the centre of Asia, the irresistible power of the Mongol cavalry had once again been graphically demonstrated. For it was just ten years since Timur (often known as Tamburlane) had swept away every state, every army and every city that stood in his way, in a continuous series of cam-paigns fought between 1367 and 1405. At the Battle of Ankara in 1402 the army of the young Ottoman Sultanate – which had emerged as the most dynamic of the half-dozen emirates that now ruled over Anatolia – was swept away. Only the Mameluke Sultans succeeded in defending Egypt.

In an obscure westernmost corner of Europe in 1415, a Portuguese fleet was being prepared to raid the coast of their Muslim neighbour. It was believed that a foreign invasion would be good for national unity. This expedition, which sailed south from Lisbon to the Moroccan city of Ceuta, begins the epic of the Last Crusaders.

PART ONE

Birth of New Powers

1

The Crusader Prince
of Portugal

Henry the Navigator, 1415–60

Treason doth never prosper; what's the reason?
For if it prosper, none dare call it treason.

John Harrington

Two vast limestone outcrops guard the union of the Atlantic with the
Mediterranean. The sea that runs between them divides the continents
of Africa and Europe. In fine weather the Strait of Gibraltar can be
crossed in just a few hours, the habitual wind cutting up elegant crescents of white foam. But even on such a day you sense the power,
strength and depth of the Strait, where beneath you run seven separate
levels of ocean current. There are ancient rumours of drifting islands,
subterranean tunnels, treacherous sandbanks left behind after the
destruction of Atlantis and the ghostly tale of a lighthouse of copper
and stone built by a heroic king.

From the summits of either of the two limestone mountains you can,
in principle, make a watch over the whole Strait, though the silhouettes
of the Pillars of Hercules (as they are known) are liable to be half-hidden
in a pale banner, a tell-tale slipstream of muggy cloud known as the
Levanter. The mountain on the southern shore is known as Jebel
Moussa – the mountain of Moses, a western counter-balance to the
mountain in Sinai where the Prophet of God was spoken to through a

The Straits of Gibraltar, with the fortress ports of Gibraltar, Ceuta and Tangier. Drawn for Sultan Suleyman by Piri Reis between 1524 and 1528.

burning bush. On its slopes are a number of caves and caverns, one of which is believed to have been used by the 'Seven Sleepers', who escaped the persecution of the pagan Roman Emperors and woke up after a sleep of a hundred years into the newborn world of Christendom. It is a miracle that is attested to by both Christian tradition and a verse of the Koran but also stands on ancient traditions of numerology. In the eastern lee of this sacred mountain stands an ancient trading city with a well-guarded port, situated on a long strategic promontory. It is known as Ceuta (Septem by the Romans) in honour of the Seven Sleepers, and is one of those urban survivals that, over two thousand years, passed from Phoenician to Roman to Byzantine and latterly Islamic rule in an unbroken heritage of the trading civilisation of the Mediterranean seas. Ceuta grew prosperous over the medieval centuries, for into its narrow streets poured every Moorish, Saharan and Jewish trader with an ear for business, both to exchange the goods of eastern and western Islam (the Mashraq and the Maghreb) and for the more animated barterings over the exotic products brought up by camel caravans from the far south: that precious litany of ebony, tusks of ivory, bales of ostrich feathers and quills of gold dust. It was a place of legendary activity, where twenty thousand merchants could be found seated in the honeycomb of booths that lined the alleys of the city's marketplace.

In times of peace, merchant-captains from the nations of Rum (the Christians) were allowed to base themselves in rented courtyards beside the harbours of Ceuta, so that men who sailed the Atlantic came here from Galicia as well as nearby Granada, Castile and Portugal. From the Rum of the Mediterranean came the merchants of Catalonia, Aragon, Valencia and Majorca, as well as their competitors from Pisa, Florence, Marseilles, Naples and Sicily. So, as well as the exotic scents and precious goods sold by well-established Moorish merchants in the market square, the harbour was also filled with ships bringing timber, pitch and barrels of salted cod from the Atlantic, along with the habitual staples of Mediterranean coastal trade: olive oil, corn, livestock and dried fruits.

Ceuta's strategic position and rich levy of customs dues meant that the high politics of its citadel was keenly fought over. From its earliest days Ceuta bent with the wind, saluted the new lord, the new empire, the better to get on with its own concerns. Some of this flavour of political finesse is remembered in the tale of Count Julian, the Byzantine governor of Ceuta who had made a tactical alliance with the Muslim Arab invaders in the eighth century. He had, so the story goes, sought to avenge the dishonour done to his daughter at the hands of a Visigothic king. So he lent his squadron of ships to Tariq, the young commander of the Muslim army based in Tangier, who began the invasion of Spain by landing on the other Pillar of Hercules, which henceforth bore his name: Jebel Tariq ('Tariq's Mountain'), Gibraltar. In the days of the Almohad Empire (which stretched throughout Spain and north-western Africa from 1060 to 1150), Sultan Abdel Moumen saw the Strait of Gibraltar as the centre of his power. To bring together all his governors, judges, feudatory tribal lords and vassal Christian princes in one great Royal Court, he built a glittering showpiece of power: the Medinat al-Fatih, 'City of Victory', which cascaded down the rocky slopes of Gibraltar, ornamented with gardens, aqueducts, towers and windmills. It was designed by the team of architects whose work at the Giralda in Seville and the Hassan Tower in Rabat still endures, though of the

Medinat al-Fatih and its great centrepiece, the Tower of Homage, there is nothing left but a dream.

By the middle of the thirteenth century the fundamentalist Almohad Empire had fractured into half a dozen dynastic states. Two of its political heirs, the Merenid Sultanate of Morocco and the Nasrid rulers of Granada, kept a close watch over the Strait of Gibraltar – and each other. They liked to keep a toehold in each other's territory, both as a military bridgehead to help each other in times of need and as a secure exile for inconvenient members of their own families and an outpost for diplomatic intrigue and intelligence. By the end of the fourteenth century the Merenids of Morocco had turned Gibraltar into their northernmost naval base while the Nasrids of Granada kept control of Ceuta as their southern base. In both of these trading fortress cities changes of Sultan, as a result of dynastic schisms, military coups, mercurial alliances or counter-coups, were frequent. Except for a minor alteration in the script of a new minted coin or in the bidding prayer of the Friday sermon, these were changes that the population could ignore.

On an August day in the year of 1415 such a transfer of power is once again being effected in Ceuta. Three young princes, who have fasted and spent the night in prayer, stand to the fore of a procession of noble young warriors. They are of the bloodline of Avis mixed with that of the English warrior king Edward III. They have processed through the city to the great mosque, which, having been scrubbed with salt, has been rededicated as a church. They advance to stand before their father, the fifty-year-old King of Portugal. John I, known to his people as both 'the Great' and 'the Bastard', is a powerfully built man with a squat frame that well matches his black eyes, dark complexion and determined chin. One by one the young princes advance and drop to their knees before their liege-lord father to be knighted. They are dubbed with swords that their English mother, Queen Philippa, had specially prepared for the event. She had not lived to see this day but on her deathbed the dying Queen had bestowed these bright new swords on her children and also requested them to renew their oaths to be good Christian knights, to honour justice and protect the weak. After she slipped away the Portuguese royal family very nearly cancelled the launching of the 'great enterprise' of the crusade against Ceuta, in grief at her death, though they knew she would have scorned such weakness.

Philippa may not have been a beauty but she always cut an impressive figure: tall, willowy, fair-haired and armed with commanding authority. She was the daughter of John of Gaunt, niece of the Black Prince (England's Achilles) and granddaughter of Edward III, the founder of the first order of English chivalry, the Garter. She set an uplifting example to her children, her husband and her adopted Kingdom of Portugal, which had been through confusing times before her arrival. It was her unvarying custom to begin each day with a recitation of her Book of Hours (which followed the Salisbury ritual) and on Friday mornings she habitually worked her way through the entire Psalter before touching her breakfast.

How proud Queen Philippa would have been of this moment, the knighting of her sons on the field of battle. Right from the start she had thrown her whole support behind the 'great enterprise', which had now proved a triumphant success. The Moorish trading city of Ceuta had been seized by her three sons, Dom Duarte (Edward),[1] Dom Pedro (Peter) and Dom Henrique (Henry), all serving under their father's command. None of the boys would ever forget this defining moment in their lives, but what tangled fates awaited them: one became an obsessive scholar-hermit and patron of navigators, another died of grief at what he had inflicted on his brother, and the third would be murdered by his own nephew.

From the citadel at the top of the city on that same day in August 1415 you could survey the rooftops of Ceuta's packed, narrow streets and pick out the mosque towers, the area of the two ports and the silhouette of the great mountain that stands to the west. Over the previous three days you would have observed the slow death of a city and a civilisation. Ceuta had not been consumed with flames but with cries of anguish as its places of worship were defiled, the strong front doors of the houses were broken down and rooms methodically looted. The inhabitants were hunted down, dragged from the rooftops and attics, hidden cellars and old cisterns in which they had hidden, then abused, brutalised and the women repeatedly raped. Later many of the captives were tortured, mostly for the sheer inexpressible pleasure of watching the enemy dance in pain, but also to find out who was worth keeping alive (to sell as a skilled slave or to be ransomed) and where they might have hidden their treasures – be it coin, a bin of dry corn or some pretty child. Ceuta was rich in treasures. In the words of one of the astonished Portuguese soldiers, 'Our poor house looked like pigsties in comparison with those of Ceuta.'

The sack of Ceuta took place over three days, its tortures and cruelties not only sanctioned by law and tradition but underwriting the whole mechanism of war. The peasants who had been recruited to serve as foot-soldiers in the invading Crusader army relished the sack most intensely, for all the accumulated abuse, humiliation and victimisation that they and their families had endured could at last be repaid. As a famous French general, Marshal de Saxe, would candidly confess many years later, 'The thing that keeps all soldiers so cheerful and makes them work with superhuman energy is the promise I made to them that they could plunder the town, if they took it by storm.' Three days was hardly long enough to balm the invaders' ancient hurts, but what deep pleasure they must have derived from this long-awaited reversal of roles. Those proud inhabitants of a great city, those tithe- and rent-collecting, mortgage-possessing merchants, those clever lawyers and men of letters at last learned what it is to suffer, to be forced to remain quite still and powerless as they witnessed the suffering of their loved ones. Even Grotius, that principled Swiss lawyer, one of the first Westerners to try to improve and codify the practice of war in order to reduce its horrors, had to allow that 'the slaughter of infants and women is allowed to have impunity, as comprehended in that right of war'.

The sacking of a city was like a containable medieval revolution. A monarch recruited all the toughest, most vicious and ambitious men from the peasantry and the impoverished gentry and, once in a while, gave them permission to play out all their otherwise unattainable erotic dreams and desire for power. There were no prohibitions during the sack. But, just as in a fairy story, such magical departures from normality have to end promptly, in this case with the strike of the bell at the end of the third day. But there were always some who had forgotten the rules, or who had progressed from the hurting of humans to the damage of buildings (which belonged by the act of conquest to the King) or who were too drunk or delirious with the glow of unaccustomed power to hear the tocsin ringing out. So it was also quite the custom for the commander of the army to hang a few soldiers to show that social order had returned. The gallows might be a tree, gatehouse or tower. Another act of returning order was the solemn procession, for

which everyone reassembled in their rank and place, so that thanks for
the victory could be offered to God. In Ceuta this also entailed the
conversion of the great Friday prayer mosque into a cathedral dedicated to Our Lady of Africa.

Only then could King John start taking firm possession of his property,
by positioning guards on the gates of looted warehouses and palaces and
tidying up the defences that had been slighted during the siege. The
streets, recently witness to such scenes of horror, waited for the memories of carnage to fade away. Ceuta's old bustling market square lay
empty, flanked by the city's great Muslim edifices: the mosques and
their associated bath-houses, the covered alleys of the bazaar and the
elegant series of interconnecting courtyards where merchants lodged
and students had been taught to follow the example of the city's celebrated sons, the scholar-geographer El-Idrisi and the 'St Francis' of
Morocco, the much-loved saint of the poor, Sidi Bel Abbes (who we
shall meet again right at the end of this tale, this time as an angelic
force, wrapped in a grey cloak, riding a grey horse and urging his followers into one last battle against the Portuguese Crusaders).

Commercial life was far from dead. There were frantic scenes of trading in the camps and on quaysides as victorious soldiers disposed of
their bundles of loot and strings of captives for ready coin. For those
with an eye and ready cash there were great bargains to be picked up
and many a great aristocratic collection of art treasures owes its existence to the flea markets which arose among the army tents after the
sack of a city.

News of this great victory spread quickly around the Christian world.
It was the habit of the time for victors to send letters filled with the
news of their success to the other courts of Christendom. And since
there had been no crusade from Western Christendom against the
Islamic world for well over a century, despite much talk, there was
rejoicing that Portugal, the poorest, most southerly, most westerly, most
isolated of all the Christian kingdoms, had shown that this chivalric
ideal was not lost. And, most crucially, the Portuguese had won the day.
Crusading had fallen out of fashion in Christian Europe simply because
of a critical lack of success. After two centuries of activity the Crusades
had stopped not for any lack of men or money, or any diminution of
zeal for conquest and gold, let alone guilt for the murderous crimes of

the Fourth Crusade (1202–4), the scandal of child slavery or the rivalries exposed between Genoa and Venice, England and France, Emperor and Pope. They had ceased because of a long string of significant and painful defeats. In 1244 Jerusalem, after being held by Christians for twenty-six years by treaty, was reconquered by a Muslim army. Five years later Louis IX of France and his invading army were defeated and taken prisoner at Mansura in Egypt by that country's army. Military catastrophe struck again in 1270, when Louis IX and a second army of Crusaders landed outside Tunis and then melted away into the sands of Carthage suffering from chronic dysentery. Twenty years later these two experiences were shown not to be chance instances of ill fortune but a true reckoning of military capability. For in 1291 the best-defended city, the triple-walled citadel of Acre (on the coast of the Holy Land near today's frontier between Lebanon and Israel), which could be endlessly resupplied and reinforced through its closely guarded port, defended by the flower of Europe, fell to the direct assault of a besieging army led by the ruler of Egypt, the Mameluke Sultan. It was such a straightforward test of military power that the last remaining Crusader fortress ports along this coast, at Tyre, Beirut and Sidon, were abandoned in the immediate aftermath. If Acre could fall, nothing was safe. This was also the period when the last remnants of the Crusader duchies established by the Fourth Crusade were formally dissolved by the Palaeologue dynasty of Byzantium.

It was in reaction to this series of decisive military defeats that many of the leading monarchs of Christendom had sought out a convenient scapegoat. Edward I of England persecuted the Jews while in France King Philip IV destroyed the Crusading Order the Knights Templars using a familiar pattern of private torture and public confession at showpiece trials for treason. The two monarchs were enriched by their crimes, both in material goods and as a result of debts which they no longer had to pay, for the Jews of York and the Knights Templars in Paris had both foolishly acted as bankers to kings.

The Portuguese victory at Ceuta was all the more welcome in that it came after the dismal fate of Christendom had been aggravated by the Black Death and such ruinous internal conflicts as the Hundred Years War (1337–1453), which had wasted France with civil war and brought armed bands of murderous English to her lands. But that victory had been a very close-run thing. There was nothing preordained about the success of Portugal's great crusading enterprise. The resources of most of King John's key supporters had been locked up in loans to equip a fleet which had been weakened by plague just before it was about to sail. His careful attempts to keep the destination of the attack a secret, at a time when rumours were being disseminated about an intended Portuguese strike against the Dutch, were undermined when the invasion fleet advanced rapidly towards North Africa but was then becalmed off the Algarve coast for a week. When they did at last catch a wind that took them to the shores of Ceuta, the Portuguese had but half a day to land an advance guard, before the wind transformed itself into a storm which blew them straight back towards Europe. Yet this shattering misfortune was transmuted into their greatest stroke of luck, for the Muslim garrison at Ceuta, having destroyed the small Portuguese invasion force, watched the scattering of the fleet and relaxed their guard. But instead of accepting defeat, the Portuguese had decided on one last effort. Prince Dom Henrique led an armada of small boats straight for the beach and swiftly seized control of the port gate, losing just eight men. The city's defences then fell apart like a ripe fig as the rest of the Portuguese army stormed ashore, pouring though the captured gatehouse to fight its way up through the streets to the citadel.

On 2 September the victorious Portuguese fleet set sail for the return journey to Lisbon. Accounts differ as to its size, putting it at between sixty and two hundred ships. King John had appointed Dom Pedro de Meneses to be the commander of Ceuta and left him with a garrison of three thousand men. Dom Pedro had been given an olive wand as his staff of office, a ritual that continues to this day in the Spanish-ruled city. Despite this saving on regalia, the garrisoning of Ceuta was a big commitment for the Portuguese in terms of both men and money. But to have done otherwise, to have torched the city or sold it back to its Sultan, would have diminished their great victory. And King John was shrewd enough to see that there were many ways in which to make political capital out of the success of the 'great enterprise' against Ceuta. The affecting scene which he presented to the courts of Europe, of himself as a valiant old Crusader knighting his sons on the field of battle against the Moors, was a promising start.

Up until this time King John had not been considered much of a brother monarch by the other rulers of Christendom. He had reached the throne of Portugal in an unorthodox, if not Macbeth-like ascension. As the illegitimate son of a Portuguese prince he had broken into the royal palace, killed the regent of the day, expelled the widowed Queen and seized power for himself. He had managed to sustain himself on the throne only because the two principal cities of Portugal, the bustling ports of Lisbon and Oporto, had enthusiastically thrown their support behind the young adventurer. They had seen him as a national saviour who might stop the inevitable, a sell-out by the landed nobility of Portugal to their powerful neighbour, the Spanish kingdom of Castile–Leon. In due course the expected counter-attack against young John's usurpation took place. An army composed of heavily armoured Castilian and Portuguese knights advanced into Portugal, supposedly marching in support of the legitimist heir. But on 14 August 1385, in a day that has often been compared to Agincourt, King John and the Portuguese archers shot down this army of knights on the field of Aljubarrota. It was the single, decisive act that confirmed John's hold on the throne. The victory of the humble bowmen of Portugal, gathered around their young king, over foreigners and 'treacherous nobility' also confirmed John the Bastard as the popular national champion.

In the aftermath of this military success John was able to complete the destruction of his enemies by confiscating the estates of many noble families who had sided with Castile–Leon. This allowed him to reward his allies. So he created a new governing class largely drawn from the citizens of Lisbon and Oporto, the enterprising merchants, educated clerks, guild officials and lawyers who had first backed him. In short John proved himself to be a thoroughly Renaissance prince. As well as posing as a folk hero to the *arraia-miuda*, the peasantry who had fought for him, John also set his lawyers to retrospectively smooth his assumption of the throne. They cleared a legal path to his usurpation by deciding that all his dynastic rivals were illegitimate too. Indeed, being a bastard at this time proved a useful start to a career at court. The Constable of Portugal, John's chief military officer, had two such blots on his family history. And he was not alone. During the King's reign two archbishops, five bishops, nine deans, seventy-two canons and six hundred priests received official dispensation to legitimise their bastard children. John himself had a pair of children, born out of wedlock to his mistress Ines Pires.[2]

King John the Bastard's reputation as a successful Crusader was particularly relevant in the Iberian Peninsula, where the various different kingdoms gloried in the centuries-long reconquest of territory from the Moors. Portugal, one of the five Iberian kingdoms (alongside Navarre, Leon, Castile and Aragon) had played a vital role. However, from the late-thirteenth-century Castile–Leon had extended its power and excluded any of its neighbours from any further chance of territorial expansion by pushing its own frontiers right down to the Mediterranean and Atlantic shores. So, after 150 years of Portugal's being elbowed out of the limelight by Castile, its capture of Ceuta put it back at centre stage. This may also have helped to keep at bay a slight sense of unease caused by too great a knowledge of Crusading history. For, though its people tried to forget it, Portugal owed its origin to Castile–Leon: back in the eleventh century the 'County of Portucale' had been given as a feudal grant to an adventurous Crusader by a king of Leon.

The victory at Ceuta also gave a renewed sense of purpose to Portugal's Crusading Orders. In the rest of Christendom the Knights of St John of the Hospital of Jerusalem (or Knights Hospitallers) and the Knights Templars had emerged as great land-owning forces. In Portugal, owing to the proximity of Muslim neighbours, these two pan-European knightly orders had been reinforced by two local versions, the Knights of Avis and those of Santiago. The commanders of these orders held positions of great military importance in Portugal. Indeed it was from his position as Commander of the Knights of Avis that young John had first launched his murderous *coup d'état* against the regent. The victorious crusade allowed the King to fulfil his destiny as the Commander of Avis and to strengthen his control over these powerful institutions. And he had made certain that one of his younger sons, Prince Henrique (Henry), had been appointed Commander of the Order of Christ, a new Portuguese Crusading Order created in 1319 to absorb all the knights, priories, castles and traditions of the Templars, after their formal suppression in the rest of Europe.

But how was possession of the Crusade-conquered Ceuta to be paid for? The Kingdom of Portugal was one of the poorest in Europe, so much so that it was incapable of striking a gold coinage. There was no shame in making use of the Florentine florin or the Venetian ducat – which all the world treasured – but having to use the coinage of its all-too-powerful neighbour, Castile–Leon, had many unsatisfactory connotations, ancient and modern. No, if Portugal was to survive at all, it had to make its own future. It was the genius of King John to recognise the futility of engaging in a border war with Castile–Leon and to look instead to the maritime horizon for its future.

All sorts of mercantile treasures found their way back to Lisbon from Ceuta with the victorious army, but the Portuguese soon found that Ceuta's role as the great entrepôt of the western Mediterranean had been killed off by their occupation. The city was besieged by the surrounding tribesmen of the mountains, and the Moorish merchants of North Africa were quick to divert the trans-Saharan caravan trade to other ports, such as the anchorage of Badis, sheltered by the Rif mountains to the east of Ceuta, and to the neighbouring city of Tangier, just two days' ride to the west of Ceuta. Although Morocco was used to the threat from seaborne northern invaders, be they Vandals or Visigoths or Vikings or Crusaders, the Portuguese were the first to place a garrison on African soil rather than sail away with their loot.

There was enormous pressure on the political leaders of North Africa to lead an army to expel these murderous invaders, a real, clear and unanswerable case for a just struggle, for *jihad*. Although the popular will was tangibly manifest and reflected by a series of thunderous sermons in the Friday mosques, political realities delayed any effective immediate response. The Portuguese had seized Ceuta not from the fractured Moroccan Merenid state but from the Nasrid dynasty of Muslim Granada. The Nasrids, who also held Gibraltar in this period, had made themselves many enemies in Morocco, for their interference had reduced the great Merenid Sultanate into three rival emirates, based on the cities of Fez, Meknes and Marrakesh. None of these rival emirs cared to lead an army away to the far-northern coast, giving their rivals an opportunity to stab them in the back. Also to be worked out was the question of future sovereignty. And who would become the master of a reconquered Muslim Ceuta? Should it be returned to the Nasrids of Granada or transferred to Morocco? While these issues were being resolved, the Portuguese had time to upgrade their defences.

Over the winter of 1418 the old Merenid Sultan of Fez, Abu Said Uthman, finally succeeded in patching up a truce with his uncle in Meknes and his cousin in Marrakesh. They agreed not only not to attack him while he was engaged in Holy War but to allow troops to be recruited from their territories. So in the spring of 1419 Sultan Abu Said himself was able to ride out from the walled city of Fez to take the field against the Christian enemy. He had also successfully negotiated with the Nasrid Sultan of Granada, who had waived all claims to Ceuta in the cause of religious unity. Abu Said's siege of the city had the appearance of a genuine holy war. As the chronicler Gomes Zurara reported, 'There came against Ceuta a great host of Moors, one hundred thousand strong . . . including peoples of the Kings of Fez and Granada, Tunis and Marrakesh and Bugis, with many engines of war and much artillery with which they thought to take Ceuta, encircling it by land and sea.' The tribes of the northern mountains were well represented in this counter-crusade, led by their caids (local governors) such as Muhammad of the Anjera and Yusuf of the Beni Arus, each in command of two thousand highlanders. But they were not alone in their ardour. Even the Moroccan ports on the Atlantic coast as far away as Safi and Anfa (as Casablanca was once called) sent five-hundred-strong regiments of volunteers, while from such rural provinces as the Haha (the western edge of the High Atlas mountains) a holy sheikh led ten thousand mujahidin volunteers into battle.

But the tide of history had turned, and the conflict was not to be won by the passions of thousands but by the skills of the few. Zurara reports on a decisive artillery duel right at the start of the siege: 'They tried to wear them down with that violent invention – the bombard. The Moors had two, a lot for them, the mainstays of this diabolical offensive. They shot at the walls but with no success because we brought up our own, and they were able to continue inflicting real damage . . . and as the enemy was repairing, a wily engineer fired his piece off so well that he bested the enemy's main gun, killed the gunner, and so adroitly suppressed the fire of the other that the Moors lost their guns.' Nor did it help that the commander of the Granadan force serving in the Moroccan army, Ali Ahmad, was ordered to return by his new emir, Muhammad VIII, who had just come to power through an army coup. The old Merenid Sultan, Abu Said, continued the siege deep into the winter. Many brave young warriors lost their lives during the repeated assaults on the city's walls, but the peculiar geography of the peninsula of Ceuta concentrates all possible landward attacks on a narrow neck of land where the Portuguese concentrated their bombards.

When the old Sultan at last rode back over the Rif mountains to Fez in midwinter, this city rang with the mourning cries of the women as they greeted the vanquished columns of men returning with news of many deaths. The Sultan retired to his palace outside the walls of the ancient city and never showed himself to his people until the day he was carried out, wrapped in a white shawl, to join his ancestors in the Merenid tombs whose roofless halls still overlook the city. He left a one-year-old son, Abdul Haq, as the last tragic scion of this talented dynasty. The real victor of the failed siege of Ceuta proved to be an ambitious young general named Abu Zakariya, who was at once a cousin of the infant Sultan, chief of the Beni Wattas tribe and governor of the Atlantic port of Rabat-Sale. He moved quickly to establish himself as regent in 1420, defeating a rival candidate whom the new Nasrid Emir of Granada had backed.

Prince Henry, who had just been made governor-general of Ceuta by his father, King John the Bastard, had been summoned to the aid of the besieged fortress in 1419. He arrived just after the fighting was over, but his delay had been for a good cause, for he brought with him the most up-to-date weaponry that Portugal could afford, '*bombardos, colobreta, beeistoris*' – cannon, wall-mounted light cannon and arbalesters – as well as '*troos*', the giant slings of medieval siege-craft. It was an impressive commitment and with it, and the arrival of Prince Henry, the heavy annual cost of the garrison passed from the royal treasury to that of the Order of Christ, the Crusading Order formed from the wreck of the Knights Templars.

The defence of Ceuta in 1419 had further boosted the reputation of Portugal in the eyes of Europe, and confirmed Prince Henry in his own sense of a peculiar destiny on this far frontier. In the aftermath of the siege he spent three months in the city which were partly devoted to questioning various Moorish and Jewish merchants about the nature of the lucrative trans-Saharan trade, most especially in West African gold. Where had it shifted to? And where did it originate? This was not the idle speculation of a theoretical geographer but the interested enquiries of a prince on the lookout for cash. In preparation for an imagined time when the trade returned to Ceuta, certain measures were put in place. The Casa de Ceuta was established to oversee all trade and check that the crown received its full due of customs. It was part of an attempt to make the new conquest 'wash its face', but unless trade returned to the port all would be in vain. Poor Portugal, which exported only olive oil, wine and salted cod, could not hope to compete with the merchants and manufactures of Catalonia, Venice and Genoa (who held a near-monopoly on the trade with Moorish Granada) nor with the keen-eyed traders of Flanders and the Hanseatic League in the Northern Seas. However, if it could secure access to the trans-Saharan gold trade this imbalance would be corrected at a single stroke. As Prince Henry looked south from the fortified walls of Ceuta he imagined a glowing future for

Prince Henry the Navigator. (Museum of Ancient Art at Lisbon)

his family and the kingdom. Surely it was Portugal's destiny, and its chance, to find out what lay just beyond the southern horizon?

Prince Henry pursued this line of inquiry all his life with a persistence, a sense of inner confidence and a dogged, pragmatic perseverance that is rare in princes, who by their very nature are distracted by a thousand different fashionable concerns. But his interest in exploration would now be no more than an intriguing footnote to maritime history (to be set beside England's two-hundred-year obsession with discovering a non-existent North-West Passage through the polar seas) if it had not borne spectacular fruit a hundred years later. For Portugal did succeed in carving out a great commercial empire for itself in the

Indian Ocean and the southern Atlantic, rising meteorically from being the poorest to become one of the richest kingdoms in Europe. In retrospect Prince Henry would be dubbed 'the Navigator' in honour of his laborious efforts which laid the foundations of this future achievement. Yet his personal travels were confined to the short stretch of water between Portugal and Morocco. His central motive was to tap into the gold trade while also hoping to find an ally in his fight against the Moroccans and so continue with his youthful crusade which had begun with the capture of Ceuta. A contemporary chronicler, Diego Gomes, states, 'At the time of the conquest of Ceuta, Prince Henry gained information from Moorish prisoners and others which led him to believe that the gold-producing lands lay south of the Sahara', which he tried to reach 'in order to trade with them and sustain the nobles of his household' (an opinion echoed in 1539 by the Portuguese chronicler John de Barros).

It was in the year after the successful defence of Ceuta that Prince Henry launched his first expedition to the south. As Commander of the Order of Christ he was doing in the Atlantic waters just what the Commander of the Knights of St John of the Hospital was doing in the eastern Mediterranean from their base of Rhodes. Each year he sent out the young knights and squires of his household to wage a form of naval war on the Muslim enemy. The surviving accounts of the first two decades of these expeditions reveal that their enthusiasm for the profitable activity of slave-raiding quite outdid their interest in geography. Prince Henry's genius lay in his ability to build with what he had to hand, so that the local boats of the Algarve coast were gradually strengthened in response to tougher conditions, while his crews became more confident. There was certainly no shortage of sailors in Portugal. It has been estimated that in this period at least 1 per cent of the active male population earned most of their subsistence by fishing, providing a pool of some thirty thousand experienced sailors from which to recruit.

There was also the expertise of the past upon which to draw. Prince Henry acquired maps and itineraries not only from Jewish and captive Moorish merchants, but also bought them directly from the Catalan and Majorcan map-makers who were working for Christian, Jewish and Muslim clients in the late fourteenth century. These cosmopolitan draughtsmen had already mapped the coast of North Africa and the Sudan to the south of the Sahara. And the Genoese, though potential rivals in this arena, had discovered (but not developed) in the twelfth and thirteenth centuries most of the nearby Atlantic islands which in an earlier era had been visited by the Carthaginians and the Romans. So much so that the Portuguese and Spanish captains only modestly claimed to have 'rediscovered' Madeira (1419), the Azores (in or around 1439) and Cape Verde (between 1456 and 1460).

Prince Henry also possessed sufficient resources, not through his royal birth but through the Order of Christ, which from 1319 had absorbed all the Templars' land-holdings and assets. In addition the order was awarded lucrative national monopolies, such as the right to trade in soap and fish, which could be profitably auctioned off to sub-licencees in a land where olive oil (the raw material of soap-making) and salted fish were the two staples of Portuguese trade.

So, between 1419 and 1434, Prince Henry was able to part-finance, part-commission some fifteen separate attempts to push the trade frontiers of Portugal to the south. After each attempt his young captains were interviewed about their experiences and discoveries, and the following year maps would be issued reflecting the new state of knowledge. But side by side with the formal knowledge that could be marked on charts and written up in *roteiros*, sailing directions, and followed by dead reckoning and compass, there was also a growth in the craft of the navigator. For example, how the cast, run and colour of the sea was a barometer of latitude to the experienced eye, and how debris drifting on the sea's surface could be read and the movements of fish, birds and seaweed analysed.

The Arab merchants settled on the coast of Morocco had little interest in exploring the Atlantic, which they called the 'Sea of Obscurity' and the 'Green Sea of Darkness'. For them the land route across the Sahara was more direct and safer. The progress of a series of freebooting Portuguese squadrons sailing south down the Moroccan coast during these years must have further discouraged any Arab trading ship from sailing too far from its haven. But it was not all one-sided, for the roles of prey and predator could be easily reversed. Indeed maritime records show that in this period some forty-six Portuguese ships were captured by corsairs on the Atlantic.[3]

For their part, the Portuguese sea captains were reluctant to cross the southern threshold marked by Cape Bojador (about two-thirds of the way down modern Morocco's long Atlantic coast), and with good reason. The last known expedition, by the Vivaldi brothers of Genoa in 1291, had never returned. It was widely feared that the very strong southern current that sweeps along the shore would frustrate any return. And to this day Cap Bojador marks a climatic, cultural and emotional frontier. For once Cape Noun is passed on the way south towards Bojador, all recognisable signs of Mediterranean life – trees, cultivation, farmland, villages, houses, man and goat – are gradually bleached out of the landscape, to be replaced by the savage intensity of the empty lands of the western Sahara. The region even lacks the customary grandeur of the desert, that romantic juxtaposition of dark mountains and golden sand dunes, and is instead composed of a series of bleak gravel uplands. The shoreline is awesomely sterile, overlooked by wind-eroded cliffs, protected by reefs and with the tidal reach of the rocky shore everywhere presenting a razor-like surface. In addition the whole region is made even more dangerous and impenetrable by salty sea mists, a dense, muggy intensity of climate and erratic compass fluctuations.

However, by 1434 one of the young squires of Prince Henry's household, urged on by words of affection from his master, rather than threats, did manage to break this psychological frontier. Throughout

A fifteenth-century Portuguese galley and caravel. A detail from the 1482 map drawn by Gratiosus Benincasa. (Bologna University Library)

the subsequent century of seafaring nothing halted the spread of Portuguese mariners across the oceans of the world, as Cape Bojador had. The breakthrough was the cumulative achievement of decades of unaccounted and unacknowledged work by shipwrights and observant sailors who had slowly transformed the traditional Arab-derived coastal craft of the Algarve into the lateen-rigged caravel. Together they created a craft strong enough to ride out oceanic storms but light enough to navigate estuaries and river mouths. It had the tactical ability to make use of the Atlantic winds and yet it could also be manned by a scratch crew of a dozen hands. This was the tool with which all the first great European explorers – Columbus, Magellan, Vasco da Gama – opened up the sea lanes of a new world.

In 1433 old King John the Bastard died, on the anniversary of his youthful victory. The accession to the throne of Henry's elder brother, the scholarly inclined Dom Duarte (Edward), allowed the two brothers to once again plot an 'enterprise' that would mirror the first dazzling success of their youthful crusade against Ceuta. Edward was the more cautious of the two, but Henry, as Commander of the Order of Christ, had little difficulty in securing a Bull of Absolution from the Pope for all who should die in the coming crusade. He also had an ally at court, in the shape of his sister-in-law Queen Leonor, a princess of Aragon, who wholeheartedly supported the plan. The brothers resolved to expand their dominion out of Ceuta and advance to conquer the neighbouring port of Tangier, as this would give them control of the whole southern shore of the Strait of Gibraltar. Otherwise, they feared, it would one day be totally dominated by Castile.

As in their youth, when their English mother had blessed them on her deathbed, this was to be a family affair. King Edward had responsibility for the fleet, Henry for the army and young Dom Fernando (Ferdinand) held command in Ceuta. Edward was as good as his word. The fleet sailed from Lisbon and landed the army on the wide bay of Tangier. It then took up position immediately off Tangier, to isolate the ancient white city, one of the great landmarks of the Strait of Gibraltar, perched within its walls on the edge of a rocky escarpment that overlooks a five-mile-long beach to the east. Prince Henry was in command on the ground, and his army gradually surrounded the city, occupying the low ground opposite its gates as well as the scrubby, wooded, higher land to the west. His cannon pounded away at the land walls, and a series of direct assaults were attempted. After the third attack was repelled it was realised that many more men and cannon of greater power were required.

Prince Henry requested his younger brother, Prince Ferdinand, to march to his support from Ceuta, having stripped the city's defences of its cannon, including two impressively large bombards. On a map this looks a straightforward enough request, though Henry should have known better than to suggest they advance overland. He was sending his brother to his death. The Portuguese column was forced to travel at the slow pace set by the ox-drawn cannon carts, which laboriously trundled their way across the convoluted foothills and mountains of the Moroccan coast. The Anjera tribes, who had two decades of experience in sniping at the Portuguese from behind their walls, rose to a man to oppose this invasion of their homeland.

Meanwhile the astute regent of Morocco, Abu Zakariya, recognised that the hour for revenge had arrived. He led the main Moroccan army up from Fez to assist the Anjera. Prince Ferdinand's advance ground to a halt, but there was no turning back. Isolated in the hills, his force was cut off, attacked and overwhelmed. The prince and all his artillery train were captured. During this time a veteran Moroccan officer, Caid Salah ibn Salah, who commanded the defence of Tangier, had also begun to organise the resistance of the neighbouring hill tribes. Raids were launched against the Portuguese siege lines much assisted by the loan of some light cannon from Granada. As the triumphant army of Abu Zakariya advanced from the east, the five-thousand-strong Portuguese army, which had once encircled Tangier, was itself surrounded. The besiegers were besieged; not only from the walls of Tangier, but by the hill tribes and Abu Zakariya's army. The situation only became desperate when their escape route to the fleet still standing off the Bay of Tangier was threatened. Moroccan cavalry raided the foreshore and a battery of cannon began to find the range of the Portuguese ships and drive them from their anchorages.

Facing the prospect of annihilation, Prince Henry was forced to sue for terms. Given his complete and utter vulnerability, he agreed to the shameful abandonment of all his siege artillery and a solemn undertaking to surrender Ceuta back to the Moroccans, a pledge guaranteed by the retention of Ferdinand as a hostage. Although these concessions bought off the Moroccan royal army, the Portuguese still had to suffer the vengeance of the Berber hill tribes. The humiliated Crusaders were forced to fight their way down through lines of Anjera before they reached the safety of the shore and their boats.

In the autumn of 1437 the Moroccan army and its tribal allies marched back to a triumphant welcome from the citizens of Fez. Abu Zakariya, the victorious regent, formally resigned his powers, returning them to his charge, the Merenid Abdul Haq. The first decision of the new Sultan was to appoint the old regent his grand vizier, an office which he successfully filled until his death in 1448. The captive Prince Ferdinand was lodged in the guard chamber above the main gateway into the royal palace of the Sultans. Here he patiently waited for his elder brothers to fulfil their treaty oath and arrange his release by returning the fortress of Ceuta to Morocco.

In Portugal, King Edward was too overwhelmed by the catastrophe of Tangier to make decisions. Having waited all his life as a powerless crown prince in the shadow of his charismatic father, King John, who had reigned until his seventy-seventh year, Edward was ill prepared for the reality of statecraft. He had filled those long years studying political philosophy, creating in his book *Leal Conselheiro* a blueprint for an ideal society in which each order harmoniously performed its allotted tasks under the bright dominion of a scholar-king. Now his dream lay shattered. His soul was tortured by the fate of his younger brother held in Fez, yet he was incapable of compounding the defeat outside Tangier with the surrender of Ceuta. Sickened with remorse and regrets, he was buried within a year, leaving behind a six-year-old son, Afonso, and a widowed queen. Prince Henry also felt the disgrace most bitterly and retired to the seclusion of his villa at Sagres on the Algarve coast. It was left to the fourth brother, Dom Pedro (Peter), to contest for the royal authority with the Count of Barcellos (a bastard but a true heir to the vitality and energy of old King John). Peter emerged as regent for young Afonso and tried to console his half-brother by raising him to become Duke of Braganza,[4] in northern Portugal.

Peter was well travelled: as a young man he had voyaged north to England, staying with his cousin Humphrey, Duke of Gloucester, before crossing the Channel to visit the cities of Flanders. He then spent two years at the court of the Holy Roman Emperor Sigismund which included serving in a campaign against the Ottoman Turks. From there he made a tour through Italy, picking up a Papal Bull for his father, a copy of Marco Polo's travels and some brand-new maps in Venice, where he was also given an extensive tour and a training session in the Arsenale, the naval dockyards. He returned to Portugal with just a day in hand to prepare for the wedding of his elder brother Edward. His travels had shown him enough of the world for him to ever after oppose military adventurism, and champion trade and diplomacy.

He also worked with tact and enthusiasm to assist and extend his brother Henry's work. His travels had shown him how well the city-states of Venice and Genoa had prospered by following an adaptable policy of peaceful trade rather than armed crusading. These were to be the role models for Portugal under Peter's regency. Signed agreements were made to allow trade with a string of towns on the Atlantic coast of Morocco. Maghrebi textiles, embroideries, weavings, fine leatherwork and the superb breed of Barbary horses were in constant demand throughout Europe, as were the more exotic staples of the caravan trade: slaves, gold dust, ebony, ivory, African spices, scents and peppers. At this time Morocco also exported its surplus wheat, sugar and saltpetre, the vital ingredient of gunpowder.

Peter might have been enlightened but he also remained a realist. Portugal would keep Ceuta come what may, and while Genoa might be a role model he was also quietly determined to elbow the Genoese out of the burgeoning Atlantic trade. The skills of the Genoese captains and merchants were too vital to ignore, but they would sail under Portuguese licence and under the Portuguese flag, not the Genoese Cross of St George. Where capital and expertise were needed, he also looked to Flanders to balance the enormous influence of Genoa. This policy worked so well that the new Portuguese territory of the Azores was soon nicknamed 'the Flemish Isles'.

In the far south, Prince Henry's captains at last struck rich by making contact with the West African gold trade. We know that gold dust was being bartered from Saharan traders in 1442, and just five years later a regular trade in gold and Negro slaves had been opened up along the coast of Senegal. By 1457 there were sufficient stocks of gold in Lisbon for the Portuguese to strike their own coinage. For a hundred years the *cruzado* (crusade) was a coin of quite exceptional purity and quality, standing proudly beside the Florentine florin (first struck 1252) and the Venetian ducat (first struck 1280). Portugal could now acquire any-thing it needed or desired from the rest of the world.

It is estimated that in the next hundred years as much gold dust was bought by Portuguese merchants in West Africa as was being acquired by the Moorish merchants of North Africa in such Saharan trading cities as Timbuktu and Gao. The captains of the caravel achieved parity with the emirs of the camel caravan. Between 1450 and 1500 some 150,000 slaves were shipped out of West Africa in Portuguese hulls. Before the plantation estates of Brazil and the Caribbean had been established slaves were sold into the domestic market of Europe, to become prestige household servants, nursemaids, footmen, guards and concubines for the fashion-conscious citizens of Flanders and Italy. Within a few years the bloodline of the West African coast would mingle with that of the *haute bourgeoisie* of Christendom, be it the Fuggers, the Medici or the Sforza, all of whose family trees feature scions nicknamed 'El Moro' from the handsome mix of blood. At this time the household of the Spanish Duke of Medina Sidonia boasted forty blacks among a staff of ninety-five slaves. In this period there was little prejudice against the offspring of mixed-race marriages, be the household slaves sourced from Africa, southern Russia or the Levant. Leonardo da Vinci can be numbered among the many such successful mulatto children of this period, for he was the child of a master-crafts-man named Piero and Caterina, who came into this Tuscan household as a foreign slave girl.

The Portuguese, buoyed up by these profits, attempted to develop the coastal trade in West Africa by progressing into the interior. A long and sustained attempt was made to send embassies and explorers up-country, much as the British tried some three hundred years later with Mungo Park, a young Scottish doctor. But these envoys died off in their droves, killed by disease and the distance. They quested after the source of the gold, but in truth there was no great central mine waiting to be discovered. The gold dust was mined from alluvial beds in small jungle clearings in almost inaccessible regions of the headwaters of the Upper Volta, Upper Niger and Upper Senegal rivers. The gravel of these ancient riverbeds was panned, and some subterranean shafts were sunk to extract the richest deposits of gravel, though the broken nature of the ground frustrated more ambitious endeavours. There was no need for the expensive mills, chemical slakings and furnaces which would have attracted the attention of interested outsiders. As a result the miners kept their liberty and their freedom to work where and when they desired. The tiny grains of gold were customarily packed into quills and sold downriver, down the slow-moving Niger towards the great Sahelian kingdoms such as Songhai or such coastal kingdoms as Benin.

Some of the very toughest of these early Portuguese explorers (especially those recruited from the *degredados*, exiled criminals) survived and many decided to bid farewell to Europe and settle in up-country villages, working beside the chiefs and headmen, taking local wives and learning the language and customs. Known as *lanados*, these predecessors of Kurtz in Joseph Conrad's *Heart of Darkness* became a vital link in the chain of trade that connected the coast to the upriver communities. The pidgin Portuguese they used became one of the *linguas francas* of West African trade. The Portuguese crown, fearing a loss of income owing to the success of local traders, decided to build a fortress at Arguim, with a governor and a garrison to watch over the West African coastal trade. The local chiefs, who did not like this development at all, made it clear that they liked the Portuguese best when they came to do business and then returned home quickly. They liked them when they came ragged and ill-dressed, hungry for profits, and instinctively distrusted this new type: this castle-building breed of elegant, salaried officials with their well-armed guards. But the primary purpose of the new fort was to discipline the Portuguese, not the native chiefs. It was an impossible task. A generation later Lisbon would formally condemn to death all unlicensed free traders in West Africa as 'apostates', though their crime, other than the failure to pay tax to the crown, was not heretical.

The 1450s and 1460s were the financial heyday of the court of Prince Henry the Navigator, supported by his clever brother, the Prince regent, Peter. For in this period the Crusading Order of Christ continued to keep a careful and watchful eye over the African trade that it had nurtured. This position was confirmed by a Papal Bull of 1456 which recognised that the conquest, commerce and spiritual jurisdiction of the Saracens of the West remained a monopoly of the Portuguese Order of Christ. Prince Henry, for his part, remained true to the complicated heritage of Iberia by retaining a fifth of all profits, a tradition he inherited from the Moors, who in turn had followed the example established by the Prophet Muhammad.

It is in the last decade of his life that we can best imagine Prince Henry in his legendary role. The hermit prince, divorced from public life at Lisbon yet running a state within a state, the fledgling maritime empire of Portugal. According to the traditional account, he constructed an academy of navigation and exploration as well as a chapel beside his villa at Sagres, which stood within the walls of an old Moorish fort. This outpost of Europe, at the extreme south-west corner of Portugal, overlooking Cape St Vincent, was the destination of a steady trickle of outlandish scholars, adventurers and tyro explorers coming to make a pitch for funds or to meet the living legend. One can but try to picture this extraordinary man, conversing with map-makers from Majorca, captains back from the African coast, shipwrights from the neighbouring ports of Algarve, gay young squires of his household, sombre celibate knights of the Crusading Order of Christ, gun-masters returning from a spell of duty keeping watch on the walls of Ceuta, envoys from his brother the Prince regent, ambassadors from the Moroccan Sultan in Fez and delegates from the Portuguese traders based in the Moroccan port of Safi. In the background wait astrologers, astronomers, designers of compasses and star charts, publishers of travel narratives, while his clerks stare mournfully at correspondence from veterans wounded at Tangier or the pitiful letters of his imprisoned younger brother.

There are eyewitness accounts of Henry from Venetian writers such as Cadamosto, who described meeting the Prince: 'When he had news of us, he sent one of his secretaries . . . with samples of sugar from Madeira, dragon's blood and other products of his domains and islands. These he displayed in my presence to many on the galleys. His Lord, he said, had peopled newly discovered islands previously uninhabited and caused seas to be navigated which had never been sailed. He had discovered the lands of many strange races, where marvels abounded.' Then Cadamosto was taken into a corner and invited to become a merchant venturer under the Prince's flag. Henry would take a quarter share in all the returning cargo if Cadamosto provided his own ship and trade goods, or half if the Prince lent him a caravel. Fortunately Cadamosto took up the offer, not just once but twice. He has left us a description of early West Africa trade, free from the official-speak of the Portuguese royal chroniclers and full of enchanting details. He describes the taste of elephant flesh, gives us the first Western description of the Tuareg males' veil, tells of the poor pickings of a merchant confined to the River Gambia, 'just cotton cloth and thread', and the spectacular abasement, crawling naked through the dust, expected of those who approached the great Negro kings of West Africa with a petition to trade.

The Prince was also preoccupied with finding Prester John, a Christian monarch of the lands of the South or the East, who was greatly desired as a potential ally in the fight against the Moors. There was much confusion about this near-legendary Christian Lord, for there was always a wished-for element of deliverance which never matched the known diplomatic facts of the time. For there was a real-life Prester John already in existence, the embattled Christian King of Abyssinia, who for years had been in correspondence with various Iberian monarchs (one such letter is known to have been sent from Abyssinia to Afonso of Aragon in 1426). Yet at the same time there was a temptation to conjure up another, more powerful Prester John, some Timur-like conqueror coming out of the East at the head of an army of hundreds of thousands of knights to slaughter the armies of the Grand Turk, the Saracen and the Moors. This Prester John of the dreamworld fed thirty thousand people a night at his table, with twelve archbishops seated on his right hand and twenty-four bishops on his left. He was the creation of a hundred years of wish-fulfilment, married to reliable reports from Franciscan missionaries reporting on the Nestorian Christians of Central Asia, from Syrian Thomasite Christians in India and from Monophysite Copts in Egypt, the Sudan and Ethiopia. But dreams can inspire even more powerfully than the truth. When the Portuguese did reach India, they met on the harbour front two Moorish merchants from Tunis who asked in astonishment, 'What the devil has brought you here?', for they knew them of old from travelling among the ports of the Mediterranean. They answered, 'We seek Christians and spices', for the Portuguese, even after the death of Henry the Navigator, still sought out Christian allies with whom they might continue the crusade that had started at Ceuta.

Henry the Navigator's lifelong quest for the friendship with the mythical Prester John remains a potent story but it must be balanced, for Henry was also a man of his own time. Although he spent much time at Sagres and the Algarve, there were other demands on his time. He visited the royal court at its countryside retreats outside Lisbon, in Santarem and Setúbal; he needed to inspect his agricultural estate at Raposeira, stayed at another favourite villa – that of Nossa Senhora de Guadalupe as well as his town house in Lagos, not to mention some time spent with the bastard he fathered (whom he eventually rejected in favour of a nephew in his will) and needed, as active Commander of the Crusading Order of Christ, to regularly attend its headquarters at Tomar.

The rivalry for the regency that had existed between Peter and the Duke of Braganza was reignited once Afonso assumed the crown for himself on his fourteenth birthday. Like young Prince Hamlet, Afonso found himself speculating about the death of his father, which he was persuaded had been the work of his uncle, the regent. Peter was banished from court and when he tried to return to argue his case in Lisbon before the young King, in a city in which he was well loved for his good governance, the Duke of Braganza feared the result. An incident was arranged near the banks of the River Tagus which left Peter and his chief companions dead on the road after they 'resisted arrest'.

Prince Henry, despite his affection for his brother, adapted to the new regime with ease. Indeed he and his nephew, young King Afonso the African, found that they shared a great passion for the concept of the crusade, and anything that smacked of knightly daring and chivalry. The pair of them were totally enchanted by the descriptions of the courtly behaviour of the Duke of Burgundy, and vowed to join him on the crusade. All Christendom was astir with the news of the fall of Constantinople in 1453. The fortunes that were pouring into Lisbon from the West African trade were invested in the very latest arms, for descriptions of the fabulous artillery of Sultan Mehmet had also been circulated in Christendom. The standard wrought-iron ordnance was rejected in favour of the brass and bronze casting that Sultan Mehmet's engineers had achieved. Range, rate of fire and accuracy were all greatly improved, and a new post at court, Constable of the King's Artillery, was created to oversee the expanded arsenal, the gunpowder mills and the training of both foundry-masters and artillerymen. Initially these were all highly paid foreign technicians mostly recruited from Flanders and Germany on fixed contracts.

Prince Henry and the young King composed a letter to the Ottoman Sultan in the form of a knightly challenge, with which they were delighted. They worried that it might not be delivered in its entirety, so they had it copied in triplicate and sent by different routes. There was no reply. They made approaches to the great Italian city-states. The Venetians and Genoese, then under enormous pressure from the Ottomans, had no wish to be involved in the scheme. Deprived of their principal adversary, Prince Henry and King Afonso wished nevertheless to make use of the army they had assembled. Tangier was suggested as an objective, but memories of the recent defeat blew a breath of ill-omened air over such an enterprise. Instead an armada of two hundred ships, carrying twenty-five thousand men, struck at the little settlement of Ksar es Seghir (Alcazar Seguir), the 'Castle of the Crossing'. This was celebrated as the site of Tariq's invasion of Spain some seven hundred years before, but was otherwise a pretty but insignificant town, sited above a lovely bay and overlooked by hills.

The Portuguese invasion of Ksar es Seghir in October 1458 was an instance of massive overkill. Gunfire from the fleet devastated the Moroccan troops who had massed amid the surf to defend their home-land. Prince Henry was among the first to land as the light cannon were efficiently trundled ashore. A beachhead was established and in the morning cannon blew apart the gates, though it would be another three days before the last Moroccan soldiers were cleared from the town and its walls. Surviving descriptions clearly give credit to the overwhelming fire-power of the Portuguese, their wall-smashing bombards supported by ship-borne cannon. The technical efficiency of the victory was so complete and decisive that King Afonso the African was able to be back in Lisbon within the week. The old Moorish town was then rebuilt as a fortress.

The very splendid ruined castle that still sits in the bay is entirely the creation of the Portuguese, who carefully raised a new church over the ancient old mosque with its brick-tiled floor. It is a masterpiece of late-medieval architecture, with its long, double walls reaching right down to the shore. It was guarded by towers that were sturdy enough to house much of the expensive new ordnance that Afonso had com-missioned. The new governor, Dom Duarte de Meneses, mounted thirty-two new bombards on the castle walls, cutting brutal and devas-tating swaths through the ranks of the Moroccan army when it attempted to recapture Ksar es Seghir in 1459. This was not such an unequal contest, for the Moroccans attempted to divide the resources of their enemy by mounting a simultaneous attack on Ceuta and were able to bring up an impressive siege battery against Ksar es Seghir which included some of the Portuguese cannon they had captured outside Tangier in 1437. They also had the resources to sustain a two-month bombardment, with an average of thirty shots a day from each of their cannon. However, they were kept out of effective range, for, as Dom Duarte de Meneses reported, '[we] taught the Moors to fear the artillery on our walls'.

The year of the Moroccan counter-attack saw Prince Henry once again back in the Algarve, organising and overseeing the departure of caravels to West Africa, one of which took an abbot for the conversion of a useful West African ally, Numimansa, who expressed genuine enthusiasm for the Christian faith.

The following year, 1460, the old Crusader Prince died at the age of sixty-seven. After his death Henry's financial affairs were found to be such a morass of debts, mortgages, advance pledging of concessions and private loans that it is said to have taken nine years for the full extent of his liabilities, assets and investments to be unravelled and reconciled. In the meantime an enterprising merchant took out a lease from the King. Eventually the Prince's and the Order of Christ's trading empire was transformed into the Casa da Mina, the House of Mines, a highly lucrative branch of the crown's estate which was lodged on the ground floor of the Royal Palace in Lisbon, alongside the Tagus, so that the Kings of Portugal could personally oversee the loading and unloading of the caravels from West Africa.

Prince Henry was buried in the monastery chapel of Santa Maria da Vitoria, in the Abbey of Batalha, a monument to his father King John's day of grace on the field of Aljubarrota. It had been partly designed by Henry's mother Philippa, who imported masons from her homeland. Their exuberant carving brings a touch of English Gothic to the cloisters and chantry chapel. Henry lies beside his cultured English mother and his talented father, founder of the Avis dynasty and quite literally a murdering bastard. To both he was a faithful son.

2

The Navigator's Nephew

King Afonso the African, 1455–81,
and King John II, 1481–95

I charge thee, fling away ambition;
By that sin fell the angels

Shakespeare, *Henry VIII*

The last act of Prince Henry the Navigator had been to assist his young
nephew, King Afonso V, in the conquest of the Moroccan port of Ksar
es Seghir in 1458. The successful defence of its new fortress against a
determined attempt to recapture it furthered Portugal's reputation
within Christendom. Most especially as the news from other frontiers
of Christendom was all bad – be it the smoking ruins of Constantinople,
the Black Sea coast, the Aegean islands, the Greek mainland or such
Balkan kingdoms as Serbia. The armies of the Ottoman Empire under
the leadership of Mehmet the Conqueror were pursuing a near-inexo-
rable advance. So that one by one, many of the most famous Christian
cities, crowns and thrones were falling into the hands of the Muslims.

King Afonso was never able to recover from the glory of this successful crusading enterprise, so much so that he would be nicknamed 'the
African' by his people. His old uncle seems to have bequeathed his own
obsession with crusading to the young King, who for his part encouraged his court chroniclers to expunge the achievements of the late
prince regent, Peter, and heap all the credit for the Portuguese discoveries and growth in trade on Uncle Henry the Navigator.

Historians, moderns as well as the old chroniclers, cannot but disapprove of Afonso the African, who was obsessed with knight-errantry, indifferent to the class of merchant venturers who were transforming the Portuguese economy and over-zealous to appear charming and generous to the nobles of his kingdom. In this he was the antithesis of his tough-minded grandfather and his uncle, the regent, both men of great talent, purpose and achievement. But it was not how Afonso was rated by contemporaries in the first half of his reign. Then he appeared to be one of the defining heroes of Christendom. He was the one monarch who had been genuinely sincere in his vow to march east at the head of his knights in an attempt to recapture Constantinople. Indeed it was said that, despite the defection of all the other kings of Europe, he remained steadfast in this desire until the death of Pope Callixtus III on 6 August 1458 ended all hope of this Crusade. Only after this was confirmed did he turn his army south and (right at the dangerous end of the sailing season) seize Ksar es Seghir from the Moors that October. Enterprising young men from the length and breadth of Europe made their way to his court and volunteered to fight beneath his flag.

The travel diary of one of these gentleman adventurers, Jorg von Ehingen, has survived to offer us a vivid insight into the mentality of King Afonso's contemporaries.[1] Ehingen, despite his ardent desire to advance himself in the world by killing people in wars, comes across as an endearing individual. He was born in 1428, growing up as one among a hundred young cousins who were packed into the old family castle of Hohenentringen. It had been subdivided into a rabbit warren of apartments by the five different families of heirs. It was said that when the Ehingen children walked out to take mass in the village church, the first child was already in his seat before the last had passed through the castle gates. Jorg sought his living in the outside world, serving as a page in various ducal courts in Austria before advancing to the status of a free knight with his own string of three horses. He then served with the Knights of St John in Rhodes on his way to take the pilgrimage to Jerusalem. If a mathematical calculation can be made between the spiritual and martial motivations of such a journey, the fifteen days he spent as a pilgrim in the Holy City should be set against the four hundred days he spent as a volunteer soldier with the Knights.

Jorg's travels eventually took him to Finisterre, where, guided by the

Jacobsbrüder, a professional group of backpacker-like pilgrim guides who walked the roads that led to and from Compostella, he took ship to Lisbon with his precious war-horses. Here he was overwhelmed by the courtesy of the people and their young King, who asked Jorg to stay on 'in order to learn something more of his country' before they went to war 'against the infidel king of Fez'. Jorg's account excitedly recalls:

> he caused us to be escorted back to our Inn, and commanded the lords and nobles to lend us their company, which also happened. And such were the honours and merry-makings that the like can never be seen by any king or prince. We were also introduced frequently into the apartments of the Queen's ladies, where many beautiful dances were held. Then to the chase, with jumping, wrestling, throwing, fencing, and racing with horses and jennets, and there was also much feasting. It was indeed delightful to be there. The King was named Afonso. He was a handsome, well-grown prince, the most Christian, the worthiest, the most righteous King I have ever known . . .

Before they left for the front line

> the King gave each of us a strong jennet, and to each of our attendants a suit of tilting-armour called *brigadin* . . . On the night we arrived at Ceuta the whole company assembled in a vast square with armour and weapons at hand, and that night many messages were received, reporting that the infidels were approaching in great numbers. But though by day and night we heard the noise of many troops, and we could see them before the town, the main army had [still] not arrived.

Jorg was then sent on a dangerous scouting mission, to try to work out the size of the besieging army, before returning to the fortress to make his report. He tells us:

> it should be known that Ceuta is a great and broad town and three parts of it face the land, and one part lies on the water[2] . . . on the land side are dry ditches, in which a citadel has been erected with a number of separate towers, provided with embra-

sures below and protected above with tin, and surrounded on the
town side by a wall . . . The Captain was stationed there with a
vast number of light horsemen, while a host of the ablest footmen had been placed between the citadel and the wall, with
orders, if need arose, to spring mines and proceed as they might
be directed . . . at sunrise, the watchers on the towers gave warning and cried aloud that the infidels were drawing near in great
numbers. At this each man seized his weapon. Then we saw the
infidels crossing a mountain, which lay in front of the town, and
indeed the whole mountain seemed to be covered with men. We
shot at them with our bombards . . . but they drew near to the
ditches, being armed with hand-bows and curious long crossbows . . . They assailed us with these and with bombards, and
shot at us all that day whenever any one exposed himself, and
while they engaged us, they set the main army in array. They had
also many drums, great and small, and strange horns, and banners and flags without number. Thus we fought all day, and many
of the infidels were shot, and we also had many wounded, for the
enemy approached quite close to us into the ditches. The night
was even more disturbed, for then they came closer still, with
long wooden implements . . . they stormed us for three days in
succession, commencing at daybreak and continuing into the
night. Then, indeed, there was much labour on both sides, and
although countless numbers of infidels were shot and thrown
down about the town, in the ditches and by the walls, it happened also frequently that the Christians were repulsed by attacks
when the Captain was not ready with his counter-attack, and we
were therefore in great difficulties. But when the infidels had
assailed us for three days, as before mentioned, and had lost an
extraordinary number of men, an evil stink arose from the dead
bodies, and they ceased their attacks and withdrew.

The Portuguese cavalry, topped up by volunteers and quick-marching
foot-soldiers, then sallied out of the walls to follow the Moroccans into
the hills, who turned back frequently to skirmish. At one point the
Portuguese force, which numbered about fourteen hundred men, was
camped on one hill and the vanguard of the Moroccans on another,
with a fine level plain stretching between them. Then, like some unbe-

lievable scene of chivalry from a Book of Hours, a champion rode out
from the Moroccan lines, and Jorg took up the challenge: 'I rode from
our army . . . Our captain also sent out a trumpeter, who blew a blast
and gave the signal. Then very speedily one of the infidels appeared,
riding across the plain on a fine Barbary steed.' First they jousted at
each other, and struck such fearsome blows they were both forced to
dismount, though the horses were uninjured. The two beasts stood side
by side, having been worked hard all day, and were quite quiet. The two
warriors then hacked away at each other with their swords, but their
armour was excellent and neither received any injury. 'We then gripped
each other and wrestled so long that we fell to the ground side by side.
But the infidel was a man of amazing strength. He tore himself from
my grasp, and we both raised our bodies until we were kneeling side by
side.' Eventually Jorg managed to land a cut on the face of his opponent, who, half-blinded with blood, was then hurled to the ground and
stabbed to death through the throat. Jorg was the hero of the hour,
though the duel was in fact no more than the opening round to a day
of brutal fighting in which 'great numbers of men and horses were
wounded and shot down'. At the end of it he was paraded through the
streets of Ceuta, preceded by a trumpeter and his adversary's head,
which had been hacked off and impaled on his own spear. When King
Afonso read the Portuguese captain's report of this heroic deed he summoned the young knight back to Lisbon and presented him with 'a
bowl filled with Portuguese *gilden*, which bowl I brought back with me
to my fatherland'.

It would seem to be a classic traveller's tale – entertaining but surely
embellished – if we hadn't by chance also got independent evidence.
The memoirs of another volunteer from Middle Europe, a doctor from
Nuremberg named Hieronymus Münzer, corroborate Jorg's account,
for he recalled a Georgius de Echingen who 'divided with his sword a
certain Saracen, a very strongly armed knight, through the middle and
took his sword away from him, leaving another to the Portuguese'. This
commentator also tells how there were eight hundred Christian volunteers at Ceuta that year, how the besieging army of forty thousand[3]
made use of shield-ladders made of the bark of oaks and how a man
from Salzburg 'with his subtle mind' made what sounds like shrapnel
bombs by packing iron triangles and gunpowder into large jars of semi-
baked clay. These 'he caused to be cast outside the walls into the midst

of the Saracens [who] received great damage'.

The fearsome siege of Ceuta, which drew thousands of heroic volunteers from the length of Europe and the breadth of North Africa to fight to the death in the ditches and moats, was just one of many hundreds of such conflicts taking place at this time. Despite the carnage we have just heard about, it hardly merits a mention in the histories of either Portugal or Morocco, but probably took place in the year which the Portuguese chronicler Ruy de Pina dismissed as a siege in which 'the King of Fez did no more than look at Ceuta'. Some look. But what the world deems worthy of remembering is so often a matter of chance, some colourful detail, such as a mid-morning duel, rather than the killing of thousands of innocents. For Jorg von Ehingen briefly reports how, in the wars against the Moors, 'We had therefore to storm the majority of the towns and castles, and we slew all the infidels. The rank and file had orders to kill the women and children, which was done.' What ghastly scenes of mass murder lie behind such crisp, taciturn sentences? And how often such acts must have occurred if even a passing volunteer like Jorg remembers in his memoir that 'during this time

King Afonso V of Portugal. From a set of nine coloured drawings, probably made in 1455 to embellish the manuscript of Jorg von Ehingen's travel diary.

there were many knightly enterprises in Africa, wherein I and my companion did our best against the infidels and Moors'.

In 1460, in 1463 and in 1464 King Afonso led or directed invasions in repeated attempts to seize the city of Tangier. These were supplemented by a series of destructive, Viking-like descents upon the coastal cities of Morocco, their merchants and citizens, at Asilah, Larache, Tetouan, Massa and Safi. In 1467 Tangier was once again bombarded, and the following year he hit Anfa, on the pretext that the city fathers had placed an embargo on selling grain to Portuguese merchants. As Leo Africanus reports, it 'always had great commerce with Portuguese and Englishmen . . . it was too free-spirited . . . Fifty sail, armed with big guns, were sent against Anfa . . . The fleet-commander . . . took his soldiers into the city which – in one day's time – they so defaced, burning house and flattering walls, that Anfa remains a ghost town now. I could hardly hold back tears when I saw its ruin.'

In August 1471 Afonso, at the head of a vast armada of four hundred ships carrying an army of thirty thousand, fell upon the port-city of Asilah. In a rerun of the events of Ksar es Seghir, the ships' cannon cleared the shore to allow for the safe landing of the invaders. But a sudden shift in wind threatened to dash the fleet on to the offshore reefs, which, flecked with foam and breaking surf, can still be seen off the port. Several of the small landing boats were broken on these rocks, and two hundred soldiers were drowned, before a safe landing was effected. But then the well-drilled invasion force swung into action. As depicted on a series of tapestries still hanging in Lisbon, by the end of the day twelve large bombards (their gunners protected from enemy fire by wicker drums packed with earth) had begun to pound the walls. After four days they succeeded in breaking a way through the walls and the gatehouses of Asilah. That model of Christian chivalry, King Afonso, refused to countenance an offer of surrender from the governor, so the city fell by storm, the garrison holding out in the Kasbah and the neighbouring mosque until the last man was cut down. In what was becoming something of a Portuguese tradition, Afonso dubbed his son Prince John a Knight of the Order of Christ among the smouldering wreck of a sacked Muslim city.

The leading Wattasid Emir, who had left both his family and his treasure in Asilah, hurriedly marched his men from Fez when he heard of the attack. But news of the sack of the city and the massacre of its garrison reached him while he was only halfway to the coast – and Afonso had the ideal bargaining counter. The Emir's family was returned to him in exchange for a truce which left each side in possession of what they held. Once Afonso was certain that the Emir had kept his word and was once again deeply embroiled in internal affairs back in Fez, he broke his. He ordered the Portuguese army to race north at a double-quick march towards Tangier. Although the city had successfully resisted half a dozen Portuguese attacks over the past thirty years, the terrifying stories of what had befallen the people of Asilah during its sack, and the pseudo-truce with the Wattasid Emir, had undermined its warlike spirit. Tangier sued for terms and opened its gates to the vanguard of Portuguese cavalry under the command of the Duke of Braganza's young son. King Afonso's triumph was total, and he returned to Lisbon as master of four Moroccan cities: Ceuta, Ksar es Seghir, Asilah and Tangier. He had even negotiated for the successful return of the bones of his imprisoned uncle, poor old Prince Ferdinand. He took the epithet Africanus, was compared by flattering courtiers to a second Scipio and rejoiced in the title 'King of Portugal and the two Algarves, both on this side and beyond the sea'.

Yet even in Ruy de Pina's sympathetic description there is a hint of instability lurking within this passionate Crusader King:

> Dom Afonso was a little overburdened with flesh, to conceal which he was wont to wear loose garments. He had a round face with a strong black beard, and all his body was hairy save his head, for he had began to grow bald as soon as he was thirty years old . . . He was the first king of these realms who collected good books and formed a library in his palace. He was also the first king who made himself a familiar sight to all in public places of the cities and towns of his kingdoms . . . he had so much confidence in his own judgement that he would with difficulty let his will be crossed by the counsel of others, especially in the matter of the war against the Moors, to which he was so eagerly inclined that his wishes seemed to him to be urgent reasons . . . And being a most courageous and stout-hearted prince, he was ever eager to undertake some arduous enterprise, to be achieved by arms as became a knight, rather than to busy himself as a king in the civil and political government of his kingdom.

Another report, by a visiting noble from Bohemia, might suggest either that Afonso was losing his grip on reality or that the visitor never quite understood the point of a siesta: 'The King was not easy to approach, for when the sun was up he lay indoors, and when the sun had gone to rest he rode abroad with his counts and lords until after midnight. Their clothes and appearance are after the Spanish and infidel fashion . . . boots to the knee; his sword was hung over his neck by a broad band, and his mantel flung over his shoulder.'

In 1474 a call for help came to King Afonso, who, being inclined to knight-errantry, could not resist responding to this dangerous invitation. Henry IV of Castile died and left a will which called upon Afonso to champion the cause of his presumed daughter and heiress, Princess Juana, marry her and govern Castile in her name. There were, however, a number of complications of comic-opera complexity. To begin with, Henry IV had been divorced by his first wife for sexual impotence and his second wife (Afonso's sister) was a light-hearted, fun-loving Portuguese princess. When she had given birth to Juana only a few believed that the child had been fathered by Henry IV. Instead Juana was widely referred to as 'La Beltranja' after her likely father, Don Beltran de la Cueva, a handsome and attentive courtier.

To add to the disgust of the Castilian nobility, Henry IV appeared to be as infatuated with the man who had cuckolded him as his wife was. Don Beltran was showered with honours: after being made Count of Ledesma, then Master of the Crusading Order of Santiago, he was promoted to become Duke of Albuquerque. An opposition faction tried to force the King to divorce his Portuguese wife, repudiate Juana and formally accept his half-sister Isabella as the legitimate heir to the kingdom. He half-agreed to do this, but was then so annoyed by his half-sister's secret marriage to the crown prince of Aragon that he changed his mind, then relented, then, in 1474, died leaving a will that called on King Afonso of Portugal to sort it all out.

So when Afonso decided to invade Castile to champion the rights of his niece Juana against the already crowned Queen Isabella, it did not require a political genius to see that all would not end well. Portugal and Aragon were dragged on to opposing sides of the Castilian War of Succession of 1474–9. Not that this Spanish civil war was particularly bloodthirsty, for despite the military columns that criss-crossed the Castilian countryside from both Portugal and Aragon, on both sides

there was a distinct lack of zeal to bring the matter to the decisive conclusion of a battle. Two armies, assisted and distracted by their various
Castilian allies, circled round each other (in the region framed by
Burgos, Toro and Zamora) for a year and a half. The contrast with the
bloody devastation that Afonso had inflicted time and time again on his
other neighbour, Morocco, could not have been more acute. As was his
behaviour at the Battle of Toro.

This was not a set-piece battle but a highly confusing series of broken
engagements fought over a misty day and night around a rain-drenched
river crossing. At the end of the second day the famously bellicose
Portuguese King was found to have left the field of battle to take refuge
in a castle. Fortunately Prince John took command and saved the
honour of Portugal and managed to turn Toro into a stalemate. Afonso's
desertion was just the beginning of an ever more bizarre pattern of
behaviour. First he abandoned his army to go and talk to King Louis XI
of France. Having pursued his increasingly embarrassed host around
France for a year, he then decided to give up everything, not just his
pursuit of the crown of Castile for his niece Juana, but his own throne
as well. After giving his courtiers and companions the slip in the
Norman port of Harfleur, Afonso set off for Jerusalem as a humble
pilgrim. He was eventually discovered fast asleep in a modest wayside
inn.

The Castilian War of Succession was eventually decided, not by
battle but by the bedroom. After a series of miscarriages and a daughter,
Isabella gave birth to a son in June 1476, which effectively put an end
to the dynastic rivalry between the two half-sisters.

In Lisbon, as on the battlefield of Toro, Portugal's crown prince John
had assumed power after his father's surprising departures, but he
behaved with perfect manners once his father had been returned home
by the French. He formally stepped down from the throne to act as
regent for his father, who, despite the odd flash of animation, was clearly
incapable of ruling. The Treaty of Alcacovas, which the Prince had been
instrumental in drafting, was ratified the following year at Toledo. A
masterly document whose clauses included a clear statement of present
interests and future intentions, it helped define a permanent peace
between Portugal and Castile. The Canary Isles were reserved to Castile
but the Lordship of Guinea and all its regions, lands, markets and gold
mines, including the islands of Madeira, Azores and Cape Verde, were

henceforth adjudged to belong to the Portuguese crown. It was agreed that Portugal had the exclusive right to wage a crusade against the King of Fez and to conquer Morocco, just as the Moorish Kingdom of Granada was reserved as the victim for a Castilian crusade.

With a touching dignity and restraint, Prince John continued to pretend to do no more than assist his father. However, Afonso spent ever more time in retreat in a Franciscan monastery near Torres Vedras, where he died in the summer of 1481.

After the uncertainty of the last years of his father's reign, King John II was determined to re-establish the power of the monarchy of Portugal. John had proved himself a tactful, kind and considerate regent. Once king he would prove himself to be one of the most far-sighted, tough and ruthless of rulers; a monarch every bit as able as Sultan Mehmet, the great eagle who had transformed the Ottoman Empire. The first problem that the new monarch faced was the growing power and insolence of the shadow dynasty of Portugal, that of the Dukes of Braganza (the family descended from King John the Bastard's own swarthy bastard), who hovered just behind the throne. They had benefited greatly in lands and prestige from the open and kind-hearted patronage of King Afonso the African. Once John had buried his father in dignity, he realised that it was time to strike down his over-mighty subjects.

At his coronation he insisted on a rigorous feudal oath of allegiance from each of the *fidalgos*, the noble lords of Portugal. They were also required to provide documentary proof of title for the lands which they occupied, and to listen to the complaints of the populace, who demanded more royal officials to protect them from the rapacity of the feudal lords. Two years later, having created the constitutional framework for the return of a strong monarchy, he struck. The Duke of Braganza was suddenly arrested and accused of conspiring with Castile during the previous reign. The most powerful man in the kingdom, after the monarch himself, was then summarily executed, on 20 June 1483. But the lesson had not been attended to by everyone. So John repeated it. In 1485 Dom Dioga, the royal Duke of Viseu, was summoned to a private audience with his cousin the King. The meeting was short and to the point. The three councillors present at this summit meeting held Dom Dioga fast so that John could stab him to death.

There was to be room for only one master in Portugal. John was determined to continue the great overseas adventure of his ancestors. As a corollary to this, peace with his Christian neighbours within the Iberian Peninsula was absolutely vital. The peace that John had negotiated with the monarchs of Castile and Aragon after the Castilian War of Succession was respected and strengthened. The Treaty of Toledo of 1480, which attempted to settle all disputes between the overseas provinces of Spain and Portugal, was endorsed the following year within a papal decree, that of Aeterni Regis. The conquest of Granada and Columbus's discovery of the Caribbean islands in 1492 would call for some updating of its sub-clauses. This was achieved in the Treaty of Tordesillas, when the Borgia Pope, Alexander VI, divided the islands of the Western Seas between Spain and Portugal on a line 370 miles west of the Azores. This notion, of a Roman pontiff dividing up whole continents to the exclusive benefit of two small European kingdoms, seems incredible now, a celebrated instance of the arrogance of the West. Indeed it can be seen as the starting gun for the cruelties of all subsequent colonial empires. Yet in its day the Papal Bull was no more than an official seal to the decade-long negotiations between two neighbours. Portugal, it was reaffirmed, was to have a free hand on the Moroccan and African coast, and it would also control the Atlantic islands with the exception of the Canaries. The small print even attempted to sort out where the two countries' zones of influence started and ended along the length of the Mediterranean coast of North Africa. But it was not quite small enough, for in 1508 one of the most enterprising of the Castilian corsair captains, Pedro Navarro, discovered and then occupied an island off the coast of Morocco which subsequently became known as the Penon de Velez de la Gomera (which is still occupied by Spain). Back at the diplomatic drawing board, the Treaty of Cintra, of the following year, footnoted Spain's rights to this rocky outcrop. This series of pragmatic understandings allowed both Portugal and Spain to push ahead with their aggressive foreign adventures.

In the first months of his reign King John II sent Dom Diogo de Azambuja to build an additional centre of Portuguese power in West Africa. The fortress of Sao Jorge da Mina (in present-day Ghana) lay due south of the kingdom of Ashanti and could watch over the flow of gold and slaves from the interior. The local African chief, Caramansa, preferred the Portuguese to visit his land as seasonal traders, and instinctively distrusted the great stone walls, gun portals and power-dressing ritual of the new fortress garrison. Sao Jorge da Mina was designed by

Fernao Gomes, who, as a veteran of the Moroccan sieges of both Ceuta and Ksar es Seghir, knew all that was known about defensive artillery works at that time. But, after his initial reluctance, chief Caramansa found that trade under the sure protection of this royal fortress had increased exponentially. Portuguese merchants bought up the traditional trade goods carried by the trans-Saharan camel caravans in the Moroccan ports on their way south and were able to ship them down to West Africa at a fraction of the cost of trading them by land. In one such year of trading, the thick, blanket-like shawls, woven kilims and ornate leather horse harnesses from Morocco paid for 40 per cent of the gold that was hauled back to the royal treasury in Lisbon.

The fort's purpose was not to act as a base from which to conquer the inland kingdoms but to guard the coastal trade against European rivals. For whatever the Portuguese, Spanish and papal embassies might agree, among the quays and dockyards of mercantile Europe the Treaty of Tordesillas was not worth the paper it was written on. As early as 1479 a French merchant ship had been arrested for trading in these waters and a few years earlier a ship from Flanders had been wrecked on this coast. Whether there was any truth to the story that the entire Flemish crew had been devoured in a cannibalistic feast, the Portuguese made certain that this tale received the widest possible circulation.

King John II also used the fort as a forward base for the exploration of the African coast. He wished to find more gold and the way to the rich spice trade of the Indian Ocean. Diogo Cao was one of the heroic captains who mapped the coast south of the fort of Sao Jorge da Mina, exploring the River Congo, dispatching an embassy to the ruler of the hinterland, King Manicongo, as well as leaving some visiting cards in the form of stone columns bearing the arms and title of his sovereign. Having been knighted for his exploits in Lisbon, he was sent on a second expedition by his master in 1485. Although he again charted new territory and made direct contact with Manicongo by sailing up the Congo to the Yelala waterfall, he appears to have lost the confidence of his inscrutable monarch.

In 1484 the King had received a Genoese captain named Christopher Columbus who proposed that a voyage of westward exploration would have a greater chance of reaching the Indies than the methodical exploration of the African coast. Having listened very carefully to this plan, he dismissed Columbus but gave secret orders to three different

Genoa, the city of Christopher Columbus.

Portuguese captains to sail west from the Azores for forty days to find 'the island of the Seven Cities' which Columbus had been so foolish enough to tell him about. However, the prevailing south-westerly winds from the Azores made this difficult to achieve. Perhaps because of his own deceit in his dealings with Columbus, John became increasingly concerned about European competitors. Secrecy and stealth surrounded all the subsequent Portuguese expeditions. Indeed the next fifteen years are a blank: we still don't know what John was up to or what his captains achieved during this period. It seems probable that the coast of Brazil was first discovered then, perhaps even settled, well before the 'official' announcement in 1500, when it was formally named Vera Cruz ('True Cross') by Pedro Cabral. It is no coincidence that this public declaration of Portuguese exploration only occurred after Christopher Columbus's discovery of the Caribbean in the journeys he undertook in the 1490s. Indeed John's insistence that the line of demarcation drawn on the map of the Atlantic between the Portuguese and Spanish regions be moved some six degrees further west rather indicates that he already knew there was something there.

Meanwhile the more public exploration of the western coast of Africa continued. Bartolomeu Dias was given the command of a squadron of three ships and at last succeeded in rounding the Cape of Good Hope at the southern end of the African continent, journeying just three days into the Indian Ocean before turning back and reporting his discoveries to Lisbon by the end of 1488. Despite this vital achievement, Bartolomeu Dias was neither honoured nor rewarded by his master, for King John's attention had returned to the Portuguese positions in Morocco.

At just this time the influence of the Portuguese within Morocco was enjoying an unexpected expansion, owing to the activities of their Spanish neighbours. For the ten-year war of conquest against Muslim Granada of 1482–92 had a number of unexpected repercussions for Portugal. To prevent any reinforcements coming across from North Africa to help defend their Muslim brothers in Granada, the Spanish had launched a series of maritime raids along the length and breadth of the North African coast, sinking every boat, raiding every harbour and burning every town within their reach. In the words of one such raider, 'We disembarked stealthily, early in the morning, and destroyed and burned many villages where we took eight hundred souls, killed many more and cattle as well.' In this atmosphere it became quite impossible for any Muslim merchant to venture on to the sea or risk the transportation of any goods. The income from customs collected from the traders at ports (which traditionally had been such a vital element of state revenue) dried up overnight.

Suddenly the Moroccans began to see their old Portuguese enemy, locked up behind the walls in the fortresses of Ceuta, Tangier and Asilah, in a new light. Moroccan merchants could continue to trade with Europe and West Africa if they made use of the Portuguese as middlemen. In 1486 the Moroccan Atlantic trading city of Azzemour, sited just upstream from the sea on the banks of the River Oum er-Rbia, formally petitioned for Portuguese protection. King John II was delighted to accept and soon the neighbouring Beni Hanai tribe also bought themselves into the deal. They were followed by the Moulay Bel Gaji tribal federation, who were very keen to renew their traditional trade in horses. Two years later the port of Safi, which sits in a bay just south of a stern line of cliffs, joined this growing Portuguese commercial union. On 16 October 1488 John wrote a nice letter back to Caid al-Farhun 'and the peaceful Moors of Safi-city', and to prove their good intentions both Azzemour and Safi permitted the resident Portuguese to build fortified *feitorias*, trading posts, on their territory. This suited the Portuguese traders who wanted to acquire Moroccan trade goods as these could then be profitably shipped down to Sao Jorge da Mina and traded with the West Africans.

A further twist to this bizarre rapprochement between old enemies occurred outside Ceuta. Here the Moroccan tribes tried to persuade the Portuguese garrison to join them in an attack on the Andalusian refugees who were pouring into their country to escape the Spanish conquest. The tribes had become very suspicious of the 'two daughters of Granada' that had been set up in their lands, at Tetouan on the coast and deep in the Rif mountains at Chechaouen. Even though the nascent city of Tetouan was ruled by the saintly warrior Al-Mandari, the hero of the siege of Beza, the tribes wanted nothing to do with him. For it is a sad truth that the refugees from the fall of Granada were not always welcomed with open arms by their Muslim brethren in North Africa. It was not just that the Nasrid Emirs were seen as complicit quisling traitors in the destruction of Muslim Andalusia, but that the refugees were believed to harbour secret Jews, Spanish spies and a sexual plague. There was one note of truth in this: syphilis, then in its newest and most violent form, was rapidly spreading around the Mediterranean coast from its American homeland.

Encouraged by these promising signs, John decided to strengthen the Portuguese position in Morocco. In February 1489 a squadron of Portuguese caravels made their way up the River Loukkos, passing the white Muslim city of Larache on the south bank and then the old Roman hilltop ruins of Lixus on the north, as they progressed further inland. After continuing for another ten kilometres they built a fortress beside the river. They named the earth walls and wooden stockades Fort Graciosa. Although protected by cannon and supporting fire from the squadron of caravels anchored in the river mud, it was a truly disastrous site. The Loukkos is a sluggish river which has carved an eccentric path through the marshy valley floor, a series of elaborate serpentine coils and dead-end ox-bow lakes. As summer approached, the Moroccan military leader, Muhammad al-Wattas, who aspired to lead his country after the fall of the Merenid dynasty, tightened his control over the river valley. The Portuguese within Fort Graciosa were surrounded by the tribes of the Middle Atlas region, who poured down from the hills to harass the enemy.

In July Muhammad al-Wattas himself arrived to direct the siege, dragging with him his carefully marshalled collection of cannon to give an answer to the Portuguese guns 'who fired from the fort and off-shore vessels day and night'. By mid-August casualties had mounted on both sides, and the river mud was stained with blood of both Portuguese and Moroccans. On the 27th a ten-year truce was declared, the Portuguese agreed to abandon the fort and the Moroccans allowed them to depart in honour with all arms, horses, guns and their flags flying. King John II's forward policy was abandoned for the moment, but Portugal managed to keep all her other fortresses and local allies.

John was disappointed but not overwhelmed with despair at this reverse. For he had a number of other irons in the fire. He had been simultaneously searching for Christian allies in Africa who could help him outflank the Muslim kingdoms. In 1487 he had sent two priests on a pilgrimage to Jerusalem in the hope that they could make friends with the Christians of Ethiopia and return with them to Abyssinia to make contact with their Emperor. Since they travelled openly as official delegates of the crusading King of Portugal, it is not surprising to find that they were not given permission by the Muslim authorities for this mission. So John tried again, choosing a pair of well-travelled merchants, small-time traders and adventurers from a humble village background who had plenty of experience of Muslim society and spoke Arabic.

These two secret agents, Pero de Covilha and Afonso de Paiva, were given purses of gold (containing two hundred of the splendidly minted *cruzados* of Portugal) and sent east. They travelled first to Barcelona, then took ship to Rhodes (the customary entrance gate for Westerners travelling to the Holy Land), from where they made their way to Alexandria. Joining up with a company of merchants from North Africa, they made their way down the Red Sea coast to Aden. Afonso doubled back to Cairo to make a report while Pero managed to talk himself on to an Arab dhow that was following the monsoon winds in order to make the crossing to India. He then visited all the important spice-trade ports of the Indian Ocean, criss-crossing the seas to look at the Malabar coast, the Swahili trading cities of East Africa and then those in the Persian Gulf. After this extraordinarily successful five-year odyssey he made his way back to Cairo. There he linked up with one of John's confidential agents, a pair of Jewish merchants, who passed his report to Lisbon, replenished his purse and sent him south with orders to report on the strength of the Christian kingdom of Ethiopia. Pero, this most remarkable of confidential agents, then journeyed back down the coast and struck inland from one of the Red Sea trading ports. Iskandar, Emperor of Abyssinia, was delighted to receive him and hear of his extraordinary travels and the state of the Christian monarchies of the West. So much so that he persuaded him to take a local wife and awarded him lands and cattle. There Pero de Covilha remained, an honoured figure at court and the contented father of many children. He was still alive and well when the formal Portuguese embassy of Dom Roderigo de Lima finally made its way into the mountains of Ethiopia in 1521. Pero enjoyed hearing the Portuguese tongue again but decided to stay on, for he had made a home in Africa and found a monarch who rewarded his subordinates.

King John II of Portugal.

There were many other agents of King John II whose travels and confidential reports were never published. His most spectacular foreign policy success was, however, to be a more much public affair. In 1490, with the ecstatic backing of his parliament, which promptly voted one hundred thousand gold coins to cover the cost, he offered his daughter Princess Isabella as the bride of the son of Ferdinand and Isabella of Spain while asking for one of their daughters for his own son. This match sealed the peace policy with his neighbours that had been an essential accompaniment to his external adventures. The double wedding, held at Seville in Spain and Evora in Portugal, was a hugely popular national event. John even offered his subjects an interest-free loan so that the streets of Evora could be filled with colourful, freshly tailored wedding outfits.

But the following year John's son, the newly married crown prince Dom Afonso, fell while out hunting near a river in Santarem. His broken body was cared for by the family of a poor fishermen who discovered him. Just before nightfall he died. His father never recovered from the news, his bright chestnut hair turning white overnight. A mysterious dropsy possessed him which drained him of his habitual energy as his body swelled into a grotesque bloated version of itself. He was persuaded to try the cure at the holy well of Monchique in the Algarve, but it was to no avail. He died on 25 October 1495, just forty years old. His secrecy, his brutal, rational intelligence and the harsh way that he had dealt with both his own family and his most trusted servants meant that few tears were shed at his grave by those who knew him. He was, however, adored by the people. Dom Manuel, a young cousin of the King, the only one of a brood of nine royal children to have survived his suspicions, inherited the throne. He had led an arduously blameless life, agreeing with anyone and everything as he obediently travelled around in the immediate entourage of the King. Dom Manuel had performed this act of lifelong self-effacement in order to survive, for he never forgot that John had personally stabbed his elder brother to death for his perceived lack of loyalty. But he proved himself intensely alive once he ascended the throne as Manuel I.

The new King, like most of Portugal, had been in love with the young Spanish princess who had come to marry the crown prince amid all the celebrations at Evora. One of his first actions was to petition Ferdinand and Isabella for the hand of the young widow. The dowry they set was very high – in suffering. Portugal must follow the lead of Castile and Aragon and expel all the Jews and Muslims in order to become a 'clean land'. So on Easter Day 1497 the King secured the wife of his choice by ordering that all Jewish children under the age of fourteen be separated from their families and adopted by Christians. All those Jews who had failed to convert by October were to assemble in Lisbon so that they could be expelled. Similar orders were made to the Muslim population of the Algarve, though these were conveniently 'lost in transit' lest the promising commercial position of Portugal within Morocco be compromised.

In the meantime one of King John II's more audacious foreign schemes lay awaiting instructions at the docks of Lisbon. The reports of his agents in the Indian Ocean, the secret advances into the south Atlantic, the rounding of the Cape of Good Hope, had all led up to this expedition. Four ships, the brand-new *Sao Gabriel* and the *Sao Rafael*, plus the refitted *Sao Miguel* and a store-ship, lay ready. A hundred and seventy tough, experienced men were aboard. They were to be paid danger money for this expedition into unknown lands; seven *cruzados* a month, plus a signing-on fee of between forty and one hundred *cruzados* so that married men could leave something behind for their families in case they never returned. The trade goods they carried were suitable for the tropical coast of West Africa but would prove to be almost worthless in the sophisticated markets of the Indian Ocean. The one thing they carried that would hold them in good standing were the cannon on the deck, well-cast bronze bombards, the result of continuous technical evolution during Portugal's long crusading war against Morocco.

The aims of the King of Portugal had not changed much since the 'great enterprise' against Ceuta back in 1415. King Manuel himself declared that his ambition, 'after the desire to rule my people in peace and justice, is to increase the wealth and renown of this my kingdom'. His chosen captain was not some swaggering, proud *fidalgo* but an experienced sea captain, Vasco da Gama, whose family worked the land and fished the seas around the Atlantic port of Sines. The night before the little squadron made its departure in July 1497 Vasco da Gama knelt before his sovereign and received a silken banner embroidered with the Crusading Order of Christ, an emblem based on the ancient heraldry of the Knights Templars, whose traditions had, alone in

Europe, been conserved in Portugal. King Manuel was highly conscious that he had 'inherited from my predecessors a sacred mission. Both my great-uncle, Dom Henrique and my father, Dom Fernao, devoted their lives to the cause of exploration overseas and their labours must not be brought to naught.' That evening, like a crusading knight of old, Vasco da Gama retired to spend the night at the chapel at Restelo, which Prince Henry the Navigator had built in his role as Commander of the Order of Christ.

The next day, 8 July 1497, they left Lisbon. Less than a year later, on 18 May 1498, they reached the western coast of India. Emblazoned on their sails was the blood-red cross of the Order of Christ and their ships bore the names of the three archangels who have served as the great messengers of mankind: Michael, Gabriel and Raphael. One angelic name, Azrael, the bringer of death, had not been chosen. But it was with death that the Portuguese were soon to be associated throughout the coast of Africa, India and Asia. Back in Lisbon, thousands of Jews had been successfully expelled from the land, so that the marriage of Donna Isabella, the young widowed Queen, and Dom Manuel, the new King of Portugal, could now proceed.

3

The Great Eagle

Mehmet the Conqueror of Constantinople, 1450–80

The spider spins his web in the palace of the Caesars
And the owl sings her watchsong on the towers of Afrasiab

Saadi

At the other end of the Inner Sea, the second great power of this period, the Ottoman Empire, would expand her dominions to control the entire eastern half of the Mediterranean. At about the same time that the court chroniclers of Portugal were recording the death of old King John I, the birth of a third male child to Sultan Murat II was recorded by Ottoman palace officials on 30 March 1432. This child was born in an island palace in Thrace; a scattering of pavilions and courtyard apartments had been erected between two beds of the Tunca, one of the streams which flow through ancient Adrianople, known as Edirne by the Turks. He was born in the spring, a time when the heaths and dark woods of Thrace are alive with flowers. It was always a favourite time of the year for the sultans to reside in Edirne, for they loved to hunt in the surrounding hills with hawk and hound. The birth of young Mehmet was not at the time considered to be an important event, for Murat already had two healthy sons, one from his official wife, a Turcoman princess. Mehmet's mother was a concubine, a captive Greek slave who had briefly caught Murat's eye. However, with the birth of a son her status in the household improved, she was now referred to as Hunan Hatun and acquired her own suite of rooms and small staff of servants. For the first three years of his life Mehmet lived in this earthly paradise, in the same room as his mother and his beloved wet-nurse Daye Hatun (who as an honoured, extremely wealthy and pious nanny would outlive her master).

By the end of his life Mehmet, 'the Great Eagle', was freely equated with Alexander the Great. For, aside from the scale of their victories, the two men shared a relentless energy and a restless ambition that could not be slaked. Both possessed an intriguing combination of a gentle, enquiring humanity and a ruthless, almost sensual cruelty. Both led kingdoms that they had inherited from their fathers to greater glory, and both aspired to create empires founded on a federation of peoples. Even as children they had a lot in common: both were adored by their Greek mothers and ignored by their charismatic royal fathers, who openly showed their love for other women and other children.

At the age of four Prince Mehmet became both a boy and an Ottoman official, and his life was henceforth a confusing series of sudden arrivals and departures at the whim of his father. He was sent to Amasya and Manisa in Ottoman Anatolia to understudy his elder brothers, for the governorships of these two towns were customarily reserved as training grounds for young princes. The accidental death of first one brother, then the murder of the other, meant that he was at last summoned in to the presence of his father in Edirne. At this point Sultan Murat worried that he had made a mess of Mehmet's training. His only surviving son was on the point of maturing into a feckless truant and was in desperate need of attention. A fearsome Kurdish tutor was appointed and Mehmet responded extraordinarily well to the new discipline, and no doubt to the returning influence of his mother and the longed-for attention of his father. He became a model student, reading his way through the prescribed courses of Islamic studies and quickly branching out to read the Persian, Greek and Latin classics of history, science and philosophy.

In the summer of 1444 Murat led his army to wage war on the Emirate of Karamania, roughly speaking the southern chunk of modern Turkey that lies next to Syria, which had once again shifted in its reluctant allegiance to the Ottoman state. A political storm broke out in Edirne. A wild preacher from the eastern frontier started to publicly announce the esoteric doctrine of the Bektasi brotherhood. Twelve-year-old Mehmet was fascinated to discover the speculative mysteries that lurked behind the wild circular stomping dances of the Bektasi

Sufis of Anatolia. To what did the candle and the sharing of food, the four, the nine and the forty, allude? Rather than discipline this dervish preacher, the young prince asked to listen to him and offered him his protection, which scandalised all the mainstream Islamic judges and Koranic scholars. For the Bektasi were on the heretical edge of Islam and had a secret political agenda. When Mehmet moved to correct his public stance, he found that the clerics used this as a sign of weakness and whipped up an excited urban mob who hunted down the followers of the dervish before lynching the poor preacher, who suffered horribly before being burned at the stake. This greatly agitated the janissary soldiers guarding the palace, for they tended to be followers of Bektasi teachings. In their distress they petitioned Mehmet for more pay, before themselves moving out of their barracks on to the streets to loot and burn the city's elegant covered market. To make matters worse, the rumours of a Christian attack on the Ottoman Balkans (always a pos-sibility once it was known that the main Ottoman army was marching east to the Asian frontier) began to seem real. The lord of the Transylvanian mountains, Janos Hunyadi, had joined King Ladislas I of Hungary, a host of Burgundian knights and Italians under Cardinal Cesarini to create an impressive Crusading army. This he now led south towards Edirne. Defence had never been a priority to the expansionist Ottoman mentality, so a labour corps was marshalled of all the city's able-bodied men, who made emergency repairs to the walls and scoured and deepened the beds of the river-filled moats.

The chief minister, already bemused by the number of things that had gone wrong since his master had left, dispatched his most trusted messenger to catch up with the Sultan. Murat turned around and hur-ried his men back to defend Thrace. To make the situation even more perilous, a Christian fleet (working in alliance with the Hungarians) had simultaneously sailed into the Dardanelles in a daring attempt to frustrate the Sultan's crossing of the strait. It was a potentially brilliant plan, but it proved impossible for the Christian fleet to keep to its sta-tion and Murat made a safe crossing.

When the two armies met on the field of Varna, it was at the very end of the campaigning season, the 10th November. Varna was one of the most ferocious and fiercely fought battles of the era, for the Crusader knights succeeded in breaking both of the Ottoman wings, before they were themselves felled by the Janissaries attacking under the personal leadership of Sultan Murat. The battle had been too closely fought for the aftermath to be merciful, and in the words of the Turkish chronicler 'they made prisoners only of the fresh faced youths, all the older captive soldiers were put to the sword'. As winter closed in, Sultan Murat led his exhausted but triumphant army back to their capital at Edirne.

Young Prince Mehmet learned a lot that year. He knew that an Ottoman Sultan had to rule by the strength of his arms and keep his thoughts to himself. Despite their grand titles, they had no claim to any spiritual authority within Islam. They had not a drop of the pure Arabic blood of the Caliphs, let alone of the exalted family of the Prophet, in their veins. It is true that they were considered the war leaders of the western Turks but within the vast brotherhood of the Turkic peoples (whose homeland stretched across all of Central Asia, southern Russia, northern India and western China) they had no exceptional status. They were neither descended from Genghis Khan nor Timur (the two archetypal Turkic patriarch-conquerors) nor even connected to any of the successful medieval dynasties, such as the Seljuks. The Ottoman Sultans, by the standards of both Islam and Turkic Central Asia, were new men. They ruled through the power of their army or not at all.

The Ottoman Sultans traced their origins to Osman, one of the many dozens of freebooting border lords who had nestled against the medieval frontiers of Byzantium. Many of these lordships had been established after the break-up of the old Seljuk Empire, when not a few of the old noble families of Byzantium seem to have taken the opportunity to reposition themselves with new identities. Indeed, whether it is actually true or not, the rulers of such 'Turkish' emirates as Karamania (which held the Taurus mountains and the southern coast of Turkey) were widely believed to be Armenian converts to Islam. In Cappadocia in central Anatolia art historians have been able to trace the Islamisation of powerful local lords, who can be seen depicted as traditional patrons of a Byzantine church and are then, thirty years later, to be found on the dedicatory inscription of a new mosque. Viewed from the door of a tent of a tribal leader of a nomadic tribe, it was questionable exactly how Turkic any of these border lords were thought to be. The Ottomans, although undoubtedly of Turkish blood themselves (Sultan Murat claimed descent from the Kayi tribe of the Oguz Turks of Central Asia), had first emerged and flourished in such a confusing milieu, marrying a Byzantine princess in one generation and the daughter of a Turkic nomadic chieftain the next. They were also past masters at using Christians to fight Christendom. It was Osman's son Orhan who first propelled the family to eminence by capturing Prusa, the capital of the Byzantine province of Bithynia, which was transformed into the Ottomans' first capital city, Brusa. When their power was confirmed by the capture of another important city, Nicomedia, it was time for the Ottomans to show that they had created a separate state. A new currency was issued, while a flattened version of the old Phrygian cap, a red fez of brushed felt, was chosen as an Ottoman symbol, to unite this new Sparta – this state dedicated to war.

The Ottomans, whatever their origins, proved themselves magnificent war leaders, and they ruled their empire as contentedly from a tented marching camp as from any walled city. Indeed when you look at illuminations of their beautifully organised tent cities you at once realise the true origins of their domestic architecture. On the periphery of the Ottoman army were the *akindshci*, or light troops, who were little more than freebooting border raiders. Then came the army proper, composed of feudal levies of men under the command of their tribal Turkic chiefs, and at the centre of the Ottoman military regime two renowned corps of professional soldiers: the spahis, the 'riders', or the cavalry, and the janissaries, the 'new army' of infantrymen.

It was said that at the height of his power Sultan Orhan had command of one hundred thousand warriors, though at least a third of these would have been light troops and half brought in under the command of his allies. It was this same sultan who had the quick-witted prescience to respond to a schism within Byzantium by seizing the strategic Dardanelles crossing and establishing a permanent base at Gallipoli and from there extending his realm into Thrace. Right from the first years of their Imperium, the Ottomans had to be capable of waging war on two separate frontiers, eastwards into Anatolia and westwards into Europe (still known as Rumelia, the lands of the Romans). But rather than weaken their energies, this habit of war on two frontiers against two varieties of enemy allowed them to hone their tactical skills, so that they combined the skills of both east and west: the furious élan of the Turkish cavalry was married to the technical expertise of a professional corps of infantry trained in firearms, artillery, siege-craft and logistics.

The master stroke in the creation of this new militant state was to make the rapid transformation from swashbuckling border raiders to state-builders, who protected rather than despoiled the towns, their craftsmen and their merchants. The Ottoman Sultans progressed from warlords to peace makers with admirable speed and won acceptance by providing troops to police the markets and uphold the decisions of the lettered judges, building secure caravanserais in the countryside and covered markets in the towns. How else were they to uphold the state and equip a modern army, if not by the regular flow of rents from the peasantry and customs duties from the merchants?

They also quickly learned that the Dardanelles Strait was not just a vital bridge between East and West, but a finger on one of the jugulars of world trade. If you had artillery on the shore and men who knew how to use it, even the fabulously rich, inventive and resourceful merchants of Italy, be they from Genoa, Venice or Florence, were obliged to dip their flags and offer up a toll for the privilege of safe passage. Money was absolutely crucial in the success of the Ottoman state, for, practically alone in the Mediterranean at this period, it was wealthy enough to pay for a permanent standing army: the janissaries. In the end this cost the dynasty much more than they had bargained for, but initially

A janissary at the time of Sultan Mehmet II. Drawn by Gentile Bellini during his time in Istanbul (1479–81). (British Museum)

this professional corps of highly trained soldiers who were the personal slaves of the sultans seem to have come cheap.

The Christian subjects of the Ottoman state were obliged to offer up a certain percentage of their male children to become slaves of the Sultan. Rounded up by officials at puberty, they were marched to the capital to be converted en masse to Islam through the bloody rite of circumcision and the simple proclamation of the *shahada*. They were then sent out to work for Turkish-speaking masters for three years, so that they came back with an understanding of the Turkish language, manners and cuisine. On returning to the capital they were allotted to the different branches of the Sultan's court: the brightest became highly literate administrative clerks, while the strongest were entered into one of the regiments of the janissaries or, if they failed to achieve selection, were welcomed into the corps of gardeners and boatmen. Although they were slaves, and the Sultan could order them where and whence he willed, they were also Muslims, with the rights that this entailed. Yet they always remained members of the Sultan's personal household, clothed, fed, housed and paid a quarterly salary in coin. Thus the Ottoman Sultans acquired a professional standing army some centuries before any of their adversaries. This placed them at an extraordinary advantage over those who relied on feudal levies of soldiers, who lacked training and discipline and owed distracting seasonal commitments to flocks, fields and families. Nor did the janissaries, like the mounted knights of both Islam and Christendom, disdain the use of gunpowder lest it deafen their horses and stain their gorgeous uniforms with grease and black powder and distract from the heroic glamour of the charge. As the Chevalier Bayard, an epitome of French chivalry, so frankly put it, 'we do not like the idea of fighting alongside cobblers, farmers, mechanics and the like, who do not hold their honour in the same regard as gentlemen'. The janissaries suffered from no such class fault lines. Like the Roman legionnaires of old, their core skills were discipline, training and adaptability. They were schooled in the accurate use of the latest weapons, in how to lay out entrenchments, organise a marching camp, store ordnance, guard forts and build. Indeed one of their number, trained as a pragmatic engineer building military bridges and storehouses to order, would emerge as one of the greatest of all architects – Sinan, known only through his works and the humble tomb he designed for himself beside one of his masterpieces, the Suleymaniye.

The curious phenomenon of a slave army owed its existence to an old Muslim tradition, dating back to the first years of the Arab conquest, not to allow subject nations, be they Christian Syrians, Jews from Tiberias or Zoroastrian Persians, to bear arms. The *dwimmi*, or 'protected states', paid a poll tax to the Muslim community but were not required to bear arms themselves. For as part of the contract of surrender they were thereafter to be defended by Arab Muslim armies. This deal kept the Muslim armies supplied with the prestige of a salaried class apart and also kept the recently conquered peoples in a demilitarised state. When the Ottoman Sultans wanted to benefit from the manpower of their predominantly Christian-occupied provinces, they had to make recruitable Muslims from the many young Christians over whom they ruled. The janissary levy was a brilliant response to this imbalance, which was at first assessed on the old Muslim principle of a fifth, so that each Christian community was required to surrender a fifth of its teenage boys from each generation to the Sultan.

There was already ample traditional precedent for creating slave armies within Islam. From the earliest days the Abbasid Caliphs recruited outsiders – white slaves from the lands of the north, black slaves from the African south, brown slaves from the Berber west and tan slaves from the Turkic east – to form rival regiments of palace guards. They always tried to balance the strength of these regiments, so that none felt themselves indispensable. This was not always possible and in Egypt, for instance, the white slaves exported from Caucasia and southern Russia gradually took control of the state and became the ruling Mamcluke elite, though curiously they never grew into a distinct class (disinheriting their offspring as half-breeds unfit for military service) but instead retained their regimental loyalties, preferring to hand over authority to fresh batches of military slaves who had proved themselves in the ranks. Such was the extraordinary everyday background of the Mameluke Sultans of Egypt, who were regarded as the strongest state in all Islam at this period. It was a living example of how militarily successful armies composed of boy-soldier slaves could be, but also how politically dangerous they were. For the theoretical sovereign rulers of Egypt, both the Ayyubid Sultans and the Abbasid Caliphs, had been kept like exotic caged birds for centuries, the genealogically praised prisoners of their palaces. The more astute of the Ottoman Sultans were always aware that the janissaries needed careful watching. The feudal levies of tribesmen were encouraged to remain apart from them, as were the spahis, who maintained a hearty professional rivalry with the 'new army' corps. It helped that the spahis were very similar to the janissaries but just different enough for some powerful prejudices to take root, for in the early years they were recruited from Christian adults who had voluntarily become Muslims, not Christian boys made Muslim.

The conquest of Thrace that had been started by Orhan was completed by his son Murat I with the capture of Adrianople (Edirne) in 1362. Constantinople, formerly the capital of the Byzantine Empire that ruled over the whole of the Balkans, Greece and the Middle East, was now reduced to a city-state surrounded on all sides by Ottoman provinces. The first round of Christian counter-attacks, which swept through the Balkans to relieve the fabulous city of Constantinople, was felled by the Ottomans in a series of hard-fought battles over the following six years, such as the First Battle of Kosovo, the 'Day of the Blackbirds', which was a killing field for the knights of Serbia.

In 1396 a formal crusade was summoned by the combined energy of King Sigismund, the Holy Roman Emperor, and the passionate encyclicals of both Popes (in Avignon and Rome), which created an impressive confederation of Christian talent. A fleet made up of the ships of Venice, Genoa and the Knights of St John would sail up the Danube from their Black Sea bases to meet up with an army of German, French and Hungarian knights assisted by the soldiers of Wallachia and Transylvania. It offered up a vision of an extended Holy Roman Empire under the ancient House of Luxemburg, healing the traditional division between German, Magyar and Slav. By July some ten thousand knights had ridden from western Europe to join the assembled German and Hungarian army. By September this Crusader army was in good position, having crossed the Danube and besieged the city of Nicopolis on the river's southern bank. But the gorgeous tapestry of united Christendom, led into the field of battle by their elected Holy Roman Emperor, would soon unravel. It was perhaps too much to expect that the chivalry of France and Burgundy (led by John, Count of Nevers) would obey a German King-Emperor. Nor would either the French or Germans listen to commanders from the Balkans, who had generations of useful tactical experience of the Ottoman army to share, nor even wait for the allied fleet and their water-borne artillery that was sailing upstream to meet them. On 25 September thousands of French and Burgundian knights set off on their own, riding up the hill above Nicopolis to do battle with the Ottoman army. Depending on your point of view, the Transylvanian and Wallachian divisions either deserted the field or refused to join a suicidal frontal attack which they had advised against. The knights trotted forward and then spurred their way into a glorious frontal charge across the length of a plateau, cantering on firm, dry ground that made good going for their war-horses. It was a parade-ground exhibition of magnificence, like the glorious tourneys that they had so often executed in front of admiring galleries of ladies and courtiers. Their attack smashed through the irregular skirmishers and cut deep into the Turkish infantry. But they had been expected.

In the words of one of the survivors:

When the Saracens saw that we were near enough, the whole cavalry battalion wheeled away in tight formation like a cloud and moved to the rear, behind the stakes and behind their infantry . . . The Saracens began to shoot . . . so thick and fast that never hail or rain fell more heavily from the sky than the arrows now flew, in a few minutes they had killed great numbers of our horses and men . . . Jean Boucicaut, who was unable to see the sharp stakes so wickedly set just in front of them, began to speak like the valiant warrior he was and said, 'Hurry, let us attack them boldly, and in this way we shall avoid their arrows.' At once they spurred on to charge the Saracens, and rode straight in among the stakes, which were strong, rigid and sharp, so that they drove into the horses' bellies and killed many of them and injured the men who fell from the horses.

To make matters worse, Sigismund advanced to give support to the shattered remnants of this attack, so that the German and Hungarian soldiers who had remained obediently under his command shared in the slaughter. The aftermath left the Balkans riven between local warlords, many of whom were forced to become tributaries to the Sultan. Constantinople, instead of being rescued, now hung in the background like a ripe plum ready to drop into the hands of the patient Ottomans. The way seemed clear for the capture of the great city of the Caesars. It had been under a blockade since the spring of 1394; after the Battle of

Soldier on horseback, 1498. By Albert Durer.
(Grapische Sammlung Albertine, Vienna)

Nicopolis this became a siege.

The French knight who helped lead the doomed attack at Nicopolis, Jean Boucicaut, did in fact survive the slaughter. His horse was shot down and he was made captive and later ransomed. Rather than tell sad stories of the death of brave knights, the moment he returned home he started on preparations for a second crusade. With a force of just eight hundred knights and soldiers he managed to cut his way through the Ottoman siege lines and enter Constantinople in the autumn of 1399. But this was all that this gallant body of adventurers could achieve. Brought face to face with the vast scale of their endeavour, they were forced to leave the beleaguered city that winter in the comparative safety of a Venetian boat. Boucicaut did not, however, give up. He volunteered to be the guide for Emperor Manuel II, as the Lord of Byzantium toured the royal courts of the Kings of the West to seek their aid. This diplomatic tour began in the winter of 1399 and ended with Manuel's return in the spring of 1403. The English were much struck by the piety, simplicity and discipline of the embassy: 'The Emperor Manuel always walked with his men, dressed alike and in one colour, long robes of white cut like tabards . . . These Greeks were most devout in their church services, which they were joined in as well by soldiers as by priests.' Of the money that was enthusiastically donated by the citizens of London for the relief of Constantinople not a penny would reach the intended beneficiaries – for the usual reasons. The siege had ended by the time Manuel sailed up through the Sea of Marmara and once more caught sight of the great domed churches of Constantinople. And what of Jean Boucicaut? He used this golden opportunity to launch himself against the Holy Land. Although his cruise over the summer of 1403 completes the picture of him as a very true and perfect knight, it also left a trail of burned and devastated ports along the Syrian coast. This may have quietened his conscience but had no tactical benefit whatsoever, as this coast belonged to the chief rivals of Ottoman power, the Mamelukes of Egypt.

Boucicaut's Crusader raid had also proved unexpectedly easy – which was not due to any new battle tactics of the Christians but to cataclysmic events further east. For an even greater Turkic warlord had ridden into Anatolia from the East, in a manner that had not been seen since the Mongol hordes of Genghis Khan swept all aside some 150 years earlier. In one day in 1402, outside Ankara, the patient achievements of five generations of Ottoman Sultans was cut away, like a field of ripe corn before the reaper. The Ottoman army led into battle by Bayezid I was overwhelmed by that of Timur. So much so that the Sultan himself was captured and in the aftermath of battle confined in a barred cage as an ornament to the court of the conqueror, forced to watch the degradation of his wife before it was his turn to die.[1] Before that favour was granted him, he accompanied Timur's army in an iron cage perched on top of a camel's back as it advanced ever further west into the heartland of the Ottoman state, remorselessly destroying all that had been so laboriously achieved in the cities of Iznik and Brusa. Only in its European provinces did the Ottoman Empire survive. It is claimed that Timur was contemplating the invasion of Europe and the destruction of Constantinople on his way to flatten Rome. But instead he led his army through southern Anatolia in order to march into Syria and Egypt to fight the Mamelukes: the one force left in the world that could put up a good fight.

*

So it had been left to young Prince Mehmet's father, Murat II, to begin the slow re-establishment of Ottoman authority in Anatolia once Timur and his heirs returned to Central Asia. The victory of Varna against the Crusader army led by King Ladislas I of Hungary and Janos Hunyadi in 1444 had been achieved when Murat II was aged forty. It seemed to make promise of greater events to come. The court and the victorious army was in a mood to celebrate that November, after the year's many tribulations.

Instead Sultan Murat II resigned. He put aside his military and political authority, which had never stood higher, in favour of his teenage son. Nor did he linger to receive the many hundreds of courtiers, generals and allies who begged him to reconsider this action. Instead, by 1 December, young Mehmet was acclaimed Sultan and Murat II had ridden out to his chosen retirement town, Manisa. It is still not fully understood what Murat II intended by this action. Was it an attempt to remove himself from the moral corruption of politics and prepare his soul to seek God? Was it a shrewd device to encourage the enemies of the dynasty to expose themselves? Was it a sham, like that practised by the Roman Emperor Augustus, whose many resignations were an attempt to get the crowds to clamour that much louder for his return? Power was, in any case, effectively left in the hands of his chief minister, the grand vizier Halil Pasha, who sent a stream of messages seeking advice from Murat in Manisa and obstructed young Mehmet's plans for the siege of Constantinople. After two years of this chicanery, Murat returned as Sultan and his son, disgraced and humiliated by the whole experience, was persuaded to resign and exchange places with his father. To make Mehmet's rejection by his father even more intense, it was made known that the Sultan had already made plans to be buried beside his beloved son Aladdin. And it became common gossip at court that the old Sultan's attempt at resignation had been due to his frustration at the loss of this beloved son.

There was, however, to be one last chance of reconciliation on the battlefield, in 1448. The redoubtable lord of the snowy passes and forested mountains of Transylvania had once again patched together a crusading army from among the Balkan princes and peoples. Over the summer Janos Hunyadi advanced south and in September forced a crossing of the Danube. Prince Mehmet responded to his father's summons by bringing troops from Anatolia, who paraded through the streets of Edirne before the whole army marched north to do battle. The two forces met at Kosovo, the same field of battle where the Serbians had been destroyed by the Ottomans in 1389. The Christian army was eager for vengeance and the Second Battle of Kosovo was hard fought, ranging over three days, at the end of October, of attack and counter-assault. Mehmet had been given command of the troops from Anatolia, who formed the right wing, while his father held the centre. The young prince proved himself well in this, his first baptism of fire. But divisions among the Christian allies once again allowed the Ottomans a decisive advantage. The test of arms achieved by the Second Battle of Kosovo also bore fruit on the Ottoman eastern frontier, for a number of Turkic Emirs now came forward with offers of alliance. This was celebrated exactly a year after Kosovo, in a spectacular double marriage held in the Ottoman capital of Edirne. For two months in the autumn of 1449 the city was filled with processions, public banquets and concerts to celebrate the event. The Sultan was to wed a Turcoman princess from the Candaroglu tribe and his son Mehmet the daughter of the Emir of the Dulkadirli.

Far from its being a bridge between father and son, Mehmet was insulted that he had not been consulted about his own marriage, and by a tragic coincidence his beloved mother died just before the munificent state-funded celebrations started. Mehmet was forced to attend, though his heart was elsewhere, concentrated on a tomb which bore the simple but poignant inscription 'Built by her son Mehmet for his deceased mother, queen among women, may the earth of her grave be fragrant'. He never could tolerate the company of the bride whom his father had inflicted upon him during that season of grief. He preferred the company of a simple Greek concubine – just like his mother – who bore him the only children he cared for, Bayezid and Mustapha.

When the messenger arrived at Manisa in February 1451 to inform Mehmet that his father was dead, there were no tears, regrets or bashful false steps. It took the nineteen-year-old prince just fifteen days to ride through the mountains, cross the Sea of Marmara and make his way to Edirne. He had been through all the rituals of coronation once before, and so again he received the *bayat*, the personal oath of loyalty from his chief ministers and officials, and was ceremonially girded with the simple sword of his ancestor, the border raider Osman Gazi, by a dervish sheikh.

Mehmet moved with circumspection. The humiliating mistakes of his regency and his first reign would not be repeated. The men he had every reason to fear and hate, the powerful ministers of his father who had frustrated him throughout his life, were confirmed in their positions. The demands of the janissaries were once again acknowledged and their dissident spirit appeased and forgiven. The time for the settling of old scores could wait, though there was one task that could not. While Mehmet formally received the members of his father's harem, he arranged that his younger half-brother be strangled while he was given his bath.

Mehmet knew that if he was to lead the Ottoman state he needed to be certain of one thing above all, the loyalty of his army. Once he had that the rest would follow. He was not going to prove himself with a new war against Serbia, Hungary or one of the Turkic emirates to the east. The gradual bite-by-bite expansion of the far borders could wait. He was going to go for Constantinople itself, which in his day was known as 'the red apple', the conquest of which was the very symbol of worldwide dominion. The apple is of course an image beyond cultural frontiers, an icon for something sweet, tasty and out of reach that ripens slowly beneath your longing glances. It may also relate symbolically to the formal orb held by emperors on both coins and statues, a tradition that perhaps goes back to the mythic divine gifts awarded by the heavenly powers to their favoured individuals, as in the judgement of that prince of Troy, Paris. There was also a very particular apple known to all visitors to the great city, the orb held in the hand of the giant statue of Emperor Justinian, which stood on a great column in the public square in the formal centre of both the city and the empire. It was twice red, red from the Porphyry granite of Egypt from which it was carved, and red from the undercoat over which it had once been gilded. It was now weathered by the centuries, fragile but still potent, like the city that stretched beneath it.

Mehmet knew that he had to be quick. Quick to establish his authority and bury his childhood failures, quick to bury the fame of his father with his own bright renown and quick to seize the hour which was at hand. Who could tell when another great crusading army might not emerge from out of the West and reverse the run of four decisive Ottoman victories: Kosovo I, Nicopolis, Varna and Kosovo II? Or if another great Turcoman lord would not thunder out of Central Asia?

Or if Genoa and Venice would forget their rivalry and agree to share command of the seas?

The siege was always going to be a make-or-break affair. For it would surely attract the attention of Christendom, even if merely vengeful after the event. And while the army was concentrated on the city the frontiers of the rest of the Ottoman state would be vulnerable. If the siege failed, Mehmet would find his own prestige crippled, the army mutinous and his finances wasted, and provincial rebellions might well shake the foundations of the state, allowing another of the Turkic lords, be it the Emir of Karaman, or Kastamuni or the rival Emirs of the White Sheep Turks and the Black Sheep Turks, to topple the House of Osman.

The resources needed would stretch the Ottoman state to near breaking point. Money was required to hire the world's most talented men, to attract allied emirs, to pay vast armies, build fleets and forge an army confident of victory. It was acquired through the usual short-sighted royal expedients: devaluing the silver content in the coinage and taking cash in advance by pledging tax and customs revenues and auctioning off long leases of mines.

Despite the scale of the endeavour, it also remained highly personal. That winter the Sultan challenged his four chief ministers to each design, build and pay for a tower in the new castle that he was designing. The joint effort was to stand on the northern shore of one of the narrowest reaches of the Bosporus. For it was a critical first step to a successful siege for Mehmet to be able to cut the supply lines from the Black Sea to Constantinople. The group of towers, named after their builders, still forms one of the great monuments of Istanbul. The castle of Rumeli Hisari is impressive at a distance but brutal and inelegant at close range: the massive thick walls, formed from crude chunks of black volcanic stone set in great beds of mortar, lack all the elegance associated with medieval masonry. Put up in six months, just five kilometres north of Constantinople, it was a potent emblem of a new age. It was built by a thousand masons for a single purpose, to withstand attack from ships using the Bosporus and protect a vital sliver of shore from any assault. For the real biting edge of the fortress of Rumeli Hisari – the Bogazkesen ('Cutter of the Strait') – was a humble-looking, low embankment in front of the castle's walls. Here, just a metre above sea level, two dozen cannon could rake the waters through open sites. It was the noose that would strangle the city of the Caesars. When a Venetian ship attempted to force the passage unaware of the latent power of the castle's artillery, she was holed, dismasted and rendered rudderless within minutes. Those sailors who survived the cannonade were initially imprisoned. Later they were taken down to the water's edge and held down while a pointed fence post was driven into the rectum and up through their guts. The posts were hoisted up into place. Eventually the wriggling of the half-impaled victim allowed the sharpened stake to penetrate further, pierce the chest cavity and put an end to his agony. It was a cheaper method of execution than crucifixion for it required no nails or crossbar, and also involved the added psychological humiliation of inflicting death by anal penetration.

Meanwhile the Sultan made certain that the most likely allies of the city, the younger brothers of Emperor Constantine, who ruled as joint despots of central Greece from the walled mountain city of Mistras, should be kept busy. An Ottoman army invaded the Peloponnese in the autumn of 1452 with orders to extend the campaigning season deep into the winter.

Mehmet's spies knew that the Byzantine Emperor Constantine XI was in negotiation to persuade Janos Hunyadi to come once more to the rescue, riding south at the head of an army of Hungarian knights. Other potential allies included the King of Naples and Pope Nicholas V. Venice appeared to be hiring out part of her navy to the Emperor – though the Sultan doubted he had sufficient cash to gain much from this – and what of Genoa? Genoa had too much to lose in the region to find it easy to choose an ally and in the end the city-state decided to play on both sides. It secretly negotiated with the Sultan so that the town of Galata (which looked at Constantinople from the other side of the Golden Horn creek) would declare itself neutral, thereby greatly weakening the Byzantine defences along the Golden Horn. At the same time a resourceful commander, Giovanni Giustiniani Longo, had taken a well-equipped company of Genoese volunteers to come to the aid of the Byzantine Emperor.

All this made it ever more urgent that the young Sultan should act while he could. There was, however, one more vital preparation that had to be done, but it could not be hurried. Mehmet had brought the service of one of the world's great master magicians of armament making, a Hungarian in whose person were fused the craft secrets of bell-founder, blacksmith and armourer. Urban, as he was known, had first offered his services to the Byzantine Emperor, but the fee he named and the quantities of metal he required were completely beyond the resources of Constantine. He found a better reception at the court of Mehmet, who tripled his salary and made certain that his viziers and financiers supplied Urban with all that he could require. Expensive metals had first to be stockpiled and then turned into liquids in vast crucibles and blended with other liquids that glowed the colour of the setting sun. But the true magic of the calling was in the art of cooling, of slaking and refiring, of working the liquid metals so that they simultaneously filled a mould in equal streams. A clot of carbon, a seam of ill-mixed alloy that had cooled at a marginally different rate, was a weakness waiting to destroy its owner. In the making of a medieval bombard, twisted lengths of wrought-iron rods were embedded within a deep mould-poured crust of bronze. If the making of a cannon was so very far from being an industrial process, so too was the making of the shot: spheres of stone fashioned by masons were in this period much preferred to iron. They required half the gunpowder charge of a cast-iron ball but had a shell-like impact, splintering into thousands of

Artillery park. Drawing by Leonardo, 1487.

shrapnel-like fragments which could clear whole trenches and ramparts of men.

Technology such as this was extremely expensive, and only available to those rulers who could afford superpower prices. As the Duke of Guise wrote advising another wealthy ruler, the Pope, on the true costs of a modern war, 'You know that when you want to take a fortress of any strength, you have to think of taking along twenty-four cannon to form two batteries, and six or seven powerful culverins to fire at the (upper) defences. You must also have at hand eight or ten thousand shot and two hundred thousand pounds of powder.'

As the spring rains finished towards the end of March in 1453, the Ottoman army was ready for this most famous of sieges. It was almost the exact opposite of how it is customarily imagined by many Western writers. No nomadic horde of Turks rode in from the southern and eastern horizons. Instead a well-disciplined army marched 150 miles from the north-west. In terms of numbers there was no question as to where the advantage lay, for there were at least ten Ottoman soldiers to every active defender. This sort of a proportion was vital for the successful prosecution of any siege. The city's position, astride a long peninsula, overlooking the entrance to the Bosporus channel but also opening out over the Sea of Marmara, has always benefited its defence. For it concentrated an attacker on the comparatively narrow landward walls, a mere fraction of the whole circumference. Even today the time-wrecked walls of Constantinople remain impressive, truly one of the wonders of the medieval world: a great triple line of ascending walls cunningly interspersed with towers and embellished with moats and fortified gates. They were made of quarried stone interlaced for greater resilience with courses of the distinctive flat bricks of the late Roman Empire. They had, in over a thousand years of very active history, repelled literally a hundred sieges, largely because the city could be supplied by sea against a landward assault, or by land against an assault from the sea. But Mehmet was leaving nothing to chance. He was attacking by land, having first sealed the sea routes with fortresses along the Bosporus and the Dardanelles. In order to further increase the odds in his favour, he had a small flotilla of ships dragged across the hills so that they could operate in the closed waters of the Golden Horn: not that he imagined he could breach the city walls with a marine assault, but so that his enemy could not concentrate their defences.

On 5 April Sultan Mehmet pitched his tent within clear view of the walls and by the following day the first of his batteries had begun to speak. The cannon fired at almost point-blank range to break down the walls, bombards dropped shells in mortar-like trajectories and culverins kept up a steady fire to clear the battlements, lest the Byzantine forces have the opportunity to rain fire back on the Ottoman artillery bastions. In the meantime, like a line of a hundred moles, the first trenches began to zigzag their way towards the walls, bending after each 160-yard approach. These were designed not to sap the walls' strength, but to allow troops to muster out of harm's way, virtually invisible to the defenders, for the trenches were protected with earth ramparts held together by hurdles. They also helped to mask the progress of the real mines, as the mining engineers snaked their underground shafts towards the foundations of the walls. These skilled workmen were not renegade Christians but Armenian and Orthodox Christians paid a salary for this non-military service. The Ottoman army was to prove itself masterful in its use of sappers, who at this period were transforming their battle tactics. The old practice had been to sink a shaft underneath a wall and then burn away the wooden shafts that propped up this underground chamber, so causing the defences to subside or crack. The new technique borrowed from the advances in gunpowder technology to create a truly explosive subterranean mine. The job was dangerous, not only from collapsing walls but from counter-mines sunk to intercept them; these were directed by dead reckoning but also by the use of delicate bells which tracked minute underground vibrations. A mine was a powerful and feared instrument of war but the miners remained outcasts who, like a spy, could expect no mercy if captured, not even in a general surrender.[2]

The main assault point was never in question. The Lycus valley causes a slight but noticeable depression in the long landward march of the walls of Constantinople. Even though their original height and breadth was increased to compensate, and no landward gate was permitted to breach this section (known as the Mesoteichion) it was the obvious weak point. It was here that Mehmet placed the bulk of his artillery, and further emphasised his slight tactical advantage by building a siege tower which could spray the upper battlements with musketry and light cannon fire. For seven weeks the batteries pounded this section of the walls with relentless dedication. There were pauses, to allow forays to probe the shattered defences, but then the cannonade would start again. There was also a constant movement of ordnance, for some of the lighter cannon were required to subdue outlying fortifications that remained on the Princes' Islands and along the Bosporus channel, but at the concentrated height of the siege the Sultan had collected together the largest artillery park ever assembled in the world: some seventy cannon.

The longest silence in the bombardment prefaced the arrival of the cannon that was the masterpiece of Mehmet's foundry. It had been specially cast by the Hungarian engineer Urban at Adrianople, twenty-six feet long with an eight-inch-thick barrel. Like the pregnant queen at the centre of a hive, it was surrounded by its own court of attendants. Some two hundred engineers prepared the road for the advance of the sixty oxen that pulled the great cannon's gun carriage. It was named 'Urban' after its maker. It was extraordinarily cumbersome, difficult to manoeuvre and could fire just seven shots a day. But once it had been embedded on vast chocks in its own earth bastion it quickly proved its worth. It could throw a twelve-hundred-pound ball over a mile, but at a quarter of that distance it crushed walls. It joined the fire-play directed at the Lycus valley, then shifted its sites to the south, to break open the Byzantine gate of St Romanus. Behind their shattered walls the Byzantine defenders had been busy, clearing houses and constructing a low inner wall, an earthen barricade laced with gun points. These were in place for the first all-out assault, so when Ottoman soldiers poured through the gaps made in the walls, they stumbled into a killing field and were raked with crossfire.

It was a victory of sorts. But even more encouraging to the defenders was a naval battle that had been watched by cheering crowds on the walls, in which a squadron of Christian ships, three Genoese and one Byzantine, not only broke through the Ottoman blockade of the Dardanelles but fought their way through a line of Turkish ships to reach the safety of the walled harbour. If this was the vanguard of a Christian fleet, which could outflank the Turkish siege lines from two shores, even Mehmet's scrupulous preparations would have proved inadequate. At this critical moment the young Sultan's spiritual confidant, Sheikh Aksemseddin, came to bless the troops and soothe Mehmet's concerns with reports of divine signs that prophesied victory. The discovery of the tomb of one of the Prophet Muhammad's standard bearers, Eyup Ansari, who had died during the first Muslim siege of Constantinople back in the seventh century, was a further boost to morale. As a Companion of the Prophet from the ancient oasis-city of Medina in the heart of the Arabian Desert, he had saintly status in the eyes of the Muslim army, while the banner that he carried had been embroidered by the wives and daughters of the Prophet Muhammad, which gave the discovery a further glow of holiness in the eyes of the Bektasi-influenced janissaries. However, memories of the two failed sieges by Muslim armies six centuries ago, and the two Ottoman failures over the past sixty years, had their own depressing context. As has often happened in such critical times, a number of inspirational but made-up *Hadith*, or sayings, of the Prophet began to circulate throughout the camp. Such false sayings can be easily spotted, as they are concerned with politics and material success, while the Prophet Muhammad's true sayings are concerned with mans relationship to God and suffering. Most of the '*Hadith* prophecies' that were circulating in the camp turned around the idea of the success of a third attempt to counteract the previous failed sieges. 'In the struggle against Constantinople, one third of Muslims will allow themselves to be defeated, which God cannot forgive, one third will be killed in battle, making them wondrous martyrs, and one third will be victorious.' Another popular siege prophecy was:

> Have you heard of a city with land on one side and sea on the other two sides? The Last Hour will not dawn before it is taken by seventy thousand sons of Isaac. When they reach it, they will not do battle with arms and catapults but with the words, 'There is no God but God, and God is great.' Then the first sea wall will collapse, and at the second cry the second sea wall, and on the third time, the wall on the land side will collapse, and, rejoicing they will enter in.

But the most popular one, still quoted in modern Istanbul, is 'Verily they will conquer Constantinople. Truly their commander will be an excellent one. Truly their army will be an excellent one.'

Despite these popular prophecies of victory, the spiritual and political leadership of the Ottoman siege remained quite sanguine and rational about the motivation of their army. Sheikh Aksemseddin himself had written privately to Mehmet, 'The number of those who are ready to sacrifice their lives for the love of God is extremely small . . . and you well know how many of the soldiers have in any case been converted by force . . . On the other hand, if they glimpse the possibility of winning booty they will run towards certain death.' The prospect of a sack, not salvation, underwrote every successful *jihad* or crusade. Be it Ceuta or Constantinople.

By 28 May every soldier, whether attacker or defender, knew that the moment of destiny was at hand. Two determined assaults had been driven back by the heroic soldiers of Byzantium, reinforced by the volunteers from Genoa. But each of these counter-attacks had been achieved only at the cost of a further reduction in the numbers of the defenders and a shattering renewal of the bombardment by the Ottoman artillery. They knew they could man the broken walls one last time, but there were only three or four men left to each tower and they no longer had reserves to hold the second line of ramparts, which had proved so murderous to the enemy. The end was at hand. A solemn fast was decreed, the holy icons and relics were solemnly processed along the city walls, and all day and night the great bells and tocsins of the city's churches rang out, calling the people to one last act of repentance, so that God might once more send the Virgin to the rescue of the city, or their souls would be shriven for the great test of the morrow.

As the cannon spoke out through the night, 'so heavy that to us it seemed to be a very inferno', Emperor Constantine took the opportunity to ride back into the centre of the city. He wanted to take mass one more time at the hallowed altar of the great church of Ayia Sophia. Then, according to an eyewitness account left us by the historian Phrantzes (as translated in Caroline Finkel's superb history *Osman's Dream*), he stopped off briefly at the Palace of Blachernae, which was built into a corner of the walls:

> Constantine assembled his household and said goodbye to each of them in turn, asking their forgiveness for any unkindness he might have ever shown them. 'Who could describe the tears and groans in the palace, even a man of wood and stone could not help weeping?' The Emperor then rode out of the palace in the company of the historian, who watched him dismount and ascend one of the towers in the darkness as the noise of the massed kettledrums and

horns prepared the Turks in their advance trenches for the sign of the attack. Three hours before daybreak, one of the giants within the janissary corps volunteered to lead an assault, and fought his way to the summit of a gate tower. His silhouette was glimpsed, urging on his brethren, before he was cut down. In the confused but evocative words of an Ottoman eyewitness, Tursun Bey, 'And from the furthest reaches below to the top-most parts, and from the upper heights down to the ground level, hand-to-hand combat and charging was being joined with a clashing and plunging of arms and hooked pikes and halberd in the breaches amidst the ruin wrought by the cannon. On the outside the Champions of Islam and on the inside the "wayward ones", pike to pike in true combat, hand-to-hand; now advancing, now feinting, guns firing and arms drawn, countless heads were severed from their trunks . . . presented to the bastion their hooked pikes, drawn, they were knocking to the ground the engaged warriors; as if struck in the deepest bedrock by the digging of a tunnel, it seemed that in places the city-walls had been pierced from below.

Constantine's post was in the tower above the fifth military gate in the cannon-shattered section of the Lycus valley. Beside him stood his cousin, Theophilus Palaeologus and his brothers-in-arms, the Spanish knight Don Francisco of Toledo, and the Serbian John Dalmata. It may have been this tower that was first ascended by Hassan of Ulubat at the head of a detachment of forty men, but none of the garrison survived. It is known by the Turks as Hucum Kapisi ('Gate of the Assault'). The body of the last Emperor of Byzantium, Constantine XI, was never found. Some claimed that it was last seen laid out in the Ayazma of Blachernae, where a walled garden sheltered a sacred spring beside a revered chapel where the mantle of the Virgin had been venerated. Others believed that the gypsies, who were given shelter within the walls by the Emperor, and who still frequent this quarter of the city, repaid their debt by spiriting his body away before it could be defiled. Wherever his body lies, Constantine's bravery and fortitude have for ever fused him with the identity of his city. In the manner of his death he ensured that the last hour of Byzantium was equal to its thousand years of past glories. In the words of a Turkish chronicler, 'The ruler of Istanbul was brave and asked for no quarter.'

In the afternoon of 29 May the young Sultan rode through the Adrianople gate, along the road that led directly from the edge of his capital of Edirne to the centre of the city, to receive the acclamation of his troops as 'Fatih', the Conqueror of the city of Constantinople, as they believed had been prophesied by the Prophet. Then he returned to his camp and his men had their much-dreamed of reward, the murderous, erotic, money-making, world-turned-upside-down delirium of the sack of a city. In the words of Chalcocondylas, 'The whole city was filled with men killing or being killed, fleeing or pursuing.' Kritovoulos Imbros, a near-contemporary Greek historian, tells of newborn babies hurled into the squares, and how the weak-minded, the old, the lepers and the infirm were slaughtered mercilessly, women and boys raped, 'dragging them out savagely, driving them, tearing at them, manhandling them, herding them disgracefully and shamefully into the crossroads, insulting them and . . . ten thousand other terrible things were done'.

On Friday 1 June the Sultan re-entered the city, riding on a white horse along the central avenue. The roadside was lined by thousands upon thousands of his troops, drunk with victory and elated by the sack. Behind them the stink of despair hung over the city – a foul memory concocted by tens of thousands of deaths, of rapes, of days of pitiless torture – mingled with the real stench of half-buried corpses and stagnant pools of glistening fluid rotting in the cellars and burned-out buildings. The aftermath of siege was always loathsome; an eyewitness of the death of another city at another time wrote, 'The dead bodies, having been thrown by heaps into holes, and but ill-covered. Broke out again, in so much that the streets ran with gore and matter, which issued from those disinterred carcasses.'[3]

In the words of Kritovoulos Imbros:

> The Sultan entered the city and looked about to see its great size, its situation, its grandeur and beauty . . . and the costliness of its churches and public buildings . . . When he saw what a large number had been killed, and the wreckage of the buildings, and the wholesale ruin and desolation of the city, he was filled with compassion and repented not a little at the destruction and plundering. Tears fell from his eyes as he groaned deeply and passionately, 'What a city we have given over to plunder and destruction.'

He rode towards the great domed church of Ayia Sophia, or Holy Wisdom, before which he dismounted and solemnly stooped to pour dust over his bowed head. The blood of the Christians who had been slaughtered in this last sanctuary had been cleaned from the marble floors and walls, braziers of incense burned in the outer courtyards, rows of prayer carpets tastefully indicated the direction of Mecca and from the great upper balconies hung the long trailing silk banners of the victorious army. Sheikh Aksemseddin acted as Imam, lead the prayers and gave the Friday sermon. Afterwards the twenty-one-year-old Sultan rode out to inspect the battered shell of the old palace of the Caesars, which overlooked the junction of the Bosporus and the Sea of Marmara, its ancient marble-framed balconies perched high above the sea walls. Looking out over the ruin – which had stood like this for many centuries and had nothing to do with either the violence of the recent sack or his artillery – he quoted the Persian poet Saadi:

> The spider spins his web in the palace of the Caesars
> And the owl sings her watchsong on the towers of Afrasiab

It was a beautifully timed couplet, for Saadi, as both a Muslim and a Persian, was referring to a time of mixed emotions for his people. When the Arabs occupied the capital city of Ctesiphon they were on their way to destroy the ancient Persian Empire but spread the gift of Islamic faith. For Mehmet – like Wellington sunk into an exhausted huddle wrapped up in his cloak after Waterloo, and Scipio foreseeing the eventual destruction of Rome as he watched Carthage burn – could now taste both the exhilaration and the tragedy of conquest.

Before autumn arrived the vast army had returned to Edirne and been discharged back to its home provinces. That winter the great bejewelled bride of the eastern Mediterranean, the capital city of the Caesars, long protected by the mantle of the Virgin, was an empty peninsula inhabited by rats, cats, feral dogs and bored guards. Above this ghostly miasma rose the edifices of a thousand years of imperium: dark palaces, broken walls, empty churches, closed markets, vast cisterns, triumphal arches, isolated columns and solemn gatehouses, now abandoned, locked and empty.

Because the Ottoman navy had, to a man, also joined in the excitement of the sack there had been no guard boats left on patrol. In the resulting confusion some refugees managed to escape from the city by crossing the Golden Horn and begging passage on one of the few ships moored in the safe harbour of Galata. When this small flotilla, which included Venetian ships and a galley from Byzantine Trebizond, nosed its way cautiously out of the Golden Horn, they were then free to hoist their sails and catch a stiff northerly wind which carried them rapidly out into the safety of the Sea of Marmara. On one ship alone the presence of four hundred refugees would have rendered her unsailable if the wind had not been so perfectly favourable, while the passenger list of another resounds with the chief families of Byzantium: six members of the House of Palaeologus, two Lascaris, two Notaras, two Comneni and two Cantacuzenus. Some seven Genoese ships followed this example before the commander of the Ottoman navy restored sufficient order among his fleet to capture the last fifteen ships as they stood in the docks, swamped with refugees clamouring to gain a footing aboard. They were fated to join the lines of manacled slaves, who over the next few days were marched out to the soldiers' camp, where the trade in flesh and goods reached a climax of speculative activity.

Most of the senior captives, once identified, were brought before the Sultan. He struck hard at the Western leadership, ordering the immediate execution of the Consuls of Venice and the Catalans and their chief counsellors, but was business-minded enough to accept ransoms for the lesser officials and merchants. With the native Byzantine nobility he proved exceptionally clement, offering freedom and advancement to all who would convert, while others were ransomed. Michael Cammariotes's experience may have been typical in that he 'ransomed my sister from one place, my mother from somewhere else' but found that his father and brother had been killed and three of his four nephews had already accepted the offer of conversion to Islam. One of Mehmet's other political master strokes was to immediately appoint the great adversary of the union between Greek Orthodoxy and the Latin papacy, the monk Gennadius, as the new Orthodox Patriarch. Gennadius, for his part, publicly declared that it was better for the Orthodox to be ruled under the Turban than the Tiara (of the Roman Catholic papacy) and dutifully received his appointment at the hands of Mehmet, just as if the Sultan was the legitimate heir to the old spiritual responsibilities of a Byzantine Emperor.

But not all received such grace. The Sultan initially befriended the

Byzantine chief minister, Grand Duke Lucas Notaras, who had been greatly opposed to any alliance with the Latin West, and thought long and hard about appointing him as the new prefect of the city. During their discussions Notaras revealed that Mehmet's grand vizier had been on the Byzantine payroll. This was of course music to Mehmet's ears, for he had long resented his father's favourite minister and now in his hour of triumph he no longer stood in any need of his services or cautious advice. The Sultan's delayed revenge for the many slights of his youth was pitiless. Halil Pasha was tortured for forty days before he was executed. Notaras remained in high favour with the Sultan and a frequent guest at his banquets until the day he was commanded to send his youngest son, a handsome fourteen-year-old, to join the Sultan in his bedchamber. The Grand Duke refused and paid for his high sense of honour with his own life and those of all his sons. It is a good tale but seems unlikely, for surely anyone with any talent for political life, let alone holding the office of prime minister, would not have held the art of pimping in such low esteem. It seems more likely that the Sultan found out that he had been lied to about the actions of his grand vizier. Not that there is any need to draw a puritanical cloak over Mehmet's free-ranging sexuality, which appears once again to have had much in common with that of his alter ego Alexander. In the words of a Turkish historian of the sixteenth century, after he returned from a campaign, 'Mehmet spent many nights in debauchery with lovely-eyed, fairy-like slave girls, and his days drinking with pages who looked like angels.' This easy sensuality has been misinterpreted by hostile historians anxious to besmirch Mehmet's character, which needs to be seen in the context of the freedoms of earlier centuries. Think for a moment back to such books of wisdom as the highly esteemed *A Mirror for Princes*, which the Muslim Sultan of Tabaristan, Kai-Ka'us Ibn Iskandar, wrote for the moral guidance of his son, and reads like an eleventh-century Persian Lord Chesterfield. In it he counsels, 'As between women and youths do not confine your inclinations to either sex, thus you might find enjoyment from both kinds.' Elsewhere in this fascinating guide to proper conduct he indicates that there might be a seasonal pattern to such inclinations, 'during summer let your desires incline towards youths and during winter towards women'. But whoever you slept with the most important rule was to maintain good manners. A nobleman, wishing to lie with his slave page-boy one afternoon, was reproved by the boy for crudely asking him to turn his arse towards him, when he could have framed the request with greater elegance: 'That you ask me to turn my face the other way.' The nobleman in question was so impressed by this lesson in manners that he gave the slave his freedom. Although we cannot be certain that Mehmet read this seminal work,

Page at the court of Mehmet II. Possibly by Gentile Bellini at the request of Mehmet II in 1480. (Isabella Stewart Gardner Museum, Boston)

there is a very good chance, for a Turkish translation had been made from the original Persian for the library of his father, Murat II.

For a year Mehmet appointed no one to the office of grand vizier, before selecting Mahmud Pasha Angelovic, a recent convert to Islam descended from both a distinguished family of Byzantine civil servants and the Serbian nobility. This was part of a conscious policy to balance the power of the old Turkic emirs with converts personally loyal to the Sultan. Another of Mehmet's favourite ministers was the convert Murat Pasha, a Palaeologue cousin of the last Byzantine Emperor.

The following spring the Sultan returned and explored the city in much greater detail. Winter had washed away the stink of despair and now it felt possible that the city could be made anew. There was much to be done and undone, and though the Sultan made frequent inspection tours, it would be five years before he moved his court and his women from Edirne to Constantinople, known colloquially by its Greek nickname 'to the city', Istanbul. Suleyman Bey was appointed in command of all the works, and beneath him laboured the Sultan's share of a fifth of all the surviving captives. So it is no cultural accident that the feel of the masonry – especially those regular courses of tile-like bricks – that was built during Mehmet's reign is nearly identical to that of his Byzantine predecessor. First the walls were repaired and a potential weakness that Mehmet had contemplated during the siege, the junction of the land walls and the sea walls along the Marmara shore, was plugged. The seven towers of Yedikule Castle, architectural brood sister to the hulking mass of Rumeli Hisari on the Bosporus Strait, rose to anchor this corner of the city walls, including the suburban Roman triumphal arch within its structure. Yedikule was designed as a military strong point and only later acquired notoriety as a state prison. Then Mehmet decided on the site of the central market which fronted one of the formal squares of Byzantium (Forum Tauri) and spilled downhill towards the docks. The multi-domed Bedestan, which is still the most impressive single structure in Istanbul's covered bazaar, dates to this period. Nearby, on the summit of one of the city's seven hills, he ordered a palace to be raised. Then, some ten years after the Conquest, he rounded off this central government block by laying out a vast mosque over the site of the Church of the Holy Apostles – perhaps in a conscious appropriation of the tomb of Constantine, the founder of the city. Around it were built all the caring elements of the state, following the personal example of the Prophet Muhammad: schools and colleges for students, charitable kitchens, fountains and hospices for wandering dervishes.

So, within two decades, a highly visible Ottoman core was placed on the high ground right in the centre of the city, astride the main avenue. This model was to be copied by Mehmet's ministers and later by his royal heirs, to the great benefit of Istanbul's skyline. So that hill after hill would be capped with a formal architectural mosque whose perpetual upkeep was funded by a landed trust in the form of an endowment of rent-paying shops, baths and markets established around it. Meanwhile on the shore the dozen distinctive villages of old Constantinople gradually re-emerged, becoming the natural home of the Ottoman Empire's vivacious minorities of trading peoples: Italians, Greeks, Jews, Armenians, Syrians and Egyptians.

As the years passed Mehmet began to better appreciate the unique topography of the city and realised that the government block in the centre of the city was a dull place in which to live. The end of the peninsula of Constantinople (the site of the pagan Acropolis) framed a most wonderful variety of views, up the Bosporus, along the Golden Horn, towards the Asian coast and south across the Sea of Marmara. It also allowed for easy boat access so that the Sultan could make quick and private use of the hunting palaces, pavilions and picnic sites that are strewn along the Bosporus shore. Not much of his original palace has survived the centuries of improvements and rebuilding by later Sultans, except the lovely tiled pavilion with its elegant upper balcony that was built to overlook the polo field: a delicate fusion of Turkoman and Persian taste. Here the court poets recall the intimate gatherings of his companions, where 'the Sultan drunk wine under the stars with his pages, and of the evenings he was entertained by the women of his harem'.

Mehmet also developed an increasing eye for symbolism, and it no doubt pleased him that his new palace of Topkapi ('The Cannon Gate') had been a centre of sovereignty for over a thousand years of history, for it overlooked Ayia Sophia and the great square of Justinian and abutted the ancient palace: the three formal centres of the old empire. It must also have helped that by this period the Ottomans' hold on the Black Sea seemed secure and the other maritime gateway into Istanbul, the Dardanelles, had been greatly strengthened by the construction of two new artillery forts, Sultanhisar on the eastern shore and Kilitulbahr ('The Lock Put on the Sea') on the western shore.

By the end of his reign the revitalised city had almost doubled in size from its pre-siege population of forty thousand. This was the conscious policy of the Sultan, who for the rest of his active reign sought to recreate the old frontiers of Byzantium and to pour new life into its capital. To chronicle his actions is a lesson in statecraft and a testament to his extraordinary energy, dynamism and discipline.

The fledgling navy that he had assembled for the siege of

Constantinople, and which had been dragged across the hills to dominate the walls along the banks of the Golden Horn, was at once put to
work. The following year a fleet of fifty-six ships was sent on a tour of
the Black Sea coast, harassing and threatening the Venetian and Genoese
strong points (such as Caffa in the Crimea), though none was actually
taken. Having shown his strength, and digested his admirals' reports on
the respective strengths of his enemies, he began to divide them.
Although he knew that one day he would have to fight the Venetians
for mastery of the Aegean, he put 'La Serenissima' to one side, the better
to concentrate on the marginally more vulnerable Genoa. The Venetians
were encouraged to sign a beneficial trade agreement, permitting them
to operate in the Black Sea in exchange for their ships calling into
Istanbul and paying a tariff of customs. They were also permitted to
establish a permanent storehouse and legation for this purpose in the
city. Their control over the Aegean island of Naxos was acknowledged
in return for a modest tribute.

All Ottoman forces could then be concentrated on the Genoese.
Mehmet did not waste his energies, for he knew exactly what to attack
and in which order. In 1455 the Alum mines at Phokaia, just north of
Smyrna, were seized. The export of barge-loads of this ground crystal
powder was not the most glamorous element of the Levant trade but it
was certainly among its most lucrative. Alum (aluminium sulphate) is
vital for the successful curing of leather and the cleaning of raw wool
and could be sold to all the leading cities of Europe, year in, year out,
be it Florence, Antwerp, Valencia, London or Lübeck. As the Phokaia
mines then represented about 90 per cent of the world's resources, you
could also pretty much name your own price.

Next Mehmet picked off the Genoese trading cities on the Black Sea
coast. This was not done in one over-ambitious imperial armada but
one by one, in well-planned specific operations. Genoese Amasra
(Amastris) was attacked in a pincer movement by an Ottoman naval
squadron, while the Sultan himself led his army on the long overland
march to break down the city walls. Nor did he upset his northern
neighbours. Many of the operations were planned in alliance with the
Tartar Lords of Krim (Crimea) and there was absolutely no deluded
attempt to dominate the vast hinterland of the steppes – as other impe-
rially minded outsiders, be they Cyrus, Napoleon or Hitler, all lived to
regret. The Sultan was content with possession of the key trading cities

of the Black Sea coast, through which all the southbound trade of Poland, Lithuania and Moscovy naturally flowed. Nowadays, when it has become fashionable for white politicians to apologise for the crimes of past centuries, most especially that of slave trading, it is fascinating to look back to this period. To a time when white Christians were to be numbered among the most miserable victims, their villages sacked and sad defiles of the survivors rounded up for the long march to the ports that specialised in this inhumane trade. In this period the soft steppe-land underbelly of Poland, Lithuania, Ukraine and southern Russia was milked of about twenty thousand sad souls a year by Tartar raiders.

Far from setting himself up with delusions of world dominion, Mehmet was scrupulous to treat the Tartar Khans with respect: a tradition which was continued by all his descendants. For everyone versed in the proud genealogy of Central Asia knew that the House of Ottoman was descended from a mere border lord on the frontier of the Byzantine Empire, while the Tartar Khan of Krim was of the direct line of Genghis Khan. Alone of all leaders of the 'protected states' within the frontiers of Ottoman hegemony, the Tartar Khan was asked not for tribute but given an annual gift from Istanbul.[4]

No such restraint was shown to the Christian kingdoms of the Balkans. Here Mehmet revealed himself at his most expansionist, ruthless and persistent, seemingly determined to create a bulwark of conquered tribute-paying provinces against the expected Christian counter-attack. Year after year the Ottoman army was assembled at Edirne in the spring and launched west into the Balkans. When other frontiers, in Anatolia, the Black Sea or the Aegean islands, called for the Sultan's personal presence he made certain that a trusted vizier led the annual assault into eastern Europe. By the end of his reign Mehmet had accumulated a vast host of border raiders, obedient to hardly any authority except his annual instructions to raid the Christian kingdoms of the West. Some experts reckon that there were as many as fifty thousand of these licensed freebooters drawn from every creed and race. So that the hammer-blow invasions of Serbia by the main Ottoman battle army in 1453 and 1454 were duplicated by thousands of lesser raids that gradually drained the vitality of the kingdom. In 1455 Mehmet struck decisively at the economic jugular of the old medieval kingdom of Serbia by annexing the silver-mining district of Novobrodo.

The Sultan's attacks on Hungary were less successful, owing largely to the leadership of Janos Hunyadi. There has always been something unexplained about this great Hungarian hero, the William Wallace of the Magyars. He first emerged, like some personification of their ancient god of war, at the Battle of Semendria in 1437, riding into the battle as an unknown knight, on his shield a black raven with a golden ring in its beak. By the end of the day Hunyadi had proved himself an heroic warrior and he eventually rose to become the chosen commander of the Hungarian army, the darling of the people, though loathed by the magnates and nobles. He was a master tactician, energetic in victory but also a determined leader of the resistance in defeat. His greatest test was in 1456, when he organised the defence of Belgrade against a powerful army led by Mehmet himself. Belgrade was then the southern gate of Hungary, a fortress city astride the junction of the rivers Danube and Sava. Deserted by the jealous Hungarian nobility, Hunyadi resisted the invaders by leading fifteen thousand men out of the mountains of Transylvania, aided by a volunteer army of peasant crusaders that had been raised by the passionate oratory of the monk John Capistrano. Armed with little more than scythes and poll-axes, this peasant army won a conspicuous victory, using small boats in a series of near-suicidal assaults on the wide-bottomed Ottoman river barges that accompanied the Sultan's army. But Mehmet was not discouraged from the siege by the sinking of his river navy. Instead the siege lines were tightened for eight days of intensive bombardment. On the dawn of the ninth day the Sultan ordered wave after wave of attacks to be launched against the city's broken walls. His persistence seemed to be on the very point of success, with the moat and lower slopes all in the hands of his infantry, when Hunyadi struck back. He gave the order that the reserve stock of fascines (wattle-like bundles that were filled with earth and used to bolster broken walls) should be drenched in oil and pitch, and then ignited as they were rolled down on to the enemy. Immediately behind this wall of fire, Hunyadi led the defenders in a last, all-out counterattack. The Ottoman line broke and in the near-panic of an unexpected retreat Mehmet was himself wounded by a pike thrust deep into his thigh. Whether by treachery or chance, Hunyadi was also struck down at this time. The wound proved mortal. He was mourned by all Hungary and even by his bitterest enemy, for the Sultan sent a message of condolence to Budapest on the death of 'the ablest general in Europe'. The Ottomans would not invade Hungary for another seventy years.

Although Mehmet was famously well disposed to employing converts from Christianity and trusting them with the highest offices of state – from admiral to general to grand vizier – the Ottoman state was not interested in missionary activity or mass conversions. Never is that false image of Islam being spread by invading armies, with the sword in one hand and the Koran in the other, less applicable. For it was vital for the finances of the Ottoman Empire that the peasants and town-dwelling merchants of the conquered western provinces remained Christian. The poll tax on non-Muslims was the backbone of state income, greatly assisted by the annual tribute sent by the Ottoman vassal kings of Christian Wallachia, Moldavia, Transylvania and Bosnia-Herzegovina. In their dealings with its own Muslim subjects the Ottoman state was bound to follow hallowed Islamic tradition which laid out a modest system of tithes on livestock and gathered crops.

Mehmet also made skilful use of the schism that still exists between the Catholics and the Orthodox of the Balkans, always favouring the latter. But for all his posing as a protector of Orthodoxy against the papacy, the last remaining political pockets of Byzantine authority were ruthlessly hunted out and squashed. The Sultan himself led his army deep into the Peloponnese to crush the last fortresses of the Palaeologue dynasty in 1460, and again took a personal lead to destroy the even more reclusive enclave of the Comnenian dynasty, Trebizond. Recalling this campaign, a soldier told how the Sultan had to beg 'the janissaries to make an effort to get the camels down to the plain and we had to go back up the mountain with great effort and struggle all night before we got them down to the plain. The Sultan stayed there that day resting and gave the janissaries fifty thousand gold coins to divide among themselves and he raised the wages of the soldiers.' Mehmet made certain that sooner or later he extinguished these rival dynasties. The more attractive of the daughters of the Palaeologi and Comneni entered his harem and their officials and cousins passed with an extraordinary ease into his service, so that his court soon boasted convert princes from Bosnia, Serbia and Herzegovina as well as the Byzantine princes we have already noted. The grand vizier Mahmud Pasha's unconverted Christian brother, Michael Angelovic, ran the pro-Ottoman faction within Serbia, and the easy way in which Trebizond capitulated suggests a similar network. The high treasurer of Comnenian Trebizond was Georgios Amirutzes – another cousin of Mahmud Pasha – who, having 'handled' the surrender of Trebizond, went on to a dream of a job at Mehmet's court. He was commissioned to pull together all the contemporary European travel reports and marry them up with Ptolemaic geography and the accounts of Muslim scholars to create a state-of-the-art Ottoman research institute bristling with detailed maps and route plans. Here the achievements of the Portuguese Crusaders in exploring the coast of Africa and the islands of the Atlantic were watched with great interest.

Some ten years after the fall of Constantinople the Sultan was faced with the long-expected counter-attack from Christendom. He had, as we have seen, immeasurably improved his position, but the threat was still potent. The papacy and the Duke of Burgundy promised aid but the immediate tactical threat came from the army of the Kingdom of Hungary and the fleets of the Republic of Venice. In 1463 they struck simultaneously, Venice reoccupying most of Greece and Hungary advancing into Bosnia, while Gjerj Skanderbeg, the wily lord of the mountains of Albania, once again changed allegiance (and faiths) to join this promising alliance. The Sultan recognised the danger presented by the alliance between Hungary and Venice, especially if they could unite their forces in Albania. In 1466 he repeated the spectacular achievement of his youth by leading an army into Albania and in just twenty-five days throwing up the castle of El-Basan on the strategic pass that linked the Adriatic with the Balkans. This coup was followed by a series of Ottoman invasions and by 1468 Skanderbeg had been thrown out of the mountains and sought refuge as a pensioner of Venice. But the Venetians had a surprise of their own in store. Working in alliance with a Turkic tribal leader from Central Asia, Uzun Hassan, they delivered a two-pointed attack. As the Ottoman army rushed east to protect their Central Asian frontier, Venice struck at the Ottoman fleet at Smyrna (now the Turkish city of Izmir) and Antalya and burned the naval base at Gelibolu (deep in the Sea of Marmara), having fought its way up the Dardanelles. It was a spectacularly successful maritime campaign, but the Venetian ally in Central Asia failed to repeat the terrible destruction that had been unleashed on the Ottomans by Timur. In 1473 the Ottoman army of Mehmet proved as decisive on the battlefields of its eastern frontier as it had before the Crusader armies of the West and the walls of Constantinople. Uzun Hassan's ambitions were blown apart as the vast hordes of tribal cavalry under his command were mown down by the shrapnel and gunfire of the Ottoman army.

This dangerous double attack blunted, Mehmet and his generals once again took to the offensive, conquering the Emirate of Karaman and raiding deep into the Adriatic until the Venetians were forced to sue for peace in 1479. Like all great rulers, Mehmet knew how to befriend his enemies. Within the first year of the new peace he had invited the Doge to attend the month-long circumcision ceremonies that he was staging to honour the manhood of his grandson, young Selim, who went on to prove himself a chip off the old block. The Doge made the customary excuses, much regret unable to come owing to pressure of work and family commitments, but he did respond to one particular request, to send a 'good painter'. It is thus that today we can look upon the face of Mehmet in London's National Gallery. The portrait was executed in the last year of his life, when he was described as of 'medium height, fat and fleshy, he had a wide forehead, large eyes with thick lashes, an aquiline nose, a small mouth with a round copious reddish-tinged beard, a short, thick neck, a sallow complexion, rather high shoulders and a loud voice'. What this slightly hostile description by the Venetian Angiolello fails to mention is this Sultan's nimble, highly intelligent eyes.

The year after he made peace with Venice the Sultan felt free to concentrate his forces on a particularly obstinate enemy. The Crusader Knights of St John of the Hospital of Jerusalem were a worthy opponent. They were sovereign lords of the island of Rhodes, which sat squarely on the principal maritime routes both east–west and north–south and was used as a base for piratical raids all over the Aegean. A militant thorn in the side of Muslim coastal trade, they had in the past allied themselves with any and every enemy of the Ottomans, be it Venice or one of the rival Turkic emirates within Anatolia. Their history, as one of the Crusading Orders that had brutally occupied the Holy Land and enslaved many pious Muslim pilgrims on their way to the Haj, made them an especially inviting target for any Muslim leader who wished to win the praise of his co-religionists. It was also vital to unpick the Knights of St John from their fortress home before any further Ottoman advance could be made east along the coast of Turkey, or an attempt be made against any of the major island bases of Venice in the Aegean such as Crete, Corfu and Cyprus.

But that year Mehmet seems to have made one of the few strategic mistakes of his career, though at the time it seemed a dramatic and outwardly successful venture. No one can quite understand why he ordered his admiral, Gedik Ahmed Pasha, to assault the Italian fortress town of Otranto that summer. For in the past he had been scrupulous to concentrate all his available resources on each target and to presume nothing was worth undertaking unless it had been planned down to the last detail. He had also, for all the wide-ranging concerns of his fast-expanding empire, made certain that every military effort had been backed up by diplomatic activity to isolate his chosen target. Gedik Pasha, yet another of Mehmet's highly talented and trusted renegade commanders, made a fine job of this operation, swooping down on the Italian coast within a day of leaving his harbour base, landing unopposed and then surrounding and subduing the fortress in a two-week siege. It was said that the slave market in Istanbul was glutted with twenty thousand Italians from the Kingdom of Naples. An Ottoman garrison remained to overwinter in Otranto and continued to raid the surrounding countryside. This action, more than any other, sent shock waves throughout western Europe, alerting its peoples to the proximity of the Ottoman threat in a way that the loss of a Balkan kingdom, a Greek island or a Venetian fortress had never achieved. Rumours of the barbarity of the Turks grew ever more monstrous in the telling: how twelve thousand Christians had been marched out of town and driven over cliffs to be eaten by dogs or how the old Archbishop had been sawn in two over his altar.[5] The move also antagonised a new enemy, the Kingdom of Naples and Sicily, which had so far remained outside the conflict. Nor was this designed to be a bridgehead for a subsequent invasion of Italy, for we now know, from the evidence of his ministers and courtiers, that Mehmet was much more interested in the annexation of southern Turkey and Syria.

The Knights of St John in Rhodes, unlike the Neapolitan garrison at Otranto, had long expected an Ottoman siege. Indeed it is not too much of an exaggeration to say that they lived for such a thing. To the Order of St John, peace was always a much greater danger than war. In order to justify their productive portfolio of monastic estates, scattered across the length and breadth of Europe (all neatly subdivided into priories and commanderies) it was vital for the Knights to preserve their reputation as the shock-troops of Christendom. Wherever the fight was on, they had to be involved and be seen to be in the thick of things.

The example of what befell that other Crusading Order, the Knights Templars, did much to inspire them. Their old rivals in the Holy Land had not been quick enough to reposition themselves after the fall of Acre in 1291. It did not help matters that the Templars had also become overexposed by holding too many foreign bonds. One of their leading clients, King Philip IV of France, found it much simpler to arrest and torture a public confession of heresy out of the Templars' leaders, whom he grabbed off the streets of Paris, than repay the interest on his debt. A pain-engulfed mind will always reach out to find what it is the police-man-torturer wishes to hear, so in the cold light of the courtroom the indicted found themselves facing the charges dreamed up by their inquisitors: to arse-kissing, sodomy, secret oaths, kissing on the lips, a mysterious talking head and blasphemy. It didn't matter that they later retracted them in public. They paid an appalling personal price for their bravery, for they were not so much burned at the stake as slow-grilled on an isolated islet in the Seine, after which the order was destroyed.

The Knights of St John paid very close attention to this example. They refused all offers from princes and kings to relocate their head-quarters into their kingdoms. Instead they revealed a most insistent desire to remain their own masters. They also found themselves the unexpected beneficiaries of the burning of the Templar leadership for, despite the backstairs diplomatic manoeuvres of the French King, the Templars' vast international holdings were not sequestered as a 'profit of justice' by their torturers but were passed on to other 'brother monks militant'. Throughout most of Christendom this meant the Knights of St John, though, as we have seen in Portugal, a new knightly order, the Crusading Order of Christ, was especially created to provide a new identity for the Knights Templars, their castles and landholdings.

The Knights of St John, like most of the refugees who escaped the fall of Acre in 1291, first moved to Cyprus.[6] But just seven years later they embarked on the conquest of the island of Rhodes, fighting not the Saracens but the local Byzantine Greeks. The order was weak in men and ships in those first years of exile. They rowed out from the harbour of Limassol in just two galleys, supported by four smaller ships. This little squadron stopped off for a month at Castelrosso (Kastellorizo), a little fortress island just off Kas on the Turkish coast, to recruit more fighters. The whole operation was nearly blown when their spies were arrested in Rhodes but they managed to talk themselves out of trouble.

On 20 September they struck, the thirty-five armoured knights now supported by a considerable body of freelance infantry. They seized the old acropolis turned fortress of Pheraclos (beneath which the modern village of Heraki lies along its pebble beach), followed by that of Phileromos just up the coast. The city of Rhodes proved quite beyond their resources, so that there was a curious two-year interval in the conquest, which allowed the order's Grand Master to go on a fund-raising tour of Venice, Rome and Genoa. He returned in the spring of 1309 at the head of a handsome squadron of a dozen galleys with which the Knights finally enforced the peaceful surrender of the city of Rhodes. The cost had been minimal in terms of blood, though the Knights of St John had been forced to mortgage twenty years of island revenue to their financial backers. But it was money well spent, for they were safely established as masters of their own island and destiny, which they protected against both the Muslim foe and 'other' powers, by building forts all along the coastline of Rhodes and slowly acquiring strong points on neighbouring islands (Leros, Piskopi, Nisyros, Symi, Calymnos and Cos) and the mainland coast.

Above all they continued to prove themselves warlike, seizing Smyrna in 1334 and repeatedly raiding the coast of Mameluke Egypt, sacking, burning and looting the ports. In 1365 a Crusader fleet, led by King Peter of Cyprus, assembled in the harbour of Rhodes to descend on Alexandria on 9 October, at the very end of the sailing season. They sailed straight into the harbour and sacked the city with such savagery that it even appalled their contemporaries, while the Egyptians (Jews, Copts and Muslims alike) were still seeking their revenge two generations later.

They were not just a nuisance to the Mamelukes of Egypt. After one piece of piracy the Genoese paid the nearby Turkic Emir of Mylasa to put 'pressure' on the Knights to release one of their merchant ships. On another occasion the Venetians allied with an Egyptian Sultan to put together a thirty-six-ship blockade of Rhodes in order to recover three galleys that had been illegally seized. The Knights also had a more pacific line to their business. They were specialist travel agents. Rhodes operated as a useful stop-off for the Holy Land and they kept permanent consuls at Ramleh, Beirut and Jerusalem who looked after the travel arrangements of the pilgrims. Much of this income was ploughed back into the most spectacular charitable achievement of the Order of

the Knights of St John: the maintenance of a hospital where the poor
and ill were treated with skill, charity and dignity, to the extent that
they were served their meals on silver plates.

After losing their castle at Smyrna to Timur – the only Western
Christians who could claim that they had fought the great Tartar warlord – the Knights relocated further south. They ransacked the classical
ruins of Halicarnassus, demolishing one of the Seven Wonders of the
ancient world in the process. The Mausoleum was quarried for building
stone and its marble veneer burned to make lime mortar with which the
Knights constructed St Peter's Castle (also known as Petronio) on an
offshore islet overlooking the harbour at present-day Bodrum. Whatever
their politics, and regardless of their deformation of the example of the
life of Christ into one of snobbery,[7] racism and violence, they had an
unwaveringly good eye for a site, adding their own texture to many a
classical acropolis, creating the sort of landscapes that you can sometimes observe as the backdrop to a Renaissance miniature, a rocky cleft
crowned with the pinnacles of a Gothic tower. The castles they built at
Lindos, Archangelos, Symi, Kastellorizo and Bodrum would certainly
allow them to be acquitted of many of their crimes if they came up
before a jury of architects and travel writers.

Their reputation as rulers was not so good. When they were invited
by a cabal of crusading princes, popes and emperors to bolster the fortifications of Byzantium by taking over the defence of Mistra and
Monemvasia in the Peloponnese, the local population rebelled at the
thought. They instinctively preferred to fight the Turk unaided than be
'protected' by the Knights of St John. After the fall of Constantinople
the Knights sent delegations to the Sultan offering peace as they hurriedly prepared for the coming war. In 1476 the Ottomans tested the
island's defences by attacking the outlying forts on Symi and Kos. The
next year they landed a raiding party at Archangelos on the east coast of
Rhodes. The Grand Master had started evacuating the outlying possessions to concentrate all strength, in terms of men and money, in that
island. The Knights also tried to mend fences with their old adversaries,
signing non-aggression pacts with their Muslim neighbours, the
Mameluke Sultan of Egypt and the Hafsid Sultan of Tunisia and Libya.
In 1478 Sophianos, an Ottoman ambassador, arrived at Rhodes with
proposals for a peace. It was, like much formal diplomacy, a farce. For
both sides knew that he had come to spy out the land in order to make

a personal report to the Sultan and that his presence meant that an invasion was imminent. The ambassador's report was backed up by a small group of renegade converts who identified the weak points of the Rhodian defences on a map for the Sultan in Istanbul. In the autumn of 1479 a flotilla was dispatched to reconnoitre the island, looking for possible anchorages as well as landing some raiding parties. This naval force overwintered in the protected haven of Marmaris, just eighteen nautical miles from Rhodes, on the Turkish coast. The following spring the Ottoman army marched south to Marmaris so that it could embark for the short crossing in May.

On the morning of 23 May the lookouts on the watch-towers of Rhodes saw the seas to the north-west gradually fill with sails, as a fleet of 170 ships blotted out the horizon. They made their landfall later that evening on the Bay of Trianda, its long, shelving beach a perfect landing place for the galleys and narrow-keeled coastal barges. Exact numbers are difficult to pin down: some chroniclers talk of an invading army of one hundred thousand, some of half that number, but the important figure to bear in mind is that of the professionals. The entire janissary corps, even in the heyday of the Ottoman Empire, numbered around twelve thousand men, the Knights never more than eight hundred. Their sergeants, allies, conscripted serfs and hired mercenaries would have topped up the defending force by another two and a half thousand armed men.

The discipline and organisation of the Ottoman force was immediately impressed upon the defenders. The morning after the landing, the first battery began bombarding the sea tower of St Nicholas. This was in itself a near-miracle of advance planning and staff work, but also indicated a coherent strategy right from that very first dawn. The tower was the key to the harbour defences of Rhodes, into which the Knights had poured much of their expertise and energy. The funding for the Tower of St Nicholas had come from the rich Duchy of Burgundy, a handsome stone memorial to the Burgundian volunteer knights who had sailed to Rhodes to help repel the revenge assaults of the Egyptians in 1440 and 1444. It sat on the end of a mole which divided the naval harbour (the Mandraccio) from the commercial harbour. The tower's lower walls were twenty-four feet thick and ringed with cannon portals. Above rose an artillery tower whose field of fire commanded the two harbours. It could also rake the backs of any besieging force that attacked the sea wall, for the tower stood some five hundred metres proud of these defences. Closer to the city walls stood the more striking silhouette of the Tower of Naillac, a tall, vertical piece of medieval showmanship with overhanging galleries and corner turrets. It had been built in 1400, just before the rapid advance in artillery technology made it obsolete. Behind it stood the sea wall, and it was an open secret that this sector was the weak point, for it was a mere medieval curtain wall. By contrast the land wall that stretched around the city of Rhodes had been upgraded into a state-of-the-art defensive network with moats, ramped foundation walls and squat, protruding bastions that could cover every inch of ground with artillery fire. If St Nicholas fell into Turkish hands, or was even neutralised, the Turks would be free to bring their entire fleet into the two harbours and fall upon the weaker sea wall.

So the Ottoman commander-in-chief, no less a figure than the former Palaeologue prince Mesikh Pasha, threw the full force of his artillery, including sixteen bombards which fired stone shot eleven inches in diameter, against St Nicholas. Watching his every move and disposition was a fifty-seven-year-old Frenchman, the Grand Master of the Knights of St John, Pierre d'Aubusson. He knew every inch of the island and its surrounding waters, having first come to Rhodes aged twenty-one as a swashbuckling novice. D'Aubusson stood at the pinnacle of a lifetime's experience, having served as a junior commander, a European fund-raiser and most recently as the mastermind behind the modernisation of the defences. He rushed a line of earthen ramparts along the length of the mole to ensure that the tower of St Nicholas could be resupplied from the city. Each night a battalion of labourers reinforced the foundations of the lower walls of St Nicholas. The tower's upper part, with its thinner walls and battlements, looked seriously scarred after a fortnight's relentless bombardment. In one six-day period three hundred direct hits were recorded to have struck the tower. This must have encouraged Mesikh Pasha to launch his first major assault.

Just before dawn on 9 June the seas around St Nicholas were churned into foam as dozens of low galleys turned the point and rammed themselves into the lower works. A frenzy of fire from their decks attempted to clear the lower ramparts of defenders and allow ladders, ramps and grappling hooks free passage. Marine landings are difficult to organise even in calm, unopposed waters and this was to be no exception. For d'Aubusson had also been at work on the seaward defences, so that lines of underwater palisades kept the galleys from beaching too close to the walls while submerged stakes, planks studded with nails and spiked iron balls skewered the brave Ottoman soldiers who leapt into the surf. Despite the bombardment-smashed silhouette of the upper floors of the tower of St Nicholas, the lower battlements remained well manned and well prepared. That morning the Turks were caught between the devil and the deep blue sea, and the wooden walls of the galleys, overlooked by the light cannon and arquebuses on the walls, provided precious little defence. After one of the tightly packed ships was set alight, the remainder of the squadron was forced to withdraw as best it could. It was thought that as many as seven hundred Turks might have died during the assault.

To revenge this public reverse Mesikh Pasha ordered a massive artillery bombardment that very afternoon. The huge mortars, though they took an age to load, were brought into play. For two weeks an extraordinary intensity of fire was maintained: the Knights later assessed that a thousand cannon rounds were fired each day at this time. St Nicholas remained the principal target, for its sea position made it almost invulnerable to mine and the galleys remained vulnerable to the Knights' shore batteries. But Mesikh Pasha also directed his cannon at the well-defended Akandia Gate and the area beyond it, the small section of the sea wall that stood outside the two harbours, near the line of harbour-wall windmills that were such a feature of the approaches to Rhodes. This coastal section was the Jewish quarter of the city. Mesikh Pasha had succeeded in feeling out another potential weak point and, as these old walls began to crack under the strain, he began to shift more and more cannon to this sector. D'Aubusson recognised that nothing could be done to prop up these defences and immediately started to clear the damaged houses behind, so that a second moat could be dug and the accumulated earth, reinforced by fascines, would create a second, low, internal wall. Mesikh Pasha moved more and more troops to this sector, massing them in nearby trenches for the expected attack. But under the cover of these well-observed manoeuvres he was actually planning a second surprise attack on St Nicholas. Instead of the earthen ramp that Alexander the Great had laid across the sea to assault Tyre, his ordnance corps had been secretly constructing a wooden pontoon formed from a line of stout barges.

On the night of 18 June, as the cannonade against the Akandia Gate attracted all attention, the barges were quietly but methodically manoeuvred into position. D'Aubusson had no time to construct any counter-defence but nevertheless reacted with speed to this new threat. Every spare cannon and grenade-lobbing mortar was directed to rain fire down upon the Ottoman pontoon. The Turks brought up thirty light ships to give close support. All night the attacks came, continuing past dawn. By ten that morning the sea around the Tower of St Nicholas was veined with blood and the bodies of hundreds of dead and wounded bobbed around four burned-out hulls. The pontoon was damaged but remained an open track, without protecting trench or rampart, that was swept by cannon fire. It also sagged and buckled, for a Greek sailor had dived down and cut through the cable that linked it to one of its supporting anchors.

By noon the thunder of the Ottoman artillery was once again focused on the area beside the Akandia Gate. Having been a Palaeologue prince of the ruling dynasty of Byzantium, Mesikh Pasha was in a good position to make peace overtures to the Orthodox Greek population. They would be permitted to keep their lives and property if they withdrew from the fighting, otherwise they would share the fate intended for the Knights. To drive his point home, eight thousand stakes were prepared outside the city walls to impale every male defender over the age of ten. At dawn on 27 July, Mesikh Pasha was ready to throw his all into a massive frontal assault that spilled out in wave after wave of soldiers advancing from trenches that had crept ever closer to this landward section of the walls. At the same time he had once again decided to risk a marine assault on the smashed sea wall beside the Jewish quarter. This his men easily took but were caught in the deathtrap of the second moat. Then, in mid-morning, one of the assaults on the Tower of Italy, which stood beside the Akandia Gate, forced its way through to the broken summit and planted the Ottoman battle flag on the ramparts. It was at this critical psychological moment that d'Aubusson knew he must lead from the front. He rushed forward to take command of a body of a dozen Knights in a direct assault on the Ottoman guard who were defending their flag and this toehold on the city walls.

D'Aubusson's attack failed to regain the Tower of Italy and the Grand Master was dragged back to safety after receiving a lance in his chest, his

fifth wound of that day. The public collapse of their commander and
the loss of a tower should have been enough to crack the spirit of the
defenders, but d'Aubusson managed to prop himself up on a staff and
order a second counter-attack. It was one of the Knights' great strengths
that they fought in language groups, each under their own elected commander, which meant that they were used to operating as independent
regiments. Then, like a turn in the tide, when the city's defences seemed
on the very edge of collapse the situation was reversed. A counter-mine
was exploded in the moat below the Tower of Italy, which was packed
with Turkish troops who had rushed to join their brethren defending
the battle standard. On the other side of the city a sally of mounted
Knights had charged out through one of the land gates, cut their way
through the siege lines and briefly penetrated the Turkish camp. It was
a time of utter confusion but after three hours of hand-to-hand fighting
it became clear that the Knights remained in possession of all their
towers and walls. Whether they had the strength to fight another day
was not to be tested. For over the next three weeks the Ottoman army
kept to its siege trenches. A threshold had been passed.

The Knights were not to know it, but the three ships that had come
to Rhodes from Naples at the end of July were feared by the Ottomans
to have been the vanguard of a much larger reinforcement from the
West. If a Christian fleet arrived and severed the lines of communication with Marmaris, Mesikh Pasha's entire army would be cut off in
Rhodes. With Gedik Pasha and his army in Otranto that winter, the
Ottoman Empire was critically over-committed to exposed beach-
heads.

In the third week of August, Mesikh Pasha, after a flurry of messages
between him and his master, ordered the withdrawal of the army from
its siege lines. The island of Rhodes had been devastated, but the battle-
wounded d'Aubusson survived to become a hero to all Christendom. In
due course he was made a Prince of the Church and legate of all Asia by
the Pope, but that winter his attention was focused on emergency
repairs to the walls, an issue of free wheat to the island's impoverished
Greek peasantry and a decree exempting them from any tax or tithe.
Only the Knights knew how close the issue had been. Their victory
celebrations were muted and pious and combined with strident calls for
a moral rearmament. This spiritual self-examination had reached a
climax of fasts, penances and self-recrimination when a second devasta-

Profile of Mehmet the Conqueror. Medal struck by
Costanzo of Ferrara in 1481.

tion hit them. The city's already damaged defences were totally flattened
by an earthquake. According to an eyewitness, Rhodes was reduced to
rubble in half an hour. The whole city lay open.

It was rumoured that Sultan Mehmet was planning to lead the army
himself against Rhodes the next year. This was confirmed when reports
started filtering in that he been seen to cross the Bosporus in April and
had established his standard at the landing of Uskudar, on the Asian
shore of the straits. This meant his target for the year stood to the east.
On 1 May the Ottoman army began its first day's march. At the camp
of Maltepe, thereafter called 'Sultan's Meadow', Mehmet collapsed, possibly from a stroke brought on by his increasingly severe gout and
abdominal swellings. Despite the care of his devoted Jewish physician,
Maestro Iacopo, who had looked after Mehmet's health since his childhood, he died just before midnight on 3 May, aged forty-nine. Mehmet
had held all political authority for the past thirty years, he had personally led eighteen military campaigns and directed another thirty, and so

his death was kept a state secret until one of his heirs assumed the throne. But, despite the packed ice, the braziers full of incense and the vast scented candles, the truth could not be concealed. Their master was dead and his superbly obedient and well-directed army began to unwind its tightened coils within a few hours.

The janissaries might have been prepared to listen to their Sultan's entreaty but they were not interested in that of one of his slaves. His prime minister, Grand Vizier Karamani Mehmet Pasha, ordered the soldiers to stay in their camp, so they killed him. In the great new capital of the Ottomans, as the corpse of the conquering Sultan rotted in the hidden courtyards of his palace, his troops rebelled outside the gates for more pay, the populace rioted and Mehmet's court of ministers and administrators were paralysed without a single directing voice. A former grand vizier came out of retirement to replace the slaughtered one and wrote to tell one of Mehmet's sons 'to hurry' while simultaneously trying to establish some order by declaring an eleven-year-old grandson regent. Prince Bayezid rode day and night to halt the meltdown of authority. On 22 May he solemnly escorted his father's now embalmed body through the streets of Istanbul from the Topkapi Palace to the burial ground behind his father's new mosque. As father-in-law to the military governors of both Rumelia and Anatolia, Prince Bayezid was well placed to succeed his father. His position was trebly confirmed when Gedik Pasha responded to his orders, abandoned Otranto and took his still-disciplined Ottoman army off to fight a rival army that had been recruited by Bayezid's brother, Prince Cem. A battle fought between the two armies outside the old capital city of Bursa determined that Bayezid II would indeed be the next Sultan.

Mehmet in death as in life proved to be imaginative and unorthodox. He was buried in a monumental tomb, not the unmarked grave of the true believer, open to the skies and known only unto God. Also of great significance was the situation of his tomb, in the middle of a city (rather than the customary burial place beyond the city walls); and the company he kept (for it was here that Constantine the Great had been buried, surrounded by the relics of the twelve other Apostles), while the rest of the Osmanli dynasty lay in the hills outside Bursa. He was once again an innovator. To say Mehmet was of both the East and the West is misleading, but there is in him some vital element of fusion that truly represents the beguiling spirit of Turkey, half European and half Asian, half

Byzantine and half Turkic, half Aegean and half Anatolian, a Muslim nation that sits on the throne of Orthodoxy. Of all the Ottoman Sultans Mehmet is the only one to remain a genuine national hero, in part because the man who would renew the Turkish nation in the twentieth century, Kemal Ataturk, shared many of his dynamic contradictions.

Mehmet had formally instituted the practice of fratricide, not only by his disposal of his infant half-brother on his own accession but also by a retrospective legal decision. It was written that it was 'appropriate for whichever of his sons became Sultan to do away with the others for the sake of the good order of the world'. This chilling *realpolitik*, which reversed the universal exaltation in 'brotherly love', was of course a crime by any moral code, let alone the intense family-centred spiritual vision of Islam. The Sultan papered over this by citing a few *Hadith* sayings of dubious provenance and little legal relevance, before having this infernal decree rubberstamped by a 'majority' of religious scholars. But the background to his decision was firmly rooted in history, especially the disastrous imploding of Ottoman power after the death of Bayezid I, when prince fought prince and pretenders emerged as puppets of foreign powers or were borne aloft at the head of an angry mob.

Still, he stopped somewhat short of the absolute logic of this policy by leaving his own two surviving sons to fight for mastery after his death. Was this intentional, a further twist of Darwinian-like survival of the fittest to rule? We will never know, though many of his contemporaries believe that he lost any specific interest in the succession after the death of his favourite son, Mustapha, in 1474. 'He was inconsolable, weeping over the death of his beloved son for three days and three nights . . . and the entire city was filled with loud lamentation because Mustafa was especially beloved of his father and of all those who had dealings with him.' There are always rumours of poisoning around the death of a young prince. Usually these complicated plots so beloved of street gossips and soap operas can be ignored, but not, it seems, in this case. The chance unearthing of legal documents from an Ottoman court archive some five hundred years later have given a touch of unexpected credence to these habitual rumours. For these documents show that Sultan Mehmet's trusted prime minister of twenty years' standing had divorced one of his wives after she had been accused of inappropriate behaviour with Prince Mustapha. It may be that the slighted honour of an Ottoman grand vizier had resulted in Mustapha's death by a subtle poison. Certainly on 18 July an explicit message was sent to the constable of Yedikule Castle that the grand vizier be strangled with a bowstring. However, the next day his body was buried with full honours beside the mosque that still bears his name.

The Sultan was fascinated by the histories of great conflicts. According to the contemporary Venetian writer Niccolo Sagundino, a native of the Greek island of Euboea, he was well versed in the wars between the Spartans and the Athenians, as well as the struggle between Rome and Carthage. These are classic studies in conflict between a land power and a sea power, which must have been of obsessive interest to the leader of that great land power, the Ottoman Empire, against the

Mehmet II. By Gentile Bellini, probably painted in 1480. (National Gallery)

centuries-long dominance of the sea by Venice and Genoa. He was also interested in the lives of Julius Caesar and Alexander and had the basic biographies (such as Arrian) copied out for his personal library.

We know too that he took time to view the monuments of Athens while on campaign in Greece and looked over the ruins of Troy while on his way to capture Lesbos in 1462. Here he searched out the tombs of Achilles and Ajax, where he had a melancholic shudder about the likelihood of his own posthumous fame, remarking that they had been 'fortunate indeed to have been extolled by a poet such as Homer'. Yet again he was acting, consciously or not, like Alexander, who shed a tear at the transitory nature of fame when he visited the neglected tomb of Cyrus. Comparisons with Alexander do not imply that Mehmet suffered from any delusions of appearing like an Occidental monarch as well as being a Turkish Sultan. For uniquely Alexander the Great had been absorbed as a hero within Islamic culture (especially its Persian literary core), where Iskender, as he is known, is a familiar figure testing the limits of mankind's achievements and is frequently depicted in miniatures comfortably dressed in kaftan and turban. Mehmet's interest in Western culture was not to copy it, but to help him conquer it. Although, along with his many other titles, he styled himself 'Caesar' after the conquest of Constantinople, he also delighted in the conceit that he had at long last avenged the death of Priam and the fall of Troy.

In Venice, when a messenger from Istanbul burst into the meeting hall to find the Doge and the senate in council, he cried out, 'The Great Eagle is dead.' No one doubted for a second who the 'Great Eagle' of the age had been. In the peace that fell upon the Aegean that following year, Otranto was abandoned by the Turks and quietly reoccupied by a Neapolitan garrison[8] and the Knights of St John, sitting completely defenceless among the ruins of their fortresses in Rhodes, were left in peace.

4

Reconquista

The Crusade of Ferdinand of Aragon and Isabella of
Castile against Muslim Granada, 1480–1510

Insanity in individuals is something rare – but in groups, parties,
nations and epochs it is the rule.

Nietzsche

There has never been a double act to match the physical and political
union of Queen Isabella of Castile and King Ferdinand of Aragon.
There is something about the size of the kingdoms of the Catholic
Monarchs, their shared values and their very different natures which
makes this partnership one of the most fascinating and politically successful in history, surpassing even that of Justinian and Theodora,
William and Mary or Victoria and Albert. Their influence, for better or
for worse, is still potent. The discovery of America, the conquest of
Muslim Granada, the creation of the Spanish Inquisition, the expulsion
of the Jews, the unification of Spain and the creation of the first extra-
territorial European colony were all their achievements. Nor did they
simply preside over these vital events. They were the prime directors,
architects and technicians of these successful policies, all of which were
part of a shared political vision. The united Spain which they created
became the third of the great powers competing for dominance in the
story of the Last Crusaders.

The couple have never lacked admirers. Ferdinand of Aragon, 'El
Catolico', was Machiavelli's acknowledged role model for the perfectly

capable prince, while there have been repeated campaigns within Spain to canonise Isabella. More controversially, they were the chosen role models for the historians and ideologues of Spanish fascism. Their early interest in such matters as Spanish purity, in monitoring loyalty and correct thought, in national unity, in the creation of secret courts, in extracting evidence by torture, in public confession and execution, in the creation of a police militia and in the victimisation of minorities resonates in many of the great political crimes of our own age. In Spain their political legacy, the creation of a Castilian, Catholic and central-ised authority over the divergent languages, kingdoms, cities and cultures of Iberia, has still not been overthrown, though generations of politicians, freedom fighters, poets and artists have struggled in a brave attempt to revive the lost heterodoxies. Despite such twentieth-century heroes as Lorca, Goytisolo or Almodovar their cultural edifice still stands.

Friar Alonso de Palencia was dispatched from the Castilian capital, Valladolid, on a secret mission. He travelled east into Aragon, where he was to seek out Prince Ferdinand and inform him that a certain young lady was impatiently awaiting his attentions. For just as in the plot of Romeo and Juliet, Isabella had put her trust in a friar when it came to discreetly sorting out matters of love. Ferdinand accepted this romantic challenge and made his way to Castile in disguise, as one of a gaggle of eight strolling minstrels. It was a liberating experience for him to be freed of the bodyguards who normally accompanied the crown prince of Aragon, though it had its own dangers, like the time when this band of young Catalan musicians were driven out of a Castilian town by a hail of stones.

The secret assignation between Ferdinand and Isabella was to be at the Castilian town of Duena, dominated by the Archbishop's brother, who was also in on the love plot. Isabella, though she had never met her distant cousin, is said to have picked him out at once from among his travelling companions. Her cry, '*Ese es, Ese es*' ('This is he, this is he') was appended by Ferdinand as a badge to his coat of arms. The two cousins desired each other in many ways but chiefly for the political support they could exchange. There was an immediate rapport and an instinctive insight that they, alone in the world, could understand each other. Isabella, two years older than her young cousin, wanted to

strengthen her hand as the heir of Castile against the prior claims of her
niece, Juana (La Beltranja). Ferdinand was already an experienced military commander and as crown prince of Aragon he also had the resources
to fight her cause. Although he was just sixteen, he had already proved
himself a man, having fought in two wars and fathered two bastards. He
was also a possible heir to Castile itself (if one excluded all women and
looked for the nearest male), so marriage to Ferdinand also protected
Isabella from Ferdinand. Their marriage would both heal enmities
between the neighbouring kingdoms but also open up vast possibilities
for the future. And if Isabella didn't set the pace in such matters, then
her elder brother, King Henry IV, most certainly would have done. She
rightly feared that he was plotting to marry her off to some despised
Frenchman (in Isabella's own words, 'a country abhorrent to our
Castilian nation'), which would have removed her from Spain and
denied her any hope of gaining the throne.

A notary was on hand at Duena to record their pledges, and soon
afterwards they journeyed back to Valladolid, where they were married
in January 1469. The ceremony was not exactly secret, though it was
undeniably quick and modest. They also had to fake a papal dispensation, for they were within the proscribed degrees of close-cousinage.
Isabella's brother the King was furious, not only because it was a form
of treason for those of royal birth to marry without the monarch's permission but because it had wrecked his own plans to marry his daughter
Juana to Ferdinand. An army was sent to besiege Valladolid, Isabella
was denounced and Juana was again proclaimed the official heiress. But
Isabella suspected that Henry's fury would pass, and after some thirty-
six secret messages had passed between them, a family peace was
brokered. In 1474 Isabella was invited to spend the feast of Epiphany
with Henry in the newly restored apartments of the Alcazar of Segovia.
She was still at the castle when he died that December, so she was well
placed to take immediate control of the royal treasury and, after a whole
day of mourning, to proclaim herself Queen.

For the next five years Ferdinand was forced to campaign against the
Portuguese, who backed the candidacy of Juana in the War of the
Castilian Succession. The Battle of Toro and the increasing eccentricity
of King Afonso V of Portugal, but above all the birth of a boy to
Ferdinand and Isabella in 1476 allowed the couple to triumph over the
opposition. And after the death of his own father in 1479 Ferdinand

found himself King of Aragon as well as Prince Consort to Queen Isabella of Castile. Even so, he had to swallow his pride in the harsh marriage settlement that the Castilians had insisted upon, but the man whose personal motto was 'Like an Anvil I Keep Silent Because of the Times' knew how to hold his tongue.

Ferdinand had been born on 10 March 1452, in the high valley of Sos on the edge of the Pyrenees, a place beloved by the nobles of Aragon for its clean water and air. His mother had taken a house there so that her child could be born in the ancient heartland of the kingdom. She was an impressive, commanding presence in her own right who once directed the successful defence of a city during one of the recurring civil wars that afflicted Aragon. Ferdinand, although the son of a king, had an elder half-brother, so he escaped the obsessive scrutiny and fawning attentions that so often conspire to undermine the character of a crown prince. He was educated for the life of a warrior, trained in the exercise of arms from the earliest age and to hunt and to fight throughout boyhood. He was given his first horse at eight years of age and his first experience of battle at ten. He was brought up to be constantly on the move, a small cog within the peripatetic medieval Aragonese court, which moved through the three Kingdoms of Aragon, Valencia and Catalonia as well as through the almost independent city-states on the coast, such as Barcelona, and the Balearic Islands. The death of his mother in 1468, her body progressively broken by cancer, may have helped to cauterise Ferdinand's emotions. His own self-description, 'seen much but read little' is a telling example of his noncommittal reserve. Although attractive to women, socially easy-going and full of humour, he was incapable of giving love. This lack of passion allowed him to function as a prodigiously hard-working, efficient, calculating and ruthless political animal, for ever 'hovering between gravity and laughter', between the absurdity and the opportunities of life.

Isabella, like Ferdinand, was the child of a king and like him had no expectations of ruling, as two boys (an elder half-brother and a brother) stood between her and the throne. Indeed she was hardly noticed at court, so much so that the astrologers forgot to note down the date and hour of her birth, though it is known to have been in April 1451. She was three when her father died, but this presaged one of the happier periods of her life, when she lived with her mother in the comparative simplicity of a widow's court in the Castilian city of Arevalo. She was given an adequate, though not a testing, education, being groomed to be a good wife and mother at the court of some foreign prince. This happy, gentle, familiar life was snapped when Isabella's half-brother Alfonso died in 1468 and she was thrown into the centre of Castilian court intrigue. It was an interesting but disturbing experience. For the court kept by her brother King Henry IV and his Portuguese queen was a wild, intellectually liberated and free-speaking environment. Henry's wife had a joyful approach to life, with uninhibited manners and openly took lovers. The accepted Christian pieties of provincial life were laughingly scorned, and the moral tone set by a clever, creative but lazy monarch who affected Moorish customs and dress. The King's private life was the focus of much private speculation and public enquiry. He had been divorced by his first wife on the grounds of the non-consummation of their marriage and it was thought that he was not the biological father of princess Juana, his second wife's daughter. However, doctors had testified in court that, according to their own manipulations and inspections, the monarch's sperm did flow, and certainly he had a large number of mistresses and courtesans. Some historians speculate that Henry may have been homosexual, others that his personal preference, perhaps not that rare among men, was for highly sexualised women rather than a virtuous, virgin princess.

When Isabella was finally in control of her own court as Queen of Castile, her experience of her brother's court stood her in good stead. She knew all too well how the lack of confidence in the parentage of her niece had allowed her to take the throne from Juana. There would never be any doubt in her court who the father of her children was. She could do little to stop the philandering habits of either her husband or any of the powerful men at her court (the cardinal-archbishop included) but she made certain that her immediate circle was beyond suspicion. Her maids of honour slept in a dormitory, and when a gallant from Galicia was arrested climbing up a tower to an enticing window, she had the unfortunate young nobleman sentenced to death and then took her time before relenting to the tearful entreaties of her little court for clemency.

Though renowned for her piety Isabella was no ill-lettered puritan. She delighted in music, supporting a choir of twenty-five that followed her on her annual progress, and by the standards of her time was extremely well-read. Her library of four hundred books ranges from the *Imitation of Christ* by Thomas à Kempis to the bawdy chronicles of Boccaccio and that anonymous Spanish master of the salacious tale, the arch-priest of Hita. But there were also plenty of shelves filled with tales of chivalry, the highly imaginative mythic world of such characters as Roland, Charlemagne, Arthur and Alexander the Great. In art she delighted in the quiet realism of everyday life and its occasional instances of spiritual transfixion, collecting a very fine gallery of over five hundred Flemish pictures, and had no interest in the idealised bodies then being invented by Italian Renaissance artists. She was an enthusiastic supporter of the new medium of print, so that Spanish printers were soon in business in Seville, Valencia and Segovia, even if the technical knowledge had to be imported from Germany and Flanders. Though Isabella was not renowned for her humour, it was sometimes suffered to escape. Once, with her big, round eyes stretched wide open in mock concern, she asked her confessor if the sins of the Cardinal did not seem very pretty? For at that moment there passed by Rodrigo, the young Count of Cid, known to be the product of one of

A free concert held at the steps of a cathedral, around 1497. From the personal prayer book of Queen Isabella of Castile.

the Cardinal's many lapses, in this case with a wild maid of honour at King Henry's court of reprobates.

The first five years of Ferdinand and Isabella's reign was completely over-shadowed by the Castilian War of Succession, which, in engendering hundreds of different armed rivalries between nobles, towns and cities, consumed the kingdom of Castile. The Moors of Nasrid Granada also enjoyed a holiday from paying tribute, and took the opportunity to raid their neighbours on the borders. For instance, in April 1478 the Murcian town of Cienza was stormed, the Granadan raiders slaughtering eighty of its defenders and carrying off the rest of its inhabitants into captivity.

When a fine and lasting peace was concluded with the clever young crown price of Portugal at the Treaty of Toledo in 1480, there was no doubt what was to come next. Everyone in Spain could read the signs, be they Moor, Jew, Genoese or crusading knight. Ever since the fall of the powerful Almohad Empire in the middle of the thirteenth century, the Emirate of Granada owed its continued existence to the mountains, the prompt payment of tribute and to its warriors, but above all it had been preserved by the jealousy that existed between the Iberian Christian kingdoms. With Castile–Leon and Aragon–Catalonia united for the first time, and Navarre and Portugal at peace within their own natural frontiers, it was time for a popular, local war against the traditional enemy. It would only take another round of frontier warfare to break out with France over the kingdom of Navarre, or the county of Roussillon in the Pyrenees, for this window of opportunity to be closed by the strategic nightmare of a war on two fronts. And Castile had been shamefully eclipsed as a crusading nation over the past seventy years by Portugal, whose successful enterprises had earned it new territories, wealth and honour. Yet the Portuguese attacks had also served a beneficial purpose for Spain. They had so damaged the Moroccan Sultanate that it was most unlikely that it would be able to come to the aid of Granada. This was an important consideration, for over the previous seven hundred years the determined support of the bellicose peoples of North Africa had time and again been decisive in maintaining Muslim presence in Spain. The Ottoman intrusion into the territory of Naples, seizing hold of Otranto in 1480, had also served as a warning to Ferdinand and Isabella. Who knew if the emergence of the newly assertive Ottoman Empire, with its strong navy and vast artillery, might not soon be able to support Granada? Indeed we know that one particular embassy sent by the Granadans to the Mameluke Sultan of Egypt in 1487 so alarmed the Catholic Monarchs that they sent their best man, Peter Martyr of Anghiera, with an open brief to keep the Mamelukes out of the war at any price. Most especially as the Mamelukes at this time had built up a navy.

The war against Granada would also give the monarchs the perfect opportunity to strengthen their throne. In the words of Machiavelli, 'Nothing buys a Prince more prestige than great campaigns and striking demonstrations of personal abilities.' No longer would they be seen as merely the lucky victors in a messy war of succession with a lingering odour of illegality and oath-breaking about them. Instead they could emerge as the leaders of their people in a crusade against 'the other', the Muslim outsider. It would also provide the ever-fractious nobility with a common enemy, a valid reason for the grandees to put aside their own feuds. Even the Marquess of Cadiz and the Duke of Medina Sidonia, who lived for their sworn enmity towards each other (as if they were the Montagus and Capulets of Andalusia), would fight together against the Moor. If successful it would also give Ferdinand and Isabella vast new territories, both to the benefit of the crown estate, but as a way of rewarding the nobility, binding them into loyalty to the dynasty. The two monarchs would indeed prove conspicuously generous in this way, freely dispensing with half the lands of the conquests to those who had fought beside them. It was also a golden opportunity for Ferdinand, the commander-in-chief, to win a good name, and not be treated as the interloper from Aragon. In much the same way that Henry V of England, a usurper's son, had tried to heal the civil-war wounds of the Wars of the Roses by invading France.

The Moors of Granada were so aware of the coming storm that they struck first. On a moonless night in December 1481 they advanced to seize control of one or two vital border fortresses. At Zahara, wrote the Marquess of Cadiz's chronicler, 'they scaled the castle and took and killed all the Christians whom they found within, save the commander, whom they imprisoned. And when it was day they sallied forth and opened the gates of the castle and descended to the town and made captive 150 Christian men, women and children, and sent them bound to Ronda.' Ferdinand and Isabella were honest enough to declare, 'And if it can be said that we take pleasure in what has passed (at Zahara), we say so only because it gives us the chance to put in hand forthwith what has long been in our minds . . . but now that this event has happened, we are taking counsel to determine how war shall be waged against the Moors on every side.' In due course their formal request for the resumption of tribute was answered with the now celebrated reply from Sultan Abu al-Hassan (which may alas be a retrospective creation, an historical *esprit de l'escalier*): 'The Kings who used to give tribute are dead, and the palaces in Granada where they used to strike the coins to pay the tribute are now being used to forge lance-heads to prevent it from ever being paid again.'

Ferdinand used his new position as Crusader-in-chief against the Moors to gradually assume control of Spain's three orders of knightly chivalry. Rich and influential, with their vast landed estates, castles and priories, these orders had been a dangerously powerful weapon in the hands of the fractious nobles. But once the war was well under way they would be quietly annexed to the crown. In 1485 the Order of Calatrava led the way by agreeing not to elect a new master and to pass its resources and leadership to Ferdinand. And after Ferdinand had proved himself victor he was able to annex the Order of Santiago in 1493, a move repeated the following year when the last master of the Order of Alcantara was encouraged to resign in favour of the King. This annexation of Church real estate, which had been steadfastly resisted for centuries, was formally confirmed by a Papal Bull issued by Alexander VI (the Borgia Pope) in 1501. For Ferdinand to be able to achieve this while still remaining a hero for the Catholic Church was impressive. (To put it in an English context, it was as if King Henry VIII had been able to sequester half the wealth of monasteries but still remain 'defender of the faith'.) But this was only possible because of Ferdinand's close understanding with the Borgia papacy. Before their ascent to high ecclesiastical office, the Borgia were to be numbered among the nobility of Aragon, for they were cousins of the Dukes of Gandia from Valencia. The Borgia wished to retain a good relationship with their old Spanish homeland and its monarch. One of the keys to the authority of the Borgia papacy was that Pope Alexander VI's illegitimate son (Cesare Borgia) had been made captain-general of the papal forces and had enforced control of the Romagna of central Italy for the papacy. Much of the strength and discipline of Cesare Borgia's army rested on a contingent of Spanish troops that had been loaned to the Holy Father by

King Ferdinand at the same time that he received that valuable Papal Bull confirming his authority over the Crusading Orders of Spain.

The old Crusading Orders of knights were a role model for the new national militia which Ferdinand and Isabella created, the Santa Hermandad (Holy Brotherhood). A home guard recruited from the free peasants and impoverished gentry of Castile, it had been set up by Ferdinand and Isabella to counter the prevailing lawlessness during the five years of the Castilian War of Succession. Initially it had the authority to apprehend and shoot down criminals, murders and rapists but as royal justice was gradually reimposed this police function was removed. After 1498 it became simply a militia, which could be mobilised against foreign invasion and corsair raiding parties as well as a recruiting ground for the army.

When it came to providing troops for the war against Granada of 1482–92, the Santa Hermandad could field fifteen hundred lancers to the fifteen hundred knights that each of the three Crusading Orders could still summon from their lands. In addition it provided about twice as many footmen and led the way in providing trained arquebusiers, men who could fire muskets. The crown lands supplied another fifteen hundred lancers and an equal number of footmen, as well as the fifty hand-picked crossbowmen, who were charged with guarding the monarchs by day and night. So the Spanish crown could call upon twelve thousand troops at full stretch, while the rest of the eighty-thousand-strong army marched into the royal camp under the pennants of the noble families, the grandees of Spain. Some, like the leader of the Guzman clan, the Duke of Medina Sidonia, were very powerful subjects indeed. On the scale of military force they were but a very short step beneath the throne. The Duke's personal contribution to the siege of Malaga, a fleet of a hundred ships, was a vital element in the success of the endeavour.

Just as in the creation of the new army of the Ottoman Empire, there was a massive royal expenditure on the recruitment of gunners and artillerymen. These were painstakingly picked from the cities of Flanders, Germany and northern Italy, especially Ferrara, Brescia and Milan, which in this period had acquired a formidable reputation for expertise in artillery. They had to be paid promptly in good coin or they melted away to find service with a more reliable master. The story of the Hungarian cannon founder Urban, who first offered his service to the last Lord of Byzantium before moving on to Ottoman service, was echoed a thousand times. As well as hiring foreign technicians, Ferdinand and Isabella also commissioned the creation of a national arsenal of artillery. At the forges set up at Ecija, halfway between Cordoba and Seville, the mineral wealth of the nation was poured into the manufacture of some two hundred pieces of artillery. These foundries coincided with another turning point in the science of war, for the master casters had perfected the casting of gun bronze, from a new version of the old alloy of copper and tin. The Holy Roman Emperor Maximilian turned his agile mind to a proper classification of these deadly instruments. He realised that the weight of shot fired, not the weight of the artillery piece itself, was the vital determinant. So he classified siege artillery, designed to smash walls, not men, by its ability to fire shot that weighed either twenty-four, thirty-six or forty-eight pounds which had a direct proportion to a cannon's calibre, the width of its mouth. Below this were the basilisks, firing shot of between twelve and twenty-four pounds, which could also be mounted on walls and would soon become the cornerstones of an active siege defence. Field artillery was designed to kill men and horses in battle, so it was lighter. A culverin was the heaviest cannon in this range where manoeuvrability was absolutely vital to battlefield success. It could fire either a sixteen-pound shot or a casket of shrapnel for a lethal spread of small shot at close range. The half-culverin was an eight-pounder, with falcons (four pounds) and falconettes (two pounds) the weapons of choice for use on board ship.

But Ferdinand also commissioned a weapon that was out of the ordinary. The 'Lombard' was twelve feet long, with a barrel two inches thick and further reinforced by a series of stud-like wrought-iron rings. When directed by a skilled crew these cannon kept up a rate of fire of 140 shots a day, sending 175-pound balls or exploding mortar shells into a besieged city. On the march, the King would make certain that he travelled immediately in front of this virtually irreplaceable artillery train, his lancers providing a protective screen behind which a great creaking caravan of hundreds of ox-drawn artillery wagons processed. The Moors soon realised that this was when the Castilian army was at its most vulnerable, and learned to wait in their mountain fastness until the siege train was strung out before launching a raid.

Attention has always been focused on the melodramatic set-piece of the war, the final siege of Granada in 1492. But, like the methodical expansion of the Ottoman Empire by its seizing control of the trading cities of the Aegean and the Black Sea, the war was all about the efficient exercise of logistics. First the Emirate of Granada was shaved of its borderlands, then it was cut in two, half of which was neutralised by a truce, then each isolated region was subdued in turn, until all that was left after ten years of war was the city of Granada itself. It was a merciless process, for the year before the designated siege of a city the surrounding region would be devastated by cavalry raids and feudal war bands who had been ordered to destroy all resources that would enable the Moors to feed and water their population. This was a time of opportunity for the companies of knights, often ranged in bands of between 150 and 300 men, to acquire booty, slaves and celebrity in countless fiercely fought skirmishes. It was the heyday of the *hidalgo*, the poor gentleman determined to reverse his fortune by his daring, his resourcefulness and his conspicuous bravery. One such was Alonso Manrique, a poor knight of Salamanca, who could boast, 'My lineage is for me enough / content to live without expensive stuff.' It was to be the training ground for all of those ruthless but brilliantly self-determining conquerors of new worlds such as Cortes and Pizarro and their fictional counterpart Don Quixote.

But even when the Castilians dug in for a formal siege, they did not always have it their own way. The successful defence of Loja in 1482 by Ali al-Attar ('Scented Ali') so inspired the Moors that Sultan Abu al-Hassan summoned up a relief army from other garrisons and triumphantly descended on the Castilian siege lines, chasing them back to Cordoba. The following year they had another success. They lit small fires on the mountain tops so that the Moors could follow the progress of a Castilian military column as it made its slow way through the Ajarquia mountains to the east of Malaga. When it reached a narrow defile the Moorish army struck in force, massacring the column and sending a thousand prisoners to Malaga, where the streets echoed to the victorious ululated war cries, the *alaridas*, of the Moorish women.

But even when fighting for its continued existence, the Moorish leadership was hopelessly weakened by divisions within the Emirate. The Nasrid dynasty was plagued by *fitna* (division), with Sultan Abu al-Hassan restricted to Malaga while his son Boabadil (Muhammad XII) took command of the city of Granada in a bloody coup in which the civil-war fighting spilled out from the palace into the narrow streets. This infamous division of the Emirate in its final hour is supposed to have been the result of harem rivalry between Abu al-Hassan's two wives. One was a noble princess of Nasrid blood (the daughter of Muhammad IX and the widowed bride of Muhammad X), known as Aisha or Fatimah; the other, Boabadil's mother, was a ravishingly beautiful Christian captive named Isabel de Solis but known as Zoraya after her conversion to Islam. For all the satisfying melodrama of this tale, which so fulfils the expectations raised by the spectacular architecture of Granada's Alhambra – and which touches upon the ubiquitous passion of mothers for their sons and the envy of stepmothers – there are other possible explanations.

The Nasrid Emirate of Granada, for all its great fame and glory, had always been based on a historical dichotomy. It had first emerged from the ruins of thirteenth-century Muslim Spain through tactical co-oper-ation with the Christian enemy. Indeed the very first Nasrid Emir to appear in history, Muhammad from the town of Arjana, had risen to power as a sworn military ally of the Christian King of Castile back in the 1240s. Muhammad had even assisted in that decisive event, the fall of the Muslim city of Seville to the Christians, by leading a force of five hundred cavalry in support of the siege. The founder of the Nasrid Emirate of Granada could be seen as a traitor to the Muslim culture of Spain. Once he was sure of 'protection' as a sworn tribute-paying ally of Castile he withdrew from any further conflict. It was Nasrid policy then quietly to watch as the various other rival Muslim emirates in southern Spain, be they in Murcia or the Portuguese Algarve, were overwhelmed at the end of the thirteenth century. The result was that Granada would emerge as the single Muslim successor state, much strengthened by all the refugees arriving from the fallen lands.

So when Prince Boabadil seized control of Granada and sought for a peaceful truce with the Christian kings, he was doing no more than fol-lowing a tried and successful dynastic policy. How much a pensioner of the Castilian court he might have been, or how much he might have been working within a subtle understanding with his father the Sultan on the lines of 'You take the road to war, I will take the road to peace and we will see which one leads our people to safety,' we will never know. The story is further complicated by Boabadil's history of captiv-ity, for he seems to have been captured at least three times by the

Castilians. The first ransom paid for his release was met by his mother Zoraya, and as this consisted of a tribute of twelve thousand *doblas* and the release of sixty prisoners a year for five years, it did little to increase his popularity. His father, the old warrior Sultan Abu al-Hassan, was suffering from a creeping blindness, so Boabadil's half-brother, Muhammad al-Zagal, effectively governed for him.

By 1484 the war had assumed a more systematic pattern. Piece by piece the old fortresses of the late-medieval age were destroyed by Ferdinand's artillery train, which had to be moved, guarded, entrenched and constantly supplied with sufficient shot and powder. There were fewer surprises for, as in the taking of Alora, foot-soldiers had previously 'advanced over the mountains and passes of that region to flatten the roads and rough sections so that the [siege] wagons could get through.'[1]

The fall of Stenil in September 1484 was followed by that of Ronda, which collapsed after an intense fourteen-day bombardment. As the Spanish chronicler Hernan Perez de Pulgar writes:

> The bombardment was so heavy and continuous that the Moors . . . could only hear one another with great difficulty: they did not have the opportunity to sleep . . . in one place the cannon knocked down the wall, in another the siege engines destroyed the houses, and if they tried to repair the damage wrought by the cannon they could not, for the continuous hail of fire from the smaller weapons killed anybody on the walls.

The news of the devastation wrought on Ronda now preceded the royal siege train, so that as the Spaniards approached Moorish Marbella the city fathers sued for peace. Once he was east of Marbella the rapid rate of Ferdinand's advance was halted as the fighting intensified. A cavalry battle outside Granada, won by the Moors, was outweighed by the crushing of three fortress towns by the Castilian artillery before the end of the year. The second siege of Loja in 1486 prepared the way for the greatest testing of the balance of power.

If one has to pick just one engagement in the whole ten-year war, the siege of Malaga of 1486–7 was the linchpin. Ferdinand was well aware that nothing must be left to chance. Abundant supplies of iron were brought up 'to forge picks and trenching tools and spades and other iron implements necessary to dig away hills and . . . construct ditches and embankments in the military camps'. A maritime blockade was placed around Malaga to stop supplies and reinforcements being sent into the city from North Africa. As part of this strategy an aggressive forward policy was once again let loose on the North African shore: the harrowing of the Muslim coast of the Mediterranean to create a no man's land of smashed harbours, burned-out fishing boats and devastated coastal towns. In fact Malaga had already received a subvention of Berber troops from Morocco, the *gomeles*, who stiffened the defence of the city and its interconnected fortresses, the Alcazaba and the hilltop Gibralfaro. The city's walls, like those of Constantinople, had been considered almost invincible before the development of siege artillery in the fifteenth century. The two heirs to the dwindling throne of the Nasrids, Boabadil and Muhammad al-Zagal, were left to bicker over possession of Granada, leaving the local governor of Malaga, Ahmad Zeli, to organise the defence. He proved himself to be an inspiring commander. It was noticed that the Moors 'have a greater desire to kill Christians than to preserve their own lives . . . the desire for vengeance predominated over the desire for gain, and nobody made any attempt to take prisoners, only to kill and maim'. The hand-to-hand fighting over possession of the lower of Malaga's fortresses, the Alcazaba, 'went on for six hours, and the sounds of the trumpets, the shouting, the alarms, the clash of weapons, the noise of the matchlock guns and the crossbows on both sides were so loud that the hills re-echoed the ceaseless strife'.

After the fall of the Alcazaba, the surviving Moors withdrew up into the Gibralfaro to continue the fight, leaving the Castilians at last free to encircle the city. The circuit of walls from sea to sea was too long to entirely wrap up with trenches, so Castilian engineers threw up fighting platforms, *estancas*, along the length, linked by trenches and patrolled by cavalry. The *estancas* supported a mixed garrison of soldiers, some armed with matchlocks, some with crossbows and some with sword and pike. Once this line seemed secure, the siege settled into a long artillery duel, though technically the Moorish garrison proved more than a match for the Christians. Their artillery silenced many of the Castilian batteries, and even found the range of Ferdinand's tent, which was forced to withdraw behind the safety of a hill. The rate of fire was so intense that the King's arsenal, patiently accumulated over the year, was rapidly depleted. Merchant captains were commissioned to buy what they could where they could. And this they did, unloading their merchandise – shot, powder and naval cannon – directly on to the beaches beside the siege lines. The weight of fire eventually began to crack the walls but not the morale of the defenders, who won the esteem of their enemies, for 'although they saw their fellows fall dead and wounded in the fighting, it was noteworthy how bold this barbarous folk was in battle, how obedient to their commanders, how hard-working as they repaired their walls, how astute in the ruses of war'.

The Nasrid Emirs in Granada never attempted a relief of the city, nor did any other Muslim power come to its aid, though we can nevertheless pay testimony to a brave band of volunteer warriors. They came from the island of Djerba, off south-eastern Tunisia. Under the leadership of a villager named Ibrahim they sailed halfway across the Mediterranean and then slipped through the Castilian naval blockade. Supported by local scouts, they marched across the hills and worked their way down so that they could launch a dawn raid on the eastern edge of the Castilian siege lines. They managed to storm an *estanca* and though half lost their lives, some two hundred broke through the siege lines to add their strength to the people of Malaga. Ibrahim deliberately courted capture in the hope that he would be interrogated by the Christian King and might then be able to strike a dagger into the heart of the man who was strangling Muslim Granada. And he very nearly succeeded in his wild plan but made his lunge too early, having mistaken a finely dressed noble for Ferdinand. He was cut down immediately, his body hacked to pieces and catapulted into Malaga. Here these were reassembled, lovingly washed, sewn back together with silk, anointed with myrrh and escorted to the grave by thousands of warriors.

Fear of plague, the escalating cost and mounting casualties put immense pressure on Ferdinand to lift the siege, but he knew he had to persevere. Since his cannon and men never quite managed to storm the city, he placed his faith in subduing Malaga by blockade. The citizens and the garrison were slowly starved into surrender. They had been too brave and steadfast for there to be any room for negotiation. In August 1487 the army of the Catholic Kings finally entered Malaga, and organised the clearing of the entire city. Tens of thousands of inhabitants were enslaved, a third given as rewards to the besiegers, a third put aside as slaves for the crown and a third reserved for prisoner exchanges. The

first task of the enslaved was to clean the city of the corpses of the slain
and the thousands who had died of starvation. Still the garrison in the
hilltop Gibralfaro would not surrender. They were Berbers from the
mountains of Morocco and preferred to die than endure slavery. The
war machine of Castile-Aragon was tested to its very last degree by
defenders who were in every degree their equals in courage, determination and technical ability.

After the fall of Malaga the shadows rapidly lengthened over the
Emirate of Granada, for there was now no port in Muslim hands which
could receive any reinforcement or aid from the sultans of North Africa,
Egypt or the Ottoman lands. The fearless Berber garrison in the citadel
of Malaga and the brave band of volunteers from Djerba give a sugges-
tion of how different the war could have been if the Nasrid Emirate had
found allies. Malaga was itself a potent symbol at the time, though its
fame has been eclipsed by that of Granada. For five hundred years the
city had stood beside Ceuta as the great multicultural entrepôt of the
western Mediterranean, the chosen marketplace for Moorish merchants
who had acquired the gold dust and rich products of the trans-Saharan
trade from their brethren in North Africa. Now it was emptied of its
citizens.

The next year it was the turn of the city of Baza to be besieged by the
Christians: to first have its lands burned out, then be embraced in siege
lines before the bombardment started in midsummer. Once again it was
the blockade and the determination of the Castilians to maintain the
siege deep into the winter months that brought submission. In negotiations Ferdinand was careful to respect the honour and position of the
ruling class, who throughout the war were offered the choice of conversion to Christianity or emigration. Only peasants and craftsmen were
encouraged to remain as Mudejar, protected Muslim subjects whose
faith and traditional laws were guaranteed within the Christian
Kingdom. In such a manner did Boabadil's warrior half-brother,
Muhammad al-Zagal, finally depart in 1489, though it was then his
turn to be labelled a traitor, for he surrendered the citadel-cities of
Guadix and Almeria to make the cash with which to fund the emigration of his people. Boabadil stayed on as Emir in Granada and surprised
his subjects by leading an attack that recaptured the city of Padul, while
a small army of volunteers from North Africa succeeded in evading the
Castilian naval blockade. Once in Andalusia they quickly went on the

offensive, recapturing the harbour of Adra, which they hoped could function as a supply base through which reinforcements might yet relieve Granada. It was a brave but doomed last burst of militant energy.

For in 1490 Ferdinand directed the operations that would at last bring the war to the walls of Granada. The surrounding hamlets and farmland were progressively destroyed by marauding patrols of lancers. Six miles from the city, on the burned-out ruins of the village of Atqa, a base camp was formed. Over time this became a town of stone, Santa Fe. It was laid out in the shape of a cross, like some vast set-piece for a court masque. It had stables for a thousand horses and each of the four entrance gates was crowned with a chapel. By 1491 an army of eighty thousand men had assembled to witness the last act in this crusading enterprise, achieved by, in the words of Juan del Encina, 'she with her prayers, he with many armed men'.

The myth of Ferdinand and Isabella was being turned into stone before the approving eyes of all Christian Europe, as the siege camp filled with visiting ambassadors, volunteer knights and delegates. Here the combined totems of the Iberian crusade could be revered: the silver cross sent by Pope Sixtus IV, the ancient ensign of Santiago the Moor-slayer, the sword of King Ferdinand (the sainted conqueror of Seville) and the banner of St Isidore, a bishop of Seville from the pre-Islamic period of Visigothic Spain. The Pope saluted Ferdinand and Isabella with the titles of 'Catholic Monarchs' and 'Athletes of Christ' while the 'third King' of Spain, the cardinal-archbishop Mendoza, paraded in armour fastened over his scarlet vestments. The Queen, dressed in black, was already being treated with some of the reverence given to a living saint, for it was whispered that neither of the sieges of Malaga or Baza had been successful before her presence brought grace to the military camps. Isabella was never considered a beauty, for her face was too round and plain, with a slightly pouting mouth and an irregular nose. But her eyes, though shrouded by bags of care, flashed with conviction. She was undeniably of the Trastamara dynasty, with the pale skin, fair hair and blue eyes of the family which prided itself on its pure descent from the German tribe of Visigoths who had ruled for hundreds of years between the fall of Rome and the coming of the Arabs. In subduing Granada, Ferdinand and Isabella never thought of themselves as conquerors, but as the dispossessed heirs who had at last, after some seven hundred years, come to take back what was rightfully theirs. Peter Martyr described Isabella as a 'mirror of all virtues'. The poet Montoro considered her 'worthy to have given birth to the son of God'.

The outcome of the siege of Granada was never in doubt, largely because Ferdinand seems to have reached a basic understanding with Boabdil right from the start. So Santa Fe was always more of a courtly parade ground than a battlefield, though the thunder of the cannon and the cavalry skirmishes in the surrounding hills added greatly to the colour of a siege that was otherwise determined by negotiations, payments and insider deals. These were all finally completed by November 1491. In January 1492 Castilian troops quietly entered the gates and took up their positions on the walls and in the citadel. The terms of surrender were fantastically generous. The Catholic Kings promised to protect the property, faith, mosques and legal traditions of their new Muslim subjects. There was to be a three-year tax holiday, a general pardon for all crimes committed during the war and a release of prisoners. On 2 January, as the last Nasrid Emir formally presented the keys of the city to the Catholic Monarchs, and stooped to kiss Ferdinand's hand, the silken red and white banners of Castile and Leon were unfurled from the towers of the Alhambra.

The terms of the surrender were too good to be true, though to be fair to Ferdinand and Isabella they did not immediately break their word, merely reneged on it year after year. Pressure was put on the old ruling class to emigrate, which most of them had done by 1495. Even the ex-Emir Boabdil, who greatly enjoyed hunting on the estate in the Alpujarras mountains given to him by Ferdinand, eventually sold up and took ship for Tlemcen in Algeria. A Spanish historian, Marmol, would later create the enduring story of the 'Moor's last sigh', which has Boabadil turning around in his saddle to take one last lingering look at the city of Granada.

Boabadil would later end up an exile in Fez, dying at a ripe old age in a battle between the Wattasid and Sharifian dynasty of Morocco which 'made a mockery of fortune, for death struck him as he was defending the kingdom of somebody else when he had not dared defend his own'. Within fifty years of his death his impoverished descendants were dependent on the charity of their Moroccan neighbours.

Yet how had this vast enterprise, a ten-year-long crusading war, made possible by the creation of the world's largest and most extensive artillery park, been financed? In a good year the crown's income was barely enough to cover the annual expenses of the court. This basic income came from the royal lands, assisted by port customs, a tithe on cattle in May and on crops in the autumn, a salt tax and the profits from justice and the coining of currency. Subsidies could be advanced by vote of the Cortes, the parliaments of the different kingdoms of Spain, and by the grant of a crusading tax by the papacy (with a third deducted for expenses) while the native Church could grant the crown 'tenths' of all clerical income. But all this would have produced only a fraction of what was consumed by the ten-year war. It was said that all Spain shared in the experience of the siege of Malaga, 'for the villages were drained by the tax-farmers because of that siege' as they tried to supply a siege army which ate up thirty thousand pounds of wheat and barley a day.

Since there was a formal prohibition on usury, Spanish people could only lend to their monarchs without interest, and so would normally only be persuaded to do so by holding something tangible in pawn, be it a crown, a sword of state or a vineyard. But even this could not account for much. So the war was financed by floating vast loans on future income, conquered lands, customs duties and monopolies and mortgages on existing lands. These were contracted with Spain's foreign merchants, especially the half-domiciled Genoese and the ancient community of Jews. Exact sums and modern conversions are an almost pointless exercise, but a figure of some eight hundred million *maravedis* can be imagined.

Whether it was because these bills were now coming in, or for the safety of their subjects' souls, Ferdinand and Isabella turned on their chief creditors after the war was over. This made them extremely popular, for the Genoese and the Jews were loathed by all classes in Spain as crafty, clever, rich, clannish foreigners. The powerful Genoese trading dynasties, such as the Centurione of Malaga, who had specialised in the gold trade, the slave-trading house of Fornari, the Grimaldi (then mostly interested in the wheat trade), the great wool-broking Castiglione, or the olive-oil and soap kings of Seville, the Ripparolo, were made to pay heavily for the right to remain in Spain. The same pressure was put on the Jews, whose civic leaders came up with a staggering collective offer of three hundred thousand ducats (about 122 million *maravedis*) for the right to remain. But a trial expulsion of the Jews had already been made in one of the regions (in Andalusia between 1484 and 1491) and had been shown to be extremely lucrative to the crown, not only in wiping out debts, but in property confiscations, paid-for permits, speculations and benefiting from the dramatic price shifts that occur when a community that has lived in a country such as Spain for seventeen hundred years is ordered to pack up and go within a few months, especially as in this case the Jews were also prohibited from taking any gold or silver out of the country. The offer of three hundred thousand ducats was very briefly considered, but rejected, and Ferdinand and Isabella published their expulsion order on 30 March 1492. All Jews who converted to Christianity were to be permitted to stay, and both Ferdinand and Isabella seem to have been personally delighted by the baptism of Jews with whom they were associated, and their court was full of talented *conversos*, some of many generations' standing. For the Jews had been under intermittent pressure to convert, and perhaps two-thirds of their number had already done so over the previous two hundred years.

Even so, by the end of 1492 about half of the two hundred thousand Jews in Spain had been forced to leave their property, their homes, their language, their graves and their cherished landscapes behind in order to keep their faith. It was a torturous and highly personal decision which ripped tens of thousands of families and communities apart. Many of these journeys of exile were never to be completed, and there are court records that preserve the terrible testimonies of those who survived: how sorry columns of exiles were abused and plundered by Old Christian communities, how their children were abducted from them at the ports and their women raped. In one notorious case a ship's crew killed all seventy of their passengers in order to seize their property and in another the exiles 'were plundered and slain and their women taken from them' the moment they landed on the foreign shore, so that these wretches then begged to be allowed to convert and return to Spain. Yet others told a different experience, of being safely escorted by royal troops to a nearby port where chartered galleys awaited to take them to their destination.

The *conversos* must have made the choice to accept baptism with extreme trepidation. For even before the infamous and sudden expulsion order of 1492 there had been a hundred years of riots, persecutions and massacres, directed as much against the *conversos* as the professing communities of Jews who had been herded into ghettos and made to wear distinctive clothing. So, while the armed crusade was being fought in the streets and fields of Granada, another crusade had been launched to shore up the security of the homeland. It began modestly enough, in 1480, when the Pope gave permission for the monarchs to set up an Inquisition into the true practice of the faith in Seville. Ominously the first action of the two Dominican friars charged with this task had been to set up a prison on the edge of the city, on the other side of the River Guadalquivir at San Jorge in Triana. Using torture, sudden arrest, rumours and secret trials in which the accused were not even allowed to know the charge, let alone the evidence or the name of the witnesses, the Inquisition proved itself a wildly profitable success as all profits were remitted to the crown. Rich *conversos* were the target right from the start and it was soon noticed how few Old Christians were ever brought up before the tribunals. Even the innocent could be fined and publicly humiliated, usually by being ordered to join street processions in long, pointed hats and yellow surcoats before they publicly attended mass.

While the war raged on in the south, a cultural revolution was being unleashed within Spain. Some thirteen thousand people were found guilty by the courts of the Inquisition, five thousand of these were publicly punished and seven hundred were handed over to the secular authorities to be burned alive. Pope Sixtus IV was appalled at what he had unwittingly set in motion, but control of the Inquisition had now effectively passed out of the hands of the papacy into that of the Catholic Monarchs, who had no interest in suppressing such a vital, profitable and powerful new instrument of state power. Ferdinand even started to suggest to the Inquisition that treason and defying one's monarch might also be considered a form of heresy. The populace adored the public humiliation of rich, intellectual city-dwellers by the Inquisition, so much so that anyone who proved good at business or who cooked lamb on a Friday stood in danger of being denounced. The Spanish national cuisine, based on the triumphant consumption of ham, raw garlic and sausages by Old Christians, all of which were repugnant to Jew and Muslim alike, began to gain strength at this time.

A few heroic men of conscience stood up to the madness of crowds and the prevailing wisdom of the times. Juan of Lucena argued that the

The public burning of Arabic books in Granada.

Inquisition actually endangered souls, for in 'their confusion and anguish [of torture] men confess to heresies they did not practise'. Hernando de Talavera, the principled Archbishop of Granada, argued that Muslim converts should have forty years' grace from any inquisition as they made their own slow cultural transformation. The celebrated case of 'the holy infant of La Guardia', in which a group of Jews were accused of crucifying a Christian child on Good Friday over a disfigured host, gives a unique insight into the mindset of the torturers. They were so incapable of understanding anything about the nature of Judaism that their accusation took the form of a simple negative of their own beliefs. As any Rabbi will explain, a professing Jew does not believe in original sin and so has no need for a redeeming sacrifice.

Spain would ultimately suffer from this internal terror. The combination of the expulsion order against the Jews and the Inquisition's obsessive inspection of those who had converted would transfer hundreds of thousands of able, clever and well-informed Jews into the territory of Spain's Muslim enemies, especially that of the Ottoman Empire. Sultan Bayezid II was astonished that the most powerful Christian kingdom in the Mediterranean should have made such a catastrophic mistake, impoverishing its own provinces and so enriching his. Entire Ottoman cities were to be created by the exodus of Spanish Jews. The most dramatic renewal was that of Thessaloniki, which had remained an empty circuit of walls after its sack by the Ottomans in 1432 but became almost overnight one of the great mercantile powerhouses of the Ottoman Empire sixty years later and, incidentally, won the concession to create all the uniforms for the janissary corps. By 1520 at least half of the city's thirty thousand inhabitants were Spanish-speaking Jews, who wore turbans of saffron yellow (their Greek neighbours sported blue, their Muslim neighbours white). Within Thessaloniki there emerged twenty rival synagogues, which resisted Ottoman pressure to elect a chief rabbi. Instead this vocal, argumentative community of exiles proceeded to create a parliament of representatives from the synagogues, who raised money for a redemption fund (buying back Jewish captives from corsairs) as well as running

The public burning of heretics by the Spanish Inquisition.

a school, a hospital and a hospice. One of the rabbis got so bored with his congregation dwelling on the evils of the past that he demanded that they 'stop cursing the Almighty and accept everything that has happened'. The Sultan's government also gradually gained the respect, thanks and grateful dependency of the exiled Jews, who every year were joined by a further trickle of *conversos* fleeing from the intensifying internal terror within Spain. Without so much as lifting a finger, the Ottoman viziers found that they had access to the most astute intelligence-gathering service in the Mediterranean, some of the best metalworkers and the world's most acute financiers.

Once the war was over and the war loans had begun to be paid off, the Catholic Monarchs were free to look at other concerns. Some of their more bookish counsellors had been championing the proposal of a Genoese sea captain who sought royal support. The man was vastly experienced at sea, having already sailed to Tunis, Chios, Iceland, Ireland, Madeira and West Africa. This practical experience was backed up by theoretical knowledge of navigation, partly gleaned from his Portuguese wife (whose father had been an adviser to Prince Henry the Navigator) and partly from his own sideline in dealing in new maps and travel books of the day, such as the 1477 Bologna edition of Ptolemy's *Geography*, lovingly enriched by the publisher with twenty-six maps, or *Description of Asia* by Aeneas Silvius Piccolomini, a brilliant Renaissance scholar and diplomat who became Pope Pius II.

Although this Genoese captain had impressed all the sovereigns he had met, Portuguese, French, English and Spanish alike, his ideas had been crushed by the various sub-committees appointed to report on his proposal. These councils of worthies tended to agree in principle but not in practice, bringing up so many questions about supplies, distance and the projected morale of the crews that the simple enough project – to sail west in order to reach the markets of the East – was always buried in paperwork and forgotten. But Queen Isabella, encouraged by her advisers and her own wit, placed her full support behind it. Among the most enthusiastic supporters of the Genoese sea captain were a group of Franciscan friars who were fascinated by the prospect that they might discover a back door to Jerusalem and so help usher in 'the last age of humanity' of the Book of Revelation. Others even dreamed of discovering the gates to paradise or the fortunate isles of the immortals.

So it was that Captain Christopher Columbus was given the

resources to charter three caravels which would unleash the crusading zeal of Castile on the New World. If it is true that Christopher Columbus's family mixed Jewish and Genoese blood it is one of the ironies of history that the two communities of traders that Isabella and Ferdinand had so ruthlessly despoiled should yet lead the Catholic Monarchs towards even greater wealth. What is even more tragic is that Columbus was planning to explore the world in the style of the Genoese, which was to build a fort or a town as a safe base for trade. What a different vision of the world we would have now if the goods of Europe had been traded to the Aztecs of Mexico or the Incas of the Andes through a Genoese trading colony. Instead Ferdinand and Isabella insisted that, like all crusading ventures, the expedition be dedicated to the specific goal that 'Our Holy Faith is extended and our realms increased'. The triumphant example of the crusade against Granada was to be the role model for Europe's very first overseas empire and for all those that followed.

In Granada, the benign policy of the peace treaty and first two years of Christian rule would soon be twisted out of shape. The militant new primate of Spain pushed forward with a campaign to convert the Muslims. The redoubtable Jimenez de Cisneros had first risen to power when he was appointed confessor to Queen Isabella in 1492. His zeal and fiery resolution had led him, as a young friar, to be imprisoned for six years by the Church authorities. But when, just three years after his appointment as royal confessor to Isabella, he was made Primate in 1495, the Church in Spain was plunged into a dramatic and purifying reformation. The habitual failings of clergy – the keeping of concubines, nepotism (jobs for nephews and other boys), simony (the buying and selling of offices), absenteeism – and the inadequate vocations of lazy, aristocratic placemen were purged. Frequent synods, a pyramidal system of confession and the foundation of Church colleges and universities completed the transformation of the religious landscape of Spain. It is no exaggeration to claim that if Jimenez de Cisneros had been made Pope or Friar Martin Luther had been trusted with a Cisneros-like reformation of the German Church, there would have been no social grounds for the Protestant Reformation. Indeed such Protestant martyrs as William Tyndale, who translated the Bible into English, would have been cherished by Cisneros. For the Spaniard himself commissioned the first polyglot Bible, with side-by-side translations in

Hebrew, Greek and Latin, to better understand the truth of the Gospels. At first he tried to convert the Moors through preaching and granting fiscal privileges to those who converted. However, this mild process soon gave way to the well-tried methods of the Inquisition and to ever-tightening political 'pressure'. In 1499 the first mosques were forcibly converted into churches, while the old network of Muslim neighbourhoods was deliberately broken by the construction of a rigid grid plan of new roads. A handful of leading Muslim citizens were tortured and cajoled into accepting a public baptism. This led, as Cisneros's own chronicler so candidly reports, to the public burning of books:

> all the books of the Mahometan impiety, of whatsoever author or kind they might be: more than five thousand volumes of ornamental bindings, even of gold and silver and of admirable artistry. These caught the eye of some who asked for them as gifts, but he would give none to anybody, and all were burned together on a great bonfire – with the exception of certain books of medicine.

When the Moors of the Alpujarras mountains took to arms again to protect their religion and their faith, supposedly guaranteed to them by treaty, this was in itself made the excuse for the formal suspension of the generous peace terms. In 1501 the Catholic Monarchs repeated the terms that they had enforced upon the Jews: the Moors could stay in Spain only if they converted to Christianity. All their mosques and shrines were to be turned into churches. The revolt spread, especially in the mountain districts behind Ronda and Almeria, but this was suppressed with savage efficiency by Spanish troops who had just returned from a victorious campaign in Italy. There were widespread rumours that an emir was being summoned from North Africa to lead the rebellions and the Castilians certainly took the possibility very seriously. All along the coast of North Africa they established a string of outposts where they could listen out for news and to which they could ship into exile Moors who refused to convert. This process of expulsion was continual, both from local pogroms but also as a result of the regional nature of Spanish law. The Andalusian Muslims who would not convert were formally expelled in 1499, those in New Castile and Old Castile in 1501 and 1502, but it was not until the 1520s that this was enforced upon the Moors in Aragon, Valencia and Catalonia.

So it was that, almost by default, the Spanish Monarchs established a chain of fortresses, forts and garrisoned islands along the North African shore. Since they had devastated the coast opposite Andalusia for ten years during the conquest of Granada, and had profited by shipping Jews and Moors to North Africa in the aftermath, the venture had none of the history of crusading zeal that shaped Portuguese possessions such as Tangier and Ceuta. Indeed, rather than the future landing points of a Castilian crusade, these forts were no more than advance customs posts where refugees could be conveniently disembarked, some trade conducted and an eye kept on the locals in case any counter-crusade against Spain was being planned. Melilla was occupied almost peacefully in 1497, after a Spanish fishing boat had reported that the citadel was virtually deserted. In 1505 a series of squat artillery towers were constructed to overlook some of the more strategic harbours in western Algeria, such as Mers-el-Kebir and Qassasa. In 1508 one was placed opposite the old port of the Rif mountains of Morocco, at Badis. The Spanish watch was placed on the island of Penon de Velez de la Gomera, which over the centuries would be turned into a fortress – so much so that today it looks as if a stone battleship has been moored half a mile offshore. In 1509 towers were built on a rocky islet outside the harbour of Algiers, and around the edge of the domains of the great territories of the Hafsid Sultans of Tunis, at Bejaia (now in eastern Algeria) and at Tripoli (now the commercial capital of Libya), followed the next year by one on the island of Djerba. It will be remembered that the men of Djerba had rallied around one of their village elders, Ibrahim, and a body of volunteers had bravely broken through the Spanish siege lines to try to assist their brother Muslims during the siege of Malaga. They are a recorded instance of a deep-rooted fear that would remain long implanted in the guilt-ridden Spanish mindset: 'Moros en la Costa' ('The Moors have landed').

The one exception to this police-like presence on the North African shore had been the Crusader-like invasion of Oran. This had been personally financed by Primate Archbishop Cisneros, who had employed Pedro Navarro to lead the military expedition in 1509. Cisneros had passionately argued with King Ferdinand that Oran should be the springboard for a full-scale Spanish crusade into North Africa with the desert as the ultimate frontier. The King had listened but refused to back this mad plan, whereupon Cisneros had threatened to resign and retired to Alcala to teach. Nevertheless, after Ferdinand's death he would rule Spain as regent while the young Charles V remained in the Duchy of Burgundy.

*

In Italy the prestige of Ferdinand and Isabella had reached its apogee. The late 1490s were a dynamic period, highly charged with hidden expectations of a cataclysmic new age to be unleashed with the dawn of the new half-millennium. In Florence the threat of a financial crash helped usher in the evangelical storm of Savonarola's call for repentance. Even among otherwise sane and business-minded Europeans, the crimes of the Catholic Monarchs were imitated, with Jews being expelled from Portugal and Nuremberg. Buoyed up by the Christian victory in Granada, Pope Alexander VI received promises from all the great monarchs of Europe, including Emperor Maximilian and Charles VIII of France, to personally lead a crusade to reverse Mehmet's great conquests. This spirit did not last many months. Instead in 1494 Charles VIII, with his eye firmly fixed on possessing the Kingdom of Naples and the Sforza Duchy of Milan rather than Constantinople or Jerusalem, passed down the spine of Italy at the head of a small but well-disciplined army. Superbly equipped with new artillery of the same type that Ferdinand had created for the conquest of Granada, he swept south like a hot knife through butter. The old duchies, margraves and principalities of Renaissance Italy, whose previous conflicts had been stage-managed by celebrity mercenaries, were seen to now belong to a vanquished age.

King Ferdinand watched with interest, quietly biding his time. He too had plans. He waited until the King of France had become embedded in the mercurial politics of Italy and bogged down with this war, before efficiently occupying the strategic Kingdom of Navarre which sat astride the Pryenees frontier and placing it under a Spanish military protectorate. He then gave enthusiastic backing to a papal Holy League, a pan-Italian and anti-French alliance, under an acceptably benign banner. Next he pretended to support a crusade that was being equipped and sent out into the Aegean, heavily supported by both Venice and France and which also drew heavily on the artillery resources of the Kingdom of Naples. This crusade aspired to reconquer Greece and the Aegean and did indeed fire off a considerable weight of shot and powder while off the coast of Lesbos. Its real purpose, how-

ever, was to allow Ferdinand the perfect opportunity to seize control of
the Kingdom of Naples and Sicily from his cousins, already weakened
by the French invasion. The King of Naples had been foolish enough
to send the best of his artillery on this fool's errand of a crusade in the
Aegean. Naples, emptied of artillery, proved very easy to occupy. In the
treaty of Granada, secretly signed in 1500 by France and Spain, the
two powers had agreed to divide the territory of the Kingdom of
Naples between them. Ferdinand's diplomacy was ruthless, cunning
and duplicitous to a degree. Beneath the front of a Europe-wide holy
crusade he had plotted the annexation of two neighbouring Christian
states and betrayed both his cousins and his allies. No wonder that he
had no time for the Cardinal-Primate's obsessive interest in a crusade
into North Africa.

His sure political touch had been evident even after he had been
badly wounded by an assassin's blade. His murder had been attempted
a number of times, during both the siege of Granada and Malaga, by
Moorish warriors. But in fact the assassin who got closest to him was a
true maverick, working without confederates or policies but at the
urging of an inner voice, believed to be the Holy Spirit. It had happened during one of Ferdinand's regular Friday audiences, which
despite his other commitments he managed to sustain, in which the
populace spoke their concerns and presented their petitions to the
monarch. So it had been in his own kingdom, in the city of Barcelona,
at the height of his glory, in 1492, that a dagger held by a Christian
subject of the King of Aragon had penetrated Ferdinand's chest. The
blow was deflected by a golden chain, but even so, in the startled
words of his wife, it was 'four fingers deep'. The King, as usual, had it
both ways. His personal appeal for clemency for the mad would-be
assassin was publicised as further proof of the 'faith and devotion, constancy, indefatigability, amity, patience and many other and great
virtues which repose in his Highness'. But the Royal Council 'rejected'
his appeal and condemned the assailant. The hand that had done the
deed was sentenced to be cut off, the feet that had borne him to the
crime were to be pulled off, the eyes with which he had taken aim were
to be torn out and the heart which had conceived such villainy was to
be plucked out. Before this sentence was performed he was tortured to
check if he was truly insane. Afterwards his mutilated corpse was
stoned, burned and the ashes thrown into the common sewer.

Ferdinand made an excellent recovery.

If Ferdinand and Isabella can be seen to have triumphed on every imaginable frontier of political life – conquering Granada, banishing Jews and Muslims from their lands, annexing the Kingdom of Naples, pacifying Navarre, silencing all religious and political dissidence through the Inquisition and commissioning Columbus to discover America for them – there was yet a threshold where the gleaming canvas of perfection was turned to ruin, like the true face behind the mask in Oscar Wilde's *The Picture of Dorian Gray*.

Indeed Queen Isabella, towards the end of her life, began to believe that her family had been punished for her political crimes. Her daughter Isabella, after almost twenty years of negotiation, had been married to the crown prince of Portugal, Afonso, who had then promptly died in a hunting accident. Their second daughter, Juana, was betrothed to Philip the Handsome, the Habsburg heir of Emperor Maximilian. Juana, who loved her husband, was driven insane by his infidelities and lack of reciprocal feeling. Ferdinand and Isabella's son, Prince John, had been married to Emperor Maximilian's daughter, Margaret, in a double-marriage pact. Their experience was to be the very opposite, for the young couple were so madly, so ardently in love, so delighted by the mutual freedom of their bodies, that they wore each other out. The court physicians grew alarmed at the amount of the time the lovers spent in bed. By July the crown prince of Spain knew he was dying of love. His published will, providing a million *maravedis* to house poor orphans and half as much again to ransom prisoners, might indicate that he was too good for the world into which he was born. His father, in a deathbed scene recorded by the Spanish chronicler Bernaldez, tried to comfort him in the only way he knew: by acquiring more kingdoms: 'Very beloved son, be patient since God has called you, Who is the greatest King of any, and has other realms and lordships greater and better than this which would have been yours and for which you were prepared. He will give them to you.' By tragic coincidence, John passed away the week that his widowed elder sister, Isabel, was married to the new King Manuel of Portugal, so that 'the rejoicing of the wedding were exchanged with lamenting and mourning . . . within a single week'. Then, like some triple-twisted Gothick tale, Princess Isabel died giving birth to a male heir, the infant Miguel, who stood to inherit every throne within the Iberian Peninsula. When he died two years later he delivered the 'third stab of pain to pierce the Queen's heart'. To keep the border between Portugal and Castile peaceful, King Manuel was now presented with a second Spanish bride, Princess Maria, the fourth daughter of Ferdinand and Isabella. It was just as well that Isabella could not look into a glass that revealed the future and see the fate of the one child she considered to have been happily married off, her daughter Catherine. This Princess of Aragon had been shipped north to marry Arthur, the crown prince of England, and then after his early death was wed to his surviving brother, Henry VIII.

In 1503 Isabella's daughter Juana returned home on a state visit after her marriage to the wealthy, charming, erudite Philip the Handsome, the Habsburg Lord of Flanders and Duke of Burgundy.

> The Princess's condition is so grave that not only to her to whom she is so important and who loves her so much does it cause much anguish, but to anyone, even to strangers. For she sleeps little, eats little or at times nothing at all; she is very sad and very thin. At times, she refuses to speak so that in this respect as at other moments when she seems to be transported, her sickness is very advanced.

The prolonged separation from her husband had exposed the depths of Juana's passion to the world for the first time, as night after night she stalked the gatehouse of the castle of La Mota (outside Medina del Campo), peering through the lowered portcullis as she waited for the arrival of her lover-husband. No one dared interfere with the night walks and ravings of the Infanta until her mother, Queen Isabella, stumbled upon the ranting heiress herself. Although already frail, Isabella cast aside the cares of state in order to try to personally nurse her child back to sanity. Juana was eventually considered strong enough to return to her husband in Burgundy, from whom she quickly conceived another child. But 'her boundless jealousy and eccentric actions' such as the time when she launched herself on a pretty Flemish maid at court, savagely disfiguring her with scissors less she win her husband's favour, disturbed the polished equanimity of court life.

Queen Isabella had gradually turned her back on political affairs so that she could nurse her mad daughter. Isabella became convinced that the madness was just punishment for the way that she had deposed her niece Juana and the way she had taken Ferdinand to the altar. Her spirit seems to have rejoiced at this decision, for her body began to collapse and she expired at Medina del Campo in the winter of 1504. Ferdinand had his own way of expressing his distress at his daughter's condition. When his son-in-law Philip had died, instead of mourning him in a suit of black he selected a celebratory scarlet, set off with white ermine trimmings.

Juana was, however, inconsolable after the death of Philip, which removed the last traces of conventional behaviour from the Infanta. Like some dark heroine from a Gothic novel, she refused to be parted from his body and would night after night set forth on a torchlight procession to the crypt chapel, where she would command the coffin once again to be opened so that she could embrace her true love and assure herself that he had indeed departed from her. Her royal father eventually persuaded her to allow the corpse to be buried. It was also Ferdinand who gently encouraged her to retire from the strains of public life and take up residence within the towers of the castle of Tordesillas, outside Valladolid. Here she gave birth to Philip's posthumous child, Catherine, who grew up to become a nursemaid, friend and companion to her mad mother.

After Isabella's death Ferdinand helped perpetuate the cult of the Queen, most especially in his dealings with Castile, when he would become loquacious about her virtues. He had not been sexually faithful to her in her lifetime, and there was no need to be so after her death. In 1505 he took Germaine de Foix, the pretty young niece of the King of France, as his second wife. Ferdinand survived Isabella by twelve years, successfully interfering with the politics of Christendom until his dying day in January 1516. Towards the end of his life he developed a fondness for his grandson Ferdinand, who though born in Flanders had been brought up by his grandfather in Spain. Ferdinand was the younger brother of Charles V, who was set to inherit half of Europe. The old King began to suggest that the crown of Aragon should be broken off from this inheritance and given to his favourite grandson and namesake, which allowed him to make mischief and court intrigue until the last.

In Chapter Twenty-One of his definitive guide to statecraft, *The Prince*, Machiavelli wrote:

we have now in our days Ferdinand, King of Aragon, the present King of Spain: he in a manner may be termed a new prince, for from a very weak King, he is now synonymous with fame and glory, the first monarch of Christendom, and if you shall well consider his actions, you shall find them all illustrious and every one of them extraordinary . . . in the beginning of his reign he assailed Granada, and that exploit was the foundation of his power. At first he made that war in security and without suspicion . . . and thereby kept the nobles of Castile busy, who were so engaged upon that war that they never minded any innovation . . . and was able to maintain with the Church and the people's money all his soldiers, and to lay the foundation for his military strength with that long war . . . serving himself always of the colour of religion; he gave himself to a kind of religious cruelty, chasing and despoiling those Jews of the Kingdom . . . under the same cloak [of religion] he invaded Africa and went through with his exploit in Italy: and last of all he hath assailed France.

Ferdinand used 'the colour of religion' to bind the Spanish people in obedience to him, leading them to war, then despoiling a wealthy minority and further increasing his authority by exploiting the fear of the stranger within society as well as that without. He is the very model and exemplar of how a ruthless leader can bridle the religious feelings of his people to further his own authoritarian ends. But he could not have achieved any of this without Isabella, who not only brought him the resources of Castile but whose genuine religious convictions and personal morality helped mask his own cynicism and duplicity. As an adventurer, there are very few who can equal Ferdinand in skill, personal bravery, audacity and charismatic charm. God protect us from such men.

5

Barbarossa

The Emergence of the Muslim Corsairs, 1480–1510

To prepare for the future, examine the present. To understand the
present, study the past.

William Ward

The newly united kingdom of the Catholic Monarchs of Spain emerged
to stand beside Portugal as the second spearhead of Christian expansionism in the period of the Last Crusaders. And in the lands of Islam
there would be a similar pattern. For, just when the power of Spain was
waxing, the corsair fleets of the Barbary coast emerged from the harbours of North Africa to fight the Christian powers as the sworn allies
of the Ottoman Empire. The corsairs were a totally new power on the
chessboard of Mediterranean politics. At first they were nothing more
than a freewheeling confederation of piratical sea captains, but they
would soon enough meld into a coherent force that would almost sin-
gle-handedly open up a second front against Christendom. There were
many corsair leaders but we can best understand their importance, and
their story, by following the career of the Barbarossa brothers.

Barbarossa, the merciless, red-bearded admiral of the Muslim corsairs, is a name still loaded with resonance throughout the waters of the
Mediterranean. You can swim in waters once turned blood-red by his
butchery or walk across the limestone plateaux of an island that he had
once cleared of all traces of mankind. You can find many an empty cove
and isolated bay where his squadrons of galleys once anchored. Local
traditions recall the cliff-top lookouts where his men were posted to

scan the faint junction of sky and sea for the distant trace of a mast. Whether travelling down the coast of Spain, Italy or North Africa or on to islands such as Majorca, Gozo or Sicily, it is impossible not to cross his historical as well as his legendary path. The place where Barbarossa tried to abduct the most beautiful duchess in Christendom from her palace, the port he burned to the ground, the town he sacked or the island across which he dragged a net to drive thousands of innocent villagers towards a beach and a life of damnation in the galleys. Even when you leave the shore and explore the mountain regions overlooking it, you continue to touch his legend when you are shown the high walls that were built to repel his raiding parties, or hear of the populations that for ever abandoned their old way of life on the sea to seek refuge from Barbarossa in the hills and forests.

Some of these tales touch on true facts, but others have crystallised centuries of brutal experience around one identity. For the story of piracy in the Mediterranean is ageless and corsair and crusading raids scarred both the shores of Islam and Christendom for over a thousand years. Legends from the Christian shore commonly fuse the experience of the so-called Saracen raids of the ninth century with that of the cor-sair captains in the sixteenth century. Even when we enter the pages of recorded history there is room for confusion. There were, for example, two Barbarossas – Uruj, the elder, was succeeded by his younger brother, Khizr. It is also easy to muddle both these men with their colleagues and successors, men such as Dragut and Uluj Ali. One other detail is worth remembering: in Muslim cultures the angel of death is often imagined as an intemperate, red-bearded man with blue eyes. Whether Barbarossa, which means 'red beard', fitted into this schema, or helped cause it, we will never know.

The Barbarossa brothers were born in Mytilene on the island of Lesbos in the reign of Sultan Mehmet the Conqueror. Standing on the harbour front, you look across a ten-mile tongue of water to the hills of Anatolia. Their father was an old Ottoman soldier, named either Mohammadi or Yacooub, or rejoicing in both names, who had settled here, built up a small business and raised a large family. Two daughters and four sons – Uruj, Elias, Isaac and Khizr – survived into adulthood. It was the wise habit of the Ottoman Sultan, while the empire was in its prime, not to allow the janissaries to marry while they received his coin, paid out four times a year and all properly accounted for. For the Sultan wished the disciplined core of his standing army to remain absolutely mobile, capable of being sent on long campaigns without worrying about the behaviour of their wives or the fate of their children while they were away. Nor did he wish his soldiers to be softened by domestic life, but to remain edgy and alert. However, when their time of service was up he also did not want them to remain dependent on the state, filling the streets of the capital with their political opinions and needs. The answer was to formally discharge them (and examples of these signed discharge papers survive to remind us how efficient the Ottoman Empire was in its clerical administration), and to dispatch them to the provinces, where they were at last free to marry, to breed, to support themselves and to act as an occasional home guard in times of danger. Such is the background of Yacooub, though neither his papers, nor a record of his actual regiment, his *orta*, survives. He is believed to have been recruited into the janissaries as one of the draft of Christian children from the Balkans and then to have been sent to bolster the local garrison in Lesbos.

The island was not an old Ottoman possession, for it had only been conquered in 1462. When the Ottoman army crossed the strait that year, the locals headed to the hills, while the ruling Giustiniano duke, Nicholas, tried to sit it out within the walls of his five-sided castle which stands above the harbour of Mytilene. The janissaries selected a site to the east of the castle, where an earthwork was thrown up with space for six cannon to operate independently of one another. Throughout the summer these pounded the walls of the castle, which from the outside looked most impressive. It was, however, an old structure, based on a Byzantine fort, and the walls were no more than a medieval curtain wall that had been embellished and reinforced through the centuries with apartments, battlements and with odd pieces of antique sculpture (like that of a gladiator) that had been dug up by ploughs. By the autumn Duke Nicholas knew that the walls had had enough. He negotiated his own departure and formally handed over the castle's keys on 17 September. There were few regrets among the population, for Nicholas had not been a popular ruler and had murdered his own brother to acquire the throne.

Once the drama of the siege was over, the Ottoman army made the short crossing back to the mainland. The small garrison left behind, which probably included Yacooub, had its work cut out. They had to man all the strong points of the island and also prepare the old castle for modern warfare, which they did by shifting the main gate to the east and wrapping the whole complex in a new defensive outwork. They were kept on their toes. Two years after the siege young Orsano Giustiniano landed on the island and tried to raise a local rebellion, for though Duke Nicholas had been personally despised, the Giustiniano dynasty had grown into the fabric of Lesbos over the centuries and become more than part-Hellenised through intermarrying with the imperial family of Byzantium. In 1501 there was another alarm, as a Crusader fleet was led into the northern Aegean by the Knights of St John.

Whatever the nature of his military duties over these years, Yacooub had time to take a wife. Catalina, a local woman, was the young widow of a priest, Orthodox parish clergy having always been allowed to marry. Yacooub settled down to work as both a potter and a trader. The two tasks were not incompatible in the economy of the Aegean, for over the winter months pots could be made and fired, then the stock of goods traded when the ports were officially open between March and September. In his day Yacooub took his merchant boat north to Constantinople and as far south as Antalya. His sons accompanied him as they grew up, getting to know the names of the straits and the ports, not just through charts and compass bearings but with their own eyes. Later they were trusted to take the boat out by themselves and started to make their own way among the islands. They grew up to be highly versatile, though Khizr was most adept on the pottery wheel, Uruj had the sea stamped on his face from a child and Isaac advanced from patching up boats to become a carpenter. Only Elias seemed a bit apart, the scholar of the family, who absorbed the love of learning and religion from both his mother and father. He seemed set to memorise all 114 verses of the Koran and perhaps one day would become the Imam of Mytilene's new mosque.

One summer Uruj asked Isaac to crew for him on a trip in the family boat. They would sail south from headland to headland until they reached the coast of Lycia, where huge pine trees that grew in the mountains were sent down to the coast when the rivers briefly ran as torrents in the spring. There they were sawn into crude thick planks and seasoned beside the salt marshes. Boats from all over the Mediterranean flocked to buy these ships' timbers. Isaac's practised eye was well employed sorting out the more desirable and commercial lengths of timber, which were then bargained over and loaded up. Then began the long haul back up the straits and sea lanes, using their lateen sail whenever possible but also rowing when necessary: when the wind slacked or it proved impossible to tack around an awkward headland.

It was during some such simple everyday manoeuvre that they suddenly came into full view of *Our Lady of the Conception*, one of the largest war galleys of the Knights of St John, as it paddled its way through these coastal waters looking for something upon which to prey. On its long deck, under canopies raised to aft and stern, loitered the military Knights and sergeants of the order, while a predominantly Greek crew handled the craft. From below decks protruded long, flexible oars powered by galley slaves. All at once the midday indulgence of an Aegean summer's day was interrupted by the clamour of the ship's bell, and urgent blasts by the junior officers on their silver whistles. The galley sprang into action like a lean sight-hound let off its leash, the whistles and whips encouraging a fast new rhythm among the oarsmen, while the helmsman swung the rudder around so that the galley was set on a course that would cross with that of the merchant ship weighed down with its cargo of timber. The men at arms sprang to action, tightening the breastplates of their armour, securing helmets and greaves and preparing the small, light swivel cannon that were mounted on the fore and after decks. Here was action at last. Every apprentice Knight or high-spirited noble youth who came south to earn his spurs with the Order of St John during his 'year off', or who wished to qualify as an administrative prior for one of the properties in the rich portfolio that the order possessed throughout Europe, had to serve two years on the caravans. These water-borne caravans were the whetstone that kept the crusading Knights as bright and keen as their swords. They were the active lance of Christendom which jabbed again and again at the enemy, be it raiding the coast, sacking a port or seizing any ships they could find on the high seas. Despite their fame in Christian Europe and their notoriety within Islam, their permanent fleet was surprisingly small: between six and ten galleys. These criss-crossed the southern Aegean from the various strong points held by the Knights, whose headquarters was the city of Rhodes, though they also maintained castles elsewhere on the same island, at Lindos and Archangelos as well as at Bodrum on the mainland and on other islands such as Kos.

Uruj urged his crew on, and they rowed with a desperate strength, but in his heart he knew their only hope was that a sudden wind would fill their sails. But despite their prayerful entreaties, the canvas sails hung sullen and empty.

As the galley pulled alongside the merchantman, rather than risk any of his men unnecessarily, the commander of *Our Lady of the Conception* ordered that it should be raked with gunfire. For in these waters you never knew who was armed with what. Many fell, both those wounded and those simply in search of protection. A boarding party swung aboard, a line secured the boat and a huddle of manacled prisoners was led down to the pens in the lower decks of the galley.

Uruj had watched as his bright-eyed younger brother, the skilled carpenter Isaac, stretched his arms up in surrender only to crumple under the Knights' broadside. He was then put to work as a galley slave: after being stripped naked and searched he was chained to a bench by one leg alongside half a dozen other luckless captives. Galley slaves were treated worse than dogs, beaten by the Christian overseers and disposed of without scruple if they should weaken or show any sign of resistance. They were forced to eat and defecate in their filthy, dark bilge of a deck, in almost an exact antithesis of the practice of their customary Islamic life with its insistence on cleanliness, modesty and respectful decency. The sudden descent from the bright memories of family life on Lesbos to the realities of a galley slave's existence helped forge the character of Barbarossa.

Two stories are told about his release from slavery. One is that he was ransomed, the other that he escaped while his galley was in Egyptian coastal waters. This would have been almost impossible while he was rowing: the galley decks had no direct access to the sea as the oars passed out through rowlock-like portholes, sealed with a padded leather washer, like the collar worn by a plough horse. Moreover, the rowers worked together as a chained unit, with between four to six men on each of the benches handling a fifty-foot oar. In a fair-sized galley of, say, 150 feet in length, there would have been twenty-five benches on each side of the ship. Two narrow walkways, often no more than two feet wide, were raised above the rowing benches, as was the much sturdier platform that ran down the length of the central deck connecting the poop and stern decks. The soldiers on guard duty used these three raised walkways to patrol the benches, while others kept an eye out while seated on their sack-like kitbags. A system of minor privileges also kept the rowers under their own form of self-discipline. For life became more bearable for the slaves if they were permitted to have on the bench a leather cushion packed with cheap flock wool and to hang ox-hide curtains from the benches to make a tiny covered bunk-house below. In addition the central of the three raised walkways could be used to house hundreds of pigeonhole-like boxes where they might be allowed to keep their kit dry and safe. For, aside from the simple loincloth worn on the benches, a galley slave's kit might also include a shirt, a shepherd-style smock and a long woollen cloak which doubled up as a blanket. Normally they rowed under a system of watches, half at work while the other half rested, this system controlled by distinctive blasts from the bosun's silver whistle.

Galley slaves.

Food was another key element by which an experienced captain could exercise almost complete control of a galley full of three hundred hardened slaves, for the daily subsistence diet of twenty-six ounces of hard biscuit and four ounces of cooked beans (dressed in a little oil and with a pinch of salt) could be lowered or raised as punishment or reward. Another reward was to be permitted to share the richer mess prepared for the crew, which would include the tempting flavours of salted beef, fish, rice, olive oil and wine. This was a most effective currency in which to reward slaves, who could become either a trusted strokes-man (the leading rower of each bench) or the headman of a section of benches. If there was a sprinkling of Christian criminals or press-ganged islanders among the larger mass of captive galley slaves, they were most likely to find favour. These trustees could be distinguished by being allowed to wear their own clothing and to sport a moustache, instead of being restricted to the crude loincloth and shaven head of the rest of the slave crew. These were the men that in a well-run ship might also be permitted to run cash-earning light industries that employed rowers during their rest-watch, such as knitting stockings, aside from such formal duties as scrubbing the deck, mending the sails or the pathetic task of polishing cannon balls. Behind all these privileges lay the lash. For, as well as being used by the overseers to keep time and urge the rowers to greater speed at critical moments of battle, the lash was the formal punishment for some instances of disobedience. The victim was draped across one of the walkways, his hands held down by one bench, his feet by another, while he was flogged with an inch-thick rope that had been dipped in the sea. Twenty or thirty strokes was the habitual punishment for a slight offence, while between eighty and a hundred strokes was effectively a death sentence.

This seaborne regime came to an end as winter set in and the sailing season finished. The gunpowder would be sent ashore to the arsenal stores in the small rowing boats before the ship was itself allowed into the safety of the harbour. There it would be stripped of all tackle, sheets, sails, armaments, stores and fittings and then sunk beside the docks to remove the accumulated filth from the bilges. Even the ballast of goose-egg-sized pebbles that kept an even keel even would be removed and scrubbed clean. Then the ship would be raised, beached, scrubbed, repaired and the bottom re-pitched in March, ready for its tackle to be fitted once again in preparation for the spring campaign.

During the winter the galley slaves would be moved to bagnios, slave barracks often sited in old quarries or casements, those subterranean cellars set within the thickness of a city's walls. Here they were at hand to labour on improvements to fortifications or to the harbour works, if not needed for the overhauling of the galleys. Or they could be rented out to local farmers a month at a time, to split wood, clean drains, break stones and clear fields. Those with a useful skill would pay small rents to the captain of the guard and be permitted to set up booths at the bagnios and work as tailors, cobblers, barbers, carvers and engravers, while the literate found work as secretaries and scriveners or astrologers casting fortunes and telling horoscopes. This was the slaves' opportunity to send letters and to alert relatives and close neighbours that a ransom paid to some trusted Jewish, Genoese or Venetian middleman would restore them to freedom. Now and then, instead of waiting for these negotiations to be completed, a slave would use the greater freedoms of the winter months to try to escape. Such attempts were seldom successful. The alarm would be given from a watch-tower, five guns firing in close succession, the signal for all huntsmen, bored soldiers and peasants in possession of a good pair of working hounds to join in the fun of the chase. In this were spurred on by the customary reward of twenty silver coins for the return of an escaped slave.

However it was accomplished, by daring escape, prisoner exchange or ransom, by 1490 Uruj was working as a ship's captain in Egyptian waters. Around that time he and his younger brother Khizr made a journey to the far-western end of the Mediterranean, where their education in the ways of the Christians continued. It gives some idea of the scale of the displacement then going on in Catholic Spain that for the next eight years the two brothers ferried the Jewish and Muslim refugees who were being driven out of that country to new homes and identities within the lands of Islam. All along the coast of southern Spain there was work for sea captains. Streams of refugees, clutching their possessions and hidden stores of coins, clattered down from the hills towards the sea. The ports were filled with tens of thousands of victims of Ferdinand and Isabella's nation-building. Many fell into the hands of unscrupulous captains, who overcharged and packed them into unseaworthy boats. There are horrific stories of Jewish women being raped onboard ship, fleeced of all their possessions and then dumped on an alien shore, where they were abused all over again by the natives. But there were also good men afloat, who considered it an honourable duty to convey the exiled Moors and Jews of Spain to new homes. Those who have travelled along the shore of North Africa will know that there is hardly a town, let alone a city, that does not share in the honour of having been part-settled by these refugees at the end of the fifteenth century, be it Derna in the lee of the Green mountains in eastern Libya, Testour beside the Mejerda valley in Tunisia or the city of Tetouan, overlooked by the Rif mountains in northern Morocco.

It is impossible to fully understand the bloodthirsty career of the Barbarossa brothers without appreciating this unrecorded and thus unsung period. The process of shipping refugees to North Africa made them intimate with thousands of suffering Muslims and Jews and taught them the maritime geography of the Maghreb by giving them first-hand experience of the hundreds of bays, harbours, headlands, off-shore anchorages as well as the pattern of seasonal winds. It also created a body of supporters who would come to their aid time and time again. Wherever the Barbarossas were driven along the coast of North Africa, they seem to have found men prepared to fight for them, even after the most crushing defeats and changes of fortune. They may have possessed an invincible charisma, but they also shared with the people of the ports a burning desire for revenge. And these allies could not have been more useful, for they knew their way around their old homelands and their familiarity with the Christians' languages and dialects made them highly effective raiders. Unwittingly these years of shipping refugees won a constituency for these sons of a Greek woman of Lesbos and an Ottoman soldier, and for better or for worse bound them emotionally to North Africa.

But the Barbarossa brothers were not alone in this struggle. In the years when Uruj and Khizr had but a ship each under their command, the corsair admiral Curtogali could call upon thirty ships and was co-ordinating raiding parties of thousands of men. The walled city of Bizerta, on the northern reach of the Tunisian coast, was his base of choice. Surrounded by well-wooded mountains, even today renowned for game and every possible variety of waterfowl, it sits astride a canal that had been first cut by the Phoenicians to link the sea with a succession of internal lakes some two thousand years before. Bizerta had always made a superb harbour: long before the corsairs began to gather here at the end of the fifteenth century, it was used by the admirals of Carthage, Rome and Byzantium. Curtogali also had the advantage of always being very well informed. When the Genoese could bear his raids no longer and fell upon Bizerta with a great fleet, he had slipped out of harm's way just a few days before. On another occasion he seems to have been intimately aware of every movement of the papal court at Rome and landed a snatch squad on the shore which missed kidnapping a Pope by only a few hours. He also knew how to work with the powers-that-be and would end his days in the service of Suleyman the

Magnificent, who appointed him the first Ottoman governor-general of Rhodes. While based in Tunisia Curtogali was scrupulous in paying his 'dues' to the ruling Hafsid Sultan, who for his part liked to pretend that Curtogali had imposed himself by force on Bizerta, a stance which allowed him to both take the corsairs' money and honour his old trading pact with his ally Genoa. As a Franciscan brother, Alberto Gugliemotti, records, the Hafsid Sultan

> desired peace with all and prosperity for his own interests. Friendly to the merchants in their commerce; friendly to the corsairs in their spoils. Let all hold by the law: the corsairs handing over a fifth part of their robberies and the Sultan – their common friend – would ever keep at peace with them all. Outside his ports the merchants and the pirates might fall by the ears if they would: that was no reason for him to trouble his head. On the contrary, he would joyfully await them on their return either with custom dues or tribute of the fifth as the case might be.

On the northern coast of Morocco an exile from Andalusia, Ali al-Mandari, had set up an independent corsair base at Tetouan to fight back against the Spanish. Al-Mandari had left in 1491, a year before Granada had surrendered, taking with him his fortune, family and followers. Tucked into the fold of a hill and overlooked by some of the most dramatic silhouettes of the Rif mountains, Tetouan was an evocative choice, for it had been a complete ruin since 1399, when a Castilian crusading army had landed there to slaughter or enslave the population and then burn the city to the ground. Al-Mandari's brave stance was strengthened by a steady stream of refugees leaving Granada, which became a flood after the expulsions and forced conversions that followed. Tetouan was a few miles from the shore, but in the shallow waters of the River Martil's estuary al-Mandari's corsairs had their harbour. What they lacked in numbers they made up for in proximity to the Spanish coast. Every summer the men of Tetouan, the 'daughter of Granada', took the *jihad fil-bahr*, the 'Holy War at Sea', to avenge the fall of the mother city. The raids were so successful that al-Mandari accumulated a slave army of three thousand Christian captives who, chained and in woollen smocks, laboured on rebuilding the ancient walls of Tetouan. A marriage with Fatimah bint Ali Rachid confirmed al-Mandari's working alliance with her father, the Emir of Chechaouen. This principality in the mountains had been recently established by an Idrissid descendant of the Prophet Muhammad. It was a stronghold of the faith, sited deep within the territory of the bellicose Berber tribes of the western Rif. It too had been reinforced by a flood tide of skilled refugees from Moorish Spain who transformed the mountain village of Chechaouen into another vengeful 'daughter of Granada'. The warriors of Chechaouen left Tetouan to pursue the Holy War at Sea while they concentrated on building up cavalry armies that skirmished with the Portuguese garrisons planted on the Moroccan coast.

In the last years of his life the blind old warrior Ali al-Mandari relied on his literate wife to be his secretary and his eyes (which by coincidence is what 'tetouan' means in Berber). When he was buried in the cemetery that stretches to the north of the city's walls, in 1512, she assumed leadership of the town and for thirty-three years dominated the northern coast of Morocco as the corsairs' *Hakima*, or governess. She was a resourceful ally to anyone who participated in the *jihad* against Spain and Portugal, accepting a symbolic offer of marriage from the Sultan of Fez and always worked in full concert with her brother in the mountains, Ibrahim, who succeeded their father as Emir of Chechaouen. She corresponded with the Ottoman Sultan and on more than one occasion sent supplies to aid Barbarossa, though she was too cautious an operator to trust him with the use of her fleet. It is tempting to speculate whether the *Hakima* might have been an inspiration for some of the other female pirate admirals of her day, such as the celebrated Irish pirate Grace O'Malley who operated out of the Burren hill country of County Clare and corresponded with Queen Elizabeth I of England.

In 1500 Uruj and Khizr were just two among many dozens of independent corsair captains operating along the North African coast with volunteer crews that were customarily assembled for the season. A modest-sized galley was known as a galleot, which is what they would have initially commanded, usually powered by nineteen or so oars on each side of the boat. Each oar would have between two and four men working it on the rowing bench, which would mean crews of around a hundred. They would row, fight, fish and form raiding parties by turn. Uruj could speak Turkish, Arabic and Greek, and knew the fusion of Spanish and Italian which was the *lingua franca* of the western

Mediterranean.

Their first base was in Djerba, a beautiful, rather mysterious and totally flat island tucked away in the shallow tidal waters of the far-southern reaches of the Gulf of Tunis. From a distance it looks like one

Barbary corsair galley.

vast wild palm grove, though up close it reveals itself as a carefully worked land at the southernmost edge of possible cultivation before the Sahara. Its inhabitants are famously industrious and self-sufficient, for they have always had to supplement the meagre subsistence extracted from their gardens by other means, be it trading, weaving or fishing. It was not on any of the principal trade routes and was always a place apart, where the sheikhs of the scattered village communities (all belonging to an ancient schism within Islam known as the Ibadi or Kharajites) formed a virtually self-governing community. But for a pirate captain starting out in the world, all this would have had its own distinctive appeal, far away from the eyes and ears of the sultans and city governors. The many sandbanks, rocky islets and tidal channels also made it a safe haven for those who had acquired local knowledge of its water, as we shall see.

In 1504 Uruj and Khizr decided to move further north into the cockpit of the Mediterranean and sailed to Goletta, just a few miles south of the ruins of Carthage. They petitioned for an audience with the Sultan, who for official business resided in the Kasbah (the citadel-palace) overlooking the white city of Tunis. They had prospered enough to bring acceptable gifts to the court and were received graciously and given official permission to make use of the port. This was a great boon, for a narrow canal leading from the sea created a completely protected harbour basin within Goletta, guarded by a royal fortress. Here in the bustling docks the two young captains could sign up well-trained crews, buy and sell galley slaves and trade in everything, anything and anybody. All they had to agree to was to accept the Sultan as their commander, and in doing so they implicitly accepted a tradition which reached back to the days of the Prophet Muhammad himself and which obliged them to present a fifth of everything they captured to the Sultan.

The next spring Uruj and his crew worked their way diligently up the coast of Sicily and across to Sardinia and tucked themselves away in a rocky cove in the lee of Elba. In a long ordeal of patience the crew took turns to fish and cook, but the vital task was to keep watch from the cliffs for any sign of movement on the horizon. They needed to observe but also to remain constantly alert lest they themselves were being marked out as prey.

After weeks of inaction two galleys were spotted a few miles off the coast of Tuscany making their way south from Genoa to one of the ports of Rome. There was just time for Uruj to make a plan: to move, shadow, then race ahead to take up a position where the seas narrow to a five-mile strait. At last the planning, the tense, half-silent weeks of waiting, were over, to be replaced by a time when strength and fierce energy would flow through every vein. The first rush must carry all, for in a long race the bigger Christian galleys, with twice as many oars and twice as many men to each oar, would win.

So Uruj's men pulled as one, swept down on the first boat and raked the terrified decks with arrows and fire. Watching the panic among the galley's banks of oars, they heaved in their own blades at the last possible moment, certain that their momentum would sweep them alongside the enemy vessel and allow them, a hundred strong, shouting in the name of God and fallen Granada, to storm its higher decks. Their captain, undaunted by the magnificence of their prize, one of the papal galleys owned by Pope Julius II, turned his new weapon on the second galley, which, having seen the bloody disaster that had befallen its brethren, meekly hove to and surrendered.

When Uruj brought these dazzling prizes safely back through the Christian seas to Tunis's harbour of Goletta, he returned as the hero of the hour. Among the warrior sailors in the harbour he was now saluted as *Rais*, captain, while in Italy they started naming this audacious young captain Barbarossa, 'the red-bearded one'. There was little need for spies in the ports of the Mediterranean, for the lucrative business of ransoms necessitated accurate and detailed reports from both sides. As the near-contemporary historian Diego Haedo has it, 'The wonder and astonishment that this notable exploit caused in Tunis, and even in Christendom, is not to be expressed, nor how celebrated the name of Uruj Rais was become from that very moment; he being held and accounted by all the world as a most valiant and enterprising commander.'

Each season Barbarossa's activities only added to his fame. But, like many a 'fortunate' *Rais*, he made his own luck, by dogged perseverance through foul weather and by the length of his cruises, criss-crossing the strategically vital triangle of water that stretched between Tunis, Sicily and Sardinia. Within this triangle a scattering of islands, such as Malta, Gozo, Lampedusa, Pantelleria, Meretimo, Ustica and Stromboli, allowed his crews access to fresh water, fresh meat and food cooked over a fire. It was on a seemingly fruitless mission in May 1505, when a five-day storm had blown every other ship in to shelter, that Uruj came across his greatest prize. A large Spanish galleon was wallowing in the waters off the coast of Lipari. His flotilla of galleys encircled the powerful boat but there was no fighting that day. The corsairs were welcomed as deliverers by the Spanish crew, drained of energy from keeping their ship afloat in the aftermath of the storm. The detachment of soldiers on board were so seasick that they could no longer stand, and the bilge pumps, which had alone kept the ship afloat, were about to collapse after weeks of continuous use. On board were chests, within chests within chests, all stamped with the signed and counter-signed seals of Ferdinand, King of Aragon, Valencia and Catalonia. Uruj had intercepted the coin with which the Spanish garrison at Naples was to be paid.

That winter Barbarossa put this fortune to good work, not, as other captains would do, on building a courtyard palace in the old city of Tunis, or acquiring an estate among the beautiful orchards of Cap Bon

to the south, but by breaking up some of his old prizes and designing
and laying out the hulls of two sleek new galleys. By the beginning of
their sixth season in Tunis, in 1506, the two brothers commanded a
fleet of eight ships. Fast, seaworthy but small, especially when compared
with the great galleys of Genoa and Venice, they nevertheless proved
their worth even in the most testing conditions. In one ferocious
engagement three of the corsair galleots, rather than retreating to the
safe shelter of Goletta, pitched themselves against a Christian battleship, *The Galley of Naples*, which was patrolling the straits. This bitter
conflict, likened to a bull baited with three hounds, raged over two days
and a night, until a synchronised attack by Uruj on the port side and
Khizr on the starboard allowed the third captain, Hasan Ali, to smash
his way through to the stern and carry the day. It was the practice of
Uruj to lead from the front, but that day his wounds were so serious
that for the first time he asked his younger brother to assume command. It was after this trial of strength that the Ottoman Sultan
dispatched an envoy with a splendid document, embellished with his
tugra, or formal signature, addressing the brothers with the honorific
Khayr-al-Din, Protector of Religion.

That winter the brothers were summoned many times to the palace
on the hill. Over the past years the stream of tribute and slaves that they
had sent to the Hafsid Sultan of Tunis had greatly endeared them to
him. Now he had taken the brothers into his confidence and talked to
them about the problems and challenges that were facing the Muslim
community of believers. Whether out of their own crusading aggression, to guard their new conquest of Granada or in reaction to the
corsairs, the Spanish were hitting back, not just with naval patrols and
coastal raids, but by building artillery forts at key points along the
North African coast. The Hafsid Sultan was not over-concerned that his
old dynastic rivals, the Sultans of Fez in Morocco and the Zayyanid
Sultans of Tlemcen in Algeria, were being inconvenienced. Indeed he
may have harboured faint hopes that the Spanish outposts established
at Mers-el-Kebir, Quassa and Oran, and the garrisons at Ceuta, Melilla,
Penon de Velez de la Gomera, Tangier and Asilah, might direct the
lucrative trans-Saharan trade exclusively towards Tunis. But in the
winter of 1509 or the spring of 1510 the Sultan was informed that three
Spanish garrisons had been established within his extensive Hafsid
domains. At Bejaia (now in modern Algeria), at Tripoli (now in Libya)

and on the island of Djerba, Spanish forces had begun the construction of fortified outposts. These artillery towers, usually sited on an offshore islet or a rocky tide-washed peninsula, were clearly designed to keep a watch on the corsair anchorages and any unusual mustering of volunteers planning to come to the aid of the Moors of Granada.

But might they not be a toehold from which a future invasion could be achieved? What could be done? For the past twenty years Spanish ships had aggressively controlled the sea lanes, sinking any North African or Moorish craft they could find. It would be easy for them to supply the garrisons in these watch-towers with munitions and food. Would the brothers accept the Sultan's invitation to lead the holy war against these invaders and expel them from the lands of Islam? Surely, if the catastrophe of Granada and the brutal expulsions that had followed it had taught them anything, it was that there was no room for compromise with such people? Despite the most solemn oaths they had proven themselves determined to destroy the Muslims, their language and their religion. They had made bonfires of the Holy Koran in the public squares of Granada. They had converted the ancient mosques, hallowed by centuries of prayer, into churches and they had forcibly converted the believers and compelled them to eat the flesh of swine and drink wine.

The brothers Barbarossa accepted the invitation to drive the Spanish back into the sea.

6

The Just and the Grim

The Transformation of the Ottoman Empire under Sultans Bayezid II and Selim I, 1480–1520

Every morn my hosts of fancies ride o'er streams of tears to war:
O'er the one-piered, two-arched bridge my brows have builded,
    forth they fare.
Veiled in airy webs, bespangled with each good and evil star:
Every evening fickle fortune winds me in her wanton hair:
Still alone, a lonely stranger, in strange lands I roam afar,
While around me march the sullen guards of grief and pain and
    care.
Till I've read life's riddle, emptied its nine pitchers to the end
Never shall I, Sultan Selim, find on earth a faithful friend.

Sultan Selim I

With the death of the Great Eagle, Sultan Mehmet, the discipline by which he had held together the machinery of the Ottoman state snapped. Like a taut steel cable suddenly released, it whipped round in lethal frenzy, awaiting a master strong enough to reapply the tension.

Within hours of Mehmet's death in May 1481 the janissaries had lynched the grand vizier, Karamani Mehmet Pasha, and streamed out of their camp to join the rioting mobs and dissident soldiery who had taken over the streets of Istanbul. The Sultan's palace, source of all orders and decrees for the past forty years, was paralysed, incapable even of burying Mehmet. In the Islamic tradition, even a pauper can be expected to be washed and buried within twenty-four hours of his death by his community, but not so a Sultan.

Mehmet's sons, who ruled over distant provinces as governors, moved to secure their rights, though since the death of the beloved Prince Mustapha none had been chosen as heir. Prince Bayezid was best placed to succeed, for not only had he healthy adult sons of his own, Ahmed and Selim, but he had made politically astute alliances, marrying off one daughter to the military governor of Anatolia and another to the governor of Rumelia (the Ottoman Balkans). He was also the first to physically reach Istanbul, where he took immediate charge. He escorted the now-embalmed body of his father out of the courtyards of the Topkapi Palace and along the processional road, the Divan Yolu. Sultan Mehmet the Conqueror was buried behind the prayer wall of the magnificent new mosque he had had built over the foundations of the Church of the Holy Apostles.

Bayezid's principal rival for the throne was his younger brother Prince Cem. This conflict would be settled by battle, a crude but necessary contest for their fitness to rule over this warrior state, like some political adaptation of Darwin's theory to palace life. But once Gedik Pasha, the Ottoman general whose army held the Italian port of Otranto, had formally declared his support for Prince Bayezid, and brought his soldiers back to the mainland, the outcome was already half resolved. The tribal levies that Prince Cem had been able to summon up from the central plains of Anatolia were no match for Gedik Pasha's disciplined regiments. After a battle fought outside Bursa, Cem was defeated and forced to retreat into the east before crossing the Taurus mountains to escape Ottoman territory. He passed into Syria and Egypt before deciding, in a superbly romantic gesture, to sidestep from any dynastic ambition and join the Haj, the pilgrimage across the Arabian Desert to Mecca. On his return he made one more attempt against his elder brother Bayezid before drifting off into exile. To everyone's surprise he chose none of the neighbouring Muslim lands but took ship to the Christian pirate haven of Rhodes. The Knights of St John could hardly believe the rapid transformation in their fortunes. Sitting among the ruins of Rhodes, smashed first by siege and then by earthquake, they were in sorrowful expectation of a second Ottoman invasion, which they stood very little hope of opposing. But then, like political manna from heaven, in dropped Cem. He may not have been the most astute political animal, but he was clearly charming company as well as a practised poet and womaniser. This exiled Bonnie Prince Charlie of the Ottoman romantic imagination wrote to his brother from Rhodes:

> *With a smile on a bed of roses dost thou lie in all delight,*
> *While in darkened cellar mid the ashes couch I – why is this?*

To which couplet Bayezid replied with a quatrain:

> *To me was Empire on the fore-eternal day decreed,*
> *Yet to destiny why wilt though yield not, why is this, why is this?*
> *A pilgrim to the holy shrines and thus content dost thou declare,*
> *And yet thou dost for earthly Sultan-ship sigh, why is this?*

He also enclosed a note to the Commander of the Knights, offering to pay them forty thousand ducats per annum to keep Cem out of the Ottoman Empire. Given the usual offer made by a successful Ottoman prince to his defeated brother – an oiled bowstring tightened around the neck by a pair of deaf-mutes – it was also quite exceptionally generous. The Knights later subcontracted their role as hosts, and Cem was sent on a tour of some of the most lovely Renaissance courts and chateaux of western Europe. Sultan Bayezid II kept true to his word and never changed the terms of his deal. He sent a succession of ambassadors and spies to check on his brother's health and whereabouts (such as agent Barak, who tracked down Cem in France) but never an assassin or a subtle poisoner.

For his part, Cem refused to be won over by any of his hosts' offers to provide him with an army to recover his throne if he would only convert to Christianity. In private conversation with Pope Innocent VIII he confessed that he could not abandon his faith, 'even for the rule of the whole world'. He is perhaps best known now as the author of a number of verses charged with the anguish of exile, for the land, sounds, memories and loves of his youth. Even if it now seems unlikely that they are all his own work, his example has encouraged generation after generation of Turks to compose in the melancholic mood of Prince Cem. But all was not regret, as this couplet about the freedom one could enjoy on the Riviera suggests:

How wondrous nice a town, this town of Nice
Where none is questioned, whatever his caprice.

Cem died of the plague in Naples in 1495 and his body was taken back to Istanbul, saluted by cannon as it passed below the forts on the Dardanelles and then escorted up to Bursa, where he was buried in his grandfather's mausoleum beside his elder brother Mustapha.[1]

Bayezid, for all the mercy he had shown to his younger brother, was capable of pragmatic decisions when he needed to be. The military backing of Gedik Pasha had been crucial to his accession to the throne, but it is a rule of political life that it is insupportable for any leader to be reminded that they have ever been dependent on any one of their subjects. The steps to the throne must always be cut away so that no other may observe a path to power. Gedik Pasha was first honoured and flattered, and then summarily arrested in one of the pavilions of the palace at Edirne and quickly executed, his reputation subsequently blackened by insinuations that he had been in treasonable correspondence with Prince Cem. Another enemy of state, Cem's son Oguz, was also disposed of. An order was dispatched that he should be strangled, though out of pity the means was mitigated to a phial of poison.

Sultan Bayezid had long experience of government. He had served his apprenticeship as governor of the north-eastern province of Amasya during his father's long reign. While Sultan Mehmet had delighted in the company of clever converts, especially from the old Greek, Bosnian and Serbian royal families, Bayezid's court had been quite the reverse. It was composed of members of the old Turkish dynasties, Islamic scholars, mystical poets, wandering teachers and philosophers. While Mehmet spent the bulk of his career fighting the Christians in the Balkans, the Aegean and the Black Sea, Bayezid's experience of war had been garnered in the plains and high plateaux of the eastern frontier. One can imagine that it was always a cause of regret to him that he had been fated to fight brother Muslims rather than the enemies of his faith.

When Sultan Bayezid assumed control of the state, he at first pursued a careful policy of non-engagement. On the eastern frontier this was based on a genuine desire for peace with his co-religionists, which was fully in keeping with the message of the Koran. It wasn't his style to know about, far less care to measure himself against, the historical heroes of pagan history in the manner of his father. Nor did he seem to be interested in pursuing the campaigns of conquest mapped out in the last year of Mehmet's life. The Kingdom of Naples was delighted to make peace with the new Ottoman Sultan, just as the Knights of Rhodes had been effectively pacified by the annual pension that he awarded them. When the French King Charles VIII invaded southern Italy in 1494, to the great consternation of the European balance of power, Bayezid resisted the temptation to benefit from the political confusion, apart from commissioning a thorough overhaul of the defences of the Dardanelles forts and the walls of Istanbul. He concentrated the empire's resources on the creation of a stronger navy.

As the Ottoman navy grew ever stronger, the swashbuckling Knights of St John in Rhodes and the crusading dynasty within the Kingdom of Cyprus grew ever more respectful. But they were spared any direct intervention because yet another border war broke out between the Ottoman Empire and the Mameluke Sultanate of Egypt. This conflict lasted from 1485 until 1491. A truce had already been signed before the Ottoman battle fleet was broken up by a vicious storm and fortunately the peace held. Sultan Bayezid was in any case not deterred. He used the disaster to look into the creation of lighter, more seaworthy craft, which were produced that winter in a fierce drive of production at the naval arsenals that stretched along the northern bank of the Golden Horn. Once again the islands of Rhodes and Cyprus braced themselves for an expected attack, though the Sultan had a much tougher foe in mind.

It seems that, as early as 1477, delegates from the Emirate of Granada had aspired to create an alliance with the Ottoman court. As a prince, and then as Sultan Bayezid II, he never flinched from his stated policy, of freely offering asylum to all emigrants from Andalusia while never affording them the slightest hope of any military assistance. With the length of the Mediterranean studded with Christian islands and fortress ports – Rhodes, Cyprus, Crete, Sicily and the Balearics – standing between the docks of Istanbul and Malaga, it would have been reckless to imagine that the Ottoman Empire could have at this time offered any effective aid to Granada. But when Ferdinand and Isabella expelled all Jews who refused to convert to Christianity, Bayezid once again made certain that the doors of his empire were open to the refugees. While Christendom hailed Ferdinand and Isabella as the great monarchs of the day, the Sultan protested, 'How can they call such a king wise and intelligent? He is impoverishing his country and enriching my kingdom.' Bayezid was a lone voice of reason in his age and from 1492 to 1512 he was also the wise and merciful as thousands upon thousands, followed by tens of thousands of skilled merchants, artisans, bankers, weavers, potters, dyers and jewellers, made their way to the safe haven of the Ottoman Empire. He was also aware that there will always a backlash by the indigene against the energy of the immigrants. So the refugees were initially prohibited from settling in the capital but welcomed into provincial cities, especially barely populated Thessaloniki, which rose to fame and fortune just as rapidly as Malaga had been emptied.

In 1499 Bayezid's preparations were complete. He struck against Venice by land and sea in a brilliantly conceived campaign which isolated her Aegean and Adriatic fortresses at the same time as Ottoman cavalry armies carried out raids within a few days' ride of the fabled city itself. Distracted by this direct threat in their homeland, Venice's fortress outposts in the mainland of Greece fell to Ottoman sieges one by one. By 1501 her maritime empire had been stripped back to Corfu, Cyprus and Crete. Although the Venetians, urged on by some unscrupulous Christian allies, counter-attacked with a raid on Lesbos and the sack of Fethiye, they sued for peace in 1503.

Bayezid was also aware of the wider Islamic world. His agents had been monitoring with alarm a new threat to the economy of the lands of Islam: the progress of the Portuguese. Just a few years after Vasco da Gama's first journey to India in 1498, they had returned to the Indian Ocean and methodically burned and sacked their way along the cities of the trading coasts. Their conquests uprooted the centuries-old pattern of the spice trade. Such was the threat to what had hitherto been a Muslim trade lake that in 1510 Bayezid offered to put aside all the old animosity and provide the Mameluke Sultans of Egypt with free access to Ottoman naval materials. For the Portuguese had in this period established fortress bases on the periphery of Arabia, at Ormuz and Socotra, and had tried to force an entry into the Red Sea.

Within his domains Bayezid II also championed the cause of Islam. He reduced the predominance of slave-converts in his court, encouraging the return of native Turks to the administration, traditional Islamic scholars to the law courts and holy men to the mosques. He tried to balance the strength of the army by preferring native-born cavalry to the converted Christian renegades whom his father had employed, using the nomadic tribes in the east as a balance to the growing predominance of the janissaries. He also reversed his father's suspicious ban on the popular mystics who regularly appeared from out of Iran and Central Asia. The Halveti dervishes, for instance, were welcomed in Istanbul, where this Sufi brotherhood flourished. The great mosque that Bayezid raised up in the centre of the city seems to encapsulate some of his spirit. Flanking the main prayer hall of the mosque there is a pair of pavilions built especially for the use of dervish mystics and as lodgings for pious travellers. The mosque is strong rather than sublime, enduringly well made, with an affectionate fusion of Byzantine, Persian and Turkish traditions in its welcoming open-air courtyard, fringed by university colleges, beneath which shelters the courtyard of the dealers in old books, odd Sufi itinerants and an exchange market in prayer beads. A park-like umbra of ancient plane trees now surrounds it, so that this quarter established by Bayezid remains one of the most enchanting in all Istanbul. It is difficult not to warm to its creator, who seems to have been one of the more humane and principled rulers of his terrifyingly competitive age. It is no surprise that it was Bayezid who initiated the first Ottoman diplomatic missions to the Christian powers, to the King of France in 1483, the Duchy of Moscovy in 1495 and to the King of Poland and the Holy Roman Emperor in 1496. Considering peace to be at the heart of the Islamic message as revealed to the world in the Koran, the Sultan worked hard and consistently to fulfil this obligation. His compassionate concern for fellow believers, be they exiles from Granada or the hard-pressed Sultanate of Egypt, should have been an uplifting example to his brother monarchs. It may be that Sultan Bayezid II was the most genuine Muslim ever to have sat on the throne of the Ottomans.

But what have the proper exercise of religion and the leadership of men ever had to do with each other? Bayezid II was to be punished by the world for his piety and his moderation. The Ottoman Empire had been created as an instrument of war, fine-tuned by annual campaigns of conquest, not as an institution for putting the teachings of Islam into practice. Its leaders had no God-ordained right to rule: they were descended neither from the Prophet nor any of the Arab dynasties of Caliphs that succeeded him, nor had they been freely acclaimed by the faithful as successors. They were an upstart Turkic dynasty established on the cosmopolitan frontiers of Byzantium and their authority had only been established by the successful prosecution of war. Sultan Bayezid II, in his immersion in the practice of Islam, overlooked the essential nature of the Ottoman state.

Ironically it was a threat from within Islam which almost destroyed Bayezid II. A threat led by a charismatic genius, who could blend together a perfect cocktail of holy war and personal ambition, fire it up with terror, mystical prophecies, drama, poetry and death. In 1501 Ismail, a handsome, young Safavid sheikh, announced his rule as Imam-Shah over the city of Tabriz. He had deposed a cousin in the process but his accession was enthusiastically welcomed, for the sheikhs of the Safavid Sufi brotherhood had come to be regarded with religious awe by the surrounding tribes. They were not the only ones to be impressed, as Caterino Zeno's description of Ismail shows:

> Of noble presence and a truly royal bearing, as in his eyes there was something, I know not what, so great and commanding, which plainly showed that he would one day become a great ruler. Nor did the virtues of his mind discord with the beauty of his person as he had an elevated genius, and such a lofty idea of things as seemed incredible at such a tender age . . . he had vigour of mind, quickness of perception and personal valour, never equalled by any of his contemporaries.[2]

This opinion was shared by his fellow Italian, Angiolello, who described Ismail as 'fair, handsome and very pleasing. He is almost worshipped, more especially by his soldiers, many of whom fight without armour, being willing to die for their master.'

The Safavids, like so many influential Sufi brotherhoods, were devoted to the teaching of Islam in regions which were effectively beyond the reach of urban civilisation. Sufi centres have often been compared to Christian monasteries as they have much in common. Many originated as the hermitage of a single holy man which progressively expanded into a place of learning and healing where travellers and merchants could feel secure. Initially they would be supported by the charity of the surrounding tribes, and so their benevolent hospitality had none of the hated connotation of a royal palace, paid for by the extractions of soldiers, taxmen and judges. These unworldly Sufi sheikhs, as their leaders are often called, followed the Islamic practice of poverty and hospitality and, as respected outsiders, were often asked to arbitrate in tribal wars and clan vendettas. In due course the tomb of the peace-making sheikhs became centres of pilgrimage in their own right, neatly dovetailing with the traditional respect for the shaman-healer that ran through most of the Turkish societies of Central Asia.

The Safavid brotherhood grew to be especially influential in the Kurdish mountainous region that stretches between Anatolia, Syria and Iran. It had been founded at the time of the Mongol destruction of Baghdad in the middle of the thirteenth century, when the traditional patterns and instinctive loyalties of Islamic society had been broken asunder. The Safavids were no more than one element within a very wide movement, mirrored by Rumi's teaching in Konya and the creation of the Naqshabandi in Central Asia, to mention those who still have great influence today, though there were many others, among them the Sradabar, Hurufiya, Dhahabiya, Nurbakhshiya, Kubrawi and Halveti.

The first recorded Safavid sheikh is Safi al-Din Ishak (after whom the order was named), who was buried at Ardabil in the mountains of north-western Iran in 1334. He was succeeded by his son Sadr al-Din, who set about organising his father's teachings into a coherent movement with a chain of command stretching from *Murshid* (the head), through director-agents, missionaries and assistants, to students and novices. The Safavids had apparently become respected enough for the great Timur to visit Ardabil on his way back from his victory over the Ottomans and he released a number of prisoners of war in their honour. A half century later the preaching of Sheikh Junayd propelled the Safavids to greater prominence. As their leader from 1447 to 1460 he gave the order a militant direction, preaching a holy war, first against the Christians who remained in the East, in the mountains of Georgia, Armenia and Trebizond, but later against anyone who opposed his rule. Otherwise pious Muslims who questioned his reasoning were denounced as infidels. The local ruler eventually tired of this noisy and bloodthirsty sheikh and had him expelled, but instead of weakening his influence, this merely fanned the flames. For a poor, wandering, persecuted sheikh was just the sort of figure that most appealed to the wild tribes. Safavid

influence soon spread beyond its Kurdish core, south into Syria and
north into Azerbaijan. Sheikh Junayd received another boost when he
was welcomed into the court of the greatest Turkic warlord of Central
Asia, Uzun Hassan. This alliance was confirmed when one of Sheikh
Junayd's sons, Sheikh Haydar, was married to a daughter of this powerful warlord.

Ismail, born in 1487, was the fruit of this union. He was the seventh
sheikh of the Safavid house through his father, and a descendant of
Timur and Genghis Khan through his mother. As a Safavid he traced
his descent from the seventh Shia Imam, which placed him among the
Sharifs – the 'people of the house', or lineal descendants of the Prophet –
through his daughter Fatimah and her husband Ali, who was considered
by all Shia Muslims to be the first disciple and spiritual heir of
Muhammad. To this exalted ancestry were added the fervent preaching
of his father and the poetry of the young Ismail himself. Speaking in
riddles and in rhetoric, using the most potent imagery and allegory, and
working within the traditional messianic imagery that is always latent
within popular Islam. The Shiite tradition taught that Ali should have
governed the Muslim community, for it believed that he had been
appointed by the Prophet as his heir just before his death. It also taught
that this blessing had been passed down the line of his descendants
(rather as Christians believe in an apostolic succession rippling down
through the generations from Christ's first designation of St Peter).

Ismail's followers were encouraged to see him as the true Imam: the
legitimate spiritual leader of the entire worldwide community of Islam.
In addition, enduring Central Asian traditions of reincarnation (which
had absolutely nothing to do with Islam), meant that as well as being
saluted as Ali's heir he was also considered the manifest spirit of Ali in
his age. Not only touched with the power of interpreting the holy book,
he was also the holder of generations and generations of accumulated
ancient wisdom. In the imagery of the Zoroastrian-influenced poetic
culture of Persia he was the bearer of the divine fire, to the Shia the
incarnate Imam, to the mountain tribesman he was *el-Khidr*, the inde-
structible warrior saint, the green-hued St George of Islam. To his more
ardent disciples it seemed that he must also be the reincarnated spirit of
Issa (Jesus), who as the Mahdi would return to earth to usher in the
divine kingdom at the end of the world. His followers, who became
known as the Kizilbas, wore red hats as both a badge of identity and a

mark of potential martyrdom. Ismail offered these not just rewards on this earth but inclusion in the holy cult of martyrdom which was revisited every year during the month-long Shia commemoration of the death of Husayn, son of Imam Ali and grandson of the Prophet Muhammad. When he wrote to his followers that 'no one can be a Kizilbas unless his heart is pure and his bloody entrails are like rubies', he demanded nothing less than total obedience and offered a martyr's death as a reward.

When Ismail, the brilliant fourteen-year-old prodigy of a poet-sheikh, first declared himself Imam at Tabriz, he also unleashed thousands upon thousands of devoted Kizilbas warriors upon the world. Within just nine years they had conquered in his name all the mountains, oases and plains of Persia. By 1510 Ismail was hailed as the Shah of Iran as well as the *Murshid-I Kamil* ('perfect master') and 'Shadow of God on earth'. Architects, artists, poets and engineers were drawn to his new court and to its youthful imaginative ruler, who knew how to use talented men.[3] For instance, Bahzad, 'the greatest painter of his day', left Herat in 1510 in order to meet Ismail, who appointed him director of the new royal library.

At times Ismail's passion and fierceness engendered a terrifying cruelty, as when he avenged the death of a Sufi mystic by surrounding the city where he had been murdered with an entire army to ensure that no one would escape the massacre. It was also Ismail who instituted the childishly partisan habit of publicly cursing the first three Caliphs (who are revered by Sunni Muslims) and who would publicly drink from the skull of one of his old rivals, which he had mounted like rare porcelain with a gilt tracery. Having once charmed the Ottoman ambassadors with his attentions and manners, he then made them witness the execution of a learned scholar whose only crime had been loyalty to the Sunni traditions. Yet his own writings, under the pen-name Hatayi/Khatai, 'the Sinner', are still numbered among the masterworks of Turkish mystical verse:[4]

> *My sign is the Crown of Happiness. I am the signet ring on*
>   *Suleyman's finger.*
> *Muhammad is made of light, Ali of mystery. I am a pearl in the sea*
>   *of absolute reality.*
> *I am Khatai, the Shah's slave full of short-comings, at thy gate I am*

the smallest and the last servant.
I am the living Khidr and Jesus, son of Mary. I am the Alexander of
my contemporaries.

Sultan Bayezid II was so personally intrigued by the Sufis' teachings, their charismatic sheikhs and their secretive brotherhoods that he proved an almost embarrassingly supportive neighbour to Ismail. Delighted by the prospect of a reformed and revitalised Islam, he quite failed to concentrate on Ismail's political agenda. Much to the fury of some of his less spiritual advisers, he even acceded to Ismail's request to march an army across the Ottoman eastern territories. Nor did the scare-story that Ismail had secretly planted in Istanbul five thousand Kizilbas secret agents ready to rise up at a moment's notice seem to adversely effect the old Sultan. Some of Bayezid's children (he fathered eight sons and seventeen daughters) were less confident. One of the oldest and toughest of his sons, Prince Selim, became convinced that his father's indulgence of Ismail would bring down the whole edifice of the Ottoman Empire. Acting as governor for his father in Trebizond (a modest governorship on the mountainous Black Sea coast), Selim took it upon himself to march into the eastern frontier provinces in 1505 to stop the gradual leaching of loyalty towards Ismail. For this he was reprimanded by his father for overstepping his own authority and this charge was repeated in 1510, after Selim defeated an army led by Ismail's brother, even though it had advanced within Ottoman territory.

Selim's worst fears were to be realised the following year. At the time of the annual celebration of Husayn's martyrdom, when the mood of even a moderate Muslim drifts towards an emotional sympathy with the disinherited family of Ali, the Kizilbas struck out in Ismail's name. Responding to the call of a holy man to whom Sultan Bayezid in his kindness had been in the habit of sending annual gifts of alms, four and a half thousand rebels rose up and attacked the retinue of the local Ottoman governor. This uprising was not on some far-distant eastern frontier, but deep within Ottoman Turkey, just outside the Mediterranean port of Antalya. As the Kizilbas advanced through Anatolia they were joined by thousands of volunteers, not just other secret Kizilbas cells but also disaffected members of the regime, embittered by the leading role Christian renegades and the Christian-origin janissary corps had acquired in the Ottoman state. The Ottoman governor of Kutahya led his troops out to quell the revolt, but they deserted him and he was impaled and roasted on a spit. If the rebels succeeded in storming their way to Bursa, the old seat of the Ottomans, it seemed possible that the whole empire might fall to the lure of Ismail's millenarian promises. Stirred into action by the report of the local judge, who placed no faith in the loyalty of Bursa's population unless it was stiffened by the presence of the army, the grand vizier personally rushed there at the head of a column of janissaries. Not for the first time the discipline and equipment of the janissary corps proved triumphant over mere enthusiasm. The Kizilbas army was driven off and then routed on the field of battle at Sivas. Its leadership was hunted down and killed, but there were just too many captive common soldiers for a massacre to be enforced. Many sought refuge after the battle by escaping east towards their Shah, Ismail, in Iran, while many of the prisoners were deported to the Ottoman Empire's Balkan frontiers, where it was considered they could do no harm.

The suppression of the revolt by the Kizilbas brought to a head the succession crisis in the family of Bayezid II. It was clear that Selim was now set upon deposing his father and pushing forward with an aggres-

Ottoman woman of Istanbul. By Gentile Bellini, 1479–81. (British Museum)

sive policy against Ismail. This forced his other brothers, Ahmed and Korkud, among others, to declare their candidacy. The actual details of the fighting between the various brothers is highly confusing but as only Prince Selim had the confidence of the janissaries, the outcome was certain enough. He eventually defeated all his rival brothers in battle. Some of his brothers would appeal to Shah Ismail for assistance, while others seem to have been genuinely 'infected' by missionary preaching, so that at least one of the Ottoman princes, Selim's nephew Murat, openly wore the red cap of the Kizilbas.

Selim's ambition had never been far from the surface, but the violent infighting during the succession war hardened his resolve. No male relative of his would be suffered to survive. In this, as in so much, he was a true heir to his grandfather, Mehmet the Conqueror. All his brothers, nephews and great-nephews were eventually to be throttled by a greased bowstring and dispatched to the family mausolea to be buried with honour. The final act was when Selim's victorious army of janissaries returned to Istanbul in the spring of 1512. They backed the formal deposition of the pious old Sultan Bayezid II. Selim's father died just a month later, on the road to the village where he had been born in Thrace, which had been chosen as his place of retirement.

Sultan Selim knew that a great test lay ahead. If he failed to force a resolution against Shah Ismail, it was almost certain that the disaffected population of his state would rebel again and again in favour of the bright, new world being predicted by the Shah-Imam in the east. He acted with a fierce and violent logic. His allies among the traditional Sunni Muslim establishment of Istanbul were encouraged to condemn the new regime. They solemnly declared that the Kizilbas were 'unbelievers and heretics. Any who sympathise with them and accept their false religion or assist them are also unbelievers and heretics. It is necessary and a divine obligation that they be massacred and their communities be dispersed.'

But this was only a paper victory, for even those close to Selim knew that a sizeable majority of the population, and possibly even his own army, favoured the passionate millenarial teachings of the Kizilbas to a state that depended on the salaried obedience of a janissary army composed of ex-Christian slaves.

Selim knew that he had to strike quickly and ruthlessly or not at all. He sent out a Muslim 'Inquisition' to make a register of those suspected of loyalty to the Kizilbas. Their first mission was to make safe the military road leading from Istanbul towards Iran. To cleanse this, forty thousand suspects along the route were first registered and then marched off to be resettled elsewhere in the empire, though many were killed on the way. At the same time the Sultan informed his ministers that he needed peace treaties with all of the empire's traditional enemies: the Mamelukes of Egypt, the Republic of Venice and the Kingdom of Hungary. He must have a completely free hand to deal with this principal threat. Selim had also become aware that Ismail had been attempting to forge an alliance with Venice, not only to distract the Ottomans in the west, but to provide his Persian army with the modern field artillery that they so desperately lacked. Later Ismail even turned to the Portuguese, despite their brutal activities among the Muslim trading cities in the Indian Ocean and Persian Gulf, to try to fill this gap in weaponry.

In 1514 Sultan Selim led the Ottoman army across the breadth of Anatolia. It was an exhausting progress. The public proscription of the Kizilbas and the brutal evidence of their massacre in village after village helped make the campaign deeply unpopular with the rank and file soldiers. At one marching camp mutinous shots were even fired into the Sultan's tented enclosure. On 23 August the two armies finally confronted each other at Caldiran, north-east of Lake Van. Selim wished to delay fighting so as to assemble all his troops, but one of his advisers pressed him to attack immediately whatever the terrain or tactical difficulties, for he feared that otherwise the bulk of the Ottoman army might be persuaded to defect to the enemy by Kizilbas missionaries. Ismail had a vast force of volunteer cavalry recruited from the Turkic tribes under his command, but the battle was decided by Selim's field artillery. Some five hundred light cannon had been chained together in a long line, defended by twelve thousand janissaries. This line of artillerymen and infantrymen blasted the Shah's army into oblivion, despite a series of desperately brave frontal attacks.

The slaughter at Caldiran achieved by shrapnel, cannon and musket fire shattered the myth of Ismail's God-given invulnerability. He escaped but Selim moved quickly to follow up his surprisingly decisive victory. He rewarded his troops by letting them sack Tabriz on 6 September, thereby recovering some popularity among the soldiers. Even so his army absolutely refused to advance any further east that year.

The next year Selim, aware of how tenuous the loyalty of his army was in any campaign fought against Ismail, decided to take his revenge on the allies of the Shah. The Turcoman tribes of eastern Anatolia were conquered in detail and the heads of their various emirs sent as grim trophies to their allies, both Ismail and the Mameluke Sultanate of Egypt.[5] Having returned to Istanbul for the winter, Selim once again marched eastwards in the spring of 1516, as if determined to renew the struggle against Ismail. Then, without any warning, he wheeled his army south and crossed the frontier to invade Mameluke Syria. There was absolutely no pretext, no reason to wage war on this fellow Muslim state, especially one which shared the Sunni tradition. The Koran forbids such aggression, but Selim must have privately reasoned that sooner or later Ismail and the Mamelukes would be forced to combine to protect themselves against him. It also seems probable that he had received reports that Egypt was pouring its resources into creating its own artillery arsenal. In May 1512 seventy new Egyptian cannon, cast in both bronze and iron, had been publicly tested, and the following month a batch of fifty-seven had successfully completed their test firings at Raidanya. They were designed to defend Cairo and were too heavy to accompany a field army but it seemed clear to Selim the Grim that any technical advantage that the Ottomans had possessed might soon be cut.

So Selim, threatened by his neighbours' new weapons, decided on 'preventive action'. Just outside Aleppo, the fortified city that commands both the trade and the physical approaches to northern Syria, the Ottoman army destroyed 250 years of Mameluke rule in a battle lasting just a few hours. At Marj Dabiq on 24 August 1516 the bravery of the Mameluke cavalry, which had once halted Timur's advance not far from Aleppo, had not diminished. At one moment an impetuous cavalry charge surged through the line of cannon on the Ottoman left wing. But this was not enough. The Ottoman line held and Selim's armoury swept his brave adversaries from the battlefield. His political agents had also been at work. The Mameluke governor of Aleppo, who commanded the left wing at Marj Dabiq, had been 'turned' and was acting as a paid agent of the Ottomans by the time of the battle. Someone may also have been paid to poison Sultan Qansuh, the seventy-eight-year-old Mameluke leader, who collapsed at midday with a stroke and fell to the ground from his saddle before he could be offered so much as a sip of water.

That very evening Selim dined in the tent of the dead sultan. Four days later he stood on the balcony of the fortress gateway of the citadel of Aleppo, looking out over the vast extent of the city. As Damascus and then Jerusalem fell without a fight, Selim's advance turned into a triumphal progress. The Mameluke ruling class of Egypt and Syria had been respected but never loved by the populace. They were an ossified version of the janissary army, for all recruits to the Mameluke regiments were by purchase, chiefly white slaves acquired from the far Christian north, from the Caucasus mountains and the Russian forests. They had no support from the indigenous Arabs of Syria and Palestine, who were encouraged to greet the Ottomans as their liberators. In two further battles fought during that blisteringly successful campaign, outside Gaza and then at Raidanya just outside Cairo (January 1517), the Mamelukes were again routed by the superior fire-power and discipline of the Ottoman army. Cairo should have surrendered and been peacefully occupied like Aleppo, Damascus and Jerusalem, but after such an epic series of victories which had given Sultan Selim vast new territories and doubled his annual tax revenue, his soldiers were hungry for their own reward. The sack of Cairo they saw as their just desert: to rape its women and youths, to slaughter whom they wished and to pillage this densely populated, rich city. A sudden counter-attack on the Ottoman camp by diehard Mameluke officers, who then withdrew into Cairo, dragged the war into the maze-like alleys of the old city. This gave Selim's soldiers the excuse they were looking for. Every house was searched and the streets were soon filled with the headless corpses of soldiers, suspects and those who were deemed to have resisted the search. Selim knew the limits of power, and reining back his victorious soldiery from the sack of a city was a step to be taken with great caution. The great medieval capital city of Islam, the seat of the Caliphate (the leadership of the Muslim world) since the destruction of Baghdad, adorned by generations of Mameluke Sultans, by Saladin himself and by centuries of Fatimid Caliphs before him, was handed over as mute victim to their hunger and lust.

Blame for the sack of Cairo was subsequently heaped on the Mamelukes, who were hunted down like mad dogs across the length and breadth of Egypt, not just through the city's alleys, tombs and courtyards. The last ruler, Tuman Bey, was tracked down and brought before the Sultan. He was held in the Ottoman camp for two weeks, then paraded in his misery through Cairo before being crucified above the Zuwayla Gate for all to see. The area of the city to the south of this gate was cleared of all its inhabitants to make way for new Ottoman army quarters.

The search for remnant Mamelukes allowed the Ottomans to take a full inventory of their new conquest, and to quietly occupy all the outlying provinces of Egypt. The Ottoman Empire now included the entire Red Sea coast of Arabia and Africa, as well as the mountains of the Yemen, Nubia and the oases of the western Sahara. It also inherited the tradition of guarding the Haj route and protecting the two holy cities. Selim now ruled over all three of the holiest cities of Islam: Mecca, Medina and Jerusalem. The Ottoman Sultan was no longer just the commander of war bands of Turks and slave armies of Christians on the westernmost frontier but could glory in the proud Islamic titles of 'servant of the two Holy Cities' (khadim al-haramayn ash-Sharifayn) and 'guarantor of the Pilgrimage routes'.

The Sultanate was well on its way to becoming the official backbone of Sunni Islam, a role that at last gave it a sense of moral purpose and religious orthodoxy. In the battle for Islamic legitimacy that would accompany the long drawn-out war against Ismail's Shiite Iran, these were vital tools. It is, however, an error copied by all too many historians to claim that Selim ordered the murder of the last Caliph and took this title to himself. For this would indeed have played straight into the hands of Shah Ismail, who could have made telling parallels between the Ottomans and the enemies of Islam. Ever since the destruction of Baghdad in 1258 by the Mongol hordes and the murder of the last Abbasid Caliph al-Mustain (his body was wrapped up in a carpet and galloped over by Mongol cavalry, according to popular tradition), a cadet branch of the ancient dynasty of Abbasid Caliphs had been sheltered in Cairo.[6] They had no religious, let alone political, function, but earned a stipend and their position of hereditary honour by serving as the official title-bestower to the swift-changing cast of Mameluke Sultans. Selim identified the reigning member of this remnant Abbasid clan, al-Mutawakkil, who was sent to accompany and authenticate the totemic treasures of Islam that were kept in Cairo: the Prophet Muhammad's patched and tattered cloak, his simple bow, the swords of the first four Caliphs and a modest little agate signet ring – all of which were sent in great honour to Istanbul. And from court records we know that this last recognised member of the Abbasid dynasty accompanied these treasures to Istanbul and was alive and in receipt of a pension throughout Selim's reign and well into that of his son, Suleyman. Selim never claimed the title Caliph for himself, but nor did he bother to get this last Abbasid to authenticate his title as Emir or Sultan.

In September 1517 Selim and his army marched out of Egypt. The following year he led them to secure the frontier of his empire on the Euphrates, but once again he thought twice about testing their loyalty in a direct confrontation with Shah Ismail. This was no instance of royal paranoia. For in 1519 and 1520 a series of Kizilbas revolts, all led by well-respected local holy men, broke out again in central Anatolia, proof that even after the catastrophic defeats at Sivas and Caldiran, and the sack of Tabriz, the Kizilbas message of a divine Shia monarchy remained a potent alternative to the Ottoman Sultanate.

Selim might be known in the West as 'The Grim',[7] but despite the savagery of his campaigns against Ismail and the Mamelukes, his reign was actually a period of peace with Christendom. The truce that his father had made with Venice was consolidated into a mutual peace and the borders with the kingdoms of both Hungary and Poland were also quiet. Christendom could have taken advantage of the desperate Muslim civil war that sapped the energy of Ottoman Turkey and Shiite Persia, set against each other as they were, though in fact these internal divisions were replicated in the West. The rivalry between Francis I of France and Charles V of Spain consumed the attention of those young monarchs for the first twenty years of their reigns.

The only Christian power that had reason to be immediately alarmed about the expansion of Selim's empire was the Knights of St John at Rhodes. They and their small fleet of galleys now lay directly astride the sea route between Istanbul and Egypt. Surely no Sultan would allow this nest of maritime raiders, these Christian corsairs, to freely prey upon the rich cargoes of spices as well as the boatloads of pious pilgrims who would now sail between Istanbul and Alexandria? Indeed it seems likely that the fleet-building Selim had ordered while in Istanbul in 1520 was specifically designed for use against Rhodes. But on the evening of 21 September the Sultan, driven by a sudden premonition, decided to leave his hunting palace in Edirne for Istanbul. He died at midnight, struck dead, according to a superstitious story, by a stroke at the same place where his father had died among the witch-haunted heaths of Thrace. Whatever the truth of this tale, he must have been a haunted man. His conscience is almost beyond conception. The acknowledged murderer of all his brothers and nephews, the deposer of his father, a man directly and personally responsible for at least a hundred thousand violent deaths aside from the sacking of two great cosmopolitan capital cities, he was loathed by half his subjects and feared by the rest. And, to those who followed the Shiite tradition within Islam, he must have appeared a near-diabolic spirit.

He was, however, genuinely mourned by his son, Suleyman. They had trusted each other implicitly. It was to his son's household that Selim had first fled when he was about to defy his own father for the first time. By the time of his death Selim had so tamed the body politic that his son achieved the first peaceful succession in centuries of Ottoman history. The janissaries and the court of viziers attended on the new Sultan without so much as a whisper of dissent. It must have helped that Selim had performed an horrifically ugly task on behalf of his son. For though the Sultan had six acknowledged daughters from his many wives, no boy had been permitted to survive infancy to create difficulties for Suleyman.

In the autumn of 1520 the young prince rode through the high portals of the Topkapi Palace and on through the thronged streets of Istanbul in order to be girt with the sword of Osman, the founder of the Ottoman Empire. Even his enemies admired him, and a Venetian envoy reported on this great public occasion that 'he was only twenty-five years old, tall and slender, but tough, with a thin and bony face. Facial hair is evident but only barely. The Sultan appears friendly and in good humour . . . enjoys reading, is knowledgeable and shows good government.'[8]

PART TWO

Struggle

7

Conquest of Commerce

King Manuel, Hammer of Morocco, Lord of Guinea and of the Conquest of the Navigation and Commerce of Ethiopia, Arabia, Persia and India, 1499–1515

In nine tenths of the written treaties between the Kings of Portugal and the various reigning Princes of Hindustan, the matter of pepper came up in the first clause.

Admiral Ballard

Four new militant powers – Portugal, Spain, the Ottoman Empire and the corsair admirals of North Africa – had emerged, each expansionist, each hungry for power and glory, and all headed into a contest for absolute dominion. Portugal, a poor, weak state that had been on the point of being absorbed by its powerful neighbour, had suddenly catapulted itself into fame and wealth. Instead of becoming a province of Spain, it had emerged as an expansionist Crusader kingdom, carving out a trading empire along the Atlantic coast of Morocco and on the gold coast of West Africa. Yet the Portuguese crusade – as last we saw three ships leaving Lisbon for India – would become something much more: the very first worldwide trading empire.

On 10 July 1499 Vasco da Gama sailed up the River Tagus to be greeted by King Manuel, the court and the whole jubilant population of Portugal. The news of the discovery of a passage to India, after a century of effort, could not at first be believed. It was only when the spices were displayed on the dock that the doubters were finally silenced.

Vasco da Gama spent nine days recuperating and offering up prayers of thanks in the chapel at Belem before entering Lisbon in triumph. Church bells were rung, jousts, bullfights and other entertainments decreed by the exultant monarch.

The return of Vasco da Gama's voyage of exploration (on which he had set out in 1497) was the first direct contact between western Europe and India. Right from the first it stank of success. The cargo of spices that Vasco da Gama unloaded on the docks of Lisbon reaped a 600 per cent dividend. In grateful thanks King Manuel used part of his share to turn the simple chapel of Prince Henry the Navigator into a dazzling Gothic abbey. The spices had been bought in the open market from the merchants of Cochin but, by cutting out the complicated chain of middlemen that had previously controlled this trade, the Portuguese hit trading manna. Pepper was the ideal commodity: light, valuable, inimitable and in constant demand. It is the dried seed of an ivy-like creeper that grows only in the Tropics. It was bought from the cultivators by travelling agents of the Hindu merchants of the Malabar coast, where it was sorted and graded before being sold in the royal markets of Cochin and Cranganore. Traditionally it had been carried across the Indian Ocean by Muslim merchants (especially those from Gujarat) and transshipped through trading cities such as Ormuz in the Persian Gulf. There the cargoes were broken up and sold on to Persian, Swahili, Yemeni and Syrian traders who took it inland, passing through the customs houses of such states as the Mameluke Sultanate of Egypt before it first touched European hands, probably those of a Venetian merchant from one of the dynasties of Levant traders, as much at home in the caravanserais of Aleppo and Cairo as the Adriatic. All this was now cut out.

The newly ennobled, honoured and promoted Vasco da Gama was put to work, using his experience to equip a trading fleet for the next year. As soon as the sailing season opened, a fleet of thirteen ships with a complement of twelve hundred men set sail from the Tagus on 9 March 1500. The profits had been so good that even the casualty figures from the first journey (for less than a third of da Gama's crew returned) did not discourage recruitment. Indeed it had been possible to recruit a better class into this second enterprise, with fewer convicts enrolled to bolster numbers, and also on board were some sixteen monks and chaplains.

In the first few delirious years of the new trade the cargoes were auctioned on the wharves, but the Portuguese crown then decreed that the spice should be sold through the courtyards of its official monopoly, the Casa da India. Europe's foremost banking houses soon moved in to expand and develop trade. They started to buy in advance, forwarding to the Portuguese crown irresistible sums to take up leases and percentages of this staggeringly profitable trade. So that Lisbon would very quickly become just the first port of call while the bulk of the crop was moved swiftly north to Antwerp, where the brisk financial action – sales, auctions and futures – was further fed by the ever-expanding demands of the English, German and French markets. The Portuguese crown initially tried to cut in on this, but realised that its salaried agents at the *feitoria*, or trading post, in Antwerp were no match for the fiscal agility of the men from the trading houses. The bankers were not predators but an integral part of the trade from the start. For the Hindu spice merchants of Cochin were not interested in acquiring any of the sub-standard manufactured products of western Europe. They insisted on being paid in just one material, gold coin, which only the banking houses could supply. So it was entrepreneurs like the Florentine merchant banker Bartolomeo Marchione[1] became a vital link in the Portuguese pepper boom. They provided coin for the merchants and the two-year financing of ships and their crews, as well as marine insurance. As the sixteenth century progressed, other spices grew in importance as the European markets became more sophisticated and developed a taste for mace, nutmeg, cinnamon bark and ginger root.

Within a few weeks of Vasco da Gama's return to Lisbon, King Manuel wrote to his agent in Rome, the Cardinal-Protector of Portugal, to reconfirm and extend his exclusive possession of this trade. In the summer of 1499 Manuel was already writing of himself as 'Lord of Guinea and of the Conquest of the Navigation and Commerce of Ethiopia, Arabia, Persia and India'. It was an absurdly grandiose claim for a small nation that had so far managed to put just three trading ships into an ocean that had buzzed with thousands of merchant vessels for thousands of years, but that is beside the point. The real target of this diplomatic activity was his fellow Christians in Europe, especially his Spanish neighbours and the cities of Venice and Genoa. King Manuel was determined that the trade with India would remain in Portuguese hands. When he heard that the Castilian settlers in the Canary Islands had established an outpost on the Moroccan shore of the western Sahara, he moved quickly and decisively. In 1504 the Portuguese encouraged, and probably provided the arms for, a massed attack of Moroccan tribes that wiped out this settlement. That same year Manuel proclaimed the Indian Ocean a royal monopoly, another outrageous assertion unless one reads it as an official announcement that any rivals found trading in these waters would be inspected and their goods and ships confiscated.

Playing on the existing local rivalries between the two rival powers along the Malabar coast of western India – the Samorin ('Sea Rajah') of Calicut and the Rajah of Cochin – the second Portuguese fleet managed to get permission to build a fortified trading post at Cochin. In a similar manner the Portuguese had also succeeded in exploiting rivalries between the Swahili trading cities of the East African coast (especially that between Mombasa and Malindi) to give them a foothold on this shore. But two facts soon became abundantly clear, and threatened to undermine the whole Portuguese venture into the Indian Ocean. No Muslim community, along either the African or Indian coast, was going to be converted to Christianity by a Portuguese Franciscan friar, just as no merchant (of any faith or creed) was interested in any of the trade goods carried by the Portuguese merchants – other than gold.

A new strategy was needed, and so a third convoy was dispatched from Lisbon to India in 1502. This had grown to a fleet of twenty well-armed ships, five of which were to be permanently based in the Indian Ocean. The days of polite salesmanship in an indifferent market were over. With a cannon-bearing fleet at his back, Admiral Vasco da Gama was going to demand tribute from the free-trading cities of East Africa. Thus would the trade with the East be financed. When his outrageous first demand for an annual payment of fifteen hundred meticals of gold from the city of Kilwa was slow in coming, he had the Swahili ambassadors stripped naked and flogged within an inch of their lives. They were then bound hand and foot and thrown into an open boat to bake in the sun as they drifted back to their native harbour. The treatment worked, and to drive the point home, when he had at last extorted sufficient coin from the city fathers, da Gama let his crew on to the streets of Kilwa, raping, pillaging and abducting two hundred women to their boats for their continued pleasure. From the proceeds of the sack of the city, a fifth of which would be presented to the crown, King Manuel instructed the master jeweller Gil Vicente to make a monstrance for the

A marauding galleon.

new Abbey of Belem as 'the first fruits of the conquest of the East'.

Three years later, having extracted as much protection money as could be squeezed out of Mombasa, the Portuguese decided to destroy the city. As the tearful local ruler wrote to warn a neighbour:

> May God protect you, Sayyid Ali. I have to inform you that we have been visited by a mighty ruler who has brought fire and destruction among us. He arrived in our town with such might and terror that no one, neither man nor woman, neither the old nor the young, nor even the children, however small, was permitted to live . . . the stench from the corpses is so overpowering that I dare not enter the town . . . pray hearken to the news of these sad events, that you yourself may be preserved.

When the Portuguese fleet anchored offshore from the reefs of Lamu, the ruler of this East African town promptly sued for peace, formally subjugating himself to the overlordship of Portugal, embracing its flag and a stone column cut with the royal coat of arms that had been sent to him. The Sultan of Lamu had also prudently prepared in advance for the costs of such unstinting loyalty. He was able to pay the first instalment of 'tribute' then and there, in cash, in the attractively recognisable form of a chest full of fresh Venetian-minted silver coins.

But the suffering that would befall the Swahili city of Barawa appalled even a Portuguese chronicler, who was otherwise respected for the 'moderation of his reports'. Having driven the men out of the town in a hard-fought street battle, the Portuguese commander, Tristao da Cunha, then ordered that all the town gates be closed, 'to keep his men together'. The resulting sack of the city, the rape and murder of the women and children who were trapped in the streets, exceeded anything that had yet been witnessed. Eight hundred women had their hands and ears cut off their still-living bodies so that bracelets and earrings could be removed more quickly. In the square outside the central mosque, the commander of this massacre, Tristao da Cunha, chose to have himself formally knighted. He was dubbed by one of his subordinate captains, Afonso de Albuquerque, who bore the rank of Commander of the Crusading Order of the Knights of St John. It must have brought a tear to the eye to the more historically inclined among the Portuguese to see the example first set by King John the Bastard and Prince Henry the Navigator among the ruins of Ceuta repeated at Barawa. The spot chosen for the ceremony was where da Cunha had been wounded in the leg by an arrow, just before the defenders of Barawa, a mixed force of household slaves and townsmen plus some warriors hired from Somalia, were cleared from the streets by grenade and cannon fire. The sack of the town continued for three more days. Then the surrounding villages were raided to provide provisions for the fleet. As the last boats left the shore it was decided to set the whole place on fire. One of the boats was so laden with loot that it failed to cut its way clean through the breakers and was rolled on to the rocks by the surf. Even their comrades took it to be a judgement of God.

These triumphs of arms in East Africa encouraged the Portuguese in Morocco to become more imperious. One of the first signals of this new wave of authoritarianism came in 1504, when the city fathers of the trading city of Azzemour, hitherto free allies of Portugal, were ordered to pay an annual tribute. In 1505 a Portuguese force was sent ashore in the far south of Morocco. On a hill overlooking the estuary of the River Souss, as it twists itself behind sand dunes to reach the Atlantic, they built a new fort. The low silhouette of the walls of Santa Cruz (broken by earthquakes, subsequent occupations and sieges) still overlooks the Moroccan city of Agadir. To confirm her influence along Morocco's central Atlantic coast, Jorge de Mello was instructed to start laying out another new fort where the rocky peninsula of Mazagan overlooks a long beach.

The following year, yet another fortress was built by the Portuguese on the Moroccan coast. Diogo de Azambuja, the man who had created the fortress base of Sao Jorge da Mina to guard Portugal's trade on the gold coast of West Africa,[2] was commissioned to create the Castello Real, or King's Castle, at Mogador. Right from the start he found his workmen 'greatly harassed and attacked by hordes of Arabs and Berbers who united to combat him'. Mogador, a broken archipelago of rocky islets set off the Atlantic coast of Morocco where the western High Atlas mountains reach the ocean, was one of the most physically dramatic but challenging places for empire-building. Just offshore stand a pair of inhospitable islands which had been used by both Carthaginian and Roman gold merchants, with good reason, for the proud tribes of the region, the Haha, would never accept the presence of the Portuguese on the mainland. Ultimately even the masonry of the Portuguese castle at Mogador would be hacked away.[3]

The rate of imperial expansion, fuelled by the profits of the pepper trade, was to remain relentless. King Manuel ordered his agent in the Moroccan port of Safi, which had welcomed the Portuguese sea captains with open arms and become a hard-working partner in the West Africa trade, to expand Portuguese influence. So in 1507 Captain Diogo de Azambuja deposed the old governor of the town and installed a pro-Portuguese candidate, who immediately authorised the Portuguese to expand their *feitoria* into a self-contained fort. In response the local leaders of the town, fearing a complete take-over, began to buy up arms and recruit mercenaries to recover their position. But this was just the excuse that Manuel was looking for. He authorised a full-scale military occupation, his aggressive intent reinforced by an operation directed against Azzemour a month later. These two cities, the leading centres of the 'Moros de Paz' ('Moors of Peace'), were thus made into enemies.

Central authority in Morocco at this time rested with the Wattasid Sultans. The dynasty had first come to prominence in the spectacular military victory that had been won by the Wattasid grand vizier against the Portuguese outside Tangier in 1437. They were also close cousins of the old dynasty, so when the last of the Merenid Sultans perished in 1465, they gradually assumed control over what was left of the country. One of their most important tasks was to oppose the gradual Portuguese take-over of the Moroccan coast. So the year after the Portuguese occupied Safi, the Wattasid Sultan had prepared a counter-attack. He had sent messengers to all the tribes calling for a simultaneous assault on all the Portuguese positions in Morocco, against their fortified positions in the north, such as Asilah, Tangier and Ceuta, as well as their new southern strongholds such as Safi and Mogador. As a Portuguese observer reported:

> In October 1508 the King of Fez [the Wattasid Sultan] came with all his forces which we confirmed included twenty thousand horseman and one hundred and twenty thousand foot-soldiers, ten thousand of them crossbowmen and riflemen, with plenty of bombards . . . the next morning, our men saw the fort surrounded on all sides with an infinite host and, all along the beach, a series of dug-out redoubts, armed with bombards, to block the port entrance.

Despite the probable exaggeration of numbers in this report, the Moroccan counter-attack was certainly impressive that year. Asilah might have fallen had it not been reinforced by the arrival of a Portuguese fleet. But this was not to be a one-off counter-attack.

The very next year, 1509, a Wattasid-led army again struck against Asilah and the following year Safi was besieged. Here the Portuguese commander, in his desperation, was forced to recruit and arm those Jews who had settled in Safi after being expelled from Portugal by King Manuel just a few years before. In between formal sieges, a tit-for-tat pattern of border raids devastated the rural hamlets and villages. In a similar way to that in which the *hidalgo*, the Castilian gentry, had 'softened up' Granada with fire and sword, the Portuguese garrisons were now ordered to scour the land in a succession of *rebato*, 'raids'. The Wattasids, for their part, also began to scorch the land around the Portuguese positions, in an attempt to deny them any local allies or trading partners. Whole towns and many villages were evacuated to secure, inland positions, to such walled cities as Tetouan, Ksar el Kebir and Meknes or the mountain strongholds within the western Rif such as Ouezzane and Chechaouen. Local leaders were blessed with war banners by the Sultan and encouraged with tactical advice and the occasional loan of specialist troops, who had been trained in the use of artillery, handguns and the laying of underground mines.

In the Indian Ocean, the Portuguese aggression directed by King Manuel would bear much more promising fruit. To push forward with his plans for expansion, the King appointed Dom Francisco de Almeida as his viceroy. Each viceroy was provided with a detailed blueprint of strategic objectives but, given the vast distances and delays in communication, he was also granted the authority to act as he saw fit. Through the informal reports of country traders, embassies and returning mercenaries, the Portuguese became aware of the immensity of the task of imposing themselves in the East. One of the earliest Portuguese to penetrate into the hinterland of India, Domingo Paes, was astonished to observe the wealth and extent of the Hindu Vijayanagar Empire. Paes reported back to Lisbon that the Emperor, Krishna Deva Raya, could field an army of a million men. On later journeys he assessed in greater detail the Vijayanagar capital, Hampi, a city of one hundred thousand houses with a population of five hundred thousand supplied by lakes, aqueducts and markets that spread over thirty square kilometres. It was 'the best provided city in the world', he reported, and he was right. Even after four centuries of ruin Hampi remains one of the wonders of the human world, in extent, in the happy fusion of cultural forms, in the detail of its carvings and in its architectural exuberance.

The Hindu Emperor had need of a powerful army, for to the north a squabbling pack of five rival Muslim Sultanates fought one another for dominance over the Deccan (the great internal plateau of southern and central India) and the chance to conquer the south. The good news, as far as King Manuel was concerned, was that the Vijayanagar Empire was disposed to look kindly on the anti-Muslim crusading notions of the Portuguese, especially if it could continue to manage the ancient trade in horses (shipped across to India from Arabia and East Africa) and provide trained artillery crews for hire. Also by a stroke of good fortune for the Portuguese, their arrival had coincided with the overthrow of most of the major Muslim powers in India. For in the snow-capped mountains of the far north, the armies of the warrior prince Babur (the founder of the Mughal Empire and himself a Muslim) were descending from their base in Afghanistan to rip the heart out of the old Muslim powers in a series of brutal campaigns that devastated Gujarat, Delhi and Bengal between the years of 1504 and 1526. Persia was similarly disabled in this period, as it was being transformed from within by the Shia revolution launched by Ismail, the charismatic Safavid Shah.

It was against this interesting and highly confusing background that Afonso de Albuquerque, the second Portuguese governor of India, launched his campaign of determined expansion. Armed with just a small naval squadron based on the three allied ports (Cochin, Sofala and Mozambique) he struck quickly, decisively and with devastating aggression. With a total homeland population of a million, there was not the faintest chance of the Portuguese being able to impose themselves as rulers on the teeming hundreds of millions of southern Asia. The one advantage they had, and it seemed a small one, was their sturdily built ships and the cannon mounted on them. These had been tested and refined by three generations of oceanic exploration and intermittent warfare with the Moroccans. In the spring of 1509 the Portuguese squadron of eighteen ships met the combined fleets of the Sultan of Gujarat and the Mameluke Sultan of Egypt. These were the two great commercial and nautical powers of their day, united by their Muslim faith and a desire to protect their trade routes. They were also supported by practically all the Muslim Sultanates along the Indian Ocean, so that an allied fleet of well over a hundred ships stood gathered against the Portuguese interlopers, led by a dozen new ships of Egypt and half a dozen from Gujarat. The vast Muslim fleet was, however, hampered by a lack of offensive vision and a complete absence of central command. All that could be agreed was that they should fight at anchor, guarding Diu, a seven-mile-long island just off the coast of Gujarat. It was a truly disastrous decision, allowing the highly manoeuvrable Portuguese to blast this long line of sitting ducks from midday to nightfall of 3 February. In the dawn light, the allied Muslim fleet was seen to have been literally blown out of the waters. The Portuguese left Diu alone, indeed they may have already reached a secret understanding with its governor, the perspicacious Malik Aiyaz (who had began his life as a Russian before he had been enslaved by a Tartar raiding party and sold into slavery, rising rapidly through the ranks of the Gujarati Sultanate). But, to demonstrate the scale of their victory, the Portuguese naval squadron made a slow tour down the west coast of India, stopping at each port to execute another batch of prisoners of war and fire the limbs and heads back into their native cities. The Portuguese fort at Cochin was reached on 8 March.

The absolute and decisive extent of this Portuguese naval victory over the assembled fleets of the Indian Ocean established the world's first maritime empire. But the Portuguese fleet still required a secure naval base in foreign waters. And its numbers were growing. In early September that same year another squadron of fourteen ships, sailing out as further reinforcements for the viceroy under the command of the Marshal of Portugal, arrived in southern India. They also carried papers, relieving the hero of the Battle of Diu, Francisco de Almeida, and confirming his deputy Alfonso de Albuquerque in command as both Captain General and Governor of the Indies. King Manuel had complained of being left out of touch and in consequence had taken pleasure in subdividing the commands to weaken any individual's authority. Albuquerque made certain that the trust that had been placed in him would not be weakened by any lack of communication. He established a chancellery of half a dozen mobile secretaries, who followed the Captain General by foot, by horse and by sea, copying out accounts, orders and counter-assessing the state of every ship and fortress, to provide their distant royal master with a stream of written and counter-signed reports. The result was that Albuquerque could loyally assert: 'There is nothing in India or within myself that I do not report to you, save only my own sins.' This stream of correspondence[4] also left him free to plot the next conquest unhindered by new commanders being sent out from Lisbon.

Taking the advice of a Hindu pirate, the corsair Timoja, Albuquerque attacked Goa, a port that belonged to one of the squabbling Muslim Sultanates of the Deccan. The Governor's first assault failed, but in 1510 he launched a second attack. Goa was seized from the governance of the Sultan of Bijapur, whose real power base was inland, east of the imposing mountain barrier of the western Ghats. In the aftermath of victory nineteen Portuguese soldiers were identified among the captive Muslim garrison. They were deserters who had converted to Islam and who had been well-paid by their new masters on account of their inval-

uable skill as gunners. Albuquerque had already sworn that all who
surrendered would have their lives spared. He was true to his word, and
so gave these Portuguese deserters a mild sentence of mutilation. First
their beards and eyebrows were torn out, then their ears, nose and left
thumb were clipped off. Those who survived these operations had their
right hand cut off. Seventeen died, but two managed to survive, one
ending his days as a hermit on the island of St Helena, growing vegetables which he traded with the crews of passing ships. Albuquerque was
always severe with deserters, in part because it was absolutely vital that
Portugal retain the technical superiority of its ship-borne cannon. Three
years later, on one of his ocean cruises, his fleet came across a small
rowing boat with four Portuguese sailors trying to scull their way to
freedom. This time he was not hampered by any scruple about having
to keep his word. The deserters were arrested and clapped in irons in
the bilge tanks. Once ashore at Goa they were paraded through the
streets before being burned alive in the boat in which they had made
their attempted escape.

In seizing possession of Goa, the Portuguese at last acquired a secure
base for themselves on the Indian Ocean and a centre for their operations for the next five hundred years. Goa was ideal for their purposes:
an island surrounded by two wide estuaries, which could provide safe
anchorage for a thousand ships, as well as affording an easy trade route
into the immediate hinterland. It, and the surrounding headlands,
were embellished by a series of great artillery bastions whose architectural features, cut into the dark volcanic rock of the region, survive
magnificently intact, even if their gun ports are now softened by the
presence of palm trees. Later Goa become the seat of an archbishopric
and a branch of the Portuguese royal mint was established here which
struck gold coins.

Goa quickly took over as the central command base from the island
of Socotra, which had, in April 1507, been one of Afonso de
Albuquerque's first conquests. On a map Socotra looks perfectly formed
to act as a naval base, lying just south of Arabia and almost midway
between the entrance to the Persian Gulf and the Red Sea. In practice it
has always proved just too distant from the main coastal routes to work
as a lookout, and this problem, compounded by a lack of ground-water,
any really convincing harbour, the island's cliffs and recurring banks of
sea mist, has always helped perpetuate its end-of-the road isolation. The

Portuguese, when they first waded ashore on to this isolated island community, were surprised to find themselves in contact with native
Christians. For the last communities of Jacobite Arab Christians had
emigrated to the two Arabian islands: Bahrain and Socotra. Having
witnessed the slaughter of the Muslim garrison that resisted the
Portuguese invasion, the Christian Arabs of Socotra were determined to
avoid being either blessed or freed by these invaders. They evacuated
their villages and fled to the central hills, to hide in the labyrinth of
caves and among the ghostly silhouettes of the indigenous forests of
Socotra: the Island of Dragon's Blood.

Having secured Goa and Socotra in addition to Portugal's commercial bases in southern India and East Africa, Albuquerque authorised an
attack on the Far East trade routes. In 1510 his fleet seized control of
Malacca from the Muslim merchants of Indonesia. The subsequent
destruction of a fleet of Indonesian war junks by a naval squadron completed the astonishingly rapid creation of the Lusitanian thalassocracy:
the Portuguese maritime empire. In March of 1513 Albuquerque led an
attack on Aden, the Yemeni port that stands just south of the Red Sea.
It was one of the few strategic positions on the shore of the Indian
Ocean that managed to successfully resist him. Two years later his fleet
finally seized control of the famous trading port of Ormuz, situated on

Portuguese fortresses at Muscat in the Arabian Sea.

an island at the entrance of the Persian Gulf.

This string of fortified bases, Goa, Cochin, Ormuz, Malacca and Mombasa, allowed Albuquerque to create a self-financing naval empire. He instituted a system whereby all the merchants of the Indian Ocean were required to purchase licences to trade on the seas, the infamous *cartaz*. These could only be acquired at the three naval bases of Ormuz, Malacca and Goa. Merchants not only submitted to this official protection racket, but were also simultaneously required to pay duty at these three 'command' ports. Thus were the Portuguese, without so much as a single trade good to barter in the vast markets of the east, able to fund and police their vast new maritime empire. The crews and captains of the Portuguese ships were kept keenly interested in the system of patrols, for they were free to confiscate any ship and its merchandise that they found at sea without a valid *cartaz*.

As Albuquerque now wrote to his royal master, the maritime empire that he had created could be held with 'four good fortresses and a large well-armed fleet manned by three thousand Portuguese'. There were, however, limits to the eastward growth of this sea empire. When a Portuguese naval squadron tried to extend its dominion into the China Seas it was driven off by the coastguards of the 'Middle Kingdom', as China called itself, in 1520 and again in 1521. Denied imperium, the Portuguese quickly learned to adopt a more flexible, submissive and mercantile attitude to the Chinese Ming Empire, and eventually received permission to establish a small trading post at Macao. This naval victory of the Chinese against the Portuguese opens up one of the many intriguing questions of modern history. What if the Portuguese fleet had been thrown out of the Indian Ocean right at the start of the careers of Vasco da Gama and Afonso de Albuquerque? What if Asia had never fallen victim to European aggression? For the role model established by the success of the Portuguese in the East would be followed, almost step by step by those who came in their wake, first the Dutch, then the French and English, then the Japanese and the Americans.

What if the Chinese navy, which defeated the Portuguese in the Far East, had maintained a Pax Sinaica over the Indian Ocean? The dates are tantalisingly close. For in 1405 the Ming dynasty, somewhat buoyed up by two near-miraculous events – the death of Timur just as his army was about to invade China and the one and only submission of Japan to Imperial Chinese rule – had started to explore the outside world in a methodical way. The western travels of Chen Cheng, who crossed the Gobi Desert to establish peaceful relations with the heirs of Timur in Central Asia, showed how useful this could be. This was coupled with a series of peaceful naval expeditions which sailed off to inform the world, from Java to Ceylon, from East Africa to the Red Sea, of the greatness of the Middle Kingdom. If either Vasco da Gama or Afonso de Albuquerque had met the full magnificence of any one of these seven imperial expeditionary fleets under the command of an admiral like Zheng He,[5] they would surely have learned very quickly to trade in the East in peace, instead of setting themselves up as Crusader sea lords.

After the failure to capture Aden in 1513, the Portuguese naval squadrons of Afonso de Albuquerque were effectively barred from entering the Red Sea. To have penetrated this inner highway of the Near East and to have connected with the Christian fleets in the eastern Mediterranean (such as those of the Kingdom of Cyprus and the Knights of St John of the Hospital in Rhodes) must have seemed but an ace away. But King Manuel, although greatly encouraged by the success of Portuguese arms in the Indian Ocean, had decided to throw all the new wealth and resources of his kingdom against Morocco. As he wrote to the newly elected Pope, Leo X, he would win the kingdoms of Fez and Marrakesh for Christianity.[6]

This policy began with the appointment of an ambitious new generation of captains to oversee the Portuguese garrison forts in Morocco. The appointment of Nuno Fernandes de Ataide to Safi and Dom Francisco de Castro to Santa Cruz at Agadir was followed by the extension and expansion of these bastions. The ruins of an elegant Gothic chapel, still hidden in one of Safi's side alleys, reveal the confidence with which the Portuguese treated their long-term presence in Morocco. Larger contingents of Portuguese cavalry were established in the stables formed within the casements of the walls. They poured out through the city gates, in ever more ambitious patrols that rode into the Moroccan countryside. Generous supplies of coin allowed the recruiting and arming of local tribal lords to aid Portugal's cause. As one young Portuguese officer in the Santa Cruz garrison wrote approvingly of their local ally, Malik ibn Dawud of the Zirara tribe, 'he routinely served in the forward scouts of our captain. He would send them ahead to spy out the country, and they assured the security of the Christians in the region. He also used the Moors in large scale raids, ravaging the area to such a degree that none dared go foraging.'[7]

In Safi a tough-minded Berber warrior, Yahya-ibn-Tafuft, came to the fore as the 'local ally' of the Portuguese. Back in 1506 he seems to have been an accomplice in the assassination of the Muslim governor of Safi, before betraying his allies by becoming a double agent simultaneously acting for both the Portuguese and the Wattasids. When things got too hot he took ship for Lisbon, but returned a few years later as the gazetted lieutenant of the Portuguese governor. For the local inhabitants wanted 'a Muslim to serve as an intermediary between the Muslims and the Christians'. Using his new position Yahya gradually built up a client state for himself in the lands to the south and east of the city of Safi. It was undoubtedly easier for a Muslim to collect the traditional taxes, the tithes on crops and herds, which were sanctified by the Koran, rather than a foreign Portuguese cavalry commander working in the name of the Christian King Manuel I. Yahya, well supplied with arms by the Portuguese, was able to expel any forces sent against him by either the governor of Marrakesh or the Wattasid Sultan in Fez. The historian Leo Africanus was sent to meet Yahya by the Wattasid Sultan Muhammad al-Burtugali in 1512, to sound him out on various policy options. But nothing came of it. These were confusing times. Even Leo Africanus was secretly serving two masters, both the Wattasids in Fez and the recently established Sharifian dynasty in southern Morocco. At this point in his varied career Leo was officially working as a diplomat for the Wattasid Sultan and would later be sent across the Sahara to meet the ruler of Timbuktu. He would write his famous description of North Africa some ten years later, after he had been captured by Christian corsairs and sent to Pope Leo in Rome as a gift, after which he converted to Christianity.

In 1513 King Manuel sent an army of eighteen thousand men into Azzemour, which was already under Portuguese control. This force raided the hinterland with impunity and in the following year clashed with a Wattasid detachment which was driven from the field at the Battle of Doukkala. By the end of the year it seemed possible that the independent-minded governor of Marrakesh, Nasr al Hintati, was on the point of defecting from his nominal allegiance to the Wattasids and declaring for King Manuel. To conclude the stirring succession of adventures of this most promising of years for Portugal, a cavalry force made a celebrated ride across the steppes, right up to the red walls of Marrakesh. They drew their names in chalk on the ancient fortress gates of the Bab Dukalla but did not force their way into the city. This act of Christian bravado would not be bettered until Colonel Mangin finally entered the city at the head of a column of the French army some four hundred years later.

The following year King Manuel, once again overriding the requests for reinforcements to the Indian Ocean, dispatched another force into Morocco. The crusade against the Moors had now been waged for a hundred years and this expedition was designed to be a permanent annexation of a province. A force of two thousand cavalry and eight thousand foot-soldiers was landed up the muddy waters of the River Sebou's estuary at Marmora. The Portuguese garrison at Azzemour controlled the sea mouth of the great southern river of Morocco, the Oum er-Rbia. This new plantation aspired to seize the mouth of the main river of northern Morocco, the Sebou, which led inland towards the political capital of Fez. There was nothing temporary about the Portuguese advance, which included a small colony of farmers and cattle to provide a permanent population within the fort. In June the Portuguese were busy throwing up the first earth walls, reinforced with stockades, ditches and moats, the whole riverbank settlement being protected by ships' cannon.

The Moroccan counter-attack came in July 1515. It was led by the Sultan's younger brother, grand vizier Moulay Nasr, who invested the fort from the north bank. The Sultan himself led another army, which swept through the southern provinces of Morocco to make certain that none of the tribes intended to assist the Portuguese invader. He then marched up to take position on the south bank of the Sebou, but allowed his younger brother to concentrate on the fort while his artillery concentrated on the Portuguese ships. The discipline and accuracy of the Moroccan gunners, which had been noted in the siege of Asilah, now seemed even more impressive. The Sultan, who had spent much of his youth as a captive in Portugal, knew exactly what he was doing. He watched carefully over the activities of his hand-picked battery of five bombards. They struck an unexpected bull's-eye when they hit one of the Portuguese ships, which sunk into the estuary mud at such an angle as to block all river traffic. Within that hour the whole nature of the siege changed. For the escape route downriver from Fort Marmora was blocked, as was the progress of any Portuguese reinforcements coming upriver. No longer being threatened by ships' cannon, the Sultan ordered twelve light field artillery pieces to be trundled straight to the river shore, while an old whitewashed saint's tomb, which occupied a slight hill near the fort, was fortified and the Moroccans started lobbing explosive grenades at close range into the Portuguese lines. The whole operation had uncanny parallels with the failed attempt to establish the fortress of Graciosa on the River Loukkos half a generation before.

At Graciosa the Moroccan Sultan of the day had allowed the Portuguese to withdraw, and once again it seemed that the Moroccans would give their enemy the opportunity to evacuate in peace. The Moroccan batteries held their fire as the Portuguese garrison began to dismantle the fort and filed into small boats. Only then did the Sultan gave his signal. By the end of the afternoon the waters of the Sebou ran red. Leo Africanus witnessed the siege and wrote that for 'three days the sea spouted waves of blood'. When the Sultan returned to Fez, his victorious column of soldiers escorted some fifty-two captured cannon.

That winter the Sultan's emissaries were welcomed with renewed respect as they visited the tribal leaders and sheikhs. Another joint attack was to be orchestrated against the Portuguese, while the Sultan used his much-reinforced artillery corps against the walls of Asilah yet again. But the campaigning season of 1516 did not reward him with a second victory like that of Marmora. Protected by their fleet, the Portuguese fortresses all held firm and the captains of those fortresses had orders to recover lost prestige by hitting back. Raid after raid was sent into the interior to prove that Portugal's power had not been diminished by the disaster of Marmora. Captain Nuno, the governor of Safi, was killed in a cavalry battle fought that May, but his redoubtable Moroccan ally remained undiminished. Yahya took his cavalry army deep into the Haha hills and then east into the fertile hinterland around Marrakesh.

8

Sharifs, Sheikhs, Sufis, Sultans and Smugglers

The Moroccan Struggle against the Portuguese Crusade, 1515–50

The condition upon which God hath given liberty to man is eternal vigilance, which condition if he break, servitude is at once the consequence of his crime and the punishment of his guilt.

J. P. Curran

The Battle of Marmora marked a hundred years of almost continuous war between Portugal and Morocco. Ever since the fall of Ceuta in 1415, followed by the loss of Ksar es Seghir, then Asilah, then Tangier in 1437, the Moroccan tribes had been called forward season after season by their sultans and sheikhs in the *jihad* to repel the enemy. Although the Moroccans had never recaptured Ceuta or Asilah it was nevertheless something of an achievement that the Portuguese invaders were still confined within the strong walls of their coastal citadels. And when they had tried to push inland, in the attempt to establish a fort upriver, first at Graciosa in 1489, then at Marmora in 1515, the Moroccan resistance had proved triumphant. It is ironical that this hero-Sultan had been nicknamed 'al-Burtagali' by his people, which means 'the Portuguese'. Arguably it was only his youthful captivity in Portugal that gave him sufficient understanding to outflank this most resourceful and implacable of enemies.

The resistance of the Wattasids was an astonishing achievement. Portuguese domination of all the major ports of the country should have crippled the Moroccan sultans but Morocco had a third shore in the far south: the sand sea of the Sahara Desert. The Portuguese were never able to interfere with the great southern trade routes that led across the Sahara to the West African kingdoms on the River Niger. Similarly an inland caravan route existed across the length of North Africa, across the semi-arid steppe-lands – some hundreds of miles south of the Spanish garrisons that had also been established all along the Mediterranean coast in this period. In terms of carrying trade this route was laborious and expensive, but in spiritual and intellectual terms it linked Morocco with all the recent developments in Shiite Persia, Ottoman Turkey and the Far East. For the pilgrimage to Mecca was like an unofficial summit held every year, which drew together the savants of Islam as well as the most up-to-date gossip about military, political and commercial developments, be it in Indonesia, China, India, West Africa, East Africa or Morocco.

Another great resource for Morocco was the black economy, that murky world of smugglers, arms dealers, renegade deserters, hungry exiles and commission men. Morocco produced much that was exportable (cattle, cloth, wheat and sugar) as well as selling on the rich products of the trans-Saharan trade. Some of this was funnelled through the enemy-held ports in order to be securely shipped out to European markets on Portuguese boats. But a simultaneous trade co-existed in the innumerable sandy bays and secretive coves of the Moroccan coast. Here Catalan, French, Castilian and Genoese traders would operate free from the customs duties and interference of the Portuguese governors. The Moroccans for their part were free to acquire from these traders the technical instruments of war that the Portuguese were keen to prevent them from acquiring. Nor was Morocco just a dependent petitioner in this secretive arms trade, for it held one of the trump cards in the game. Morocco possessed saltpetre (potassium nitrate), the rare and vital component of gunpowder. Each and every war, siege, summer campaign and counter-siege that was waged throughout the fifteenth and six-teenth centuries had to be costed by financial officials and paid for in advance. For each military season required tons of gunpowder and shot to be stockpiled. As the earliest Arabic recipe for gunpowder (by Shams ad-Din Muhammad in 1320) has it, 'a description of the mixture put into the cannon is ten parts saltpetre, two parts charcoal and a measure and a half of sulphur. You grind them into a fine powder and fill one third of the cannon, do not put in more or it will burst . . . push the mix in by force, insert either ball or arrow and put fire to the primer . . . Be careful!'

Charcoal was freely available the world over and sulphur deposits are reasonably well spread around the globe in old areas of volcanic activity, but Morocco sat on the world's largest and purest source of saltpetre and the one most accessible to western Europe. For the other major deposits are found in Iraq, Syria and Egypt. This was no secret, for there are Andalusian references to the trade in *barud*, as saltpetre is known in Arabic, that date back to 1240. The quantity of saltpetre shipped out of Morocco in this period was immense, and the expulsion of the Jews from both Castile and Portugal assisted the development of this illegal but vital trade. Converted Jews who remained in Iberia were able to correspond with their cousins and business associates who were among the flood of forty thousand exiles who poured into Morocco between 1480 and 1510. The trade was undocumented and will for ever remain so, but Jewish merchant families such as the Ruti, Zamiro and Bocarro were known to be able to operate in both Morocco and Iberia. They and such cosmopolitan trade barons as Joseph Rosales supplied both governments with the munitions they needed to fight each other. They could clearly provide other services, such as when one of the Ruti family recruited a Portuguese gunner of Jewish ancestry, one Master John, to work as a *bombarderio* cannon for a Wattasid Sultan. The Ruti are a good example of how these family networks crossed political and faith frontiers. One cousin was the official Sheikh al-Yahuddin ('Mayor of the Jews') in Fez, another was close to the royal court in Lisbon, while a junior cousin served as provisioner to the Portuguese garrisons in Morocco. Similar networks connect the skilled Jewish exiles of Iberia with the armament industry within the Ottoman Empire. Rabbi Elijah Capsali (1467–1523) observed that Sultan Selim 'loved Jews very much because he saw that by means of them he would beat nations and kill great kings, for they made cannon and weapons for him'.

By the end of the sixteenth century many of these resourceful traders were able to come out of the shadows. The Rosales, the Pellaches and the Levies openly established businesses as licensed munitions contractors on behalf of their sovereign, the Sultan of Morocco. The career of the Portuguese-born Dom John Miquez was even more spectacular in the scale of its internationalism and breadth of contacts. He was a cousin to a powerful clan of Spanish bankers, the House of Mendes, who had publicly converted to Christianity while privately keeping true to their faith and traditions. The family, aware of the gathering dangers to rich *conversos* in Spain of Jewish origin, especially to those whom the crown owed vast debts, began to methodically diversify its holdings and spread its assets. Although young Dom John Miquez had been born in the comparative safety of Portugal he was sent to study at the celebrated University of Louvain before entering the dizzy world of Antwerp finance in the last days of the old Duchy of Burgundy. Here, as Joseph Nasi, he became a familiar and welcome figure at the court of the regent Mary, Emperor Charles V's clever sister, as well as a close friend of the Emperor's nephew, Maximilian, and young Prince William of Orange-Nassau. Later he moved to France and then on to Venice before opening negotiations, through the good offices of Moses Hamon, Suleyman the Magnificent's doctor, who secured him and his entire family an official invitation to move to the Ottoman capital. After arriving in Istanbul in 1554 Joseph publicly took up his faith and married his cousin, the daughter of his charitably inclined aunt, the very wealthy Dona Gracia Mendes-Nasi. Safe in Istanbul, he started collecting Hebrew manuscripts and set up a bank and a printing press. He was by then known as Yusuf Nasi who became a recognised figure at the court of Sultan Suleyman and later became one of the inner counsellors to Sultan Selim the Sot. It was just these sorts of intimate connections that allowed trade, finance, letters and intelligence to pass with dazzling speed across the war zones of the Mediterranean and which allowed the Wattasid Sultanate to continue to exist despite the loss of all its principal ports to the Portuguese.

The Wattasid Sultans had no illusions about the nature of their political authority. They occupied the throne of Morocco through their military ability. Although they were allied by generations of intermarriage to the old medieval Merenid dynasty, it was the victory achieved by the head of the clan, Abu Zakariya Yahya, against the Portuguese attack on Tangier back in 1437 that had first propelled the family into the limelight. They were also well aware what could happen to a sultan tarnished by too many defeats. Abdul Haq, the last of the Merenid Sultans of Morocco, had been denounced in the mosques of Fez and then formally disowned as the commander of the faithful. When he tried to enforce his authority on the people, his own soldiers turned against him. He was dragged through the streets so that the elders of the city of Fez could pass judgement. After this he was taken out to one of the rubbish tips beyond the gates, where his throat was cut and his head was hacked off. The populace then chose one of the descendants of the Prophet who lived like one of them in the city, Muhammad al-Juti, to exercise authority, advised by a council of learned sheikhs and sharifs. Other surviving members of the old dynasty were hunted down, and their palatial tomb complex (which still stand roofless on the hillside to the south of Fez) was sacked. This experiment in Islamic democracy would last half a dozen years but it was too saintly to fully engage with the commercial and military realities that underlay the exercise of power. This gave the Wattasid general, Muhammad al-Shaykh (one of the sons of Abu Zakariya Yahya), his opportunity. He had held on to his post as governor of one of the Moroccan port-cities and slowly won over the local dynasts and the servants of the old regime. By 1472 he had reimposed his authority over the capital city of Fez, but was tactful enough to give the sheikhs time. His rule over northern Morocco would be confirmed when he expelled the Portuguese from Fort Graciosa in 1489, just as his son Sultan al-Burtugali's authority would be confirmed by the victory at Marmora in 1515. Authority within the Wattasid Sultanate of Morocco always remained a patchwork affair. Their relationship with the dynasty of old royal governors who ruled over Marrakesh, the Hintata, was never clearly defined, but a nod of acceptance and an occasional trickle of tribute seems to have suited the needs of both parties. For the Wattasids were realists, and preferred to use their resources with caution, content to keep an effective hold of the inner core of the nation defined by the block of territory around the walled cities of Meknes, Fez, Taza and Ksar el Kebir.

On to this confused political situation was poured the aftermath of the destruction of Muslim Granada. Wave upon wave of refugees poured into the country; some brought a determination to fight back against the Christian Crusaders but many arrived exhausted, humiliated and filled with doubt over the future structure of their whole world. The Muslim intellectuals of Fez, working within the gorgeous medieval courtyard colleges of the University of Qarawiyyin, tried to make some sense of it all. Ahmad al-Wanshari was at work on a great compilation that would rescue a thousand years of learning from the flames of the Christian book-burnings. He created a multi-volume compilation of the legal and spiritual decisions that had come out of Andalusia, which were then compared with those of North Africa. This was no academic cul-de-sac but a vital resource for the tens of thousands of Moors scattered across the Mediterranean who desired to see how their traditions fitted in with the rest of Islamic society. Which could they keep, which must they discard? At the same time Ibn Ghazi was a hugely popular lecturer instructing generations of students on history, the *Hadith*, poetic metre, biography and Koranic studies while corresponding with a wide range of rulers and judges on the great issues of the day. How did one define an 'unbeliever'? Could one employ skilled Christians and Jews in a Muslim army? How should one relate to the different sects within Islam, to renegade-converts or the even more problematic issue of Muslims who had converted to Christianity? To whom should a ruler seek legitimacy after the last Abbasid Caliph had been deported to Istanbul in 1517? The professor-sheikhs were also called on to comment on a fatwa that came out of Oran (western Algeria) permitting Muslims in Christian lands to practise *taqiyya*, which permitted them to remain Muslims in their heart even if they were forced to attend mass, drink wine and eat pork. It rested on a very old tradition within Islam, much used by the Shia during bouts of Sunni persecution, soundly based on a specific Koranic verse, 'excepting him who has been compelled but his heart is still at rest in his belief'. These were very live issues. For the line between expediency and treachery, between dissimulation and apostasy, was wafer-thin. When Sultan al-Burtugali found that he held a prisoner of war who was revealed to be a Muslim who had turned Christian and then served the Portuguese, he had the man burned alive. Yet he had himself spent many years as a captive guest in Portugal and his own grand vizier's mother was a highly honoured Muslim convert from a Castilian Christian family.

Another key thinker of the day from these years was the Sufi teacher Zarruq. Despite his own pursuit of the mystical path, he retained a pragmatic, commonsense caution. He advised believers to stay clear of such popular forms of devotion as the ecstatic trance dances and ascetic disciplines taught by some charismatic sheikhs. He also warned about the pious fads of the day. At this time there was an obsession with prayer rugs and pilgrim rosaries, and Zarruq argued that these practices had nothing to do with the example of the Prophet. Even with the Portuguese Crusaders hammering at the gates of Marrakesh, the savants of Fez kept to the true path of Islam. When a preacher of political Islam, al-Maghili, came to deliver his sermons of hate, denouncing the Jewish refugees who had fled from Spain and labelling all Muslims who had dealings with the Jews and Christians as apostate infidels, his audience dwindled away and he was expelled from the land. Sadly, he managed to find listeners for his hate-filled message in the Saharan oasis of Tuat, but the population there later regretted that they had allowed themselves to be stirred up by his sermons and had attacked their own ancient community of Berber Jews. Al-Maghili's opportunist career as a political preacher then took him south to Timbuktu, where the new ruler of the Empire of Songhai, Askia Muhammad (who had just deposed the legitimate Sultan, Ibn Sunni Ali), looked with interest on this preacher's *jihad*-filled rants. Emperor Askia could see that they had a very practical use, not only legitimising his own usurpation, which could now be seen to be part of a necessary *jihad*, but also identifying previously harmless Muslims as 'apostate unbelievers' who could be attacked, robbed and then sold on as slaves. His voice was not the only one to be heard in the Sahara. For a scholar from Egypt, al-Suyuti, had taken service under the Tuareg ruler at Agades and carried on urging the Sultan 'to rule with justice in the compassionate spirit of the Prophet'.

Within the vivid intellectual life of Wattasid Morocco it is possible to identify other fundamentalist preacher-politicians. Al-Sayyaf was such a man, who had been one of the many disciples of sheikh Muhammad al-Jazuli as-Samlali. Al-Jazuli was a gentle Sufi scholar, cherished by the people as one of the spiritual ornaments of Fez. Although born in the Sous valley (south of the High Atlas mountains) he pursued his life's work in Fez, where he taught and put together a collection of mystical teachings, including a book about the Sufi search for God, *Dala'il al-Khayrat*. He died during the dramatic political events of 1465 when the last Merenid Sultan was toppled from his throne. Whereupon one of his more excitable followers, young ibn Suleyman, nicknamed al-Sayf, 'the sword', accused the political authorities of poisoning the revered sheikh. He then spirited his master's dead body out of the city, so that in a mummified state it accompanied al-Sayf on his missionary journeys, swaying like a blind seer within the howdah of a camel, a poignant symbol of a revenge unfulfilled.[1]

Al-Sayyaf journeyed south into the Berber mountain regions of the High Atlas, Anti-Atlas and the Sous, which at this time had passed beyond the effective control of the Wattasid sultans. Here he taught versions of al-Jazuli's spiritual practices as well as preaching a vehement hatred of the Merenid dynasty and their Wattasid successors. Upon their heads was heaped the shame that had befallen Islam with the fall of Granada and the Portuguese invasions of Morocco. Al-Sayyaf was condemned by the scholars of Fez as 'a demented fake' and a 'murderous brigand', though his charismatic style of preaching attracted a devoted following in the mountains. It was with al-Sayyaf in mind that Zarruq spoke against the excesses of certain apostles of the luminous al-Jazuli:

> They started gathering the ignorant and the vulgar, male and female, whose hearts are black and whose minds are immature. They instilled in them . . . the belief that repentance is to be had by shaving the head, gobbling up food, gathering for banquets, invoking by turn utterances and cries, using mantles and beads, making a show of themselves, and holding that so and so is their master, and there is no other master save him . . .

Al-Sayyaf eventually moved the centre of his cult to his home town of Afughal in Haha, on the western edge of the High Atlas mountains as they drop into the Atlantic. It was a good place to plot rebellion, for there lived some of the most free-spirited of all the Berbers, among them al-Sayyaf's own Shayazima tribe. It was also well placed to benefit from illegal trade with European merchants, such as the Genoese and Castilians from Cadiz, who bought sugar and saltpetre from the many coves, beaches and harbours along this coast, of which Tarkuku was an accepted meeting place. It is also a region celebrated for magic and herbal lore, where such unique species as the Argan tree (a curious mixture between an olive and an African thorn-tree) grow. Sarmak can also be found, a potent aphrodisiac of those times, which could be identified for it gave a man an erection by just accidentally walking over a plant. In this environment al-Sayyaf grew increasingly tyrannical and divorced from normal standards of morality, which would lead to his death in 1485. He was poisoned by one of his wives after she found out that al-Sayyaf had also been secretly sleeping with her own daughter. At long last both he and the body of his old master, al-Jazuli, were buried. Their tombs were soon covered by a domed shrine which transformed Afughal into a pilgrimage town for their followers.

In lawless regions such as the far south of Morocco, a Sufi brotherhood fulfilled most of the roles of government without benefit of either soldiers or tax officials. So long as the brotherhood retained its reputation for sanctity and holiness it was offered respect and the charitable tithes indicated in the Koran. The brotherhood offered hospitality to travellers, merchants and pilgrims, set up schools for the pious, worked as an arbitrator between quarrelling tribes and issued safe conducts to allow travellers to pass inviolate through war zones. The Portuguese soon recognised this, and when they wished to arrange the exchange of prisoners-of-war or an opportunity to trade locally (such as the Wednesday market that developed in neutral land south of their fortress of Santa Cruz at Agadir) they went to the sheikh of a Sufi brotherhood to help them arrange this. It was just such a need, to settle the ransom price for some tribal dignitaries whom they had captured in a cavalry raid, that led a Portuguese embassy to send a letter to the door of a revered Sufi sheikh, Sidi Barakat. He lived in the oasis trading town of Akka, which is perched in the foothills of the Anti-Atlas mountains and looks directly out over one the principal routes across the Sahara. Sidi Barakat politely declined the opportunity to abandon his desert hermitage to become an intermediary for the foreign Crusaders, but was able to recommend for this task a revered local family who were descendants of the Prophet Muhammad. This family of Sharifs had dwelt in the Kasbah of Tagmadart for generations, where they overlooked some of the beautiful palm orchards of the oasis valley of the Draa. They had come from Mecca in the thirteenth century, their presence petitioned for by a delegation of Moroccan pilgrims anxious to break a decade-long drought with the presence of a member of the holy family of the Prophet Muhammad, who might bring *baraka*, divine blessings. There is a biblical purity about this region, with its extraordinarily powerful landscapes, where gorgeous scented, palm-shaded gardens are over-looked by the denuded slopes of sun-baked, barren mountains. The family were widely respected for their sanctity and the honour of their word. As Sharifs they stood outside the fierce rivalries of the local tribes. As the chronicler Ziyyani explained, 'The people would go to him [the leader of the family] in the most essential matters because of his knowledge, his piety, his zeal for *jihad* and his devotion to his heritage of virtuous ancestors who commended good and resisted evil.' In contrast the local chieftains knew enough about local politics to freely confess to Ziyyani, 'If we choose among ourselves [as a leader], rivalries between our tribes will explode.' So in 1510 the head of this house, Sharif Muhammad ibn Abd ar-Rahman, was publicly acknowledged by many of the tribes of southern Morocco as their judge, commander and mediator. He would become known by his most ardent supporters as 'Al-Qaim', 'the awaited one'. They asked him to leave his home and take up residence in the centre of the Sous valley. He, for his part, asked each tribe to appoint ten elders to liaise with him, which was framed in the poetic idiom of the Maghreb as 'to stand when I stand and sit when I sit'. The people of Sous, 'tired of living in a constant state of war, paid the Sharif enough money to feed five hundred horsemen. Using his money to hire even more soldiers and winning great renown from the struggle, he came to dominate the region. I know this for a fact for when I came to his court, he had assembled three thousand cavalry, innumerable numbers of men and vast amounts of money.'

The Wattasid Sultan worked with many such powerful sheikhs who were scattered throughout the mountain regions of Morocco. He acknowledged the local leadership of Al-Qaim and invited his two sons to study at the University of Fez and sent the Sharif a white war banner to bless his endeavours against the Portuguese Crusaders in the far south.

For their part, this Sharifian family from the desert south moved with speed and confidence to confirm and strengthen their position. Al-Qaim accepted the Wattasid Sultan's invitation to his sons to visit Fez, but advised them not to dwell there too long and to continue to Mecca and return with the added dignity of a Haji. Local traditions about the emergence of the Mahdi began to circulate. These were quite specific: the Mahdi would first emerge from an ancient mosque, whose beams were built of whale bones, on the Moroccan beach at Massa. There is nothing canonical about any of the traditions associated with the Mahdi, which have allowed them to proliferate.[2]

Al-Qaim's first attack on the Portuguese fortress of Santa Cruz at Agadir was a bloody reverse, though the Crusaders' advance post at Tamarakht was overwhelmed. It had, however, been taken as a serious enough threat by the Portuguese, for soon afterwards the wooden stockades and compacted-earth walls of the fortress were replaced with ones of stone, mortar and brick and reinforced with arms and artillery in 1513. That year Al-Qaim also accepted the invitation to become sheikh of the Jazuli brotherhood, who had always taught their disciples the greatest respect for the descendants of the Prophet. The holy town of Afughal became his new base, and while preaching the practice of holy war also made certain that the highly profitable regional trade remained unaffected. War was waged in the north against the walled positions of the Portuguese at Safi and Azzemour and those of their Moroccan clients, while clandestine trade with foreign merchants in such anchorage as Massa and Tarkuku boomed. A report by the Portuguese governor to King Manuel described the roaring business by Castilians and Genoese along this coast, and how he tried to put a stop to this, even catching a Frenchman in the act of selling cannon balls.

In 1514 Sharif Al-Qaim's two sons, Sharif Ahmad (al-Aruj) and Sharif Muhammad (esh-Sheikh), returned from their pilgrimage to Mecca and joined the army of the Wattasid Sultan for the summer season as he besieged Asilah. The following year witnessed the triumph of Wattasid arms at Marmora, followed by their direction of a nation-wide assault on the Portuguese positions. As we have heard, the Portuguese garrisons were ordered to recover prestige with a general assault of their own. In the far south the Moroccan ally of the Portuguese at Safi, Yahya ibn Tafuft, led a force that sacked Sharif Al-Qaim's forward base at Amagur in May. Later in that same year Yahya and the Portuguese rode side by side into the central plains of Morocco. Al-Qaim met them at the head of two thousand lancers, divided into three regiments commanded by him and his two sons. As a Portuguese eyewitness reported, one brother 'led the main formation, the Sharif commanded the left, and the other [brother] the right. The centre hurled itself upon our advance guard encircling it completely. Coming to the rescue, our side struck their exposed rear while the "loyal" Moors attacked the Sharif and the other flank with savage zeal.' Yahya and the Portuguese cavalry were once again left in control of the field of battle.

Sharif Al-Qaim played a long game. Tafetna, one of the few contraband ports that had remained outside his control, fell to his men. Elsewhere in the country the tribes were organised to place the Portuguese fortresses under a loose siege, which, while it never threatened their walls, isolated them from all trade. And one by one the leading Portuguese Crusaders were taken out. Captain Nuno Fernandes was shot down in an ambush, then the new governor of Safi, Lopo Barriga, was kidnapped, and in 1518 Yahya ibn Tafuft was himself finally struck down.

Al-Qaim did not live to hear of the death of his chief adversary. He had been buried in Afughal in 1517, but his two sons continued the struggle. Sharif Muhammad was based in the region south of the High Atlas, his brother Sharif Ahmad to the north of the mountains.

Inspiring though their leadership may have been against the Portuguese Crusaders, it was not these military exploits that brought the Sharifs such fervent support throughout the south of Morocco. It was their role as good Muslims. For during this period Morocco was hit by a series of famines, in 1514 and 1515, followed by a catastrophic drought in 1517, and a string of bad harvests in 1520, 1521 and 1522. Throughout this testing period the Sharifs emptied their treasury to feed the poor and the starving. The Sharifian garrison headquarters and the branches of the Jazuli brotherhood were all co-ordinated in the struggle to feed a desperate population. Behind this generosity lay their absolute command of Morocco's southern export trade. Neither the Hintata regime in Marrakesh nor the Wattasid Sultan in Fez could achieve such spectacular charity. Indeed it seems clear that from the 1520s onwards there was a gradual migration south from their towns and cities towards the food distribution centres controlled by the Sharifs. The Portuguese chronicler Diego de Torres (who was no partisan for the Sharif's cause) reported, 'They spared no effort, no expense, to provide food at reasonable price, and those who fared best were those of Marrakesh, Taroudant and their other dominions.'

Compassionate concern for your brother Muslims, though exhorted in verse after verse, chapter after chapter of the Koran, has seldom been exercised with any conviction by the rulers of Islam. But when it occurs it draws irresistible comparisons with the golden days of the 'rightly guided rulers', the first generation of Caliphs who governed the community after the death of the Prophet. Times when Caliph Abu Bakr refused to eat before he had patrolled the streets and observed for himself that all his people had been fed; and when Caliph Omar carried sacks of grain to the destitute on his own back and privately refused to taste either butter or honey while the people of Syria suffered famine. It also struck a chord with the great biblical example of the wisdom of the Prophet Joseph (Moulay Yusuf in Morocco), so wisely using the seven good years to allow his people to survive the seven lean years.

Such generosity came with a price. In the words of Santa Cruz, a Portuguese nobleman, 'The Sharif seized the entire countryside through his own campaigns and as he conquered, he decapitated the caids and the sheikhs in order to grab their property and fill everyone with terror and all the people feared him greatly. In this manner, he subjugated all the mountain villages to his will, mastered them and pacified them.'

In 1524 Sharif Ahmad was ready for his political masterstroke. He summoned a large tribal army for an advertised assault on the Portuguese garrison at Azzemour but, having slowly skirmished his way across the coastal plateau in the summer months towards this objective, he suddenly switched towards Marrakesh. The Hintata dynasty of Marrakesh had ruled for over a century, but in just one night it was over. Idris, the Hintata chieftain who rejoiced in the title of Lord of the Mountains, and his cousin Muhammad, Lord of the City, were felled. That autumn Sharif Ahmad entered the southern city as if by the acclamation of its citizens. He at once set about upgrading the defences and mounting detachments of arquebusiers and light artillery on the walls. He was right to do so. Up until this point the Sharifians had been just another dynasty of governors, but their seizure of Marrakesh, one of the ancient capital cities of Morocco, threw down the gauntlet to the Wattasid Sultan.

Once the news of the fall of Marrakesh reached him, the Wattasid Sultan al-Burtugali knew he had to act. He broke off from besieging Asilah and marched south, gathering allies and field artillery as he went. He was able to reach the walls of Marrakesh, but the opposition to his advance from the nomad tribes of the central plateau of the Middle Atlas warned him that a decisive shift in loyalties had already occurred. He did not attack the Sharifian brothers and died a few months later. His son, Ahmed al-Wattas, inherited the throne, which he ruled with the active support of his brother-in-law, Ibrahim ibn Rashid, the powerful dynastic governor of the western Rif who ruled from the mountain-top base of Chechaouen. A series of border clashes, in 1527 and again in 1530, established a division of the country into the Wattasid Sultanate of the north and Sharifian southern Morocco. This amicable solution had been brokered by the leading Sufi masters and tribal sheikhs, who were determined to halt a war between Muslims while the greater threat of the Portuguese Crusaders on the coast went unchallenged.

Sharif Ahmad proved himself an inexhaustible leader of the *jihad*. In 1530 and again in 1531 he directed attacks against Fort Santa Cruz at Agadir, switching to an assault on Azzemour in 1532 before plotting a surprise attack on Santa Cruz the following year. An agent of his managed to assassinate the governor, a breach was blown in the walls and the beach beneath one of the towers of Santa Cruz was so thick with Moors 'that it was impossible to see the ground'. Once again Portuguese wall-mounted artillery created devastating crossfire from the protruding bastions. But the Portuguese were having to take notice of the increasing accuracy of the Moroccans. For, as was reported during this campaign, when defenders rushed to fill the breach in the wall they were shot down by marksmen: 'Two soldiers, each pushing a cask into position, were shot dead, the bullets passing clean through their heads. This is no exaggeration.'

In the background there was a consistent and clear-sighted arms race. The Sharifian brothers were establishing arsenals in both Marrakesh and Taroudant which could cast munitions and grind gunpowder to the new extra-fine specifications of 'corning' as well as forge their own cannon. In that way they never need be totally dependent on the imports of foreign merchants, though the free ports were as busy as ever. Tarkuku passed under Sharif Muhammad's control while his brother Sharif Ahmad opened up Tafetna as his own harbour. A Portuguese ambassador passing through Marrakesh reported that 'there are a great many merchants in this country and artisans talented in all crafts and practices for making firearms . . . among these merchants are many "new Christians [forcibly converted Jews]" extremely skilled in making lances, crossbows, and arquebuses, who work here [so that they may] return to Judaism'.

The Wattasid Sultan was similarly busy with upgrading the arsenal workshops in Meknes and Fez. The Sultan had also found a new ally in the corsair captains and French smugglers who used the port of Badis on the Mediterranean shore of Morocco. Once again the vital need for Moroccan saltpetre seems to have cemented friendships. This new alliance scored its first tactical success when the Spanish outpost of Qassasa,

just west of Melilla, was overwhelmed in 1533 by a joint attack of corsairs, Rif tribesmen and a Wattasid regiment. This opened the door for
a wider alliance and Sharifian spies were soon reporting that the arsenal
at Fez held three dozen fine new bronze cannon, serviced not just by
Christian renegades but also by Andalusian refugees. The Sharifian war
machine had also been upgraded to new levels of efficiency. In 1534 a
disciplined army of ninety thousand men surrounded the walls of Safi
with a web of entrenchments and earthen bastions. Among the artillery
pieces that pounded the walls of Safi that year was a '*maymuna* which
fired a cannonball so big that a man could scarcely get his arms around
it'. The new King of Portugal, John III, had received sufficient warning
to reinforce the garrison, but as the siege tightened over the summer he
was forced to borrow troops and munitions from other outposts to
reinforce Safi.

In 1536 the two rival Sultanates of Morocco broke the truce and
their campaigns against the Portuguese to test their new strength against
each other. The Wattasid Sultan himself took command of the snaking
procession of artillery protected by infantry commanded by his brother-
in-law. The vanguard was led by the last Nasrid Emir of Granada,
Boabadil, riding beside the young Wattasid crown prince. The Wattasid
equipment was superior to the Sharifians' and seems to have been reinforced by a regiment of Turks. The Sharifian brothers lay in wait for
them at Wadi Abid, or 'White River'. Ahmad himself led a crack corps
of arquebusiers, trained to fire in a sequence of ranks if they could get
close enough to the enemy. This they achieved and poured a devastating
rate of fire 'as their enemies were passing through the river or climbing
the banks, they fell upon the Wattasid advance guard'. The Sharifians
shot down the crown prince and 'his adjutants, throwing the troops
behind them into a panic, sending them tumbling over those coming to
their aid, down the banks and over the ford with the enemy on their
heels. In an instant, the river was choked with men, horses, and baggage
wagons.' In the confusion the Wattasid second battalion fired on their
own side before the whole army broke and withdrew north. The Sharifs,
their army bolstered by the possession of all these fine new bronze field
cannon, were now clearly in the ascendant.

As a direct result of this shift in power, the Portuguese and the
Wattasids agreed a three-year truce and suspended their former ban on
trade. John III briefed all his ambassadors, 'Do not allow the King of

Marrakesh to overcome the King of Fez . . . for all beside becomes secondary if this serious and disturbing business begin. The King of Marrakesh is very astute and wealthy. I am told intelligence contacts with the Turks exist . . .'

The Sharifs were once again visited by a suppliant council of holy men from Fez including most of the revered Sufi sheikhs and professors of Islamic science. They were begged to continue respecting the north-south division of the country and to desist from waging war on fellow Muslims. They were listened to with respect but the Sharifs give no absolute commitment.

With the northern frontier secure, Sharif Muhammad wanted to secure his mastery of the trans-Saharan trade by subjecting the far south and the strategic oasis valley. Having done so, in 1541, he summoned a vast tribal army of twenty thousand cavalry and seventy thousand infantry. Assisted by his own skilled corps of arquebusiers, engineers and gunners, they enclosed the fort of Santa Cruz at Agadir. The range and power of the Sharifian call to arms was impressive to observe, for there were blue-veiled Tuaregs from the central Sahara, lean Wolofs from Senegal, white-veiled Moors from the western Sahara as well as regiments of Turks, Andalusians, ex-Mamelukes from Egypt and Christian renegades. A promontory named the Pic was turned into a secure forward base from which trenches and covered ways snaked out across the land. Within just two weeks of the start of the siege an earthwork had been set up from which fourteen heavy cannon pounded away at the weak point in the walls, keeping up a consistent crushing rate of fire for thirty-two successive days, while fifty smaller artillery pieces kept the Portuguese sheltering behind their walls. A separate battery of nine long-range cannon was sited to cover the entrance to the harbour anchorage should a Portuguese squadron try to come to the assistance of the fort, but these were never to be put to the test. On 11 March one of the main towers of Santa Cruz exploded after a direct hit on a gunpowder store. This breach in the walls was filled by a rush of Moroccan soldiers, while covering fire kept the garrison pinned down.

The Portuguese fought on, defending their individual stations but section by section the internal terraces and towers of Fort Santa Cruz were stormed. Discipline among the victors was such that several hundred prisoners, of both sexes, survived the fall of Santa Cruz to adorn the court of the Sharif. As the King of Portugal wrote in the immediate aftermath, 'We must recognise that warfare in Morocco has changed. The enemy is now very adept in the arts of war and siege craft.' Elsewhere a Portuguese chronicler would write with more emotion and in the true spirit of a Crusader knight, 'It is as if Jerusalem had fallen again.'

It was indeed a testing time for Portugal. That very summer the other Sharifian brother, Ahmad, mounted a siege of Azzemour, in the aftermath of which the Portuguese garrison mutinied. Improvements in artillery meant that many of the Portuguese positions, including Safi and most especially the riverbank position of Azzemour, could no longer hold their own. For the increasing range and sophistication of Moroccan siege artillery kept the docks and port entrances permanently closed. That September King John III reviewed his options in an emergency council meeting in Lisbon. The figures no longer added up. The upkeep of the string of Portuguese fortresses in Morocco now consumed three-quarters of the amount that was spent upholding the entire Indian Ocean empire. Their maintenance ate more than the entire annual profit from the West African gold trade: the initial impetus behind Portugal's emergence as a major commercial power.

Orders were sent to abandon both the fortresses and the walled towns of Azzemour, Mogador and Safi, along with a number of outlying forts and local allies. Portuguese strength was henceforth to be concentrated at just Mazagan. Here the fortifications were perched on a promontory that looked straight out to sea. The defences were upgraded, walls were strengthened, two new bastions were constructed and the one hundred bronze cannon released from service at Azzemour, Mogador and Safi bristled along its walls. A permanent garrison of seven hundred men proceeded to show the flag with vicious, vindictive energy, storming out of the land gates to sack and burn. Mazagan also made diplomatic sense perched somewhere near the border between the rival domains of the Sharifian and Wattasid Sultans.

The abandonment of Safi, Azzemour and Mogador may have been impeccably rational, but it in no way disguised the fact that the fall of Santa Cruz in 1541 was a critical watershed in a Portuguese crusade against Morocco that had lasted for 125 years. The southern Sultanate of Morocco ruled by the Sharifians no longer needed to evade Portuguese naval and cavalry patrols. Shipping from France, Castile, Genoa and England flocked to the open bay of Agadir, where the customs dues helped pay for a standing army of sixty thousand men, including five units of five thousand horsemen, each under the command of a royal prince.

Success breeds discontent among allies. The first accord to be weakened was between the two Sharifian brothers. The failure of Sharif Ahmad's siege of Azzemour had been all the more odious in view of his brother's great triumph at Santa Cruz. A spat about who owed whom what from the fall of Santa Cruz led to a cavalry skirmish fought in one of the passes over the High Atlas. Sharif Muhammad proved magnanimous in victory, sparing his elder brother's life but requesting the surrender of the Draa valley and the Tafilalt oasis to round off the borders of his southern state. Ahmad was even permitted to return to his throne in Marrakesh, but in exchange sent his eldest sons to serve as honoured hostages at their uncle's court. Two years later the brothers fought again, though this time Sharif Muhammad secured his control over both Taroudant and Marrakesh for himself. News from the north was critical. The Middle Atlas tribes were in rebellion, the Wattasid peace treaty with Portugal was condemned as a national disgrace and it seemed possible that Fez and the Mediterranean coast might fall under the control of the Ottoman Turks.

The armies of the two rival Moroccan states clashed once more in the borderlands of the Middle Atlas. The Battle of Darna confirmed Sharif Muhammad's reputation as a brilliant tactician. He divided his army up into its customary five units, but each of these self-functioning battalions maintained its own mobile field artillery and arquebuses. This flexibility perfectly suited the broken landscape of the hill region of central Morocco. Furthermore he had also concentrated on the training of new regiments of dragoons, mounted fusiliers, who were taught to fire in four sequential volleys. These crack regiments were recruited from the Jazuli Sufi brotherhood in the Berber mountains of the High Atlas, and had the Sharif's complete trust. The dragoons' deployment proved to be such a devastating success that they broke the spirit of the Wattasid army within the first hour of battle. Sharif Muhammad proved merciful in victory, packing his opponent off to internal exile while recruiting whole corps of his army into his own military formations. This included a well-travelled professional mercenary, a Persian named Sufyan, who had fled the Shia massacre of the Sunni in his homeland. He had ended up in command of four hundred Turks and four hundred renegade fusiliers at Algiers which he had led west in the service of the Wattasid Sultan. He had sat out the confusion of the Battle of Darna on a hilltop and now entered the service of the Sharif, bringing with him the welcome gift of artillery. He also brought a wealth of diplomatic experience and may have opened his new master's eyes to the potential for stirring up rebellion against the Ottoman Empire.

After the defeat at Darna, the Wattasid Sultanate fragmented into its component parts. The corsair republic at Tetouan, the Emirate at Chechaouen and a tribal chieftain who had proclaimed himself 'King of the Rif Mountains' split off and started to intrigue with external powers. At one point the Wattasid rump state, now composed of little more than the city of Fez, even implored the Holy Roman Emperor Charles V to intervene, while ambassadors simultaneously took a similar message to the Ottoman Sultan.

Sharif Muhammad knew he could control any battle field but was determined to resist the brutalities of a siege, especially one that pitted Muslim against Muslim. This was as much policy as piety, for he wanted to lead his nation, not destroy it. So he encircled Fez but did not attack it, sending in agents to see if the leading sheikhs of the city could not be persuaded to declare in his favour, while quietly seizing control of all the supply routes. The common citizens were completely confused: 'Some cheered for the Beni Merin, some for the Sharif, but most for bread.' Al-Wansharisi, one of the most respected of the city's scholars and long-serving judges, remained obdurately impervious to either threats or bribes from the Sharifian party. His example held the rest of the *ulema* and *shurafa*, the council of the learned and the holy dynasties, steady in their old loyalty. It also helped that Al-Wansharisi and his followers controlled the markets, law courts, tax inspectorate and *shurta*, the police. There was very little scope for compromise as the Sharifians had, from the very start of their endeavours, refused to recognise the tax-exempt status of the Sufi sheikhs, the Islamic scholars and other Sharifian families. They had also enforced new taxes and levies to fund the *jihad* that had no Koranic precedent.

Having failed to win over Al-Wansharisi with gifts and with words, Sharif Muhammad struck. Al-Wansharisi was assassinated and the walled palace of Fez, which stood to the west of the old city in its own distinct quarter, was attacked. The explosion of an underground mine coupled with an artillery barrage crumpled a section of the medieval palace wall. Three days later the entire city was his, and the last Wattasid passed into captivity. There was no purge, no hunting down of the members of the fallen dynasty, no reprisals, no looting, no sack. Very few of his contemporary monarchs could have exercised such restraint or held his men under such close command.

King John III of Portugal instructed his ambassador to 'put before the Emperor [Charles V's] eyes the great concern he ought to feel about the victorious Sharif – did he expect to find a prince ruling two power-ful states, so well provided with artillery, with munitions, with infantry and cavalry, with funding, and already so arrogant and self exalted by his recent victories to be peace-loving?' Or, as the Moroccan historian al-Ifrani put it, the Sharif 'lived for dominion and protection of his subjects. His restless spirit never ceased its vigilance in that regard. He did everything vigorously and was not shy about shedding blood. He was the first to levy the tax commonly known as the *naiba*, and he put all kinds of duties and fees on people without exempting a soul from these charges.'

The Sharif reorganised his army to include those members of the Wattasid military establishment who wished to serve him. The new rates of taxation were pasted up so that all could read of the new inclu-sive order. Here was a Sultan indeed.

Within the Islamic world of the Mediterranean there was only one other man who equalled him in power and determination and they both wrote verse. Sharif Muhammad's were a highly individual develop-ment of personal moral responsibility. All mankind was created with an equal soul: the difference between one mortal and another was in the energy and determination with which that individual grappled to improve and understand his inner self. Those who controlled the desti-nies of this world and its imagination were those who struggled most fiercely with themselves.

In 1550 the courts of Portugal and Spain waited anxiously for the next move of the dynamic new Sultan of Morocco. An alliance between the disciplined, battle-tested Sharifian army and the Ottoman fleet based at Algiers was rightly feared. It would have had every chance of expelling the last Portuguese and Spanish garrisons from North Africa and then perhaps proceeding in an attempt to reconquer Andalusia. But in truth the chances of such an alliance was never strong – any more than the wished-for friendship between the two great Christian monarchs, Francis I and Charles V. The Ottoman Empire was in no position to indulge in military adventures in the western Mediterranean in the year of 1550. Suleyman the Magnificent had signed a peace treaty with the Habsburgs just three years earlier and in the same year he had lost his closest European ally, King Francis I of France, as well as his great naval commander, Barbarossa, whom alone could have co-ordinated such a complicated operation. Furthermore the simmering rivalry between the Sunni Ottoman Empire and Shiite Empire of Persia had once again broken out into open war. From 1548 the resources of the Ottoman Empire were concentrated on its eastern front.

It may have been knowledge of these campaigns that tempted the Saadian Sharif into his totally unexpected next move. In 1551, rather than besiege the Christian Crusaders in Ceuta or Tangier as might be expected from the celebrated leader of a thirty-year-old *jihad*, he sent an army east to invade the territories of the Ottoman Empire. The Sharif appointed his eldest son, Muhammad al-Harran, to lead a force of thirty thousand men into western Algeria. The city gates of the old Zayyanid capital of Tlemcen were not defended. Instead they were thrown open to celebrate the liberation of the city from the Turkish garrison in a manner that suggested a well-laid conspiracy. Proclamations were issued that suggested that this was the start of a campaign of liberation that would chase the Turks from all the positions they held in North Africa and Egypt. The Sultan of Fishermen, as the Ottoman leader was insultingly addressed, would be expelled and authority restored by the Sharifian Muhammad, the true descendant of the family of the Prophet Muhammad. For those who knew their history this was no empty boast, for the Fatimid Caliphate had arisen in just such a manner, from out of the mountain tribes of North Africa. The similarity between the charismatic claims of the Sharifian Sultans of Morocco and the Shiite Shahs of Persia threatened to squeeze the Ottomans from both the east and the west, while denying them the right to claim to be the legitimate rulers of the old Islamic heartland. This was a serious threat to the heart and soul of the Ottoman state.

Events on the ground further widened the gulf between the two Muslim states. For the local commander of the Ottoman janissaries, Hasan Qusru, proved himself an effective leader. Summoning help from the local tribes he struck back at the Sharifian army, which was crippled by the sudden death of their leader, crown prince Muhammad al-Har-

ran, from a disease picked up at Tlemcen. The Sharifian army was
forced to withdraw in some disorder back into Morocco, while the
enterprising janissary commander reoccupied Tlemcen, formally banishing the last of the native Zayyanid princes and annexing the city to
the Ottoman Empire. Worse was to follow. In the spring of 1554 a
column of Turkish janissaries marched across the eastern plains and
occupied Fez. A Wattasid Sultan was placed as a puppet ruler on the
throne, and for the first time the call to prayer in the ancient mosques
of Fez was called out in the name of the distant Ottoman Sultan
Suleyman the Magnificent. It was a brief enough period of Ottoman
power, for that autumn Sultan Muhammad led the Moroccan counter-
attack himself, recapturing Fez in September. The old privileged class of
scholars and Sufi sheikhs had welcomed the return of a Wattasid Sultan,
even though he was now upheld by a foreign army. The Sharif was once
again merciful but he confiscated the lands and properties of all those
who had co-operated with his enemies. Elsewhere in Morocco, the
application of the new Sharifian tax system had been widely resisted,
which was why the Sharif had been unable to defend Fez when the
Turks first invaded: he was embroiled in suppressing a rebellion in the
far south.

The prospect of an alliance between the two Islamic powers against
the Christian enemy had now totally receded from the diplomatic picture. So much so that the Sharif started negotiating with the commander
of the Spanish garrison in Oran, and openly talked about joint operations against the Turks. The local Ottoman military commander struck
back before this potential alliance could be put into practice. The
Spanish fort at Bejaia, which had resisted the siege attempts of both of
the Barbarossa brothers, was finally stormed in 1555. The following
year they attacked the main Spanish base at Oran by both land and sea,
though the effectiveness of this siege was much diminished when an
order came through to send back men and galleys to reinforce the
Ottoman army on the eastern front. The Sharif, for his part, made good
use of this opportunity and once again established a Moroccan garrison
in Tlemcen.

In 1557, having signed a peace treaty with the Persians at the field of
Amasya, the Ottoman Empire was able to turn its full attention back to
the Mediterranean. Hasan, the son of the second of the two Barbarossa
brothers, was appointed as the new commander-in-chief at Algiers.

Using such battle-experienced officers as Hasan Qusru, they drove the Moroccans out of Western Algeria once more and penned the Spanish garrison into Oran. A crack squad of Ottoman secret agents infiltrated the Sharifian army, an easy enough process, for it had been Sharif Muhammad's open-hearted policy to absorb the soldiers of any defeated opponent into his army, if they swore to serve him. They proved themselves to be such exemplary and efficient soldiers that they soon won the personal commendation of the Sharif. They were even selected to accompany him on one of the frequent armed inspections of the mountainous interior with which an active Sultan of Morocco exercised his personal authority over the tribal lords. While he was on one such patrol in the Atlas mountains his bodyguard of young cavalry officers suddenly revealed their true loyalties to their distant master. The Sharif, master of a dozen battlefields, was struck down, his head severed and stuffed into a leather satchel lined with salt. The young soldiers then rode fast to the east to the frontier fortress of Tlemcen. From there they rode on to Algiers, where the gory satchel was opened for inspection in the governor's palace before being sent, packed in ice, on a fast war galley to Istanbul.

The following year, to drive home the message of the long reach of the Ottoman Empire, an army was sent into Morocco to threaten Fez. Later that same year the Spanish governor Count Alcaudete was lured out of Oran on a fool's errand: to seize the town of Mostaganem, which he had been informed was on the point of accepting Spanish rule. Instead the twelve-thousand-strong Spanish military column found themselves surrounded outside the town's walls by Algerian tribes strengthened by a detachment of Ottoman janissaries. The Spaniards attempted to fight their way back to Oran in the heat of midsummer. Half of the men, including their commander, were killed, the rest taken prisoner and marched into Algiers as slaves.

The Ottomans were content to stabilise their far-western frontier after this double triumph. The Sharifians never doubted that the Turks had now become a much greater threat to their sovereignty than the Spaniards and Portuguese on the coast. The cities nearest the Algerian frontier, such as Oujda, Taza and Fez, were reinforced with new walls and artillery forts, while Marrakesh, too far south to be threatened by any janissary army, became the preferred capital. The Sharifians did not always remain on the defensive, and when the political situation seemed to warrant the risk, struck back. There was another determined attempt to seize control of Tlemcen in 1560, though the frontier that was drawn between the Ottoman and the Sharifian state in these years is the one that still endures between Morocco and Algeria to this day. Although the Moroccans managed to preserve their independence, the influence of the Ottomans was felt in a number of ways.

Most obvious and repugnant was the reaction to the news of Sharif Muhammad's assassination. In a clear and bizarre salute to the Ottoman practice of fratricide, six Sharifian princes were slaughtered. Their sad little line of tombs can still be seen in the necropolis of the dynasty: that gorgeous pointillist confection of mosaic tile and carved plasterwork in the heat of Marrakech known as the Saadian Tombs.[3] Two sons of Sharif Muhammad survived this family massacre and resisted the blandishments of their ruling half-brother to return to the safety of his court. They chose well, for the two of their brothers who did accept an offer of safe conduct and a prestigious post in the government were both dead before the end of the year. The surviving brothers fled east in the company of their talented mother, Sahaba Errahmania, and sought exile in the lands of the Ottoman Sultan. First they lived among the Turkish garrison in the old royal citadel of Tlemcen before moving to Algiers. After the death of Suleyman the Magnificent they were permitted to travel east, to Istanbul. Assisted by their mother, they learned to speak and read many languages, but, in keeping with the sad life of exiles, pinned their hopes of returning home on frequent petitions to the Court of the Sultan. Their half-brother meanwhile stabilised the Sharifian regime, suppressed the last of the independent emirates, such as Chechaouen in the Rif mountains, and wisely refused to interfere in the last doomed rebellion of the Moors in Andalusia in 1568. Although it would have been wildly popular with his subjects, it would have been a political endgame, irritating the one ally, the Catholic Kingdom of Spain, which could help Morocco remain independent from the ever-expanding Ottoman Empire.

It was out of a sense of exasperation at their petition-obsessed lives that the two Moroccan princes volunteered to serve in the Ottoman navy in the campaigns of 1571 and 1572. A Muslim fleet had left Istanbul to fight the Christians, who had briefly united their navies under a confederate Holy Alliance. Most of the Ottoman fleet was sunk at the Battle of Lepanto in 1571 and their crews slaughtered by cannon fire, but the two Moroccan princes managed to survive the battle, albeit as captives of the Christians. They were treated well by the young commander of the Christian fleet, the chivalrous Don John, and would in due course be returned to Istanbul. This adventure was to be the making of them, and the first link in the chain of bizarre incidents that led to the final battle of the Crusades.

But before we meet these exiled princes again, right at the end of this book, we must first understand the wars and crusades that had been waged by the Holy Roman Emperor Charles V as well as those led by Sultan Suleyman the Magnificent.

9

The Rivals

The Division of Christendom between
Charles V and Francis I

But these thoughts had taken a rather peculiar turn; it seemed to
me that I myself was the immediate subject of my book: a church,
a quartet, or the rivalry between Francis I and Charles V.

Proust, *Du côté de chez Swann* (from *À la recherche
du temps perdu*)

Charles V always knew that one day he would inherit the crowns of
Spain from his grandparents Ferdinand and Isabella, and the lands of
the Habsburgs in southern Germany from his grandfather Maximilian.
That was in the future. What he was born into in 1500, and lived
among for all the impressionable years of his infancy, boyhood and
manhood, was the fabulously rich and complicated inheritance of a
Duke of Burgundy. These lands sprawled like a half-finished jigsaw
puzzle between France and Germany, a rich conglomerate of some two
hundred industrious cities, of which Bruges, Ghent, Antwerp, Louvain,
Brussels and Amsterdam were the most conspicuous, dotted across agricultural provinces such as Flanders, Picardy, Holland, Burgundy,
Zeeland, the Rhineland and Luxemburg. The Dukes of Burgundy were
rulers of a society that, in industry, ability, artistry, diversity, sophistication and wealth, could only be equalled by the cities of northern Italy.
Though independent of both the elective Holy Roman Emperor of
Germany and the hereditary King of France, none of the dukes were

content with their status. They wished to be kings, and constantly aspired to create a unified state that would stretch in an unbroken line from the mouth of the Rhine to the Mediterranean. Tangled up amid these ambitions were the strong currents of trade, which linked the cities of Flanders with the primary wool producers, England and Spain, and the financial centres of Italy. These were their natural allies, while France and Germany were the neighbours to be watched.

The Dukes of Burgundy, for all the talented commercialism of their

Duke Philip the Good of Burgundy accepting the first presentation copy of the History of Hainault. His son and heir Charles the Bold stands to his left.

lands, were extravagantly committed to the old ideals of feudal life, courtly behaviour and knight-errantry. Indeed one can read into their enthusiasm a need to preside over a court more regal than that kept by any mere king. So it is typical of this Burgundian mood that the most senior order of knighthood in all of Catholic Christendom is their Order of the Golden Fleece. This was created by Duke Philip the Good on his wedding day, 'out of his love for chivalry and to protect and propagate the Christian faith'. In the charming traditions of those days, fragments of classical mythology, dark-age legends and antique heroes were woven together to make a seamless cloth of fifteenth-century enthusiasms. Troy, Merlin, Alexander, Roland, Arthur, King David, Solomon and Julius Caesar all co-exist in this tapestry of heroic adventures. The Knights of the Golden Fleece thought of themselves as modern Argonauts being led by a new Jason towards Jerusalem. For their ceremonies they wore robes of scarlet set off by a golden chain from which hung the badge of the golden fleece. But it was not all a fancy-dress parade that processed from chapel to chapter-house and then on to dinner, for they also succeeded in functioning as a military brotherhood. For instance, it was the Duke of Burgundy who paid for the construction of the great sea tower of St Nicholas in the fortress city of Rhodes, held by the Knights of St John during the first Ottoman siege. And it was Duke John who rode at the head of a host of Burgundian and French knights to join the army of Emperor Sigismund in Hungary – though in truth their arrogant conduct seems to have brought on the disaster of the Battle of Nicopolis back in 1396.

Although it happened a generation before Charles V was born, it's worth looking at the celebrated Fête du Faisan to get a feel for the atmosphere of medieval Burgundy. In order to encourage a fresh generation of young knights to risk their lives in another crusade a great pageant was held in 1454, in direct response to the news of the fall of Constantinople. Presided over by the Duke of Burgundy, the festival was an outrageously gorgeous panoply of tournaments, jousts, parades, feasts, masques and spectacles. The vast wealth of the duchy was on show: in the damasks hung over the banqueting tables, the rich and dazzling succession of courses, the relic-lined chapels, the heavy gold and silver vessels, the imported rock crystal, embroidered vestments, coloured glass and near-perfect vintages. Exquisite tapestries were hung in the audience and withdrawing chambers to set the mood for symbolic presentations, such as when the Lord of Ravestein, young Adolf of Cleeves, made a breathtaking appearance as the Swan-Knight, glistening in silver armour and white silks from head to foot. On another occasion a fiery dragon flew around the room pursued by a heron. This arresting scene was eclipsed in its turn by the unveiling of a statue of a naked woman who presided over a wine-filled fountain encrusted with jewels and guarded by a lion. Other nights were devoted to symbolic presentations of the labours of Hercules and the adventures of Jason complete with their biblical analogies. Fierce sermons were preached on the immorality of the times, the decline of virtue and the spread of vice.

In this emotional climate, young men swore to take the cross of the crusade over a succession of the noble birds: peacocks, swans, doves and on the penultimate night, a golden pheasant. As this feast of feasts drew to its climactic closure, a herald mounted on an elephant appeared and called forth the individual knights by name and challenged them: 'Dear son, draw thy sword, for the glory of God and for thine own honour.' The knights responded by vowing to fulfil the challenge by 'God, the Virgin Mary, his lady and the Pheasant', after which a maiden labelled 'God's Mercy' made her appearance with a dozen equally elegant figures, embodying the twelve virtues. These ladies blessed the knights, thanked them and challenged them to stay true to their word. After this there was dancing in which the twelve virtues were persuaded to join in.

Charles knew the love neither of a mother nor a father. His mother Juana was a mad queen locked up in a distant castle, while his handsome and much-loved father, Philip, had died before he could retain any memories of him. Grandfather Ferdinand was considered to be the cleverest monarch in all Christendom, but he lived in Spain and also clearly preferred Charles's younger brother. Maximilian, his paternal grandfather, had a much stronger presence in Charles's life and proved himself a dutiful correspondent and a candid counsellor. Emperor Maximilian was intelligent, charming and passionately engaged with life, but he was always short of money and patience. It was said of him that a hundred concepts revolved in his brain, but this kaleidoscope never allowed him to concentrate on any one particular plan for long.

The most important and positive character in Charles's youth was his loving and attentive aunt Margaret. She seems to have been a genuinely kind and inspiring woman, clever, enquiring and tempered by her own experience in life. Charles and his three sisters, Eleanor, Isabella and Mary, were all lodged in the old ducal palace at Malines. Opposite it, their aunt Margaret, the reigning regent of the duchy, constructed a modern, light-filled palace, arguably the first Renaissance building in northern Europe (though it also had vaulted Gothic wings). Margaret had been passionately loved by two young husbands, and despite offers of matrimony from many grandees, including Henry VII of England

and the Duke of Norfolk, she had no desire to disfigure their memories with a third partner. Her court attracted some of the most interesting men of her times, be it the clever Italian lawyer Mercurino Gattinara, who would later be Charles's Chancellor, or Adrian of Utrecht, a gentle scholar-mystic who would become Pope. When Albrecht Dürer passed through, it was Margaret who volunteered to be his guide, walking him round on a tour of palaces and art collections.

Although Margaret's salon was enchanting it would have bored a young man, so she made certain that Charles grew up in a boisterous household of like-minded companions, such as young Henry of Nassau (who was excellent on a toboggan), plus one of the high-spirited sons of the Duke of Saxony and one of the Sforza boys from Milan. Charles's tutor-governor was the dashing French nobleman William of Chièvres, who owed his appointment to the personal recommendation of Charles's grandfather, Emperor Maximilian. Chièvres had fought in many a war and was able to teach the young Charles how to ride, fight, hunt and behave like a man. He was the perfect counterfoil to the intellectualism of his aunt, and Charles, deprived of a mother and a father, poured all his love on his tutor. They shared a bedroom for the first twenty years of Charles's life.

On 5 January 1515 Charles came of age. He was formally acclaimed duke in the Parliament Hall of the castle of Brussels. In the very same year, month and week, Francis I succeeded to the throne of France. Like Proust in one of his youthful reveries, it is almost impossible not to indulge in wistful day dreams about the failed relationship between these two young monarchs: 'But these thoughts had taken a rather peculiar turn; it seemed to me that I myself was the immediate subject of my book: a church, a quartet, or the rivalry between Francis I and Charles V.' For though Francis I and Charles V bestrode their age, they also very nearly suffocated it. The succession of wars that was fought between them forms one of the great spoliations of Christendom. They fought over the mastery of the Low Countries, of Italy (especially the Duchy of Milan and the Kingdom of Naples) and indeed wherever their kingdoms touched upon each other, be it in Provence, Savoy, Roussillon or Navarre. This vast and useless destruction of cities, this devastation of provinces and the massacre of hundreds of thousands of lives, eventually so exhausted the two states and their treasuries that a peace would have to be signed, but time and again this turned out to be no more than a temporary truce, a mere pause for rearmament before the next round of conflict. But was this inevitable? Could Charles and Francis not have forged a friendship that touched upon the youth, idealism and the romantic yearnings that they both shared? There was certainly an opportunity for such a friendship. Chièvres, Charles's beloved tutor, never failed to promote a pro-French agenda – to the extent that some believed him to be a confidential agent of France.

Francis I invited the young Duke of Burgundy to his coronation, but Charles did not come. Had he already supped too deeply from the history of his Burgundian ancestors to be able to attend? Was he afraid that because he was destined to be a king of many lands, he would in some way be dishonoured by giving a feudal oath of loyalty to Francis for his French lands and dignities? Was he not in awe of being overshadowed by the character of the young Frenchman? Charles was a serious, pious and reserved young man who kept his own counsel and was constantly aware of the need to guard himself from the sexual passions that had destroyed the life of his Spanish uncle and the sanity of his own mother. In almost total contrast, Francis was a tall, physically confident, sensual and handsome man, given to sudden changes of policy, to laughter and to adventure. He was a witty conversationalist who revelled in the company of women, be it his vivacious mother and elder sister, who had poured their adoration on him in his youth, or one of his many mistresses. If opposites attract, here indeed were the ingredients for a profound friendship.

But there was to be no youthful meeting – and even Charles's delegation of courtiers (geographically the closest) arrived too late to witness the French coronation. But the prospect of the two young princes working in tandem was a tantalising one. As Charles's chosen ambassador, Henry of Nassau, put it in addressing Francis I, 'Your Majesty is as young as our prince; you are both blank pages and could together do much for Christendom.' Francis agreed passionately and swore by his honour as a knight, that 'he was not second to Charles in his care for the weal of Christendom'.

But perhaps no amount of the idealism of two young princes could have restrained the tectonic forces of national rivalry within Europe. Francis for his part had been brought up to regard the young warrior knights who had fought for France in the Italian wars of his predecessors, Charles VIII and Louis XII, as his true role models. Indeed, arguably France has never quite recovered from the examples of such living D'Artagnans as Gaston de Foix or the Chevalier Bayard, whose actions in the Italian wars became a living exemplar of the romantic, spirited hero.

The following year, 1516, the Burgundian regime moved to strengthen its alliance with its natural allies. For reasons of politics, they had to pretend to snub the Venetian ambassador in public – though in private he was doubly cherished with intimate dinners and candid conversations. No one bothered to camouflage the strong understanding between the Duchy of Burgundy and the Kingdom of England, which was further enhanced by the warm friendship that existed between the Burgundy-born genius Erasmus and a member of the English delegation, Thomas More.

Then came the black-clad heralds from Spain. They came to announce the death of a king, but also the eclipse of the Duchy of Burgundy.

On a cold, dark wintry day in March Brussels was ablaze with light, for thousands of citizens armed with fiery torches, had lined the streets. Through this double column of flickering orange flame passed the sombre procession of mourners on their way by foot from the palace of the dukes to the cathedral of St Gudule. The interior of the cathedral had been bedecked with all the textile glory of Burgundy, a priceless cascade of brocades, silks and tapestries, whose gilden and scarlet threads reflected the intimate flicker of thousands of candles and scented tapers. At the culmination of the funeral the preacher thundered out from the pulpit, 'This is the dance of death which all must tread, even Kings and Princes. This is the irrevocable law of life! Sceptres and crowns must fall. Let us not forget how swiftly joy and feasting turn to mourning and lamentation!'

Directly opposite the pulpit sat the thin figure of the young Charles, the throne of Burgundy draped in black. Then the herald of the Golden Fleece emerged to stand below the carved chancel screen. With a lone voice he questioned the echoing vaults of the ancient church, 'Don Ferdinand?'

From the assembly came the slow growl, 'He is dead.' Three times the enquiry was framed, and as the sound of the last answer echoed away, the royal standards of Aragon were lowered to embrace the dust. Then once the silence of the grave had been tasted the herald rose up again from his knees to announce, 'Long live their Catholic Majesties, Queen Juana and King Charles!'

The heavy mourning cloak that enveloped the young prince was then unfastened by his pages. Charles was free to advance towards the altar and to climb on to a raised platform. There he took hold of a dagger that the Bishop of Badajoz had solemnly fetched for him from its place on the altar. As Charles raised the dagger towards the heavens, the cathedral rocked to the sound of a mass acclamation: 'Long Live the King!'

In such a style was the ancient Duchy of Burgundy to be gradually extinguished by the greater light of the kingdoms of Spain, and so was the almost otherworldly zeal of a courtly Burgundian knight to be transferred south towards the Mediterranean war zone. There was need of a new direction, for with the death of King Ferdinand in April 1516, political events across the western Mediterranean were once again on the move. France had reawakened. Sicily was in revolt. The Spanish command of the sea lanes was being aggressively challenged. A fleet that had been dispatched by the regent of Spain, Cardinal-Primate Cisneros, to Algiers had been defeated. In Spain the old crusading tax on Church income, the *cruzada*, was once again imposed to enable a new fleet to be built in double-quick time. This was not just a question of pride: the vast coastline of southern Italy, Sicily, Aragon and the Balearic Islands was now a frontier that had to be protected from the Muslim corsairs operating out of the anchorages of Algiers, Bizerta, Tetouan and Tunis. Granada was being avenged through the Holy War at Sea. It was reported that the old Cardinal was extracting fifty-three thousand ducats a month from the Church's coffers to fund the ship-building programme for this.

It was to be another year before sufficient money had been borrowed (from the English in this instance) for Charles's court to afford to move south with the splendour required of a new king. On the dawn of 8 September a breeze at last lifted the sails of the royal squadron of forty ships that lay waiting off the harbour bar at Flushing. The wind picked up as they sailed down the Channel, so they made good speed into the challenging waters of the Bay of Biscay. Here the wind grew into a gale, and then broke into a storm which scattered the squadron. Each captain was left to pick his own course in order to make the safe havens along the Galician shore. Charles's ship made a landing just ten days out of Flushing. Its sudden arrival at the fishing village of Villaviciosa threw the locals into such alarm that they rushed to arms to protect themselves against what they presumed to be a corsair – but fortunately they were informed that it was their new king before any blows had been struck. The sea-tossed Burgundian court gradually reassembled itself, and began a laborious wagon-laden journey across the high mountains of northern Spain. Their route was highly irregular, deliberately skirting all the ancient cities – such as Santander, Leon, Valladolid and Burgos – that were expecting to greet their new monarch. It was whispered that there was a conspiracy underfoot, that the King was being deliberately kept away from an audience with Cisneros, the Cardinal-Primate and regent of Spain, who aged eighty was approaching his end.

But the reason for this circumspection was locked away in a tower of the castle of Tordesillas. Charles (and his sister) were determined to visit their mother and see her mental condition for themselves, before accepting the crowns of Spain that theoretically belonged to her. The condition of Queen Juana was a state secret, and not even the trusted courtier Vital (who accompanied Charles and his sister Eleanor to the very threshold of the Queen's room) was allowed into her presence, though by offering to bring a light, then a jug of water, then a plate of food, Vital did all he possibly could to be allowed to catch a glimpse of the Queen. But each time Vital was driven away from the room by Charles, though these visits of long-separated son and daughter to their mother were repeated many times over the following days. At length they realised that nothing could be done for their mother, but, having grown up in the luxury and ornament of Burgundy, they were appalled at the state of their little sister Catherine, who had grown up to become a child-servant to her mad mother. They tried to persuade Catherine to leave the battlemented towers of Tordesillas but this idea so appalled the old Queen that Catherine volunteered to stay on and fulfil her duty. Charles for his part set up his youngest sister with a household and an income of her own.

Four days later Charles was brought the news that Cardinal Cisneros had died. Cisneros could have supplied him with a lifetime of knowledge about Spain, the true character of his mother and that of his celebrated grandmother Isabella. Charles then met for the first time in his life his fifteen-year-old-brother Ferdinand, the native-born, fluent Spanish-speaking namesake and favourite grandson of King Ferdinand.

In the way the world works, young Ferdinand was immediately packed off to exile in the Duchy of Burgundy, to be 'finished' in the civilised court of his Aunt Margaret under the guidance of Erasmus (from where he would migrate further east to eventually become a highly accomplished Archduke of Austria). Charles then felt free to finally make his entrance into Valladolid. It was, in the words of a chronicler, as if King Arthur had finally returned, his horse harness ablaze with gems, 'clad in shining armour and priceless stuffs'. His shields bore two devices, the famous 'Plus Ultra' ('Even Higher') but also 'Nondom' ('Not Yet'). These symbols were widely taken to be a reference to the great Christian crusade of the Burgundian imagination when both Constantinople and Jerusalem would be conquered.

But it was also a prescient statement of Charles's distracting range of

Charles V aged twenty-two. (Museum of Fine Arts, Brussels)

responsibilities. For when news reached him of the death of his other grandfather, Emperor Maximilian, Charles halted his personal progression, and, having ransacked the treasury of Spain for funds, dashed back

to Germany to organise the acquisition of this branch of his inheritance. Although he was already the acknowledged heir, the formal
election of a Holy Roman Emperor was always an expensive process.
His old grandfather had candidly warned him that 'much money' would
be the best argument among the seven German electors. Nor would
anyone be won over by mere promises: hard cash was required. Call it
what you wished: gift, loan, bribe, present, fee or indemnity, the spirit-
ual-electors wouldn't even begin to discuss where their vote might be
placed before they had received a sweetener of four thousand gulden,
while for the prince-electors you needed to add a nought. Then the real
bargaining could start. Fortunately the Fugger brothers and their allies
among the other bankers of that great financial city, Augsburg, were at
hand to advance such enormous sums. The bidding, egged on by both
Henry VIII of England and Francis I of France's ambition to be elected
Emperor, went through the roof. From the surviving account books we
can trace the final deals that were struck. One hundred and eighty-four
thousand gulden paid to the Count of the Palatinate, 52,800 gulden
paid to the Bishop of Cologne. Only then could the tocsin be sounded
thrice, the signal for pious citizens to fall down on their knees to pray
to God to send down his grace on the Electors that they might choose
a worthy Emperor. Charles was then acclaimed by the massed trumpeters of the Count Palatine and the Margrave of Brandenburg. His
election 'expenses', at nearly a million gulden, broke all existing
records.

But, in Charles's own words, 'it is so great and sublime an honour as
to outshine all other worldly titles'. His Burgundian ancestors would
have been thrilled to see how very far the Duchy had risen. In May
1520 the young Emperor Charles V crossed over to Dover and then on
to Canterbury, where young King Henry VIII and his Queen Catherine
of Aragon (Charles's aunt) awaited him. This court was also embellished
by Henry's sister, Mary, who, having served her stint as a Queen of
France (in a desperate attempt by the dying King Louis XII to father an
heir), then married England's leading sportsman of the day, the lusty
young Brandon, a heroic figure on the international jousting circuit.
This meeting was to be but a prelude of magnificence before the June
gathering of the two Renaissance courts of France and England in a
summer camp, 'The Field of the Cloth of Gold', on the coast of northern France. Fantastic entertainments, a duel of extravagant showmanship

and some loose talk about crusading helped, just a little, to mask the deep mutual distrust between France and England. King Francis I's high spirits encouraged him to ambush the young King of England while still asleep in his tent, after which he insisted on acting as his valet and helping him to dress and take breakfast. Beneath the convincingly broad smiles and little intimacies brought upon by these high jinks, it seems clear that Henry VIII and Charles V had already plotted to dismantle King Francis I's kingdom of France between them. It was a new version of the old alliance between England and the Duchy of Burgundy that had underwritten the Hundred Years War. Henry and Charles met immediately after the Field of the Cloth of Gold for a post-conference assessment of their intended victim.

For Charles there were tours of Germany and Austria, a coronation at Aachen and German Diet to attend, plus a second agreeable visit to England in 1522. Then, recalling the adventure of his first alarming crossing of the Bay of Biscay, he settled down to make provision. Sitting in the great flint-built halls of the Bishop of Winchester's Waltham Palace, which looks over the clear waters of a moat fed by a Hampshire chalk stream, he wrote out his will before taking ship from Southampton. The wealth from Cortes' conquest of Mexico had already begun to flow back to Spain in useful quantities, and Charles had proudly shown off pieces from the golden treasury of Montezuma on his progression. The English were dazzled but so too were the master artist-designers of Middle Europe, and Dürer is said to have stood back in wonder at the 'subtle ingenuity of men in strange lands'.[1]

The gold had been sent to Charles V by Hernan Cortes, the conqueror of Aztec Mexico. Cortes was a classic by-product of Spain's militant crusading traditions. His father had been a typical *hidalgo*, a poor knight, who had seen active service in the conquest of Granada as a cavalry officer. However, he had encouraged his son to turn away from knight-errantry and study at the University of Salamanca so that he could enter the new class of '*letrados*', lettered government officials. Hernan had escaped this bureaucratic fate by jumping on board a ship bound for 'the West'. He arrived in the West Indies aged just nineteen but was befriended by the Spanish governor, who entrusted the young *hidalgo* with the task of administering a plantation. But Hernan was not interested in cultivation, even of such a lucrative crop as sugar, and soon set about recruiting all the most desperate diehards on the island in order to lead a freelance raiding expedition into the Mexican coast-lands in 1519. It was thus that the celebrated conquistador, the conqueror of Mexico, started his career, as the self-appointed captain of a freebooting raiding party; in other words, a pirate, a corsair. But he was also acting in the manner in which his father and his comrades had been sent by King Ferdinand to scorch the earth of the Emirate of Granada as a prelude to its conquest. It would be Hernan Cortes' genius that, once his raid had started to snowball into such an aston-ishing success, he deftly started to cover his tracks, making duplicate copies of treaties and proclamations that loudly trumpeted that he was acting in the name of 'the greatest King of the world, Don Carlos, and his all-highest will'. These reports, backed up by a steady remittance of golden treasure and conquered provinces, would eventually help him clear his name and provide for an honourable return to Spain. But Cortes had in fact sailed extremely close to the gallows. Only the size of his conquests saved him from a court of inquiry, not only for desert-ing his post but for launching a direct military assault on the official Spanish expedition to Mexico.

By the time Charles V finally returned to Spain in July 1522, some three years after his sudden departure, the conquest of Central America had already been achieved without any assistance from Charles's 'all-highest will'. And by now the machinery of state was already striving to replace the era of freebooting entrepreneurs with the dead hand of sound administration. A young Spanish friar, Bartolome de las Casas, had in 1515 come back to make his passionate report on the reality of the new empire, the ruined civilisations of the natives, the uncontrolled brutality, violence and the endless frontiers of greed. When Charles looked over the correspondence – which included the casual but epoch-making decision to start sending African slaves to replace the Indians as they proved better agricultural workers – he realised that his new sub-jects had been treated 'not as men but beasts'.

They were not the only subjects to feel deeply dissatisfied. The Spaniards were infuriated by the absence of their young monarch and even more with the Burgundian courtiers he had appointed to rule over them. Rebellions consumed the land, most savagely in Valencia, where a civil war had broken out between the wealthy classes of rural nobles and urban merchants set against the peasants and artisans. As so often, it was the powerless who suffered the most, especially those considered to be foreign. The *conversos*, those who only a decade before had to choose between conversion and exile (the recently baptised Muslims and Jews of Spain), were driven from their lands, and their leaders lynched.

In eastern Europe, at the same time that Emperor Charles had been visiting the royal courts of western Europe, a series of hammer-blows had transformed the frontiers. So that while the Field of the Cloth of Gold was being spread out over the meadows of Picardy, the great fortress of Belgrade, which had already withstood half a dozen sieges, was on the point of finally falling to an Ottoman army led by the young Sultan, Suleyman, son of Selim the Grim. And while Charles was showing off the golden treasures of the Aztecs to the astonished court in Windsor Castle in a clement English June, the Sultan of the Ottomans was on the point of capturing the other great stronghold of Christendom, the fortress city of Rhodes. Then came the news that the great breeding ground of Christian cavalry armies, the Kingdom of Hungary, was to be assaulted by the full force of the Ottoman Empire.

Francis I of France. The perfect Renaissance prince. (Louvre, Paris)

All in all, the pressures for some sort of decisive response from the idealistic young King-Emperor Charles V mounted day by day, year by year. From Germany came letters and delegations that begged Charles V and Francis I to put aside their rivalry and lead a crusade to come to the rescue of Belgrade. The brilliant Venetian Ambassador Giovanni Contarini greeted Charles V the moment he landed back in Spain, with a heartfelt plea that he would one day carry his victorious arms as far as Constantinople. The equally talented ambassador of the Pope, Baldassare Castiglione (the author of that elegiac description of the perfect year-long country-house party and book of manners, *The Courtier*) also pressed the same cause. He mixed it in with a new form of potent flattery, born from the renaissance in Latin learning, that sought to see the young Charles as a new Roman: 'Sacra Caesarea Majestatis', Holy Imperial Master. It was also a time when the young Emperor and old Pope could have banished all the suspicions of a thousand years of Guelf and Ghibelline rivalry (over the leadership of Western Christianity), and walked hand in hand through the states of Italy, as they had so often done literally in the walled gardens of Burgundy. For the reigning pope at this hour was Hadrian VI, none other than Charles's old tutor, Adrian of Utrecht, who had loyally served him as his regent in Spain during his three-year absence. Charles himself, writing in his own diary, felt animated by 'simple and vivid emotions of honour and fame' and confessed, 'I cannot but see and feel that time is passing, and I with it, and yet I would not like to go without performing some great action to serve as a monument to my name . . . what is lost today will not be found tomorrow and I have done nothing so far to cover myself with glory and cannot but blame myself for this long delay.'

So by 1523 the stage was set, and Charles was ready to direct his 'Great Project'. Armies were raised in Spain and Germany and even the English were to be involved.

But instead of unfurling the banners of Christ and standing at the head of Christendom and advancing to the aid of a stricken eastern Europe, the Holy Roman Emperor's Great Project had a narrower focus. Charles V intended to use this opportunity to stab King Francis I in the back, to encourage the English to take back Aquitaine, to support the treasonous rebellion of the Bourbon branch of the French royal family and therefore expand the Duchy of Burgundy and grab what he could of the French possessions in Italy.

The war raged across every frontier and province of western Europe. After three years of siege, march, sack and counter-siege, one February morning the two armies blundered towards each other outside another besieged city in northern Italy. The flower of French chivalry, led by their own young King Francis I, seemed to carry all before them. Meanwhile the Imperialist army of Charles V, led by a Neapolitan soldier of fortune, was almost on the point of deserting their camp in fury at the lack of pay from their distant master. But, under the inspired leadership of their commander, Pescara Ferrante, the tide was reversed, and in just two hours the Battle of Pavia turned into the total route of the French. Francis I was captured, and Charles V was elevated to the mastery of Europe. It was his twenty-fifth birthday, but he forbade noisy celebrations and feverishly planned a series of thanksgiving services and bouts of personal prayer. Though eternally grateful to his God, he proved himself less attentive to his fellow men. Pescara Ferrante, to whom he owed the victory of Pavia, had been so badly

The Battle of Pavia, 1525. From a contemporary German print.

wounded that he would die later that year from his wounds despite being nursed by his devoted wife, Vittoria Colonna (who in her widowhood became a friend to Michelangelo). Pescara Ferrante expired on the night of 2 December, still patiently waiting for any sign of thanks or reward from his Emperor.

King Francis was also surprised to find that his captor showed no interest in arranging a personal audience but instead made outrageous demands for the dismemberment of France through his courtiers. Neither Francis, nor his capable mother, who ruled as regent during his absence, could agree to listen to any of these demands. The peace that Francis was eventually forced to sign, that of Madrid in 1526, was immediately repudiated once he gained his liberty. And as the rest of Europe had now grown alarmed by the increase in Charles V's military power, he was able to go back to the battlefield with new allies.

In the east of Christendom, the chivalry of Hungary and Bohemia once again stood ready to oppose the advance of an Ottoman army. Sultan Suleyman himself led the Ottoman field army north of Belgrade into central Hungary. At the end of August the two armies confronted each other. The knights of Christendom, called into conclave by their monarch, King Louis II (also known as Ladislas or Lewis), King of Hungary and Bohemia, refused to wait for the expected reinforcements from Transylvania. Instead, at five o'clock on 29 August 1526, a silver helmet was placed on the head of their monarch, who was surrounded by his entire court: a sea of bishops, treasurers and great magnates in armour. The chief justice of the land, John Dragfy, claimed as his right of old the honour of carrying the national standard into battle on a white horse untouched by spurs. Around this armoured court clustered a thousand mailed knights arranged like a mobile bodyguard. As this crescent of glittering horseman advanced towards the enemy, they brought the entire fifteen-thousand-strong cavalry army of Hungary in their obedient wake. Then the drums and the horns were sounded, and they advanced from an obedient trot into a canter and lowered their lances towards the enemy. As they sped across the field of Mohacs they chanced all on one mad, brave charge at the disciplined ranks of the Ottoman army. No commander had been chosen, no tactical plans had been drawn up, while the actual decision to choose between death and glory seems to have been a response to the taunts of some Turkish outriders.

They were all doomed. Three hundred light cannon, supported by disciplined regiments of janissaries, lay primed and ready for them behind the screen of Turkish outriders. It was not a battle but slaughter, achieved with the very first round of cannon fire. The Hungarians still number as martyrs those who fell on the field of Mohacs. Among the dead were a thousand nobles, five hundred magnates, thirteen lords of the lands, seven bishops and one king, Louis II himself. To add to the slaughter that day, Sultan Suleyman gave the order that no prisoners were to be taken. As he would note in his diary for 31 August (writing dispassionately in the third person), 'The Sultan, seated on a golden throne, receives the homage of the viziers and beys; massacre of two thousand prisoners, the rain falls in torrents.'

As the ravens pecked their way over the corpses of the slaughtered Magyar and Moravian nobility, the perpetually fortunate Habsburg dynasty would once again benefit from the heroism of others. The crown that rolled off the head of King Louis of Hungary and Bohemia would be a symbol of lost sovereignty. For the next four hundred years after the catastrophe of Mohacs, the kingdom of Hungary would be ruled by German-speaking strangers, only recovering its independence after the Habsburg-ruled Austro-Hungarian Empire had been broken by the First World War of 1914–18.

On 2 September the Sultan ordered great trenches to be dug and wrote, 'twenty thousand Hungarian infantry and four thousand of their cavalry are buried', for he had ordered all the prisoners of war to be executed. In the immediate aftermath of Mohacs the army of Suleyman just marched their way through a fallen kingdom. On 10 September they poured through the defenceless gates of Buda, which fell to sack.

When Charles V's younger brother Ferdinand did advance his troops into the East, he made no move against the Ottoman invader but concentrated on mopping up his Christian neighbours. He arranged to have himself declared King of Bohemia in 1526 and denounced the Hungarians for choosing one of their own (the principal Magyar magnate, the Voivod of Transylvania, John Zapolya) rather than backing his own candidacy for this crown as well. The Habsburgs' good fortune was confirmed when, to the astonishment of all observers, the Ottoman army withdrew back to the south of the Danube – as if to indicate the limit of their western ambitions. After a year of watching behind their fortress walls Ferdinand ordered his soldiers to occupy this open terri-

tory and declare it his own. Such was the cautious beginning of the
Habsburgs' Austrian Empire in eastern Europe, and it was combined
with ever-more violent denunciations of the native-Hungarian monarch, who was stigmatised as an usurper. So much so that John Zapolya
(much encouraged by France) was forced to seek the friendship of the
Ottoman Empire.

Turks inspecting an abandoned cannon, Austrian-Hungarian frontier.
By Albert Durer between 1515 and 1518.

   The following year, 1527, Charles's Imperialist generals felt sufficiently free of exterior threats to marshal their forces to try to subdue
one of the independent cities of northern Italy. German soldiers
recruited by Georg Frundsberg would be marched down to join the
Duke of Ferrara's artillery and the Imperial garrisons already based in
Italy. But once again the Imperialist army grew querulous: unnoticed,
unpaid and ravaged by the ingratitude that had been shown to them
over the years. Sniffing imminent mutiny, General Frundsberg walked
down into the camp to have a heart-to-heart talk with his fellow German
soldiers, and in his customary bluff style asked his comrades of the bat-

tlefield to form a circle and talk out their troubles in confidence, man to man. But they had had enough with promises, and the disdain and neglect of their distant Emperor. Frundsberg's appeals to loyalty were drowned by one insistent reply, 'Give us the money we are owed' – and when his tone became threatening they silenced him by raising their lances.

This momentary crack in discipline would become a flood. The so-called Imperialist army had been largely recruited from German peasants (many with Lutheran sympathies) but all of a sudden they became aware of their own power and the weakness of their masters. Like a great herd of oxen that has long been used to being driven by an officious young herdsman, they looked for the first time at their oppressor and started to move at their own speed, in their own direction. They moved quickly. From their tented encampments in northern Italy they streamed rapidly down through the Tuscan hills, bypassing Siena and Florence, for they knew their enemy: they were marching on Rome. But it was not for them the Eternal City, a place of pilgrimage and absolution. Instead it was a place synonymous with the oppression of well-connected bankers, tax gatherers, absent bishops, corrupt foreigners and corpulent cardinals. By 5 May this revolutionary army had arrived before the gates of Rome.

The following day they stormed its walls. In their minds, the dogs of war had entered a cellar full of rats. The adventurer Charles du Bourbon was among the first to scale the summit of the walls and was shot down by a crossbow bolt – fired, so the traditions tell us, by the goldsmith Benvenuto Cellini – like Paris's bowshot that brought down great Achilles. The 'Saccio di Roma', the sack of Rome, lasted for months, though its most awful murder and rapine were concentrated in the first ten days. In the words of a contemporary witness, 'We have seen practised upon priests tortures from which a victorious Carthaginian or Turk indisputably would have abstained.' Among the observers of these ten days of rape, torture and extortion were the Pope and thirteen cardinals, sheltering behind the battlements of Rome's Castel San Angelo. By mid-June the troops, enriched by plunder and the ransoming of hostages and glutted by power, were in a more tractable mood. Many drifted north back to their German homeland, while others were slowly marshalled back into camps. Through the breakdown in order, the half-buried corpses helped to encourage a further catastrophe, as the plague swept through both survivors and soldiers that September. As the returning soldiers spread the word about what had happened in Rome, a new confidence in political action reanimated the German people. The Hanseatic port-city of Lübeck turned itself into a radical democracy just two years later, while the Anabaptist citizens of Münster, who referred to themselves as the Children of God, attempted to create a heaven on earth.

By 1528 the struggle between Francis I and Charles V had swung in favour of France. The Imperialist army had been driven behind the walls of Naples and its navy had been virtually destroyed in a desperate attempt to guard the supply ships that were bringing in Sicilian corn to the blockaded city of Naples. The ridiculous circular nature of the rivalry between Francis I and Charles V was, however, once again to be exposed. For now that the wheel of fortune had lurched forward and raised France up, her confederacy of Italian allies (Florence, Milan, Genoa and the papacy) grew secretly alarmed at her re-emergent ambitions. The annexation by France of some border towns on the Ligurian coast (which Genoa claimed to be within her traditional sphere of influence) proved to be the decisive act. It also did not help that France had proved incapable of paying its debts to its subcontracted Genoese allies, whose navy had just proved so decisive in the bay of Naples. So, on 4 July 1528, the admiral in charge of the Genoese fleet changed sides. Andrea Doria's defection to the cause of Charles V reversed the balance of power overnight, isolating the French army in Italy and reconfirming Spanish control over Sicily, Sardinia and Naples.

A truce was called between the two adversaries, greatly assisted by the energetic diplomacy of the Women of the Royal Courts, especially Francis I's mother (Louise of Savoy) and Charles V's aunt (Margaret of Austria) and the near-bankruptcy of both monarchs, so that the 'Ladies' Peace' of Cambrai could be signed with much emotion in 1529. In his inimitably gallant style Francis I concluded the peace-making process by offering to serve as commander of the vanguard in a great crusade to be led by Emperor Charles V. Francis sketched out a happy daydream of how this pan-European force would number sixty thousand men, equipped with the very latest artillery and protected by the finest cavalry. But he also concluded this flurry of speculative crusade-making with the deep regret that it was, alas, impossible, for he had no money and already owed the English too much.

This last explanation was at least true, for both monarchs had consumed every last source of available funds, otherwise they would never have signed a peace treaty together. Yet, despite the debacle of the Genoese defection, two factors meant that in 1529 the wind stood very fair for the future diplomacy of France. First, the understanding between Henry VIII of England and Charles V was on the point of being totally wrecked by the prospect of Henry divorcing Catherine of Aragon. Charles, ever loyal to the extended family which had supported him as a child in the absence of parents, had already written to his wife, asking her to summon 'theologians, lawyers and men of learning from the universities with all care and activity' to defend the honour of his aunt, Queen Catherine of England.[2] The second piece of good fortune for France was that Germany was about to split asunder between Protestants and Catholics. For, that very April, the Chancellor of Saxony had framed a 'Protestation' that 'In matters concerning God's honour and the salvation of our souls, each man has the right to stand alone and present his true account before God. On the last day no man will be able to take shelter behind the power of another, be it small or great', which, for all the sincerity of its language, would help break apart the very fragile unity of Germany for the next three hundred years.

In the immediate aftermath of the defection of Genoa, France had need of a new ally if it was to combat the power of Charles V. The year of 1529 identified the only military ally that could possibly make a difference in the coming struggle. For in the summer of 1529, an army had pushed west and besieged the city of Vienna. Although the Ottoman siege of Vienna is one of those flashpoints of European consciousness — the very image of the enemy at the gates sits beside those of the Mongol horde and Attila the Hun — it was a much less dramatic event at the time. The Ottoman attack was part of well-established and tactically logical process, for Vienna sits on the banks of the broad Danube, which provided the only easy route across eastern Europe for any army equipped with siege weapons. The Ottoman army was well drilled for this sort of campaign, which was indeed part of the annual ritual of their state. Troops would assemble at the great gathering grounds outside Istanbul and then march north-west along the old Roman roads to the banks of the Danube, where were waiting the fleets of river boats which could then supply the army with all the food, munitions and transport of heavy ordnance that it required. Indeed all the notable battles fought out between the Ottoman Empire and Christendom over the previous hundred years – be it at Mohacs, Nicopolis or Belgrade – had taken place along the banks of the Danube.

Although it may be doubted that Francis and his French court ever honestly wished that Vienna would be sacked by the Ottomans, they must have been hugely satisfied at the diplomatic muddle that subsequently befell Charles V. For although his role as Holy Roman Emperor meant that he must take a lead in the defence of Vienna, which stood on the far-eastern edge of the empire, it also meant that he was unable to discipline the Lutheran princes while he needed their help to repel the Turkish invasion. To add another twist to the conundrum, the Habsburg lands of the Emperor and his brother were scattered over Austria and stood like a bulwark between the Ottoman Empire and the rest of Germany. But, despite the gravity of the Ottoman siege of Vienna, Charles V did not exactly rush to defend this endangered frontier himself. Instead the campaigning season of 1529 was dedicated to processing through Italy so that he could formally have the iron crown of Lombardy bestowed upon his head in Bologna. Most of 1530 was consumed with diplomatic talks with various German princes (and his bankers) at Augsburg. A grand reunion of the Order of the Golden Fleece in Ghent, the old capital of the Dukes of Burgundy, was staged in 1531. It wasn't quite as magnificent as the Fête du Faisan of his ducal forefathers but all the absent stalls were filled by the creation of new knights. So it was not until early summer of that year that Charles V was free to ride out from Ghent, escorted by 150 knights, to lead an envisaged German army into the east. But while the Emperor and the princes talked more about this event, first at Regensburg and then at Nuremberg, the campaigning season ebbed away.

Instead military action was concentrated upon a little-celebrated engagement in western Hungary. The Ottoman army, having already collected the keys of sixteen fortified castles that year, were advancing upon the artillery fortress of Koszeg (Guns in German). But, instead of evacuating his position, Nicolas Jurisics, a Hungarian officer in charge of just twenty-eight hussars and ten cuirassiers, decided to hold his ground. Six hundred refugees were seeking protection within its walls, so he decided to arm these peasants and hold the line of its walls. They held out for three critical weeks, 7–28 August, before they were overwhelmed. The Ottoman commander then realised that no useful advance could be made with what was left of the campaign season. To add to this conviction, he had just received news that Charles V's new ally, the Genoese admiral Andrea Doria, had gone on the offensive in the Adriatic and seized the fortresses of Patras and Castelnuovo from the Ottomans, creating a distant threat to their supply lines.

There was, however, to be a further clash of arms that year, at Fernitz in Austria. German troops stumbled upon the Ottoman rearguard on 13 September, but after an exchange of fire they could not be persuaded to harry the Ottomans any further. Even less so after the enemy withdrew beyond the frontiers of the Holy Roman Empire into Hungary. Charles V finally entered Vienna on 23 September. There he advised his younger brother, Archduke Ferdinand, who ruled the Habsburg lands in Austria, to make peace with the grand vizier of the Ottoman Empire 'at any price'. Thus was Vienna defended by her Holy Roman Emperor, some four years after the Ottomans had abandoned their siege.

On 22 June 1533 a peace was agreed between the Austrian court of Archduke Ferdinand and the Ottoman Empire. The Habsburgs had been forced to dispatch a delegation to Istanbul and the Ottoman ministers had much pleasure in teasing the Habsburg officials during the negotiations, revealing just how well informed they were of everything that went on in Europe. They were openly scornful of Emperor Charles V's impotence against both the Protestants on one side and the Pope on the other. They also delighted to explain how clever France had been in outflanking the Emperor's plans for a new Holy League in Italy by marrying the younger brother of the Dauphin (the crown prince) to Catherine of Medici, who just happened to be the niece of Pope Clement. Then there was the matter of Henry VIII's formal excommunication by the Pope, which had broken asunder the ancient understanding between the Duchy of Burgundy and England. It was also always amusing to talk to any Habsburg embassy about Wittelsbach Bavaria. It was no secret that this ancient dynasty loathed the (comparatively) upstart Habsburgs. The Ottoman viziers also liked to make the Habsburg ambassadors uneasy by confidentially hinting that they were prepared 'to make peace with Ferdinand but not with Charles'. This was their one mistake, for whatever else one might like to throw at the Habsburgs, they never lacked family loyalty. Nor was there any mistaking who stood at the head of the house.

Charles V had advised his brother Ferdinand to make peace with Turkey on the Austrian borderlands for two very good reasons. It would allow him to be much tougher with the Lutheran princes when it came to the next round of discussions. It would also allow him to concentrate his resources and attack the Ottoman Empire where it mattered: on the Mediterranean shore.

The French court had come to a similar conclusion. Using the services of one of the many talented exiles who had been driven out of Spain, Rincon, they had opened talks with the Ottoman court back in 1528. An understanding of mutual interest had been made in 1532, leading to an exchange of formal embassies three years later and a treaty of alliance in 1536. Before this, King Francis I had come to an arrangement with Muslim corsair captains of North Africa, allowing them to use such French ports as Toulon and Marseilles as safe havens. Such a public military alliance between France and the Ottoman Empire brought the King a degree of notoriety which still echoes to this day. From a humanist perspective, it can be celebrated as one of the critical dates in which the notion of a christian-wide crusade was finally buried. A landmark treaty in which the rational interests of politics and trade at last triumph over any concept of an inherent clash between civilisations. The cultivated society of France certainly took to the Ottoman embassy with a passion. The fashion for things Turkish was even permitted to affect that sense for which France has always held the greatest respect. For whether in truth or in historical fantasy, the excellence of French cuisine is credited to the influence of the first Ottoman cooks arriving in the sixteenth century, aided by the experiences of returning French ambassadors from Istanbul. It was said to be the enlightened patronage of Francis I's mistress, the cosmopolitan Diana of Poitiers, which encouraged the rapid spread of the science of the Ottoman kitchen. It is a curious reflection on national myths that in the Austrian imagination such recognisable symbols of Turkish influence as coffee and a crescent of pastry is claimed to have entered the national gut though the proximity of an Ottoman siege, while in France it comes as the gift of a foreign embassy popularised by a monarch's mistress.

The Habsburgs tried to make political capital out of France's treaty with the Ottomans but they were in no position to blacken their French enemies for initiating alliances with the Muslim 'enemy'. They had been energetically pursuing their own *realpolitik* for some years, though their attempts to forge a military alliance with Persia had just been foiled. For in May 1530 the Ottoman and Safavid dynasties had signed a peace. It was a valuable achievement for both courts. The Safavid Shah was free to turn his attention to his enemies in Khorassan (the frontier province of eastern Persia where it meets Afghanistan), while for the Ottomans it freed them from the anxiety of waging a war on two fronts. They would instead be able to commit themselves fully to the testing struggle ahead, the battle for the control of the Mediterranean.

The opening rounds of this battle could already be heard. In the spring of 1530, after his success against Patras the previous year, Charles V asked Andrea Doria to clear Cherchel, a port west of Algiers, of the pirate fleet operating from its harbour. Then, in 1531, Alvaro de Bazan was commanded to seize control of the port that served the old Zayyanid capital city of Tlemcen in western Algeria.

At the same time Charles V planted an offensive force on the maritime frontiers of his empire. The most easterly posts that his viceroys controlled, the North African harbour-city of Tripoli in western Libya, and two strategic islands due south of Sicily, Malta and Gozo, were handed over to the command of the Knights of St John of the Hospital of Jerusalem. The order had been homeless since it had evacuated Rhodes in 1520, and though reluctant to take charge of such poor and difficult frontier territories, it had no choice. Prolonged failure to take up a military position would have undermined the existence of the order and led to its eventual suppression. The example of the fall of the Templars was ever to mind, as was the recent annexation of the Spanish Crusading Orders by the crown.

In the spring of 1533 Charles V finally returned to Spain. It is clear from the orders that he posted elsewhere in Europe (ordering his ambassadors in France and England to be compliant, and that his brother should try the unenviable task of trying to befriend Bavaria and not kick up a fuss about the loss of their ancestral homeland at Württemberg) that his mind was already focusing on some great action in the Mediterranean. Was this the fulfilment of all those childhood dreams of a Duke of Burgundy leading a crusade? Was it a desire to gain some credence in the eyes of the great Spanish nobles and the Cortes of his Spanish kingdoms? Had he realised that in order to aspire to the great fame won by his grandparents, Isabella and Ferdinand, he would have to achieve something to stand beside their conquest of Granada? Or was he just trying to fulfil his role as the paternal king of his people and protect them from the ravages of the North African-based corsairs? Or did he just wish, having witnessed the success of the maritime campaigns of his new ally, Admiral Andrea Doria, to embark on a similar winning adventure? Or did his erudite Italian chancellor Gattinara finally succeed in transforming Charles's chaotic scattering of feudal inheritances into an intellectual blueprint for the restoration of a united Europe, a renewed Roman Empire?

Given the complex pattern of events and expectations that crowded in upon Charles V, it was a fusion of many such influences. But one must not overlook the influence of love and Portugal. Charles was always cripplingly aware of the potential for madness in his family through over-heated emotional engagement but his marriage to Isabella, the Infanta of Portugal,[3] seems to have broken down his carefully constructed reserve. They had been married in an Andalusian spring, a halcyon period of imagined resolution for Charles just a year after the great victory over the French at Pavia. They had met for the first time on the very morning of their marriage in the great Mosque-Cathedral of Seville, but the tumultuous welcome that the city had freely offered up to the delicate twenty-three-year-old Portuguese princess Dona Isabella would never be forgotten by either of them.

All spring and into the sultry heat of summer, the royal couple continued their progression through the enchanted landscape of the Moors, passing slowly from riotous Seville to the magnificence of Cordoba[4] and then finally Granada. In the environment of the royal Alhambra Palace, the timid, reserved nature of the two was merged into a trusting love. It no doubt helped that they were both very devout and thought nothing of rising from their beds on the evening after their wedding to thank God by hearing mass together. Sandwiched in between the Alhambra's most characteristic chambers, the Court of Lions, the Tower of the Ambassadors and the Court of the Myrtles you can still find the nest of cramped little chambers that were added to the palace as their honeymoon apartment. In later years, burdened by a large court, they would lodge in the monastery of San Jeronimo while that exquisite counterfoil, that disciplined marble Renaissance courtyard, a Doric circle inserted into an Ionic square, was being raised.[5] 'Profound and tender was the love he learned to feel for his frail, feminine little Empress.' He may also have desired to one day win her approval by acting like one of the crusading kings of recent Portuguese history. It may be an irrelevant detail, but I have always thought it was a telling act that their 'honeymoon' apartments within the Alhambra would later be hung with tapestries and frescoes that recounted Charles's adventures in North Africa, in action during one of the Last Crusades.

In 1529 Charles brushed aside the opposition of many of his most trusted officials and officially received the reprobate conqueror of Mexico, Hernan Cortes, at his court in Toledo. Cortes was honoured, ennobled and made into a respected figure at the Emperor's court. But Charles was no fool. He had carefully digested the reports from his officials about the man's past behaviour and quietly determined that he should never be allowed to return to the Americas. The conquered territories would be brought under control by more obedient servants. The old Aztec Empire, along with its allies, tribal opponents and neighbours, was to be ruled as the province of New Spain. Additional seats of government were established on the coasts of Panama and Guatemala, while the Caribbean islands were ruled from Columbus's first foundation of San Domingo. A daughter settlement of San Domingo soon emerged on the northern shore of the lagoon of Maracaibo. The bustle of merchants and the wooden piles driven into the muddy shore to support the commercial warehouses (and in imitation of the native houses) irresistibly suggested a Little Venice and soon earned the affectionate nickname of Venezuela. Although the city of Seville (then located within the province of New Castile) had secured a trading monopoly with the Americas, it is clear from the surviving records that it was not just Castilians who were employed to exploit this vast new commercial horizon.

Who would have thought that the landlocked city of Augsburg (which sits pretty much plum in the centre of Germany) would be among the first into this new market? But as early as 1528 the Welser family of merchant bankers from Augsburg had a signed concession and had acquired their own portion of dockyard space along the muddy banks of the Guadalquivir at Seville. They had also recruited twenty-four expert miners from the famous silver mines in the Joachimstal valley (on the border between Saxony and Bohemia), who were sent out to South America and assisted by a formidable workforce of four thousand slaves freshly brought in from West Africa. To protect their financial investment from any political risk, the Welser family decided to include Charles V's influential secretary of state, the Andalusian Francisco de los Cobos, as a minority shareholder of their enterprise. They employed agents of proven worth, men such as Heinrich Ehinger, who had already shown his mettle by buying up a large chunk of the lucrative cargo of spices that came into Spain when the one surviving ship of Magellan's round-the-world expedition docked in 1523. Another Ehinger brother was sent to attend the viceroy's court at San Domingo as the Welser agent and proved to be such a useful man of parts that – when it was decided that Venezuela should become a province on its own – he was appointed the first governor.

The energy of this first generation of emigrants is still astonishing to behold. One of the officials that Cortes had so memorably slighted, the deputy governor Panfilo Narvaez,[6] would later prove an equal in fortitude to any of the more celebrated conquistadors. His expedition, which explored the vast extent of the shoreline of northern Mexico, Texas, Mississippi and Alabama right round to Florida, was on one level a catastrophe. Of the original expeditionary force, only three men would limp back, having survived 'naked among the Indians like one of them', yet this makes this six-year odyssey all the more of an astonishing personal achievement.

The most extraordinary adventure was yet to come, though the Spanish court would be spared the truth about an emperor who was kidnapped, ransomed and then burned alive by a ruthless band of marauders. For the real story of how a band of armed men had murdered the Inca Emperor Atahualpa in the spring of 1533 would not fully emerge for another decade. This story of cold-blooded and calculating wickedness, of dogged determination and reckless, bold bravery is like a page ripped from mythology. That they were only 180 strong, with just twenty-seven horses under the command of a wizened sixty-year-old, only intensifies the diabolical nature of the enterprise. But, like many a robber band, they were destined to fall out among themselves, and the violent civil war they would fight over the ruins of the Inca empire ended with the murder of the conquistador Francisco Pizarro in 1541. By this time, however, the vast treasure that had been solemnly brought back by Pizarro's younger brother, Hernando, and conveyed to the astonished Spanish court at Catalayud in Old Castile in 1535, had done its work. Pizarro was saluted as a hero, not a brigand.

In a mirror to Spain, with its different kingdoms and history of conquests, the new territory would be christened 'New Granada'. Like that of the inhabitants of Old Granada, the suffering of the conquest would be but a foretaste of horrors to come. The old Inca Empire would be transformed into a slave state, whose original inhabitants would be worked to death in order to export a river of millions upon millions of silver coins to the docks of Seville. It is now known that the great financial presence of Charles V's court, Francisco de los Cobos, skimmed off at least a tenth of this flow before he neatly remitted it to the treasury. Roughly a tenth was spent on fortifications to defend the coast, a tenth on the navy, a tenth on upholding the court and a tenth on servicing the debt. The rest, at least half this treasure, was spent on the Emperor's wars, topped up by new rounds of borrowing. That a new province of this empire – Venezuela – had been immediately leased off as a territory to be exploited by some of the Emperor's German bankers provides a powerful, prophetic and haunting image of how South America would be treated by its new masters for the next four hundred years.

10

The Ottoman Golden Age

Suleyman the Magnificent and the Five Victories:
Belgrade, Rhodes, Mohacs, Tabriz and Baghdad, 1520–
36

> History is little more than the register of the crimes, follies and
> misfortunes of mankind.
>
> Gibbon, *Decline and Fall of the Roman Empire*

The Holy Roman Emperor Charles V personally led two great crusading armies across the waters of the Mediterranean. Yet the career of his Ottoman rival, Suleyman the Magnificent, would prove just as epic, with its own string of military victories. In 1520 Prince Suleyman had succeeded to the throne of the Ottoman Empire, whose borders had been almost doubled in size by the wars fought by his father, Selim the Grim. After his father's vicious and contentious series of campaigns against all his Muslim neighbours, be they the Turks of eastern Anatolia, the Shiite Safavids of Persia, the Mamelukes of Syria and Egypt or that internal enemy of the Ottoman Empire, the Kizilbas, it was a highly popular move to once again lead the army west against the Christians. The new Sultan would be stepping back into the familiar role of the House of Ottoman by battling it out against the traditional enemy on his western frontier.

The young Sultan's first campaign, in 1521, was a triumph. First the fortress of Shabatz was stormed and then he brought his army up against the Hungarian and Serbian-held fortress of Belgrade. Even his most acclaimed ancestors, from Murat II to Mehmet the Conqueror, had failed before these walls. Suleyman was fortunate that year. The two commanders of the seven-thousand-strong Christian garrison had left their posts in order to press for overdue payments due from the Hungarian court at Buda. In their absence a dispute broke out between the Serbian and Hungarian regiments within the garrison of Belgrade which seems to have caused one of the deputy-governors to go over to the Ottoman camp. After a two-month siege the fortress was stormed in August. To mark this victory Suleyman allowed himself the dignity of full manhood and grew a beard.

While the army was tied up in Serbia, one of his father's old governors rebelled and attempted to establish himself as the independent Sultan of Egypt. All at once the young Sultan was faced with war on two fronts, and a third threatened to erupt when the rebels in Egypt tried to enlist the Knights of St John in Rhodes to their cause. Rhodes stood halfway between Istanbul and Cairo as well as midway between Syria and Greece. It pressed like a thumb on the twin arteries of Ottoman communication and maritime commerce. It might look small on the charts, especially compared with other islands in the region, such as Christian-ruled Cyprus and Crete, but these were both dominated by Venice, which in the interests of its Levant trade could always be relied upon to keep the peace. By contrast, the Knights of St John in Rhodes had to be seen to be constantly at war to fulfil their crusading mission. In this period this meant raiding the harbours and plundering the shipping on the nearby Turkish coast, as well as seizing pilgrims en route for Mecca. If the island fell, the young Sultan would also have succeeded in fulfilling one of his illustrious great-grandfather's unfinished projects. By the winter of 1521 the Venetian envoy in Istanbul was reporting that an invasion fleet was clearly being prepared. Although disinformation was released that its likely target was Otranto, this was most unlikely. A Turkish invasion of Italy might be the one thing that would succeed in embarrassing Charles V and Francis I into refraining from their relentless rivalry across the breadth of Europe, a rivalry that was otherwise so convenient to Ottoman interests.

The Knights of St John were in no doubt about the young Sultan's intentions. They redoubled their energies, deepening Rhodes's moats and strengthening its walls, and stockpiling food and munitions. Their agents recruited mercenaries, though the wars between Charles V and

Francis I meant that most of the available soldiers were already pledged to one master or another. The Knights' outlying strongholds on the island, the ancient towns of Lindos and Pheraklos, which look east towards the Turkish mainland, were also reinforced, as was Monolithos, perched alone on the mountainous west coast.

The island of Rhodes, with the fortress city of the Knights of St John
of the Hospital of Jerusalem. Drawn for Sultan Suleyman
by Piri Reis between 1524 and 1528.

That summer the sea between Marmaris and Rhodes began to fill with hundreds of Turkish sails and it was clear that only a miracle could save the Knights from this armada. But Suleyman had already closed most of the possibilities, for he had made peace on the eastern frontier with Persia and on the west with Venice. By the end of June 1522 the first Ottoman regiments had begun to disembark on the shores of Rhodes.

Suleyman's second vizier, who was also his son-in-law, Mustapha Pasha, organised the first round of the siege. The Ottomans had learned from the experiences of 1480. No bloody marine assaults were attempted by ship or pontoon and the activity of the navy was restricted to blockading the harbour. Instead, right from the first week of the siege, the land-based Ottoman artillery pounded away at the land walls. These had been completely restructured since the first siege and the subsequent earthquake. The annual pension sent by Sultan Bayezid to the Knights to secure the neutrality of Prince Cem had been poured into defensive stone and mortar designed by a leading military engineer, Fabrizio del Carretto. Wide moats were designed to keep the besieging artillery at a distance while their impressive depth discouraged the placing of underground mines. Angled counterscarps were placed to absorb the impact of an artillery bombardment, while protruding bastions had been built with thick enough foundations to enable the Knights to mount effective counter-fire from the summits of the towers and portals in the basements. When the Turks tried their first two assaults against the positions guarded by the Tongue of England (each sector of the walls was defended by one of the old crusading nations of Europe) they were cut down in their hundreds by the angled crossfire unleashed from every level of the bastions.

In late July the Sultan arrived with reinforcements and began to directly supervise the operations. After another blistering, month-long bombardment a general attack was mounted at dawn on 24 September. It was towards the end of the traditional sailing season. In the bitter hand-to-hand fighting of that day the tower at the centre of the section of the city wall, defended by the Knights of the Tongue of Spain, changed hands twice. At dusk it was the red cross of the Knights that still buckled in the evening wind. The corpses of thousands of young warriors filled the trenches and some 350 Christians (from a total force of around seven thousand defenders) would never fight again. As a measure of his increasing concern that there were enough men fit to take their place on the walls, the Grand Master of the Knights sent out signals to evacuate the outposts of the order, including their proud castles on Kos and at Petrumi (Bodrum), so that Rhodes would be reinforced. Whether it was true, or just a paranoid product of a siege, the Grand Chancellor of the Knights, Andrea d'Amaral, was accused of treasonable reports to the Sultan. He and his Albanian manservant were executed on 5 November.

Despite the approach of winter the Sultan decided not to strike camp, and relying on the frequent and confidential reports of his agents and ambassadors, took the colossal gamble of continuing the siege. Not that the generally mild winter of Rhodes threatened his army. It was more that he would be powerless to respond to an insurrection or rebellion elsewhere if the seas were made unnavigable by storms. The fact that his father had suffered no male Ottoman princes to survive, and that Shah Ismail was known to be drawing towards the end of his life, must have played a part in Suleyman's calculations. There were rumblings about a joint rescue plan being mounted by the Pope and the Emperor, but once again it proved to be just a volley of words. Towards the end of November a second attack was launched and once again repelled. But the Ottomans knew that if they could maintain the blockade (already five months old), Rhodes would eventually fall.

Suleyman wooed the largely Greek civil population with peace proposals shot into the city on blind arrows. Freedom of religion and residence for the Orthodox was promised in exchange for a peaceful surrender. If the walls had to be stormed, the city would be sacked. The Metropolitan was persuaded that he must talk to the Grand Master and explain that his people, increasingly enfeebled by their wounds and starvation rations, were on the point of breaking. He alone could risk the anger of the Grand Master, who knew that the Knights, just three hundred strong at the start of the siege, could never hope to stand alone. In addition they were now critically short of powder and shot. A truce was declared for three days, but when the Knights asked for some guarantee other than the Sultan's word, Suleyman at once ordered a resumption of the siege. It became clear that the city's defences were at breaking point. So, on 22 December, a delegation filed its way out through the land gates and across the siege lines to the tented compound of the Sultan. Here they begged to accept his proposals and placed complete trust in his word.

The terms given by Suleyman were astonishingly mild. The Knights had twelve days to quit the city of Rhodes and were permitted to take their weapons, ships and banners with them. The Orthodox Greek citizens had three years to make up their minds if they wished to become Ottoman citizens or refugees. No church would be desecrated and there would be a tax holiday for five years. It was an incredibly peaceful culmination to a siege that was rumoured to have destroyed a quarter of the forces of both the defenders and the attackers. It is true that the city's streets were looted on Christmas Eve and Christmas Day, but it was not given over to the full appalling horrors of a sack. On New Year's Day all the Knights and about three-quarters of the surviving citizens of Rhodes embarked at dawn and set sail for Crete.

Suleyman proved many things with this peace. He had achieved absolute command over his army and he had also showed that Christians need not fear becoming citizens of the Ottoman state. At later sieges and in battles, this example of the Sultan who kept his word and offered generous peace terms would bear abundant fruit. But his army was annoyed at being denied the sack of a city and it is difficult to understand quite why he let the Knights of St John sail off into the west to fight another day. For this was an enemy he surely knew he would have to fight again. Perhaps he had already become aware that a second revolt was about to break out in Egypt.

Rebellion in Egypt caused Suleyman to call a halt to all other military operations for the coming year and a half. To crush the revolt he sent the man he trusted most implicitly in all the world, Ibrahim Pasha. Ibrahim had come into Suleyman's life as a young slave page-boy when he himself was the same age. While Suleyman had served as a provincial governor for his grandfather Bayezid II, they had become inseparable companions, sharing meals and illegal drinking sessions. Ibrahim slept across the threshold of the prince's door as his night-time bodyguard. When Suleyman became Sultan he promoted his page-boy companion to be chief of the royal bedchamber, then grand vizier of his empire. He gave him dignities, wealth and a splendid palace which overlooked the old Byzantine circus track in the heart of Istanbul, close to his own. The following year Ibrahim was given an Osmanli princess (Suleyman's sister Hadice) and a fifteen-day-long celebration was held where, the Turkish historian Ibrahim Pecevi (1572–1650) recorded, 'spread before the eyes was such an abundance and merriment as had never before been observed in the wedding of a princess'.

It was a bizarre, fairy-tale ascent to power for a humble Greek boy from a Venetian city who had been scooped up by a corsair galley while out fishing. Ibrahim, who had been given to the palace by these corsairs, must have been recognised for his abilities and, as well as learning the precepts of Islam, was taught many languages and skills.

In the wake of the successful conquest of Rhodes, Ibrahim Pasha

travelled to Egypt in the ship of one of the most promising young captains in the Ottoman navy. Eight years earlier Piri Reis had been in
charge of the naval squadron that had shadowed Sultan Selim's initial
conquest of Egypt. He knew every inch of the coast, as those who have
studied his beautiful maps of the Mediterranean know all too well. As
well as these exquisite charts, he had prepared for his master a complete
summary of the importance of a navy entitled *Kitab-i-Bahriyye* ('The
Book of Those Who Sail the Seas'). This was designed as an explanatory
companion to his charts but it was also an acute summary of the strategic situation at the time. During this voyage Piri Reis had time to
explain the state of play to grand vizier Ibrahim, who became a keen
devotee of a forward naval policy. Ibrahim even got Piri Reis to create
an updated addendum which he was able to bring back to show
Suleyman on his return. Together they gave orders for the creation of a
strong Egyptian squadron that would be able to defend the Red Sea.
There was even a five-year-plan sketched out to build up the fleet to
sufficient strength to contest the control of the Indian Ocean. It was
imagined that by 1531 this Red Sea fleet would be strong enough to
take on the Portuguese. In conjunction with other Sunni Muslim trading powers, such as the Sultanate of Gujarat, they would expel the
Portuguese Crusaders from their naval bases at Ormuz, Goa and
Socotra. This would restore the full flow of trade and customs revenue
from India back to the Levant and it would also break up the chance of
an alliance between the Christian Portuguese and Shiite Persia. It was a
grand vision and could have had enormously beneficial consequences
for the Ottoman Empire and the entire Middle East had Suleyman
dedicated the resources, zeal and men of imagination to fulfil it.

When Ibrahim returned to his master he left behind in Egypt a legal
code to govern the region and protect it from the abuses of the colonels
of the army of occupation. The administration in Egypt had also been
primed to watch over the security of the Red Sea and Hejaz coast and
the safety of the route of the Haj. All this had been achieved while yet
arranging for a surplus of revenue to be forwarded to the Sultan at
Istanbul.

Once back in Istanbul, Ibrahim Pasha immediately set about organising a military campaign for the following spring. The old eastern
enemy of the Ottoman Empire was no more, for Shah Ismail had just
died. A ten-year-old prince had succeeded him on the Persian throne.

Ottoman diplomats had been busy creating useful understandings with other Muslim Sunni states in this part of the world, such as the Mughals in Afghanistan and India and the Uzbeks in Central Asia. They all shared a desire to contain the threat to their thrones which a dynamic Shiite state in Persia represented. So the Ottoman court could be quietly optimistic that the empire would not be threatened by Persia for a number of years, and this allowed Suleyman and his vizier to once again look to the western frontier.

Thus it was that, in 1526, the traditional invasion road that led into the Balkans was taken once again. Most such annual campaigns had culminated in the siege of some Danubian fortress town, but this year was to be different. For the Hungarian army composed of King Louis II, his bishops, magnates, nobles and knights, had advanced to give battle. At five in the afternoon a feint by Turkish cavalry drew a counter-attack from the massed ranks of heavily armoured Magyar nobles. The Turkish light cavalry then opened their ranks, so that the Hungarian knights charged straight into a prepared line of some three hundred Ottoman cannon, lined hub to hub, backed by several thousand janissaries. A large portion of the Magyar cavalry fell at the first cannonade. Within two hours the fighting was over. The Hungarian ruling class, all mounted up and clad in obsolete armour, was blown apart. It need not have happened, for the Hungarians were on the point of being reinforced by two experienced allies. Peter Frankopan was leading to their aid an army recruited from Croatia and Slovenia, as was John Zapolya, who was marching down from Transylvania.

The political vacuum caused by the slaughter of the Hungarian nobility on the field of Mohacs would take some six years to sort itself out. The Habsburg Archduke Ferdinand (Charles V's younger brother) and Sultan Suleyman each tried to absorb chunks of the ancient kingdom of the Magyars. This dispute over Hungary would culminate in the Ottoman siege of Vienna, which still echoes through the European subconscious, although the essential truth was that the two opponents were geographically too far apart to do each other much damage. It took the Ottoman army four months to march from Istanbul to Vienna in 1529, so there were only two weeks left for the actual siege. When you compare this with the six months that it took the Ottomans to reduce the city of Rhodes, the seriousness of the attack on Vienna is put in perspective. There was, however, another time for the Ottomans to show the Austrians how efficient they were as an army of engineers. The siege trenches were cut in double-quick time and artillery batteries established, but then it was time to pack up tools and return home. Nor was there any great disparity in armaments or siege-craft between the two sides. If anything, the Germans alone had a slight technical edge over the Ottoman janissaries, for they were the acknowledged world leaders in mining and smelting.

Archduke Ferdinand was, however, able to transform the Turkish threat against Vienna into a political godsend. Although the history of Austria and the Habsburg dynasty might now be thought of as inseparable, this was not always so. The origin of the Habsburgs was not in the Austrian Alps but in the upper valley of the Rhine (in the southwest corner of Germany that borders modern Switzerland and Alsace), but the Turkish threat of 1529 gave them the opportunity to forge a unitary kingdom out of the jumble of lands they had long possessed in the east. This patchwork of counties, bishoprics and hereditary duchies, within Tyrol, Styria, Carinthia and the Windish Mark, would be transformed into the Osterreich ('Eastern Kingdom'), or Austria. This was just what the Dukes of Burgundy had tried to achieve in western Europe, but despite centuries of effort had failed. And this was not all. The death of King Louis II at the Battle of Mohacs allowed Archduke Ferdinand to aspire to two other crowns, those of Hungary and Bohemia. For a passed-over second son, Ferdinand was doing well. But perhaps it is no surprise, for he was brought up in the court of his grandfather, Ferdinand of Aragon, one of Europe's most brilliant, opportunistic, cynical and successful monarchs.

There were deeper currents at play which help explain the meltdown of Hungarian military strength at Mohacs. For Hungary was at war with itself. Just twelve years before Mohacs, in 1514, a crusade had been summoned by an ambitious Hungarian archbishop. Once again, just as in the days of Janos Hunyadi, the nobility showed no interest. Leadership passed into the hands of George Dozsa, a poor Transylvanian gentleman. His call brought a response from the peasants, who had soon formed a massive forty-thousand-strong crusading army which rapidly turned radical, purging the land of the hated class of idle nobles, who were exempt from every form of tax, tithe and labour. The Hungarian nobles had armed themselves to meet this threat to their existence and lifestyle. In a brief but terrifyingly violent civil war that left fifty thousand dead on the two sides they reasserted their military control over the nation. Dozsa and his inner council of peasant commanders were punished in a manner which was designed not to be easily forgotten. They were all starved for fourteen days in solitary confinement. Then Dozsa was killed in a manner befitting a peasant king. He was placed on a red-hot iron throne, a heated crown was then hammered on to his skull and a red-hot sceptre pushed into his lap. His starving confederates were then let out of their cells and tore his charred flesh from his bones to assuage their desperate hunger.

Dozsa's brutal execution would find its legal equivalent in the Tripartite Code that was made law that winter at the Diet of Nobles. This declared that the Hungarian peasants had 'forfeited their liberty and become subject to their landlords in unconditional and perpetual servitude'. The peasant had no right over his master's land save bare compensation for his labour. Every species of property was judged to belong to the landlord and the peasant was to be denied the right to ever invoke justice or law against a noble. It has been called 'the most inhuman measure in European history, dictated by a savage vindictiveness'. So when the Hungarian nobles were shot to pieces on the field of Mohacs, it was not just the Ottoman Sultan who had something to celebrate. To the peasants of Hungary the Turkish victory came as a form of liberation.

Sultan Suleyman personally commanded the second invasion of Hungary in 1529 (which culminated in the two-week siege of Vienna), as well as that of 1532, which confirmed what everyone suspected, that an Istanbul-centred Ottoman Empire had reached its logistical western limits. The truce that the Sultan signed with Archduke Ferdinand's ambassadors in 1533 was a direct manifestation of this geopolitical fact.

By the summer of 1532 the Sultan had also become seriously concerned about the actions of the Genoese admiral, Andrea Doria, who had seized the ports of Nafpaktos and Coron in western Greece in a brilliantly orchestrated operation. If this had been the action of a Venetian squadron it would have been irritating but containable, but Doria's master was Charles V. The King of Spain, Sicily and Naples now held two bridgeheads in eastern Europe that were supported by an aggressive fleet. Fortunately there seemed to be a ready solution at hand, for the Sultan and his grand vizier had plans which would allow him to acquire an aggressive fleet manned by an equally brilliant sea captain. Barbarossa, the celebrated corsair of the North African shore, was going to be transformed into the Lord High Admiral of the Ottoman Navy.

Clearly the Sultan thought this action, the destruction of the Christian fleet in the central Mediterranean, was going to be but a small sideshow. Nothing else can excuse him of the greatest mistake of his life. For just as he was preparing to strike against Christendom he also committed his empire to a war on a second front. No sooner had a truce been signed with Ferdinand, Archduke of the Austrians, than he dispatched his trusted grand vizier, Ibrahim Pasha, to initiate a war of conquest in the East. In the winter of 1533 the Ottoman army advanced into the Kurdish mountains that occupy the borders of the two rival empires. In the spring he advanced ever further east, taking the Safavid capital of Tabriz that summer. It was then that the Sultan asked his grand vizier to hold the army in this exposed frontier position while he made a three-month progression across the centre of Anatolia. So that the Sultan and his grand vizier could together lead the Ottoman army south to occupy Baghdad and central Iraq. It was a great moral victory, for now all the great medieval seats of the old Muslim Arab Caliphate: Medina, Damascus, Cairo and Baghdad were within the frontiers of the Ottoman Empire. Suleyman was never to make an official claim to the Caliphate before a council of the scholars of Islam but henceforth it started to creep into official correspondence. Although he was the acknowledged leader of orthodox Sunni Muslims in the Middle East, it is astonishing to see how the more extravagant, quasi-religious, mystical claims of the Shia now started to be borrowed by the Ottomans. Even in such a hallowed place as the new mosque that he would build in Istanbul one finds these extraordinary claims:

> The Caliph, resplendent with Divine Glory, Who performs the Command of the Hidden Book and executes its decrees in regions of the inhabited Quarter: Conqueror of the Lands of the Orient and the Occident with the Help of Almighty God and His Victorious Army, Possessor of the Kingdoms of the World, Shadow of God over all Peoples, Sultan of the Sultans of the Arabs and the Persians.

The claim to be the 'Shadow of God' is in itself an almost unspeakable heresy to any Muslim with even a passing acquaintance with the message of the Koran. The madness of power would have seemed to have already began to warp the mind of the young prince, who, when he had ascended to the throne in 1520, had been observed to be 'a wise lord, and all men hope for good judgement from his reign'.

That judgement was to decay further. He had already commissioned a quadruple crown from a Venetian goldsmith, a bizarre piece of regalia one-upmanship to the tiara worn by the Pope in Italy, which was displayed at state receptions. It was of course completely against the known teachings of the Prophet, who poured scorn on the pomp and pride of kings and their golden ornaments. Worse was to come.

For shortly after he returned from his great victory in Iraq, Suleyman invited Ibrahim Pasha to the palace to enjoy a private supper in his rooms in the Topkapi Palace. This was normal practice for the two friends and indeed a room was always kept furnished within the Sultan's palace for the grand vizier's personal use. In the middle of the night of 15 March Suleyman stood outside the doorway of this room and made a signal with his hands. A squad of his deaf-mute slaves then advanced into this chamber and strangled his childhood friend. Ibrahim did not go quietly into the night but put up a ferocious struggle, and 'for long afterwards bloodstains could still be seen on the walls of the room in which he had been sleeping'. His lifeless body was taken out through the palace gardens to a boat which conveyed it to a secret burial place.

The city awoke to find that the Sultan's own men stood at guard outside the grand vizier's sprawling palace, instantly recognisable as its terraces had been decorated with statues of marble and bronze. All exits were sealed so that his wealth could return back to his master's treasury. By breakfast the quip of the wits had already circulated around the city, that the *makbul*, the favourite, had been transformed into the *maktul*, the executed. In death all Ibrahim Pasha's faults were aired: how ruinously expensive the two-year-long Baghdad campaign had been, what a botch he had made of the siege of Vienna and how he had been so loathed by the janissaries that they had even sacked his palace in 1535 though it stood right in the centre of the city. It still stands, though now transformed into a museum of Turkish art where you can walk the terraces that overlook the great monuments of the Hippodrome which Ibrahim would also have gazed upon, the obelisk of Pharaoh Thutmose

III and the brazen serpent-headed column that came from Delphi. The bronzes that Ibrahim had brought back as part of the victory spoil from Hungary were smashed up after his death, though the massive candlesticks fetched out of the cathedral at Budapest remain where he placed them: beside the prayer niche apse in the Ayia Sophia.

The Sultan had destroyed his best friend and his most brilliant adviser. Later, when we look at Suleyman's emotional and family life, we will begin to understand some of the reasons behind this murder. But there was never a political justification for it. Ibrahim Pasha had a profound understanding of the uses of naval power and the vital role of commerce in strengthening the state. The second half of Sultan Suleyman's reign would not be lacking in grandeur, but after Ibrahim Pasha's death nothing ever worked out so well as when the two childhood friends had governed the empire together. The gap would, however, be filled. A pair of brothers, corsair captains from the shores of North Africa, would rise to become the swords of Islam and champion the Ottoman Empire against the Christian Crusaders.

11

Corsair Kingdom

The Barbarossa Brothers, Uruj and Khizr, and
Condottiere Andrea Doria, 1512–34

Whoever serves his country well has no need of ancestors.

Voltaire

When we last observed the Barbarossa brothers, Uruj and Khizr, they were wreaking havoc on Christian shipping from their base at Goletta, the port of Tunis. They had used the profits of ten years of corsair raids to build up a small but formidable squadron of eight galleys. In the winter of 1510 they had been invited by their master, the Hafsid Sultan of Tunis, to expel the Spanish from his lands, as they had just set up a chain of artillery forts along the North African shore. A half-built Spanish outpost at Djerba was the first to be toppled. Then, in the summer of 1512, they sailed around the coast of Tunisia, recruiting volunteers for the attack on the Spanish outpost outside the medieval city of Bejaia (also spelled Bujeya or Bougie) from where the Hafsids had been used to sending a governor to watch over the coast of eastern Algeria. By the time they reached Bejaia the Barbarossa brothers sailed at the head of a fleet of a dozen galleys and had a thousand 'Turks and Moors' under their command. They were welcomed by a Hafsid prince with a force of three thousand warriors recruited from the surrounding mountains. These fierce tribesmen had placed the town under a blockade but were totally lacking in the artillery and technical skills to effect a breach of the walls. The Spanish bastion that had been erected just under two years earlier under the supervision of Count Pedro de Navarro was the key to the position. It was not quite finished and lacked the full complement of both armaments and men.

When the Barbarossas' galleys intercepted and then captured a Spanish ship that had been sent to supply the tower at Bejaia, they struck a double blow. Khizr advised that the demoralised garrison would fall sometime that season if they maintained a tight blockade. It was sound advice but somewhat lacking in the heroic glamour that was one of the vital ingredients in his older brother's leadership. Uruj prepared for a dawn assault with a hand-picked team of just fifty warriors. The idea was that they would scale the walls but they were observed and repulsed by the light cannon that the Spanish garrison had managed to mount on the walls. Uruj led from the front, and received another battle wound that day, for a piece of shrapnel smashed up his left forearm. A surgeon had to amputate the arm above the elbow, and alarmed at the subsequent loss of blood, Khizr insisted that he should be taken back to Tunis to recover. The siege was over, but the tribes promised to continue harassing the Spanish garrison and to keep them hemmed in within its walls until both brothers were fit enough to return.

Operating out of Tunis, Khizr managed to seize a galley off the island of Tabarka. It was not a popular move, for Tabarka acted as a neutral free port. It was leased to the Genoese, who did a good trade in the bright pink-red fossilised coral from these waters, but made an even more successful living by arranging the finance for the ransom of wealthy captives from both Christian and Muslim corsairs. To show their displeasure, the Genoese struck back at Tunis, sending a squadron to bombard the fortress of Goletta, sink what they could find and tow away the rest. Although they were not officially expelled by the Hafsid Sultan of Tunis after the Genoese attack, it was agreed that it would be better for all concerned if the brothers found another port out of which to operate. While Uruj was permitted to stay a while longer in Tunis to recover from his wounds, Khizr led the operation that would secure them a new base. He picked on the harbour of Jijil (also spelled Jigelli or Jejel), sixty miles east of Bejaia. By chance it was held by a Genoese, not a Castilian garrison, which allowed for a double sense of revenge. This time Khizr was left to make his own dispositions. Supported by a mass of volunteer tribesman who poured down from the hills, he placed the garrison under such a close siege, by land and sea, that they were cut off from any supply. As the trenches of Khizr's methodical siege crept closer and closer, the garrison grew ever more weak and beleaguered. As a last desperate resort the commander of the Genoese garrison determined to lead a break-out, sallying forth from the walls in the dead of night. It was a recklessly brave but doomed adventure. They were cut down to a man and the tribes poured in to sack the castle, now empty of all but the wounded. The next day, bearing the grim trophies of five hundred heads impaled on pikes, the tribes saluted Khizr as their commander.

Shortly afterwards Uruj sailed into Jijil harbour and was hailed as Emir. He showed characteristic mettle by besieging the Spanish fort at Bejaia once again. The Castilian garrison stood firm but he had the satisfaction of fulfilling his promise to the tribes that he would return. It may be that he had also been promised help from the Sultan of Tunis which failed to arrive. Whether by design or not, the Hafsid Sultan of Tunis was now publicly seen to be failing to lead his people in the struggle against the foreign Crusaders. Uruj decided to make a decisive political break with the past. A delegation was dispatched from Jijil to Istanbul to offer the loyalty of the corsairs, tribes and the two brother-commanders to the Sultan. It was a dangerous gamble. If the Ottoman court had looked askance at this uninvited delegation, which had after all come from the freebooting sons of a retired ex-janissary from their garrison at Mytilene, Barbarossa would have been left exposed to revenge from the Hafsids and an unanswerable charge of treason. But the court and the Sultan had been following the careers of the brothers with great interest. The delegation was welcomed, honoured and given a going-away present of fourteen Ottoman galleys. It was a generous gift, especially as in 1516 the Sultan must already have been deep in his secret plans for the invasion of Mameluke Syria and Egypt. The death of old King Ferdinand of Aragon that same year seemed to indicate a further turn in fortune for the brothers.

For the people of the port of Algiers, Ferdinand's death seemed just the opportunity that they were looking for to expel the Castilians. The Spanish did not control the city of Algiers, though the artillery fort that they had built on an offshore islet did command the anchorage and access to the town harbour. The fort had been well constructed, a key point in the chain of forts that Count Pedro Navarro had imposed on the coast of North Africa between 1504 and 1510, and was usually guarded by at least one Spanish ship. Salim al-Thumi, the local sheikh, had promised the support of the townsmen if Uruj Barbarossa would take command of the siege of the Spanish fortress. That spring Uruj advanced at the head of a fleet of sixteen galleys and six thousand men. On the way there they put in at the harbour of Cherchel, where a corsair captain had set himself up as leader, after deserting Barbarossa when his arm had been blown off at Bejaia. Kara Hasan was invited on board Barbarossa's flagship but this was not to be an amicable reunion of old comrades. After a short interview he was taken away and beheaded. His deputies now quickened to obey the orders of Barbarossa, lest they also be judged to have shared in their master's desertion. The siege of the Penon of Algiers, 'Navarro's bastion' held by a determined garrison of two hundred Castilians, proved to be beyond the capabilities of Barbarossa's artillery. A twenty-day-long bombardment made little impression on the thick, angled walls of the distant bastion and Barbarossa's offer of safe conduct and a ship with which to return to Spain was rejected by the commander, who staunchly replied that 'neither threats nor proffered courtesies availed aught with men of his kidney'.

Some of the leading citizens of Algiers now began to reflect more closely on the situation, and they did not like what they saw. It seemed to them that Barbarossa would fail to clear the Spaniards out of the Penon at Algiers, just as he had failed at Bejaia, and they would be left to suffer revenge at the hands of the Spaniards when the corsair fleet sailed away. They began to plot, what exactly we don't know, but almost certainly to get rid of Barbarossa and make peace with his enemy. But Barbarossa got to hear about their machinations. He made certain that for the midday Friday prayers the central mosque was packed with his men. After the prayers were over, he gave a signal. Twenty-two of the leading conspirators were seized and dragged before him and solemnly upbraided for their cowardice and treachery. They were then taken out of the mosque, through a jeering crowd of corsairs and citizens, to a summary execution just outside the city gates. Sheikh Salim al-Thumi was not among their number, for he had been more discreetly disposed of. While washing himself for the Friday prayers in the local *hammam*, or steam bath, as was his habit, he was drowned in a bucket of water by a pair of strong masseurs.

It was a savage action and led Barbarossa towards establishing himself as the uncrowned king of the coast of Algeria, for now the people of Jijil, Bejaia, Cherchel and Algiers all acknowledged his absolute leadership. Nor had the beheading of two dozen rich citizens ruined his standing among the locals. In fact it proved to have been a highly popular action. Barbarossa was acclaimed as the leader of the *jihad* by both the Berber tribes of the mountains and the Moors in Algiers.

This leadership was to be tested soon enough. The regent of Castile and Aragon, the old Cardinal-Primate Cisneros, had reacted with customary speed and efficiency to the news of the corsairs' siege of the Spanish fort at Algiers. Cisneros had long pushed for an aggressive crusading invasion of North Africa. Now he was free to act. He appointed Don Diego de Vera to command an expedition of fifteen thousand men for the relief of the fort at Algiers. Don Diego had already proved himself to be a resourceful officer in a war against the French that had been fought just three years before. He was even '*bien aprovado con el Conde Pedro Navarro*': he enjoyed the good opinion of Count Navarro. Two supply ships, escorted by a powerful naval squadron, would have done the job just as well, but the Cardinal-Primate knew what he was doing. He hoped to provoke another crusade. For while his old master, King Ferdinand, had been alive, his attempt to interest the King of Aragon in prolonging the conquest of Granada with a crusade into North Africa had failed time and time again. It was not that Ferdinand objected in principle (for he could hardly object to his saintly wife Isabella's last will and testament, which clearly stated, 'I beg my daughter and her husband that they will devote themselves unremittingly to the conquest of Africa and to the war for the Faith against the Moors') but in conference after conference with the Cardinal-Primate he rattled him on the details. Where would they stop: at the North African coast, or in the mountains, or the arid steppe beyond, or should they plan to advance right to the edge of the Sahara? How many men, how many ships, how much would this cost and who would pay? Now the King was dead, and the old regent could pursue the vision of a prolonged holy war that he so avidly shared with the dead Queen Isabella. Even if it was rumoured that the Queen's old confessor had been a little too influential in the drafting of that clause in her last will.

So it was that, on the day of St Bartholomew, thousands upon thousands of Spanish soldiers were landed on the shore just outside Algiers. Within a few hours this highly disciplined body of men had started to throw up entrenchments. By the end of the day the first cannonade had been fired at the walls of Algiers, echoed by that of the Spanish fleet.

Barbarossa seems to have learned nothing from his bitter experiences at Bejaia, for once again he planned to stand at the head of his men and lead a frontal attack on the Spanish lines. Nor did he delay, but launched his desperate assault that very first day of the siege. At the head of 'one thousand Turks and five hundred Moors . . . he flung his forces upon them with loud cries. And so great was the fear inspired by Barbarossa that they were routed almost without loss to the Moors; and with much ease did these slay three thousand men and capture four hundred', as the Spanish chronicler Sandoval dispassionately has it.

It was considered a great mystery how the finest army in Europe had been routed so decisively in September of 1516. De Vera managed to evacuate about half of his expeditionary force to the safety of the ships. In the confusion of night, fighting on a foreign shore, this was in itself an astonishing achievement, but his career was finished. To its eternal credit the garrison of the fort at Algiers continued to defy Barbarossa, despite having watched the destruction of the Spanish force sent to their relief.

Once he heard the news of this victory, Barbarossa's brother Khizr at once sailed from Jijil to assist, bringing with him six galleys. The following year Barbarossa took a momentous decision. In 1517 he turned his back on the sea and marched inland, towards the capital city of one of the three independent sultanates of North Africa. The Zayyanids had ruled western Algeria from the medieval city of Tlemcen for hundreds of years. Their capital stood beside Tunis, Fez and Cairo as one of the great cultural centres of North Africa. In their heyday they had ruled all of western Algeria and controlled the central crossroads of the trans-Saharan trade. But in their decay Sultan Abu Hammu III had accepted a tributary alliance with the Spanish and it was to strike a blow against the Crusaders on the coast that Barbarossa now marched against Tlemcen accompanied by a disaffected Zayyanid prince, Abu Zayyan. A battle was fought outside the walls and Barbarossa's victory was welcomed by the sheikhs and merchants of Tlemcen, who were at once freed from the ignominious demands of paying tribute to the Christians. Guided by his new ally, Barbarossa also struck out against another treacherous Zayyanid, Hamida al-Awda, who planned to carve out an emirate with Spanish military support. The eastern coast of Algeria was within the domains of the Hafsid Sultan of Tunis, but even here a Hafsid prince, Ahmad, now sought the protection of the Spanish lest Barbarossa advance in his direction.

Thanks to the zeal of Barbarossa, 1517 was a time of ceaseless diplomatic activity as the political boundaries and alliances were redrawn across North Africa. Barbarossa had always enjoyed good relations with the corsair ports of the Moroccan coast, especially that of Badis, tucked into the folds of the eastern Rif mountains, as well as with Tetouan, overlooked by the wild Alp-like summits of the western Rif. His agents now made formal contact with the Moroccan ruler in Fez, the Wattasid Muhammad al-Burtugali, a Sultan much more to Barbarossa's liking. Having tasted the humiliation of foreign captivity like himself, the Sultan now led his own armies and was currently locked in a struggle to oppose the relentless advance of the Portuguese on his kingdom's Atlantic coast.

The invasion of Algiers may have blown up in the face of the Spanish regent, but Spain did not remain idle while Barbarossa embroiled himself in the murky world of North African dynastic politics. The new monarch, Charles V, had responded to the urgent entreaties of the Spanish governor of Oran. Ten thousand Spanish veterans were sent to the Marquis of Comares so that he could wipe out the memory of the disaster at Algiers. Oran was the urban linchpin of Pedro Navarro's advance upon North Africa. But even the capture of this city back in 1509 had been achieved without King Ferdinand's support. All the money and men for the expedition had been recruited from Church lands and from the revenues of Cardinal Cisneros. Advised by Girolamo Viannello, a Genoese captain who knew these waters, the Count and the Cardinal had occupied the city in May 1509 at the head of an army, the latter reciting the verses of Psalm 115 as he processed through the streets. Cisneros had returned in triumph to Spain, burdened with trophies of his victory: bronze candlesticks and libraries of books looted from mosques, as well as slaves and a picturesque troop of camels. He later commissioned a fresco of the uplifting scene of his triumphal procession, which was painted on the walls of the Mozarabic side chapel in the cathedral of Toledo. But after the first rush of this surprise victory, things had not all gone Spain's way. A substantial proportion of the invading force had been left behind to continue the crusade. Under the command of Diego Fernandez de Cordoba they ventured out of the city walls. On their first expedition inland, they were isolated by tribesmen and cut down at the debacle of Las Grebes.

King Ferdinand had been right to be wary of the problems of exporting the crusade against Granada to North Africa. But his seven-teen-year-old grandson, Charles V, was desperately proud of the crusading traditions of both his Burgundian and his Spanish ances-tors. He would order thousands of the best soldiers of Spain to replace those who had fallen. The governor of Oran had also confidentially written to the young king that 'now was surely the time to unseat them . . . before the Barbarossa brothers were able to gain complete control of their kingdom'. The governor was right, for Barbarossa's dramatic rise to power was bitterly resented by many of the tribal chiefs and regional power brokers who decided to back Spain in this venture, if it meant that they could be rid of the corsair king. So when the new Spanish army marched out of Oran to attack Barbarossa and return the old Sultan to the Zayyanid throne at Tlemcen, they found themselves being escorted, not opposed, by a host of tribal cavalry.

Cut off from his supporters, his corsair allies and his brother, who were all on the coast, Barbarossa nevertheless decided to organise the defence of Tlemcen against the Spanish. Only when he realised that Tlemcen's citizens could no longer resist the siege and blockade, did he decide on a characteristic undertaking. With fifteen hundred men at his back he broke out of the city, cut his way through the siege lines and made a forced march towards the safety of the coast. The Spanish, aided by his Algerian rivals, set off after him in hot pursuit. At one critical moment Barbarossa ordered that his store of gold coin be thrown down a mountainside, knowing that the pursuing soldiers would be long delayed by their treasure hunt. At another, he hurried back on his tracks in order to escort his rearguard, which was being harassed as it struggled across a river. It was in just such an encounter that the old sea wolf found himself cut off from his men, trapped the wrong side of a dry-stone wall that was used as a pen by mountain goatherds. The one-armed warrior made a rush at the Spanish soldiers who had cautiously encircled him. He seemed on the point of breaking through when a savage jab from a pike caused him to stumble, whereupon he was quickly struck again and felled. With Barbarossa pinned to the ground but still struggling, it was left to Lieutenant Grazia de Tineo to behead the tough corsair but even then the Spaniard received a deep wound that he proudly bore for the rest of his life. In the words of Morgan, the valiant Barbarossa had 'resided in Barbary for fourteen years, during which the harms he did to the Christians are inexpressible'. He was but forty-four years old when stabbed by that fatal Spanish pike,

> not very tall of stature but extremely well set and robust. His hair and beard was perfectly red; his eyes quick, sparkling and lively . . . he was a man excessively bold, resolute, daring, magnanimous, enterprising, profusely liberal and in no-wise bloodthirsty except in the heat of battle, nor rigorously cruel but when disobeyed. He was highly beloved, feared and respected by his soldiers . . . and when dead was by them most bitterly regretted and lamented. He left neither son nor daughter.

Barbarossa might have fallen, but a second Barbarossa immediately arose to take command of his inheritance. Selim the Grim had awarded the title Khayr-al-Din (or Kherredine or Kheyr el-Din), 'Protector of Religion', to both brothers, but it is usually applied to Khizr, who, after the death of his elder brother, assumed leadership of all the soldiers and seamen who had so devotedly served Uruj. The fragile alliance with the local tribes that had supported the Spanish army in its assault on Tlemcen dissolved with the news of Uruj Barbarossa's death. The Marquis of Comares was later criticised for failing to advance on Algiers at this time of uncertainty but acted prudently in withdrawing his army safely back into Oran. He had received a report that the Moroccan Sultan had dispatched an army to rescue Barbarossa and relieve the siege of Tlemcen. This rumour turned out to be correct, though it arrived just fifteen days too late.

Khizr Barbarossa moved quickly, dispatching an ambassador, Haj Hussayn, to renew his oath of loyalty to the Ottoman Empire. Sultan Selim the Grim, who had just returned from the conquest of Syria and Egypt, was delighted to accept yet another vast new province for the empire. Barbarossa was saluted as Beylerbey (Lord of Lords) and sent the official insignia of the horsetail banner, which preceded an Ottoman governor on his journeys. Accompanying this insignia was the loan of two thousand janissaries, trained in the use of artillery and the arquebus. They arrived in time to reinforce the city of Algiers from the threat of a second enormous Spanish invasion.

The viceroy of Sicily, Admiral Hugo de Moncada, had been directed by his master, Charles V, to bring together a fleet of some fifty-eight galleys, troop ships and men-of-war. All Charles's Italian allies and the Spanish soldiers garrisoned in Naples and Sicily were to furnish contingents for this great venture. Indeed, with soldiers drawn from Genoa, the Knights of St John, the papacy and the Gonzaga rulers of Mantua, it had more than something of the air of a real crusade about it. Admiral de Moncada succeeded in getting the whole of the Armada into the bay of Algiers in mid-August, which is usually a period of sultry fine weather. It was, however, the very same day that the first expedition, under de Vera, had landed at Algiers, the ill-omened day of St Bartholomew. True to these premonitions, the weather started to worsen. The Crusaders attempted a forced landing but the bad weather rapidly turned worse. The Algerians watched in delight as their sea took on that characteristic northward swell that so often precedes violent winds blowing in from the north-west. As the storm was unleashed, Barbarossa ordered an assault on the vanguard that had been landed. Four thousand men of the twenty-three-thousand-strong invasion force would be killed or drowned that day and twenty ships would be wrecked as the storm worsened. Admiral de Moncada would eventually lead his storm-battered armada back to the safety of Ibiza. Here the men would mutiny for lack of pay.

To avert the ill omens now associated with St Bartholomew's Day, the Spanish made the saint a gift. They had triumphantly born away the fine Maghrebi cloak that Uruj Barbarossa had been wearing when they killed him outside Tlemcen. They reverently embroidered it and turned it into a vestment which was then draped over the statue of St Bartholomew. 'La Capa de Barbarossa' become a relic in its own right.

The Turks, Moors, Berbers and citizens of Algiers were triumphant. Twice now they had driven the brutal Crusaders from their shore. It wasn't quite revenge for the fall of Granada, but this double victory was the very next best thing. Apart from the odd island fortress with an isolated Spanish garrison, all of Algeria, be it Constantine, Bona,

Meliana or Mostaganem, now offered loyalty to the victorious Beylerbey. Barbarossa, for his part, acted with greater clemency and circumstance than his elder brother had done, forgiving rebels and confirming many of the existing princes as rulers. Thanks to the patronage of the two brothers, Algiers, from being one of many middle-ranking ports along this coast, gradually rose to become the capital of a new nation. The frontiers established by Uruj and Khizr Barbarossa still define the modern state of Algeria.

The entire coastline of Algeria was now a springboard for raid upon raid to be launched against the northern coast of the Mediterranean. This was the golden decade for the Algerine corsairs, as the 1520s saw the two powers of western Europe, the Emperor Charles V and Francis I of France, locked in a relentless series of wars. The war of 1521–6 was followed by that of 1526–9, fought across Italy and the Low Countries. At the same time Spain and Germany were racked by social rebellions, Rome was brutally sacked by a mutinous army and in eastern Europe, first Belgrade, then the fortress of Rhodes, surrendered to the new young Ottoman Sultan.

This was the time when the captains who had served under the Barbarossa brothers emerged in their own right to win their laurels: men such as Dragut, Salih Reis*, Black Hassan and Sinan ('The Jew of Smyrna'), as well as Aydin Reis, nicknamed Cacha-Diablo by the Spanish. The North African shore had been burned, sacked and raided by the Spanish for the past thirty years; now was to be the time of many revenges. Yet it was not only the Spanish coast that was attacked but also that of more innocent Christians along the southern Italian shore, and the islands of Majorca, Menorca, Ibiza, Sicily, Sardinia and Corsica were hit time and time again by the hungry corsairs.

But even in this heyday Khizr Barbarossa could be tripped up by local ambitions. A group of rivals, a triumvirate formed by a Hafsid Prince, a sheikh of the Berber tribes of the Kabylie mountains, Ahmad ibn al-Cadi, and one of his own corsair captains, Kara Hasan, managed to take over the city of Algiers in 1520. But Barbarossa, making use of his old base at Jijil, contained this local coup, bided his time and in 1525 returned to Algiers as its ruler.

These local disputes did not affect the corsair raids, and indeed Kara

---

* Rais or Reis can be translated as 'captain'.

Barbarossa, Kapudan Pasha (Lord High Admiral) of the Ottoman
Navy and Beylerbey (Governor-General) of Algiers.
Woodcut by Agostino Veneziano, 1535.

Hasan remained one of the most effective of the corsair captains. But
none of their operations would quite match that of the summer cruise
of 1529 commanded by Cacha-Diablo and Salih Reis. Using the network of lookout islands spread across the western Mediterranean, they
worked their way up to the southern coast of Majorca at the head of
fourteen galleys. They had already made two armed landings on this
shore when word reached them that a party of Moors who had been
forcibly converted to Christianity but had renounced their conversion
were desperately trying to make contact with them. A bounty of ten
thousand coins had already been offered for the capture of the Moors,
who would be turned over to the Inquisition. Knowing their fate, a
corsair raiding party landed a third time, made contact and fetched
them away under the cover of night. Then a swift sailing boat brought
news that a small squadron of Christian galleys, returning to Spain
from Genoa, might cross their path. After catching an early glimpse of

the power of the enemy squadron the captains decided to land the civilian refugees on a deserted island before they engaged the Spanish in action. It was a merciful decision, but must have been highly alarming to the stranded refugees. For no one could doubt their fate at the hands of the Inquisition if the Spanish ships won. In the vicious naval battle that followed the corsairs managed to seize seven Christian galleys. That autumn they sailed back into Algiers as the heroes of the hour, their decks burdened with hundreds of Moorish refugees, plus the one thousand Muslim galley slaves they had released from the Spanish ships.

For the next season's cruise, Barbarossa numbered thirty-six galleys under the command of his various captains. They drew upon a reserve of seventy thousand Moorish volunteer soldiers from all the different harbours and anchorages of Algeria. But before the raiders set out there was one piece of unfinished business to attend to: the Spaniards still held the fortress off the harbour of Algiers. So that spring the corsairs were summoned to assist in yet another attempt to break down the Tower of Navarro. Every inducement had been offered to the governor of the fort, Don Martin de Vargas, who, according to the traditional account, replied, 'I spring from the race of the De Vargas, but my house has never made it a practice to boast of the glory of their long descent; they professed merely to imitate the heroism of their ancestors. So I wait with calmness all your efforts, and will prove to you, with arms in my hands, that I am faithful to my God, my country and my King.'

The cannon of the Beylerbey, now directed by experienced janissary gun crews and reinforced by some heavy cannon acquired from the French, then spoke their own message. They pounded the little offshore fort for fifteen days, from the shore and from a sea filled by a fleet of galleys. On 16 May 1530 the corsairs made their assault, some thirteen hundred warriors swarming over the cracked and broken walls of the fort. Barbarossa proved merciful in victory and the Spanish garrison was spared massacre. Instead they were put to work. It was their task over the next two years to hack down every last stone of the Tower of Navarro and to put this rubble to good use by building a new harbour mole. Thus the four rocky islets off Algiers were to be joined to the mainland by a causeway so that they could never be occupied by an enemy again.

It was a timely victory, for the golden decade of Muslim victories at sea was at ebb. In 1529 the Emperor Charles V and Francis I had at last made a peace, and that same season the army of Sultan Suleyman reached its westernmost zenith with the two-week siege of Vienna. But of much greater importance to the Beylerbey than either of those distant and important events was the entrance of Andrea Doria into the service of the King of Spain. Charles V now had an admiral and a navy with which to strike back at the corsair fleet.

Andrea Doria was a Genoese soldier of fortune, a freelance Christian corsair. He was born in 1468 into an impoverished branch of a noble

Andrea Doria, the condottiere admiral.

family. Like many of the poor gentry of Italy, he sought fame and fortune as a mercenary soldier. His first training was in the Papal Guard, where one of his distant cousins was recruiting young men that he could depend on. A change of pope saw the Genoese expelled from the guard, whereupon Andrea took service under one of the great mercenary captains of his day, the Duke of Urbino, before being embroiled in

King Ferdinand of Aragon's treacherous invasion of Naples. At this
stage in his youthful career he had risen to the command of a platoon
of twenty-five soldiers. Later he drifted into the employ of a Sforza
Duke of Milan, before switching to the galleys, thus taking, in his for-
tieth year, a new path in his military career. He proved to be an
exceptional captain, and in the freewheeling habits of the time changed
masters and allegiance with bewildering ease, serving first Genoa, then
the King of France, from 1522, before being 'turned' by an envoy of
Charles V.

For by 1528 Doria was weary of the French, whose arrogance had
grown in proportion to their victories. When they started to occupy
some Genoese border fortresses to 'confirm and strengthen' their alliance with the city-state, and then went on to fine Doria for not
plundering Sicily after winning a naval battle for them, he was easily
persuaded to switch sides, even though it was mid-war. The Emperor
offered him a fortune – an annual salary of sixty thousand ducats – but
kept the loyalty of this soldier of fortune by the absolute trust which he
placed in him. All of Charles V's governors and commanders in Italy
were told to answer Doria's requests without double-checking with the
Emperor. But Doria's squadron of twelve galleys was never just an
Imperial navy. It continued to double as a personal venture, a freelance
Christian corsair fleet, always on the lookout for profit for its *condottiere*.

Barbarossa first became aware of the winds of change threatening his
control of the western Mediterranean in 1531. In that year Andrea
Doria launched a sudden raid on the Algerian port of Cherchel, releasing seven hundred Christian prisoners from the citadel. It would have
been a triumph if only the soldiers he had so efficiently landed had
obediently responded to his orders to re-embark. Instead they ignored
the sound of his signal gun and attempted to break into and sack the
town. The admiral was not used to being disobeyed. He ordered his
ships to cast off and left the soldiers to their fate. He was heavily criticised, for the abandoned soldiers failed in their attempt to take the
town and were pushed back on to the beach and all slaughtered. But
Doria argued that he could not risk his squadron, upon which the
defence of Christendom now rested, because of the greed of disobedient
soldiers.

The next year he showed his critics what he meant, and this time his signals were most promptly obeyed. His attack on the coast of Greece in 1532 would check the whole western advance of the Ottoman army which was recalled to defend this region. Doria led his fleet to the very foot of the Greek fortress of Coron in the midst of a hostile bombardment and succeeded in landing an army. It was a manoeuvre that required meticulous timing and complete confidence between the individual ship captains and their admiral. Coron was successfully stormed. Then he moved on. Patras was seized in a similarly impressive, co-ordinated marine landing before he finished this campaign by seizing the artillery forts that controlled the Gulf of Corinth. The following year he again proved himself a master tactician, by running supply ships through the Turkish naval blockade and siege that was intended to recapture Coron. They were small enough victories on the great tapestry of Mediterranean-wide conflict, but they were welcomed as the first real ebb in the tide. For his part, Suleyman the Magnificent was sufficiently concerned by these developments to rethink his whole strategy. So much so that in the autumn of 1533 he sent a message requesting a personal conference with the Beylerbey of Algiers. That winter Barbarossa appointed a trusted renegade from Sardinia, Hasan Agha, to govern Algiers and the North African coast in his absence, while he gathered together his ships and prepared to sail east for Istanbul to pay court to his Sultan.

12

Emperors and Sultans

Conquests, Crusades and Family Killings

He was a man, take him all in all.
I shall not look upon his like again.

Shakespeare, *Hamlet*

The cavalcade of the Ottoman state on the march exceeded anything that we can now imagine in the magnificence of orchestrated humanity. Istanbul and Edirne might have been used to royal weddings, to the Friday processions when the Sultan formally rode out to prayer in one of the great mosques and to the formal receptions awarded to allied embassies. But way beyond these state celebrations was the awesome spectacle of the Sultan and his army marching off to war. We have several eyewitness accounts, written by critically minded foreign ambassadors as well as by loyal court historians, reports and painted miniatures which catch snapshot details for us: a drummer striking both of his kettledrums while perched on the high saddle of a camel or the swirl of ostrich feathers in the cap of a janissary.

At the head of the vast column were the corps of water-carriers, who both provisioned the city on the hoof that followed behind them and also sprinkled scented water to settle the dust and perfume the air. Next came the baggage train, which could stretch for miles as nine hundred horses, two thousand mules and five thousands camels filed past. After them came the siege corps, five hundred sappers recruited from the mines of Bohemia and Armenia, a thousand blacksmith armourers in their leather aprons, eight hundred bombardiers trained in the new and exact science of the cannon and an equal number driving forth the cumbersome creaking gun carriages themselves. Watching over this most vital and expensive unit of the army were the palace officials – the treasurer, the keeper of the pantry, the head doorkeeper – all surrounded by their own officials, clerks and strongboxes of filed accounts and correspondence. Champing at their heels, or riding out to watch their flanks, was the gorgeous swirl of two divisions of Turcoman cavalry, composed of two thousand mounted men on each wing. Behind them, riding in closer rank, were the two rival regiments of palace horse guards, watching over the paymaster's heavy chests of coin. Then rode the chief officers of state, the members of the Sultan's Divan, or council, including the two fearsome military judges of Europe and Asia and the four viziers each accompanied by their staff officers and slave servants. Then, in a moment of light relief, came the palace huntsmen with their hounds, falcons and runners, followed by a great herd of royal horses, led, ridden and accompanied by farriers, saddlers, leather-workers and three hundred mounted chamberlains under the direction of the Master of the Horse.

Then, finally, one's eye fell on the first of the regiments of the new army, the Oda of the janissaries. They carried their own side arms – swords, lances and bows – but the silence of their disciplined stride and their distinctive, long, flowing white headdresses were what the spectator never failed to remark upon. The finer points of their precise ranking system, all based on bizarre details from their mobile kitchens, such as soup-bearer and spoon-holder, was lost on a beholder dazzled by the almost endless spectacle of twelve thousand men advancing as if they were one – and in total silence. Behind them, like an integral part of the march of the janissaries, were the one hundred trumpeters and one hundred kettledrummers of the Sultan's entourage. The horse-tail banner that indicated a Pasha or the three horse-tail banners of the grand vizier now gave way to the seven gilded staffs of the Sultan's yak tails. Then it was the Sultan himself, like a queen at the centre of a migrating hive of hornets, surrounded by four hundred mounted life guards, flanked by 150 pursuivants who ensured a clear passage with their silver staffs. Among them were an equal number of golden lances, brandished by the fast-footed *peyk* runners.

Ahead of this vast host, a smaller army of engineers, baggage animals,

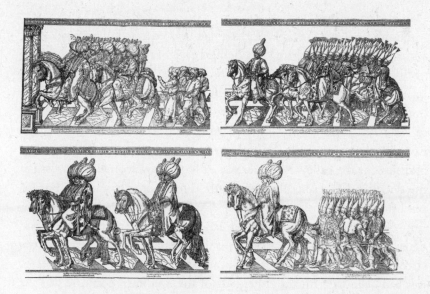

Ottoman procession in Istanbul. Venetian woodcut, circa 1563.

tent-makers and workmen was already constructing a city in canvas, felt, appliquéd cotton, silks, velvets and rush mats overlaid with carpets. Here the hierarchy of the army on the march was replicated by a series of tented courtyards, linked with screens and guarded enclosures. At the centre was the Sultan, surrounded by his court, then his chief ministers, lesser officials, guards and regiments. Something of this tented city can still be felt by any visitor entering the Topkapi Palace in Istanbul, whose three successive courtyards, that of the janissaries leading to that of the viziers (the Divan courtyard), which in turn leads to the inner palace of the Sultan, have usefully been compared to an Ottoman military camp petrified in stone.

The terraces that surround the Topkapi Palace overlook the fast-running waters of the Bosporus stream, seemingly draining the Black Sea into the Aegean at a gallop. They also look south, out over the wide expanse of the Sea of Marmara. It was from here that in February 1534 the galleys of Barbarossa, the Beylerbey of Algiers, could be seen to be approaching the city. It was no surprise, for his arrival route in Istanbul had been eagerly awaited, and the squadron had already exchanged respectful signals and salutes with the Ottoman forts that guarded the

Dardanelles passage.

For his final entrance, Barbarossa had hoisted graceful long silk pennants that trailed a hundred feet behind each of the three masts on each of his galleys. On them a swirl of crescents, calligraphic Koranic blessings and exhortations were mixed with the shape of the distinctive double-bladed sword of Ali. A flurry of swift-oared caiques rowed out to escort the galleys, showering blessings and welcomes on the heroes from North Africa, while the harbourmasters tried to organise a smooth berthing for the galleys. A vizier was at hand to welcome Barbarossa at the docks and to make him a first gift, a handsome bay horse. For his part, the corsair admiral was anxious that his own last-minute preparations were in order. The city of Istanbul had seen the arrival and departure of much greater fleets, but there was a particular buzz on the streets to observe the famous red-bearded admiral. Although his victories had been won on the other side of the Mediterranean, he was yet one of them, the child of a discharged Ottoman soldier who had risen to high rank by his wit, loyalty and bravery.

In imitation of the royal progression of the Ottoman army, Barbarossa now set his own procession in order. Camels laden with the choicest pickings of the corsair war, mules laden with the exotic produce of the trans-Saharan trade, Christian war-horses decked up in the different liveries of the Christian nations – Spanish, Italian, German and Portuguese – were followed by two hundred of the most attractive young Christian slave women, arrayed in two columns, each carrying a basket overflowing with silver. Behind them came an equal number of African girls laden down with gold. Then came the parade of exotic beasts – tethered lions, ostriches, nervous gazelle, horned antelopes – followed by the bright uniforms of the corsair crews themselves, the master bombardiers, navigators and seamen bearing the armour and arms they had captured from the Spanish invaders. Lastly, riding on his gift of the Sultan's bay horse, came Barbarossa himself, surrounded by his captains.

The gifts were judged to be a magnificent tribute to their master by the crowds who lined the processional way. The Divan, the grand vizier and finally Sultan Suleyman himself received Barbarossa with every mark of honour. After the parade was over, his men were feasted in the long square before the palace gates. A palace was immediately placed at the disposal of the admiral and barracks set aside for his

Turbanned Turkish gentleman, fifteenth-century Istanbul.
(British Museum)

crews.

Barbarossa had not been summoned to Istanbul to take part in a
crisis conference. Peace treaties had recently been signed with both
Habsburg Austria and Safavid Persia, leaving Suleyman completely free
from his traditional enemies. The Sultan and his chief ministers were
now planning the next round of strategy. For it was clear that no further
advance could be planned for the Ottoman Empire without an improved
command of the Mediterranean Sea. After the first meeting, the grand
vizier advised Suleyman, 'We have set our hand upon a veritable man of
the sea. Have no hesitation in naming him Pasha, Member of the Divan,
and Captain General of the Fleet.' With the captain-generalship which
normally went with the job of commander of the forts of Gallipoli,
Barbarossa was awarded an annual salary of fourteen thousand ducats,
financed by the revenue extracted from such Aegean islands as Lesbos

and Rhodes. Barbarossa also acquired responsibility for supervising the construction of a new fleet in the dockyards that stretched along the safe anchorage of the Golden Horn of Istanbul. In the weeks and months that followed, a strategy for dealing with Christendom was slowly mapped out. Suleyman may have privately dreamed of conquering Rome, the first city of the Caesars, to put him on an equal footing with his ancestor Mehmet II. But in the meantime he listened to the patient, step-by-step advice of his admiral and his grand vizier. France had to be confirmed as an ally of the Ottomans, just as the Protestants of Germany and those emerging within Hungary were seen as gift from God, because they would help to further divide the Christian enemy already divided by the schism between the Catholic Church and the Orthodox Church of the Greeks. The naval power of Genoa and Venice would have to be confronted one day, as would the Portuguese fleet that had already pushed its way into the Persian Gulf and was knocking at the fortress gates of the Red Sea.

In the meantime there were some practical steps to be made at once. Barbarossa was given permission to do as he suggested, which was to annex the Hafsid Sultanate of Tunis to link his own area of authority with the rest of the Ottoman Empire. This would also give the empire a bridgehead for any eventual invasion of Sicily and Italy. The French would be kept on side by awarding them the trading privileges with the Ottoman Empire that only the Venetians and Genoese had hitherto possessed – which would be formally ratified just two years later. It was recognised that the Spanish were the Ottomans' most redoubtable enemy and should be weakened whenever possible but not directly invaded. When the new fleet was ready Barbarossa would try to destroy the naval power of Genoa. It was hoped that Venice might be coerced into joining the Franco-Ottoman alliance. Some diplomatic capital could no doubt be made from the fact that the Habsburg possessions in Austria and Milan encroached upon the land frontiers of the Serene Republic.

After four months this series of Divan meetings was over. Sixty-one slimmer, faster, more seaworthy galleys had been launched, and the admiral had helped train and select their crews. In July he led a fleet of some eighty galleys through the Aegean. He struck southern Italy with precision, encircling the town of Reggio and deporting its entire population as slaves to Istanbul. Avoiding the well-defended cities of the

Neapolitan coast – with their watch-towers and early warning signals – he fell upon little Sperlonga, where Tiberius's seaside palace can still be found. Like some fabled monster from a Scottish Border ballad, he sent a raiding party inland to surround the little town of Fondi, intent on seizing the most beautiful woman in Italy: Giulia Gonzaga, widow of Vespasiano Colonna. While the town was sacked Giulia escaped out of her bedroom window and rode off to safety in her nightclothes. This tale of misadventure and partial nudity has encouraged artists, poets and historians to add their little embellishments to the story. An Austrian has the Countess Giulia condemn her attendant for being overbold in his rescue, a Frenchman visualises her bare-breasted as she cuts her way through a line of lustful Turks with her cutlass, while an English chronicler imagines Barbarossa surveying the miserable selection of captives borne back from Fondi by his men and thundering out a reproof, 'I sent you to bring back a pearl without price, and you return with these cattle.'

Towards the end of the summer of 1534 Barbarossa steered his fleet towards his true objective, Hafsid Tunisia. On 16 August he stormed into his old safe haven of Goletta. Once a guest, he was now its master. The Hafsid Sultan waited for him to advance a little inland, to the city of Tunis, where he imagined that the tribal cavalry under his command would have an advantage. But his cavalry were scattered from the field by the disciplined fire of Barbarossa's janissaries. The Hafsid Sultan then decided to abandon Tunis and retreated to the old inland capital of the country, the steppe-land city of Kairouan, and left Barbarossa in charge of the coast.

It may be that Suleyman had initially intended to repeat this campaign against Italy annually, gradually softening up the country with a series of devastating raids before he contemplated an actual invasion. This had indeed been Ottoman strategy for some two centuries. But if this was the plan it was rapidly jettisoned. The bulk of the fleet and the army were recalled to Istanbul from Tunis to contribute to his new adventure, a two-year invasion of Persia and Iraq. This set the Ottoman Empire on a course that would lead it to wage war simultaneously on two vastly separate frontiers.

It also left Barbarossa dangerously exposed. He was left in command of his original forces in the Mediterranean but these were barely adequate to control a state that now stretched from the frontiers of Morocco to Libya. Furthermore his raid in force along the coast of Italy had awoken the whole of Europe to the scale of the threat. Charles V had been resident in Spain since 1533, after a long period away from the affairs of the Mediterranean, and was at last free from the concerns of Germany, Burgundy and his war with Francis I of France.

Throughout that winter of 1534 Charles threw himself into planning a counter-attack, which was to be launched not just by himself as a King of Spain but as the anointed leader of Christendom. His governor-generals in Granada, Naples, Aragon, Sicily and Castile were instructed to assemble regiments at designated embarkation ports, as were his allies in Italy and Germany. Andrea Doria was invited to guard the invasion fleet, which would rendezvous off Sardinia, a conveniently central point. The Knights of St John, recently established by the Emperor's gift in Malta and the Libyan city of Tripoli (in 1530) also hurried to profess their support. An invitation was sent to Charles's brother-in-law, the King of Portugal, to ask if he would join the crusade. Nor could the loyalty of Genoa to Charles's cause be doubted, for the recent alliance between Francis I and Suleyman was everywhere seen to mark out the Republic of Genoa as a future province of France. As part of this diplomatic war of nerves, Charles instructed envoys to make contact with Barbarossa to see if he could be weaned from the Ottoman alliance.

But behind the sealed walls of his innermost council chamber, the Emperor had to put up with strongly worded rebukes. The new Cardinal-Archbishop of Toledo, Juan Pardo de Tavera, warned his master that Spain now required his attentive presence, not another absence, and that the 'endeavour' risked starting another Europe-wide war. Indeed he classified the enterprise as 'the adventure-lust of a young nobleman', a phrase that was echoed by another trusted adviser, Cardinal de Granvelle, that Charles 'ought to avoid enterprises fit for young lordlings'. And they were right. The spirit of the Burgundian knight chivalrous burned deep within the Emperor. And despite all the battles and sieges fought in his name, he had never yet faced an enemy army himself. What is more, in launching a crusade against the corsairs in Tunis he would also be seen to be the good feudal lord, fulfilling his half of the medieval social pact, the protection of his people.

For the radicals among the Protestants of Germany were seen to be challenging the old world order. The first eruptions of revolution, unleashed by the otherwise bookish Protestant Reformation, were about to send shock waves through the establishment. The procession of three thousand self-proclaimed 'children of Israel' across the Zuyder Zee and the emergence of a baker in Harlem who claimed to be a prophet of God were early warning signs. The first full storm was unleashed in Münster, where the 'children of God' took over from the bishop and started receiving directions straight from the Holy Spirit. Throughout the summer of 1534 this revolutionary state defended itself with an unheard of confidence against its feudal masters. It was eventually destroyed but the smouldering wreck of the burned-out city left behind a reputation for savage violence. Found among the ruins was the Anabaptist *Book of Vengeance*, which prophesied: 'God will smite the ungodly and take away their strength. He will confirm the hand of David and teach his fingers how to yield the sword. He will furnish his chosen with iron claws and horns of brass. They shall fashion swords and pikes from ploughshares and reaping hooks. They shall find a leader; they shall unfurl their standard and blow a blast on their trumpets.' This sort of misdirected spiritual energy had fuelled centuries of external crusades, and soon enough would be turned in upon Europe, which would nearly consume itself in religious wars. It also strengthened Charles V in his determination to be a true and Holy Roman Emperor.

So, in late May 1535, the Emperor left the port of Barcelona, sailing with the galleys of Aragon, Castile and Portugal to join up with the fleets of Italy and Sicily, which met outside Cagliari, Sardinia, on 10 June. They left on the 13th, carried by an excellent wind that brought the entire fleet to the Tunisian anchorage of Goletta just twenty-four hours later. It is claimed that six hundred head of sail filled the gulf, the largest such congregation in living memory. The army of the Holy Roman Emperor at once disembarked, making its camp among the Roman ruins of Carthage: the circular walls of the amphitheatre, the long striding arches of the aqueduct and the subterranean vaults of the massive water cisterns. These monuments did not survive by mere accident as the crusading army soon learned. For the provision of food and fresh water, among the brackish lakes that surround and protect Tunis like a series of vast moats, soon became their critical concern, just as it had been for the Romans trying to supply the city of Carthage before them. As dysentery spread through the camps, an early assault was deemed vital. The earth banks that protected the strong stone vaults of the central fortress of Goletta were pounded hour after hour, day after day, for three weeks. The Emperor, with becoming modesty, was content to serve in the army under his appointed supreme commander, the Marquis de Vaso. The German and Spanish regiments faced the north and east walls of the fort, the Italians the west, while the Knights of St John directed a co-ordinated naval bombardment.

Barbarossa had placed the cream of his forces, the Turks and Moors, to man the fortress of Goletta, which had been well supplied. Having received word of the size of the invasion fleet, he had sent all his available craft to seek shelter in the ports of Algeria. He remained in the city of Tunis, directing a series of hit-and-run raids on the Christian camp with the cavalry and soldiers under his command. But in truth he knew that only another summer storm or a plague spreading itself over the disease-ridden camp could protect the fortress from the vast host that besieged them.

On the morning of 14 July the galleys of the Knights of St John delivered three volleys in fast succession. It was a prearranged signal that silenced all the land batteries. Christian troops from a dozen nations advanced on the fort from all sides, initially under the shelter of the trenches but then in a pell-mell dash as they rushed towards the smashed walls of the bastions. After a short resistance the Turks were forced to strike their flag, though some of them managed to survive by making their way via a causeway that led across the lake to the walls of Tunis. Among the booty that fell that day were a large quantity of cannon that had been sold by France to her Ottoman ally. It was fitting, for the honour of France in the crusading camp that night, that it had been a knight from the French Tongue of the Order of St John, the Chevalier Cossier, who had been the first to plant the standard of the cross on the battlements.

During the last days of the siege of the fort, the Hafsid Sultan, Moulay Hassan, had ridden up from Kairouan to place some three hundred tribal cavalry at the service of Emperor Charles V. After the fall of Goletta, Moulay Hassan renewed his pleas that they should advance on Tunis, expel Barbarossa and his corsairs and restore him to his native throne. This idea appealed to Charles, but the lack of water and the unrelenting heat of the North African midsummer brought its own problems. The men were forced to become their own beasts of burden as the pack animals weakened, leaving it up to the soldiers to drag the monstrous cannon through the sterile mud of the salt marshes. As Charles wrote in his own hand to his sister Mary, 'We die of thirst and heat.' The battles fought for possession of the few good wells in the region were the fiercest, for Barbarossa knew that this was the one tactical card that might reverse the imbalance of forces. In one such engagement Charles's horse was killed, as was his page-boy, who fought with desperate gallantry to protect his master. Although Charles had been proud enough of his youthful victories in the jousting grounds and tourney fields, the bitter experience of war made a man of him. He never talked about these days in North Africa.

The battle for water that was fought out over the wells that summer was never to be resolved. For something totally unexpected broke apart the walls of Tunis. In council Barbarossa and his captains had argued about what they should do with the several thousand Christian slaves that were then being held prisoner in Tunis. Under normal conditions they would have been held in the casements beneath the thick walls of the fortress of Goletta, ready to be led in chains to the galley benches, or housed in reed huts that sprawled across dozens of old quarries in the suburbs. But they had all been evacuated and packed into the city of Tunis before the Christian army had landed. Now they were not only a burden on the city's limited food and water supplies, but were a considerable security threat in their own right. As the sound of the Christian guns came ever closer, these eight thousand tough, brawny galley slaves became increasingly confident and excitable. A proposal to slaughter the lot was aired in Barbarossa's council but the decision to order such a cold-blooded massacre could not easily be agreed upon. However, news of the council's debate was reported to a group of ex-Christian renegades in Barbarossa's service. They were so horrified at the prospect of this massacre being agreed at a later date that they decided to free the slaves. With nothing to lose but their chains, the freed slaves stormed the citadel walls and opened the gates to the Christian army. Barbarossa saw at once that the city was lost, and, using one of the city's northwestern gates, led his own troops in a series of quick marches towards the safety of the Berber hills. From there they marched inland to reach the harbours of Algeria, where the corsair galleys had been withdrawn for safe keeping.

Tunis was not so fortunate. Whether at the hands of the escaped slaves or the Emperor's soldiers who now pressed in through the city gates, there was to be no pity or quarter given. 'The streets became shambles, the houses dens of murder and shame' as 'abominable outrages were committed by the licentious and furious soldiery of the great Emperor'.

The Burgundian painter Vermeyen and the Spanish poet Garcilaso de la Vega accompanied the expedition. From their sketches and descriptions a celebrated series of tapestries were made which show the Crusader fleet, the sea voyage, the siege and the camp in Carthage. They do not show the sack. But to an extent the city of Tunis still does. The medieval buildings of this capital city, the like of which you will find in Fez, Marrakesh, Granada and Cairo, do not exist in Tunis. For all its heritage was destroyed – the medieval colleges, mosques and palaces – just as libraries of Korans were broken up and used as bedding straw for the cavalry horses that were stabled in the main Zitouna mosque. After three weeks of occupation the ghost city of Tunis, a wreck framed by walls, was handed back to the Hafsid Sultan. In exchange he promised to surrender the harbour and fortress of Goletta to be a permanent bastion of Spain, to forbid corsairs to use his harbours, to pay an annual tribute and to release any Christian slaves found in his territories. It was a compromising way in which to regain a throne: a powerless Muslim ally of a destructive Christian power.

On 17 August the victorious crusade fleet set sail, landing at Trapani in Sicily just a few days later. It was the first time that Charles V had visited his Kingdom of the Two Sicilies. He came to them out of the sea at the head of a victorious fleet and was greeted as an heroic Emperor by adoring crowds, hymns, triumphal arches and acclamations. In Palermo the gate that the citizens built to welcome him into their city still stands, its two vast, Hercules-like figures sustaining the archway, a deliberate joyous salute to Charles's own heraldic symbol, the two standing pillars which represent Ceuta and Gibraltar, the Two Pillars of Hercules that watch over the entrance to the western Mediterranean. They would be used as symbols on the Spanish silver dollars that poured out of South America and thence they would migrate to the design of the US 'greenback'. Embroidered banners stretched from steeple to steeple: 'Long Live our victorious Emperor, father of the fatherland, conqueror of Africa, peace-maker of Italy.' This architectural commemoration of the Emperor's passage up Italy can still be followed through the freshly carved commemorative portals erected to him on the Porta Capuana in Naples, then along the Appian Way to be fêted by the proud women of Rome, of the Farnese, Orsini, Colonna and Pescara families.

In the Vatican he spoke to the Pope and the College of Cardinals for a whole hour in Spanish, protesting his love of peace and his desire to lead the next crusade against Algiers. Although he used eloquent hand gestures to convey his meaning, especially his continued suspicions of Francis I and the German heretics, the choice of language was not lost on the Holy Conclave. He could have chosen any one of the half-dozen languages (including Latin) in which he was fluent but he now chose to present himself as a King of Spain. It has also been noted that throughout his triumphal tour of southern Italy he had abandoned the magnificent jewelled textiles of Burgundy and wore the sober black of a Spaniard. He saw himself as a Crusader from Spain rather than the richest prince in Christendom.

At Bejaia Barbarossa and the survivors of the sack of Tunis rejoined the corsair fleet. There was consternation in the town. Would he choose to evacuate the Algerian coast, and pull back his fleet to the Levant and the safety of Ottoman territories? Were they to be left at the mercy of another Spanish-led crusade?

The admiral had no such plans. He took his galleys out of port in a north-westerly direction, away from all the familiar island lookout posts, in order to sweep straight on to Menorca's coast from the north. News of the Emperor's victory over the corsairs at Goletta and the city of Tunis was still being celebrated when Barbarossa's fleet suddenly filled the anchorage of Port Mahon. The place was looted and burned and an impressive booty of captured cannon and six thousand slaves was taken back to Algiers. It was a piece of fabulous defiance in the face of such crushing reverses and it also advertised to the cities of Algeria that the admiral remained in charge.

The following year Barbarossa set sail once again for Istanbul, undoubtedly to request resources with which to recapture Tunis or another powerful fleet with which to burn the Italian coast. But despite the bravado of the Port Mahon raid there was no mistaking the turn in the wind. In 1536 Andrea Doria took his fleet deep into the Aegean, seizing all the merchant ships that he came upon, before taking on a squadron of the Ottoman navy commanded by the lieutenant-governor of the Dardanelles. His tactical victory, greatly reinforced by the capture of several galleys, was a sharp reminder to how vulnerable Istanbul could be to any resurgence of Christian naval power.

In this light, the reconquest of Tunis was put to one side. There was to be a concentrated effort to seize full control of the Aegean and the entrance to the Adriatic. In May, as the Sultan marched west into Albania, Barbarossa commanded a fleet of one hundred galleys that streamed down through the Dardanelles into the Aegean. There may have been a wild plan to ship the Sultan, with an army, over to Italy by seizing Brindisi, but in the end a more cautious policy was followed. Corfu was invaded by the Sultan at the head of a huge siege train which included the largest cannon then in existence, capable of throwing a fifty-pound ball. But the Venetian fortress had been embellished by engineer after engineer over the past century to become one of the strongest on earth, and it withstood the cannonade. As if in revenge, once Barbarossa had ferried the army back across the narrow strait to the safety of the Albanian mainland, he scorched the Italian coast of Apulia, then proceeded to methodically wreck all the remaining Venetian-held islands. A truce had been in place since the reign of Sultan Bayezid II and the islands had benefited from this long peace, so the booty brought back to Istanbul was immense.

The admiral's progress from the landing station to the gates of Topkapi Palace to, in the words of Hajji Khalifa, 'rub his countenance against the royal stirrup', outdid even his first memorable audience. Two hundred page-boys dressed in scarlet carried alternate vessels of gold and silver, two hundred were burdened by bales of precious cloth while a thousand enslaved girls and a thousand enslaved youths brought their new master four hundred thousand pieces of gold. It was a most magnificent treasure, but seized at what cost? To make war on both the naval powers of Venice and Genoa had never been the policy of his ancestors. It is difficult to imagine that Suleyman's grand vizier, Ibrahim Pasha, would have permitted such folly. But that may have been why it happened: to celebrate the fall of the vizier it was necessary to reverse his known policies. The parade of treasures and captives, processing up the hill to the palace from the docks, also helped hide the fact that the Venetian fortress of Corfu had successfully resisted the Ottoman offensive, even when this was supported by the full muster of its fleet and led by the Sultan himself.

That same year the King of France and the Sultan progressed from their tactical understanding to a secret alliance. It was not exactly a trump card for either sovereign, separated as they were by several seas, mountain ranges, nations and languages. The only direct application of the new alliance was that a combined French and Turkish naval squadron fought a small engagement against the Spanish. Much more talked about was the fact that Turkish boats were drawn up in Toulon, where the crews out-wintered the storms before returning home.

In 1538 the Sultan's aggressive policies helped create a union of the four greatest naval powers in Italy to oppose the fleet commanded by Barbarossa. The joint fleet was composed of thirty-six galleys from the papacy (under Marco Grimani), eighty-one ships from Venice (under Vincenzo Capello), thirty galleys from Spain (under Ferrante Gonzaga) and the forty-nine galleys from Genoa. All had been placed under the overall command of Charles V's admiral, Andrea Doria. It was a unique experience in European unity, had been extremely difficult to organise and was riddled with personal and national rivalries. And it was missing one vital ingredient: a squadron of fifty sailing ships, the Spanish and Portuguese galleons, the latter of which had proved themselves to be such a formidable force in the Indian Ocean.

Barbarossa had fewer ships under his command but enjoyed an absolute command of all his subordinates. Many of his captains, such as Dragut, had loyally served him for years. The only new addition was the Red Sea fleet of Egypt, which had been patiently constructed over the past two decades to take on the Portuguese in the Gulf and the Indian Ocean. Instead the bulk of this force had been transshipped at the last moment and sent north to join Barbarossa.

A skirmish by the captain of the papal galleys just beneath the Ottoman fortress of Preveza first established that the two battle fleets were in close proximity. Barbarossa took his ships into the Gulf of Arta (the bay in which the decisive Battle of Actium had been fought between Octavian and Mark Antony in 31 BC). It was a safe anchorage, shielded by islands and overlooked by Turkish-held forts, islands and headlands. Andrea Doria, having at last assembled all the elements of the allied fleet, sailed south from Corfu on 25 September to confront them. It was later in the season than he might have wished, right on the autumn equinox, a time traditionally associated with sudden changes in weather. He was old, but the caution he displayed in the coming days was well founded. He tried to lure Barbarossa out of his very favourable, fort-defended anchorage, and on the morning of the 27th he led his fleet south. The differences between the various squadrons were as nothing to the difficulty of keeping together a fleet composed of both galleys and full-rigged galleons. The line of Christian ships soon stretched ten miles, all the way down the length of the island of Levkas (just north of Ulysses's Ithaca).

Barbarossa, observing the fleet's disorder – whether intended or accidental – raised his flag to signal for the Ottoman fleet to follow and pick off the stragglers. So it was against a long, drawn-out line of Christian ships that the compact Ottoman fleet, a tidy crescent of well-disciplined galleys, made their speedy advance. Dragut in command of the right squadron, Salih Reis of the left and Barbarossa at the centre, they soon swept up against the first Christian stragglers. This included *The Galleon of Venice*, her progress across the waters literally weighed down by the cannon she carried and an early version of armour plating. Though encircled by the entire vanguard of the Ottoman navy, her captain, Alessandro Condalmiero, maintained absolute control over his crew. Her masts were blown away by the cannonades from the pack of galleys that rowed towards her, but still he forbade his men to fire back until the enemy further closed the range. When he finally did give the order to unleash the first broadside at point-blank range, it was to be a sudden and devastating revelation to the Ottoman captains of the evolution of naval fire-power. One galley was literally blown out of the water by the ferocity of the Venetian cannonade and then immediately sunk beneath the waves, while half a dozen galleys were severely disabled. The Ottoman captains quickly backed their craft out of range of *The Galleon of Venice*, though some had been so damaged by the broadside that they required to be towed away.

The rest of that day Barbarossa and his captains quartered the waters, awaiting their opportunity to dart in and launch another attack. They swooped on a few other stragglers which trailed behind Doria's fleet but which did not share *The Galleon of Venice*'s bewildering new fire-power. Doria, for his part, refused to come to the aid of the beleaguered Venetian ship. Captains Marco Grimani and Vincenzo Capello took turns to go aboard his flagship and beg him to intervene. Dark political motives have been heaped on him for this, fired up by the usual jealousy that exists between Genoa and Venice, but the reason was simple enough. Doria aspired to lure Barbarossa's fleet out from the protection of the Ottoman-controlled shore. In the deep sea, he knew that his galleons had a chance of damaging the entire Ottoman fleet, after which the gates of Istanbul lay open. But for him to draw his fleet after him into the shore of Levkas in order to defend *The Galleon of Venice* was to hand over all the tactical advantages. Neither admiral wished to be drawn into the other's chosen battleground. So in the end Barbarossa was left in possession of seven Christian galleys that he had captured, to be set against the loss of three galleys that had been crippled by the gunfire of *The Galleon of Venice*. Incredibly enough, Captain Condalmiero's ship managed to survive the attention of the Ottoman fleet and despite being unmasted managed to work its way north to the safety of the harbour of Corfu.

In the morning light it could be clearly seen that the fleet of Barbarossa held its position on the seas while Doria had used the cover of the night to retire to Corfu. Why, remains a mystery to this day. As the French naval historian de la Gravière would later comment, 'for less than this the English shot Admiral Byng in 1756'. The Battle of Preveza was an Ottoman naval victory, but for all its individual bravery it remains a curiously unsatisfactory engagement, the Jutland of the sixteenth century.

Andrea Doria tried to recover some face by capturing Castelnuovo (north of Corfu) but the allies squabbled over who was going to garrison it and the following year it fell back into the hands of the Turks. Sultan Suleyman ordered prayers of thanks to be offered in the mosques, victorious illuminations and processions, and heaped honours and rewards on Barbarossa. But if his Divan had studied the battle reports in detail, they might have spared themselves a future shock by laying down keels and ardently copying the design of *The Galleon of Venice* for their own navy. As we have already heard, this lesson should also have been reinforced by what had happened at the first naval Battle of Diu (when Portuguese cannons sunk the Gujarati fleet in 1509). This battle was very nearly repeated a generation later. For, despite part of the Egyptian squadron being sent to join Barbarossa's fleet at Preveza, the Ottoman regional commander, Hadim Suleyman, had been left with enough ships to sail out of the Red Sea into the Indian Ocean and chal-

lenge the Portuguese. He sailed south to join forces with the navy of the
Sultan of Gujarat, who planned to expel the Portuguese from the new
fortress they had built at Diu. Admiral Hadim Suleyman took just nineteen days to cross the Indian Ocean and reach Diu but backed off from
an armed confrontation because the Portuguese were found to be
already well entrenched in their new base and supported by a well-
armed fleet at sea. Instead of fighting a second Battle of Diu, the two
powers settled on a truce. The Portuguese recognised Ottoman control
of the Yemen (including the fortress of Aden, which Hadim Suleyman
had captured in 1538) while the Ottomans recognised the possessions
of the Portuguese in India.

Venice retired from the naval alliance the next year, in 1539, though
it would be a year or more before she could accept the stringent terms
demanded by the Ottomans. Sultan Suleyman did not use the naval
victory of Preveza to allow him to undertake a second siege of Corfu.
This was not out of lack of martial energy, for he led campaigns into
eastern Europe in 1538 and 1541, and his army would also be campaigning into Iraq a few years after that.

Even before the Battle of Preveza, Emperor Charles V was having
difficulties with his Spanish kingdoms. Though he sketched out the
basic outlines of his planned crusade in lecture after lecture (one even
delivered to the collected Senate of Venice) the Spanish would not be
persuaded. Neither money nor men nor Spanish ships were pledged by
the various Cortes of the Spanish kingdoms for his prospective crusade
in the East. The Emperor had learned much from the experience of the
Tunis crusade and had all the practical details in his mind. Strong
ocean-going barges would be gathered from the Duchy of Burgundy to
transport the best Italian guns, while great quantities of Germans
would be recruited because of their steadfastness as infantry. The
Spanish were to provide the backbone of the force, the whole fleet to
be escorted by the combined navies of Venice and Genoa. But the
Spanish were not interested in joining any expedition to conquer
Istanbul. Their taciturn response was a single word, 'Algiers'. They
would gladly sail against the corsair city any year, even though two
Spanish expeditions had already failed on this shore and tens of thousands of young Spaniards had also perished in the various expeditions
that had been launched out of Oran.

Venice was soon compelled to open negotiations to establish trade with the empire and to confirm the immunity of her merchant ships against Ottoman corsairs. Though scorned by the rest of Europe for the ease and speed with which she made peace with the 'Grand Turk', she had no choice in the matter. To keep her navy afloat, to garrison and supply her fortresses cost hundreds of thousands of golden ducats a year. The city's Arsenale, the magnificent ship-building and cannon-casting production centre that stood at the centre of her military strength, alone cost some five hundred thousand golden ducats a year to maintain. These fixed costs established on the back of her booming Levant trade could not be afforded without it. But perhaps Venice's very good tactical showing at the Battle of Preveza made the Ottomans even keener to exact a humiliating settlement. They requested an annual tribute and the secession of fortresses in Greece. At least Venice now had the assistance of the French as an intermediary in the process of making a peace. Even so it took two years of negotiation. The tribute was eventually fixed at 236,000 ducats a year, a fortune that exceeded the income of many a proud monarch, but worth it given the estimated size of the Levant trade, which was around seven million golden ducats a year in this period. Soon enough all her critics, in both the East and the West, were once more choosing to dispatch their trade goods in the safety of a Venetian ship or requesting her bankers to help in negotiating bills of exchange.

As the Venetian diplomat Cavialli would comment of his city's relationship with the Ottomans, 'Clearly we must not go to war with them, but they should not be allowed to suppose that we cannot go to war.' An essential aspect of this policy of deterrence was the guided tour of the Arsenale, when both friends and enemies could be made aware of Venice's production-line efficiency. The pre-fabricated war galleys that were all ready to assemble, the massed stockpiles of hundreds of ships' cannon, the masts and tackle – these were the physical proof of Venice's latent power. It just took a vote from the Senate and the world's finest war fleet of a hundred galleys could be launched in as many days. As a Venetian ambassador so elegantly put it, the city's foreign policy could be likened to 'playing with a ball of glass which must be kept perpetually in the air with light and skilful touches but would be broken by either a fall or a violent hit'.

Emperor Charles V, being much more of a knight-errant than a figures man, could never talk with any conviction to the Senate of Venice.

It was some relief to find that the year after Preveza, the Ottoman army was not waiting on the coast of Albania, to be shepherded across the Adriatic by their victorious fleet. Instead they were on a far-distant frontier, establishing their dominance on the frontiers of Russia. On the banks of the River Dniester, north of the new tributary states of Moldavia and Bessarabia, the soldiers of Suleyman erected a proud inscription about their master, 'In Baghdad I am the Shah in Persia, in the realm of Byzantium the Caesar, in Egypt the Sultan.'

Nor the next year, for the naval victory of Preveza, combined with peace with Venice in 1540, seems to have left the Ottomans content with preserving the status quo. There was no attempt to seize an Italian port or recapture Tunis from the Spanish. The Sultan had reverted to his interest in Hungary, which allowed him to follow up on his own youthful victories at Belgrade and Mohacs. The new schism within Christianity gave the Ottomans a valuable new policy wedge, as they threw their backing behind the Protestant faction within Hungary and the candidacy of John Zapolya's infant son, John Sigismund. So, in the spring of 1541 and again in 1543, the Sultan led an army to throw the Catholic Habsburg Archduke Ferdinand out of his tentative encroachment into central Hungary. In 1541 Charles V was also in central Europe, tied up in months of negotiations with German princes at the Diet of Regensburg, to produce a compromise between the Catholics and Protestants. The well-meaning inter-faith document that was produced was ultimately to be rejected by both Catholics and Protestants.

As the Ottoman army advanced further west, the Habsburg siege of the old Hungarian capital of Buda was abandoned. The defence of Austria and the Holy Roman Empire once again rested upon a few heroic Hungarian fortress towns. Both Charles V and his brother Archduke Ferdinand were aware of the terrible danger of directly facing the Ottoman army on the field of battle. They talked loosely about the superiority of Turkish cavalry but this was disingenuous. There was not a branch of land warfare, be it artillery, infantry or cavalry, in which the Ottomans were not the acknowledged masters. The run of victories on the battlefields of Syria, Anatolia, Hungary, Egypt, Iraq and Persia painted a picture of Ottoman invincibility which was as much based on their disciplined artillery and infantry as their heroic cavalry. As the proud wearer of the crown of the Holy Roman Emperor, Charles V appears to have felt personally ashamed that once again he was not advancing to confront the Ottoman army at the head of Christendom. All the more so since the Ottoman army was once again being personally led into battle by its reigning Sultan Suleyman.

In a last-minute frenzy of diplomatic activity held through the night of 28–9 July 1541, Charles V managed to pull several rabbits out of the hat. A much-amended agreement was signed in which the Protestant princes agreed to lend ten thousand infantry and two thousand cavalry to fight the Turks on the south-eastern frontier of Germany for three months. At two in the afternoon, before the ink had dried on this document, Charles V galloped out of town – to join another crusade. This was to be another Mediterranean adventure rather than confront the huge, powerful Ottoman army that was so close to hand in central Hungary. Riding non-stop through Munich and Innsbruck, over the Brenner Pass by way of Milan and Pavia, he took ship from Genoa to join the fleet that he had ordered to be assembled at Palma, the capital of the island of Majorca. An agonising delay blew his ship to shelter in Corsica before they could be under way again, the crew rowing all day and night to make the rendezvous. Spanish troops under the Duke of Alva, the Genoese under Andrea Doria, the Neapolitans and Sicilians under Ferrante Gonzaga and thousands of German mercenaries were waiting to leave for the invasion of Algiers. But the Emperor's delayed arrival would not be the only one to afflict this polyglot, multinational force.

It would not be until 19 October that five hundred transport ships, manned by twelve thousand men and carrying twenty-four thousand soldiers, stood off the bay of Algiers. It was late in the season, but this had its own distinct advantage for it avoided any encounter with Barbarossa's fleet. For the admiral of the Ottoman navy was based in Istanbul and this late in the season would not be in a position to also guard the North African coast.

All through Friday 21 and Saturday 22 October a heavy swell made a landing quite impossible. But, after the Emperor heard mass on Sunday morning, the weather changed and he was able to lead his army ashore in beautiful weather, a few miles to the east of the city. A naval cannonade had cleared the tidal strath of tribal cavalry, and the men waded ashore through the surf to find themselves not in the blazing wilderness of Africa but in an enchanted suburb of well-watered walled gardens and orchards. Once sufficient of the regiments had arranged themselves on the shore, they marched directly on the city. The Spanish left wing took the high ground and picketed the hills, the Emperor and his German troops took the centre, while the Italians and the Knights of Malta advanced closest to the shore.

The city they looked at hungrily that evening shone at its very best, a dazzling series of white houses piled up in terrace after terrace as they climbed the hillside, the skyline broken only by the neat rectangular towers of the mosque minarets. On the high ground to the north of the city stood the citadel, a free-standing fortress which was connected to the circuit of city walls. The bastions that reinforced the sea walls and the handsome harbour mole, built by captives with stone that was once the Spanish fort, were new works, well supplied with cannon. But, between these harbour defences and the hilltop citadel, Charles V and his commanders looked with keen-eyed interest at a less well-defended, old curtain wall.

Out of a sense of almost chivalric courtesy, a messenger was dispatched to the governor of Algiers, the renegade captain Hasan Agha, demanding the keys of the city: to surrender with terms or face the consequence of the sack of Algiers. Hasan Agha, in command of one thousand janissaries and some five thousand armed citizens, including many experienced corsairs and refugees from Andalusia, held his position with defiant confidence. Five hundred sail might fill the horizon to the north, but his master Barbarossa's victory at Preveza helped his men keep their spirit, reinforced by a recent local knock to the military reputation of the Spaniards. The bellicose military governor of Oran, Count Alcaudete, had been instructed to push the authority of Spain inland. Just a year after his arrival, in 1535, he had sent an army inland to support another client Zayyanid prince trying to claim the throne of Tlemcen. This had not proved as easy as the attack on the elder Barbarossa brother, when the Spaniards had enjoyed the support of many of the local tribes. On their way back the Spanish expeditionary force were pinned down within the fortress of Tibda. Isolated from assistance, they had been overwhelmed by the Beni Rashid tribe. Only seventy men who were taken prisoner survived.

As the first lines of the Crusaders' siege trenches were being prepared that evening the heavens opened. The troops were soaked and then battered by gales while a dangerous onshore wind picked up strength and stopped all further disembarkation. No tents, no cannon, no further food and supplies could be landed. That night the army shivered, while the colonels began to fret about keeping the gunpowder sufficiently dry in the appalling and unexpected weather.

Hasan Agha, with the example of Barbarossa's elder brother Uruj before him, seized the moment to launch an attack that morning, under the cover of shrieking winds and rainstorms. They pushed the Italians back to the coast and seemed on the point of making their way through to the Emperor's post. But the steadfast resistance of the Knights of St John stemmed the first approach of panic, for they were well used to fighting in armour in the most appalling conditions. This gave the German troops time to come up and defend their Emperor. A counter-attack, once again led by the Knights, threw Hasan Agha's men out of the trench-works. Then the Crusaders ebbed forward and pushed the Algerines back to the very walls of the city. The storm prevented the fleet from assisting with a naval bombardment, so that the fighting that morning reverted to a medieval contest of sword and pike, fought hand to hand in the mud. One Knight managed to jab at the closing gates of the Bab Azun with his sword, but as soon as their brothers were safe within the walls, the defenders on the battlements felt free to open fire with their light cannon. This soon cleared the immediate approaches to the walls of Algiers of any Christians.

Then Hasan Agha launched a second stroke. As tribal warriors descended from the hills towards the embattled Crusader camp, he had the gates of the Bab Azun once again opened, and led his cavalry out at a gallop in a frontal attack on the enemy lines. This was more than just a brave gesture. The Emperor himself had to rally the troops to fight again that day. Protected by his bodyguard, the corps of gentleman adventurers that had been recruited from the grandees of Castile and Aragon, the King of Spain rode forward once more to repel an attack of Moorish knights. Even this skirmish, fought over the siege trenches overlooking Algiers, left some three hundred dead.

The rest of that day and the next, the weather ruled. Sufficient supplies for only two days had been landed, so it was with great relief that the hungry besiegers looked out on the morning of Wednesday 25 October to see that the weather had at last cleared. Over this day the invasion fleet slowly reassembled beside the beachhead a few miles to the east of the city. A few supplies were run ashore and messages exchanged.

Then, unexpectedly from the north-east, a mother of an autumnal storm broke upon the scene. There was no room for manoeuvre. The devastation was awesome, compounded by confusion as ships ran over one another's cables, snagged in one another's rigging, ran into half-sunk boats and disabled masts. This storm raged for two days, driving dozens of galleys to a splintered death on the immediate shore, while others were driven west, past the walls of Algiers, to founder on the offshore rocks. Even the Emperor took it as a judgement from God. He was seen in a long white cloak outside his tent, murmuring, '*Et Fiat voluntas kua*' ('And thy will be done'). For the Algerines, thrice rescued from the destruction of a Spanish army by 'miraculous winds', it must have imbued them with an awesome sense of the immanence of the divine.

The Emperor struck camp, and his drenched, starved, disillusioned army was led on a march west, skirting the high citadel to pass above Algiers and then to plough its way on through the foothills. They were harassed by tribesmen who now swarmed down from the mountains to join in attacking the retreating invaders, as well as by Hasan Agha, who once again lead his Turks and his Moors in attacking the rearguard. Deprived of supplies, the Crusader army only survived this desperate two-day march by plundering the suburban orchards and gardens and devouring their own pack animals. The remains of the fleet had established a secure anchorage at the Bay of Temendefust, where, under the cover of the ships' guns, an orderly camp was at last created. It was here that Hernan Cortes, one of the gentleman-adventurers who formed a marching bodyguard around the Emperor, begged him to try again, to turn adversity into good fortune by leading one more assault on Algiers. Cortes, who had conquered an empire by kidnapping the Aztec Emperor in his own capital city, might have been the man to lead such an unexpected counter-attack. But for Charles V God had spoken in the storm. The order to embark was given. On 2 November the Emperor, who wished to be one of the last to leave the African shore, waded out into the surf and was hoisted into a rowing boat. That night he settled down to write a long letter of explanation to Archduke Ferdinand about what had gone wrong. As if to remind Charles, a third storm pinned the fleet to the Algerian shore, twice driving them back south towards the North African shore, before releasing them. They reached Cartagena, which could take a day with a fair wind, a month later. Once back in Valladolid he wrote a frank appraisal to his intimate counsellor Granvelle: 'We must thank God all of us and hope that after this disaster he will grant us of his great goodness, some great good fortune . . . Nobody could have guessed the weather beforehand. It was essential not so much to rise early, as to rise at the right time, and God alone could judge what that time should be.'

In Algiers that winter a Christian slave was scarce a fair barter for an onion, though in later years the Algerines grew curiously proud of their old enemies. The grave of the Knights of St John who had held back Hasan Agha's first attack was pointed out with respect, as was a hilltop to the west of the city that was considered to have been the site of the tent of Charles V. To this day it is still known as 'Emperor's Castle'.

Both Francis I and the Ottoman court were jubilant about the reverse Charles V had suffered at Algiers. The following year the Sultan decided to lead his army back into central Hungary, for Habsburg soldiers had once again crossed the frontier and raided the Pest bank of Budapest. But the two allies also considered that something positive should be done to reinforce the victory at Algiers and to make a reality of the Franco-Ottoman alliance. So Barbarossa was sent into the western Mediterranean, and his fleet of some eighty galleys made raid after raid on the Italian coast as it worked its way up towards France. In the Gulf of Lyons, Francois de Bourbon, commander of the French fleet, awaited with his galleys dressed in a long, welcoming line. His guns sounded a salute as the white lilies of France set against a background of blood-red silk dipped in honour of the arrival of their Ottoman allies.[1] Aside from these gallantries, the practical preparations that had been made for the arrival of the Turkish fleet at Marseilles proved to be minimal, much to the disgust of Barbarossa. The central objective of the alliance was to attack the Italian city of Nice which was bombarded, besieged, stormed and sacked. The addition of this burned-out city, a small advance in the frontiers of France, came at a heavy price. The French crown had to supply the needs of the Ottoman fleet throughout the winter of 1542 and they, to all practical purposes, turned the harbour of Toulon into a Turkish enclave. Genoa's old suspicions of French intentions were revived and the rest of Europe was free to comment on this unnatural and 'impious alliance'. Not that the hypocrisy wasn't mutual. Archduke Ferdinand was certainly undertaking negotiations that would result in his having to pay a demeaning annual tribute to the Ottomans. For their part, the Ottoman navy behaved with exemplary decorum, as an astonished visitor confessed, 'To see Toulon one might imagine oneself at Constantinople, everyone pursuing his business with the greatest order and justice . . . never did an army live in stricter or more orderly fashion than that one.' The French ambassador to Venice freely confessed that 'they are more hardy, more obedient, and more enduring than us. They have one great advantage, that they think about nothing except war.'

Before settling down for the winter, Barbarossa dispatched a squadron under Salih Rais to raid the Spanish coast and then overwinter in Algiers. In the break from the fighting, it appears that the two rival admirals, Andrea Doria and Barbarossa, exchanged a series of embassies in their Riviera hibernations. Once again the chanceries of Europe and Istanbul buzzed with talk of secret plots. Was Barbarossa being approached to defect to Charles V, or was Doria negotiating the cost of bringing his fleet over to join the Franco-Ottoman accord? It is certainly true that Francis I always regretted losing Doria to Charles V. Indeed in one candid meeting with Charles he admitted that it had been the Emperor's master stroke. But the only known result of these talks between the two old corsair admirals was an exchange of prisoners and ransoms.

Among many such deals, Barbarossa paid three thousand crowns for the release of one of his vice-admirals. It seems that back in the summer of 1540 Doria's nephew, Giannettino Doria, had caught Dragut unawares. The corsair squadron of twelve galleys had been drawn up on a beach in Sardinia, where Dragut was resting the crews, drawing fresh water and repairing the hulls with molten pitch. Suddenly the corsairs found themselves totally surrounded, with soldiers on the heights and Doria's ship-mounted cannon covering the entire beach. It was a famous coup, the entire squadron taken – crew, boats, booty and all – without a shot fired. Dragut was put to work in one of the galleys of Andrea Doria's fleet, where he was visited by a French Knight of St John named Jean de la Valette. Dragut was saluted with a taciturn greeting by this Knight: '*Usanza de Guerra*' ('It is the custom of war'), to which he is said to have replied, '*Y mudanza de fortuna*' ('I see a change of luck'). When last they had met they had occupied different seats. Then it was Dragut who patrolled in majesty on the prow while de la Valette worked away at the five-man oars, chained by his ankle to a bench, amid the stink of a hundred unwashed galley slaves.

But when Barbarossa sailed away in the spring of 1543 from Toulon, Dragut had been returned to his command. After leaving France the corsairs raided down the Italian coast until they reached the Strait of Sicily. Barbarossa may have known that this would be his last active cruise. He was content with the deputy he had appointed in Algiers. Hasan Agha, though a Christian renegade and a eunuch, had proved himself a loyal and accomplished warrior. Barbarossa also had a son, Hasan, by his Algerian wife, who would prove himself a talented officer and rise to become Beylerbey of Algiers himself one day. But it was Dragut who was Barbarossa's true heir on the high seas. They seem to have shared a similar background, born to modest families who made their living by fishing and farming on the shores of the Aegean. Dragut received his first military training in the Mameluke fleet of Egypt before working west to seek his fame and fortune as a corsair in North Africa. European writers attempted to tarnish his name by claiming that he was a Greek boy who was taken into a Turkish governor's household as a page-boy. And though this was indeed a familiar enough pattern throughout the empire, owing to the levy of the janissaries from Christian families, it does not seem to be so in his case. His parents were from a Muslim village in one of the many coves of the indented peninsula west of Bodrum looking out over the island of Cos. Even in his period of captivity in a Christian galley, Dragut's experience mirrors that of the Barbarossa brothers.

Barbarossa returned to the Bosporus that summer in time to watch the construction of a magnificent waterside mosque that was consuming most of his fortune. It was built on an embankment just upstream from the Imperial cannon foundries at Tophane: Istanbul's answer to Venice's Arsenale. It was equipped with an *imaret*, an enormous kitchen which prepared food for the poor. It is a splendid if heavy building, its roof more like a great leaden helmet than a dome. Here Khizr Barbarossa would be buried in the summer of 1546 in a mausoleum that overlooks the fast-running waters of the Bosporus and the ferries that criss-cross its waters from the Besiktas landing. It became a custom among the Ottoman navy that 'no voyage is undertaken from Istanbul . . . without their first visiting his tomb, whereat they say a *Fatiha*,[2] a sort of prayer for success . . . saluting the remains of so efficacious an individual with repeated volleys of small fire-arms, both at arrival and departure. All of which is done with much ceremony and singular solemnity.'

Barbarossa had once praised Dragut as 'a living chart of the Mediterranean'. Whether as a result of conversation with him or of his own volition, Dragut made his base in Tunisia, not among the other celebrated corsair captains working out of the ports of Algeria. There remained plenty of opportunity to prosecute the Holy War at Sea against the Christians on this coast. The fall of Tunis to Charles V's invasion in 1535 had never been avenged and the Spanish were still in possession of Goletta, the port of Tunis, while the Knights of St John ruled over the Arabic-speaking island of Malta and the nearby Libyan city of Tripoli.

Elsewhere the momentum of war on the exhausted coasts of the Mediterranean had dropped. The Emperor and the French King had made yet another peace, that of Crépy-en-Laonnois in 1544, and this one seemed finally to have worked. And soon enough the architects of the relentless generation-long struggle for power fell away like leaves from the world tree. Martin Luther and Barbarossa died in February and July of 1546, Henry VIII of England and Francis I of France in February and March of 1547. That year a five-year truce was signed between Archduke Ferdinand and the Ottomans. But the fine-tuned Ottoman war machine, with its standing army of paid slave soldiers, could not function without any enemy lest it turn in on itself – or its masters. From 1547 armies were dispatched to the eastern frontier with Persia. The Red Sea fleet, free at last from the need to support naval operations in the Mediterranean, was able to direct its attacks on Portuguese positions in the Indian Ocean. For their part, the Spanish, the Italians and the island communities in between, continued working upon a massive programme of coastal defence, erecting a chain of watch-towers and signal stations that could track corsairs and warn of their approach.

In this atmosphere, Dragut was one of the liveliest of all the corsairs, with a fleet of thirty-six galleys based on the island of Djerba just off southern Tunisia. In 1550 he took advantage of a local dispute and seized control of Mahdia, to the north, as a second harbour for his fleet. It was an ideal spot, a stoutly fortified peninsula that stuck far out into the sea, creating a harbour on its northern and southern shores. It also had a certain dignity, being littered with imposing monuments from the tenth century, when it had served as the capital of a Shiite Empire.

The Europeans liked to call the town Africa, from the old Arabic name for Tunisia, Ifriqia. When Dragut set sail to maraud the sea lanes, he left his new base at Mahdia in the hands of a regiment of five hundred Turks. As reports from the watch-towers chronicled Dragut's progress, the aged admiral of Charles V prepared his counter-strike. Andrea Doria ferried the viceroy of Sicily with a siege train and many thousands of Spanish troops down to Mahdia, and then went back for reinforcements. After a three-month siege, well supplied with munitions by their offshore fleet, they finally blasted their way through the old walls. It was a successful, if not an entirely glorious, operation. A garrison was installed and the next spring renewed pressure was put upon Dragut. Doria brought a fleet of galleys down the coast of Tunisia, passing Goletta and Mahdia on his way south. He almost succeeded in hemming Dragut's squadron in the southern corner of the Gulf of Djerba. Dragut only escaped by the celebrated expedient of cutting a canal, which sounds laborious and unlikely in the midst of a battle, but was simpler than might be thought. For he simply blasted his way through an old Roman causeway that linked Djerba to the Tunisian mainland, and so escaped from Doria's encircling galleys.

The Spanish offensive against North Africa, most especially the seizure of Mahdia, hit a nerve in Istanbul. A raid against corsairs was one thing. Seizing a fortress and then holding on to it with a permanent garrison of soldiers was quite another – especially when it was rumoured that it might be surrendered to the Knights of St John as an additional base for their galleys. If you added Mahdia to their existing possession of Tripoli, Tunis and Malta, it did indeed look like an aggressive Christian advance into the eastern Mediterranean. So the new admiral-in-chief who had replaced Barbarossa, Sinan Pasha, delivered a note demanding the evacuation of Mahdia as his fleet waited off the Sicilian harbour of Messina. This formal request to the Spanish viceroy in Sicily was refused.

Having first tried to make a peace, as is the formal tradition of Islam, Sinan Pasha then felt free to wage war. Reinforced by Dragut's squadron, the combined navy went on a whirlwind campaign against the Christian positions, as if a long-thought-out strategy had at last received the necessary tactical back-up. Malta, home of the Knights of St John, was invaded on 18 July, but the walled towns, Medina, Birgu and Senglea, were too strong to be taken by a raiding party. Next Dragut surveyed the new defensive positions being constructed along the sides of the grand harbour of Valletta, before falling on the neighbouring island of Gozo. Every inhabitant, all six thousand islanders, were herded into slave pens in the bowels of the Ottoman galleys. Having set the Knights of St John off, like ants defending their nest, Dragut led the fleet due south on 31 July towards Libya. On a good wind, Tripoli is just a day's sail south. Dragut knew the land intimately. He dropped a landing party at Zuara, west of Tripoli, and one at Tadjoura, to the east of the city. These forces raised the tribes and advanced through the palmery gardens that surrounded walled Tripoli, while the bulk of the invasion fleet moved up so that it anchored off the deep harbour. Unopposed, the ships were free to land their men, who built a nest of three artillery emplacements around the key to the defence of Tripoli, an outlying artillery fort that sat on the end of the mole and overlooked the approaches to the harbour. Supplied either by land or reinforced by sea, Tripoli should have been able to put up a convincing defence. But Dragut's campaign had brilliantly isolated the Knights, both by land and by sea. Just thirty of them were resident in Tripoli at this time, backed up by a force of 630 mercenary soldiers who had been recruited from Calabria and Sicily. The Arab population of the walled city may not have embraced Ottoman rule of their own volition, but they would certainly not lift a finger to assist the Christian Crusader Knights. But before Dragut's gunners had even begun to find their range it was all over. The Italian soldiers who had not been paid, mutinied and threatened to open the gates to the fort unless the leader of the Knights negotiated a surrender.

Dragut had yet another ace up his sleeve: the presence in his fleet of the French Ambassador, Gabriel d'Aramon, who was put in charge of negotiations with the French-speaking Knights of the Tongue of Auvergne who held Tripoli. Thanks to Dragut's lenient instructions they came to quick terms. The Knights could depart with their arms and flags flying if they left the fortifications of Tripoli unslighted. This they agreed to, and took ship in the galley of the French ambassadorial delegation, who put them safely down on Malta. The mutineer soldiers were left behind at Tripoli to fend for themselves, which they did either by embracing Islam or a life of slavery. Dragut then moved quickly to secure this great prize. Murat Agha, the local sheikh of the Tadjoura, who had proved of great assistance in the land blockade of Tripoli, was made civil governor of the newly liberated city. It was a wise and popular choice.

The following year, 1552, saw the sea war swing decisively in favour of Dragut's forward policy. Sinan Pasha once more led the Ottoman fleet out of the Aegean to join up with the corsairs and a French squadron to defeat an Imperial squadron in a battle fought between the islands of Ponzo and Terrafina. The following season Dragut was appointed admiral for the campaign of 1553 and linked up with another of Barbarossa's old trusted captains, Salih Reis, who had assumed command in Algiers. Although the combined fleet numbered some forty galleys, the golden decades of the corsair raids had passed, for the Spanish coastal defences functioned ever more effectively. Dragut concentrated on the Sicilian and Italian coasts before assisting the French in once more despoiling the Genoese riviera. This time, instead of attacking Nice, they concentrated on Corsica, which they effectively occupied that year, save the Genoese strong point of Calvi. In 1555 Dragut's squadron once again joined up with the Ottoman fleet to raid southern Italy (Reggio, opposite Sicilian Messina, was hit yet again) and in response to diplomatic requests from France Corsica was once again raided. For the Genoese had managed to expel the invaders. When Dragut raided the countryside around Bastia, taking some six thousand captives, he was weakening Corsica's defences in preparation for the next French invasion. But this involvement in the endless tit-for-tat frontier war between the allies of the Habsburgs and the French held no great prospect for the extension of Ottoman power.

Two years later, in 1557, an Ottoman squadron was sent to assist the corsairs of the Algerian coast in their attempt to expel the Spanish garrison from Oran. It was potentially well timed, for in January of that year the royal treasury of Spain had declared itself bankrupt. The mountain of debt from Charles V's wars, some twenty million ducats, had exceeded the power of the crown to even service the interest. But it was not the disaster that was feared. The financial markets in Antwerp and Augsburg seem to have recognised the new king (Charles V's son) Philip II's desire to establish a new fiscal order, and the news of massive discoveries of silver in Peru had already percolated through to where it mattered. Certainly the first of the new round of lenders, who included the Genoese banker, Nicolo Grimaldi, in 1558, clearly specified that he was to be repaid in silver 'when the first ships arrive from Peru', at an effective rate of 15 per cent per annum.

It was also a highly confusing period, for political alliances cut across all the presumed confessional frontiers. A talented commander of janissaries, Hasan Qusru, directed military operations on behalf of the Ottoman Empire from his base at Algiers and worked in close alliance with the corsair captains. But the loyalty of the tribes and the old cities of the interior was very far from certain, for a charismatic new dynasty had emerged to power in Morocco. The Saadian Sharifs of Morocco not only supported the claims of the old Zayyanid dynasty to recover their position in Algeria but poured scorn on the Ottoman claims of any spiritual and legitimate political leadership over the Arabs. To add to the complexity, the old dynasty of Morocco (the Wattasids) had become clients of the Ottomans while the Spanish garrison in Oran had become the military ally of the Sharifs of Morocco. After a highly dramatic series of invasions, plots, counter invasions and a royal assassination the disputed borderland between Algiers and Morocco settled back into an ever-watchful armed truce.

In 1558 the Ottoman fleet was once again back in the waters of the central Mediterranean. The galleys steered clear of their habitual targets along the coast of Calabria and made a surprise descent on Sorrento, on the Neapolitan coast, before heading out to sea and swooping, once more with total surprise, on the town of Ciudella in Menorca. Then they joined the allied French fleet off Toulon. But the Ottoman admiral Piale Pasha made problems about assisting in another joint operation against Corsica. In the midsummer heat an epidemic had broken out among the squalid conditions of the slaves' rowing benches and had greatly reduced the speed of his galleys. In order to protect his fleet he seems to have struck a deal, accepting a bribe from the Genoese not to attack Corsica and calling a mid-season truce. Piale Pasha's fleet, with some galleys forced to tow their sister ships, sailed peacefully back down the coast of Italy, shadowed but not attacked by Christian galleys. On the North African coast the corsairs and Moors of Algiers once more repelled an attack from the Spanish fortress of Oran. The new military governor planned a raid on Mostaganem, but by the time the column marched out of Oran on 26 August any element of surprise had been lost. Instead the hills were crawling with tribesmen who harassed, attacked and finally isolated the Spaniards. That autumn twelve thousand young men were led into Algiers as captives to once again glut the slave markets. The following year the majority of the captives decided to turn their back on domestic slavery and 'turned Turk', converted to Islam and volunteered to fight under the banners of Hasan Qusru, the Pasha of Algiers, who determined to invade the tribal territories of the Kabyle Berbers.

*

In the far east of his domains, the Sultan had a much more promising use for his navy. Plans that had first been brought to his attention some twenty years earlier by his grand vizier, Ibrahim Pasha (supporting the proposals of the brilliant young Ottoman cartographer Piri Reis), were at last activated. In 1552 the now venerable captain Piri Reis was put in command of a naval squadron that would sail out of the Red Sea and expel the Portuguese from Ormuz as well as extinguish their growing influence on the island of Bahrain, where their trading outpost had grown into a fortress.

By the standards of Piri Reis's corsair navy operating in the Mediterranean, the cruise should have been counted as a success. With a fleet of twenty-three galleys under his command, he swept out of the Red Sea, sacked the Portuguese-dominated town of Muscat and besieged Ormuz. The town was captured and the nearby Persian-influenced island of Qeshm was sacked before Piri Reis brought his fleet safely back to Basra for the winter laden with booty. But back at court in Istanbul his failure to take the fortress of Ormuz was criticised, as was the accidental loss of some siege artillery in a storm. So, instead of receiving praise and promotion, Piri Reis was disgraced and executed on the written orders of the Sultan. It is difficult to understand this action. Perhaps it was nothing more than punishment for a man known to have enjoyed the support of the disgraced grand vizier Ibrahim Pasha. Certainly there was no change in policy; indeed one of Piri Reis's recommendations from his old naval policy document, the creation of a joint military and naval command for the new province of the Persian Gulf, was soon implemented, as was his proposal to expand the empire's influence along the Red Sea shore. A planned invasion up the Nile fizzled out owing to the vast distances involved, but an occupation of the Ethiopian coast from the Egyptian military base of Suez was achieved in 1555. This was part of a proxy war being fought out in the mountains of Africa between the Christian Portuguese and the Ottomans. The Portuguese had been providing military assistance to the Christian

Emperor of Abyssinia, who had been locked in a life-or-death struggle in the mountainous interior for the past thirty years. For the conversion of the Afar and Somali tribes to a violent form of aggressive *jihad*-driven Islam had swept aside the civilised sultanates of the East African interior and the old balance of power. In particular a notorious left-handed warrior, Ahmad Gragn, had seized control of the walled city of Harar after a coup against the reigning Sultan, Abu Bakr, in 1520. From this base, and recruiting his army from the famously bellicose nomad tribes of Afar and Somalia, Gragn had launched a series of savage attacks on Christian Ethiopia. In all the old Abyssinian cultural centres – at Lake Tana, at Aksum and among the rock-carved churches of Lalibella – his army was brutally victorious. As a chronicler reported:

> In every place where they had triumphed they laid waste and destroyed and turned the country into a desert. They carried off from the churches the gold and silver vessels, the precious Indian stuffs, which were sewn with gems . . . and then set fire to them, and razed the walls to the ground. They slew every adult Christian they found, and carried off the youths and maidens and sold them as slaves . . . nine men out of ten renounced the Christian religion and accepted Islam. A mighty famine came on the country.[3]

Into this desperate conflict, the Portuguese sent four hundred well-armed infantrymen under the command of one of the sons of Vasco da Gama. The Ottoman governor in Yemen replied by sending out nine hundred Turks from his own garrison. So in 1541 the rival Muslim and Christian armies of Abyssinia, reinforced by the technical help of the two rival superpowers of the day, clashed on a hillside just south of Takazza known as 'The Mountain of the Jews'. After the battle Ahmad Gragn sent the pickled head of commander Da Gama to his Ottoman ally alongside a dozen prisoners of war to announce his victory. Two years later, on 21 February 1543, this day was reversed. For the Portuguese, far from being discouraged by this defeat, had responded by sending into the distant mountains a larger force recruited from their garrison bases along the East African coast. Ahmad Gragn was shot through the chest by a Portuguese musketeer, and in the aftermath of the battle his body was identified, his head severed and impaled on a pike which was then paraded victoriously across the countryside. Three years later the most aggressive of the Afar and Somali tribes had been expelled from the Christian heartland of Ethiopia. Gragn's widow, Bati Del Wambara, urged the tribes to counter-attack and even promised to marry her young nephew if he made a vow to continue the war. Harar remained a frontier town and acquired the circuit of walls that can still be seen today.

Gragn's formal blue velvet robe, which had been seized by the victorious Christians from the field of battle, was presented to the monastery of Mertule Maryam in much the same manner that the Spanish had dealt with the cloak of Barbarossa. Like Barbarossa, he also lives on in popular lore, the giant-sized demon warrior of many an Abyssinian folk tale. It was said that his body had already absorbed four thousand musket shots before the silver bullet of the Portuguese marksman finally felled him. If the Portuguese quest for an alliance with Prester John had helped start their astonishingly successful maritime empire, they succeeded in discharging some of their debt by their rescue of the last surviving African Christian state. The Ottoman occupation of the Red Sea coast was by comparison an almost lightweight matter, for the Christian Emperor of Abyssinia was too busy trying to revive his kingdoms after the devastating invasions of Ahmad Gragn to make any direct attempt to expel them. The Ottomans occupied Massawa and Arkiko in 1557 and later fought their way inland to build the fortress of Debarw, just south of Asmara. Although they were harassed by the Tigrayans of northern Ethiopia they stayed on this coast for three hundred years, naming it the province of Habesh within the litany of the Ottoman Empire's many tributary provinces.[4]

In Abyssinia a new migration of people would transform political life, as the Oromo warrior clans of pastoralists (also known as the Galla) pushed their way south into central Ethiopia. The Portuguese remained an influence in this Christian empire for another century, providing many of the technicians and craftsmen who created the new capital. Gondar is a still mesmerising collection of walled monasteries and palace compounds draped over several hillsides. This golden period of alliance between Portugal and Abyssinia was destroyed by the presence of Jesuit missionaries, who started to try to undermine the ancient traditions of Ethiopian Christianity. A hundred years after the Portuguese had saved Abyssinia from Ahmad Gragn's invasion, Emperor Fasildas was forced to expel them lest they turn his country into a Roman

Catholic seminary.

Spurred on by their success on the Red Sea shore, in 1559 the Ottomans once again tried to expel the Portuguese from their fortress of Manamah on the island of Bahrain. This siege was outflanked by the arrival of a Portuguese naval squadron. But the maintenance of forts and a separate fleet for the Persian Gulf proved an expensive commitment for both the Ottomans and the Portuguese. Within a few years the two empires came to an understanding to quietly demilitarise the region and maintain the existing frontiers. This spirit may have had commercial underpinning. For by 1560 it is now thought that the Indian traders had become accustomed to the presence of Portuguese bases along the coast and had developed new trade routes in the interior. So after the initial dramatic redirection of the spice trade at the beginning of the sixteenth century, a new pattern re-emerged. The result was that a third of the spice trade was being shipped out to western Europe in the annual Portuguese convoy, with another third passing through the lands of the Ottoman Empire and a third through Persia. Whatever the state of play between rival armies and faith-based empires, something as useful as pepper would always get through. The fate of the ruling families of the faith-based empires was never so certain.

Leaning on the shoulder of young Prince William of Orange, the gout-crippled elderly Emperor hobbled his way into the great hall of Brussels Castle, which was packed with the knights, nobility and ministers of the Duchy of Burgundy. It was at the beginning of winter, 25 October 1555.

He spoke to the assembly of his ceaseless travels, his attempts through forty years of war and diplomacy to protect the patrimony of his fathers, and their fathers before them. Nine times he had journeyed into the German Empire, six times through Spain, four times into France, twice across England and twice he had led a crusading army on to the North African shore. But he had failed. Failed to deliver peace to his people and failed to protect the Church. Now his armies were weakened, his treasury overwhelmed with debt, his health gone and Christendom riven apart. 'He was tired even to death,' and desired only to unburden himself of his lands and responsibilities. He appealed to his brother Ferdinand and his son Philip to avoid his errors, those of youth, self-will and indolence and always to 'stand fast in the faith of his fathers, to care for peace and justice'. But he declared with pride that he had never wilfully wronged any man and, if he had, he now asked their forgiveness.

With that the exhausted old man sank back into his throne. It was some minutes before the silent congregation could collect themselves, for the cheeks of many were, like the Emperor's, streaked with tears. It

Charles V aged 48. By Titian. (Alte Pinakothek, Munich)

was true: his attempt to defend the Church, to maintain the unity of Germany, to defeat the pretensions of France, had failed. But it was also untrue: he had defended his kingdoms and dominated Italy like no one since the time of the Caesars. He ruled over new empires as well as the old and had also remained true to himself. He had aspired to be a crusading Knight, King, Emperor and a man.

Then his son Philip approached the throne. He threw himself down at the knees of the father whom he cherished as a living saint. He took a public oath before the assembly to continue his father's work as Duke of Burgundy. Charles was then raised by two attendant courtiers, so that he could embrace and bless his son. Three months later, in a private family council, he resigned to his son the kingdoms of Leon, Castile, Aragon and the two Sicilies, and the islands and the Lordship of the Indies. The Habsburg lands in Germany had long since been consigned to the care of his younger brother, Archduke Ferdinand who would also later be elected his successor as Holy Roman Emperor.

He had just begun this process of legal divestment by surrendering his mastership of the Burgundian Order of the Golden Fleece, and it would only finally be completed when he divested himself of the Grand Masterships of the Spanish Crusading Orders of Santiago, Calatrava and Alcantara. As he did so he bore witness to the fact that he belonged to an age that was now dead. He recalled one of the great moments of his life: how proud he had felt in 1536 to ride through the specially built victory arch into the city of Naples after his triumphant crusade against Tunis. But the age of the crusading knight who fought for Christendom, not a nation state, was over. And for this old relic of it, his gout was such that he could hardly move a pen without assistance or cut through the string that held a parcel of letters from France.

The following summer the former Emperor Charles V took ship from Zeeland for Spain. He was no longer a monarch and had forbidden any formal receptions. However, in city after city of his native Duchy of Burgundy, the people set lights in their windows and rung out the church bells to bid the Emperor farewell as he made his way to the port. In Spain he journeyed south one last time, to look over the enchanted cities of Seville and Granada, where he had first basked in the love of his young wife. In November he moved to an eight-room villa that had been built for him on the outer edge of the high wall that enclosed the monastery of San Jeronimo at Yuste. Here, it was as if the apartments of his youth had been transferred to the bleak plateau of Estremadura. For they were furnished with rich Burgundian furniture and tapestries, gleaming canvases (including Titian's vision of the Trinity, *La Gloria*), clocks, globes, charts and a small library. The books chosen for the villa, his own travel journals and notebooks standing beside Boethius's *Consolation of Philosophy*, St Augustine's *Confessions*, *Caesar's Gallic Wars* and a biography of his Burgundian ancestor, *The Deeds of Charles the Bold*, give us a revealing insight into his character. A Christian in need of spiritual advice who was also an heir to the classical civilisation of Rome as well as the Gothic heritage of medieval Dukes of Burgundy.

He left casket after casket of old wills, testaments and letters of advice for his son. A selection of sentences from the will he made in 1548 provide plenty of evidence of his pragmatic sensibility and the soundness of his advice to his son Philip about the inevitable tensions within Europe:

There will always be trouble with the Pope, in Naples, Sicily and in Castile.

Keep a good understanding with the Venetians.
I have done much for the Duke of Florence and he is grateful: he is also [now] our kinsman.

The Duke of Ferrara leans to France: handle him cautiously.
The Duke of Mantua is to be trusted: cherish him for he has suffered much in the wars.

Genoa is the most important of all to us. Act shrewdly and skilfully in your dealings with it.

France has never kept faith and has always sought to do me hurt. The young King seems about to follow in his father's footsteps . . . always be casting about for excuses to resume their claims on Naples, Flanders and Milan . . . defend Milan with good artillery, Naples with a good fleet . . . you can never manage without Spanish troops in Italy.

He also candidly advised his son not to waste Spanish resources by sending men or money to assist Austria in the Turkish wars, for they were the responsibility of the German Empire. Instead he should confirm the strength of Spain by continuing to cultivate a close friendship with Portugal and watching over a good fleet, the best defence against corsairs, which would also 'keep the French from interfering in the Indies'.

In an earlier draft of advice to Philip, Charles V had concentrated on reviewing the internal workings of Spain. As a general rule he had followed the lead of his grandparents and excluded the powerful dynasties of nobles from any involvement in the inner workings of government, though he allowed that the grandees could be employed as diplomats and in war. Then, with an impressively sharp awareness of character, he had jotted down notes about the leading men of his court, their abilities, aspirations and failings:

> The Cardinal of Toledo is a good man and in all serious questions you can rely on his honesty. Only do not subject yourself wholly to his influence . . .
>
> The Duke of Alba . . . is ambitious, bear himself with as much seeming humility as he may. He will do his best to make himself agreeable to you, probably with the help of feminine influence. Take heed of him; yet trust him implicitly in all military matters.
>
> The Duke of Osorno is sly and deceitful, but he speaks so little that it is very hard to see through him.
>
> Granvelle will be your best guide in international policy. He too has some private interest in Burgundy and several sons to provide for, yet I think him honest.
>
> [The Cardinal of Seville, President of the Board of the Indies] has always advised me very well. But his feeble health and his inability to get on with the Cardinal of Toledo are two great drawbacks. If he shows any inclination to withdraw from Court life, you would do well to encourage him.
>
> Don Juan de Zuniga may appear rough and harsh, but do not forget that he is a devoted servant . . . He is jealous of Cobos [Charles's financial expert] and the Duke of Alva . . . Zuniga and Cobos, you must remember come from different social stratum from the others.
>
> Cobos is growing older and easier to manage, but he is true. No one knows as much of all my affairs as he . . . the danger with him is his ambitious wife. Do not give more influence . . . and above all do not yield to any temptations he may throw in your path; he is an old libertine, and he may try to arouse the same tastes in you. Cobos is a very rich man, for he draws a great deal from the dues for smelting bullion from the Indies.

The Emperor went on to confess that the current financial mess (for the treasury was on the point of bankruptcy) had nothing to do with Francisco de los Cobos's management but everything to do with Charles's incessant wars. Yet looking back, he was aware that he had placed too much authority in his secretary of state's capable hands owing to his own ignorance and negligence. It would be better, in future, to divide such power between two men. Philip should also remember that the current viceroy of Aragon is 'wholly dependent on Cobos' and was only chosen because 'he was the least bad of all the possible candidates'.

Like a dark secret at the centre of all this advice were Charles's veiled words to his son concerning the passionate sensuality that had destroyed so many of his family. 'Let me entreat you to keep a watch on yourself and not to give yourself over too much to the pleasures of marriage. An undue indulgence may not only injure your health . . . it may even cut short your life as it did that of your uncle Don John.' He hardly needed to mention the example of his own mother, mad Queen Juana, who had remained locked up in her castle throughout Charles's whole reign.

But the family madness, the passionate overwhelming sensuality and susceptibility to love, had not been buried with the old Queen. Even the grave, earnest, totally dedicated King Philip would now and then betray himself. A crack in his iron self-discipline would give vent to the violent obscenities that were otherwise kept at bay by a life of prayer and work. In Philip's son and heir, Don Carlos (who had lost his own mother at birth[5]) all the accumulated repression of three generations found its release. Although totally dedicated to the hereditary principle, even Charles V had doubts about his grandson: 'His manner and humour please me little . . . I do not know what he will be capable of in the future.' An English ambassador, in a confidential report, was more frank: 'I have never dealt with a more dissolute, desperate and contemptible person.' It was as if Don Carlos was compelled to a passionate absorption in everything that was repressed in his grandfather and father and in their kingdoms. He had a near-obsessional interest in religious heresies, in sensuality, in proscribed beliefs and in peoples and cultures who had been driven so cruelly from the shores of Spain.

Don Carlos's tragically short life would later be immortalised by, among others, Schiller and Verdi as that of a sacrificial young hero, a romantic free-thinker on the model of Hamlet, Shelley or Byron. But he was also a deeply flawed character, a bully to his servants, boorish in his sexual demands and proud of his ability to eat nauseating foods, the sort of substances only the desperately hungry resort to – insects, rats, reptiles and boiled leather. Two things seem to have pushed Don Carlos's behaviour beyond any acceptable limits. The first was the marriage of his father to a young French princess, to whom he believed he himself was about to be betrothed. The second was an accident, when he cracked his skull falling down a stone stairway in the midst of an attempted seduction. Thereafter he began to openly rage and plot against his father. These schemes were probably no more than the working of Don Carlos's impotent rage, but he succeeded in attracting a band of desperate conspirators to his cause. On Christmas Eve they were all arrested and the details of the plot were extracted from them by torture. The tradition that King Philip personally attended and directed the 'questioning' of his son may or may not be true but it was too powerful an image to have been ignored by novelists and dramatists. The king certainly read a detailed transcript of the confessions extracted from all the conspirators. Don Carlos, like his grandmother before him, was never to be released from captivity. He died in prison, quite how no one knows, but it was noticed that after this event his father could never frame an honest smile. When he tried to, it was, his courtiers agreed, 'like receiving a stab'.

While Suleyman the Magnificent differed from his great Christian rival, Charles V, in many ways, the fates of their children and grandchildren share a disturbing similarity. Suleyman was no orphan, indeed he had not only known his own father, but had assisted him in his struggle to seize the throne. When he himself succeeded his father, his mother Hafsa (the name borne by the most intellectual of the wives of the Prophet Muhammad) was still 'a very beautiful woman . . . for whom the sultan bears great reverence and love'. It was she, the absolute monarch of the harem, who selected the young women most likely to please her son as well as directing her daughters-in-law in the way that they should bring up her grandchildren. It is a curious combination of feminine roles for a Western mind to contemplate. Imagine it being normal for a loving maternal presence to co-exist with an authoritarian grandmother who also prided herself on an acute understanding of the erotic preferences of her son. But such was the emotional background of Suleyman and most of the Ottoman Sultans: not the frenzied, eunuch-controlled orgies of an Orientalist's imagination, but a mother presenting her son with a new concubine for his bedroom, with all the decorum and elegance expected within a palace drawing room. Suleyman was already a father at the time of his accession. His son Mustapha had been born in 1515 and grew up to be described by Bragadin, a European observer, as having 'extraordinary talent, is much loved by the Janissaries and performs great feats'.

Suleyman gradually turned his back on the delights of multiple concubines and slave girls and of his own free will chose himself a single partner. By 1526, when he was thirty-two, he had already shown a marked preference for the company of Roxelana. Seven years later Suleyman freed her from her position as his slave-concubine by marrying her, and then set aside all his other concubines. This is one of the great love stories of all time, a story of enduring friendship achieved amid the adversity of the furious rivalries of the palace. Many letters and verse notes survive from a relationship in which romantic infatuation was fanned year after year by prolonged separations. As we have seen, the Sultan often led his armies in campaigns that would last from March to October, and were sometimes extended over two years.

Suleyman to Roxelana:

My very own queen, my everything,
My beloved, my bright moon;
My intimate companion, my one and all,
Sovereign of all beauties, my sultan.

Roxelana to Suleyman:

Go gentle breeze, tell my sultan, 'She weeps and pines away;
Without your face, like a nightingale, she moans in dismay.
Don't think your power can heal her heartache in your absence:
No one has found a cure for her woes', that's what you should say,
'The hand of grief pierces her heart with its painful arrow;
In your absence, she is sick and wails like that flute, the ney.'

In this last line Roxelana uses the imagery of the Sufi poet Rumi, who played with the idea of how a reed flute (*ney*) is filled with desire to return to the marshy reed-bed of its birth, just as the soul desires to return to God. Suleyman for his part showed the most delightful side of his nature in his intimate dealings with his beloved. When Roxelana

Roxelana, Queen of Sultan Suleyman's heart.
Anonymous Venetian woodcut, circa 1550.

bore him a deformed son in 1531, rather than dispose of the shameful
hunchback, he poured love and attention on the crippled child. So
much so that Cihangir became much more of a trusted companion and
friend to the Sultan than any of his healthy children.

The critical moment in their relationship came with the death of
the queen mother, the Valide Sultan Hafsa, in March 1534. Thereafter
there was no one to balance Roxelana's authority in the palace. Her
attention inevitably turned to the life-or-death struggle on behalf of
her young sons: Mehmet, Selim, Bayezid and Cihangir. For all brothers, half-brothers, nephews and male relatives of a reigning sultan were
doomed. Mustapha, Suleyman's eldest son, was capable, confident and
much admired by the janissaries, but he was not Roxelana's son. She
knew her boys were all destined to have an oiled bowstring tightened
around their necks the moment that Mustapha succeeded to his father's
throne – unless she did something about it. So she began the transfor-

mation from romantic heroine to ultimately wicked stepmother. What else could she do? To save her children from certain death, she had to make certain that all her male stepchildren should be killed. She was not a Lady Macbeth, lusting for the throne, but a mother protecting her children from the bowstring. Nevertheless her influence on her husband and the Ottoman Empire would be utterly malign.

The first to fall seems to have been the grand vizier, Ibrahim Pasha. His old friendship with Prince Mustapha and the prince's mother, Mahidevran, made of him a deadly enemy. It took Roxelana years to destroy her husband's trust in his childhood companion. That he was supremely talented, energetic and successful must have made it all the harder. It seems likely that Roxelana was able to dig up some evidence that Ibrahim was secretly receiving money from Venice, or was betraying the empire in some way. She and her ministerial allies also circulated stories of how he boasted of his power over the Sultan, and how Suleyman could never win true renown while his all-controlling grand vizier lived to steal the credit. His death in March 1536 was followed by the slow promotion of Roxelana's creature, Rustem Pasha, the Uriah Heep of Ottoman politics. From governor of an eastern province, he became a minister, then married Mihrimah (daughter of Suleyman and Roxelana) in 1539 and was appointed grand vizier five years later.

The death of the eldest of Roxelana's sons, the twenty-one-year-old Mehmet, during an outbreak of smallpox in 1543 was a devastating blow to her plans. Mehmet was adored by his father – who sat beside his body, lost in prayer, for three whole days before he would permit its burial – and was the only one of Roxelana's children who might have been able to take on his half-brother Mustapha in terms of popularity, talent and leadership. To drown their shared sorrow, Suleyman and Roxelana had a vast domed memorial mosque constructed on the summit of the third hill of Istanbul, a still beautiful building, touched with the melancholy of its foundation. The Sehzade Camii, the Mosque of the Prince, and its associated tombs are seldom to be found without an escort of veiled mothers bringing their grief and supplications to the site.

In the spring of 1553 the plot of Roxelana and her henchman Rustem Pasha reached its awful conclusion. Suleyman was once more planning to send an army against the Safavid Shah and had appointed his grand vizier as army commander. By this period all four of his surviving sons were being trained in the art of ruling and were serving as governors in the provincial cities of Aleppo, Manisa, Konya and Amasya. One of their jobs in the spring was to send the janissaries of their garrison and the local tribal levies of warriors to join the Sultan's army. But for two decades Roxelana and Rustem Pasha drip-fed Suleyman with subtle lies and innuendo in an attempt to build up suspicion between father and eldest son. This is no mere supposition or whiff of old court gossip. The whole political class of the empire observed the process, as did the various foreign ambassadors who were unanimous in their praise of Prince Mustapha. The Italian Navagero wrote that very year of how 'it is impossible to describe how much he is loved and desired by all as successor to the throne'. Ogier de Busbecq, a clever Burgundian civil servant, who was then an ambassador for Archduke Ferdinand, wrote that Mustapha was in the prime of his life and enjoyed a high repute as a soldier' and a French observer, Guillaume Postel, rated him as 'well-educated and prudent and of the age to reign'.

But, once on the eastern frontier, Rustem Pasha wrote to Suleyman requesting his immediate presence. He claimed that the army was on the point of mutiny and that the janissaries were clamouring to be led by Prince Mustapha. This may have been true, for Rustem Pasha was detested by the rank and file for his vast wealth, legendary greed and corruption. Later that summer he managed to convince the old Sultan that the lack of troops coming from Mustapha's province of Amasya was evidence of a plot. It was alleged that Mustapha was hoarding janissaries in order to stab his father and the Ottoman field army in the back, in treacherous alliance with the 'heretical enemy', the Safavid Shah. It was a scarcely believable fiction, though Rustem Pasha did not need to exaggerate the enthusiasm with which the janissaries regarded the young prince. Whatever evidence he produced, or whatever innate suspicion he inflamed, in late October Suleyman sent an order to summon Mustapha to the army camp assembled at Karaman. Some of his closest friends begged him to refuse, but the prince was aware that this would indeed be a treasonable act, and he was completely confident of his innocence.

When Mustapha arrived to discuss these matters with his father, he processed through the tented city of the Ottoman army and 'in the camp there was considerable excitement among the soldiers'. He was escorted with honour through the customary pavilions and screen-like

walls of canvas around the Sultan's compound of courtyards. But there
was to be no discussion:

> As soon as he entered the inner tent, they [the Sultan's deaf-mute
> personal guards] made a determined attack upon him and did
> their best to throw a noose round him. Being a man of powerful
> build, he defended himself stoutly . . . Suleyman fearing this, and
> being only separated by line tent hangings from the scene . . .
> thrust his head out of the part of the tent in which he was and
> directed fierce and threatening glances upon the mutes . . . [who]
> redoubling their efforts, hurled the unhappy Mustapha to the
> ground and throwing the bowstring around his neck strangled
> him.

Mustapha's body was displayed on a carpet outside the entrance pavilion to the Sultan's enclosure. 'When the news spread through the camp,
pity and grief were general throughout the army; and no one failed to
come and gaze upon the sad sight.' Thousands of highly trained janissaries made their pilgrimage past the throttled body of the dead prince
and departed

> sad and silent, with their eyes full of tears, they betook themselves
> to their tents, where they could lament to their hearts content . . .
> they inveighed against Suleyman as a crazy old lunatic; then they
> railed against the treachery and cruelty of the young man's step-
> mother and the wickedness of Rustem, who together had
> extinguished the brightest star of the House of Othman. They
> passed that day in fasting, not even tasting water; nay, there were
> some who remained without eating for several days.

All his life Suleyman had battled against the Shia version of Islam,
which mourns the death of Husayn, the son of Imam Ali and grandson
of the Prophet Muhammad. Husayn was the archetypal heroic young
prince who was pitilessly slain by the machinations of wicked ministers. Now the Sultan had given new life to this potent belief by
re-enacting the whole tragic tale in his own family. So when the soldiers gave way to an intense period of mourning and lamentation,
though they were not Shia, they were also mourning a familiar inevita-

Suleyman the Magnificent. Engraving of 1559 by Melchior Lorks.

bility of human tragedy: that the virtuous will always be destroyed by scheming power politicians.

To distract his soldiers from their grief, the Sultan ordered the army to prepare to march into Syria, to patrol the frontiers of the empire. They were also calmed by the staged dismissal of Rustem Pasha (who would soon enough recover his old position) and a generous increase in their annual salary. There were, however, a few individuals whose grief could not be assuaged by a bribe. Mustapha's half-brother, the crippled Prince Cihangir, was so appalled by this incident that he lost any further interest in living and died of grief before the end of the year. His father had his body buried on the top of a hill overlooking the Bosporus, away from the city centre and the heavy mausolea of the men of power.

Roxelana died three years later, in the spring of 1558. Despite her scheming, she was loved by Suleyman to the last. During her lifetime he had commissioned a series of public works in her name. The magnificent bathhouse outside the Ayia Sophia and the vast charitable kitchen, hospice and mosque that rose on the city's seventh hill both bear her formal name: Haseki Hurrem. These were models for the vast pilgrim kitchens and hospices that were also raised in her name at the three Holy Cities of Islam: Jerusalem, Medina and Mecca. Her body was buried in an elegant kiosk within an enclosed garden behind the prayer niche of the vast Mosque of Suleyman. She lived just long enough to witness the inauguration of this magnificent house of prayer, which was opened in 1557. But she was spared the last act in the family tragedy, when her son Bayezid and her son Selim fought each other for the succession, even while their father still reigned. Bayezid escaped from the battle he fought with his brother outside Konya, to find the protection of his father's enemy, the Safavid Shah. For he had 'resolved to try to win anyone's pity rather than fall into his father's hands'. His host was eventually persuaded – by the usual means – to execute his guest and the four infant sons who had travelled with him into exile.

Bayezid's fifth son, the youngest, who was still being nursed by his mother in Brusa, was also executed, on the instructions of his grandfather. A particularly brutal jailor, a man callous enough to commit any crime, was selected and was accompanied by a palace servant sent to witness the death of the infant. But 'when the jailor entered the room and was fitting the noose around the child's neck, the child smiled at him and lifted himself up as far as he could and tried to throw his arms around his neck and kiss him. Brutal though the jailer was, he was so touched that he could not bear to do the deed, and fell fainting to the ground.' The palace servant could not leave the task unaccomplished and 'with his own hand he crushed out the feeble life of the innocent boy'.

On that day, according to the testimony of a Venetian official, the Sultan 'looked up to heaven with joined hands and spoke after this fashion, "God be praised that I have lived to see the Muslims freed from the miseries which would have come upon them if my sons had fought for the throne; I may now pass the rest of my days in tranquillity; instead of living and dying in despair."' It was what his own father had done for him. Turning the pages of Ottoman dynastic history is like descending into the most violent dream cycle, wading through a living paranoia, fed by real fears and a need to function like a serial-killing

Herod the Great.

Suleyman was hardly being true to either himself or his empire when he thanked heaven for the death of his errant son and grandsons. For the rank outsider, the son who had kept his head down and survived to become the recognised heir, was no hero. Selim, whose interests were in poetry, women and wine, never escaped being judged as the creature of Roxelana and Rustem Pasha. It didn't help matters that he was widely considered to be a drunkard, even if this was a popular distortion, though Busbecq does describe Selim as 'naturally gluttonous and slothful'. Selim was a lesser man than his full-brother Bayezid, and was clearly never going to supplant the memory of his murdered half-brother Prince Mustapha in the estimation of the janissaries. He knew this, they knew this and he knew that they knew this. Instead he is known to history as 'the Sot', which may be a cruel exaggeration especially when compared with that awarded his father, 'the Magnificent', and his grandfather, 'the Grim'. An empire that had been forged by a succession of heroic warrior commanders faced a Sultan apparent who lacked the confidence to lead his own slave soldiers into battle. An era had passed.

We also now know, from a private conversation between Busbecq and Rustem Pasha, just how delicate was the balance of power within the state. Even in the heyday of the Ottoman Empire the grand vizier could speak of the janissaries thus: 'Avoid any pretext of quarrel with the rascals. For surely, I was well aware that it was a time of war, during which they were masters to such an extent that not even Suleyman himself could control them and was actually afraid of personal harm at their hands.'

Busbecq goes on to reflect that, although a professional standing army possesses great advantages, it is accompanied by serious draw-backs, the chief of which 'is that the sovereign is kept in continual dread of a mutiny, and the soldiers have it in their power to transfer their allegiance to whomsoever they will'.

PART THREE

Destruction

13

Skull Islands

The Battle of Djerba and the Siege of Malta, 1560–70

The knights neglected to live but were prepared to die in the service of Christ.

Gibbon

By 1560 the superpowers of Habsburg Spain and the Ottoman Sultanate had expanded to their very fullest degree, bloated with conquests, annexations and chance acquisitions. Both states were already beyond the power of any one man to rule, and would soon be rocked by inflation, revolt and internal dissension. But the power structures within both regimes would not allow the momentum of a century of violent expansionism to be halted. Fleets of galleys that were worthy of Rome in her prime would be constructed for the great trial, treasure beyond calculation consumed in the pursuit of victory and hundreds of thousands of lives thrown into an all-consuming war machine. Peaceful islands would be transformed into killing fields, and their shores are still haunted by the spectre of siege, counter-siege and violent death from these years.

In September 1558 Charles V had died at his hermitage in Yuste. While his father lived Philip II, though titular King of Spain, ruled from the Duchy of Burgundy. This was out of respect for his father and because his marriage to Queen Mary of England had offered up the tantalising prospect of the addition of another throne to the vast Habsburg inheritance. Union of the crown of England with the lands of the Duchy of Burgundy would have created a commercial superstate and completed the encirclement of France. When Mary's pregnancy turned out to be a malignant growth, the prospect of a Habsburg empire of the North Sea ebbed away. Philip's marriage to his cousin Mary, daughter of his great-aunt Catherine of Aragon, which began in the chilly stone nave of Winchester Cathedral, formally ended four years later with her death in November 1558. That winter the diplomats and councillors of Europe made a new reckoning of the balance of power. Philip II made a sincere offer of marriage to the new Queen of England, Elizabeth (despite her known Protestant sympathies), before accepting the hand of a fifteen-year-old Valois princess, also called Elizabeth, as part of a peace package with France signed at Le Cateau-Cambrésis in 1559. He appointed his sister as regent of the Duchy of Burgundy and, having freed himself from all his responsibilities in the north, he could move south to take up the vacant thrones of Spain.

One of King Philip's first acts on his return to Spain was to witness an auto-da-fé in the centre of old Castile, the Plaza Mayor in Valladolid, where he had been born some thirty years earlier. It was an extraordinary spectacle, for the streets had been packed with row upon row of benches, the great square filled with scaffolding so that thousands upon thousands of spectators could have a fulfilling view. They looked out over a column of chained heretics, dressed in gaudy yellow tunics and ridiculous tapering hats, neatly labelled with their confessed crimes, advancing at a slow pace, surrounded by a buzz of soldiers and monks. Not even the dead had been permitted to escape, for the corpses of those who had expired during the 'questioning' of the Inquisition were also included in the procession. The preachers assured the populace that it was a meritorious act to witness the humiliation of heretics, while to add a faggot to the execution pyre was as efficacious as a fully paid-up indulgence. The Inquisition's jail had been closely guarded for weeks, not just to prevent the prisoners from escaping, but to stop the ever more excited crowd from breaking in and lynching the guilty.

For in the very heart of Spain, in the royal cities of Seville and Valladolid, the Inquisition had unearthed a nest of home-grown Protestants. Or so the Inquisitor-General claimed, having first broken the bodies and then the spirits of a group of Christian mystics in his torture chambers. Others saw it as a crude demonstration of power. For, aside from the core group of heretics, collected around the family of Dr Agustin de Cazalla (a most satisfactory hate-object, a converted Jew and

an intellectual who had once been a preacher to the Emperor himself),
they also included Juan de Ulloa, a Knight of St John who was a veteran
of both the Tunis and Algiers crusades, as well as the aristocratic brother-in-law of the head of the Spanish Jesuits. There was no mistaking
these signals: no one in Spain was to imagine themselves too powerful,
too heroic, or too well connected to escape the jurisdiction of the
Inquisition.

The heretics, having endured the hysterical screams of the mob and
stones flung by children, stood penitent in the square as a Dominican
monk preached over them for an hour. Those who had been pardoned
then joined in an open-air mass, while the condemned, who included
all of Dr Agustin's tortured family, were tied on to donkeys and trotted
off to be burned alive on the pyres that had been built beside the city
walls. It is a horrific image of the new Spain: the old enemy without,
the Moors, is replaced by the enemy within. It is tempting to read the
scene as the emblematic act that separates the Renaissance era of old
Emperor Charles V from the modern, nationalistic Counter-
Reformation rule of his son, Philip II. But history is seldom so neat.
Philip had no part in the planning of this inferno of heretics, for he had
landed in Spain just a month before it, while it was his father who had
dictated a violent denunciation of his old companion Dr Agustin and
demanded punishment not mercy even in his retirement.

These were dangerous but also thoroughly confusing times. Even the
future hero saints of the Catholic Reformation were very nearly consumed by the authoritarian machinery of the Church. The spiritual
companion of St Theresa, the Spanish mystical poet St John of the
Cross, had himself been imprisoned by his own order, alarmed by the
Protestant associations of the personal prayer which he advocated; while
Emperor Charles V, who fought against Protestants all his life, had
received special dispensation to possess contemporary translations of
the Gospels for his own personal study: one of the chief planks of the
Protestant reform movement.

The peace signed at Le Cateau-Cambrésis in the spring of 1559 had
the immediate effect of depriving the Ottoman fleet of the safe harbour
of Toulon. Philip was also aware that his uncle, the old Archduke
Ferdinand (now elected Holy Roman Emperor in succession to his elder
brother, Charles V), was deep in negotiations to sign a permanent truce
with the Sultan. Reports from the various spies, merchants and ambas-

sadors in Istanbul made it clear that the succession struggle between Suleyman's two surviving sons, Bayezid and Selim, was preoccupying the Ottoman Empire. It was a perfect time in which to make, or at least practise, peace. During the summer of 1559 even the Ottoman galleys rowed only as far as the Albanian shore before returning home.

Philip II's renewal of the war against the Ottomans and their corsair allies towards the end of that year has never been satisfactorily explained. Perhaps he wished to imitate his revered father, who had twice taken the opportunity to launch a crusade against North Africa when peace with France permitted it. Certainly it had very little to do with impressing his Spanish subjects. For a close inspection reveals that it was an exclusively Italian affair, with galleys recruited from the new fleet being established by the Medici Grand Duke of Tuscany, from the Genoese, the papacy, the Knights of St John and from the lands of Philip's own Kingdom of Sicily and Naples. The prime movers behind this scheme appear to have been the new head of the Knights of St John and Philip's viceroy in Sicily, Juan de la Cerda, the Duke of Medina Celi. However, from the start the whole expedition was weakened by a lack of clear leadership and forceful direction. Even the central objective, the reconquest of Tripoli from Dragut, was altered in mid-campaign.

It was not until 1 December that the Italian Crusader fleet left Syracuse, fifty-four warships and thirty-six supply ships carrying a mixed force of twelve thousand men drawn from the garrisons and mercenaries in the service of the Habsburgs. It was a form of collective madness to sail so late in the year and the fleet only managed to get itself halfway across the Strait of Sicily before a storm forced it to take shelter in Malta throughout December and January.

In mid-February the fleet lumbered down the coast of Tunisia, landing on the low-lying archipelago of the Kerkennah Isles before reaching the island of Djerba. Here, much to the delight of the presiding general, the Duke of Medina Celi, they captured two ships, fully loaded with olive oil, spices and the elegant camel-hair cloaks of southern Tunisia which the Spanish called *barracanes*. Then they set sail for nearby Tripoli, only to be driven back by heavy weather. To make a virtue out of this setback, the Duke occupied the island of Djerba, solemnly annexing it as a new territory for King Philip. The army was kept in admirably good order, the local villages were not pillaged and supplies were purchased at the markets. Agents familiar with the tribes were dispatched to make common cause with those local sheikhs who had grown anxious about Dragut's ever-expanding corsair kingdom. Trade was initiated with the governor of Kairouan as well as with the Hafsid Sultan of Tunis, whose throne was assured by the Spanish garrison at the fortress of Goletta. The army was kept busy building a fortress on the northern coast of the island, quarrying the friable local sandstone and smashing up marble columns from the ruins of the classical city of Meninx to make lime mortar.

Agents for both Dragut and the Ottoman fleet followed these manoeuvres during the winter of 1559. To an extent, the inordinate

Spanish fortress on Djerba.

delay of the Crusader fleet served them well, for the Ottoman fleet had presumed that the operation had been called off and had headed home in October. Both Dragut and Uluj Ali sailed for Istanbul that winter with a magnificent tribute for their sultan to help press their case for an immediate and powerful response.

The Sultan instructed admiral Piale Pasha to be prepared to sail the moment the seas were safe. The fleet travelled with great speed, reaching Djerba on 11 May, having been spotted off the coast of Malta three days earlier. The lack of preparation among the allies was astonishing, and is partly explained by the divided command: the King's viceroy in Sicily pushed for an orderly withdrawal, the Genoese were concerned for the safety of their galleys and the Duke of Medina Celi was in favour of holding on to the island. In the event there was no order, just panic as the Ottoman galleys and corsair captains attacked the anchored invasion fleet. In the words of Busbecq:

> They had neither the courage to fight nor the presence of mind to escape. A few galleys, it is true, which were cleared for action, sought safety in flight; the rest stuck fast, or broke up in the shallow water, or were surrounded by the enemy and sunk. The Duke of Medina Celi, who was the military commander, took refuge in the citadel together with Giovanni Andrea Doria, the admiral of the fleet. Under the cover of the darkness they embarked in the early watches of the night . . .

Twenty-eight ships of the Christian fleet of forty-eight were sunk or captured, though most of the Genoese galleys somehow seem to have propelled themselves to safety.

Several thousand Spanish soldiers had escaped the destruction of the fleet and continued to resist from within the half-built walls of the fortress that they had constructed on the northern coast of Djerba. Under the command of Alvaro de Sande they initially held their position with grit and determination. A relief expedition, to be recruited from all Christendom, was planned with great fanfare but then quietly cancelled by Philip II on 15 June. It was piously hoped that the stores within the fortress would allow them to withstand the Turkish siege unaided. Indeed the Ottoman fleet, which had been sent out with great speed, lacked the skilled janissaries and artillery necessary for a forceful siege. But Admiral Piale Pasha was advised by Dragut, who knew the island very well. So he seized control of all the wells (even these tend towards the brackish on low-lying Djerba) and patiently waited for the one large cistern within the fortress to dry up. By mid-July the Spanish garrison had become desperate and launched sortie after sortie in an attempt to reach the wells. These were mercilessly cut down. Busbecq, reporting on the conditions inside the fort, writes:

> water was rationed, just enough being distributed to each man to keep him alive. Most of the men increased their portion by adding sea water, which had been purified of the great part of its salt by distillation – a timely device which a skilful chemist had shown them. Not all of them, however, possessed the necessary facilities, and therefore many of them were to be seen stretched on the ground on the point of death, with their mouths agape and continually repeating a single word, 'water'. If anyone took pity on them and poured a little water into their mouths, they revived and sat up and remained in that posture until the effect of the water wore off, when they fell back again and eventually expired from thirst. Many died in this manner every day in addition to those who perished fighting or from disease and the complete lack of medical stores . . .

On 29 July the Spanish commander, Don Juan de Castella, realised that his men were on the point of total collapse. So he led one last futile attack. In desperation some of his dehydrated soldiers opened the gates, though he continued to direct resistance for another two days 'and fought, together with his brother, until he was wounded and finally taken prisoner'.

Outside the fort, Dragut ordered a pyramid to be built with the skulls of the many Spanish men who had died during the three-month siege. This monument, reinforced with dabs of lime mortar, stood for three hundred years before a priest managed to persuade the islanders to allow him to dismantle it and lay the bones to rest.

Piale Pasha lost no time in pressing home his victory. His fleet raided the coast of Sicily, seizing the town of Augusta before sailing to ravage the coast of Abruzzo. On 1 September he set sail for the east, arriving exactly thirty days later to lead a victory procession up the Bosporus. Once again we have an eyewitness account from Busbecq's articulate pen:

> The first night it anchored at the rocks of Constantinople, so that it might enter the harbour by day with greater pomp and before a greater crowd of spectators. Suleyman had gone down to the col-

onnade [at the seashore of the Topkapi Palace] so that he might
have a near view of the arrival of the fleet and the Christian officers exhibited upon it. On the poop of the flag ship were displayed
Don Alvaro de Sande and the admirals of the Neapolitan and
Sicilian fleets . . . The captured galleys were towed along, stripped
of their oars and bulwarks and reduced to mere bulks, so that in
this condition they might seem small, shapeless and contemptible
in comparison with the Turkish vessels. Those who saw Suleyman's
face on this occasion declare that they could not detect any traces
of unusual elation. Certainly I myself, when I saw him two days
later . . . remarked that his expression of face was unaltered. His
countenance was marked by the same sternness and sadness so
that you would almost have thought that the victory was no concern of his and that nothing new or unexpected had happened. So
steeled was the old man's heart to accept whatever fortune might
decree, so unflinching his mind, that he seemed to accept all the
applause without emotion.

A few days later the prisoners were brought to the palace. They
were starving and half-dead: most of them could scarcely stand,
many of them were collapsing through weakness and fainting,
some were practically dying. They were made a laughing stock,
being forced to wear their armour back to front . . . The cries of
the Turks were to be heard all around uttering insults and pro-
claiming themselves the masters of the whole world; for, now that
the Spaniards had been vanquished, what enemy remained whom
they need to fear?

This same thought was exercising the minds of the Christian governors
and commanders, their fears fanned by the rumour that a hundred new
keels were being prepared in the dockyards of Istanbul. Official after
official wrote to Philip II requesting funds for coastal defence works.
The disgraced Duke of Medina Celi displayed feeling but also a sharpened sense of strategy: 'We must draw strength from our weaknesses; let
Your Majesty sell us all, myself first, if only he can become "Senor del
Mar" – Lord of the Seas. Only thus will he have peace and tranquility
and will his subjects be defended, but if he does not, then all will go ill
for us.' The same voice reached the King of Spain through other
channels. One of the resident secret agents of his far-flung intelligence

service, a medical doctor resident in Ragusa, a city on the front line of war and famous for its independence and the strength of its ships, repeated the gossip of the waterfront taverns which precisely echoed the words of the Duke. Each spring alarm was set, and gossip and the reports of ambassadors and confidential agents buzzed back and forth across the Mediterranean. The Spanish garrisons in Oran and Goletta presumed that they would be the first target of an Ottoman fleet, and, learning from the debacle of Djerba, began to strengthen their defences and the water-holding capacity of their cisterns.

But, throughout the summers of 1561, 1562, 1563 and 1564, the Ottoman fleet never sailed west to take advantage of its 1560 victory at Djerba. Only the corsairs remained on the offensive. Dragut's corsair squadron attacked the Christians from his twin bases in Tripoli and Djerba and Uluj Ali launched raids from the corsair ports along the Algerian coast. In the summer of 1561 Dragut's command of the central seaways of the Mediterranean was spectacularly confirmed when he captured the Sicilian navy's last seven war galleys, in an engagement fought off the corsairs' favourite anchorage, the Lipari islands. In the succeeding years Dragut had a fleet of some thirty-five galleys crisscrossing the inner sea. Squadrons of twenty galleys were now required to make certain that supplies of grain and munitions arrived safely at the Spanish fortresses of Goletta and Oran. The loss of what remained of the fleet, some twenty-eight galleys sunk by a storm off the coast of Malaga in 1562, seemed to confirm the eclipse of Spanish naval power. In 1563 the corsairs of Algiers felt confident enough to strike out on their own, placing Oran and its associated fortress of Mers-el-Kebir under siege during the summer. That year, in full view of King Philip II, a corsair ship seized a Spanish merchant ship just three miles off Valencia, and nothing could be done about it. The raiders no longer needed the cover of night and started their landings in broad daylight.

But why did Suleyman not order the Ottoman fleet to attack, they all wondered? After Djerba, the whole coast of Christendom, with the exception of Venice, was vulnerable. There had never been a better time. We now think we know at least part of the answer. Suleyman sat tight in Istanbul, keeping a close eye on his army, because he did not trust his janissaries not to rise against his son Prince Selim while Prince Bayezid remained alive in Persia. Apart from the unnecessary devastation of a succession war, the Sultan also feared that it might reawaken

the pro-Shia Kizilbas movement that had so often flared up during his
father's reign. The murder of his son Prince Mustapha had already led
to a number of risings by Mustapha pretenders. Suleyman's chief judge
in Istanbul confirmed the decision of his predecessors and decreed that
any Shia (or their Kizilbas supporters) found within the empire were
technically apostates and could be condemned to death or enslaved out
of hand. The massacre of tens of thousands of Kizilbas that had occurred
in Sultan Selim's reign was not, however, repeated, though the Sultan
remained implacably ruthless with preachers. It was not just the pyres
of the Inquisition that were lit in this period. The Sufi preacher Ismail
Masuki and twelve of his disciples were publicly burned in Istanbul's
Hippodrome for their unorthodox beliefs.

During 1559, 1560, 1561 and 1562 no fewer than seven Ottoman
delegations travelled east to bargain a price for Prince Bayezid with
Shah Tahmasp (Ismail's son and heir). Prince Selim was deeply involved
in these negotiations but all the cards were in the Shah's hand. Although
the quantity of gold to be paid over was at last agreed, at the last
moment the Shah added a codicil in the form of a request for a jewel-
decorated sword, a jewelled belt with matching dagger, a chestnut mare
(always highly valued owing to a Koranic reference to a dun-coloured
horse) and five stallions to be paid once Prince Bayezid and his four
sons were handed over alive and well. But Selim had had enough of this
endless upping of the agreed fee. Once the price in gold coin had been
paid over, he arranged for an agent working within Shah Tahmasp's
capital of Qazvin to kill Bayezid and his sons.

It was also during this period that the Ottoman treasury finally began
to feel the cost of endless border wars: a standing army of janissaries and
a massive fleet kept at permanent readiness in Istanbul. Spain had been
rendered formally bankrupt a few years before. This fate never befell the
Ottoman Empire, though the signs were there for all to see. The debased
gold coinage struck in 1560 saw its real value fall by 30 per cent.

By the winter of 1563 it was clear from reports coming in from
Istanbul that the problems over the Ottoman succession had been
resolved. The death of the grand vizier, Rustem Pasha, taken by one of
the plagues that periodically swept through the crowded streets of
Istanbul, had also got rid of the empire's most hated politician. Rude,
abrasive and greedy though he was in life, the fortune he had extracted
in commissions and bribes was spent on the creation of a superb series

of hospices and mosques, built in the name of himself and his royal wife. Standing on the upper terrace of the jewel-like mosque that he built above the *fondouk* (the trading courtyards) of the spice merchants in Istanbul, you are already some way to forgiving Rustem Pasha a few of his crimes. The light-drenched prayer hall built in honour of his wife Mihrimah, Suleyman and Roxelana's daughter, is such a triumphantly innovative building that it has been copied in hundreds upon hundreds of provincial mosques throughout Turkey.

In the dockyards of Istanbul it was clear that the Ottoman Empire was preparing for war over the summer of 1564. This time it was not just war galleys being refurbished and refitted, but sturdy store-ships suitable for transferring great quantities of men and artillery. The peace with Venice held. Sicily was considered too big a target, so it was confidently predicted that the blow would fall either on Goletta or Malta. Dragut's advice had been listened to. A French admiral had described him as 'a living chart of the Mediterranean [and] skilful enough on land to be compared to the finest generals of the day'. Dragut insisted that whatever the target, the operation must start promptly. The mistakes of the Spanish at Algiers and the Italian fleet at Djerba (which both only managed to set sail after the campaign season was over) must not be repeated by the Ottomans. He also requested that his corsair squadron be reinforced with fifty fast war galleys so that he could protect the invasion fleet. He and Hasan Pasha in Algiers had noticed a new tide of professionalism entering the Spanish navy. They had been impressed by a recent naval operation directed by Alvaro de Bazan, who had surrounded the Moroccan port at Martil and sunk several transports loaded to the gunwales with ballast in order to seal off the corsairs' harbour. Furthermore, from the harbour of Malta, a new generation of Knights of St John were taking their ships deep into the Aegean. In 1561 and 1563 the Chevalier Romegas took his galleys up the Nile delta to seize shipping, and later intercepted a stout Ottoman merchant ship returning from Venice. It was a tough fight to possess her, for she was guarded by some two hundred soldiers, but when the luxurious goods in her hold were unloaded it was realised that the Chevalier had intercepted goods bound for the Sultan's own daughter, Princess Mihrimah.

King Philip had indeed been pressing forward with a plan to rebuild his lost fleets. For this emergency programme he requested the grant of a *cruzada* and a subsidy from the papacy as well as from the various Cortes of Spain. Over 1563 and 1564 between five hundred thousand and one million golden ducats poured into the shipyards of Barcelona, Genoa and Messina for the construction of a new navy. It would take time for the work to be completed, but something of the new spirit of determination would again be revealed in the summer of 1563, when a Spanish expedition, reinforced by galleys from Portugal, managed to sail south and burn down the Moroccan port of Badis opposite the Spanish fortress outpost of Penon de Velez de la Gomera.

By the spring of 1565 the Ottoman campaign had been planned down to the last shipload of provisions. One hundred thousand cannon balls had been prepared, along with fifteen thousand hundredweight of gunpowder, and old sails, sacks and damaged tents had been gathered up to reinforce the siege trenches in timberless Malta. An advance guard of twenty galleys set off the day after the Spring equinox (the traditional start of the sailing season) to confirm possession of the strategic straits, reinforced by a squadron of forty and followed by another thirty galleys. Only then did the invasion fleet, consisting of some 150 hulls, set sail in mid-April. They arrived off the island a month later, on 18 May, establishing a base at the island's second harbour, Marsa Scirocco. That night the three-thousand-strong advance guard set up the perimeters of a camp, which received another twenty thousand troops the next day, so that 'a well-ordered camp was set up bright with flags and banners and sound of musical instruments'. There were no surprises, for two Ottoman military engineers, a Slav and a Greek renegade, had already made a complete exploration of the island the year before. Disguised as a pair of fishermen, they had 'noted every gun and surveyed every battery'. The Ottoman command structure was simple. Admiral Piale Pasha, the hero of Djerba, was in command of the navy while the army was led by Mustapha Pasha, an experienced general sixty-five years old.

The Knights of St John may have been surprised at the speed with which the Ottoman fleet reached their island and the dispatch with which the invading army was landed. But they had known for at least a year that they were the likely target, for they were not lacking good intelligence of their own. On the orders of the Grand Master a Greek knight had been living in disguise in Constantinople and quietly observ-

ing the construction of the new fleet. Through another source a copy of
the Ottomans' campaign strategy had also fallen into their hands. One
of their own number, a scholarly Englishman named Sir Oliver Stacey,
had made a translation, which had been sent to all the kings and princes
of Christendom with a request for assistance. At the same time a general
order had been dispatched, that all the Knights of St John resident in
foreign courts should report for duty. That winter and spring supplies
and volunteers had poured into the island: the Duke of Tuscany sent
two hundred barrels of the very finest corned gunpowder, while the
viceroy of Sicily agreed to care for all the women, children and old men
deemed unfit to fight. In the meantime wheat and water were shipped
south. The viceroy's own son, Don Federico, like many a young noblemen, was so impressed by the steadfast nature of the Knights that he
took the vow himself. In another court the illegitimate son of Charles
V, Don John (Juan) of Austria, begged his older half-brother, King
Philip, to be permitted to volunteer. On being forbidden he tried to slip
aboard a ship at Barcelona but instead collapsed with a fever.

By the time the Ottoman fleet was sighted, fifteen miles off Malta on
17 May, the Knights were as ready as they would ever be. Some seven
hundred of them, assisted by four thousand Maltese warriors and a
good quantity of gentlemen volunteers and mercenaries, held the island.
The defences were concentrated around the old town, overlooking the
magnificent natural basin of Malta's grand harbour. This was far too
large to be enclosed in a single defensive system, so three separate fortresses had been added to the peninsulas nearest to the old town and its
defences. The commander of the Knights was Jean de la Valette, who
had been elected Grand Master in 1557 and had been working on
improving the defences of Malta for some nine years. He was an old
man, toughened by life's hardships and adventures, which had famously
included a year rowing as a slave in a corsair galley. Like the majority of
the Knights of St John in this period, de la Valette was a Frenchman.
However, he did not approve of the disgraceful surrender of the fortress
of Tripoli to Dragut, arbitrated by the French ambassador, or the alliance of the King of France with the Ottoman Empire. Indeed it seems
likely that he and his brother Knights were determined that their conduct on Malta should redeem the honour of France among the
crusading knights of Christendom. Once he was sure of the arrival of
the enemy he asked a fellow Knight and highly skilled yachtsman, the

Italian Giovanni Castruccio, to take his skiff through that vast Ottoman fleet and alert the rest of Christendom. Castruccio carried a terse note from the Grand Master: 'The siege has begun. The Turkish fleet is close on two hundred ships. We request your help.'

There were not many princes disposed to provide this aid. The Knights of St John were the last of the monastic military orders to maintain their independence. Their only suzerain was the Pope and in an age of increasing nationalism they were an anachronism. After the surrender of Rhodes in the last days of 1520, their refugee Grand Master, Philip Villiers de l'Isle Adam, had wandered around the courts of Christendom for seven years. Well might Suleyman remark, 'It weighs on me somewhat that I should think to chase this old Christian from his home.' But there was no king who had a use for an order that could offer no obedience to a monarch and was forbidden to fight other Christians, and their refusal to keep to any truce with the Islamic world made them a potential embarrassment to any trading nation. Indeed such attitudes made the Knights a liability to the ambitions of any Renaissance prince. It had taken Charles V, a man who had to juggle a sufficiently complex web of loyalties within himself, to appreciate their position. He had commanded his viceroy of Sicily to give them the islands of Malta and Gozo for the annual rent of a falcon.[1] It was said that when the Knights first landed on Malta's craggy shore and looked over the thin soil of this island of stone they wept, remembering the beauty and grandeur of Rhodes.

So when the Grand Master made his terse appeal, via the governor-general of Sicily, it was in fact addressed to only one man: the King of Spain. Philip II had his own concerns, however. He wished to continue to build up a strong Spanish navy, rather than repeat the debacle of Djerba. He was also suspicious of the Knights of St John, who were French when they were not international. This opinion was intensified by the fact that the current Pope, Pius IV, loathed anything to do with Spain. Philip II was accused of dragging his feet rather than rushing to the rescue of the Knights. Others have hinted that he wished to see them destroyed before arranging to reconquer Malta for Spain.

Piale Pasha's task was the one that Dragut had requested for himself. He was to command a maritime shield that would protect the Ottoman army from the newly built Spanish and Sicilian fleets while it proceeded with the siege. Dragut was now eighty and had not been trusted with supreme naval command. Piale Pasha had never known the freedom of a corsair captain. His life had been entirely spent in the service of Sultan Suleyman. He had been discovered as a newborn babe, exposed on a broken ploughshare outside the walls of Belgrade. His victory at Djerba had crowned a long naval career but he had risked disgrace in its immediate aftermath by his less than honest dealings over the private ransoming of the Duke of Medina Celi's son. Marriage to one of Prince Selim's daughters, Genher, had restored his position at court. The stern old Sultan had publicly forgiven him, while warning that punishment undoubtedly awaited him beyond the grave. The marriage also associated him with the astute grand vizier, Sokullu Mehmet Pasha, who was married to another of Prince Selim's daughters, Esmakhan. A princess as a wife brought great distinction to a vizier and an admiral, but it also had its downside. It was expected that you would divorce your previous wives and it was also assumed that you would not embarrass the royal family by allowing any male children to survive.

Piale Pasha was rightly concerned that his ships should have a safe harbour while they guarded the Sicilian channel. He suggested that an early objective should be to take the little star-shaped artillery fortress of St Elmo Castle. This would give the Ottomans control of the rocky peninsula of Mount Sciberas, which sticks out into Malta's Grand Harbour. The fleet would be able to anchor in complete safety, allowing for a blockade of the Knights in their remaining two coastal fortresses and easy access for the fleet to assist with naval bombardments and marine assaults.

Mustapha Pasha concurred. His first, rather precipitous attack against the central St Angelo Castle had not been a success. The intelligence reports he had received were already out of date for the old curtain wall had been reinforced by two flanking bastions and a deepened moat, which had caught his troops in deadly crossfire. They were then counter-attacked by the Knights, who had sallied out during the withdrawal. It had been a punishing start to the siege.

So Mustapha Pasha gave instructions that the siege trenches below St Angelo Castle be held but that the weight of the assault be switched to St Elmo. This looked an isolated and highly vulnerable fort, alone on the end of a promontory overlooked by the higher ground of Mount Sciberas. The Turkish troops quickly cut new siege lines into the slopes of the mountain. Ten eighty-pounders, two sixty-pound culverins and one massive basilisk, which could throw a 180-pound ball, were dragged into position and started the work of smashing the walls. The Grand Master, for his part, decided to reinforce the garrison. Under the cover of night he shipped sixty-five knights and two hundred soldiers across the waters of the Grand Harbour to stiffen the defences.

When Dragut arrived in Malta he brought his fleet of fifty ships and

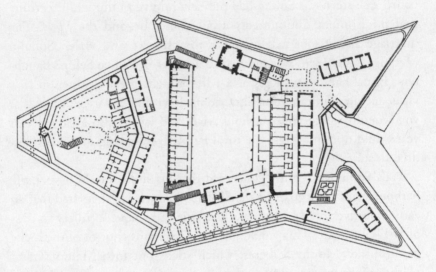

Plan of Fort St Elmo as originally designed by the Spanish engineer Pedron Pardo in 1552. (Dr David Nicolle)

some fifteen hundred battle-hardened corsairs from Djerba and Tripoli, ready to volunteer their services. He was impressed by the early start of the Ottoman siege and calculated that they had three clear months before a Christian relief force was likely to intervene. The rate of fire was increased, both as the siege trenches crept closer and as his war galleys joined in. He set up a battery on the adjacent peninsula of Marsa Muscetto to pound the sea walls of St Elmo from the north. By the end of May some six thousand shots a day were smashing into the walls. But the defenders had managed to survive this almost suffocating rate of fire by sheltering in deep, rock-cut trenches while the unimpressive, low, external silhouette of the fort absorbed much of the destruction. On 3 June the Ottomans launched an attack which was repulsed in a vicious day's fighting. The casualty figures are disputed, but it seems that two thousand attackers died or were badly wounded and eighty of the defenders perished in five hours. However, the attacking troops managed to keep possession of the ravelin, a half-finished external rampart beyond the north walls. From this forward position snipers could pick off the defenders at close range as they appeared above the ramparts. The longer Ottoman barrels gave these sharpshooters greater range and accuracy, though they suffered in close-quarter conflict, for the shorter, less accurate Christian hand guns were much quicker to load.

That night de la Valette sent two hundred reinforcements over the water to St Elmo and the critically wounded were evacuated. Even in the protective darkness it was a difficult operation, but the Maltese and Genoese sailors succeeded without serious losses. The Turkish soldiers raised the height of the ravelin by dragging forward goatskins stuffed with earth. The accuracy of these sharpshooters had a critical effect on the defenders' morale, much more so than the three days of artillery bombardment that followed. The captain of St Elmo sent a message to de la Valette, who knew enough about soldiers not to send a morale-boosting delegation of priests and officers. Instead they sent an advance on their pay and barrels of wine so that the garrison could set up bars and gaming tables. On 7 June the Ottoman besiegers managed to drag two light cannon to the ravelin and, under the cover of the close bombardment provided by these, started to construct scaffolding to bridge the moat. This was a critical development and the defenders sallied out to destroy the work, which was rebuilt and once again attacked. The following day became a continuous battle for control of the moat. The Turks were eventually beaten off, losing five hundred men, but they retained their tenacious hold on the ravelin. In their despair at the relentless casualties inflicted by the Ottoman sharpshooters, the defenders, be they Knights of St John or common foot-soldiers, wrote a petition to their commander declaring that St Elmo was now untenable. In just one day twenty-one men had been picked off at their posts. A delegation of three senior Knights came over the water that night to make their own assessment of the situation but, to the fury of the defenders, they quickly left. Morale among the garrison dropped to an all-time low.

But the next day there was a surprise when one of the three Knights returned, having volunteered to be the new captain of St Elmo, and brought five hundred volunteers with him. He offered the old garrison the chance to leave their posts for a well-earned respite. Not a soldier moved. To reward their loyalty a further advance of pay and more wine was sent across. On 10 June a sally of Knights attempted to clear the ravelin of sharpshooters, to which the Turks responded with a bombardment, so lit up by flares and incendiary shells that night was turned to day. On the third watch of that night they launched fresh troops against the walls and the attacks continued until dawn. A thousand soldiers perished that night. Throughout the 11th and the 12th St Elmo was placed under continuous bombardment, broken by brief sallies as Ottoman engineers filled the moat. On 15 June attacks were launched at dawn, in the afternoon and at night. The following day there was a general assault which lasted seven hours, the ghastly scenes partly obscured by the smoke of the incendiaries that exploded when one of the ammunition stores took a direct hit. It was said that at this point one more assault would have taken St Elmo, but with the moats blocked with a thousand dead and dying soldiers, the Turkish commanders also needed to rest their troops. That night de la Valette sent another 150 soldiers to replace those killed in the previous day's fighting. They brought with them a supply of old sails and mattresses, which were draped over the walls and soaked with sea water as fire-guards against the incendiaries.

Dragut, watching these manoeuvres that Monday morning, realised his tactical mistake. He sent orders for gun platforms to be built on the shore. These were set not against the fortress walls but trained to fire chain-shot and shrapnel into any boat that tried to supply St Elmo. By 20 June these accurately sited new positions of Dragut's prevented the defenders from even descending to the seashore beneath the walls. The main fortress of the Knights of St John was not nearly so tightly blockaded at this time. On that same day forty-two Knights, latecomers from Germany, accompanied by six hundred foot-soldiers, landed on Malta and managed to march around the edge of the Ottoman camp, slip through a gap in the siege lines and join their brethren. The Turks feared that they were the vanguard of a much larger force. Conversely the Grand Master feared that they were not the first reinforcements but the last of a trickle of volunteers. They brought with them a message.

The viceroy of Sicily requested that the Grand Master send him 'for safety' the five galleys owned by the Knights of St John that were still in the Grand Harbour. It was a modest enough request, though it came with the ominous understanding that Malta had already been written off as a lost cause.

The following day, 21 June, was the feast of Corpus Christi. Following the example of Jesus Christ, the Grand Master, attended by his senior Knights, served thirteen of the poor after first washing their feet. At the same time that this traditional ceremony was being performed, a single cannon shot, fired from one of the siege batteries, struck a mortal blow to the Ottoman cause. Dragut had been inspecting another of the shore batteries that he had set up, this one established on the Sliema promontory, west of St Elmo, and had given orders for the cannon sights to be lowered a degree. While he was observing their new range and trajectory, one of the newly adjusted cannon fired a shot too close to the rock floor so that a shower of blasted limestone ricocheted back over the gun emplacement. One of these splinters pierced Dragut's skull, and blood was seen to pour from his mouth, ears and eyes. He survived for a few more days, but death was certain. His body was taken aboard the galley of one of his lieutenants, the Italian renegade Uluj Ali, who rowed him back to an honoured burial in the walled city of Tripoli.

In the meantime Dragut's tactical preparations were all but complete. A three-day bombardment provided sufficient cover for Ottoman engineers to construct a new bridge across the moat and launch another six-hour assault. They were beaten back but at a crippling loss to the garrison, which could no longer be reinforced. No boat could survive the Ottoman gun emplacements but one of the Maltese soldiers managed to swim across with a message from St Elmo to their commander saying that there was 'not one man not covered with his own blood and that of the enemy and they had no ammunition left'. De la Valette sent a specially dismasted galley across the creek that night with muffled oars. Dragut's work in isolating St Elmo was complete. The galley was detected and his shoreline batteries erupted into fire as flares lit up the night sky above the Grand Harbour. The mastless galley was speedily destroyed and the flares revealed the silhouettes of eighty Ottoman galleys lying in wait for first light. That dawn the Ottoman assault swept the last defenders from the walls of St Elmo, who made their last stand in the garrison chapel. The janissaries slaughtered them all except for nine wounded Knights who had the good fortune to be captured by Dragut's corsairs, who knew how much these noblemen could fetch in ransom. The only other survivors were a group of nine Maltese soldiers who had even been praised by the Knights for their bravery. The Maltese escaped by slipping out of their armour and swimming across the harbour to safety. To celebrate the fall of St Elmo, every wall, tower and bastion was draped with Ottoman flags and pennants and the fleet, also dressed overall in flags, formally occupied the Grand Harbour.

The pageantry was not enough to hide the deep scars inflicted on

The fall of St Elmo.

both armies. Both Mustapha Pasha and de la Valette felt that they had lost their best men, and it was true. At least six thousand besiegers and fifteen hundred Christian soldiers had perished. A desperate savagery now entered the conduct of the siege, as both besiegers and besieged began to doubt the outcome. The ability of the Christians to mount a relief force, which was not expected by either side much before mid-July, had become the crucial factor. It only added to the madness of expectation that on a good day the coast of Sicily was just a day's sail from Malta. The bodies of St Elmo's fallen Knights were stripped and dismembered. Hands, head and genitals were removed and a cross carved into their chests. These bloody stumps were then nailed to crossbeams which were launched into the Grand Harbour. Pecked at by birds, a few drifted up to the shore beneath the walls of the old city. In savage response, de la Valette ordered that all the Turkish prisoners and Muslim galley slaves in the castle be fetched from the dungeons. All day a sad line of manacled prisoners were led one by one to the summit of a tower, where they were publicly beheaded and their heads catapulted into the trenches of the besiegers. Terror had become a legitimate weapon on both sides. For the commanders knew that the siege was now as much a test of morale as one of cannonades.

The peculiar geography of Malta also imposed its own laws on the conduct of the siege. Like Djerba, Malta is largely dependent on cisterns for fresh water, and the almost barren surface offered very little grazing and no food for the vast forces that had been brought there. The Ottoman navy and army had to be supplied from their camp. The Ottoman forces were used to having an advantage over their enemies in logistics: well-organised supplies, superior hygiene, efficient kitchens and disciplined camps. But for the first time this was not so on Malta. The Christians were usually the dirty ones, but not the Knights of St John. As 'hospitallers' they were famously zealous about cleanliness and health. They had also improved the vast cisterns that they had inherited within their fortress. So, right from the start of the siege, the Ottomans found it a challenge to supply their army and navy with sufficient water for drinking and washing for tens of thousands. The nearby islands of Pantelleria and Lampedusa are even worse off than Malta for water. By midsummer rotting corpses, half-buried in trenches and hidden beneath fallen walls and bombed-out trenches, added the final ingredient to the recipe for disease. A deserter informed the defenders that the wounds of the Turkish soldiers were not healing, that there was disease in the base camp and that they were being fed but ten ounces of biscuit a day.

Attacks on San Angelo, the Knights' main fortress, were launched with impressive speed after the fall of St Elmo, however. But the valiant resistance of St Elmo had given the Knights more than a month in which to upgrade the outer walls to a design by their resident architect-engineer, Evangelista. These were tested day after day for six brutal weeks as Mustapha Pasha bombarded, assaulted, mined and launched attacks by sea as well as land.

The general assault, on 7 August, was the high point of the Turkish siege, so much so that the Knights' seventy-one-year-old Grand Master felt obliged to personally take up position on the walls. But it was the native cavalry of Malta who proved decisive that day. They chose this critical moment to ride out from the walled city of Medina, the centre of the island, and launch a raid on the Turkish base camp. Although the Turks recovered their discipline after a moment of panic that day, it was clear they no longer believed in victory. Nevertheless they continued to besiege the walls for another thirty days. Disease, food and water shortages, the appalling casualties received in the first month-long attacks on the little fort of St Elmo, the death of Dragut and the fear of being trapped by a Christian counter-attack had finally blunted their great war machine.

Meanwhile a sufficient number of Spanish, Genoese, Sicilian and Italian galleys had been assembled to make it possible for a Christian fleet of some one hundred ships to confront Piale Pasha's 150-strong fleet and land a relief force. A two-week storm blew them straight back into Trapani in Sicily, where one thousand unpaid seasick soldiers promptly deserted, but on 5 September a five-thousand-strong force was at last landed on Malta 'without the loss of a single oar'.

The Turks were halfway through their evacuation, but nevertheless sent a regiment or two to head off this small relieving army, before completing their withdrawal in excellent order. De la Valette, whether out of admiration for his enemy, a desire to avoid the diseases that now riddled the Ottoman army or a reluctance to allow the Spanish and Sicilians to share in his victory, forbade them to attack. Escorted by the galleys of Piale Pasha's fleet, the last Ottoman troop ship left the shore of Malta on 12 September.

The news spread fast. By 6 October the city of Istanbul was in mourning, a mood which intensified over the winter as the grim extent of the casualties was fully revealed. 'One man grieved for a lost brother, while his neighbour wept for a son, another house for a husband, a father or a friend.' They heard about it in Rome on 19 September when the Pope offered public thanks, attributing the entire victory to God and the Knights of St John and making no mention of the King of Spain, his admiral, his new fleet or his troops. It is true that they were late, but the reinforcements had been decisive. It was also expected that the Turks might be back the following year, having not lost a single ship during the campaign. So Philip II lent the Grand Master six thousand troops and gave him fifty thousand ducats to repair the walls of Malta and spent a further fifty-six thousand ducats strengthening those of Goletta. He gave instructions that his precious new fleet remain in Sicily so as to be ready for a second attack.

Only the Venetians failed to join the Europe-wide celebrations of the noble defence of Malta by the Knights of St John. In Venice they had openly celebrated the fall of St Elmo, for to them the Knights were nothing but Christian corsairs who had interrupted and obstructed their trade with the East for the past two hundred years.

De la Valette knew what a close-run thing the siege had been. A third of the Knights had been killed, and the rest were all wounded to a greater or lesser degree. He had nine thousand fit men under his command at the beginning of the siege in May but only nine hundred fit for front-line service by the end of September. He accepted a sword of honour engraved 'Plus Quam Valor Valet Valette' (which was later stolen by Napoleon) that was sent by Philip II but modestly refused the cardinal's hat offered him by the Pope. Having reflected long and hard on his defensive positions throughout the four-month siege, he decided to build a new citadel and city on a site to the north of the Grand Harbour. This would include a splendid hospital, five hundred feet long, where the sick would be nursed from silver plates 'for the honour of the Hospital and the cleanliness of the sick'. It was a sign of the times that even here Christendom was rent in two, for one ward was set aside to be for Catholics only.

The Ottoman fleet did set sail the next year, but it was no more than a supporting arm for the Sultan's campaign against Hungary. A new system of defensive lookout posts linked to coastal garrisons had been extended along the corsair-battered coasts of southern Italy. That year it worked: towns and villages were evacuated inland as the fleet made its depredations and only five prisoners were taken, as compared with the usual round-up of some five thousand.

The victory of the Knights of St John in Malta did not encourage Philip II to lead a crusade into North Africa. Instead he started laying meticulous plans for enforcing his rule over his own people. The garrisons of Spain were to be marched north, out of the Mediterranean cockpit of war, to occupy and discipline the Protestant dissidents in the lands of the old Duchy of Burgundy. In the far south he also tightened the ratchet of state authority. The draconian Pragmatic Decree of Charles V which had prohibited Moorish dress, Moorish names, Moorish songs, dances and even bathhouses, was enforced for the first time. In a decree of 1 January 1567 he declared his intention to impose this state proscription of what remained of an entire culture over a two-year period. This bizarre and aggressive decision was directly responsible for the revolt in the Alpujarras hills. The uprising began, in a near-farcical way, on Christmas Day 1568, when a handsome young Granadan gentleman named Hernandez de Valor declared himself to be Emir Muhammad, a descendant of the long-dead Ommayad Caliphs, and turned himself into a bandit king of the hills. A few early successes against incompetent bands of Christian militia and the determined resistance of a few liberated towns of Muslims helped exaggerate the scale of the rebellion. In their panic the authorities licensed armed bands of Old Christian militia, who were permitted to kill any man on sight and enslave any women they found within the Alpujarras. At least twenty thousand rebels were hunted down by these lynch parties, of whom even their commander declared that they had 'not the least sense of honour among them' and 'cared for nothing but plunder and an easy life'. By 1570 a peace was declared over the devastated region. Desperate appeals for assistance were sent to the ruling Sharif of Morocco in Marrakech, the Ottoman Sultan in Istanbul and the corsair admiral in Algiers, but they were not answered. The rebels did not possess a port and the timing of their rebellion, just after the failure of the Ottoman siege of Malta, could not have been worse. The only practical assistance came from the Pasha of Algiers, who took the opportunity of emptying his jails of some four hundred criminals. They were dropped on the coast of Spain with a gun each and told to do their worst.

This Pasha of Algiers was Uluj Ali, the same faithful lieutenant of Dragut who had escorted his master's body back to Tripoli during the siege of Malta and two years later, in 1568, was appointed to take command of Algiers. He was known by many other names – Ali Pasha, Uluch Ali, El Louk Ali, Euldj Ali and Ochiali – and *Don Quixote* (Chapter Thirty-Nine) makes a flattering reference to him as Uchail. Uluj Ali was born in the poor village of Licastelli in Calabria, southern

Italy, and was captured in one of the many corsair raids on this coast. He grew into a strong, hoarse-voiced, scabby-headed galley slave. His conversion to Islam came not from any attitude of faith but as a point of Mediterranean honour. Insulted by a Muslim sailor, he converted on the spot, so that he could be free to fight and defend his name. Having killed his tormentor, he was promoted to become the whistle-blowing bosun of the galley slaves. He was allowed to grow a moustache and would now receive a share of the prize money seized by the corsair galley. Eventually he invested this in a small craft of his own. His success was a natural outcome of his easy leadership and deep understanding of how to sail, row and manoeuvre the galleys. He rose to become one of the favoured captains of Dragut, serving him with a passionate loyalty that was combined with a clear love for his men, whom he freely called his 'children'.

As Pasha of Algiers, Uluj Ali was approached by a Spanish agent who offered him money if he would agree not to assist the Alpujarras rebels any further. This he accepted, since he had no intention of doing so any more once he had cleared the jails of Algiers of criminals. More gifts followed as the agent sought to develop a special relationship with the Beylerbey. It was even suggested that he might like the Spanish title of marquis if he could bring Algiers over to the Spanish crown. Uluj Ali gave the matter his most profound attention while continuing to accept gifts. At last he decided that it was time to make his reply. In October 1569 he left Algiers by sea, landed some way to the east and marched inland through Constantine at the head of a force of some six thousand experienced corsairs and janissaries, to be joined by thousands of volunteers from the tribes. Uluj Ali was marching on Tunis against the Hafsid Sultan, Moulay Hamid, who had been put back on his throne after the catastrophic sack of the city by the soldiers of Charles V. Over the past twenty years he had done nothing to escape the tutelage of the Spanish alliance and their ever-growing military base at Goletta. This prince was not loved by his people, so when Uluj Ali's army was just two days' march away he decided to abandon Tunis and retreat to the safety of the Spanish garrison. Uluj Ali was welcomed as a hero by the citizens of the city, despite or perhaps because of his curious background as a peasant-boy renegade and a former galley slave. He appointed one of his trusted confederates, Cayto Ramadan, another Italian renegade (from Sardinia), to be the new governor of the city of Tunis and the surrounding countryside.

The Spanish garrison still held on to the fortress port of Goletta, but as Uluj Ali returned to Algiers he could feel proud that his old master's death at Malta had been avenged. Dragut rested in his tomb in Tripoli and Tunis had been returned to Dar-al-Islam. It would not be the last time that the corsair captain Uluj Ali would reveal himself to be a great warrior hero of the Islamic world.

14

A Beard for an Arm

The Conquest of Cyprus and the Holy League's Victory of Lepanto, 1570–4

There is properly no history, only biography.

Emerson, *Essays*

In the last decade of his life Sultan Suleyman became ever more pious, turning his back on the early magnificence of his youthful court, forgoing the gold and silver dinner services to eat modestly and humbly in the style of the Prophet. He forbade the public consumption of wine in his capital, even by its many Christian and Jewish inhabitants. He wrote sternly to his son Selim asking him to give up his predilection for wine and rid himself of his drinking companion. Even within the privacy of his palace compound, the Sultan decided to abstain from one of the great pleasures of his life. For he no longer cared to listen to poetry sung by boys because it gave less time for the study of the Koran. Throughout his life he struggled to prove himself to be more than just a triumphant warrior of Islam and to be seen as the acknowledged champion of Sunni orthodoxy. This Muslim tradition examined the recorded actions and collected sayings of the Prophet Muhammad and his Companions in order to interpret the Koran and foster the 'Sunna', the right path of conduct. It was a synthesis of scripture, tradition and interpretation that eventually grew into a code of conduct covering every conceivable action, from giving a dowry, eating one's dinner, wearing one's beard, cleaning oneself after sex with one's wife, to what to do on pilgrimage and how to treat a slave, a concubine or a neighbour. Suleyman and his ancestors could not match the mystical revelations or millenarian salvation that were offered by the Shiite Safavid Shahs of Iran, but he could offer law and justice. He established himself as the imperial patron of the four different legal schools within the Sunni tradition as well as functioning as the supervisor of the law courts and the judges. Suleyman had begun his reign as he intended to continue it, as the upholder of Islamic justice. He compensated the Iranian merchants who had suffered under his father Selim's draconian policies, dismissed inefficient governors and corrupt judges and started to codify a coherent body of law for his empire. At the end of his long reign a foreign observer could record, 'He has the reputation of being very just and when he has been accurately informed of the facts of the case he never wrongs any man.' Within the Ottoman Empire he was affectionately known not as a great conqueror or a magnificent builder (though he was both of those things) but as 'Kanuni', the 'law-maker'.

When you behold the astonishingly powerful domed mosque that Suleyman would create on the summit of one of the seven hills of Istanbul, you must eventually turn away from the majesty of the prayer hall and begin to observe the surrounding buildings. For here, in an elegant harmony of arcaded and domed courtyards, is the architectural expression of Suleyman's new vision of the Ottoman Sultanate. Surrounding the hallowed central mosque is a vast complex of colleges for the correct study and teaching of the Koran and Muslim law, with supplementary courtyards for the feeding and housing of legal students, travellers and pilgrims. This triumphant architectural expression of order and religious patronage would also be mirrored elsewhere in Suleyman's capital and his empire. For, aside from the *jihad* against the external enemy of Christendom that he would direct as army commander, there was a second, internal *jihad* within the empire. The engineer corps of his janissary army would wage a second war with dressed stone. Hundreds of bridges, fountains, colleges, mosques, prayer halls, dervish lodges, markets and charitable kitchens would be constructed within Suleyman's empire during his long reign. Jerusalem was walled, Mecca and Medina adorned.

The young military engineer who, through his innate skill, gradually assumed overall direction of this vast programme is now saluted as one

of the world's great architects. For nothing was beyond Sinan: not the
drawing-power of a chimney in a modest cell offered to a dervish traveller, the proportion of a supporting arch, the lead guttering of a dome,
the perfect manipulation of a spiral staircase set within a pencil-thin
minaret, the correct proportional use of the gorgeous banks of Iznik
tiling, or the correct depth of a prayer niche carved within a buttress to
diminish its weight upon the eye. You can study his growing mastery of
form all your life, or go straight to his masterworks, the Suleymaniye of
Istanbul and the Selimiye at Edirne, as well as the smaller ones he built
for Sokullu Mehmet Pasha, Rustem Pasha and Princess Mihrimah. But
beneath his endless experimentation and growing finesse, there is also a
unifying policy of permanence. He had the experience to insist on thorough foundations and, in Suleyman, a patron to match his concerns.
Their buildings were made from the very best materials, be it superbly
cut pale limestone, lead cladding, Iznik tiles, plasterwork or stained

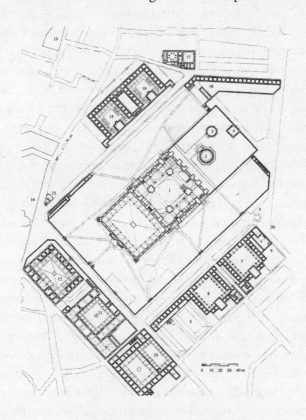

Plan of the Suleymaniye, Istanbul.

glass. Only the great public works achieved by the Roman Empire in the second century, by Justinian in his creation of Byzantium in the sixth century or the Romanesque Cathedrals of the twelfth century, are worthy of comparison with the works of engineer Sinan and Sultan Suleyman.

The Sultan's pious daughter always reminded her royal father of his constant duty to lead his people by example, not just commands. His icy comment on the failure of his army to storm the walls of Malta in 1565, 'I see that it is only in my hand that my sword is invincible,' suggested that his personal attendance was required on the next military campaign. So, in the spring of 1566, the seventy-year-old Sultan, though crippled by gout, ordered his army to prepare to march west. It was the thirteenth campaign that he had personally commanded.

Maximilian II had succeeded his father as the ruler of Austria in 1564. The new monarch had paid over none of the tribute agreed by his father, Archduke Ferdinand, while Habsburg forces were once more interfering in the Hungarian borderlands. Sultan Suleyman (backed by French diplomacy) led an army into Hungary, for he was determined to establish his candidate, the Protestant-friendly John Sigismund, on the throne. Suleyman also wished to show that whatever might have happened on an island in the central Mediterranean, the Ottoman field army remained invincible on land. This proved true enough, for no Christian army dared to confront him, and once again his opponents withdrew their forces back into the German Empire or the far mountains of Transylvania.

The summer's campaigning season was dominated by the Ottoman siege of Szigetvar fortress, a famous riverbank citadel defended with great élan by Count Zrinyi. The deeds of the Knights of St John in Malta had already spread across Europe in countless versions and cheap chapbook printed tales. Zrinyi outdid them all in his exhibition of self-sacrificial chivalry. Once the strongly fortified town had been stormed, and the inner citadel itself was on the point of collapse, he ordered the gatehouse to be opened. But no lone figure emerged bearing a flag of truce to beg terms for a surrender. Instead the Count led a desperate last charge at the enemy at the castle gate, deliberately putting aside his armour so that he could be assured an honourable death in the heat of battle. By the end of that day Ottoman banners flew from the battered towers of the citadel of Szigetvar, and the region south of Hungary's

Lake Balaton was annexed.

The Sultan did not live to see this victory. Four hours before dawn on 7 September he had breathed his last. Grand Vizier Sokullu Mehmet Pasha was fully aware of the low regard in which the Ottoman army held the heir to the throne. He knew it was vital that no gap in authority be exploited by a rebellion and so, while pretending to the victorious army that the old Sultan was too crippled with gout to attend upon them, he sent messengers post-haste to Prince Selim. From his post as governor of Kutahya, Selim rode quickly to Istanbul and was formally proclaimed Sultan Selim II on 29 September. Just three days later he left for the Hungarian front, but by now Sokullu Mehmet Pasha had began an orderly withdrawal of the army back to its winter quarters. Selim II was advised to wait in Belgrade. Here the death of Suleyman was officially announced to the army, who were also informed that Selim had already been acclaimed Sultan.

But there was a crisis within the state that threatened to undermine the smooth succession. The treasury was empty. There was not sufficient coin at hand to pay the army the expected 'donative' from a new Sultan. There was, however, just enough to make a small advance payment in Belgrade, and this dangerous deficit was camouflaged with expansive new promises of an increased annual salary and a larger 'accession donative' to be paid back in Istanbul. It worked for a bit, but by the time the army reached Edirne the janissaries were in open mutiny. They refused to enter their barracks and turned over their cooking pots: the traditional and ominous signal that the soldiers had refused the food provided by their master the Sultan. Such a universally respected figure as Admiral Piale Pasha went to personally reason with the soldiers but was knocked off his horse for his pains. It was an ugly demonstration of the harsh realities lurking beneath the grand edifice of the empire. However, the more historically minded among Selim's courtiers hastened to assure him that the reign of his brilliant ancestor, Mehmet II the Conqueror, had started in just the same way. But the janissaries would not be quietened until cash was found for them.

Fortunately in Istanbul there were men of the mettle of Joseph Nasi, able to forward the new Sultan the vast sums required. This Portuguese-born, Louvain-educated banker had moved east and found himself free at last to discard the Christian identity he and his Jewish family had been forced to wear in Spain, in France, in the Duchy of Burgundy and even in Venice, in order to be able to trade and survive. In Istanbul Nasi was free to return to the ancient faith and traditions of his family. He used his banking fortune to establish a Hebrew printing press, support a synagogue and a scholarly library and to assist fellow Jews escape from persecution within Christendom. Selim assisted him in this project, and gave him the Lordship of Tiberias in Palestine, which included seven of the surrounding villages (among them Safed, one of the acknowledged centres of Kabbalistic Jewish mysticism) as a potential place of settlement for the Jews, especially those being expelled by Pope Paul IV from central Italy. With the help of the Pasha of Damascus, the walls of Tiberias were rebuilt and mulberry groves planted in a well-meaning attempt to provide silk-weaving employment for the expected immigrants. But few of the Jews of Italy could be persuaded to become peasants in central Palestine, and most found it easier to move north into Tuscany, where Livorno was fast growing into one of the great ports of Italy.

The fate of the Jews of Pesaro had also been discouraging. The whole community had accepted Joseph Nasi's offer but had been captured as they made their way across the Mediterranean by Christian corsairs, the Knights of St John at Malta, who sold them all into slavery. Nasi remained undeterred and full of schemes. He continued to correspond with many of his old friends from his carefree days as a student in the Duchy of Burgundy, among whom were both William the Silent (the moderate champion of the Dutch Protestants) and the Holy Roman Emperor Maximilian. He was credited by both his friends and his enemies with an extraordinarily wide-ranging influence. He was said to have masterminded the election of the Polish King, cornered the beeswax market, blown up the Arsenale in Venice and monopolised the trade in wine from the Black Sea. His diplomatic skills, in helping create a truce with the Austrian Habsburgs, developing the Polish alliance and creating an anti-Spanish understanding with the Dutch rebels, made him an influential figure at the Ottoman court. As well as awarding him the Lordship of Tiberias, Sultan Selim II honoured his friend by making him the Count of Andros and Duke of Naxos.

The mutiny of the janissaries at the start of his reign marked Selim II for ever. He was determined never to risk his life again among his unruly soldiery. His palaces in Istanbul and Edirne became the twin locations of his rule, and trusted ministers were honoured with military commands on the frontiers of the empire. These were tested soon enough, for once the news of Suleyman's death reached them, Shia tribesmen in the mountains of the Yemen rebelled. This dissidence in the far south was echoed in the far north, where the Grand Duchy of Muscovy was reaching southwards, possibly opening the way towards a working alliance with the Safavid Shah. Selim II felt obliged to support the traditional allies of the Ottomans in southern Russia and Central Asia to frustrate this threat. In 1569 an Ottoman army was sent to eject the Muscovite garrison established on the River Terek in Astrakhan. At the same time Selim appointed his old tutor and adviser, Lalla Mustapha Pasha, to suppress the rebellion in the Yemen which threatened to cut off Ottoman access to the lucrative spice and pepper trade with India. This was achieved but the frontier campaign in southern Russia fizzled out because of the logistical difficulties of supplying an Ottoman army in this vast region. A victory of sorts was later delivered, however, when his ally, the Khan of Crimea, led a host of Tartar horsemen north and burned Moscow to the ground in 1571. They were, in their different ways, dramatic demonstrations of the vast range and power of the empire.

To cope with the insistent demands of his vast empire, Selim II leaned heavily on the expertise of his grand vizier Sokullu Mehmet Pasha, whose influence was freely compared to that which had been enjoyed by Ibrahim Pasha over the young Suleyman. The similarities were there for all to see, for Sokullu's palace was also on the Hippodrome, he was married to the Sultan's daughter and came from a similar background. He had been one of the Christian boys recruited by the 'youth levy' which filled the ranks of the janissaries and the palace officials. He belonged to a poor branch of a noble Serbian clan, the Sokolovic ('Children of the Falcon'), and his father was reported to have been a village priest. Sokullu was, however, not just a smooth-talking palace administrator. It was he who had led Selim's army to win a decisive victory over his brother Bayezid at Konya back in 1559, and he had also suppressed the revolt of a Prince Mustapha-pretender in 1555. Before that he had been chosen to succeed Barbarossa as commander of the Ottoman navy. Such a man was an invaluable asset to any state. Selim trusted him implicitly but was wise enough in the ways of the world to build up the power of his old tutor, Lalla Mustapha Pasha, as a rival axis of authority within his Divan.

It seemed obvious to even the non-militarily minded Selim II that he must win the obedience of his army, even if he could never aspire to win their love. This, he felt, could best be achieved by a dramatic new venture: the conquest of a new province for the empire. In that way his soldiers could acquire fame and fortune and get used to accepting his instructions. The island of Cyprus was chosen as a potential target quite early in Selim II's reign, and indeed it seems likely that he had been working on an invasion plan for his father in the spring of 1566.

The methodical first steps required for the conquest of Cyprus can be spotted very early in the Sultan's reign. He built a new fortress base on the mainland opposite the island, as well as a new supply route. In

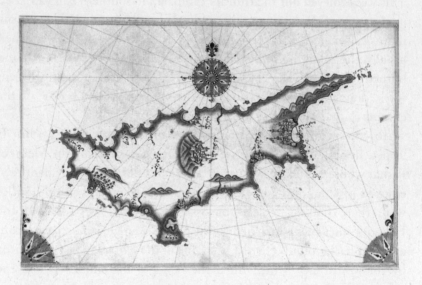

Cyprus, showing Nicosia in the centre, the smaller fortress of Kyrenia on the north coast and the larger fortress of Famagusta dominating the east coast. Drawn for Sultan Suleyman by Piri Reis between 1524 and 1528.

1568 an Ottoman squadron of some sixty-four galleys was sent to pay a friendly visit to the island, which allowed an Ottoman admiral to undertake a tour of the new defence works. By 1569 full-scale military and naval preparations were under way in the dockyards of Istanbul. That November Selim II used the hunting season at Edirne to go over the various issues with his chief advisers. By this stage Admiral Piale Pasha had joined Lalla Mustapha Pasha to form the 'war party' while Sokullu Mehmet Pasha argued on behalf of the 'peace party' and felt obliged to warn his master of some of the problems of attacking an island held by Venice. The almost bankrupt Ottoman treasury would lose its annual subsidy from Venice, the war itself would be a vast expense and there was always the potential danger of the Venetian navy to be taken into consideration.

There were also some legal issues to be overcome first. Cyprus was not a military threat, for it was ruled by Venice, who was ever anxious to maintain her trade with the Ottoman Empire. Her ambassadors had been among the first to present themselves to the new Sultan and it had always been considered illegal for a Muslim leader to be the first to break a peace treaty, even one negotiated with a Christian power. The Sultan's lawyers, however, had two ideas of how to justify any aggression. The island had been a tributary fief of the Mameluke Sultans of Egypt (after the Battle of Khirokitia in 1429), whose rights, they argued, had been absorbed into the Ottoman Empire. Their other case was that the island had once been half-Muslim, back in the early days of Islam in the seventh century, when the Ommayad Caliphs and the Byzantine Emperors had divided Cyprus between them. It was all pretty specious, but the chief legal authority in Istanbul nevertheless gave Selim II the interpretation he wanted: that, in such circumstances, to break the peace treaty 'becomes absolutely obligatory and binding'.

It was good of the Ottoman court to be so precisely legalistic, for Venetian rule over Cyprus itself rested on dubious grounds. The last independent ruler of Cyprus had been the Lusignan King James II (1460–73), known as 'the Bastard'. Although he was a bastard and had deposed his own sister, he was undoubtedly descended from a long line of legitimate Lusignan monarchs, who had lorded it over Cyprus for hundreds of years ever since King Richard I of England had sold the island to Guy de Lusignan in 1192. The Lusignan Kings suppressed the local Greek church and built themselves a series of wonderfully romantic Gothic castles, chapels and palaces whose ruins still decorate the island. Refugees from the fall of the Crusader states would later fuel a booming economy, especially after the fall of Acre in 1291 transferred most of the Levantine trading houses to the Cypriot city of Famagusta. This was the golden age of the island kingdom of Cyprus. The native Greek inhabitants, though never exactly cherished by their feudal lords, had at least got used to their ways and the feeling was sometimes reciprocated. The Lusignan King John II (1432–58) was nothing if not a Hellenophile, as his choice of women reveals: his first wife, Medea Palaeologi, was followed by Helena Palaeologina (the granddaughter of a Byzantine emperor) and he also had a Greek mistress, Marietta of Patras.

This was a period of a vibrant cultural cross-over in painting as well as in architecture. The charming fusion of Byzantine and Gothic forms can still be felt by anyone stepping into the sanctuary of the abbey at Bellapais, or of that at Ayia Napa, or the pilgrimage church of St Mamas at Morphou. However, the Genoese gradually acquired a controlling financial interest over the kingdom. When James II wished to expel these over-mighty merchants, he found that Genoa's rival, Venice, was only too happy to lend a hand. His marriage to a Venetian, Caterina Cornaro, was a grave policy mistake, however. He was dead within a year, while the birth of a posthumous son to Caterina allowed the Venetians to take over the kingdom by stealth, as advisers first to the infant James III, then, when he died, to the widowed Queen. In 1489 even this pretence at a regency was ignored and Cyprus was annexed outright. It was to be ruled by a proveditor, a governor, directly appointed by the Senate of Venice. The Venetians arrived in Cyprus as alien masters and treated the Cypriots as exploitable serfs, in contrast with the warmer relationship they enjoyed with both the Cretans and Corfiots. They even refused them permission to serve in the army or the administration.

The history of Cyprus allowed the Ottomans to suspect that the Venetians would receive very little support from its Greek Orthodox population. This opinion was shared by the Venetian governors themselves, who decided to abandon the dozen fortresses that guarded the Cypriot coastline in order to concentrate their strength on just three garrison-held strongholds: Nicosia, Famagusta and Kyrenia.

At the beginning of the sailing season Selim II's emissary, Cavus Kubad, set sail for Venice. The Doge already knew of his mission and abandoned the usual gracious hospitality that was offered to any visiting official of the Sultan. The ambassador was forced to sleep on board his boat before being permitted to land in St Mark's Square the following morning. He was taken directly to the great hall of assembly, where the Doge sat in solemn conclave, surrounded by his advisers, ministers and the full glory of the five-hundred-strong Senate. Here the Ottoman demand to surrender the island of Cyprus to the Sultan was formally and gravely rejected with the appearance of absolute unanimity: 'The Republic would defend itself against attack, trusting in the justice of God and would defend Cyprus by force of arms.' This was a considerable achievement, for the question of whether or not to fight over Cyprus had in fact been hotly debated, and the final vote had been 119 senators for peace and 220 for war.

To fund the war the Sultan had decreed the confiscation of all church and monastic lands in the European provinces of his empire in 1568. It wasn't quite as bad as Ferdinand and Isabella's expulsion of the Jews and Muslims from Spain, or even the legal robbery of Church lands by King Henry VIII of England, for right from the start the Sultan made it known that he expected the monasteries and churches to buy back their property. This the richer institutions did, often with the assistance of the Greek merchants in Istanbul, the so-called Phanariotes. It was further evidence that the Ottoman Empire was drifting towards a financial breaking point, and this was confirmed by the raising of a double levy of young Christians to fill the ranks of the janissaries. The levy, like the confiscation of Church lands, was achieved with the administrative assistance of the conquered Christians. It was a relatively easy matter for the government inspectors to tour the villages and urban parishes and use the baptismal records as a key reference point. Every four years they would make their rounds, gathering up the *devsirme*, the blood tribute, of between ten and forty thousand Christian boys. Muslims, Jews and Armenians were excluded.

The preparations for the Ottoman conquest of Cyprus were complete by the time the ambassador returned from Venice. Three naval squadrons criss-crossed the Aegean to ascertain if a Christian fleet would try to intercept the invasion. This mission accomplished, they continued to Cyprus. The army was then shipped across to make a landing on the southern shore of the island, not the closer northern coast, where the dramatic hills formed a natural fortress. As the Ottoman army landed on the beach of Larnaca on 3 July, certain Greek towns, such as nearby Lefkara, rose in rebellion against the hated rule of the Venetians. This attitude was encouraged by the Turks, who decreed an end to the ancient system of serfdom and rewarded the peasants with the freehold possession of the land that they had worked for centuries. The hated Roman Catholic bishops were abolished and the Greek Orthodox Church freed from centuries of control and allowed to return from its exile in the hills to the twelve historic dioceses of the autocephalous Orthodox Church of Cyprus. The policy worked so well that the Ottoman army was free to advance directly on the central city of Nicosia, which was reached within four days of the landings. The Venetian commander, Nicolo Dandolo, had withdrawn all his troops behind the city walls. By marshalling all able-bodied men he could theoretically count on twenty-four thousand to man the walls, stiffened with several thousand professional soldiers and a good complement of light artillery mounted in the bastions.

The Venetian Senate had decided to defend Nicosia. It was a foolish decision, especially for a maritime power, for the city sits in a natural depression in the centre of Cyprus's large agricultural plain. Nicosia would be almost impossible to reinforce, while the higher ground all round it gave the Turkish army a natural advantage. This was exactly what a military engineer, Savoragno, had reported to the Senate, but his candid advice was overruled and he was instructed to proceed with the fortification work. This he did in 1567, first toppling the old nine-mile circuit of medieval city walls, and tightening the city's defences within a concentric three-mile circular rampart. This earth bank was faced with stones and reinforced with eleven bastions which projected like arrowheads to provide fields of flanking fire. To do this, the medieval monasteries of La Cava, Beaulieu and Mangana, as well as the royal mausoleum of St Dominic and the Lusignan royal palace, were all flattened. The Ottoman siege would prove considerably less destructive to Cyprus's architectural legacy than these Venetian siege works. But Savoragno finished his work in time and on budget, making the three, tunnel-like entrances into the city, the gates leading towards the ports of Paphos, Kyrenia and Famagusta, into strong points.

By the end of July 1570 an Ottoman army of seventy thousand men was camped to the south of the city and Lalla Mustapha Pasha's headquarters was established on St Marina Hill (roughly where a Hilton

hotel stands today). Four thousand cavalry patrolled the perimeters and
the camp of six thousand janissaries guarded two hundred pieces of
field artillery. The siege began with the customary mole-like excavations
of miners and engineers. First the river, usually dry in midsummer, was
redirected away from the city, so that it would not fill the moat that
surrounded its walls or interfere with the laying of mines. Then the
artillery was distributed between three earthwork bastions and started
to lay down a barrage against the city walls. A network of trenches,

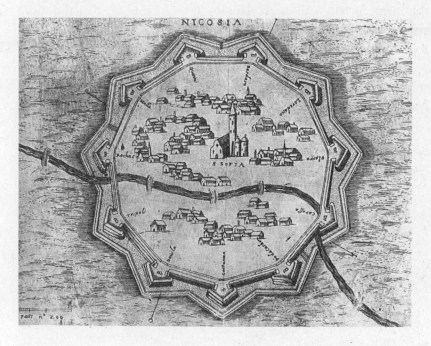

The Venetian walls built around the medieval city of Nicosia in 1567, with
eleven artillery bastions.

zigzagging to encircle the city, sealed off any escape or supply routes
before gradually inching towards the bastions. Cyprus is not like rocky
Malta, and the troops made good use of the pliable earth and rich
woodland of the island to construct parapets to shield their trenches
from Venetian counter-fire. The Ottoman commanders soon observed
that Nicosia's unimpressive, low, flat earth ramparts were absorbing the
bulk of the bombardment, and began to change their tactics. Mines and

cannon fire were concentrated on the noses of the bastions, which were gradually blasted away to form natural ramps up which their soldiers could climb. The four southernmost bastions, Tripoli, D'Avila, Costanza and Podocataro, were especially targeted. Throughout the month of August fifteen assaults were launched, picking out one bastion, or two, then all four at once, but all were beaten back. The Venetians were aware of what was being attempted and constructed internal walls within the bastions, although these had reduced their ability to protect the main curtain walls with flanking fire. To counter this the more enterprising bastion commanders launched sudden raids on the siege lines, a move which also helped keep up the defenders' morale.

In early September Lalla Mustapha Pasha received the fresh draft of reinforcements which he had requested from the Ottoman fleet. A hundred men were taken off each galley to give the general twenty-five

An improvised second line of defence after a breach in the outer walls.
From a sketch by Viollet le Duc.

thousand more men. They came with the welcome news that there was no Christian fleet on its way to bring reinforcements to the island. On

9 September Mustapha ordered an all-out attack. A standard was planted in the Costanza bastion (now marked by the Byraktar mosque) by a janissary sergeant but once again a determined Venetian counter-attack reclaimed the earthwork. The same thing occurred at the Podocataro bastion, where the fate of the city wavered in the wind as this Ottoman banner, and its knot of supporting warriors, held their position. Mustapha Pasha rushed a swarm of reinforcements to their aid. Although one outpost had fallen, the Venetian soldiers elsewhere had no thought of surrender. The adjacent Costanza and Tripoli bastions had to be taken by direct assault before Mustapha knew he had irrevocably breached the defences. Even then it took another eight hours of bitter, hand-to-hand street fighting before the city finally fell. The last-ditch defence of Nicosia's palace made a battleground of each hall and gateway. Resistance was only finally silenced by raking the yards, terraces and balconies with point-blank cannon fire. As a drunken Cypriot shimmied up the palace's flagpole to tear down the banner of St Mark, shots were still being fired as households attempted to defend their barricaded doors. The slaughter would continue as the city of Nicosia was given over to the sack: that orgy of licensed plunder, murder, extortion, rape and revenge that lay behind the zeal of all the besieging armies.

Three days later the Gothic cathedral at the centre of the city was washed clean of the last of its bloodstains. The stone floor was covered with carpets and the army assembled to sanctify the new mosque with prayer. The surviving prisoners were marched out to assist the army in burying its dead, covering up the siege lines and repairing the damage to the walls. Including those who had fallen in the sack, twenty thousand Christians were buried that week, and an even greater number of besiegers had fallen before the walls. A fifth of all the captured slaves and booty (including 160 cannon) was obediently put aside for the Sultan, and a pick of this crop was sent to accompany the victory message, which was dispatched to Istanbul in three fast ships. Lalla Mustapha Pasha's own share of the booty was later assessed at fifty thousand ducats. He shared some of the spoils with his adversaries. A silver platter was sent to the Venetian commander at Famagusta ornamented with the head of Nicolo Dandolo.

Ten days after the fall of Nicosia, mounted kettledrummers led the victorious Ottoman army out through the Famagusta Gate towards its next target. They were spared an attack on the massively thick walls of Kyrenia Castle, which stood on the island's north coast. The promise of safe conduct, combined with grim details of the sack of Nicosia, encouraged the governor to surrender. Lalla Mustapha Pasha was as good as his word, but on their arrival in Crete all the Venetian officers were clapped in irons for their disgraceful action. The Venetian Republic had spent thousands of ducats upgrading the defences of Kyrenia Castle, and it was widely thought that the governor must have been influenced by an Ottoman bribe. He was never released.

On 26 October Admiral Piale Pasha abandoned his watch over the coasts of Cyprus and took the bulk of his fleet back to Istanbul. The army remained in Cyprus, settling down for the winter in a siege camp that was being constructed around the walls of Famagusta. One naval squadron remained with them, hovering offshore in an attempt to blockade the city's harbour.

The following January a Venetian squadron of sixteen war galleys pushed its way through this blockade, escorting three supply ships. Guns, shot, powder, men and supplies were landed and the bulk of the city's women and children taken off to the safety of Crete. In spring various Ottoman naval squadrons, some based at the fortress of Rhodes, some in Alexandria, landed sufficient troops and munitions for the winter blockade to be geared up into an aggressive siege. By May five separate artillery bastions had been constructed and had started their work of pounding Famagusta and its walls. Behind the siege lines one hundred thousand men had been marshalled for the assault. It was going to be no easy task.

Famagusta was known to be one of the toughest positions in the eastern Mediterranean. It was one of the jewels in the crown of the Venetian Empire, one upon which she had lavished every possible attention. Massive walls rise up to frame the spires and churches of this late-medieval city, which looks out over a wide, well-guarded harbour. It was here that Caterina Cornaro had married King James II and here, on Thursday 26 February 1489, she formally abdicated her authority to the Republic of Venice in a magnificent ceremony. The palace of the ruling governor had been ornamented with granite columns taken from the nearby ruins of ancient Salamis to create one of the great colonnaded Renaissance piazzas of the age.[1] The scattering of half-ruined churches, once the pride of wealthy communities of merchants – Greek

Orthodox, Armenians, Nestorians, Syrian Jacobites, Copts, Franciscans, Knights Templars and Knights of St John – helped conjure up memories of the city of Acre before the fall of Outremer, the Crusade-conquered Holy Land. The cathedral was modelled on that of Rheims, for though the Lusignans had been crowned as monarchs of Cyprus in Nicosia, in Famagusta they were anointed as Kings of Jerusalem in exile.

There was only one land gate in the walls of Famagusta, the Limassol Gate, its approaches protected by a ravelin, a vast, multi-level, free-standing bastion which became the much fought-over key to the city's defence. Within three years of acquiring Cyprus the Senate of Venice had voted a monthly income of five hundred ducats to be spent for the continuous improvement of the walls of Famagusta. For twenty years a twentieth of the male labour force of Cyprus had been conscripted to work on the walls. So by 1570 they had raised a twenty-metre-high solid stone wall, set into foundations of bedrock, buttressed by eight metres of packed earth and reinforced by thirteen protruding bastions. The moat had been excavated to a width of twenty-five metres, every part of it covered by artillery mounted either on the bastions or hidden within subterranean galleries whose oval portals emerged just above the bedrock. The greatest military engineers of the sixteenth century, men such as Giovanni Sammichele and Hercules Martinego, had poured their skills into improving the defences of Famagusta.

The whole of the first month of the siege was filled with the sound of the greatest artillery duel of the age, and it soon became clear that the adversaries were well matched. Time and time again Ottoman artillery bastions were hit and put out of action. But Lalla Mustapha Pasha had at his disposal the empire's best miners and sappers, so that Bohemian renegades and Armenian mercenaries sunk shaft after shaft, snaking their way underground towards the Venetian strong points of the bastions of the arsenal and the ravelin. The first of these subterranean explosions was the signal for a massed assault, which was beaten off. At the end of this day the moat was piled high with the victims of Venetian crossfire. Again in late June, half a dozen mines were simultaneously ignited during the full pitch of a co-ordinated bombardment. Though thousands lay dead by the end of that day, for the first time the defences of Famagusta seemed to have been seriously weakened. In response Lalla Mustapha Pasha moved his artillery batteries to concentrate on four potential breach-points that had now emerged in the southern walls. As he moved his cannon ever closer to the enemy lines, they had to be continuously guarded by squads of crack troops, who were at hand to fight off Venetian attempts to sally out and spike the guns. Janissary marksmen were placed at close range behind earth ramparts to pick off defenders as they moved along the walls. Under the cover of this continuous and relentless pounding by artillery and small-arms fire, engineers directed soldiers to fill in the moat at certain points and cut their way through the banks of the counterscarp.

On 9 July simultaneous assaults were launched on all the weakest sections of the walls, though the fiercest fighting was once again concentrated around the ravelin bastion. The seventh murderous charge of the day seemed on the point of overrunning the outer bastion. If the janissaries succeeded in dragging their light artillery up to the top of this key position, they would be able to rake the parapets of the nearby bastions with their fire. So a Venetian officer took the decision to detonate an emergency mine, blowing up a hundred of his own men who were on the point of being overwhelmed by thousands of Turks. A week later a similar attack was launched, but in the meantime the Venetians had spiked this moat with small mines, which turned this assault into a bloody shambles. But these approaches were to be cleared of any further device by the Turks, who then rolled enormous oil-drenched faggots across the moat to the foot of the walls and fed the raging fires for three days.

By now the defenders had been reduced from eight thousand active men to five hundred, the same awful attrition rate that the Knights of St John had suffered five years before in Malta. The Venetian commander, in council with his officers and soldiers, agreed that they had just enough resources to hold on for another two weeks: surely time enough for one last desperate appeal to Crete to send them a relief force. On the last three days of July the siege reached its appalling, hellish climax, as a series of new underground mines were detonated beneath the ravelin and arsenal bastions and the bombardment of the southern section of walls rolled on, broken only by the sound of the kettledrums. Lalla Mustapha Pasha had succeeded in rousing his troops for one last massive sacrificial effort, and separate assaults were mounted hour after hour over a period of sixty hours. He knew that the Ottoman war strategy had provided for simultaneous raids on half a dozen positions across the Venetian Empire, including Crete, so that there was very little chance that Famagusta could be relieved. He also knew that his own army had itself reached breaking point. Too strongly staffed with young recruits, it had taken appalling casualties, some fifty thousand killed or wounded.

On 1 August an eerie stillness settled over the devastated walls. The Venetian commander, Bragadin, sent out a messenger to Lalla Mustapha Pasha to exchange hostages and discuss terms. He requested the same terms that Sultan Suleyman had offered to the Knights of St John during the siege of Rhodes: that they should be free to leave with standards unfurled to the beat of drums, taking their arms with them. The Cypriots and other Greeks from Venetian territories in the town should have two years to decide whether to quit the island or accept Ottoman rule. Lalla Mustapha Pasha agreed, except that the Venetian horses and artillery must be left behind. These were honourable terms. Ottoman galleys entered the now peaceful harbour and started embarking the surviving soldiers and townsmen in order to take them to Crete.

But on 5 August Lalla Mustapha Pasha appears to have broken his word, a rare event in the long annals of Ottoman military history. He had just discovered that a party of Muslim pilgrims on their way to Mecca had been captured by the Venetians and had all been killed during the siege. During the first personal interview between him and the Venetian commander – who had been escorted by his chief officers and was wearing the crimson of a Venetian senator, his face shielded from the sun by a scarlet parasol – Bragadin seems to have said something derogatory about the trustworthiness of the Pasha's word and did not sufficiently apologise for the fate of the pilgrims. Whether out of design, or in an instantaneous flash of temper, the Pasha ordered his troops to pin Bragadin to the ground and slice off his ears, after which the rest of the Venetian delegation were killed. This example was like a spark in a thunder-box. The bomb-shattered town was promptly sacked by Ottoman soldiers, though the Greeks and Cypriots were spared the slaughter meted out to the Venetians.

Bragadin and the other survivors of the massacre were then put to work burying the dead and clearing away the debris of the siege. Goaded and abused by his guards as the mutilated Bragadin was, his second interview with Lalla Mustapha Pasha seems to have gone even worse than the first. He called his interlocutor a 'cunning scoundrel' and asked, 'Why did you kill those poor Christians? If I offended you, then you should have killed me alone, not all the others. But these are thievish actions worthy of you . . . a dog, a disgusting fucking cuckold.' The retaliation was immediate: Bragadin was hoisted up the mast of a galley in the harbour so that all could see and recognise him. Then he was taken to one of the elegant columns of the Renaissance piazza in front of the governor's palace. There he was tied up and skinned alive by two butchers, who started with his skull, then began to remove the skin from his arms and back. He expired halfway through the operation but the flayers finished their work. His bloody hide was then stuffed with straw and dressed in the scarlet robes of a senator before, shaded by a parasol, it was placed visibly aboard a galley. This grisly example was paraded around the coastal ports of Cyprus before being sent to Istanbul.

Lalla Mustapha Pasha's actions disgusted his ministerial colleagues on the Divan. Grand vizier Sokullu Mehmet Pasha publicly referred to 'the cruel martyrdom inflicted on the most illustrious Bragadin'. The motivations of Lalla Mustapha Pasha have often been examined. Was it a pre-determined action by one of the leaders of the war party to prolong the conflict? Did he act this way because his army was close to mutiny, having suffered so many casualties? Or did this ambitious man simply lose his temper after the stress of a murderous siege? The skin of Bragadin was later recovered by his family and now lies beneath a memorial to him in the church of Santi Giovanni e Paolo in Venice.

Cyprus became an Ottoman province. In the years after the siege some thirty thousand Turks were moved from the mainland to settle among the 150,000 Greek islanders. In memory of the tens of thousands who had died beneath its walls, no Christian was permitted to live within the walls of Famagusta. Nicosia remained the administrative capital, the seat of an Ottoman governor commanding a garrison of three thousand soldiers scattered around the island's many ports and fortresses. Foreign merchants and their Greek partners were encouraged to make use of Larnaca, which had been spared the fighting. Despite his fear of the army, Sultan Selim II was now entitled to number himself among those of his ancestors who could be saluted as 'extenders of the realm'. Beside his favourite palace, so close to the good hunting grounds of Thrace, he at last felt justified in building a mosque, a permanent celebration of this victory and his reign. This, the Selimiye Mosque in Edirne, is the culminating masterpiece achieved by the Ottoman architect Sinan.

Venice had many admirers in Europe, but few of these were free of envy for her wealth, her political independence, her Levant trade, her self-determining foreign policy, her navy and her rich, clever, literate and self-sufficient ruling class. When considering the diplomatic options, the Ottoman court did not expect that any Christian power would come to her assistance. These pragmatic calculations were to be altered by a terrible explosion that followed upon one of those mysterious fires that flare up in the history of Venice. On 13 September 1569 a fire whipped through the Arsenale and blew up the vast military stockpile in one enormous explosion. At a single stroke the Republic's ability to launch a reserve fleet of a hundred half-assembled galleys was removed. Overnight Venice became a normal Italian power, not a naval superpower. In fact the damage turned out to be not nearly so bad as was first feared, but whether the explosion was arranged by an agent (a cousin of Joseph Nasi was arrested on this charge) or was an accident, it had one beneficial effect. Instead of envy of Venice throughout Christendom there was concern, strengthened by a series of bad harvests and high bread prices in northern Italy. When the Ottomans launched their attack, there were mutterings of the need for a united Christian league.

These would have remained mere diplomatic wishful thinking but for the chance collusion of three men: Philip II of Spain, Pope Pius V and Don John. King Philip II had built up a powerful Spanish navy after nearly a decade of sustained effort and now wished to reap some reward from this vast expense. The revolt of the Moors in the Alpujarra hills had been more of an outbreak of banditry than a military threat to his state, but it reawakened him to the potential dangers of an ever-expanding Ottoman Empire.

The College of Cardinals in the Vatican had also succeeded in electing a genuinely inspiring and passionately committed Pope, instead of the usual Italian career diplomat from a ducal family. It was an habitual, almost knee-jerk reaction for every newly elected Pope to call for the unity of Christendom and to summon the princes of Europe to lead a crusade. Sometimes they were sincere in this belief as they spoke from the pulpit, but more often than not their crusade would be distracted by Italian politics or the desire to gather the funds with which to enrich a nephew. Pius V proved himself to be a very different sort of Pope. He was no scion of a noble family with princely ambitions but a poor shepherd boy, the son of a muleteer named Ghisleri who had earned his living by carrying corn across the Alps. From the age of fourteen he was a passionate Dominican monk. He was the first non-fleshy Pope for centuries, a man who remained all skin and bone, who owned just two shirts and dined off vegetables enlivened by the odd egg. Far from keeping mistresses, amassing courtiers and indulging nephews, he even tried to banish prostitutes from Rome which was a step too far of course. Having ransomed his nephew Paolo from the corsairs of Algiers, he gave him just ten days to quit the holy city after he found him to be 'too luxurious an animal.' So when in mid-March 1570 the Venetians sent an ambassador-extraordinary to Spain and Rome, he did not meet with the customary evasions and counter requests. Instead the Pope, who had no personal regard for money, opened wide the treasury of the papacy and the Holy League was born. King Philip was assured that he could have both the *subsidio* (five hundred thousand ducats a year) and the *cruzada* (four hundred thousand ducats) for as long as the Holy League remained in existence. As the papal delegate explained to him, 'It is clear that one of the principal reasons why the Turk has quarrelled with the Venetians is that he thought he would find them unaided, without any hope of unity with your Majesty, who is so occupied with the Moors of Granada.'

With impressive speed the galleys of Sicily and Spain, the galleys of the papacy, the Knights of St John, Florence, Genoa and Savoy were joined with those of Venice to create a fleet capable of taking on the might of the Ottoman navy. Philip II overruled his Spanish advisers, who once more wished to attack Algiers, and gave his permission for them to sail further east. The fleet, however, had its teething problems, not least the perennial rivalries among the Italians. The joint commander, Marcantonio Colonna, was an impeccable Roman gentleman with battlefield experience but was not a seaman. Nor did the much-vaunted Venetian fleet perform well, in part because Venice, alone of the Christian sea powers, relied on citizen volunteers, not slaves, to row its galleys. It was, however, a hugely impressive undertaking: 180 galleys and eleven galleases with a total of sixteen thousand troops and thirteen hundred cannon onboard were assembled. In the summer of 1570 this fleet sailed to the strategic waters between Sicily, Corfu and Crete but failed to intervene in the sieges that were being so bloodily fought in Cyprus or to make contact with the Ottoman fleet, let alone to engage with any of their more ambitious projects such as the retaking of Rhodes or the storming of the Dardanelles forts.

The recriminations were bitter when the fleet returned to home waters that autumn, especially after it was heard that Nicosia and all Cyprus (save Famagusta) had fallen by the end of 1570. The peace party within Venice was growing stronger by the month, while the Genoese were once again criticised for pulling away from a naval showdown. The King and the Pope were both privately advised that they 'would never be well served while their fleet was commanded by ship-owners', which was a politely framed request to select a non-Italian admiral.

None of this disturbed the passionate enthusiasm of Pope Pius V. By May 1571 he had managed to convert the verbal understanding of the previous year into a signed Holy League, setting out targets and pro-portional expenses (Spain would meet half, Venice one third, the papacy one sixth), which would be reversed proportionately for the disposal of booty and captives. He had also found the man, dashing young Don John, who might be able to hold the whole enterprise together.

Philip II had only discovered that he had a blue-eyed, fair-haired half-brother after his father's death, from his careful reading of the Emperor's various wills, letters and documents. This child had been born on 24 February 1547, when Charles V was on campaign in Germany. One evening the Emperor had been entertained by the family of a war widow, and had then spent a couple of weeks with the prettiest of the daughters, Barbara Bomberg, who nine months later gave birth to Don John of Austria. The infant was whisked away to a wet-nurse and Barbara was sent off to marriage to a wealthy courtier and a com-fortable life. The young 'Geronimo' was placed under the kindly and watchful eye of one of the Emperor's Flemish musicians who had settled in Spain. Towards the end of the Emperor's life, when he was crippled by gout in his hermitage at Yuste, eleven-year-old Geronimo was sent by his musician uncle to distract the old man. He was an active child and a natural leader but he organised one too many raids on the local orchards, so that on one occasion he and his band were driven off in disgrace by stone-throwing local peasants. But he was forgiven, for Charles admired his frank, open face, which was combined with an instinctive Spanish piety.

In 1559 King Philip arranged to meet the young man out hunting, and embraced him with the words, 'King Charles V, my lord and father, was also yours. You could not have had a more illustrious sire. I am bound to acknowledge you as my brother.' He then turned to his courtiers and addressed them, 'Know and honour this youth. The natural son of the Emperor and a brother to the King.' Geronimo was henceforth to be known as Don John of Austria. Although forbidden by his brother to join the defence of Malta, Don John tried to smuggle himself on board a ship leaving from Barcelona. But he was forgiven this youthful disobedience and the following year Philip trained his ardent young half-brother for war by giving him the command of a squadron of thirty-three galleys. In this role he was watched over by an experienced Catalan vice-admiral, before being put in charge of the suppression of the Moorish revolt in the Alpujarras, a task which, by the winter of 1570, had been completed in 'fire and blood'.

So it was that in May 1571 Pope Pius V suggested that the twenty-four-year-old Don John of Austria be given the command of the fleet of the Holy League. It was an irresistible and brilliant candidacy: the handsome young son of the revered Holy Roman Emperor would lead the fleets of Christendom to war. Don John moved to take up his destiny, having spent a night in prayer before the Black Madonna at Montserrat before taking ship from nearby Barcelona. He travelled in the galley of the Genoese admiral Andrea Doria, landing in Genoa before voyaging south. In a personal audience with the old Pope in Rome, the young Crusader was blessed and warned by his second father, 'Charles V gave you life. I will give you honour and greatness.' Meanwhile his ever-cautious half-brother sent meticulous instructions and a council of lieutenants to watch over his every decision.

The allied fleet met at Messina in Sicily, where Don John's charm and good heart impressed the various factions within the fleet. The Venetian boats were still short of rowers, so he at once offered them the loan of four thousand soldiers. Privately he instructed the anxious and touchy Venetians that he had no intention of abiding by King Philip's cautious instructions and intended to attack the Ottoman fleet.

This fleet, having stood by to protect and replenish their army in

Cyprus, had, after the fall of Famagusta, advanced west to raid Crete and the Venetian territories along the Adriatic. Joined by the squadrons of the corsair admirals of North Africa, they were now sailing down to confront the Christian fleet.

They came upon each other at dawn of 7 October, two vast fleets converging in the Gulf of Lepanto to decide the mastery of the inner sea. Two hundred and thirty Ottoman warships were ranged against two hundred and thirty of the Holy Alliance, on almost exactly the same site where Preveza and Actium had been fought.

Don John ordered all the rams at the heads of the galleys to be removed to provide a clear field of fire. The heavy, ungainly galleases were then towed out to stand a mile ahead of the Christian squadrons. The Battle of Preveza had essentially turned on the fire-power of one such ship. Now, half a generation later, the Venetians had further improved both the numbers and the range of this prototype. The Ottoman fleet spread out in a great crescent opposite the Christians. The right wing was composed of fifty five galleys under Suluc Mehmet Pasha, supported by ninety-one galleys under the admiral-in-chief, Muezzinzade Ali, in the centre. The left wing was placed under the command of the corsair admiral Uluj Ali, the Pasha of Algiers, and was made up of sixty-seven galleys recruited from all the corsair harbours of North Africa. There was a small reserve held behind the central squadron. In the Christian fleet the left wing was held by the Venetians, Don John was in the centre in command of the Spanish squadrons and the Genoese were to the right.

The Venetian galleases lay like silent islands as the forest of Ottoman masts inexorably approached them. Some of the Ottoman captains mistook them for supply ships which had been mistakenly driven before the line of Christian galleys. The wind had shifted, so the Ottoman ships had stowed their sails, which allowed them to advance in a methodical order controlled by the steady beat of oars. Only when the galleys were almost upon them did the line of cumbersome galleases speak, releasing the shattering power of their heavy artillery. The first bombardment, followed by volley after volley of cannon fire, ripped the heart out of the Ottoman fleet at the very start of the battle, critically damaging at least a third of the galleys in the central squadron before the two navies clashed around midday.

Giovanni Contarini has left us a vivid depiction of the confused

Battle of Lepanto, 1571.

fighting:

> There happened a mortal storm of arquebus shots and arrows and
> it seemed that the sea was aflame from the flashes and continuous
> fires lit by fire-trumpets, fore-pots and other weapons. Three gal-
> leys would be pitted against four, four against six, and six against
> one, enemy or Christian alike, everyone fighting in the cruellest
> manner to take each other's lives. And already many Turks and
> Christians had boarded their opponents' galleys fighting at close
> quarters with short weapons, few being left alive. And death came
> endlessly from the two-handed swords, scimitars, iron maces, dag-
> gers, axes, swords, arrows . . . others escaping from the weapons
> would drown by throwing themselves into the sea, thick and red
> with blood.

Among the Ottoman commanders, only Uluj Ali instantly recognised
the transformation of naval warfare that had been achieved by the fire-
power of the Venetian galleases. As he studied in dreadful fascination
the devastating effect of their cannon, he instantly adapted his tactics,
frantically signalling to his squadron to pull away from the two sturdy
galleases that stood silent and ominous to the fore of the Genoese wing.
Doria recognised the manoeuvre and swept south to keep pace with

him. Uluj Ali, once he was totally assured that he had taken the Christian galleys quite out of the protective range of the cannon of the galleases, doubled back, striking at the centre of the mile-long line of Christian ships. It was a brilliant tactical adaptation to outflank this new technology, which allowed his squadron to fall upon a dozen straggling Christian ships, with four to five corsair galleys hitting each of the ships and taking possession of them in a simultaneous storm of boarding parties. Once Uluj Ali was in possession of ten captured Christian galleys, he signalled to his squadron to pull out of the fight. At the centre of the battle the destruction of the Ottoman fleet was growing towards its grim conclusion. Once victory looked certain after the fourth hour of battle, there was a noticeable shift in tactics. For once the Christians knew that they were 'masters of the enemy, they preferred to sack and bind, than fight and kill'. As one satisfied Venetian sailor wrote home, 'From such a victory I have gained 505 ducats, two lire and six shillings, some knives, a coral necklace and two blackamoors hardly fit to row in the middle of a gondola.'

As dusk approached, the scale of the victory became clear. All the Turkish galleys, save Uluj Ali's corsair squadron, had been sunk or captured. Ninety galleys had been sent to the bottom and one hundred and seventeen galleys were now being towed as captured prizes. The bodies of thirty thousand Ottoman sailors and soldiers bobbed among the smashed hulls and tattered sails of the sea. Three thousand captives had been taken and fifteen thousand galley slaves freed. The fearsome tenacity of the Turks, though doomed by the fire-power of the galleases, can be understood from the Christian casualty figures from that day: eight thousand dead and over twenty thousand wounded.

Don John ordered his fleet to seek safety in the numerous coves and havens of the coast, a wise decision as heavy rain clouds, which cleaned the bloody decks, were followed by a violent thunderstorm. That evening he embraced the Venetian commanders and stated 'unequivocally that the allies owed their victory to the Venetian galleases'. He appeared to be genuinely sad to hear that the Ottoman admiral Muezzinzade Ali had died in the fighting, for he had heard that he was 'a worthy and chivalrous person more loved than feared by his slaves'. So he took a personal interest in the care of the admiral's three sons, who had been made captive. He also confirmed his promise to liberate all the Christian convicts who had served in the battle, as well as those liberated from the Turkish galleys.

Pope Pius V appeared to know all about the battle before the first messenger arrived and piously murmured, 'Nunc dimittis servum tuum, Domine, quia viderunt oculi mei salutare tuum' ('Now, Lord, you can take your servant, for mine eyes have seen your salvation'). When told about Don John's role he also quoted from the Gospels, 'Fuit homo missus a Deo, cui nomen erat Johannes' ('God sent a man by the name of John'). Throughout Christendom church bells were sounded in celebration and in Venice they even forbade the mourning of their dead lest it distract from the scale of the victory.

The Holy League continued for just as long as it was directed by the animating spirit of Pope Pius V. When he died in May of the next year, 1572, the different national interests quickly reasserted themselves.

The Ottoman Empire immediately poured all its resources into a massive, ruinously expensive ship-building programme. Over the winter of 1571 and the spring of 1572 galley after galley was launched, week after week, from the docks of the Golden Horn in Istanbul, outdoing even the fabled productivity of Venice's Arsenale. Incredibly, by the start of the sailing season of 1572, the new Ottoman admiral-in-chief, Uluj Ali, was in command of a fleet of 220 galleys. They were designed to carry light artillery, for Uluj Ali had insisted on keeping the new fleet highly manoeuvrable. He took this fleet out to confront the ships of the Holy League, which were once again in the waters near Lepanto on both 7 and 10 August. Since the Christian galleys were protected by a screen of galleases to their fore, Uluj Ali did not risk trying to break through this line to fight galley to galley. He also realised that the extremely slow and heavy galleases would prevent the Christian fleet from launching any aggressive quick strikes of their own. All summer long he danced a balletic act of bluff and counter-manoeuvre. The Ottoman ships were real, as were the galley slaves and the new cannon, but there was also something brittle and ethereal about this new fleet. The testament of one of the Christian galley slaves rowing in this fleet, for the Spanish novelist Cervantes had been captured by Uluj Ali at Lepanto, tells us that when, at one stage, it seemed that a fight might be about to occur, many of the Ottoman crews deserted. They 'had already prepared their belongings and their shoes to flee ashore at once, without waiting to be attacked'. This was not known at the time, so that Uluj

Ali's accomplished handling of his fleet made it look as if the Ottoman navy had completely recovered from Lepanto. And the grand vizier did his bit to back up this illusion when he publicly boasted to the Christian ambassadors that the Holy League had 'merely singed off the stubble from my master's beard, which had only grown back stronger as a result', while they had succeeded in lopping off one of the arms of Christendom with the capture of Cyprus. It was a masterful piece of propaganda that is still much quoted today.[3]

Just a year after Lepanto, the unity of Christendom began to implode. The Protestants within the lands of the old Duchy of Burgundy were in armed rebellion against Philip II. The most hard-ened of these rebels, the so-called 'Dutch sea beggars', openly sported crescent badges in sympathy with the Ottoman Empire, so much did they loathe the rule of their Catholic King Philip II as enforced by his Spanish soldiers. The Catholic King of France, Charles IX, had also committed an extraordinary act of political suicide with the St Bartholomew's Day Massacre of 24 August 1572, when up to twenty thousand French Protestants were killed. In 1573 the Venetians, who had been hanging on to the Holy League in case it would allow them to regain Cyprus, bowed to the inevitable and made peace with the Ottomans, so that her lifeblood, the Levant trade, could once more flow through her veins. It was left to Spain to launch the last blow of the crusade of the Holy League. On 7 October 1573, the second anni-versary of Lepanto, Don John led a much-depleted Holy League fleet south from Sicily. They made a good crossing, and just two days later thirty thousand soldiers poured through the gates of Goletta and advanced towards Tunis. The city had never really recovered from the sack of Charles V and the next day it was occupied without difficulty. The troops once more set about sacking what had been revived within the shell of Tunis's walls, and the younger brother of the former Hafsid Sultan was installed as governor, supported by a garrison of sixteen thousand men who started building a fortress to link Tunis up with the stronghold of Goletta. Don John continued west along the Tunisian coast with his fleet, installing troops at Porto Farina and Bizerta. It was rumoured that the new Pope had suggested the creation of a new Christian kingdom, that of Carthage, with Don John as the first mon-arch. If this is true, Don John had the satisfaction of following in his father's footsteps, which must have been enormously appealing to this strong-willed, illegitimate prince. These rumours were certainly circulating, and they seem to have saddened and disappointed King Philip II, who was at this time grappling with the first stages of the financial meltdown which would result in the second bankruptcy of the Spanish treasury in 1575. Philip promptly removed Don John from the temptation of establishing himself as an independent Crusader monarch backed by the papacy. Don John was posted to a new command in Italy and after that sent north to fight the Protestant rebels in the Duchy of Burgundy. The Tunisians did everything in their power to remove the lifeblood of trade from the new Spanish-garrisoned forts. The caravans avoided Tunis and Bizerta and diverted to the free ports still controlled by Muslims in the south.

In Istanbul, Sultan Selim II was being encouraged by Sokullu Mehmet Pasha and Uluj Ali to strike back and reclaim some of the lost authority of the empire. Did they already know that Philip II wished for peace, that the Holy League was in tatters and that Spain was nearing bankruptcy? In the summer of July 1574 Uluj Ali led a fleet of 230 galleys into the Bay of Carthage, supported by supply ships, and unloaded an army of forty thousand men. This was much the smallest Ottoman invasion army to have been sent overseas for a generation. But Uluj Ali had been busy: the plains around Tunis were swamped by tribesmen who had come to assist the old corsair admiral of Algiers in his *jihad*. The harbours of Algeria, Tunisia and Libya were empty because the corsairs had all joined the struggle. For this was their war, as much as that of the Ottoman army. The Spanish-Italian garrisons of the Holy League in the half-built fortresses at Porto Farina and Bizerta, half-mutinous for lack of pay and supplies, were swamped. The better-led expeditionary force based in Tunis was still in the process of trying to turn the citadel into a modern artillery fortress that would defend the city and held on to their position with great courage.

Uluj Ali chose not to divide his resources and concentrated them on the old rectangular fortress whose massive walls overlooked the harbour at Goletta. Over the past twenty years it had absorbed a fortune in South American silver, spent on feeding and supplying this distant outpost from Spain. It fell after a siege of less than a month. Now cut off from access to the sea and all supplies, the commander of the citadel of Tunis, Serbelloni, was forced to concede terms on 13 September.

On 15 November the victorious Ottoman and corsair fleet once more rowed its way slowly past the Topkapi Palace, dragging the captured standards of Christendom in the waters behind them, to roars of victory from the crowds. The Christian Crusaders had been expelled by a *jihad*, a struggle by the believers, from their last and most famous outpost in Tunisia. The Spanish were also seriously considering that they might also have to abandon Oran. On the Hungarian frontier the Habsburg Emperor had just renewed an eight-year truce with the Sultan. A dispatch from Istanbul recorded that 'They stand in awe of no Christian fortress now.' But, as Braudel, the historian of the Mediterranean, asks, 'Who could have guessed that this was to be the last triumphal entry a Turkish fleet would ever make into Istanbul?'

King Philip II and Sultan Selim might have had an inkling. Under the cover of endless rounds of negotiations for the discharge of prisoners and the payment of ransoms, it appears that both monarchs had been attempting to reach a truce, an armed neutrality. For both states were being consumed from within by the staggering annual costs of keeping hundreds of galleys afloat. Venice had always known this: that, while you might be able to afford to keep three dozen galleys afloat, the rest need to be in dry storage. Anything else will ruin you. The two empires had come close to striking a formal peace deal in 1573.

In 1574 the fifty-year-old, poetry- and woman-loving Sultan Selim II slipped on the marble floor of his *hammam* and died. Not only did he build the 'noblest building I ever saw' (the testimony of the eighteenth-century travel writer Lady Mary Wortley Montagu) but he also revealed the elegance of his taste by working on the restoration of the phenomenal Byzantine cathedral of Ayia Sophia. As well as commissioning buttresses and a new minaret, he delicately inserted a Koranic library, a pair of colleges and his own tomb in the shadow of this triumphant building.

Murat III succeeded his father and the merciless bloodline of Mehmet the Conqueror and Selim the Grim was at last weakening, allowing some semblance of compassionate humanity to emerge. The new sovereign agonised for eighteen hours, at first refusing to accept the throne if it required the death of his nine brothers. Weeping as he did so, he finally followed the example of his ancestors and sent for the palace's deaf-mutes and handed them nine silk scarves for their grim task. Sokullu Mehmet Pasha remained in power as grand vizier and a truce with Spain was at last agreed in 1577. Murat III, like his grandfather

Suleyman, turned his back on the concubine-filled courtyards of the palace harem, spending most of his time in semi-retirement with his beloved wife Safiye and their three children in the provincial town of Manisa. Here he delighted in the company of an illiterate mystic, a gentle-mannered Sufi sheikh who helped him interpret his troubled dreams.

15

The Last Crusade

The Battle of the Three Kings

He had two thousand armed horse
And fourteen thousand men that serve on foot
Three hundred pioneers and a thousand coachmen,
Besides a number almost numberless
Of drudges, negro-slaves, and muleteers,
Horse-boys, laundresses and courtesans,
And fifteen hundred wagons full of stuffe
For noblemen brought up in delicate

Peele, *The Battle of Alcazar*

The fall in 1541 of the fortress of Santa Cruz, perched above the bay of
Agadir in southern Morocco, had brought down a chain of dominoes
in its wake. In the aftermath King John III ordered the evacuation of
many of the great Portuguese fortresses on the Atlantic coast of North
Africa. The abandonment of the walled cities of Azzemour, Safi and
Essaouria, which had been so laboriously won by their ancestors, was a
climactic decision for the Portuguese. Never before had the national
endeavour, the centuries-long crusade against Morocco, suffered such a
public and decisive reverse. The towers, churches and battlemented
walls, at a cost of much spilled blood and treasure, were abandoned for
ever, like some distant echo of the fall of the last Crusader fortresses in
the Holy Land. It was whispered in the streets that King John III had
betrayed the sacrifices of their ancestors. This feeling was further intensified when he ordered the desertion of Ksar es Seghir in the next round

of defence cuts. The castle occupied a strategic site overlooking the Strait of Gibraltar, halfway between Ceuta and Tangier. It had been captured by the founder hero of the Portuguese Empire, Prince Henry the Navigator, right at the end of his life, fighting alongside his young nephew, King Afonso the African.

The abandonment of the Moroccan fortresses was not, however, echoed by similar retreats in other parts of the Portuguese Empire. Indeed it soon became apparent that canny King John III had cut away the burden of the Moroccan frontier only in order to release men and money to strengthen and extend other imperial provinces. It was a total reversal of policy, for hitherto Portugal's worldwide maritime empire had merely been fuel with which to fund the bottomless 150-year crusade into Morocco. John III did not share the obsessional crusading zeal of so many of his ancestors but showed other family traits. He measured his dominions with a calm, businesslike efficiency, an equal part of the heritage of the Avis. He was the son of King Manuel, the Pepper King, who had arranged to pay the dowries of the princesses of Portugal by shipping sacks of spice to the agents of the Fuggers' Bank. John III, looking at the vast extent of the Portuguese domains in the sixteenth century, understood that Portugal was already dangerously overstretched and would need to harbour its resources if it was to hold on to some of what it already possessed.

It was during the reign of John III that the Portuguese first begun to settle and secure the coast of Brazil, which had been virtually ignored since its initial discovery. The vacuum had been filled by French traders working out of ports such as Le Havre and, on the Atlantic coast, Bordeaux and La Rochelle. Some of the enchanted descriptions of these first merchant-adventurers survive from the period when a number of up-country traders acquired the by-products of the tropical forest from the inhabitants: hardwoods, feathers, exotic parrots and monkeys. This Edenic land they described as *'sem fe, sem rei, sem lei'* ('without religion, king or law'). Its exoticism was symbolised by a red hardwood, brazil, which became a must-have accessory at the court of King Henry III of France, worn around the neck in pomander-like caskets, as well as being the source of a powerful new red dye. Not all these early ventures returned with a profit. Indeed in one notorious case a merchant ship, having loaded up with exotic parrots and caged monkeys, was becalmed in the Doldrums and the crew were forced to consume the entire cargo as they limped back to France rather than starve to death.

This trade in rainforest exotica could only be supplied by contact with the inland tribes. Like some scene from *Gulliver's Travels*, the Brazilian coastline was soon riven into two antagonistic factions: the Tupinamara traded with the French, while the Tupiniquins traded with the Portuguese. To counter this creeping French influence, John III decided to settle the land with Portuguese migrants. The coast was divided into a dozen hereditary captaincies. These were offered to some of the more ambitious gentry, who could acquire between thirty and one hundred leagues of coast from the crown and as much land inland as they could arrange to be settled. There was a rush to secure these valuable concessions though actual migrant settlers proved rather more difficult to find. Aside from the distance and dangers of Brazil, Portugal was being drained of its manpower on every frontier, by the factories in west Africa, the bases along the East African coast, the Arabian forts, the Indian coast and the East Indies, not to mention the remaining fortresses in Morocco. It was not unusual for a third of the annual pepper fleet to suffer storm damage and only a tenth of those sent out east as young men would return home at the end of decades of service. So it was the usual mixture of the broken and the desperate who were packed off to the Americas: orphans (including compulsorily converted Jewish children or those snatched from their families during the expulsion of the Jews) and bankrupts, as well as the products of a general clearing out of the jails. Of the first batch of one thousand settlers landed in Brazil, at Bahia, four hundred were classed as ex-criminals. None of them proved interested in transforming themselves into the disciplined, patriotic labourers that are continuously dreamed about in government circles. So John III and his ministers had to think again. This time they copied the successful example of the sugar plantations that had been established in Portuguese West Africa and on the offshore islands, particularly on Sao Tome and Principe, where sugar had been successfully grown since the 1530s and which shared the same latitude and climate as Brazil. So it was with the importation of sugar-cane and West African slaves that Portuguese royal authority was successfully established on the Brazilian coast. A worldwide craving for sugar took care of the economic development of this province for the next two hundred years, so much so that the munificence of the Queen of Portugal's charitable donations soon began to be measured in mule-loads of sugar whereas it had once been assessed in sacks of pepper.

In the first hundred years of exploration very few Portuguese women travelled out in the boats and the Portuguese settlers were quick to establish relationships with local women, be they in India, West Africa, East Africa, Ethiopia or the Far East. In Brazil the Portuguese gift for miscegenation reached its full flowering. Here at last the hereditary captaincies that had been established by John III found a role. The acquisition of the Captaincy of Pernambuco by the Duarte Coelho family led them to employ the conquistador Jeronimo de Albuquerque and send him out as a local agent to pacify the native tribes. Unlike his namesake in the Indian Ocean, Afonso de Albuquerque, this Albuquerque was 'naturally of a mild and friendly disposition' and had 'many children by the daughters of the tribal chiefs', whom he treated 'with consideration'. By 1584 this warrior of the bedroom was acknowledged as the grandfather of some twenty-four families, many of which still dominate the region, especially those who can also trace their descent from the Indian princess, Maria do Espiritu Santo Arco-Verde. This sort of inter-racial coupling became one of the foundation myths of the spiritualism which still pervades much of South America. The three ancestor spirits that can be appealed to by Las Madamas, the local wise women, for help seem to step out of the pages of a sixteenth-century romance. For 'las tres potestas', the three ancestral spirit powers, are commonly depicted as a white conquistador knight, a beautiful native princess and a heroic West African warrior who has escaped from the sugar plantations.

It was not just the provinces that were being transformed during the ordered years of John III's reign. The wealth of the empire, whether it was measured in pepper, sugar or gold, flowed back to enrich the capital in some form. Lisbon blossomed into a city of a hundred thousand souls and was no longer just the national capital of Portugal but part of a much wider world. Flemish, English, Genoese, Moroccan, Catalan, Florentine and French merchants flocked to the wharves of the River Lagos, which also became a new home to delegations, merchants, sailors and captives drawn from West Africa, the Indian Ocean and South America. Sixty public slave markets were doing business in Lisbon at the same time that the churches and palaces were being transformed by the playful flamboyance of Portuguese Baroque. The introduction of the Inquisition by John III (licensed by the papacy but obedient to the crown) seemed to be no more than a wise extension of royal authority over the complex and teeming masses in Lisbon. For in this period more than a tenth of the population of Lisbon were slaves, with many more descended from free slaves, not to mention the half-assimilated Jews, Moors and foreign converts. Once established in the capital the Holy Office of the Inquisition moved to set up branches across the empire. The Spanish Jesuit missionary St Francis Xavier petitioned for a branch in Goa within a few years of his arrival in India, though John III refused to sanction this during his reign. It was not until 1560 that the Holy Office began its 250-year reign of terror among the forcibly converted Hindus, Thomasite Christians, Muslim and Jewish inhabitants of Goa. The old palace of the Muslim governor was converted to become the notorious Orlem Gor, the 'Big House', whose massive exterior walls enclosed the House of Penitence, the Perpetual Prison and the House of Torture. Two hundred windowless prison cells were used to extract the truth from those suspected of deviance, whether they were guilty of using an inappropriate swear word or of a proscribed action such as throwing flowers or scented water over a newly married couple. Prisoners were fed and housed on a sliding scale of ethnicity, progressing from the *mesticos* (those of mixed blood), to the *casticos* (the Portuguese born in the east) up to the *reinoes* (the Portuguese born in Portugal).

In 1557, after presiding for thirty years over his rich, prosperous and ever more diverse empire, King John III joined his ancestors in Batalha Abbey. He had outlived his own son and was succeeded to the throne by his three-year-old grandson, Dom Sebastian. The child's mother had felt obliged to return home to Spain in order to care for her dying father, Emperor Charles V. So she left her infant son in the charge of her aunt Catherine, who was also the boy-king's grandmother and a sister of Charles V. She did her best to preside over the royal council of Portugal as the dowager queen-regent. She did this for five conscientious years before her place at the head of the council chamber was taken by another elderly relative of the boy-king. In 1562 the new regent, Cardinal Henry, placed his great-nephew in the care of a pair of Portuguese Jesuits, the brothers Luis and Martini Goncalves da Câmara. This switch in tutors and guardians coincided with exciting news from Morocco, where one of the few remaining Portuguese outposts, the fortress of Mazagan, had been besieged by the Moroccan army. To the pride and pleasure of the boy-king, his garrison of two thousand six hundred men had held off the entire Moroccan army. Or so it seemed. From a Moroccan perspective, the 1562 attack on Mazagan served quite a different purpose. The attack was organised by the Sharifian Sultan of Morocco, who had failed once again to recapture Tlemcen from the Turks some two years before. Despite this attack, the Turks had proved reasonable and Sultan Abdullah al-Ghalib was able to patch together a truce. The 1562 siege of Mazagan helped restore his standing as a Muslim leader who was seen to be attacking enemy Crusaders rather than fellow believers. It also seems to have been mere cover for the Sultan's real ambitions. The siege was combined with a determined march through the northern mountains of Morocco which allowed the conquest of the Idrisid Emirate of Chechaouen, an old ally of the previous Wattasid dynasty. This explains why during the siege there were just twenty-four Moroccan cannon available to fire upon the strong fortress walls of Mazagan. None of this *realpolitik* interested the boy-king of Portugal, who remained thrilled by the heroism of his soldiers and their commander, Rodrigo de Sousa de Carvalho. In due course De Carvalho was promoted to become the next governor of Tangier, from where his young master repeatedly urged him to launch an aggressive forward policy.

Six years later the fifteen-year-old Sebastian formally came of age. The grave, good-looking prince became a taciturn, athletic and dignified young king. His favourite possession was a suit of armour that had been manufactured for him by the master-smiths of Augsburg, the tempered steel chased with elegant gilt symbolism. When King Sebastian exercised in this armour, the four virtues on his arms moved, while the proud achievements of the Portuguese crown that were etched into the breast and backplate – Power, Victory, Peace and Navigation – remained still. It was noticed that the dark-haired, swarthy, sensual bloodline of the Avis was absent from Sebastian's make-up. The slender young man, with his pale skin, blue eyes and fair hair, seemed to be a throwback to his English and Trastamaran ancestors. The combination of Jesuit tutors and a complete lack of parental relationship burnished his nature with a clear absolutism. Sebastian possessed the bright stare of a fanatic, determined to return Portugal to the pure zeal of its crusading inheritance. He was said to be equally inspired by the victory over the Turks at Lepanto and the massacre of Protestants in France on St Bartholomew's Day in 1572. At first he imagined that he might follow in the footsteps of Alexander and launch an attack on the Muslim heartlands through India. Indeed the Portuguese garrison in Goa had to defend itself against a very determined siege made in the very same year as Lepanto. However, in due course his attention shifted back to Morocco, the traditional enemy of a Portuguese Crusader.

In 1570 a well-travelled warrior who had served in Portugal's vast empire returned home. He was a cousin of Vasco da Gama. His own father had been drowned in the Indian Ocean and he himself had lost an eye as a young man while serving in the defence of Ceuta. He went on to serve the crown in Macao, Malacca and the Moluccas. When at last he returned home to Lisbon, he found that his old city, his beloved country and countrymen, seemed to have been transformed into something unfamiliar, mercenary and unwelcome. Throughout his long, adventurous service and worldwide travels this Portuguese soldier had been composing an ode to his motherland that was inspired by Virgil's *Aeneid*. The work had been destroyed at least twice, once in Mozambique, another time in a shipwreck off the River Mekong. However, the destruction of these earlier drafts, married to the disillusionment of home-coming, made the final work much tighter and stronger. The epic poem was dedicated to the young King Sebastian, who read Camões's masterpiece, *The Lusiads*, while it was in manuscript. The defining national epic of Portugal concludes with a call to return the nation to its days of martial glory and to cleanse it of the corruption and confusion of its great wealth. Camões was rewarded for his work. His ode was printed at royal expense and he was given a small annual pension, which in those pre-copyright days was the best a writer could hope for.

In 1574 Sebastian was at last able to test himself, and his years of martial training, by leading an expedition into Morocco. Like his ancestors before him he crossed the Strait of Gibraltar and landed at Ceuta. That summer the gates of this fortress opened and the young king led a column of twelve hundred armed knights through the Anjera hills of northern Morocco. A cavalry battle was fought outside the walls of Tangier, where Sebastian proved himself a skilled and determined young commander. Those long years of obsessive boyhood training had not been in vain.

That winter the King was back in Lisbon. He started plotting with the arch-schemers and spy-masters of the Queen of England's court. Inspired by the assassination of Sharif Muhammad by Ottoman agents which had taken place some twenty years before, King Sebastian proposed establishing his own fifth column of secret agents within the Moroccan army. To do this he suggested that a handful of English corsair captains, men of the piratical stamp of Francis Drake, be employed to enslave a boatload of loyal Portuguese soldiers and sell them as military slaves to the Moroccan Sultan. It was a daring if slightly hare-brained scheme and was soon dropped. For in 1576 the young Sultan of Morocco was deposed by his uncle after just two years on the throne. The former Sultan fled to the fortress of Ceuta as the Portuguese were his only possible allies. It had become apparent that his uncle Abdul Malik's palace coup had the advance approval of both the Ottoman Empire and the King of Spain.

Sultan Abdul Malik had assembled some formidable backers for the *coup d'état* that finally put him on the throne. Born into the holy bloodline of the Sharifian dynasty of southern Morocco, Abdul Malik was one of five sons who served in the army led by their father, Sharif Muhammad esh-Sheikh. After the assassination of the Sharif by Ottoman agents in 1557, the young prince had been forced to escape Morocco. For his elder half-brother, Sultan Abdullah al-Ghalib, had begun to purge the country of all possible dynastic rivals. The fifteen-year-old Abdul Malik, in the company of his younger brother and their capable mother, Sahaba Errahmania, sought refuge in Algeria. They lived – closely watched by their hosts – first in the old medieval city of Tlemcen before moving to Algiers on the coast, the new booming city enriched by the booty of the corsair captains. Years later they were given permission to travel to Istanbul, where they petitioned the Ottoman court for assistance in taking the Moroccan throne. These petitions fell on deaf ears but the brothers made some good and unusual friends during their years of exile in Algiers and Istanbul: a Christian barber-surgeon, a Spanish priest working among the slaves and a French sea captain. It may have been the example of these free-spirited friends that encouraged the two brothers to take their fate in their own hands. They volunteered to fight in the fleet, and though Lepanto was a catastrophe for the Ottoman navy, the two Moroccan princes survived. Their fighting spirit brought them to the attention of the Ottoman court. When they also volunteered to take part in Admiral Uluj Ali's campaign to recapture Tunis and Goletta in 1574 they acquired an influential patron in the person of the corsair admiral of Algiers, turned commander-in-chief of the Ottoman navy. Two years later ministers at the Ottoman court, where Murat III had replaced his father Selim II on the throne, agreed to provide the two exiled princes with men, money and munitions. In exchange Abdul Malik promised to reward his backers with a payment of five hundred thousand ounces of gold and to lease the Moroccan port of Larache to the Ottoman fleet. The acquisition of an Atlantic port would allow the Turks to outflank Spain in any future maritime conflict and would give the corsair captains of Algiers a chance to prey on the silver bullion being shipped into Seville from Peru.

Abdul Malik's Ottoman-backed invasion of Morocco in 1576 proved to be a most efficient coup. His half-brother Sultan Abdullah al-Ghalib had died and his son, Muhammad al-Mutawakkil, had but a loose grip on the throne. Abdul Malik was well supported by his network of friends and confidential agents, many of whom dated back to his days as a refugee in Istanbul. The troops loaned by the Pasha of Algiers (then under the command of Ramadan Bey, a renegade from Venice) were handsomely rewarded and sent back home before they made themselves unpopular. The question of the lease of Larache was politely shelved, for Abdul Malik had no desire to antagonise Spain or to allow Morocco to become an Ottoman protectorate.

But it was this coup of 1576 that gave King Sebastian both a pretext and a local ally for his invasion of Morocco. He could invade Morocco under the cover of placing Muhammad al-Mutawakkil back on the throne. In 1577 he crossed the frontier to have a meeting with his cousin, King Philip II of Spain, at the monastery of Guadalupe. Philip was intrigued to meet a man even more austere, passionate, zealous, isolated and friendless than himself. It seems to have brought out the best in him and he tried to counsel his young cousin: to be cautious and not to risk his life until the succession of Portugal had been secured by marriage and the birth of an heir. It was good advice but Sebastian, too young to have joined the Holy League and fought under Don John of Austria at Lepanto, could not be dissuaded. Philip agreed to assist with the loan of an experienced Spanish regiment, but only if a rational

timetable was adopted and an achievable tactical target were set, such
as the seizure of the port of Larache. Assured of the support of Spain,
Sebastian sent his financial agents on a shopping tour of Europe to
recruit German soldiers and acquire Italian and Flemish munitions. At
the same time he licensed four proprietary colonels to tour the inland
provinces of Portugal recruiting four regiments of native infantry. The
Portuguese peasants had little understanding of the nature of modern
warfare but it was a good time to hire experienced mercenaries from
the Duchy of Burgundy. Both the Catholic and Protestant factions
within the Duchy (the Netherlands and Belgium had not yet been created from the wreckage of the Dutch Revolt) were sick of their 'own'
soldiers. The Prince of Orange was disgusted by the excesses of the
Protestant soldiery of such mercenary commanders as Duke Adolf of
Holstein, just as Catholic loyalists had been appalled by the spectacular
own goal of the sack of the royalist city of Antwerp – the so-called
'Spanish Fury' – by the very men who were supposed to be defending
them.

Munitions were another matter. The Italian powers were enthusiastic
in principle about a crusade but very exact on matters of price. The
Duke of Tuscany would be honoured to release a loan of two hundred
thousand gold ducats so that King Sebastian could acquire arms from
Ferrara, Milan and Mantua, but only after Portuguese pepper had been
landed at the docks of Livorno. So Sebastian's agents went to talk to the
Jews of Antwerp, who were less keen on listening to the broad principles of a crusade but were much more flexible on matters of schedule.
They released enough money to his agents for them to buy three thousand muskets and four thousand arquebuses on the open market. In
exchange they got a paper promising the delivery of ninety-two thousand quintals of pepper in three years' time.

The Englishman Sir Thomas Stukeley (or Stucley) came in as an
after-thought to King Sebastian's crusade. Sir Thomas had a varied
career, by turns a pirate, spy, counterfeiter, secret agent and diplomat.
Or, as Camden described him, he was 'a ruffian, a spendthrift and a
notable vapouriser'. He had, however, been one of the very few
Englishmen to fight in the Holy League under Don John at Lepanto.
He was also rumoured to be the natural son of King Henry VIII, which
helped him win the financial support of the papacy. When he sailed
into Lisbon harbour in the spring of 1578 he was supposedly leading a

scheme to land a Catholic army in Ireland and march to the aid of the Irish leader Shane O'Neill, who was struggling against the troops of Protestant England. To that end the Pope had just made Sir Thomas the Marquis of Leinster and lent him enough money to buy a ship and the loyalty of a regiment of six hundred mercenaries.

When he called into Lisbon (whether by chance or privy arrangement) Stukeley at once offered his service to King Sebastian and scuttled his ship as too unseaworthy to cross the Bay of Biscay. The Pope was appalled, Queen Elizabeth I relieved, although the subtle monarch of the English had already decided to play it safe and support both sides in this conflict. England and Morocco had a lot in common in the last years of the sixteenth century, for both countries feared an invasion by a Catholic army and needed to acquire armaments. It was not considered expedient by either the Christian Queen or the Muslim Sultan to make too much noise about their trade, but Moroccan saltpetre was liberally traded for English munitions. The one attempt to create indigenous English gunpowder had been an interesting experiment. All the earth-closets of London had been commanded to deposit their night-soil in a low pyramid covering some five acres on the edge of the city. This was then drenched with various chemicals, in the expectation that saltpetre crystals would emerge like mushrooms to be plucked from the heaving morass of rotting, rain-drenched excrement. The experiment was not repeated. Instead such well-connected arms dealers as Edmund Hogan continued their private missions to the Sharifian court. Hogan led a curious double life, publicly upbraided by the Queen when in earshot of a Portuguese or Spanish ambassador, but privately cherished in the meetings of her inner counsellors.

So, in the immediate pre-war months, we hear that captain Francis Drake had dropped in at Mogador and sent one of his crew, John Fry, to take a message to the Sultan. The Queen also arranged that an English grain ship would call into Lisbon. This was full of mercenary types who would enter the King of Portugal's service once they landed and included two trusted agents embedded among their number.

On 17 June 1578 the young King Sebastian attended a service in Lisbon's cathedral, where he was presented with a new standard embroidered with an imperial crown. It was assumed that the dignity of the Kingdom of Portugal would ascend ever higher and he would become the first Christian Emperor of Morocco. The army consisted of three thousand German mercenaries, one thousand English and Italian soldiers of fortune under Sir Thomas Stukeley, six thousand Portuguese peasant-soldiers under their four colonels, two thousand Castilian infantrymen loaned by King Philip II, two thousand Portuguese knights under the Duke D'Aveiro and two and a half thousand gentleman volunteers from Portugal under Alvaro Pires de Tavora. This army of nearly seventeen thousand would be assisted, bedded and waited upon by nine thousand camp-followers, servants, priests, women, page-boys and slaves. A thousand wagons had been prepared to transport the munitions and tents required for this mobile royal court, complete with its pavilions, chapels and royal choir. The young Sebastian looked old in the experience of war when he stood beside his cousin, the Duke of Barcellos, a ten-year-old riding to war and representing the shadow royal dynasty of Braganza.

On the feast day of St John the fleet sailed past the glittering new facades of the Church of Santa Maria and the Abbey of the Jeronimos, which had been recently adorned with pale stone hewn from the Alcantara quarries. They proceeded slowly down the coast of the Algarve, and then stopped at Cadiz, Tangier and Asilah to pick up more volunteers and fresh casks of water.

Outside the walls of the Portuguese fortress of Asilah, the King spotted a Moroccan detachment holding the hills. He at once ordered that his household cavalry be disembarked and without waiting for the rest of the army he led his six hundred knights in a charge against the enemy. They were watched by the astonished soldiers on the battlements of Asilah and the thousands still afloat on the armada, who knew that they followed in the wake of a fearless young commander who would lead his men from the front. Any remaining idea that Sebastian would be content just to seize control of Larache was firmly banished. He intended to disembark his army at Asilah and march inland to fight with the army of the Moroccan Sharif. But it took some days for the vast seaside camp that stood outside the walls of Asilah to be assembled into marching order. The private encampment of the Duke of Barcellos, with its twenty-two pavilions complete with a portable chapel with a gilt communion travelling service, was especially admired. But on Monday 29 July this city of canvas and silken pennants was struck. The crusading army didn't manage to move far that first day, just three miles in fact, but it was traditional to start a march

with a mild first day. The next day they made camp beside the neo-
lithic stone circle of El-Menorah, embedded in the Arcadian landscape
of the foothills of the Western Rif. Here they were joined by a regiment
of five hundred Castilian soldiers led by an experienced commander,
Francisco de Aldana. They had been dispatched by Philip II as a further gesture of concern for his young cousin. De Aldana brought with
him two precious relics from the court of Spain for King Sebastian: the
helmet and silk tabard that had been worn forty-three years before by
Charles V during his conquest of Tunis. Adorned with these propitious
trophies, the following day the Crusaders made good progress, marching twelve miles.

The next day they reached the Oued Makhzen stream, a tributary of
the River Loukkos. The bridge over the Makhzen was held by two
thousand Moroccan soldiers, so the Crusader army marched three miles
downstream and made use of a natural ford for a trouble-free crossing.
The ford of Mechara-en-Nedjima is a humble enough feature of this
landscape but it marked an important frontier. It was the end of the
brackish estuary waters, the geographical edge of the coastal plain,
where it gives way to the hills and plateaux of the interior. Would the
Portuguese army continue to march inland towards the walled capital
cities of the interior, or would they wheel around to secure the coast?
The port of Larache, the presumed goal of the campaign, was two days'
march from the ford. Its fortress was isolated between the Portuguese
invasion fleet, which lay at anchor off the Atlantic coast, and the
Crusader army.

Sultan Abdul Malik had been preparing to resist the invasion for the
past eighteen months. On the one hand he was the son of the great
Sharifian commander of Morocco, Muhammad esh-Sheik, preparing to
defend his homeland and his faith against an alien invader. On the
other, he was a refugee prince who had deposed his nephew just two
years before. He had been out of the country for half his life and was
acutely aware of the divisions – tribal, regional and dynastic – that
existed below the surface of his rule. Not the least of his concerns was
that the old Wattasid and Idrisid northern half of the country leaned
towards his deposed nephew and a Portuguese alliance.

On 2 July the Sultan, having heard that the Crusader fleet had defi-
nitely left Lisbon, made a formal proclamation. He summoned the
tribes of Morocco to defend their nation, their families and their faith.

Abdul Malik was acclaimed as Emir by the people of Marrakesh in the vast square before the ancient palace. On the same morning the palace gates had opened to let fly a stream of trusted officers. Escorted by soldiers bearing the holy banners of Islam, they took the Sultan's message by word and by letter to the people of the mountains, cities and plains. The Sultan then started for the north, reaching Rabat on 14 July. He oversaw the artillery train and trained corps of arquebusiers which lay at the core of the royal army. As a good Muslim he made one last conscientious attempt to avoid conflict, sending a peace delegation to the Portuguese at Asilah and instructing his ambassador to make 'a bad peace rather than a just war'. King Sebastian was not interested in anything other than a battle which would give him glory and renew the crusading zeal of the Portuguese.

Then Abdul Malik rode inland, into the forest of Marmora, and made camp at Souk el-Khemis, a clearing where the nomadic tribes of the region customarily held their Thursday markets in neutral territory. Here he waited for the tribes to respond to his summons. Any doubts he held about his right to lead the Moroccan nation to war were now silenced. Day after day the tribes poured into the camp and their sheikhs dismounted to approach the royal tent. The final accolade came when his younger brother Ahmad, who had been serving as governor of Fez, brought in the men of the northern hills. Over five thousand infantrymen and twenty thousand cavalrymen had responded to their Sultan's call to arms. They watched in silence as the pasha dismounted and hurried forward to stoop and kiss his brother's hand. But Abdul Malik was wise enough to realise that not everyone in this army wished to fight against Muhammad al-Mutawakkil, the previous Sultan, and might be caught up in an internal conflict of loyalties. So he called for volunteers to ride north. Three thousand men were assigned the task of attacking the Portuguese camp outside Asilah. This was an honourable enough task and removed those men of doubtful personal loyalty from the field of battle. The tribal sheikhs were impressed by the delicacy and discretion with which Abdul Malik had resolved this issue.

None knew, and none must be allowed to know, the Sultan's secret, which was that he was dying. The epic, 350-mile ride from Marrakesh to Souk el-Khemis had accelerated the progress of the disease. His faithful Jewish doctor had reached the end of his skills as a physician, and now repeatedly begged 'his Sultan' to rest. Abdul Malik, for his part, knew that not so much as a flicker of his illness and his inner exhaustion must be revealed to the army. Rather than rest he needed to be seen to be in absolute command, an ever-attentive father to his soldiers and a considerate uncle to the tribal sheikhs. The doctor later remembered, 'I was weeping and crying before him like a madman.' The Sultan asked for a week, but his doctor could only promise to use his art to give him two more days of vigour. The death of a sultan was always a traumatic event in Moroccan political life owing to the personal nature of the *bayaa*, the loyalty oath, and the fiercely competitive nature of the various mountain provinces. If he died before battle was joined, with Muhammad al-Mutawakkil's candidacy backed by a Crusader army, it would be a catastrophe. At the very best his country would be plunged into civil war; at worst, the experience of Granada would be meted out to Morocco, and this was not to be contemplated.

King Sebastian's Crusader army had been shadowed by Moroccan scouts ever since it left the walls of Asilah. On Sunday 3 August the commander of the scouts, Suleyman (a Moor from Cordoba), begged leave to enter the Sultan's tent. He had personally observed the vanguard of the Portuguese army crossing the ford of Mechara-en-Nedjima. There was no need to say more, for both he and the Sultan knew that the open plain that stretched out immediately beyond the ford was a perfect site for a battle. Here the Moroccan tribal cavalry had the space to manoeuvre freely, unencumbered by the salt marshes and defiles of the coast.

Abdul Malik also knew he had little time left. He must strike now or never. He summoned his younger brother and gave him command of the Moroccan cavalry, which was numbered not in thousands but in tens of thousands of horsemen. The two brothers had experienced decades of exile together. They had witnessed the victories at Tunis and Goletta and the deaths of thousands at Lepanto. They shared the same mother and the same distant memories of an exalted father. Now Abdul Malik held his brother's hands in his. He looked him in the eye and asked him 'to fight, conquer or die'. The Sultan took direct command of the centre of the army, composed of disciplined regiments of artillerymen and the arquebusiers. There were also three other regiments, one recruited from Moorish refugees, one of Moroccan townsmen and one of renegades from both Spain and Turkey. The semi-disciplined rearguard, a vast body of Berber soldiers and cavalrymen, was held in reserve. All day long the final depositions were put into place.

The Portuguese army, once it had crossed the ford, was confronted with the enemy for the first time. Until that hour its soldiers were unaware of the likely scale of the Moroccan resistance. They now looked on in bewilderment as column after column of tribal cavalry manoeuvred to take up their appointed positions during the daylight hours. King Sebastian quickly decided that there was only one tactical formation appropriate for his much smaller force, already deep inside enemy territory and now outnumbered many times over. He gave orders that his Crusader army be marshalled into a vast square. In the centre of the square the wagon train was drawn up to make a wooden village, several acres in extent, which would shelter the army of camp-followers. They would be protected on three sides by the four Portuguese regiments, interspersed with detachments of cavalry and professional soldiers to give them direction and confidence. The front of the square was composed of the experienced German and Italian mercenaries as well as the spirited gentleman volunteers of Portugal. They were arranged five ranks deep and presented a formidable force, for the arquebusiers had been trained to reload behind the protection of the stolid ranks of German pikemen and then to advance forward of this line to fire. To break up the expected force of the Moroccan cavalry attacks Sebastian also established a series of wooden forts made of wagons. These stood outside the great square and bristled with sharp-shooters.

Just before dawn lit the hills, the cries of the muezzin filled the silence of the plain. Abdul Malik, as its Imam, led his army in prayer. The shared ritual of the pre-dawn prayer – standing to address God as a rational human, then bowing down as a servant and finally prostrating oneself as a slave – helped bind the army into a single identity. When the sun rose through the mountains of the Rif and the Middle Atlas and lit up the army it also revealed the differences between the rival tribes and cities of Morocco. The Sultan retired to his tent and then reappeared as their general, ready to lead them in war. Only his Jewish doctor and his young brother knew the true personal cost of this last effort. Abdul Malik looked every inch a sultan, resplendent beneath his crimson umbrella, surrounded by five sacred banners and by the close-packed ranks of two rival regiments of bodyguards. Yet he was near the point of total collapse. His snow-white robes hung down around his horse in more than their usual magnificence, for they helped hide the fact that he had been strapped to his saddle. There could be no delaying. He must be seen to lead his army into battle that morning, 4 August 1578.

Before him lay the Crusader army arranged in an enormous square, their cannon to the fore. The Bishops of Coimbra and Oporto, assisted by the papal nuncio and a court of priests, were going about their solemn duties, blessing the troops and absolving them of their sins. They were preceded by a phalanx of tall crucifixes proudly born aloft, but now and then these dipped down, like reeds in the wind, so that an infantryman could embrace the feet of Christ.

The young king who led them into battle that day was like a vision from the dream chronicles of Christendom. A second Alexander, he was escorted by all the great lords of Portugal, the royal standards fluttering in the morning breeze at the head of a mass of silken pennants decorated with the heraldry of a worldwide empire. Like holy relics, King Sebastian wore the helmet of King Charles V and carried the sword of Prince Henry the Navigator into battle. A close escort was formed from the mounted troopers of the Tangier garrison, the most battle-hardened and experienced of all the army. The King rode up and down the lines, greeting his officers by name and saluting his soldiers.

Throughout the morning the cannon of the two armies spoke but it was only in the hour before noon that they drew close enough to find each other's range. Then, as if by prearrangement, the entire Crusader army sank to its knees one last time in prayer. When they rose they chanted the battle cry of '*Avis e Christo*'. Despite the defensive arrangement of the square, Sebastian knew that he must strike hard and decisively if he was not to be overwhelmed by the enemy's superior numbers. So, instead of standing ready and waiting, the crack troops that held the front of the Portuguese square advanced through their screen of cannon. Then they flung themselves on the centre of the Moroccan army, breaking the first Moroccan division, the Andalusians, who attempted to stand their ground. This brave frontal assault was blunted by a counter-attack by the second Moroccan division (largely composed of renegade Moors), who were in turn attacked by the crack Castilian regiments lent by King Philip. As the disciplined infantry of the two armies locked themselves in ferocious conflict, vast fields of Moroccan horsemen began to move across the surrounding plain, ready to launch the first attacks on the flanks of the Portuguese square. Like a river in spate, wave after wave of tribal cavalry descended from the hills, surrounding the whole Portuguese position and cutting them off from the ford and the road to the coast in a flood tide of horsemen.

As if in direct reply to this threat of annihilation, Sebastian launched his own surprise cavalry attack. His infantry regiments parted to allow the Duke of Aviero and the cavalry of his native ally, the deposed Sultan Muhammad al-Mutawakkil, to strike at the very centre of the Moroccan army. It was a near-suicidal charge, but if they had managed to kill Abdul Malik in clear view of his own troops they would yet have changed their fate that day. Their ferocious impetus allowed them to cut through the lines of Moroccan infantry and hack their way to within a few yards of Abdul Malik's pavilion. For a few critical moments all hung in the balance. Two of the five royal standards of Morocco were felled by the assault but the bodyguards succeeded in holding the ground around the person of the Sharif. Then, just as suddenly as it had been launched, this audacious frontal attack was destroyed as vast numbers of Moroccan cavalry swarmed in to rescue the Sultan. It may have been at this moment that the Moroccan cavalry first became aware of supernatural support. The patron saint of the fallen Muslim city of Ceuta, Sidi Bel Abbes, was seen mounted on a grey horse, moving from tribe to tribe, encouraging them in their patriotic fervour. In the words of al-Ifrani, 'Such things are not to be disbelieved, for it is known that the martyrs are ever living in God's presence.'

The Crusaders' assaults of the morning, first of infantry and then of cavalry, had been blunted and the latter overwhelmed. Yet on the ground lay proof of the ferocity of these assaults, for some two thousand Moroccan infantrymen, the disciplined cream of the army, lay dead on the field. The Crusaders now withdrew to take up their positions in defence of the original square. The field artillery of both sides had been silenced by the vicious fighting at the centre. Spiked, carriage-less or disabled, their tactical role was over and the battle took on a new shape. Throughout the long afternoon wave after wave of Moroccan cavalry launched themselves against the Crusader square. They were relentless in their courage, for where pikemen held their ground with arquebusiers embedded in the ranks, the defenders could cut lethal swaths through the ranks of the attackers.

But it was the attacks of the Sharifian regiment of dragoons, the mounted arquebusiers, which proved decisively effective that day. They were recruited from members of the Jazuli brotherhood and the Haha tribes who had formed the original core of the Sharifian army. They had been trained to discharge their weapons in the face of the enemy at the culmination of a gallop, and their horses were trained to pirouette just a few paces away from the lethal spikes of the Christian pikemen, allowing their riders to fire at point-blank range at the enemy and then double back out of danger, to reload in safety and prepare for the next attack. At first Sebastian took his place in the front rank of the front line at the centre of the square. Then he could be seen moving from regiment to regiment to inspire his men to hold their line. Three horses died beneath the King that afternoon and his magnificent bodyguard was cut down to a bare seven men.

It was the inexperienced Portuguese peasant recruits who held the rear of the square who broke first, their spirit having collapsed after the death of their valiant commander, Francisco de Tavara. But Sebastian was quick to react. He gathered together the last remnants of the Crusader cavalry and led three separate counter-attacks against the Moroccans in an attempt to give his men the opportunity to re-form their line. But it was not just at the rear that the square was crumbling. The ceaseless attrition of the mounted dragoon attacks had also broken its way through even the front line. Moroccan cavalry now poured into the centre of the square. Once they were attacked from both the front and the rear it was over for the Portuguese regiments. They retreated from their positions and fell back to the shelter of the wagon train. Effective resistance then crystallised around the sturdy German pikemen, the soldiers of Castile and the Portuguese noblemen, who alone held their positions. The last hours of the battle were long and drawn out, for the Moroccan army had started pillaging the wagon train and the victorious soldiers were now more interested in taking captives to be ransomed than in adding another corpse to the carnage of the day. In the last hour of dusk the surviving knots of Crusader resistance were subdued by the Moroccan cavalry. The Germans held their position to the end, disdaining all offers of surrender. As the sun set they were overwhelmed in one last massive cavalry charge and as the darkness thickened not a single Crusader soldier was left standing.

Of the twenty-six-thousand-strong army that had stood to arms that morning, fewer than one hundred would reach the safety of the coast. The rest were either dead, dying or captive. It was the most decisive battle of an age that was otherwise dominated by the gradual attrition of siege and counter-siege. It was the very last battle of the Last Crusade. Although it was the end of an era, it was also very much of the past: a day when monarchs led their men to war, when three kings would be counted among the tens of thousands of dead. It was a day of exhilarating bravery, where both armies displayed the utmost courage and resource. The battle had been won by the glory of the cavalry charge, and the role of artillery, the murky pre-industrial queen of battles, so decisive elsewhere, was curiously absent.

The Moroccans proved themselves impressively magnanimous. Empowered by the awesome scale of their victory, and the fortune to be made from ransoming captives, they behaved with chivalric restraint. In a bloody age so often marred by the horrendous cruelties unleashed by the sack of cities and the public torture of dissidents, it should be remembered that at the end of the Last Crusade no massacre of captives was ordered. Nor were the bodies of the dead defiled. No enemy soldiers were crucified or impaled, no heads dispatched in leather bags or jewelled caskets to horrify a foreign court. Instead, in the morning light, two Portuguese royal servants were instructed by the new Moroccan Sultan to search through the bodies of the dead and identify their king. Sebastian's body had been stripped of its valuable armour but was otherwise undefiled. His corpse was washed and bathed in myrrh and sent back in honour to his cousin, Philip II, accompanied by the Spanish ambassador, and the captive ten-year-old son of the Duke of Braganza was released without ransom. This gesture so impressed Philip II that he sent the Moroccan court a gift by return: an emerald the size of the dead King's heart and his body weight in sapphires, carried in solemn procession by forty Spanish lords.

During the daring cavalry attack that the Crusaders had launched right at the centre of the Moroccan army, Abdul Malik had used the last ounce of his strength to move forward and fight beside his bodyguard. Shortly after the enemy had been repulsed, he was seized by such a paroxysm of pain that he fainted. He recovered consciousness but briefly. Half an hour later he was taken from the world by an even more violent attack. His Jewish doctor continued to pretend to nurse him throughout the rest of the day, long enough for the Moroccan cavalry to begin their destruction of the Crusader square. Abdul Malik's young brother, as commander of the cavalry that day, was directly responsible for the scale of the Moroccan victory and was able to ascend the throne in triumph. The thirty-year-old Sultan took the title of 'al-Mansur bi Allah', 'Victorious by the Will of God'. There were no other claimants to the throne, for the former Sultan, Muhammad al-Mutawakkil, had also been found among the dead.[1] It was reported that he had drowned at the ford, caught by a broken stirrup while trying to escape from the field of battle. This is usually accepted as fact, but may be no more than the customary denigration of a so-called 'traitor'. He had certainly shown his martial qualities earlier in the day when he and his men had fought beside the Crusader cavalry. His body alone was signalled out for retribution. It was stuffed with straw and sent on a tour of his old allies among the cities and tribes of northern Morocco.

The garrison at Asilah and the Portuguese fleet anchored offshore could hear the distant noise of the Battle of the Three Kings, but they kept to their orders and held their position. As the news came in the next day with a trickle of survivors, a first wave of paralysis swept over Portugal. It seemed that all glory had been buried that day with their king. The survivors, though they may have behaved as bravely as any man, were tainted with a personal failure of feudal loyalty. They had not stood beside their king and defended him to the last. It would take ten days for a messenger to reach Lisbon. On 14 August the herald made his way to the Cistercian monastery of Alcobaca to break the news to sixty-four-year-old Cardinal Henry. The old regent was forced out of retirement and once again took up the reigns of power, this time as King Henry rather than as cardinal-regent. He was even prepared to relinquish his celibacy, and applied for a dispensation from the Pope to marry the thirteen-year-old daughter of the Duchess of Braganza.

That winter there was not a house, a cottage, a farm or a castle which did not have cause to join in the national grief. Portugal's mood at that time has been compared to that of Scotland after the flower of the nation perished at Flodden Field in 1513. In a single day the nation's proud nobility, its militant gentry, its brave young peasant volunteers, the entire court, army and administration, had perished. And with them the future lifeblood of the nation state. As Camões wrote in 1579, 'All will see that so dear to me was my country that I was content to die not only in but with it.' King Sebastian had never married, there was no direct heir and now only an ancient (and childless) cardinal sat slumped on the throne. Next in line for the throne, thrice cousin of the Avis through innumerable marriage alliances forged with the Habsburgs at every generation, was King Philip II of Spain. The old fears of being swamped by the Kingdom of Castile, which had first sparked Portugal in its crusading enterprise, were finally and inexorably coming true. Once news of the defeat had spread, it took but a second to realise that there was a second tragedy awaiting Portugal over and above the casualty figures of the Battle of the Three Kings. The country and its vast empire were fated to disappear into the vast conglomerate inheritance of the Habsburgs. There could be no doubt that Philip had the military power, money, determination and physical proximity to fulfil his legal right. He also had the moral satisfaction of recalling how he had counselled the young Sebastian against the invasion. He wrote to the city of Lisbon, 'There is no man living in the world, which hath received so great of the loss of the king my nephew . . . because I lost a son, and a friend, whom I loved very tenderly.'

Seven days later the agent for Fuggers' Bank in Lisbon sent a detailed report to his masters in Augsburg. For the commercial and financial implications of the Battle of the Three Kings threatened to topple the delicate balance of power within Europe. The King of Spain, lord of the vast silver deposits being unearthed by a slave army from the bowels of the mountain of Potosi in Peru, was fated to become the King of Pepper and the King of Sugar too.

There would be a half-hearted attempt to create a Portuguese candidate for the throne, though the cause of the claimant, Dom Antonio, would be greatly hindered by the transparent self-interest of his most ardent supporters, the dowager-queen of France, Catherine de Medici, and Elizabeth of England. Old King Henry, though he dithered about the fate of his nation, still hoped to sire an Avis child heir and was not prepared to compromise his perception of natural justice. He pronounced Dom Antonio a bastard, and in January 1580 solemnly declared in favour of the legal heir, King Philip II. Before the end of the month Henry was dead and Portugal, her empire, her wealth, provinces, fleet and fortified cities had passed into the hands of Philip II King of Castile and Aragon.

*

The Battle of the Three Kings was the last gallant but murderous epi-
sode in the 150-year Portuguese Crusade which had begun with the
capture of Ceuta in 1415. The relative position of the nations in this
vast tectonic conflict had been resolved as much by the attrition of men,
ships and treasure as by any single battle. The casualties suffered by the
Turks at Lepanto, at the siege of Malta and in the conquest of Cyprus,
the destruction of the Spanish garrisons in North Africa and their
repeated failures to capture Algiers or expand beyond the walls of Oran,
ultimately determined the conflict. The great cities of Constantinople
and Granada changed hands early on, so that the physical division
between the Muslim and Christian shores of the Mediterranean shifted
by a pair of provinces. Where it remains today. Malta and Andalusia
remain a Christian landscape, while Istanbul and Tunis remain Muslim
cities. The two empires continued to keep a close watch on each other's
intentions, but the locus of conflict drifted elsewhere. The Ottoman
Empire returned once again, in 1578, to its obsessive, doctrine-fuelled
conflict with Persia on its eastern frontier. Philip II concentrated on
trying to recover the Duchy of Burgundy and attempting to invade its
Protestant ally, England. The differences in religious authority between
Protestants and a Catholic king gave a compulsive edge to this new
frontier of warfare, just as it did to the Sunni–Shia conflict that sim-
mered beneath the Turkish–Persian wars. Even the victorious young
Sharif of Morocco turned away from the Mediterranean. He made no
attack on the Turks in Algeria or the Spanish and Portuguese forts that
remained on the coast of Morocco, but instead organised the conquest
of his southern neighbour, the Muslim empire of Songhai, whose capital, Gao, stood on the banks of the River Niger. He also carried on an
intriguing discourse with Queen Elizabeth, sketching out a plan for the
conquest of the Americas by Moroccan soldiers allied to the English
Navy.

Many Portuguese refused to believe in the death of King Sebastian
and stories began to circulate that he had been rescued from the piles
of dead on the battlefield at midnight and spirited away. He had been
taken south across the desert in a camel caravan and his many battle
wounds had eventually been mended by the mythical priest-king
Prester John. One day Sebastian, the 'Rei Encuberto' ('Hidden King'),

would ride back out of the desert, side by side with Prester John, and rescue Portugal in its greatest hour of need. For Sebastian, in the heroism of his death, had joined the company of the immortal knights, those such as Arthur of Britain, St George, Imam Husayn and al Khidr (the green knight of Islam) who are our band of once and future kings.

KEY CHARACTERS

Abdul Haq (1428–65). Last Sultan of the Merenid dynasty, which ruled Morocco from 1245.

Abdul Malik. Sharifian Sultan of Morocco 1576–8, one of surviving sons of Sharif Muhammad esh-Sheikh, who lived in exile during reign of his half-brother, Abdullah al-Ghalib. Seized throne from nephew, Muhammad al-Mutawakkil, in 1576. Fought King Sebastian of Portugal at Battle of Three Kings (1578).

Abdul Mansur. Sharifian Sultan of Morocco 1578–1603, after the death of his companion-brother at Battle of Three Kings. Veteran of Lepanto (1571), conqueror of Timbuktu and correspondent with Queen Elizabeth I of England.

Abu al-Hassan. Penultimate Emir of Nasrid Granada, aided by son Muhammad al-Zagal, though he would be succeeded by Boabadil (Muhammad XII).

Abu Hammu III. Last independent Zayyanid Sultan, who ruled western Algeria from Tlemcen, 1516–27.

Abu Zakariya Yahya. General serving Merenid dynasty, who successfully defended Tangier in 1437. Father of first Wattasid Sultan.

Adrian of Utrecht (1459–1523). Renaissance scholar from lands of Duchy of Burgundy. Born humble son of carpenter. Professor of University of Louvain and tutor, then trusted adviser, to King Charles V. Briefly regent of Spain before becoming Pope Hadrian VI (1522–3).

Afonso the African (1432–95). Twelfth Portuguese King. Minority 1438–48, reigned 1448 to 1477. Led several crusades into northern Morocco, seizing Ksar es Seghir, Asilah and Tangier before losing his wits during War of Castilian Succession (1474–9). Inherited throne as infant child of Dom Duarte (King Edward), son of King John I, 'the Great'.

Afonso de Albuquerque. Brilliant, brutal and efficient Portuguese admiral who created a naval empire in the Indian Ocean and Far East.

Ahmad, Sharif Ahmad al-Aruj. One of the two talented sons of Muhammad al-Qaim, founder of Sharifian dynasty of Morocco. Commanded northern half of southern Morocco based on Marrakesh before losing control to his brother, Sharif Muhammad esh-Sheikh.

Barbarossa. Admiral of the corsairs. See Uruj and Khayr al-Din.

Bayezid I (1354–1403), 'the Thunderbolt'. Ottoman Sultan who reigned 1389–1402, expanding empire in both Anatolia and Balkans. Conquered Bulgaria and won Battle of Nicopolis (1396) against Crusader army led by Emperor Sigismund, but defeated by Timur at Battle of Ankara (1402). Son of Sultan Murat I, father of Sultan Mehmet I Celebi.

Bayezid II (1448–1512). Son of Mehmet II, 'the Conqueror' and father of Selim I, 'the Grim'. Pious, thoughtful monarch who reigned 1481–1512. Built up Ottoman navy to sufficient strength to wage war against Venice. Deposed by own son after failing to deal with threat from *kizilbas* dissidents of Persia.

Boabadil (c.1460–1536). Last Nasrid Emir of Muslim Granada. Became Sultan Muhammad XII, surrendered Granada and died in Morocco.

Boucicaut, Jean (1366–1421). French Crusader knight, present at defeat by Bayezid I at Nicopolis (1396). Visited Byzantine Constantinople, escorted Emperor on tour of courts of Christendom and later led expeditions into Levant.

Charles V (1500–58). Holy Roman Emperor 1519–56, also King of Castile and Aragon 1516–56, Duke of Burgundy 1506–58. In France known as Charles-Quint, Prince des Pays-Bas; in Germany as Kaiser Karl V; in Spain as Carlos I (though, confusingly, King Carlos I of Spain but also Carlos V because of Imperial title). Resigned powers in 1555 and later died in a monastery.

Chièvres, William of. Battle-experienced French nobleman appointed by Emperor Maximilian to serve as tutor-companion to young Charles V.

Cisneros, Francisco Jimenez de (1436–1517). Franciscan friar, confessor to Queen Isabella, reformer of the Spanish Church, Cardinal-Primate of Spain from 1495 (after the death of his patron, Mendoza) and Grand Inquisitor from 1507. Personally funded crusade that conquered Oran in 1509 and was virtual regent to King Ferdinand and young Charles V.

Constantine XI Palaeologus (1405–53). Last Byzantine Emperor, who won approval of subjects and enemies alike by his heroic dignity. Inherited throne from brother John VIII in 1449 and only relinquished it with his life while defending Constantinople.

Dias, Bartolomeu (c.1450–1500). Portuguese sea captain and first European to round Cape of Good Hope and enter Indian Ocean.

Dragut (1495–1565). Corsair sea captain and Ottoman admiral, born near Bodrum, son of Turkish farmer. Served as captain under Barbarossa from 1520, distinguished himself in innumerable raids and marine operations and also at Battle of Preveza (1538). From 1548 most active Ottoman naval commander in Mediterranean, led campaigns that recaptured Tripoli and Madhia and helped destroy Spanish–Italian army that had invaded Djerba. Built up Tripoli as major Ottoman naval base, from which his fleet assisted Ottoman siege of Malta, where his death was major setback to campaign. Buried beside his mosque in Tripoli. Known in Turkey as Turgut Reis or Torgut Rais, and in some accounts as Darghouth.

Edward, Dom Duarte (1391–1438). Philosopher-king of Portugal, elder brother of Henry the Navigator. Succeeded father, King John I, in 1433.

Ehingen, Jorg von (1428–1508). German soldier of fortune who left description of his life, including adventures in Morocco fighting for Portuguese.

Ferdinand, Dom Fernao (1402–43). Prince of Portugal. Died in captivity in Fez after failure of siege of Tangier (1437).

Ferdinand the Catholic, 'El Catolico' (1452–1516). King of Aragon, husband of Queen Isabella of Castile. Conqueror of Granada and principal character in story of Last Crusaders. Born second son of King John II of Aragon of the ancient House of Trastamara. Ferdinand II, King of Aragon, Sicily, Naples, Valencia, Sardinia and Navarre, Count of Barcelona and Regent of Castile.

Ferdinand, Archduke (1503–64). Younger brother of Charles V, educated in court of grandfather, King Ferdinand II of Aragon. In

1521 given governance of Archduchy of Austria and married Anna, daughter of Louis (Ladislas or Lewis) II, King of Hungary and Bohemia. After death of father-in-law at Mohacs (1526) claimed both crowns. Faced Ottoman invasions in 1529, 1531 and 1541 but eventually made peace with both Turks and Protestants. Elected King of Romans in 1531 and reigned as Holy Roman Emperor Ferdinand I after brother's abdication.

Francis I (1494–1547). Elegant, clever, sensual, gallant and bellicose King of France 1515–47. Son of Charles, Count of Angoulême. Succeeded to throne because of childless reigns of two cousin predecessors, Louis XII (son of poet Duke of Orléans) and Charles VIII. Loyally followed their example in invading Italy, winning Battle of Marignano (1515) but captured at defeat of Pavia (1525). Locked into rivalry with Charles V and Henry VIII of England. His endless wars are yet a Renaissance apogee, the France of Rabelais and Ronsard and the gallant Chevalier Bayard.

Francisco de Almeida. First Portuguese viceroy of India and victor of decisive naval Battle of Diu (1509). Commander of Portuguese navy between Vasco da Gama and Afonso de Albuquerque.

Gattinara, Bartolomeo Mercurino. Italian diplomat, secretary of state and leading figure in inner councils of Charles V.

Gedik, Ahmed Pasha. Ottoman General.

Genghis Khan (1162–1227). Mongolian and Turkic super-hero, conqueror of Russia, China and his Central Asian homeland. Ruled empire extending from the Black Sea to the Pacific.

Henry, Prince Henry the Navigator, Dom Henrique (1394–1460). Son of King John I and Queen Philippa (Philippa of Lancaster). Prime motivator of initial Portuguese exploration of Africa. Duke of Viseu, Grand Master of Crusading Order of Christ (Portuguese version of Knights Templars).

Hunyadi, Janos (1407–56). Heroic Hungarian soldier-knight and military commander who died defending Belgrade (1456) against Mehmet the Conqueror.

James II. Last active Lusignan King of Cyprus, 1460–73. Married Venetian Caterina Cornaro, who ruled as regent for sickly infant son King James III (1473–4) before Venice annexed Cyprus in 1489.

John (Joao) I (1357–1433). Tenth King of Portugal. Usurper and heroic defender against Castile through victory at Battle of Aljubarrota (1385) and sacked Ceuta (1415). Father of Dom Duarte (future King Edward), Henry, Pedro, Ferdinand through his English queen, Philippa, and Beatriz and Afonso (Duke of Braganza) with mistress Ines Pires. Illegitimate son of King Pedro II and Galician mistress Teresa Lourenco. Also known as 'the Great', 'the Bastard', 'the Good' and 'John of Happy Memory'.

John (Joao) II (1455–95). Thirteenth King of Portugal. Known variously as 'the Perfect Prince' or 'the Tyrant of Portugal'. Regent for his father from 1477 and king from 1481. Brilliant and secretive Renaissance ruler who extended Portuguese exploration over coast of western and southern Africa and deep into South Atlantic.

John (Joao) III (1502–57). Fifteenth King of Portugal, who succeeded father King Manuel in 1521, aged nineteen. Almost all his nine children predeceased him and he left throne to grandson Dom Sebastian. Known as 'the Pragmatic', 'the Pious' and 'the Grocer King of Portugal', John presided over worldwide expansion of Portuguese empire, though he also ordered the abandonment of a number of Moroccan fortress outposts after fall of Agadir (1541).

Don John (Juan) of Austria (1547–78). Illegitimate son of Charles V and Barbara Blomberg. Suppressed Moorish revolt, commanded Holy League fleet at Lepanto (1571) and captured Tunis (1573). Died at Namur trying to suppress Dutch Revolt against half-brother King Philip II.

Khayr al-Din (or Kherredine or Kheyr el-Din). This honorific title, meaning 'Protector of Religion', was given to the two Barbarossa brothers, Uruj (c.1474–1518) and Khizr (c.1478–1546) by Sultan Selim the Grim, but is usually only used to refer to Khizr, the younger. Triumphant corsair captain, defender of North Africa, scourge of coasts of Christendom, admiral in chief of Ottoman Empire, victor of Battle of Prevcza (1538), creator of modern Algeria, Beylerbey (Lord of Lords) of Algiers 1520–44. After retiring in honour to Istanbul was buried just outside his own mosque and charitable foundation.

Leo. Pope Leo X (1513–21). Born Giovanni de Medici, son of Lorenzo 'the Magnificent'. Easy-going, corrupt, clever Renaissance prince, more concerned with protecting Florence and building St Peter's than reforming Church. Rome was sacked, Germany became Protestant, fiscal and spiritual treasury of papacy bankrupted.

Louis (or Ladislas or Lewis) II, King of Hungary and Bohemia. Son of Uladislaus, elected King of Poland, and Anna of Candal. Married Mary of Austria in a double marriage pact that also paired his sister with Habsburg Archduke Ferdinand. Led army of nobles into defeat and extinction at Battle of Mohacs (1526), after which south-east of Hungary was occupied by Ottomans and north-west by Habsburgs, with an independent rump left under John Zapolya.

Manuel II Palaeologos (1350–1425). Byzantine Emperor, ruled 1391– 1425. Father of last Byzantine Emperor. Toured courts of Christendom 1400–3 to appeal to France, Aragon, England and Denmark for assistance for the Eastern Empire.

Manuel (or Manoel or Emmanuel) (1469–1521). Fourteenth King of Portugal. Son of Prince Ferdinand, second son of King Duarte (Edward). Known as 'the Fortunate' or 'the Pepper King'. Succeeded cousin King John (John) II in 1495 in time to preside over conquest of naval empire in the Far East. Married two daughters of Ferdinand and Isabella: the widowed Dona Isabella and her sister Dona Maria, then a third wife, his cousin Eleanor of Habsburg.

Mehmet II the Conqueror (1432–81). Known as 'the Great Eagle'. Only surviving son of Sultan Murat II. Youthful conqueror of Constantinople, creator of Istanbul as centre of expanding Ottoman Empire. Reigned 1444–6 and 1451–81.

Mesikh, Pasha. Ottoman commander at first siege of Rhodes in 1480. Convert to Islam from a distinguished family of old Byzantium.

Moulay Hassan/Mohammed Hassan. Last Hafsid Sultan of Tunis, 1526–43. Survived as client of Charles V.

Muhammad al-Burtugali. Wattasid Sultan who repelled Portuguese invasion of 1519.

Muhammad al-Shaykh. Moroccan governor of Asilah who would later assume control of country after fall of Merenid dynasty. Father of Sultan Muhammad al-Burtugali. First Wattasid Sultan of Morocco.

Murat (or Murad) I. Sultan who first confirmed Ottoman hold over Thrace by capturing Adrianople (Edirne) in 1362. Died at First battle of Kosovo (1389), where Ottomans defeated Christian alliance of Serbians, Bulgars and Bosnians. First Ottoman Bey to style himself a Sultan, succeeded by son Bayezid I.

Murat (or Murad) II (1404–51). Son of Sultan Mehmet I Celebi, father of Mehmet II, the Conqueror. A charismatic but inattentive father, reigned from 1421 (with some attempts at resignation).

Mustapha. Ottoman prince, beloved potential heir to father Suleyman, but murdered in plot by stepmother Roxelana and grand vizier Rustem Pasha.

Orhan (1284–1359). Second of dynasty of Ottoman rulers, who greatly expanded his inheritance by invading Thrace. Reigned 1326–59 and succeeded by son Murat I.

Osman Bey (1258–1326). Son of Ertugul, founder of the Ottoman dynasty, the Osmanli House. Ruled 1299–1326 and succeeded by son Orhan.

Peter, Dom Pedro (1392–1449). Wise Prince Regent of Portugal, who supported work of brother Prince Henry the Navigator. Fell from grace when nephew Afonso the African succeeded to throne.

Philip the Good (1396–1467). Charismatic Duke of Burgundy at its fifteenth-century prime. Son of John the Fearless (killed in 1419 by French Dauphin) and grandson of Philip the Bold. Founder in 1430 of Order of Golden Fleece.

Pius V. Austere, pious Pope 1566–72. Born near Alexandria to poor family and became Dominican friar. Architect of Holy League, passionate supporter of reform decrees of Council of Trent (1545–63) and key figure in Counter-Reformation and victory of Lepanto (1571).

Selim I (1456–1520). Sultan of Ottoman Empire, 1512–20, known as 'the Grim'. Son of Bayezid II and father of Suleyman the Magnificent. Conqueror of eastern Turkey, Syria and Egypt, and destroyer of Kizilbas rebellion.

Selim II (1524–74). Sultan of Ottoman Empire, 1566–74, known as 'the Sot'. Only surviving child of Suleyman and Roxelana; a kindly man but an unworthy heir. Conqueror of Cyprus. Succeeded by son Murat III.

Sharif Al-Qaim. Founder of Sharifian power in southern Morocco after agreeing to lead *jihad* against Portuguese and to arbitrate among tribes. Father of Sharif Ahmad al-Aruj and Sharif Muhammad esh-Sheikh.

Sharif Muhammad esh-Sheikh. Son of Al-Qaim. Heroic commander of siege of Portuguese Agadir (1541) and destroyed Wattasid power in north to create united Empire of Morocco.

Sigismund (1387–1437). Of the ancient dynasty of Luxemburg. Holy Roman Emperor from 1410, King of Bohemia from 1419. Presided over creation of joint German–Slavic Empire and Church Council of Constance. His Crusader army defeated by the Ottomans at Battle of Nicopolis (1396).

Suleyman the Magnificent (1494–1566). Sultan of Ottoman Empire, law-giver, builder, conqueror of Rhodes, Baghdad, Belgrade, Budapest and Tabriz. Poet and lover of Roxelana. Only surviving son of Sultan Selim I. Reigned from 1520 until death on campaign in Hungary. Father of Princess Mihrimah and Princes Mustapha, Cihangir, Bayezid and Selim.

Timur (1336–1405). Central Asian warrior hero who conquered a world empire from his Transoxanian homeland based on twin cities of Samarkand and Bokhara. Builder of mosques, patron of literature and commander of genius who devastated India and Middle East and just before his death was poised to invade China.

Tristao da Cunha (c.1460–c.1540). Portuguese captain and commander.

Uluj Ali (1519–78). Also known as Ali Pasha, Uluch Ali, El Louk Ali, Euldj Ali, Ochiali and Uchail. Charismatic commander of Algerian corsairs, whose career began as a Christian slave boy, Giovanni Galeni, son of a fisherman, picked up off Calabria, southern Italy. After conversion to Islam rose through ranks and caught attention of corsair admiral Dragut. In 1565 appointed admiral at Alexandria, from where he joined siege of Malta. Escorted Dragut's body back to Tripoli for burial. Appointed governor of Tripoli, then in 1568 made governor of Algiers. Led left wing at Lepanto (1571), his corsair squadron being the only one to perform well and escape general destruction. Working beside admiral Piale Pasha, rebuilt Ottoman navy in 1572, recapturing Tunis and Goletta from Spanish in 1574. Died in honoured retirement in Istanbul, buried beside his mosque and charitable foundation of Kilic Ali Pasa Camii. The accidental patron of Cervantes (whom he captured at Lepanto).

Uruj (c.1474–1518). Elder of two brothers both referred to as Barbarossa. Born in Lesbos. Heroic corsair captain, leader of North African opposition to Spanish invasions. Died in combat outside Tlemcen in Algeria. Also known as Oruc Reis, Arrudye and Aruj Pasha. Succeeded by younger brother, Khizr (c.1478–1546), also known as Khayr al-Din, Kherredine, Kheyr el-Din and Hayreddin Pasha.

Vasco da Gama (c.1460/9–1524). First Portuguese sea captain to sail to India from Europe, returning to help build a trading empire through conquest.

COMPARATIVE TIMELINES

ATLANTIC AND
WESTERN MEDITERRANEAN
(British Isles, France, Spain, Portugal,
Morocco, West Africa, Algeria, Americas)

CENTRAL MEDITERRANEAN
AND ADRIATIC
(Germany, Italy, Sicily, Malta, Tunisia,
Venice, Albania, Hungary)

AD 1200–1249

AD 1250–1299

1266	Norse King Magnus of Norway sells Hebrides to Scotland.		1270	Failure of Seventh Crusade. King Louis IX of France and much of his army perish outside Tunis at Carthage.
			1282	Charles of Anjou, ambitious brother of Louis IX, had seized control of Sicily but his French troops driven out by popular rising known as the Sicilian Vespers.
1290	King Edward I of England expels Jews but welcomes instead German merchants from Hanseatic League.			

AD 1300–1349

1304	William Wallace, leader of Scottish resistance to rule from England from 1297, executed in London.			
1307	King Philip IV of France arrests Knights Templars.		1312	Order of Knights Templars formally suppressed by Pope Clemens V.
1319	Portuguese branch of Knights Templars transformed into Order of Christ.			
1339	Beginning of Hundred Years War. English invasion of France until 1453.			
1348–50	Bubonic plague ('Black Death') kills third of world's population.		1348–50	Bubonic plague ('Black Death') kills third of world's population.

AD 1350–1399

1385	King John (João) I of Portugal defeats Castilian invasion at Battle of Aljubarrota.

1399–1402	Mission of Byzantine Emperor Manuel II (ruled 1391–1425) to western Europe to seek aid.		1399–1402	Mission of Byzantine Emperor Manuel II (ruled 1391–1425) to Europe to seek aid.

WHITE SEA, AEGEAN, BLACK SEA AND RED SEA (Greece, Balkans, Russia, Egypt, Syria, Anatolia, Arabia)		INDIAN OCEAN, PERSIAN GULF AND FAR EAST (East Africa, Gujarat, Southern India, China and Far East)	
1248–54	Defeat of the Sixth Crusade. King Louis IX invades Nile Delta and seizes Damietta but is defeated at Mansura.		
1258	Baghdad, Aleppo and Damascus destroyed by Mongol armies of Hulagu, an heir of Genghis Khan.		
1260	Battle of Ain Jalut: Mamelukes of Egypt halt Mongol invasion.		
1291	Conquest of Acre: Crusaders expelled from military occupation of Palestine by Egyptian Sultan.		
1301	Osman (1281–1326) establishes Ottoman state on Seljuk–Byzantine frontier.		
1309	Knights of St John move from Cyprus to island of Rhodes.		
1326	Orhan Bey, second Ottoman ruler, son of Osman, conquers Brusa.		
1337	Orhan seizes Nicomedia (Iznik).		
1348–50	Bubonic plague ('Black Death') kills third of world's population.	1348–50	Bubonic plague ('Black Death') kills third of world's population.
1354	Ottomans seize control of Gallipoli: their first possession on European shore.		
1362	Adrianople (Edirne) captured by Ottomans and becomes their European capital. Constantinople isolated from Thracian hinterland.		
1389	First Battle of Kosovo: decisive Ottoman victory over Serbian–Bosnian army.		
1396	Crusader army led by Holy Roman Emperor Sigismund defeated by Ottomans at Nicopolis. Serbia becomes vassal state of Ottoman Empire.		
1399–1402	Mission of Byzantine Emperor Manuel II (ruled 1391–1425) to western Europe to seek aid.	1398	Timur destroys Delhi Sultanate and annexes Punjab.

ATLANTIC AND WESTERN MEDITERRANEAN (British Isles, France, Spain, Portugal, Morocco, West Africa, Algeria, Americas)		CENTRAL MEDITERRANEAN AND ADRIATIC (Germany, Italy, Sicily, Malta, Tunisia, Venice, Albania, Hungary)	
		1407	Foundation of Casa di San Giorgio: first public bank in Europe.
1415	Portuguese sack Muslim city of Ceuta in Morocco and establish garrison-fortress on coast.		
1433	Death of King John I.		
1434	Portuguese ship passes south of Cape Bojador.		
1437	Portuguese siege of Tangier ends in humiliating evacuation and capture of Prince Ferdinand.	1439	Union of Florence, decree for union between Catholic and Orthodox Churches, widely rejected by Orthodox.
1458	Portuguese conquest of Ksar-es-Seghir led by old Prince Henry the Navigator and young nephew King Afonso V (Afonso the African).	1458	Brilliant Renaissance polymath Aeneas Silvio Piccolomini elected Pope Pius II and urges Crusade throughout his pontificate (1458–64), especially at Congress of Mantua.
1460	King Afonso V grants Order of Christ monopoly on West African coast trade. Death of Henry the Navigator on 13 November.		
1465	Execution in Fez of the last of the Merenid Sultans, Abdul Haq.		
1471	Afonso V captures Asilah and advances on Tangier.		
1472	Wattasid governor advances to occupy Fez and establish new dynasty of sultans.		
1474	Isabella declared Queen of Castile after death of brother Henry IV.		
1474–9	Castilian War of Succession between Queen Isabella (supported by husband King Ferdinand) and her sister Juana (supported by King Afonso V of Portugal).		
1476	Portuguese army defeated by King Ferdinand's forces at Battle of Toro.		

AD 1400–1449

AD 1450–1499

WHITE SEA, AEGEAN, BLACK SEA AND RED SEA (Greece, Balkans, Russia, Egypt, Syria, Anatolia, Arabia)		INDIAN OCEAN, PERSIAN GULF AND FAR EAST (East Africa, Gujarat, Southern India, China and Far East)	
1402	Sultan Bayezid I defeated by Timur at Battle of Ankara. Dies in captivity.	1405	Death of Timur on point of invading China. Brief submission of Japan to Chinese Empire.
1413	Sultan Mehmet I Celebi begins restoration of Ottoman authority.	1411	Japanese rebellion against Chinese rule.
1421	Accession of Murat II (ruled 1421–51 after an early attempt to resign).	1426	Chinese defeated at Battle of Tot-Dong in Vietnam.
1422	First Ottoman siege of Constantinople.	1433	Chinese naval expedition reaches East Africa in culmination of exploratory period begun in 1405.
1439	Union of Florence, Decree for the Union between Catholic and Orthodox Churches, widely rejected among Orthodox.		
1444	Battle of Varna: Ottomans defeat Hungarian-led Crusade. Death of King Vladislav III (ruled 1440–4).		
1446	Janos Hunyadi elected regent of Hungary.		
1448	Second Battle of Kosovo lasts three days.	1449	Oriat Mongols defeat Chinese army at Battle of Huai Lai.
1451	Mehmet II (Mehmet the Conqueror) succeeds as Ottoman Sultan after death of father Murat II.		
1453	Conquest of Constantinople by Mehmet II.		
1456	Janos Hunyadi defends Belgrade against attack led by Mehmet the Conqueror and dies from his wounds.		
1457	Mathias Corvinus (second son of Janos Hunyadi) elected King of Hungary. George Podiebrad elected King of Bohemia.		
1461	Ottomans capture Byzantine Empire of Trebizond.		

ATLANTIC AND
WESTERN MEDITERRANEAN
(British Isles, France, Spain, Portugal,
Morocco, West Africa, Algeria, Americas)

CENTRAL MEDITERRANEAN
AND ADRIATIC
(Germany, Italy, Sicily, Malta, Tunisia,
Venice, Albania, Hungary)

AD 1450–1499 (continued)

1477	Charles the Bold (Duke of Burgundy 1467–77) killed at siege of Nancy. Louis XI seizes French possessions of Duchy of Burgundy.
1479	Treaty of Alcacovas brings peace between Portugal and Castile, and Personal Union between Castile and Aragon.
1482	Start of ten-year war of conquest of Granada. Inquisition established under Torquemada (1483–98). Death of heiress daughter of Duke Charles the Bold, who is married to Habsburg Emperor Maximilian.
1485	Henry VII becomes King of England, effectively ending near-century-long Wars of the Roses.
1489	Portuguese expedition to establish fortress of Graciosa expelled by Moroccan army.
1490	King Nkinga Nkuwu of Congo embraces Christianity.
1492	Surrender of city of Granada. Expulsion of the Jews from Castile. Jimenez de Cisneros (1436–1517) becomes confessor to Queen Isabella at recommendation of Cardinal Mendoza. Subsequently raised to become Cardinal Primate and Archbishop of Toledo, reforms Church, later rules as Regent. Columbus discovers Caribbean islands such as San Salvador, Cuba and Haiti after a westward sea journey of sixty-one days and expands this initial discoveries in four more expeditions to what he imagines is 'West India'.
1493	Emperor Askia Muhammad (1493–1528) establishes Songhai Empire of central West Africa, and its new capital, Gao, eclipses Timbuktu.
1494	Treaty of Tordesillas. Papal confirmation of the division of the new discoveries in the West between Portugal and Castile as already agreed by peace of Alcavolas in 1479.

WHITE SEA, AEGEAN, BLACK SEA AND RED SEA (Greece, Balkans, Russia, Egypt, Syria, Anatolia, Arabia)	INDIAN OCEAN, PERSIAN GULF AND FAR EAST (East Africa, Gujarat, Southern India, China and Far East)

1480   Ottoman siege of Rhodes.
        Simultaneous Ottoman sack (and
        year-long occupation) of Italian
        port of Otranto.
        Death of Mehmet II (Mehmet the
        Conqueror).

1489   Venice annexes Lusignan Cyprus.

ATLANTIC AND WESTERN MEDITERRANEAN (British Isles, France, Spain, Portugal, Morocco, West Africa, Algeria, Americas)	CENTRAL MEDITERRANEAN AND ADRIATIC (Germany, Italy, Sicily, Malta, Tunisia, Venice, Albania, Hungary)

AD 1450–1499 (continued)

1497	Abandoned Moroccan city of Melilla occupied by Spanish garrison. Vasco da Gama sails eastwards towards India in three ships. King Manuel I expels Jews from Portugal.
1499	Vasco da Gama returns to Lisbon from India, which was reached in 1498. Ottoman attack on Venice organised by Sultan Bayezid II.

AD 1500–1549

1500	Birth of Charles V at Ghent, into rich traditions of Duchy of Burgundy. Second Portuguese fleet sails for India.
1501	Expulsion order against Muslim Moors of Castile.
1503	King Ferdinand's annexation of Kingdom of Naples recognised by King Louis XII of France in Treaty of Arona.
1504	Spanish outpost on coast of western Sahara destroyed. Death of Queen Isabella.
1505	Spanish artillery forts erected at Mers-el-Kebir and Qassasa.
1506	Death of Duke Philip the Handsome, husband of Juana, heiress daughter of Ferdinand and Isabella.
1507	Portuguese seize control of friendly Moroccan city of Safi.
1508–12	Spanish establish coastal forts along North African coast at Algiers, Bejaia, Tripoli and Djerba.
1509	Spanish expedition led by Cardinal-Primate Cisneros and Count Pedro Navarro captures Oran. Henry VIII succeeds his father to the English throne. Rules until 1547.
1512	Barbarossa brothers, Uruj and Khizr, attack Spanish fort at Bejaia.

WHITE SEA, AEGEAN, BLACK SEA AND RED SEA (Greece, Balkans, Russia, Egypt, Syria, Anatolia, Arabia)		INDIAN OCEAN, PERSIAN GULF AND FAR EAST (East Africa, Gujarat, Southern India, China and Far East)	
1499	Ottoman attack on Venice organised by Sultan Bayezid II.		
		1499	Vasco da Gama returns to Lisbon after reaching India in 1498. Ottoman attack on Venice organised by Sultan Bayezid II.
		1500	Second Portuguese trading and naval fleet of thirteen ships sails for Indian Ocean.
		1502	Ismail I crowned at Tabriz: the first Shiite Shah and founder of Persian Safavid Empire. Third Portuguese fleet of twenty-five ships sails for Indian Ocean.
		1503	Portuguese fleet plunders cities of Swahili coast of East Africa.
		1504	Babur, a descendant of Timur, becomes Lord of Kabul and pursues conquest of northern India until death in 1530.
		1509	Portuguese naval victory over Gujarat at Battle of Diu in Indian Ocean.
1510	Revolts by Kizilbas rebels within Ottoman Empire.	1510	Portuguese seize Malacca and control strait.
1512	Selim I (Selim the Grim) wins the struggle for the succession to the Ottoman throne and in eight-year reign seizes Syria, Egypt, Arabia and eastern Anatolia.		

ATLANTIC AND
WESTERN MEDITERRANEAN
(British Isles, France, Spain, Portugal,
Morocco, West Africa, Algeria, Americas)

CENTRAL MEDITERRANEAN
AND ADRIATIC
(Germany, Italy, Sicily, Malta, Tunisia,
Venice, Albania, Hungary)

AD 1500–1549 (continued)

	Atlantic and Western Mediterranean		Central Mediterranean and Adriatic
1513	Portuguese cavalry army advances inland from Azzemour, wins Battle of Doukkala and reaches gates of Marrakesh.	1513	Leo X (a Medici) elected Pope. Rules over an artistic and intellectual enlightenment, though unable to understand demands for Reformation, until his death in 1521.
1514	Beginning of seven years of drought and famine in southern Morocco. Portuguese expedition to establish Fort Marmora up River Sebou repelled by Wattasid Sultan.		
1515	Francis I succeeds to throne of France from childless cousin Louis XII (1498–1515), who had succeeded his own cousin Charles VIII (1483–98). All three monarchs are obsessed by establishing French hegemony over Italy, especially Milan. Charles V becomes Duke of Burgundy.		
1516	First Spanish assault on city of Algiers, commanded by Don Diego de Vera, repelled.		
1517	Uruj, the elder Barbarossa brother, seizes Algerian capital of Tlemcen but is killed in following year.	1517	Augustinian Friar Martin Luther publishes his 'ninety-five theses' addressing corruption and church reform.
1518	Second Spanish assault on Algiers led by Admiral de Moncada repelled.	1519	Charles V elected Holy Roman Emperor against candidature of Francis I of France.
1520	In Mexico the Spanish adventurer Hernan Cortes kidnaps and murders Aztec Emperor Montezuma II (ruled 1502–20).	1520	Luther publishes three essays.
1521–6, 1526–9	Wars between Francis I and Charles V.	1521	At Diet of Worms Luther appears under a pledge of safe conduct. Charles V transfers Habsburg lands in Germany to his brother Archduke Ferdinand.
		1522	Luther's September Bible published in German.
1524	Sharifians seize Marrakesh from Hintati dynasty of governors. Seville made sole port for trade with Spanish discoveries in the Far West (vice-royalty of New Spain established in 1535, that of Peru in 1542, captain-generalship of Venezuela leased to Welser Brothers' bank in 1527).	1524	Beginning of Peasants' War in Germany.
		1525	Battle of Pavia, Italy: French army defeated and Francis I captured.
		1526	Battle of Mohacs: Ottoman army led by Sultan Suleyman destroys Hungarian army and king.
		1527	The sack of Rome by the unpaid, mutinous and largely German army of Emperor Charles V. End of Renaissance papacy.

WHITE SEA, AEGEAN, BLACK SEA AND RED SEA (Greece, Balkans, Russia, Egypt, Syria, Anatolia, Arabia)		INDIAN OCEAN, PERSIAN GULF AND FAR EAST (East Africa, Gujarat, Southern India, China and Far East)	
		1513	Portuguese attack Aden but fail to establish base in Yemen.
1514	Selim I wins decisive victory over Shah Ismail and his *kizilbas* army at Battle of Caldiran.		
		1515	Portuguese capture island city of Ormuz, at entrance to Persian Gulf.
1516	Ottoman victory over Mameluke Sultan at Battle of Marj Dabiq; occupation of Aleppo, Damascus, Jerusalem and sack of Cairo.	1516	Portuguese permitted to trade at Canton in exchange for annual tribute (these traders moved to Macao in 1557) but their naval ships driven from Yellow Sea in 1520–1.
1517	Selim I marches army out of Egypt and Syria. Last Abbasid Caliph deported from Cairo to Istanbul.		
1520	Suleyman the Magnificent succeeds father, Selim I.		
1521	Sultan Suleyman conquers Belgrade.		
1522	Second Ottoman siege of Rhodes. Knights of St John surrender in December.		
1526	Battle of Mohacs: Ottomans under Suleyman the Magnificent defeat Hungarian army and kill Louis II, King of Hungary and Bohemia.		

ATLANTIC AND WESTERN MEDITERRANEAN (British Isles, France, Spain, Portugal, Morocco, West Africa, Algeria, Americas)		CENTRAL MEDITERRANEAN AND ADRIATIC (Germany, Italy, Sicily, Malta, Tunisia, Venice, Albania, Hungary)	
		1528	Admiral Andrea Doria defects from service of French to Emperor Charles V.
		1529	First Ottoman siege of Vienna lasts for two weeks. 'Ladies' Peace' of Cambrai between Francis I and Charles V. Charles V formally crowned by Pope in Italy, in last such ceremony in Christendom.
1530	Younger Barbarossa brother, Khizr, finally destroys Spanish fortress of Tower of Navarro on island outside Algiers harbour.	1530	Knights of St John of the Hospital of Jerusalem (Knights Hospitallers) established in Malta and Tripoli. Charles V attempts to preserve unity of Christian faith at Diet of Augsburg.
1531–41	Between 1531 and 1534 a Spanish conquistador, the sixty-year-old Francisco Pizarro, kidnaps the Inca Emperor, Atahualpa, extorts a fortune, then strangles his captive and conquers Cuzco. He establishes Lima in 1535 before being killed by a rival in 1541.		Brave resistance of garrison in little fortress of Koszeg (Guns) holds up Ottoman advance. Charles V visits Vienna on 23 September, at end of campaigning season.
		1534	German city of Münster becomes Anabaptist.
		1535	Charles V leads Crusade against Goletta and Tunis.
		1537	Ottoman siege of Corfu.
		1538	Battle of Preveza: Ottoman fleet defeats Christian allied fleet under Andrea Doria.
1541	Charles V leads Crusade against corsair-fortress of Algiers. Portuguese fortress of Santa Cruz (Agadir) falls to the siege of the Sharifian army of Morocco.		
		1551	Dragut captures Mahdia on Tunisian coast.
1556	Charles V abdicates, surrendering power to son Philip II.		
1558	Accession to throne of England of Elizabeth I, half-sister to Queen Mary (wife of Philip II of Spain). Spanish garrison, under command of Count Alcaudete, advance out of Oran to besiege Mostaganem but are themselves destroyed.		

AD 1500–1549 (continued)

AD 1550–1599

WHITE SEA, AEGEAN, BLACK SEA AND RED SEA (Greece, Balkans, Russia, Egypt, Syria, Anatolia, Arabia)		INDIAN OCEAN, PERSIAN GULF AND FAR EAST (East Africa, Gujarat, Southern India, China and Far East)	
1533	Ivan IV, 'the Terrible', begins his long reign.		
1534	Ottomans capture Baghdad.		
1535	Killing of Ibrahim Pasha, grand vizier to Sultan Suleyman the Magnificent.		
1541 and 1543	Ahmad Gragn, backed by Ottomans, battles against Ethiopian Emperor, supported by Portugal.	1542	European armaments introduced to Japan, rapidly replacing sword, bow and lance. Fifty years later Japan attempts to conquer Korea.
1547	Ottoman army campaigns in Persia. Ottoman navy defends Red Sea shore against Portugal.		
1553	Execution of Prince Mustapha.		
		1556	In India, Akbar the Great succeeds to throne aged thirteen and starts fifty-year reign which will re-establish Mughal Empire. Succeeded by son Jahangir (ruled 1605–27).
		1560	Inquisition established in Goa.

ATLANTIC AND WESTERN MEDITERRANEAN (British Isles, France, Spain, Portugal, Morocco, West Africa, Algeria, Americas)		CENTRAL MEDITERRANEAN AND ADRIATIC (Germany, Italy, Sicily, Malta, Tunisia, Venice, Albania, Hungary)	
1560	Sharifian army of Morocco again attacks Ottoman base of Tlemcen in Algeria.	1560	Crusader army occupies Djerba in February. On 11 May Christian invasion destroyed by Ottoman fleet.
1562	Sharifian Sultan Abdullah al-Ghalib pretends to besiege Mazagan while using opportunity to destroy Idrissid rivals in Chechaouen.	1559–63	Diplomacy between Ottoman court and Persian Shah about fate of refugee Prince Bayezid.
1567	Spanish Duke of Alba establishes authoritarian Council of Blood in Brussels, which leads in 1568 to execution of Counts Egmont and Hoorn and subsequent rebellion of William of Orange.	1565	Ottoman invasion of Malta and death of Dragut in combat.
		1566	Sultan Suleyman leads his last campaign: his army storms fortress of Szigeth, defended by Hungarian hero Count Zrinyi.
	Enforcement of draconian Pragmatic Decrees against Moorish culture in Andalusia.	1567	Peace of Adrianople (Edirne) signed between Austrian Habsburgs and Ottoman Empire.
1568	Moorish rebellion breaks out in Andalusia but is crushed in 1570.		
1571	Opening of London Stock Exchange.	1571	Battle of Lepanto: Ottoman navy defeated by Holy League.
1572	Second formal bankruptcy of Spanish treasury.		
1572	Massacre of some twenty thousand French Protestants on St Bartholomew's Day.		
1573	Duke of Alba recalled from his military mission against rebels in Duchy of Burgundy (Netherlands and Belgium).	1573	Don Juan of Austria occupies cities and ports of Tunis, Bizerta and Porto Farina.
		1574	Uluj Ali recaptures Tunis for Ottoman Empire.
			Sultan Selim II dies and is succeeded by peacefully inclined son Sultan Murat III.
1576	Abdul Malik deposes nephew Muhammad al-Mutawakkil from Sharifian throne, and latter takes refuge in Portugal.	1577	Ottoman–Spanish truce signed.
1578	King Sebastian of Portugal leads Last Crusade. The Portuguese nobility destroyed at the Battle of Ksar-el-Kebir.		
1580	Cardinal-King Henry of Portugal dies and Philip II of Spain inherits empty throne of Avis dynasty and Empire of Portugal.		
1581	Proclamation of Independence of northern provinces of old Duchy of Burgundy by Union of Utrecht.		

AD 1550–1599 (cOntinued)

WHITE SEA, AEGEAN, BLACK SEA AND RED SEA (Greece, Balkans, Russia, Egypt, Syria, Anatolia, Arabia)	INDIAN OCEAN, PERSIAN GULF AND FAR EAST (East Africa, Gujarat, Southern India, China and Far East)
	1563 Chinese fleet eliminates nuisance of Japanese piracy.
1566 Sultan Suleyman the Magnificent leads his last campaign, when his army storms Szigeth fortress and overpowers Hungarian hero Count Zrinyi.	
1570–1 Ottoman Invasion of Cyprus and siege of Nicosia and Famagusta.	
1571 Battle of Lepanto: Ottoman navy defeated by Holy League.	
1571 Burning of Moscow by Krim Tartars.	
1574 Beginning of Russian conquest and settlement of Siberia.	

FAMILY TREES FOR THE RULERS
OF MOROCCO, SPAIN, PORTUGAL
AND THE OTTOMAN EMPIRE

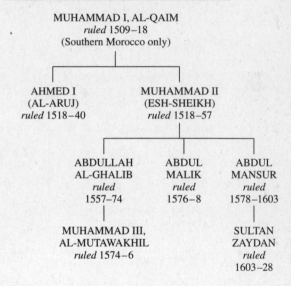

SHARIFIAN dynasty of Morocco

MUHAMMAD I, AL-QAIM
ruled 1509–18
(Southern Morocco only)

WATTASID Sultans

MUHAMMAD I
ruled 1472–1505

MUHAMMAD II,
AL-BURTUGALI
ruled 1505–24

AHMED-AL WATTASI
ruled 1524–45

AHMED I
(AL-ARUJ)
ruled 1518–40

MUHAMMAD II
(ESH-SHEIKH)
ruled 1518–57

ABDULLAH
AL-GHALIB
*ruled
1557–74*

ABDUL
MALIK
*ruled
1576–8*

ABDUL
MANSUR
*ruled
1578–1603*

MUHAMMAD III,
AL-MUTAWAKHIL
ruled 1574–6

SULTAN
ZAYDAN
*ruled
1603–28*

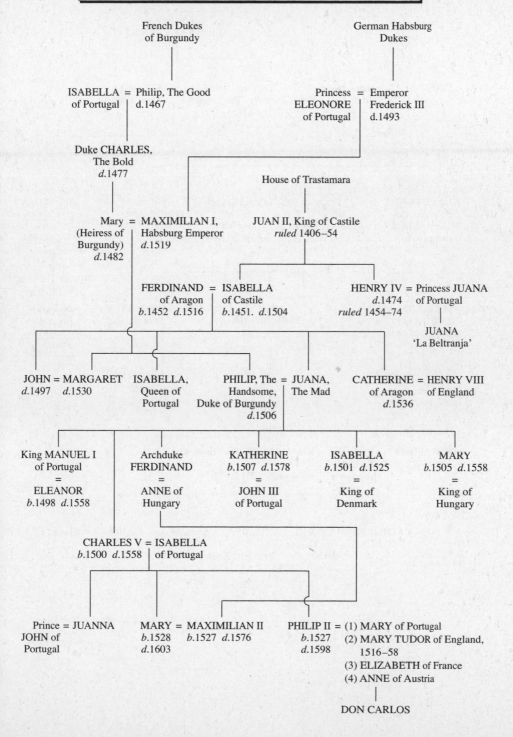

Family of CHARLES V, Holy Roman Emperor,
King CARLOS I of Spanish Kingdoms of Castile,
Leon and Aragon, King of Sicily and Naples

French Dukes
of Burgundy

German Habsburg
Dukes

ISABELLA = Philip, The Good
of Portugal   d.1467

Princess = Emperor
ELEONORE   Frederick III
of Portugal   d.1493

Duke CHARLES,
The Bold
d.1477

House of Trastamara

Mary = MAXIMILIAN I,
(Heiress of   Habsburg Emperor
Burgundy)   *d.1519*
d.1482

JUAN II, King of Castile
ruled 1406–54

FERDINAND = ISABELLA
of Aragon   of Castile
b.1452 d.1516   *b.1451. d.1504*

HENRY IV = Princess JUANA
d.1474   of Portugal
ruled 1454–74

JUANA
'La Beltranja'

JOHN = MARGARET
d.1497   *d.1530*

ISABELLA,
Queen of
Portugal

PHILIP, The = JUANA,
Handsome,   The Mad
Duke of Burgundy
d.1506

CATHERINE = HENRY VIII
of Aragon   of England
d.1536

King MANUEL I
of Portugal
=
ELEANOR
b.1498 d.1558

Archduke
FERDINAND
=
ANNE of
Hungary

KATHERINE
b.1507 d.1578
=
JOHN III
of Portugal

ISABELLA
b.1501 d.1525
=
King of
Denmark

MARY
b.1505 d.1558
=
King of
Hungary

CHARLES V = ISABELLA
b.1500 d.1558   of Portugal

Prince = JUANNA
JOHN of
Portugal

MARY = MAXIMILIAN II
b.1528   *b.1527 d.1576*
d.1603

PHILIP II = (1) MARY of Portugal
b.1527   (2) MARY TUDOR of England,
d.1598   1516–58
      (3) ELIZABETH of France
      (4) ANNE of Austria

DON CARLOS

AVIS dynasty of Portugal

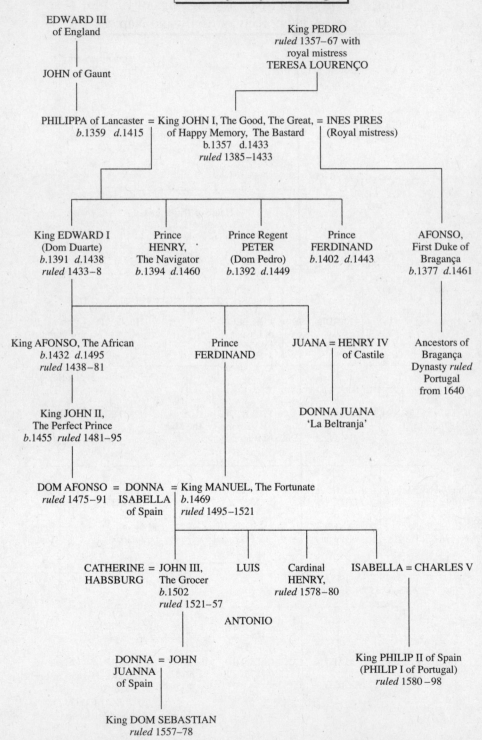

EDWARD III
of England

King PEDRO
ruled 1357–67 with
royal mistress
TERESA LOURENÇO

JOHN of Gaunt

PHILIPPA of Lancaster = King JOHN I, The Good, The Great, = INES PIRES
    b.1359 *d*.1415   of Happy Memory, The Bastard (Royal mistress)
                        b.1357 d.1433
                        ruled 1385–1433

King EDWARD I   Prince   Prince Regent   Prince   AFONSO,
(Dom Duarte)   HENRY,   PETER   FERDINAND   First Duke of
b.1391 *d*.1438   The Navigator   (Dom Pedro)   *b*.1402 *d*.1443   Bragança
ruled 1433–8   *b*.1394 *d*.1460   *b*.1392 *d*.1449   *b*.1377 *d*.1461

King AFONSO, The African   Prince   JUANA = HENRY IV   Ancestors of
   b.1432 *d*.1495   FERDINAND   of Castile   Bragança
   ruled 1438–81   Dynasty *ruled*
                                                 Portugal
                                                 from 1640

King JOHN II,   DONNA JUANA
The Perfect Prince   'La Beltranja'
b.1455 *ruled* 1481–95

DOM AFONSO = DONNA = King MANUEL, The Fortunate
  ruled 1475–91   ISABELLA *b*.1469
               of Spain   *ruled* 1495–1521

CATHERINE = JOHN III,   LUIS   Cardinal   ISABELLA = CHARLES V
HABSBURG   The Grocer   HENRY,
            b.1502   *ruled* 1578–80
            ruled 1521–57

                            ANTONIO

DONNA = JOHN   King PHILIP II of Spain
JUANNA   (PHILIP I of Portugal)
of Spain   *ruled* 1580–98

King DOM SEBASTIAN
ruled 1557–78

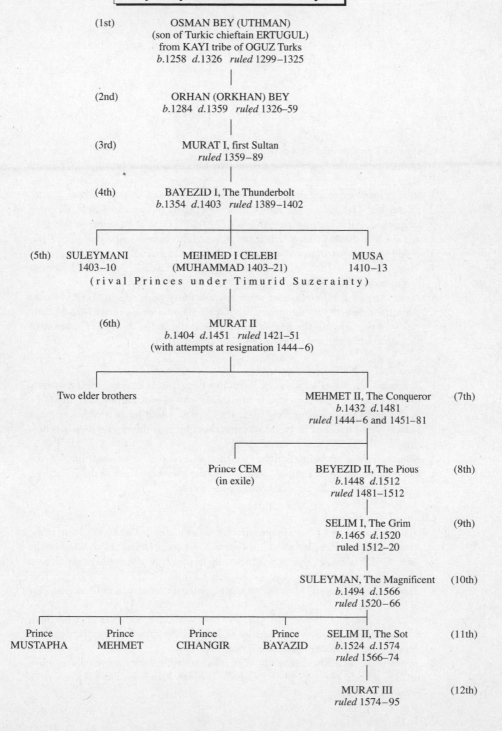

First twelve OSMANLI (Ottoman) dynasty of Sultans of Turkey

(1st)   OSMAN BEY (UTHMAN)
(son of Turkic chieftain ERTUGUL)
from KAYI tribe of OGUZ Turks
b.1258 d.1326 ruled 1299–1325

(2nd)   ORHAN (ORKHAN) BEY
b.1284 d.1359 ruled 1326–59

(3rd)   MURAT I, first Sultan
ruled 1359–89

(4th)   BAYEZID I, The Thunderbolt
b.1354 d.1403 ruled 1389–1402

(5th) SULEYMANI   MEHMED I CELEBI   MUSA
       1403–10   (MUHAMMAD 1403–21)   1410–13
       (rival Princes under Timurid Suzerainty)

(6th)   MURAT II
b.1404 d.1451 ruled 1421–51
(with attempts at resignation 1444–6)

Two elder brothers   MEHMET II, The Conqueror   (7th)
                                      b.1432 d.1481
                                      ruled 1444–6 and 1451–81

Prince CEM   BEYEZID II, The Pious   (8th)
(in exile)   *b.1448 d.1512*
                     ruled 1481–1512

                     SELIM I, The Grim   (9th)
                     b.1465 d.1520
                     ruled 1512–20

                     SULEYMAN, The Magnificent (10th)
                     b.1494 d.1566
                     ruled 1520–66

Prince   Prince   Prince   Prince   SELIM II, The Sot   (11th)
MUSTAPHA   MEHMET   CIHANGIR   BAYAZID   *b.1524 d.1574*
                                                ruled 1566–74

                                     MURAT III   (12th)
                                     ruled 1574–95

NOTES

Chapter 1: The Crusader-Prince of Portugal

1 Duarte, Edward in English, was named after his English great-grandfather, Edward III.

2 John I's illegitimate daughter Beatriz would later be married off to an English lord, to end her days among the tombs of the FitzAlans in Arundel Castle. The line established by his swarthy son, Afonso (made the Count of Barcelos), would exist as a shadow dynasty that watched the throne. This family had a dark future but would yet endure to become monarchs of Portugal after 1640.

3 These figures for 1385–1456 include captures by English, French and Flemish privateers as well as Moorish.

4 It was through this line that the seventeenth-century monarchs of Portugal would claim their descent and through which Tangier (alongside Bombay) would briefly pass into the hands of the British. Coming as it did in the dowry of Catherine of Braganza, when she was betrothed to King Charles II.

Chapter 2: The Navigator's Nephew

1 The manuscript was acquired by Raymond Fugger of the great banking dynasty of Augsburg who had it printed (embellished with nine royal portraits) in 1600.

2 In this detail either Jorg or more likely the clerk to whom he dictated his memoirs (which were published in Latin) was mistaken, for it is the reverse: Ceuta is bordered by three parts sea to one of land.

3 Soldiers from other North African countries, such as the Zayyanids (from Algeria) and the Hafsids (from Tunisia), came to help the Moroccans, just as the Portuguese were reinforced by their own Christian volunteers.

Chapter 3: The Great Eagle

1 The fate of Bayezid I has always attracted dramatic embellishments, be it at the hands of Ottoman historians, Christopher Marlowe, Handel or Vivaldi, but the sober version of events, that he was locked up in the castle of Aksehir, where he took his life, is scarcely less poignant.

2 This rule of war was still in force in the late eighteenth century in the American War of Independence.

3 Manley does not describe the sack of Constantinople but that of a northern European city a hundred years later by a Christian army, but is quoted here to illustrate that the violence of such events was consistent.

4 To enter the Tartar Khans' administrative palace of Bakhchisaray is like walking into a smaller, slightly purer sister of Istanbul's Topkapi Palace with the Rococo froth removed.

5 Pastor.

6 There you can still see still their *commanderie* castle at Kolossi, which earned a fortune from its sugar-cane plantations and export of sweetened wine, while the Templars' fort at Limassol was linked with the story of a talking head.

7 All Knights of the Order of St John had to show their unblemished descent from eight noble quarterings, but allowed those with no such genealogical background to fight as sergeants.

8 The Ottoman evacuation of Otranto after Mehmet's death was celebrated throughout Italy as the 'reconquest of Otranto' and commemorated by the striking of two elegant medals, one in honour of Pope Sixtus IV, the other for Alfonso, Duke of Calabria. On their obverse both feature a naked female figure representing Constancy and the inscription, 'To spare those who have been oppressed and to destroy the proud.' The medals are exquisite and a wonderful example of political make-believe, though they also reveal what an important incident the Ottoman occupation of Otranto had been.

Chapter 4: Reconquista
1 CCE, VI, 120

Chapter 6: The Just and the Grim
1 This is a way-station on any tour of the romantic poet-tombs of the Orient, which must also include that of Ibn Arabi in the old mosque on the hill above Damascus, al-Shabbi, hidden in the palm orchards of Tozeur, el-Mutamid's dome halfway between Marrakesh and the Atlas mountains, Rumi, beneath the high domes of Konya, and that of Hafiz in his open-aired loggia perfumed by daily offerings of roses.

2 *A Narrative of Italian Travels in Persia*, London, 1873.

3 It is not by chance that the world's finest carpet (which dominates the Islamic gallery in London's Victoria and Albert Museum) was commissioned by Ismail's son for the shrine of the Safavid sheikhs at Ardabil.

4 [Hatayi/Khatai]

5 This was a political habit which was indulged in by all Muslim rulers of the time. On 16 June 1511 Ismail's ambassador presented the Mameluke Sultan of Cairo with a casket containing the head of a great Tartar Lord, Uzbek Khan (an ally of Egypt), ornamented with a scroll of verse composed by the Shah:
'The Sword and dagger are to us as perfume
The fragrance of narcissus and myrtle
We rejoice to drink the blood of our enemies
From their skulls which we use as our goblets.'

6 Sultan Baybars, the Mameluke general who stormed Acre in 1291 and decisively expelled the last Crusaders from the Holy Land, was the first ruler of Egypt to concern himself with this family.

7 'Yavuz' is arguably better translated as 'The Stern', though to do so is to lose the evocative English of 'Selim the Grim'.

8 Caroline Finkel, *Osman's Dream*, quoting G. Fisher, *Barbary Legend, Trade and Piracy in North Africa 1415–1830*, p. 115.

Chapter 7: Conquest of Commerce

1   Marchione had a good track record with the Portuguese captains, having already interested himself in financing their trade with West Africa, the great source of gold in this pre-American period.

2   The peeling, whitewashed mass of Portugal's Fort Mina would be embellished by the Dutch and English in later centuries but still stands watch over the coast of Ghana.

3   Some lower courses of a round Portuguese tower survive, embedded in the harbour wall that a Moroccan Sultan would build in the eighteenth century to protect Mogador. The town is now known as *Es-saouria* ('little ramparts').

4   These letters home survive, for the Cartas, the letters of Afonso d'Albuquerque to his royal master, have been published in several volumes by the Royal Academy of Lisbon.

5   Apart from unnecessary expense there were three compelling reasons – Japan, Vietnam and Mongolia – why the Chinese naval squadrons were withdrawn from the Indian Ocean. In 1411, after just a few years of the experience of becoming a peaceful province of China, the Japanese turned their back on the idea in a most violent way. Indeed the ferocious raids of the 'dwarf pirates from the north' (as Ming officials referred to the Japanese) soon grew from a mere nuisance into a major preoccupation of the state. The Ming dynasty's interest in other territories beyond its traditional frontiers would also soon enough wither away. The loss of an army at the Battle of Tot-Dong in Vietnam in 1426 (after which the city of Hanoi was founded in victorious celebration) would be followed a generation later, in 1449, by the annihilation of an entire Ming army by the Oriat Mongols at the Battle of Huai Lai.

6   King Manuel also enclosed with this letter the gift of a rhinoceros, whose remarkable travels included being sent as a gift to the King of Portugal from the Sultan of Gujarat. After arriving in Lisbon in 1514, the animal was sent on to the Pope, but, sickened by sea travel, it died as it reached the Italian shore – though its form would be immortalised in a print by Dürer.

7   Weston F. Cook, *The Hundred Years War for Morocco: Gunpowder and the Military Revolution in the Early Modern Muslim World.*

Chapter 8: Sharifs, Sheikhs, Sufis, Sultans and Smugglers

1   As so often in Muslim history, this replays some vivid scene from a near-mythical past, such as the legend cycle of Antar and Abla, where the frustrated warrior hero Antar finally witnesses the destruction of his enemies, but only because his children have strapped his mummified body to a war saddle.

2   A sober historian like Leo Africanus might imagine the Mahdi as a 'Just Caliph', but others connected the Madhi with the cult of al-Khidr ('the green saint', the St George-like knight of Islam) and with Dhul-Qannayn ('he of the two horns'), who gets a cryptic mention in the Koran, Sura 18, 83–101. These two mystical heroes would conquer the world in preparation for the arrival of the Mahdi, who was often imagined as the uncrucified Jesus returning to earth from heaven.

3   After their fall from power in the seventeenth century, enemies of the Sharifian dynasty attempted to blacken their identity by claiming that they were descended from the Beni Saad tribe (to which the Prophet's foster mother belonged) rather than the pure bloodline of Muhammad through his daughter Fatimah and her cousin-husband Ali.

Chapter 9: The Rivals

1 Only the Austrian court has managed to preserve Charles V's presents intact: in the Museum für Volkerkunde in Vienna.

2 There can be little doubt that Charles's opposition was purely out of family loyalty, for despite his famous attachment to the Catholic Church he otherwise showed no doctrinal opposition to divorce. Indeed he had encouraged his loyal servant, Federigo Gonzaga, to divorce his own wife in order to marry the surviving sister of the Duke of Montferrat.

3 They were third cousins because Charles's paternal grandfather, the Habsburg Emperor Maximilian, had an Avis mother, Dona Eleonore of Portugal.

4 During their progress together Charles would give permission for a cathedral to be inserted into the great mosque of Cordoba, an act he later publicly regretted, having 'destroyed what was unique in the world'.

5 This was designed by Pedro Machuca of Toledo, who was wasting away his talent as a bored garrison officer before the Emperor's commission reignited the training he had received in Italy, which included the good fortune of studying under Michelangelo.

6 Panfilo Narvaez, the official commander of the Spanish expedition into Mexico, had been attacked by Cortes' freebooters and imprisoned so that Cortes could take control of the soldiers under his command.

Chapter 12: Emperors and Sultans

1 French war galleys retained a separate identity from the French Royal Navy until 1748, but until that time the French Royal Galley Corps sailed under its own pennant, the white lilies of France set against a blood-red pennant.

2 The short opening verse of the Koran that is often compared to a Muslim version of Christianity's Lord's Prayer, 'Our Father'.

3 Quoted in Paul Henze, *Layers of Time: A History of Ethiopia*, p. 87.

4 This period, followed by the rule of the Egyptian Khedives, is too often overlooked by Euro-centric explanations of how the Italian occupation helped create the separate identity of Eritrea.

5 At the age of sixteen Philip married his first cousin, the infanta Mary of Portugal, who died two years later in giving birth to Don Carlos.

Chapter 13: Skull Islands

1 This story gave the film *The Maltese Falcon* its title.

Chapter 14: A Beard for an Arm

1 The city is the presumed setting of Shakespeare's *Othello*, so you can walk through the locations of Acts 3 5: the citadel, the harbour esplanade and the palace.

2 J. Beeching, *The Galleys at Lepanto*, p. 273.

3 Sir Francis Drake, when he raided the Spanish fleet, would playfully allude to this famous *bon mot* by describing his operation as singeing the King of Spain's beard.

Chapter 15: The Last Crusade

1 Philip II gave shelter to the dead Sultan's family, including his younger brother, Moulay En Nasser, and his son, Moulay Ech-Sheikh, who was baptised as a Christian in the chapel of the Escorial on 3 November 1593.

FURTHER READING

Abun-Nasr, Jamil M. (ed.), *A History of the Maghrib in the Islamic Period*, Cambridge, 1987

Africanus, Leo, *The History and Description of Africa* (3 vols), London, 1896

Alvarez, M. F., *Charles V*, London, 1976

Anderson, R. C., *Naval Wars in the Levant, 1559–1853*, Liverpool, 1952

Anderson, R. C., *Oared Fighting Ships*, Percival Marshal, 1962

Armstrong, E., *The Emperor Charles V*, Boston, Mass., 2001

Atiyah, E., *The Arabs*, London, 1952

Atkinson, William C., *A History of Spain and Portugal*, Harmondsworth, 1960

Axelson, E. V., *Congo to Cape: Early Portuguese Explorers*, Johannesburg, 1973

Balbi di Correggio, Francisco, *The Siege of Malta 1565* (trans. Ernle Bradford), London, 1965

Ballard, G. A., *Rulers of the Indian Ocean*, London, 1998

Baxler, M., *Trials of the Templars*, Cambridge, 1978

Beazley, C. R., *Prince Henry the Navigator*, London, 2007

Beeching, J., *The Galleys at Lepanto*, London, 1982

Bell, Christopher, *Portugal and the Quest for the Indies*, London, 1975

Benecke, Gerhard, *Maximilian I, 1459–1519*, London, 1982

Billings, M., *The Crusades: The War against Islam 1096–1798*, [1987], reprinted Stroud, 2006

Birge, John Kingsley, *The Bektashi Order of Dervishes*, London, 1937

Blake, J. W., *European Beginnings in West Africa, 1454–1578*, London, 1970

Bovill, E. W., *The Battle of Alcazar: An Account of the Defeat of Don Sebastian at El-Ksar el-Kebir*, London, 1952

Bovill, E. W., *The Golden Trade of the Moors*, Oxford, 1958

Boxer, C. R., *The Portuguese Seaborne Empire 1415–1825*, London, 1977

Boxer, C. R., *The Dutch Seaborne Empire 1600–1800*, London, 1990

Bradford, E., *The Sultan's Admiral: The Life of Barbarossa*, London, 1968

Bradford, E., *The Great Siege: Malta 1565*, Harmondsworth, 1970

Bradford, E., *The Shield and the Sword (A History of the Knights of St John of Jerusalem of Rhodes and Malta)*, London, 1972

Brandi, K., *The Emperor Charles V* (trans. C. V. Wedgwood), London, 1939

Braudel, F., *The Mediterranean and the Mediterranean World in the Age of Philip II* (2 vols) (trans. Sian Reynolds), University of California Press, 1996

Broadley, A. M., *Tunis Past and Present*, 1882

Burckhardt, Jakob, *The Civilization of the Renaissance in Italy*, London, 1990

Burton, Richard, *Camoens: His Life and his Lusiads*, London, 1881

Busbecq, Ogier Ghislen de, *Turkish Letters*. English translations from the original Latin published 1694, 1881 and 1927. Current edns. include Eland, 2005, with an introduction by Philip Mansel.

Capponi, Niccolo, *Victory of the West: The Story of the Battle of Lepanto*, London, 2006

Caoursin, William, *The delectable news and tidings of the glorious victory of the Rhodians against the Turks in 1480* (trans. J. Kaye 1482)

Castries, H., *Les sources inédites de l'histoire du Maroc* (18 vols), Paris, 1905–36

Cheetham, N., *Mediaeval Greece*, New Haven and London, 1981

Chenier, L. S., *Cruelties of the Algerian Pirates*, 1816

Clot, André, *Suleiman the Magnificent: The Man, His Life, His Epoch*, London, 1994

Cohn, N., *The Pursuit of the Millennium: Revolutionary Millenarians and Mystical Anarchists of the Middle Ages*, London, 1993

Collis, Maurice, *British Merchant Adventurers*, London, 1942

Collison-Morley, L., *The History of the Borgias*, London, 1932

Columbus, Christopher, *The Four Voyages of Christopher Columbus* (ed. and trans. J. M. Cohen), Harmondsworth, 1969

Cook, Weston F., *The Hundred Years War for Morocco: Gunpowder and the Military Revolution in the Early Modern Muslim World*, Boulder, 1994

Cosstick, Frederick, *The Honourable Mercenary: Duke Federico and the Palace at Urbino*, 2001

Crowley, Roger, *Constantinople: The Last Great Siege, 1453*, London, 2005

Crowley, Roger, *Empires of the Sea: The Final Battle for the Mediterranean 1521–1580*, London, 2008

Currey, E. H., *Sea-Wolves of the Mediterranean*, Indypublish.com, 1991

Davis, Natalie Zemon, *Trickster Travels: In Search of Leo Africanus, a Sixteenth-Century Muslim between Worlds*, New York, 2006

Deane, Anthony, *Undiscovered Ocean: From Marco Polo to Francis Drake*, Stroud, 2005

Descola, Jean, *The Conquistadors* (trans. Malcolm Barnes), London, 1957

Duffy, Christopher, *Siege Warfare: The Fortress in the Early Modern World 1494–1660*, London, 1979

Duffy, James, *Portugal in Africa*, Harmondsworth, 1962

Ehingen, Jorg von, *The Diary of Jorg von Ehingen* (trans. and ed. Malcolm Letts), London, 1929

Elliot, J. H., *Imperial Spain 1469–1716*, London, 1963

Elliot. J. H., *The Spanish World, Civilization and Empire*, New York, 1991

Fernandez-Armesto, Felipe, *Columbus and the Conquest of the Impossible*, London, 1974

Fernandez-Armesto, Felipe, *Ferdinand and Isabella*, London, 1975

Fernandez-Armesto, Felipe, *Before Columbus: Exploration and Colonization from the Mediterranean to the Atlantic, 1229–1492*, University of Pennsylvania

Finkel, C., *Osman's Dream: The Story of the Ottoman Empire 1300–1923*, London, 2005

Fisher, G., *Barbary Legend, Trade and Piracy in North Africa 1415–1830*, Oxford, 1957

Freely, John (with Hilary Sumner-Boyd), *Strolling through Istanbul*, London, 1987

Freely, John, *Inside the Seraglio: Private Lives of the Sultans in Istanbul*, London, 1999

Freely, John, *Jem Sultan: The Adventures of a Captive Turkish Prince in Renaissance Europe*, London, 2004

Friedman, Ellen G., *Spanish Captives in North Africa in the Early Modern Age*, Madison, 1983

Fuller, J. F. C., *The Decisive Battles of the Western World 480 BC–1757*, London, 1993

Gibb, E. J. W., *A History of Ottoman Poetry*, E. J. W. Gibb Memorial Trust, 1967

Glubb, John Bagot (Glubb Pasha), *Soldiers of Fortune: The Story of the Mamlukes*, London, 1973

Goodwin, F. G., *A History of Ottoman Architecture*, London, 1971

Goodwin, F. G., *Sinan: Ottoman Architecture and Its Values Today*, London, 1993

Gravière, J. de la, *Doria et Barberousse*, Paris, 1886

Gravière, J. de la, *La Guerre de Chypre et la Bataille de Lepanto*, Paris, 1888

Grey-Jackson, J., *An Account of the Empire of Morocco*, London, 1809

Hale, J. R., *War and Society in Renaissance Europe 1450–1620*, London, 1988

Hammer-Purgsthall, J. von, *History of the Ottoman Empire* (18 vols), Vienna, 1827–35; translated into many European languages, for example into French by J. J. Hellert, Paris, 1835–43

Hart, H. H., *Sea Road to the Indies*, 1952

Harvey, L. P., *Islamic Spain 1250 to 1500*, Chicago, 1990

Hay, Denys (ed.), *The Age of the Renaissance*, London, 1967

Hemming, John, *The Conquest of the Incas*, London, 1970

Henze, Paul, *Layers of Time: A History of Ethiopia*, London, 2000

Herre, P., *Barbara Blomberg*, Leipzig, 1909

Hibbert, Christopher, *The Rise and Fall of the House of Medici*, London, 1979

Hill, G. F., *A History of Cyprus* (4 vols), Cambridge, 1940–52

Hillgarth, J. N., *The Spanish Kingdoms, 1250–1516* (2 vols), Oxford, 1978

Hitti, P. K., *The Arabs*, London, 1948

Hourani, George F., *Arab Seafaring*, expanded edn., ed. John Carswell, Princeton, 1995

Housley, Norman, *The Later Crusades: From Lyons to Alcazar 1274–1580*, Oxford, 1992

Housley, Norman, *Documents on the Later Crusades, 1274–1580*, Basingstoke, 1996

Hunt, D., and Hunt, I., *Caterina Cornaro: Queen of Cyprus*, London, 1989

Imber, Colin, *The Ottoman Empire 1300–1481*, Palgrave, 2002

Imber, Colin, *The Ottoman Empire, 1300–1650, The Structure of Power*, London, 2002

Inalcik, Halil, *The Ottoman Empire, The Classical Age 1300–1600*, London, 2000

Irving, W., *Conquest of Granada*, 2007

Izon, John, *Sir Thomas Stucley, c.1525–1578: Traitor Extraordinary*, London, 1956

Jayne, K. G., *Vasco da Gama and his Successors, 1560–1580*, New York, 2004

Jubayr, Ibn (Muhammad ibn Ahmad), *The Travels of Ibn Jubayr*, ed. W. Wright, E. J. W. Gibb Memorial Trust, 2001

Julien, C. A., *History of North Africa from the Arab Conquest to 1830* (trans. John Petrie), London, 1970

Kai-Ka'us Ibn Iskandar, *A Mirror for Princes* (*Qabus Nama*) (trans. Reuben Levy), London, 1951

Khalifah, Hajji, *History of the Maritime Wars of the Turks* (*Histoire des guerres maritimes des Ottomanes*), trans. of 1831, Constantinople, 1978

Kollias, Elias, *The Knights of Rhodes: The Palace and the City*, Athens, 1991

Kritovolous of Imbros, *History of Mehmed the Conqueror* (trans. Charles Riggs), Princeton, 1954

Ladurie, E. Le Roy, *A People's Uprising at Romans 1579–80* (trans. Mary Feeney), London, 1981

Laird-Clowes, G. S., *Sailing Ships: Their History and Development*, London, 1931–6

Lalaguna, Juan, *A Traveller's History of Spain*, Windrush, 1990

Lane, F. C., *Venetian Ships and Shipbuilders of the Renaissance*, 1934

Lane-Poole, Stanley, *Barbary Corsairs*, Boston, Mass., 2001

Lane-Poole, Stanley, *A History of Egypt in the Middle Ages*, London, 2007

Lane-Poole, Stanley, *The Story of Cairo*, New York, 2007

Lane-Poole, Stanley, *The Story of the Moors in Spain*, New York, 2007

Lapidus, Ira M., *Moslem Cities in the Later Middle Ages*, Cambridge, 1984

Lapidus, Ira M., *A History of Islamic Societies*, Cambridge, 1988

Lewis, Bernard, *The Muslim Discovery of Europe*, London, 1994

Lewis, Bernard, *The Middle East: 2000 Years of History from the Rise of Christianity to the Present Day*, London, 2001

Livermore, H. V., *History of Portugal*, Cambridge, 1947

Lomax, D. W., *The Reconquest of Spain*, London, 1978

McGlynn, Sean, *By Sword and Fire: Cruelty and Atrocity in Medieval Warfare*, London, 2008

Machiavelli, Niccolo, *The Prince*

Machiavelli, Niccolo, *History of the Florentine Republic*

Malcolm, Noel, *Bosnia: A Short History*, London, 1994

Mallet, M., *The Borgias: The Rise and Fall of a Renaissance Dynasty*, London, 1969

Mathew, K. S., *Indo-Portuguese Trade and the Fuggers of Germany*, New Delhi, 1997

Mattingly, G., *Renaissance Diplomacy*, Harmondsworth, 1973

Mattingly, G., *The Defeat of the Spanish Armada*, London, 2000

Maxwell, W. S., *Don John of Austria* (2 vols), London, 1883

Meakin, Budgett, *The Moorish Empire*, London, 1899

Mendoza, Hurtado de, *The War in Granada* (trans. Martin Shuttleworth), London, 1982

Miller, Townsend, *The Castles and the Crown of Spain 1451–1555*, London, 1963

Morgan, J., *A Complete History of Algiers*, London

Motley, J. L., *The Rise of the Dutch Republic* (3 vols), 2006

Muir, William, *The Mameluke or Slave Dynasty of Egypt, 1260–1517*, 2000

Murphy-O'Connor, J., *The Holy Land*, Oxford, 1998

Newton, A. P., *Travel and Travellers of the Middle Ages*, London, 2005

Norwich, John Julius, *Byzantium: The Decline and Fall*, London, 1996

O'Shea, Stephen, *Sea of Faith: Islam and Christianity in the Medieval Mediterranean World*, London, 2006

Parker, G., *The Dutch Revolt*, Harmondsworth, 1977

Parker, G., *Philip II*, London, 1978

Parker, G., *Europe in Crisis, 1598–1648*, London, 1979

Parks, Tim, *Medici Money: Banking, Metaphysics and Art in Fifteenth-Century Florence*, London, 2005

Parry, J. H., *The Age of Reconnaissance: Discovery, Exploration and Settlement 1540–1650*, London, 1963

Parry, J. H., *The Spanish Seaborne Empire*, London, 1966

Payne, R., *The Crusades: A History*, London, 1994

Penrose, B., *Travel and Discovery in the Renaissance*, 1952

Playfair, R. L., *The Scourge of Christendom*, London, 1884

Prescott, W. H., *History of the Reign of Ferdinand and Isabella*, Boston, Mass., 1838

Prescott, W. H., *History of the Conquest of Peru* (2 vols), New York, 2000

Prescott, W. H., *History of the Conquest of Mexico*, New York, 2000

Ranke, Leopold von, *The Ottoman and Spanish Empires in the Sixteenth and Seventeenth Centuries* (trans. W. K. Kelly), 1943

Rezette, Robert, *The Spanish Enclaves in Morocco*, Paris, 1976

Rogers, J. M., and Ward, R. M., *Suleyman the Magnificent*, London, 1988

Ricard, L., *Les Portugais en Maroc*, Coimbra, 1955

Riley-Smith, J., *The Knights of St John in Jerusalem and Cyprus, 1050–1310*, 1967

Riley-Smith, J., *The Crusades: A History*, London, 1987

Riley-Smith, J., *Oxford History of the Crusades*, Oxford, 1995

Riley-Smith, J. (ed.), *The Atlas of the Crusades*, Oxford, 2002

Rodgers, W. L., *Naval Warfare under Oars*, Annapolis 1970

Rogers, H. C. B., *Artillery Through the Ages*, London, 1971

Rogerson, B. H., *Morocco*, London, 1989

Rogerson, B. H., *Tunisia*, London, 1992

Rogerson, B. H., *Cyprus*, London, 1994

Rogerson, B. H., *A Traveller's History of North Africa*, 3rd edn., Duckworths, 2008

Roth, C., *The Duke of Naxos*, Philadelphia, 1994

Rousseau, B., *A History of the Conquest of Tunis by the Ottomans*, 1883

Runciman, S., *A History of the Crusades* (3 vols), Cambridge, 1951–4, or in paperback trilogy, Harmondsworth, 1965

Runciman, S., *The Fall of Constantinople 1453*, Cambridge, 1965

Rycault, Sir P., *The History of the Turkish Empire*, London, 1680

Sanceau, Elaine, *Indies Adventure: The Amazing Career of Afonso de Albuquerque*, 1936

Sanceau, Elaine, *Portugal in Quest of Prester John*, London, 1943

Sanceau, Elaine, *Henry the Navigator*, 1969

Sandoval, P., *History of Charles V (Historia de Carlos Quinto)*, 1614

Saunders, J. J., *Aspects of the Crusades*, Canterbury, NZ, 1961

Segal, Ronald, *Islam's Black Slaves*, New York, 2002

Seward, D., *The Monks of War*, London, 1972

Seward, D., *Prince of the Renaissance: Francis I*, London, 1973

Schimmer, Karl August, *The Sieges of Vienna*, London, 1847

Silva-Rego, Antonio da, *Portuguese Colonization in the Sixteenth Century*, Johannesburg, 1957

Slocombe, G., *Don John of Austria: Victor of Lepanto*, London, 1935

Spandounes, Theodore, *On the Origins of the Ottoman Emperors* (trans. Donald Nicol), Cambridge, 1997

Stavrides, Theoharis, *The Sultan of Viziers: Mahmud Pasha Angelovic*, Boston, Mass., 2001

Spear, Percival, *A History of India* (2 vols), Harmondsworth, 1965

Stoye, J., *English Travellers Abroad, 1604–1667*, New Haven, 1990

Strandes, Justus, *The Portuguese Period in East Africa* (trans. Jean Wallwork and ed. J. S. Kirkman), Berlin, 1899; Nairobi, 1961

Terrasse, H., *Histoire du Maroc*, Casablanca, 1950

Thomas, Hugh, *Rivers of Gold: The Rise of the Spanish Empire*, London, 2003

Thomson, Ahmad, and Ata Ur-Rahim, Muhammad, *Islam in Andalus*, London, 1996

Tmarzizet, Kamel, *Djerba*, Tunis, 1997

Tyerman, A., *Fighting for Christendom: Holy War and the Crusades*, Oxford, 2004

Tyerman, A., *God's War: A New History of the Crusades*, London, 2006

Vambery, A., *Travels and Adventures of the Turkish Admiral, Sidi Ali Rais, 1553–1556*, London, 1865

Vambery, A. (with Louis Heilprin), *Hungary in Ancient, Medieval and Modern Times*, 1972

Wedgwood, C. V., *William the Silent*, London, 2001

Weir, T. H., *The Shaikhs of Morocco, in the Sixteenth Century*, New York, 2007

Welsh, Frank, *The Battle for Christendom: The Council of Constance, 1415, and the Struggle to Unite against Islam*, London, 2008

Wheatcroft, Andrew, *The Ottomans*, London, 1993

Wheatcroft, Andrew, *Infidels: The Conflict between Christendom and Islam, 638–2002*, London, 2003

Whiteway, R. S., *The Rise of Portuguese Power in India, 1497–1550*, [1899], reprinted New York, 1967

Yahya, Dahiru, *Morocco in the Sixteenth Century: Problems and Patterns in African Foreign Policy*, Atlantic Highlands, NJ, 1981

INDEX

Figures in **bold** refer to pages with illustrations.

Abbasid Caliphs, 70, 182, 210

Abdel Moumen, Sultan, 15

Abdul Haq, Sultan of Morocco, 26, 33, 208–9

Abdul Malik, Sultan of Morocco: Battle of the Three Kings, 413–19; childhood, 228, 406; death, 418–19; illness, 412–13, 414–15; at Lepanto (1571), 228–9, 406–7; preparations against Sebastian's invasion, 411–12

Abdul Mansur, Sultan of Morocco, brother of Abdul Malik: Battle of the Three Kings, 413, 414; childhood, 228, 406; conquest of Songhai, 421; at Lepanto (1571), 228–9, 406–7; relationship with Elizabeth I, 421; succession to brother, 419; treatment of Sebastian's body, 418

Abdullah al-Ghalib, Sultan of Morocco, half-brother of Abdul Malik, 228, 404, 406, 407

Abu Bakr, Caliph, 216

Abu Bakr, Sultan, 322

Abu Hammu III, Sultan of Algeria, 278

Abu al-Hassan, Sultan of Granada, 122, 125–6, 127

Abu Said Uthman, Sultan of Fez, 24–6

Abu Zakariya Yahya, military commander, 26, 32–3, 208, 209

Abu Zayyan, Zayyanid prince, 278

Abyssinia: army, 322; Emperor, 58, 59, 321, 323; Prester John, 38; relationship with Portugal, 323

Acre, fall (1291), 20, 100–1, 376, 383

Actium, battle (31 BC), 303, 391

Aden: Ottoman control, 306; Portuguese attack (1513), 199, 201

Adolf of Cleeves, Lord of Ravestein, 232

Adolf of Holstein, Duke, 408

Adra, recapture, 130–1

Adrian of Utrecht (Pope Hadrian VI), 234, 244

Aeterni Regis, papal decree, 53

Afar tribes, 321, 322

Afonso, Dom, son of John II, 60, 144

Afonso V (the African), King of Portugal: appearance, 44, 47, 49–50; assumes crown, 39; Castilian war, 50–1; crusading zeal, 39, 42–3; death, 52; father's death, 33; Ksar es Seghir expedition (1458), 40, 42, 43, 400; mental state, 49–50, 51, 116; Moroccan expeditions, 44, 46, 48–9; reputation, 43; son's regency, 51–2; war with Castile, 50–1

Africa: gold trade, 34–5; Ottoman-Portuguese wars, 321–2; Portuguese bases, 36, 53–4, 57; Portuguese explorers, 35–6, 41, 54; sea routes, 5, 56; Spanish forts on North African coast, 140–1; Swahili trading cities on East African coast, 190–2

Afughal, holy town, 215

Agadir, 221, *see also* Santa Cruz

Ahmad, Hafsid prince, 279

Ahmad al-Aruj, son of Al-Qaim: arsenal, 218; Asilah siege, 215; Azzemour siege, 221, 222; battles against brother Muhammad, 222; battles against Portuguese, 215, 216, 218; battles against Wattasids, 219, 220; Marrakesh conquest, 217; Tafetna harbour, 218

Ahmad Gragn, 321–3

Ahmad ibn al-Cadi, 283

Ahmad al-Wanshari, 209–10, 223

Ahmed, son of Bayezid II, 166, 177

Ahmed al-Wattas, Wattasid Sultan, 217

Ahmed Zeli, governor of Malaga, 128
Aisha (or Fatimah), Nasrid princess, 126
Aksemseddin, Sheikh, 83, 84, 88
Aladdin, son of Murat II, 75
Albania, Ottoman invasions, 98, 302
Albuquerque, Afonso de, 192, 196, 197–201, 402
Albuquerque, Jeronimo de, 402
Alcacovas, treaty of (1479), 51–2
Alcaudete, Count, 227, 310
Aldana, Francisco, 411
Aleppo, fall (1516), 180
Alexander VI, Pope, 53, 122, 142
Alexander the Great, 64, 90, 106, 112, 113, 405
Alexandria: Ottoman base, 382; sack (1365), 102
Alfonso, Prince of Asturias, 118
Algeria: borders, 5, 228, 320; Zayyanid rule, 10, 320
Algiers: Barbarossa's leadership, 277; capital city, 283; capture and recapture (1520, 1525), 283; Charles V at, 2, 6–7, 309–13; commander-in-chief, 226; corsair base, 237; defences, 285; Menorcan booty, 301; Ottoman fleet, 224; Ottoman reinforcements, 282; Pasha, 407; siege (1541), 309–13; slave markets, 313, 320; Spanish expeditions, 306; Spanish fleet destroyed by storm, 282; Spanish fort, 141, 275–6, 285; Spanish fort besieged, 276, 277, 278, 285; Spanish fort captured, 285; Spanish relief expedition, 277–8, 279
Alhambra Palace, 126, 132, 256–7
Ali, Imam, son-in-law of the Prophet, 174, 176, 292
Ali Ahmad, military commander, 25
Ali al-Attar, 125
Ali al-Mandari, 57, 158–9
Aljubarrota, battle (1385), 22, 41
Almeida, Dom Francisco de, 195, 197
Almeria: Moorish revolt, 140; surrender, 130
Almohad Caliphate, 10, 15–16, 120
Alum mines, 94
Alva (Alba), Duke of, 309, 327–8
Amagur, sack (1515), 215
Amasya, treaty of (1557), 226
America: gold from, 241; routes to, 5; Spanish conquests, 241–2, 257–9

Amirutzes, Georgios, 97
Anabaptists, 250, 297
Anatolia: borders, 95; emirates, 10, 99, 179–80; Kizilbas revolts, 176, 179, 183; Ottoman campaigns, 67; Ottoman governors, 64, 110, 166; religion, 5, 66, 176; Suleyman's progress, 270; Timur's invasion, 74; troops from, 75–6, 166
Angelovic, Michael, 97
Angiolello, Giovanni Maria, 99, 172
Anjera tribes, 25, 32–3
Ankara, battle of (1402), 10, 74
Antonio, Dom, claimant to Portuguese throne, 420
Antwerp: financial centre, 189, 208, 319; Jews, 408; sack, 408
Aragon: Castilian War of Succession, 50, 53; civil wars, 117; crown of, 146; crusading kingship, 9, 23; merchants, 15; united with Castile, 120
Arguim, fort, 36
armed forces: archers, 22; arquebusiers, 123, 282; artillerymen, 123, 179, 282; cavalry, 170, 246, 290, 295, 308; crossbowmen, 123; dragoons, 417; gunners, 123; janissaries, see janissaries; knights, 22, 69, 71–2, 123, 125, 246, 410; lancers, 123; sharpshooters, 357–8; soldier on horseback, 73
Armenians, 66, 82, 93, 377, 383
Arthur, Prince of Wales, 145
artillery: artillery park, 80; Barbarossa's ship-borne, 285; at Constantinople, 82–3; costs, 81; on Danube, 71; Egyptian, 180; at Famagusta, 383–4; Ferdinand and Isabella's, 124, 127; at Granada, 132; Ismail's need for, 179; Jewish munitions contractors, 207; Lepanto battle, 391–2; at Malaga, 128–9; on Malta, 357; Moroccan, 203–4, 219; Moroccan arsenals, 218; Ottoman superiority, 308; Portuguese defences, 40, 221; Portuguese improvements, 39; Portuguese ship-borne, 40, 61; Portuguese siege weapons, 26, 31–2, 40, 48; Selim's field artillery, 179, 180; Spanish siege weapons, 124, 127; Suleyman's siege train, 302; Sultan Mehmet's, 39, 79–80, 82–3; transporting, 124; Urban's work, 79–80, 124; Venetian ship-borne, 304, 391–2

Asilah: attack on (1516), 204;
    Portuguese position, 56, 163, 194,
    205, 412, 419; sack (1471), 48–9;
    Sebastian's landing, 410, 413; siege
    (1514), 203, 215; siege (1524), 217
Askia Muhammad, Emperor of Songhai,
    211
Atahualpa, Inca Emperor, 258
Augsburg, financial centre, 257, 319,
    420
Augusta, fall, 347
Augustus, Emperor, 75
Aviero, Duke of, 416
Aydin Reis (Cacha-Diablo), 283, 284
Ayyubid Sultans, 70
Azambuja, Dom Diogo de, 53, 193
Azores, 29, 34, 51, 54–5
Aztecs, 241, 243, 257
Azzemour: abandoned by Portuguese,
    221, 399; Portuguese position, 193,
    202, 203, 215, 217, 221; siege, 221,
    222; trading city, 56, 57, 192

Babur, Mughal Emperor, 195–6
Badajoz, Bishop of, 237
Badis: port, 24, 218, 279, 352; Spanish
    fort, 141
Baghdad: campaign, 270, 271; Mongol
    destruction (1258), 173, 182;
    Ottoman rule, 270
Bahrain, 199, 321, 323
Bahzad, painter, 175
Ballard, Admiral, 187
Barak, agent of Bayezid II, 167
Barawa, sack, 192
Barbarossa, Admiral, 3, 4, 7, 148–9,
    225, 270, see also Khizr, Uruj
Barcellos, Count of, 33
Barcellos, Duke of, 410, 418
Barros, John de, 28
Basan, El-, castle, 98
Bati Del Wambara, 322
Bavaria, 253, 255
Bayard, Chevalier, 69, 236
Bayezid I, Ottoman Sultan, 74, 111
Bayezid II, Ottoman Sultan: accession,
    110, 166–8; children, 176; court,
    168, 170; death, 178; grandson
    Suleyman, 265; military career, 168;
    mother, 76; policies, 168–71, 263;
    religion, 171, 176; view of Jewish
    expulsion from Spain, 136, 169
Bayezid, Prince, son of Suleyman, 331,
    337, 338, 344, 349–50, 373

Baza, siege, 130, 131
Bazan, Alvaro de, 255, 351
Beirut: Crusader port abandoned, 20;
    pilgrim arrangements, 102
Bejaia: Barbarossa's leadership, 277, 301;
    fall (1555), 226; sieges, 273–4, 275;
    Spanish garrison, 141, 164, 273–4
Bektasi Sufis, 64–5
Belgrade: fall (1521), 243, 252, 260–1,
    283, 308; Selim II in, 371; sieges, 96,
    243
Bellini, Gentile, **68, 91, 112, 177**
Beni Hanai tribe, 56
Beni Rashid tribe, 310
Benincasa, Gratiosus, **30**
Berbers: acclaim of Barbarossa, 277;
    allies of Portuguese, 202; attacks on
    Portuguese, 32, 193; Battle of the
    Three Kings, 413; defence of Malaga,
    128, 130; Jewish community, 211;
    leaders, 283; preachers in Berber
    lands, 211, 212; slave soldiers, 70;
    territories, 159, 320
Bernaldez, Andres, 144
Bessarabia, tributary state, 308
Beza, siege, 57
Bijapur, Sultanate, 197
Bizerta: corsair base, 157, 158, 237;
    Spanish garrison, 395, 396; trade,
    396
Black Death, 8, 20
Black Sea, 94–5
Boabadil, Emir of Granada, Sultan
    Muhammad XII, 125–7, 128, 130,
    132, 219
Bodrum, castle, 103, 152, 263
Bohemia, Kingdom of, 246, 247, 268
Bomberg, Barbara, 389
Borgia, Cesare, 122
Borgia family, 122
Bosnia, 97, 98
Boucicaut, Jean, 72, 73–4
Bourbon, François de, 313
Bragadin, Marcantonio, 385–6
Braganza, Dukes of, 33, 39, 49, 52, 418
Brandon, Charles, Duke of Suffolk, 240
Braudel, Fernand, 397
Brazil, 55, 400–2
Brindisi, Ottoman plan, 302
Brusa (Prusa, Bursa), 66, 74, 110,
    176–7, 337
Buda: Habsburg siege, 308; sack (1526),
    247
Budapest, Pest bank, 313

Bulgaria, religion, 9
Burgundy, Duchy of: Antwerp finance, 208; barges, 306; Charles V's childhood, 233–4; court, 231–3; effects of Charles V's inheritance, 237; funding for Rhodes defences, 104, 232; knights, 71, 104; Protestant rebellion, 395, 396, 421; relationship with England, 236, 241, 244, 253; territory, 8, 230–1, 244
Busbecq, Ogier de, 334, 337–8, 346, 347

Cabral, Pedro, 55
Cadamosto, Alvise, 37
Cadiz, Marquess of, 121
Cairo: Islamic treasures, 182; Ottoman rule, 270; Portuguese agents, 58; sack (1517), 181
Caldiran, battle (1514), 179, 183
Callixtus III, Pope, 43
Calvi, Genoese position, 319
Cambrai, Ladies' Peace (1529), 250
Camden, William, 408
Cammariotes, Michael, 89
Camões, Luis de, 405, 419
Canary Isles, 51, 189
cannons, see artillery
Cao, Diogo, 54
Cape Bojador, 29–31
Cape of Good Hope, 56, 61
Cape Verde, 29, 51
Capello, Vincenzo, 303, 304
Capistrano, John, 96
Capsali, Rabbi Elijah, 207
Caramansa, African chief, 53–4
Carlos, Don, son of Philip II, 329–30
Carretto, Fabrizio del, 263
Carthage: destruction, 88; Louis IX's invasion, 20; ruins, 161, 297
Carvalho, Rodrigo de Sousa de, 404
Casa da India, 189
Casa da Mina, 41
Castella, Don Juan de, 347
Castelnuevo, capture and recapture, 253, 305
Castiglione, Baldassare, 244
Castile: defeat by Portugal (1385), 22; expansion, 23, 31; kingdom, 9; Moroccan settlement, 189–90; union with Aragon, 120; War of Succession (1474–9), 50–1, 116, 120, 123

Castro, Francisco de, 201
Castruccio, Giovanni, 353–4
Catalonia: expulsion of Moors, 140; Kingdom of, 117, 120, 162; trade, 26
Cateau Cambrésis, peace treaty (1559), 342, 343
Caterina Cornaro, Queen of Cyprus, 376, 382
Catherine Habsburg, Queen of Portugal, 146, 238, 403
Catherine of Aragon, Queen of England, 145, 240, 251, 342
Catherine of Medici, 253, 420
Catholic Church: in Burgundy, 231, 395, 408; in Germany, 251, 308; kingdoms, 9; Protestant revolts, 395, 408; Reformation, 343; relationship with Orthodox Church, 89, 97, 294, 378; see also Holy League, Inquisition, Jesuits, Knights of St John, Spain, Vatican
Cavialli, Venetian diplomat, 307
Cazalla, Augustin de, 343
Cem, Prince, son of Mehmed II, 110, 166–8, 263
Cervantes, Miguel de, 394
Ceuta: commercial role, 14–15, 24, 26–7, 130; history, 14–16; map, 14; Moroccan attack (1419), 24–5; Moroccan attack (1459), 40; port, 14; Portuguese garrison, 21, 24, 26, 163; Portuguese invasion (1415), 10; Portuguese position, 56, 194; Portuguese treaty obligation, 32, 33; Portuguese victory (1415), 20, 21, 23, 205, 421; sack (1415), 7, 8, 17–19; siege, 44–7, 54
Charles V, Holy Roman Emperor: abdication, 324–6; accession to Spanish throne, 236–7; acclaimed Duke of Burgundy, 234; advice to brother Ferdinand, 253, 255; advice to son Philip, 324, 326–9; Algiers siege, 2, 6–7, 309–13; appearance, 239, 301, 325; army in Italy, 248–50; arrival in Spain, 237–8; campaigns against Barbarossa, 280; character, 235; childhood, 233–4; Cisneros' regency in Spain, 141, 237, 238; crusade calls, 244, 306;

Charles V, Holy Roman Emperor –
    continued
    crusading expeditions, 260, 296, 326;
    death, 341; denunciation of Cazalla,
    343; election and coronation as Holy
    Roman Emperor, 240, 241; Field of
    the Cloth of Gold, 240–1; finances,
    240, 241, 250–1, 301, 328; Great
    Project, 244; heraldic symbol, 300;
    illegitimate son (Don John), 389–90;
    inheritance, 146, 230; languages,
    301; marriage, 250, 251, 256–7, 326;
    Mediterranean policy, 255–6, 296;
    military experiences, 2, 6–7; naval
    forces, 269, 282, 286, 287, 303, 309;
    Pavia victory, 245; reading, 326;
    relationship with Francis I, 4, 183,
    224, 234–5, 244–6, 250–1, 283,
    286, 316; relationship with Henry
    VIII, 240–1, 251; relics of, 411, 415;
    religion, 343; response to siege of
    Vienna, 252, 253; Tunisian
    campaign, 2, 297–300, 306, 326,
    395, 411; visits to England, 240,
    241, 243; wars, 229, 234, 245, 283;
    Wattasid appeal to, 223; will, 241,
    326–7
Charles VIII, King of France, 142, 169,
    235
Charles IX, King of France, 395
Charles the Bold, Duke of Burgundy,
    231
Chechaouen: corsair base, 159; Emirate,
    158–9, 223, 404; evacuees in, 195;
    governors of western Rif, 217;
    refugees in, 57
Chen Cheng, 201
Cherchel: Barbarossa's leadership, 277;
    Doria's raid, 255, 287; port, 255, 276
Chièvres, William of, 234, 235
China, Ming Empire, 200
Christianity: in Africa, 41; in Anatolia,
    66; Armenian, 82; Catholic Church,
    see Catholic Church; chivalry, 16, 48;
    Christian traders, 15; Christians in
    Ottoman Empire, 68–9; conversion
    to, 134, 135–6, 140, 164, 210,
    242–3, 284; Crusades, 19–20;
    Ethiopian, 323; knights, 16;
    Orthodox, *see* Orthodox Christianity;
    Ottoman conquests, 42; papacy, *see*
    papacy; pilgrimage, 43–4, 51, 58,
    102, 249, 376; Prester John stories,
    38; Protestantism, *see* Protestants

Cid, Rodrigo, Count of, 120
Cienza, fall (1478), 120
Cihangir, Prince, son of Suleyman, 331,
    335–6
Cintra, treaty of (1509), 53
Cisneros, Francisco Jimenez de, 139–40,
    141, 237, 238, 277, 279
Clement VII, Pope, 253
Cobos, Francisco de los, 257, 259, 328
Cochin: Portuguese fort, 190, 197, 200;
    Portuguese naval base, 196, 200;
    Rajah of, 190; spice trade, 188, 189
Colonna, Marcantonio, 388
Colonna, Vespasiano, 295
Colonna, Vittoria, 246
Columbus, Christopher, 31, 53, 54–5,
    138–9, 257
Comares, Marquis of, 279, 281
Comnenian dynasty, 97
Condalmiero, Alessandro, 304, 305
Constantine, Roman Emperor, 92
Constantine XI Palaeologus, Byzantine
    Emperor, 79, 85–6
Constantinople (Istanbul): Barbarossa's
    visit, 291–4; fall (1453), 1, 7, 39,
    86–7, 232, 421; first Muslim siege,
    83; mosques, 171, 368–70, 369;
    mourning for Malta failure, 362;
    Palaeologue culture, 7; refugees,
    88–9; shipyards, 348, 351, 375, 394;
    siege (1452–3), 81–6; slave market,
    100; Sufis burned, 350; Topkapi
    Palace, 93, 110, 166, 184, 271, 291,
    302, 397; victory procession (1560),
    347–8; walls, 81–2, 92, 169
Contarini, Giovanni, 244, 392
Corfu, siege, 302
Coron, capture, 288
corsairs: Algerine, 283; arrangement
    with France, 254; attack on Spanish
    outpost, 218; bases, 157, 158; buying
    back Jewish captives from, 137;
    development of power, 148; raiding
    parties, 157; relationship with
    Christians, 4, 254; rescue of refugees,
    284–5
Corsica, Ottoman invasion, 319
Cortes, Hernan: at Algiers siege, 2, 6–7,
    312; career, 125, 241–2, 257;
    conquest of Mexico, 241, 242, 257,
    258, 312; relationship with Charles
    V, 2, 6–7, 257, 312
Cossier, Chevalier, 298

Costanzo of Ferrara, **109**
Covilha, Pero de, 58–9
Crépy-en-Laonnois, peace treaty (1544), 316
Crimea, Khan of, 373
Crusades, 19–20; Fourth Crusade (1202–4), 19, 20; Sixth Crusade (1248–54), 20; Seventh Crusade (1270), 20; 1396, 71–4
Crusading Order of Christ, 101
Ctesiphon, capture, 88
Cueva, Don Beltran de la, 50
Curran, J. P., 205
Curtogali, corsair admiral, 157–8
Cyprus: annexation by Venice, 376; battles for, 1; defences, 375; Famagusta siege, 382–5, 389; fleet, 201; Greek inhabitants, 376, 378; Kingdom of, 201, 375–6, 383; Knights of St John, 101; map, **374**; Nicosia siege and fall, 379–82, 389; Ottoman conquest, 386, 389, 395, 421; Ottoman demand for, 377; Ottoman landing, 378; Ottoman preparations for conquest, 374–5, 377–8; Ottoman rule, 386; religion, 378; strategic importance, 168
Dalmata, John, 86
d'Amaral, Andrea, 263
Damascus: fall, 180; Ottoman rule, 270; Pasha, 372
Dandolo, Nicolo, 378, 381
d'Aramon, Gabriel, 318
Dardanelles Strait: Christian fleets, 65, 83, 98; commercial importance, 68; Constantinople siege, 83; Orhan's control, 67; Ottoman defences, 81, 93, 169, 291, 389; Ottoman fleet, 302
Darna, battle of, 222–3
d'Aubusson, Pierre, 105–8
D'Aveiro, Duke, 410
de la Valette, *see* Valette
Debarw, fortress, 323
Derna, refugees in, 156
Diana of Poitiers, 254
Dias, Bartolomeu, 56
Diu: fortress, 305–6; naval battle (1509), 196, 305
Djerba: corsair base, 160, 316, 317, 350; naval battle (1560), 346; siege and capture (1560), 2, 346–7, 349; Spanish forts, 141, 164, 273, **345**, 346; Spanish occupation (1560),

344–5; volunteer warriors, 129, 130, 141
Doria, Andrea: Aegean campaign, 301–2; Algiers campaign, 309; appearance, **286**; capture of Adriatic fortresses, 253; capture of Mahdia, 317; career, 286–7; changing sides, 2, 250, 286, 287; Cherchel raid, 255, 287; at Djerba (1560), 346; Don John and, 390; fleet, 287, 296, 303; Greek victories, 287–8; negotiations with Barbarossa, 314; Preveza battle, 303–5; relationship with Charles V, 287; successes, 256, 269; tactical brilliance, 2; Tunisian campaign, 296;
Doria, Giannettino, 314
Doukkala, battle of (1514), 202
Dozsa, George, 268–9
Dragfy, John, 246
Dragut, corsair captain, Ottoman admiral: background, 3, 315; base, 316; captured and ransomed, 314; career, 149, 283; command of Mediterranean, 349; corsair kingdom, 345; Corsica raids, 319; death, 359, 362; Djerba siege, 346, 347; fleet, 317, 319, 351; in Istanbul, 345; Italian raids, 319; Mahdia capture and loss, 316–17; Malta invasion, 317; Malta siege, 354–5, 356, 358; Preveza battle, 303, 304; relationship with Barbarossa, 303, 314–15; tomb, 366; Tripoli capture, 318, 353
Drake, Francis, 406, 409
Duarte Coelho family, 402
Dürer, Albrecht, **73**, 234, 241, **248**
Dutch sea beggars, 395

Ecija, forges, 124
Edirne (Adrianople): capture (1362), 71; Mehmet's childhood, 63–5; Ottoman army, 95, 371; Ottoman capital, 76, 86, 92; palace, 168, 183, 373; Selim II at, 375; Selimiye mosque, 369, 387
Edward I, King of England, 20
Edward III, King of England, 16, 17
Edward (Dom Duarte), King of Portugal, 17, 31, 33–4
Egypt: attacked by Knights of St John, 102; defence against Mongols, 10; Mameluke rule, 70; naval forces, 303;

Ottoman administration, 266;
Ottoman conquest, 181–2, 266;
rebellions against Ottomans, 261,
265; spice trade, 188
Ehingen, Jorg von, 43–8
Ehinger, Heinrich, 258
Eleonore, Queen of Portugal, Queen of
France, 233, 238, 250
Elias, brother of Barbarossa, 149, 151
Elizabeth I, Queen of England, 159,
342, 406, 409, 420, 421
Elizabeth of France, Queen of Spain,
342
Emerson, Ralph Waldo, 367
Encina, Juan del, 131
England: Charles V's visits, 240, 241,
243; invasions of France, 8, 20;
Philip II's marriage, 341–2;
relationship with Burgundy, 236,
241, 244, 253; relationship with
Morocco, 409, 421; Wars of the
Roses, 8, 121
Erasmus, Desiderius, 236, 239
Esmakhan, daughter of Selim II, 355
Essaouria, city, 399
Ethiopia, 59, 322, 323
Evangelista, architect-engineer, 361
Eyup Ansari, tomb of, 83

Famagusta: defences, 382–3; fortress,
374, 377; sack, 385–6, 391; siege, 2,
382–5, 389; trading houses, 376
Farhun, Caid al-, 56
Fasildas, Emperor of Abyssinia, 323
Fatimah, daughter of the Prophet, 174
Fatimah bint Ali Rachid, 158–9
Fatimid Caliphate, 225
Federico, Don, son of viceroy of Sicily,
353
Ferdinand I, Holy Roman Emperor
(Archduke of Austria): advice from
brother Charles V, 253, 255, 312,
324; declared King of Bohemia, 247;
education in Burgundy, 239; elected
Holy Roman Emperor, 343; military
strategy, 308; negotiations with
Suleyman, 343–4; peace treaty with
Ottomans (1533), 253, 270;
territorial gains, 247–8, 267–8;
tribute to Ottomans, 313, 370; truce
with Ottomans (1547), 316;
upbringing in Spain, 146, 233,
238–9, 268

Ferdinand II (the Catholic), King of
Aragon: artillery, 124, 127, 128–9;
assassination attempts, 129, 143;
birth, 117; character, 117, 147;
childhood, 117; conquest of
Granada, 1, 242; control of knightly
orders, 122–3, 255; creation of Santa
Hermandad, 123; death, 141, 146,
236–7, 275, 277; expulsion of Jews,
133–4, 169, 377; father's death, 116–
17; grandsons, 146, 233, 238;
Inquisition, 135; Malaga siege,
128–9; marriage, 50, 115–16, 117;
Naples campaign, 142–3, 287;
Navarre occupation, 142;
negotiations with Muslim ruling
class, 130, 132; refuses crusade plan,
141, 143, 277, 280; relationship with
Borgias, 122–3; religious views, 139,
147; reputation, 114–15, 142,
146–7; sex life, 118, 146; siege of
Granada, 131–2; son, 51, 116, 144;
son-in-law's death, 145–6; support
for Columbus, 139
Ferdinand III, King of Castile, 131
Ferdinand (Dom Fernao), son of John I
of Portugal, 31–3, 37, 49
Fernandez de Cordoba, Diego, 280
Fernitz, battle, 253
Ferrante, Francesco Pescara, 245–6
Ferrara, Duke of, 248
Fête du Faisan, 232–3, 252
Fethiye, sack, 170
Fez: arsenal, 218, 219; capture and
recapture (1554), 226; captured by
Sharif Muhammad, 223–4; centre of
learning, 209–12, 214; city, 209,
223; council of holy men, 220;
Emirate, 24, 52, 163, 194, 202;
fortifications, 227; Jewish
community, 207
fez, Ottoman symbol, 67
Field of the Cloth of Gold, 240–1, 243
Finkel, Caroline, 85
Florence: Duke of, 327; French alliance,
250; naval forces, 388; Savonarola,
142; trade, 68, 94
Foix, Gaston de, 236
Fondi, raid, 295
France: borders, 5; crusading knights,
71; fleet, 313; Hundred Years War,
20; invasion of Italy, 142, 169;
Ottoman alliance, 254, 296, 313;
Ottoman trading privileges, 294; St

Bartholomew's Day Massacre (1572), 395, 405

Francis I, King of France: accession, 234; appearance, 243; character, 235; captured at Pavia, 245–6; coronation, 235; crusade calls, 244, 250; death, 316; Field of the Cloth of Gold, 241; finances, 250–1; Holy Roman Emperor ambitions, 240; mistress, 254; Ottoman alliance, 254, 313, 353; relationship with Charles V, 4, 183, 224, 234–5, 244–6, 250–1, 283, 286, 316; relationship with Suleyman, 225, 296, 303; wars, 234, 283; wife, 250

Francis Xavier, St, 403

Francisco of Toledo, Don, 86

Frankopan, Peter, 267

Frundsberg, Georg, 248–9

Fry, John, 409

Fugger family, 240, 400, 420

Galata, town of, 79

Galleon of Venice, The, 304–5

Galley of Naples, The, 163

Gandia, Dukes of, 122

Gao, city, 35, 421

Garcilaso de la Vega, 300

Gattinara, Mercurino, 234, 256

Gaza, battle, 181

Gedik Ahmed Pasha, Ottoman commander, 99–100, 108, 110, 166, 168

Genghis Khan, 9 , 66, 74, 95, 174

Genher, daughter of Selim II, 355

Gennadius, Patriarch, 89

Genoa: Constantinople alliances, 79, 85; fleet, 71, 250, 303, 306, 388; Genoese in Spain, 133; Hafsid alliance, 158; merchants, 68; Ottoman attacks, 94, 319; picture, 55; relationship with Charles V, 296; relationship with France, 250, 251; rivalry with Venice, 9; Tabarka lease, 274; trading policies, 34, 139, 294

Germaine de Foix, Queen of Spain, 146

Germany: armed forces, 71; Diet of Regensburg, 308; frontiers, 8–9; Protestantism, 251, 294, 296–7, 308; social rebellions, 283

Ghassasa, Spanish outpost, 218

Gibbon, Edward, 260, 341

Gibraltar (Gebel al-Tariq), 13, 14, 15–16

Giustiniano, Duke Nicholas, 150–1

Giustiniano, Orsano, 151

Gloucester, Humphrey, Duke of, 33

Goa: capture (1510), 197–8, 199; Inquisition, 403; Portuguese base, 200, 266; siege (1571), 404

gold: Aztec, 241, 242, 243; coins, 23, 34, 58, 97, 189, 198, 280, 307, 350, 408; Genoese trade, 133; mines, 51; payment for Moroccan invasion, 407; payment for spices, 189; Portuguese treasury, 54, 221; sources, 35; Suleyman's crown, 271; trade in Ceuta, 15, 26; trans-Saharan trade, 26, 28, 34–5, 130; Vasco da Gama's demands for, 190

Goletta: capture by Barbarossa, 295; corsair base, 161, 162, 163, 273; defences, 363; fall (1574), 396; galley slaves, 299; Genoese bombardment, 274; siege and capture (1535), 2, 297–8; Spanish base, 300, 316, 345, 348, 349, 366

Gomes, Diego, 28

Gomes, Fernao, 53–4

Goncalves da Câmara, Luis and Martini, 403

Gondar, city, 323

Gonzaga, Ferrante, 303, 309

Gonzaga, Giulia, 295

Gozo: Knights of St John, 255, 354; Ottoman invasion, 317

Graciosa, Fort, 57–8, 204, 205, 209

Granada, Emirate: borders, 125; burning of Arabic books, **136**; Castilian crusade, 52, 56, 194; fall (1490–2), 1, 57, 132, 421; Malaga siege, 129; mosques, 2; Nasrid culture, 7; Nasrid rule, 10, 57, 120, 125, 126, 132; refugees from, 57, 158; relationship with Mamelukes, 121; relationship with Ottomans, 169; siege of city (1490–2), 125, 131, 143, 421; tribute payments, 120, 122, 126

Granada, treaty of (1500), 143

Granvelle, Cardinal de, 296, 312, 328

Gravière, Jurien de la, 305

Grazia de Tineo, Lieutenant, 281

Greece: Doria's victories, 269, 287–8; Venetian fortresses, 307

Gregory XIII, Pope, 395–6, 409

Grimaldi, Nicolo, 319

Grimani, Marco, 303, 304

Grotius, Hugo, 18
Guadix, surrender, 130
Guatemala, seat of government, 257
Guise, Duke of, 81
Gujarat, Sultanate, 196, 266, 305–6
gunpowder, 206–7, *see also* saltpetre

Habsburg: Austro-Hungarian Empire,
247–8; family, 253; origins, 268;
territories, 268
Hadice, sister of Suleyman, wife of
Ibrahim Pasha, 265
Hadim Suleyman, Ottoman
commander, 305–6
Hadith (recorded actions and collected
sayings of the Prophet), 84, 111, 167,
210, 367
Hadrian VI (Adrian of Utrecht), Pope,
234, 244
Haedo, Diego, 162
Hafsa, mother of Suleyman, 330, 331
Hafsids: Holy League support, 395;
Ottoman campaign against, 365;
relationship with corsairs, 158,
163–4, 273–4, 275, 279, 283, 298;
relationship with Spanish, 163–4,
273, 275, 279, 298, 300, 345, 365;
territories, 163; Tunis Sultanate, 7,
10, 103, 141, 294, 295, 300
Haha tribes, 193, 212, 417
Halicarnassus, destruction of
Mausoleum, 103
Halil Pasha, grand vizier, 75, 90
Halveti dervishes, 171
Hamid, Moulay, Sultan of Tunis, 365
Hamida al-Awda, 278–9
Hamon, Moses, 208
Hampi, city, 195
Harar, walled city, 321–2
Harrington, John, 13
Hasan Agha, governor of Algiers, 288,
310–11, 312, 313, 315
Hasan Ali, corsair captain, 163
Hasan Pasha of Algiers, 351
Hasan Qusru, janissary commander,
225, 226, 319, 320
Hassan, Black, corsair captain, 283
Hassan, Moulay, (Mohammed Hassan),
Sultan of Tunis, 298
Hassan, son of Khizr Barbarossa, 226,
315
Hassan of Ulubar, 86
Helena Palaeologina, Queen of Cyprus,
376

Henry IV, King of Castile, 50, 116, 118,
120
Henry V, King of England, 121
Henry VII, King of England, 233
Henry VIII, King of England: death,
316; excommunication, 253; Field of
the Cloth of Gold, 240–1; Holy
Roman Emperor ambitions, 240;
marriage, 145, 251; natural son, 408;
relationship with Charles V, 240–1,
251; religious role, 122, 253, 377;
seizure of church lands, 122, 377
Henry II, King of France, 253
Henry III, King of France, 400
Henry, (Dom Henrique, Prince Henry
the Navigator): at Ceuta, 17, 21,
26–7, 192; challenge to Ottoman
Sultan, 39; chapel, 188; Commander
of the Order of Christ, 23, 28, 29,
36–7, 38–9, 62; court, 36–7; death,
41; interest in exploration, 27–9, 62,
138; Ksar es Seghir expedition, 40–1,
42, 400; portrait, 27; Prester John
quest, 38; reputation, 42; sword, 415;
Tangier expedition, 31–3, 37; will,
38
Henry of Nassau, 234, 235
Henry of Portugal, Cardinal, 403, 419–
20
Hinduism, 195
Hintata governors of Marrakesh, 202,
209, 216, 217
Hogan, Edmund, 409
Holy League, 3, 142, 388–9, 390,
394–5, 408
Hunan Hatun, mother of Mehmet,
63–4, 76
Hundred Years War, 20, 241
Hungary: army, 98; civil war, 268–9;
crusade (1396), 71; elective
monarchy, 9; Hunyadi's leadership,
95–6; Ottoman attacks, 95–6;
Ottoman invasion (1526), 243,
246–8, 267; Ottoman invasions
(1529, 1532), 269; Ottoman
invasions (1541, 1543), 308;
Ottoman invasion (1566), 363,
370–1; Ottoman position, 252–3;
Ottoman relations, 179; Venetian
alliance, 98
Hunyadi, Janos, 65, 75, 79, 95–6, 268
Husayn, son of Imam Ali, 175, 176,
335, 422

Hussayn, Haj, ambassador, 281

Iacopo, Maestro, physician, 109
Ibadi sect, 160
Ibn Ghazi, 210
Ibn Sunni Ali, Emperor of Songhai, 211
Ibrahim, Emir of Chechaouen, 159
Ibrahim, leader from Djerba, 129, 141
Ibrahim ibn Rashid, governor of western
    Rif, 217
Ibrahim Pasha, grand vizier:
    achievements, 271–2; advice to
    Suleyman, 293, 294; background,
    265; death, 271–2, 333; Egyptian
    planning, 266, 321; fall, 302, 321,
    332–3; Iraq campaign (1533–4),
    270, 271; relationship with
    Suleyman, 265, 271–2, 333, 373
Idrisi, El-, scholar-geographer, 19
Ifrani, al-, historian, 224
Incas, 258–9
India: Babur's invasion, 195–6; Malabar
    coast, 190; Portuguese trade, 61–2,
    187–90; sea route, 5, 62; Vijayanagar
    Empire, 195
Indonesia, 199
Innocent VIII, Pope, 167
Inquisition: burning of heretics, 135,
    137, 342–3, 350; control of, 135; in
    Goa, 403; in Granada, 139–40;
    Moors forcibly converted, 284–5; in
    Portugal, 403; in Spain, 135–6,
    342–3
Iran (see also Persia): borders, 5; Ismail's
    leadership, 3, 175, 177, 182, 196;
    mystics, 171; relationship with
    Ottoman Empire, 182; Safavid
    Shahs, 368, 373; Safavids, 173; Shiite
    nation state, 5
Iraq, 295, 306
Ireland, 408–9
Isaac, brother of Barbarossa, 149, 151–3
Isabella, Princess, daughter of John II, 60
Isabella, Queen of Castile: appearance,
    131; birth, 117; character, 117–18,
    238; childhood, 117–18; children,
    51, 116, 144–5; conquest of
    Granada, 1; court, 118–19; creation
    of Santa Hermandad, 123; death,
    145–6; expulsion of Jews, 133–4,
    169, 377; library, 119; marriage, 50,
    115–16, 145; prayer book, 119;
    religious views, 118, 139, 147;
    reputation, 114–15, 131–2, 142;

siege of Granada, 131–2; succession
    to throne, 50–1, 116, 145; support
    for Columbus, 138–9; will, 277
Isabella, Queen of Denmark, sister of
    Charles V, 233
Isabella, Queen of Portugal, daughter of
    Ferdinand and Isabella, 60–1, 62,
    144
Isabella of Portugal, wife of Charles V,
    250, 251, 256–7
Isidore, St, 131
Iskandar, Emperor of Abyssinia, 59
Islam: angel of death, 149; conversion
    from, 135–6, 140, 164, 210, 242–3,
    284; conversion to, 7, 69, 84, 89, 91,
    96–7, 126, 170, 197, 318, 320, 322,
    365; Hadith, see Hadith; holy
    banners, 84, 412; holy cities, 182,
    336; jihad, see jihad; Kharajites, 160;
    Koran, see Koran; Ottoman Sultans,
    66, 171–2, 182, 270; pilgrimage, 99,
    166, 173, 182, 183, 206, 210, 213,
    215, 261, 336, 368, 385; preacher-
    politicians, 211–12; science, 220;
    Shiite, 174, 182, 184, 222, 225, 270,
    335, 368, 421; slave armies, 70;
    studies, 64; Sufism, 3, 64–5, 172–3,
    210–11, 220; Sunni, 178, 182, 222,
    225, 270, 368, 421; teachings, 210;
    tithes, 97, 202, 213; treasures, 182;
    values and traditions, 111, 153,
    165–6, 171, 216–17, 317
Ismail, Shah of Iran: appearance, 172;
    army, 179; background, 3, 174;
    Caldiran defeat, 179; cruelty, 175;
    death, 266; followers, 174–5; Imam-
    Shah of Tabriz, 172, 175; Kizilbas
    uprisings, 176–7, 183; old age, 264;
    Ottoman relations, 176–80; quest for
    artillery, 179; Shah of Iran, 175;
    writings, 175
Ismail Masuki, Sufi preacher, 350
Istanbul, see Constantinople
Italy: expulsion of Jews by Paul IV, 372;
    French invasion, 142, 169; French
    possessions, 244
Iznik: destruction, 74; tiles, 369–70

Jacobsbrüder, 43–4
James II, King of Cyprus, 375–6, 382
James III, King of Cyprus, 376
janissaries: at Algiers, 282; appearance,
    68, 290; armaments, 69, 268;
    discharge, 150; engineer corps, 368;

in Hungary, 267; levy of Christian boys, 69, 70, 373, 377; marriage policy, 149–50; in Morocco, 225–6; mourning for Mustapha, 335; mutiny, 371, 372; payment, 97, 149, 371; ranking system, 290; rebellion on Mehmet's death, 110, 165; relationship with Sultans, 70, 77, 170–1, 371; Selim's accession, 178; training, 69, 282; uniforms, 137

Japan, submission to China, 200

Jazuli as-Samlali, Muhammad al-, 211, 212

Jazuli brotherhood, 215, 222, 417

Jebel Moussa, 13–14

Jerusalem: fall to Ottomans, 181; Muslim reconquest (1244), 20; pilgrimage to, 43, 102, 336

Jesuits, 323, 343, 403

Jews: in Antwerp, 408; children forcibly converted, 401; conversos, 134–5, 136, 138, 207, 218, 242–3; in England, 20; expulsion from central Italy, 372; expulsion from Nuremberg, 142; expulsion from Portugal, 61, 62, 142, 194, 207, 401; expulsion from Spain, 133–4, 136, 169, 207; Inquisition, 135–6; in Morocco, 207, 211; Nasi's career, 208, 371–2; in Ottoman Empire, 93; in Portugal, 207; refugees, 156–7; in Safi, 194; in Spain, 4, 133–6, 207

jihad: against Spain and Portugal, 159, 205, 396–7; case for, 24; corsairs wage, 396; in East Africa, 321; funding, 223; Holy War at Sea, 158, 159, 237, 316; leadership, 218, 225, 277; preaching, 211; prospect of sack, 85; zeal for, 213

Jijil (Jigelli, Jejel): capture by Barbarossa, 273–4, 277; corsair base, 283

John, King of Cyprus, 376

John (Joao, the Bastard) I, King of Portugal: accession to throne, 21–2; Ceuta conquest, 16, 19, 20–1, 192; death, 31, 63; reputation, 22–3; rule, 22; sons, 16, 33; tomb, 41

John (Joao) II, King of Portugal: African policies, 53–4; agents, 58–60; Alcacovas treaty, 51–2, 53; American expeditions, 54–5; at Asilah, 48; coronation, 52; death, 60; Moroccan policies, 56–8; portrait, 59; regency for father, 51–2; Toro battle, 51

John (Joao) III, King of Portugal, 219, 220–1, 224, 296, 399–403

John, Master, gunner, 207

John, Prince, son of Ferdinand and Isabella, 144

John (Juan) of Austria, Don: attempt to join Knights of St John, 353, 390; Burgundy campaign, 396; childhood, 389–90; Holy League, 387; Holy League fleet command, 390–1, 393–4, 395; Lepanto victory, 2–3, 229, 391–4; relationship with brother Philip II, 390, 396; Tunisian campaign, 395–6

John the Fearless, Duke of Burgundy, 232

John of the Cross, St, 343

John of Gaunt, 17

John Sigismund, son of John Zapolya, 308, 370

Juana, Princess (La Beltranja), 50, 51, 116, 118, 145

Juana (the Mad), Queen of Spain, 144, 145–6, 233, 237, 238, 329

Juanna of Spain, mother of Sebastian of Portugal, 403

Julian, Count, governor of Ceuta, 15

Julius II, Pope, 162

Junayd, Sheikh, 173–4

Jurisics, Nicholas, 252

Justinian, Emperor, 77, 370

Kai-Ka'us Ibn Iskandar, Sultan of Tabaristan, 90–1

Kairouan, city, 295, 345

Kara-Hassan, corsair captain, 276, 283, 284

Karaman, Emirate of, 64, 66, 98

Karamani Mehmet Pasha, Grand Vizier, 110, 165

Kemal Ataturk, 110

Khalifa, Hajji, 302

Kharajites, 160

Khayr al-Din (Kherredine, Kheyr el-Din), 163

Khidr, al (green knight of Islam), 172, 422

Khirokitia, battle of (1429), 375

Khizr (Barbarossa, Beylerbey of Algiers, Khayr al-Din): Aegean campaign, 302; at Algiers, 278, 283; appearance, 284; background, 149, 151; bases, 160, 161; Bejaia campaign, 273–4; Charles V's campaign against, 298;

Charles V's overtures to, 296; clemency, 283; death, 316; ferrying refugees, 156–7; fleet, 163, 273, 285, 303; Goletta defence, 298; Hafsid campaign, 295; independent corsair captain, 159; in Istanbul, 291–4, 301, 302; Italian campaigns, 294–5, 313; Jijil capture, 274–5; meetings with Suleyman, 288, 291–4, 302; Menorca raid, 301; mosque building, 315; negotiations with Doria, 314; Preveza battle, 303–5, 310; relationship with Hafsid Sultan, 161, 163, 273, 274, 294; relationship with Ottomans, 275, 281–2, 288; son, 226; successor, 373; titles from Ottoman Sultan, 163, 281; tomb, 315; Tunis loss, 299

Kilwa, Portuguese pillage, 190
Kingdom of the Two Sicilies, see Naples
Kizilbas, 4, 174–9, 183, 260, 350
Knights of Avis, 23
Knights of St John (Knights Hospitallers): Algiers siege, 310, 311, 313; appeal for help, 354; campaigns, 102–3; castles, 103; Cem's visit, 166–7; conquest of Rhodes, 101–2; crusade (1396), 71; crusading mission, 261; evacuation of Rhodes, 255, 264–5, 354; hospitals, 102, 363; intelligence, 352–3; in Malta, 2, 255, 316, 317, 351; naval forces, 152, 201, 388; North African campaign (1559–60), 344; Ottoman attack on Rhodes (1480), 104–8; Ottoman attack on Rhodes (1522), 261–4; principles, 354; regiments, 108, 263; relationship with Bayezid II, 167, 169, 263; relationship with Pope, 354; rent for Malta and Gozo, 354; in Rhodes, 2, 28, 43, 99, 100, 113, 183, 261; as rulers, 103; sale of Jewish refugees, 372; standard, 2; in Tripoli, 296, 316, 317; in Tunis, 317; Tunisian campaign, 296, 298
Knights of Santiago, 23
Knights Templars: banner, 6; Crusading Order of Christ, 23, 29, 61, 101; destruction by Philip IV, 20, 100–1; Henry the Navigator, 2, 23, 29; heraldry, 61; landholdings, 23, 29, 101; suppression in Europe, 23
Konya, battle (1559), 373

Koran: blessings, 292; destruction of copies, 164, 300; memorising, 151; message of, 168, 171, 216, 271; prohibitions, 180; study of, 210, 367, 368, 397; tithes sanctified by, 202, 213; verses from, 14, 210
Korkud, son of Bayezid II, 177
Koroni, capture, 269
Kos, castle on, 152, 263
Kosovo: first battle of (1389), 71, 76, 77; second battle of (1448), 76, 77
Koszeg, siege, 252
Krishna Deva Raya, 195
Kritovoulos Imbros, 87
Ksar el Kebir: evacuees in, 194; walled city, 209
Ksar es Seghir (Alcazar Seguir), 40–1, 42, 43, 54, 205, 399–400
Kubad, Cavus, 377
Kyrenia, fortress, 374, 377, 382

Lampedusa, island, 361
Lamu, submission to Portugal, 191–2
Larache, port, 48, 57, 407–8, 410, 411
Larnaca: Ottoman landing, 378; trade, 386
las Casas, Bartolome de, 242
Las Grebes, debacle, 280
Lefkara, rebellion, 378
Leo X, Pope, 202
Leo Africanus, 202, 204
Leon, 9, 22, 23, 120
Leonardo da Vinci, 35, **80**
Leonor, Queen of Portugal, 31
Lepanto, battle of (1571): celebrations, 394; Cervantes at, 394; description, 391–4, **392**; destruction of Ottoman fleet, 228, 393, 395, 406, 421; Don John's leadership, 2, 391, 393–4, 407; Englishmen at, 408; location, 1, 391; Moroccan princes at, 228–9, 406, 413; Sebastian inspired by, 404
Lesbos: Barbarossa brothers, 149, 293; Ottoman capture (1462), 112, 150; Ottoman position, 150–1; revenue from, 293; Venetian raid, 170
Libya, borders, 5
Lima, Dom Roderigo de, 59
Lipari islands, battle (1561), 350
Lisbon: slave markets, 402; slave population, 403; spice trade, 187–9; support for John, 22
Lithuania, elective monarchy, 9

Livorno, port, 372
Loja, sieges (1482, 1486), 125, 127
Longo, Giovanni Giustiniani, 79
Lopo Barriga, governor of Safi, 216
Louis IX, King of France, 20, 51
Louis XII, King of France, 235, 240
Louis (Ladislas, Lewis) II, King of
    Hungary, 246–7, 267, 268
Lübeck, city, 250
Lucena, Juan of, 135
Lusignan, Guy de, 375
Luther, Martin, 139, 316

Macao, trading post, 200
Machiavelli, Niccolo, 114–15, 121,
    146–7
Madeira, 29, 37, 51
Madrid, treaty of (1526), 246
Magellan, Fernand, 31, 258
Maghili, al-, preacher, 211
Mahdi, 3, 174, 214
Mahdia: capture by Doria, 317; capture
    by Dragut, 316
Mahidevran, mother of Prince
    Mustapha, 332
Mahmud Pasha Angelovic, 91, 97, 111
Malacca: capture (1510), 199;
    Portuguese base, 200
Malaga: commercial role, 130; fall, 129–
    30; rule, 125; siege (1486–7), 2, 123,
    127–9, 131, 133, 141, 143
Malik Aiyaz, 196
Malik ibn Dawud, 201–2
Malta: Christian relief force, 362;
    defences, 353, 361, 363; Grand
    Harbour, 353, 355, 356, 363;
    hospital, 363; Knights of St John, 2,
    255, 296, 316, 317, 351, 352–3;
    Mount Sciberas, 355–6; Ottoman
    evacuation, 362; Ottoman invasion,
    317; Ottoman siege, 1, 352–62, 363,
    421; St Angelo Castle, 355, 361; St
    Elmo Castle, 355, 356, 357–8, 359–
    61, 360; water supply, 361
Mameluke Sultans: background, 70,
    181; battles with Timur, 74, 180;
    coast raided by Knights of St John,
    102; Cyprus fief of, 375; defence of
    Egypt, 10; Granadan embassy, 121;
    naval forces, 121, 196; non-
    aggression pact with Knights of St
    John, 103; Ottoman relations, 170,
    179; Ottoman victory over (1516),
    180–2; Ottoman war (1485–91),

169; trade, 188
Manamah, fortress, 323
Mangin, Colonel, 203
Manicongo, King, 54
Manrique, Alonso, 125
Manuel I, King of Portugal: accession,
    60; African policies, 193; expulsion
    of Jews, 61, 62, 194; Indian policies,
    195, 197, 201; marriages, 60–1, 144;
    Moroccan campaigns, 201–3; spice
    trade, 189–90, 400; Vasco da Gama's
    voyages, 61–2, 189–90
Manuel II Palaeologus, Byzantine
    Emperor, 73–4
maps: Columbus's enterprise, 138;
    drawn by Piri Reis, 14, 262, 266,
    374, 379; Ottoman research, 97–8;
    Portuguese collection, 28–9, 33
Marbella, surrender, 127
Marchione, Bartolomeo, 189
Margaret of Austria, regent of the Duchy
    of Burgundy, 144, 233–4, 239
Margaret of Parma, regent of the Duchy
    of Burgundy, 341
Maria, Queen of Portugal, daughter of
    Ferdinand and Isabella, 144
Maria do Espiritu Santo Arco-Verde,
    402
Marietta of Patras, 376
Marj Dabiq, battle (1516), 180
Marmol, historian, 132
Marmora: battle of (1515), 203–4, 209,
    215; fort, 203, 205
Marrakesh: arsenal, 218; captured by
    Sharif Ahmad (1524), 217; city, 203;
    control of, 222; Emirate, 24; Hintata
    governors, 202, 209, 216, 217;
    Saadian tombs, 228; Sharifian capital,
    227
Marseilles: defences, 313; port, 254
Martil, port, 351
Martinego, Hercules, 383
Martyr, Peter, of Anghiera, 121, 131
Mary I, Queen of England, 341–2
Mary of Hungary, Regent of the Duchy
    of Burgundy, sister of Charles V, 208,
    233, 299
Mary Tudor, Queen of France, 240
Maximilian I, Holy Roman Emperor,
    124, 142, 144, 233, 234, 239–40
Maximilian II, Holy Roman Emperor,
    208, 370, 372
Mazagan, fort, 193, 221, 403–4

Mecca: adornment by Suleyman, 368; direction for prayer, 88; holy city, 182, 336; pilgrim kitchens and hospices, 336; pilgrimage (Haj), 166, 182, 206, 214, 215, 261, 385; Sharifs from, 213

Mechara-en-Nedjima, fort, 411, 413

Medea Palaeologi, Queen of Cyprus, 376

Medina, holy city, 182, 270, 336, 368

Medina Celi, Juan de la Cerda, Duke of, 344, 346, 348–9, 355

Medina Sidonia, Duke of, 35, 121, 123

Mehmet II (the Conqueror), Ottoman Sultan: accession, 371; appearance, 99, **109, 112**; Balkan campaigns, 95–7, 168; birth, 63; building works in Istanbul, 92–3; campaigns against Hungary and Venice, 98; childhood, 63–6; conquest of Constantinople, 1, 39, 86–8, 91–2; Constantinople siege 81–6; Constantinople siege plans, 75, 77–81; coronations, 75, 76; court, **91**, 92, 93, 97, 168; death, 109–10, 113, 165; Genoese policies, 79, 94; harem, 77, 92, 97; historical interests, 112–13; Kosovo battle, 75–6; marriage, 76; military career, 168; mother's death, 76; murder of half-brother, 77, 111; naval forces, 93–4, 96; Peloponnese campaigns, 79, 97; relationship with father, 75–6, 77; relationship with Tartar Khans, 94–5; religious policies, 64–5, 96–7; Rhodes expedition, 108–9; sexuality, 90; sons, 111; tomb, 110, 168; treatment of captives, 89–90; Trebizond campaign, 97; Venetian policies, 94, 98–9; victories, 42; wounded at Belgrade, 96

Mehmet, Prince, son of Suleyman, 331, 333

Meknes: arsenal, 218; city, 209; Emirate, 24; evacuees in, 195

Melilla, Spanish fort, 141, 163

Mello, Jorge de, 193

Mendes-Nasi, Dona Gracia, 208

Mendoza, Cardinal-Archbishop, 118, 119–20, 131

Meneses, Dom Duarte de, 40–1

Meneses, Dom Pedro de, 21

Menorca, Ottoman raids, 301, 320

Merenid dynasty: end of, 57, 194, 208–9, 211; in Morocco, 10, 24;

Nasrid relations, 24; naval base in Gibraltar, 16; tombs, 26

Mers-el-Kebir, Spanish fort, 141, 163, 349

Mesikh Pasha, Ottoman commander, 105–8

Mexico, 2, 6, 241–2, 257

Michelangelo, 246

Miguel, Prince, son of Manuel I, 144

Mihrimah, Princess, daughter of Suleyman, 333, 351, 369

Milan: arms from, 408; artillerymen from, 123; Charles V's policy, 327; French alliance, 250; Sforza family, 142, 234, 287

Miquez, Dom John, see Nasi

Mogador, Castello Real fort, 193, 194, 221, 409

Mohacs, battle of (1526), 246–7, 252, 267, 268, 269, 308

Mohammed, see Muhammad

Moldavia, 9, 308

Mombasa: destruction, 191; Portuguese base, 200

Moncada, Hugo de, Admiral, 282

Mongols, 9–10, 74, 173, 182

Montagu, Lady Mary Wortley, 397

Montezuma, Aztec emperor, 241

Montoro, Anton de, 132

More, Thomas, 236

Morgan, Joseph, 281

Morocco: Battle of the Three Kings, 3; borders, 5, 228, 320; coastal navigation, 29; coup (1576), 406, 407; famines, 216; Jewish refugees, 207, 211; Merenid rule, 10; Portuguese campaigns, 3, 4, 6, 201–3, 221; Portuguese position, 56–7, 201, 205–6;

Morocco – *continued*
refugees from Granada, 209; relationship with England, 409, 421; Sharifian dynasty, 3, 132, 202, 217–21, 224–9, 320, 404; trade, 206; Wattasid resistance to Portuguese, 206, 215; Wattasid Sultanate, 209, 211, 214, 216, 217, 219–21, 223–4, 226, 320

Moscow, destruction (1571), 373

Moulay Bel Gaji tribal federation, 56

Moulay Yusuf (Prophet Joseph), 217

Mozambique, Portuguese base, 196

Muezzinzade Ali, Ottoman admiral, 391

Mughals, 195, 267
Muhammad, Prophet: Companions,
    83–4; death, 216; descendants, 3,
    159, 161, 174, 209, 213, 215, 225;
    example of, 92, 211, 367; grandson
    Husayn, 175, 335; *Hadith*, 84, 111,
    167, 210, 367; relics, 182; teachings,
    271; traditions, 161; wives and
    daughters, 84, 330
Muhammad VIII, Sultan of Granada, 25
Muhammad IX, Sultan of Granada, 126
Muhammad X, Sultan of Granada, 126
Muhammad XII, Sultan of Granada, *see*
    Boabadil
Muhammad al-Burtugali, Wattasid
    Sultan, 203–4, 205, 209, 210, 217,
    279
Muhammad al-Harran, 225
Muhammad al-Juti, 209
Muhammad al-Shaykh, governor of
    Asilah, 209
Muhammad al-Wattas, military leader,
    57–8
Muhammad al-Zagal, 127, 128, 130
Muhammad al-Mutawakkil, Sultan of
    Morocco, 407, 412, 413, 419
Muhammad esh-Sheikh, Sultan of
    Morocco, son of Al-Qaim: army,
    220, 224, 227, 406; arsenal, 218;
    Asilah siege, 218; battles against
    brother Ahmad, 222; battles against
    Portuguese, 215, 216; battles against
    Wattasids, 219, 220, 223; death, 227,
    228; Fez conquest, 223; Fez
    recapture, 226; relationship with
    Ottomans, 225–7; rule, 224, 226;
    Santa Cruz conquest, 220, 222; sons,
    228, 406, 411; Tarkuku port, 218;
    Tlemcen capture, 225
Münster, Anabaptists in, 250, 297
Münzer, Hieronymus, 46
Murat, Ottoman Prince, 178
Murat (Murad) I, Ottoman Sultan, 71
Murat (Murad) II, Ottoman Sultan,
    63–6, 75–6, 91
Murat (Murad) III, Ottoman Sultan,
    397–8, 407
Murat Agha, governor of Tripoli, 318
Murat Pasha, minister of Mehmet, 91
Muscat: Portuguese fortresses, **199**; sack,
    321
Muscovy, Grand Duchy of, 373
Mustapha, Prince, son of Mehmet II, 76,
    111, 166

Mustapha, Prince, son of Suleyman, 330,
    332–5, 338, 350
Mustapha Pasha, Lalla, Ottoman
    commander and adviser to Selim II:
    Cyprus invasion, 375, 382;
    Famagusta siege, 383–6; influence,
    374; Malta siege, 352, 360, 362;
    Nicosia siege, 379, 381; Yemen
    campaign, 373
Mustapha Pasha, Ottoman commander
    at Rhodes siege, 263
Mutawakkil, al-, last Abbasid, 182–3
Mylasa, Emirate, 102

Nafpaktos, port, 269
Naples, city, 250, 301, 326, 344
Naples, Kingdom of (Kingdom of the
    Two Sicilies): Charles V's visit, 300;
    Ottoman capture of Otranto, 100,
    120; peace with Ottomans, 169;
    slaves from, 100; Spanish garrison,
    162; Spanish invasion, 142–3, 287;
    territory, 9
Naqshabandi order, 173
Narvaez, Panfilo, 258
Nasi, Joseph (Yusuf, Dom John Miquez),
    208, 371–2, 387
Nasr, Moulay, grand vizier, 203
Nasr al Huntati, governor of Marrakesh,
    202
Nasrids: Ceuta base, 16; family divisions,
    125; first Emir, 126; in Gibraltar, 24;
    in Granada, 10, 24, 120, 125, 126;
    last Emir of Granada, 132; policies,
    126; relationship with Merenids,
    24
Navagero, Bernardo, 334
Navarre, 9, 22, 120, 142
Navarro, Count Pedro, 53, 141, 274,
    275, 277, 279
navigation, 29
Naxos, island of, 94
Nevers, John, Count of, 71
Nice, siege and sack, 313
Nicholas V, Pope, 79
Nicomedia, capture, 66
Nicopolis, battle and siege (1396), 71–3,
    77, 232, 252
Nicosia: administrative capital, 386;
    defences, 377, 378–9; fall, 381–2,
    389; garden city, 7; garrison, 377;
    maps, **374**, **379**; siege, 378–81
Nietzsche, Friedrich, 114

Notaras, Grand Duke Lucas, 89–90
Novgorod, republic of, 9
Novobrodo, silver mines, 95
Numimansa, Portuguese ally, 41
Nuno Fernandes de Ataide, governor of
　　Safi, 201, 204, 215–16
Nuremberg, expulsion of Jews, 142

Oguz, son of Prince Cem, 168
Oguz Turks, 66
O'Malley, Grace, 159
Omar, Caliph, 216
O'Neill, Shane, 409
Oporto, support for John, 22
Oran: fatwa, 210; invasion (1509), 141,
　　279; Ottoman capture (1558), 227;
　　siege (1556), 226; Spanish outpost,
　　163, 226, 227, 279, 310, 319, 320,
　　349
Order of Alcantara, 122, 123, 326
Order of Calatrava, 122, 123, 326
Order of Christ, 23, 26, 28, 29, 36–7,
　　38–9, 62
Order of the Golden Fleece, 231–2, 236,
　　252, 326
Order of Santiago, 122, 123, 326
Orhan, Ottoman Bey, 66–7, 71
Ormuz: capture (1515), 199; fort, 170;
　　Ottoman attack, 321; Portuguese
　　base, 200, 266, 321; spice trade, 188
Oromo (Galla) clans, 323
Orthodox Christianity: in Cyprus, 378,
　　383; married clergy, 151;
　　principalities and kingdoms, 9;
　　relationship with Catholic Church,
　　89, 97, 294, 378; relationship with
　　Ottoman Sultans, 82, 89, 97, 107,
　　264; under Venetian rule, 376–7, 378
Osman Bey (Osman Gazi), 66, 76, 184
Osorno, Duke of, 328
Otranto, capture and siege (1480),
　　99–100, 108, 110, 113, 120, 166
Ottoman Sultans: capital city, 76, 92;
　　extent of Empire, 182; finances, 350,
　　371, 375, 377; French alliance, 254,
　　296, 313; origins, 66–7, 171;
　　procession in Istanbul, 291; religious
　　role, 182, 270; state, 67–8, 171–2;
　　tradition of dynastic murder, 111,
　　167, 178, 184, 264, 332, 337, 350,
　　355, 397–8
Ouezzane, evacuees in, 195
Oujda, city, 227

Our Lady of the Conception, war galley,
　　152–3

Padul, recapture, 130
Paes, Domingo, 195
Paiva, Afonso de, 58
Palaeologue dynasty, 97, 376
Palencia, Friar Alonso de, 115
Palestine, 181, 372
Panama, seat of government, 257
Pantelleria, island, 361
papacy: Borgia popes, 122; Bulls and
　　decrees, 31, 33, 36, 53, 122–3;
　　crusades, 71, 133, 388; French
　　alliance, 250; funding for Spanish
　　fleet, 352; Holy League, 142, 388,
　　389, 390, 394; Inquisition, 135, 403;
　　Knights of St John, 354; military
　　forces, 282, 286; naval forces, 161–2,
　　303, 344, 388; Orthodoxy and, 89,
　　97; Ottoman Sultans and, 98;
　　relationship with Holy Roman
　　Emperors, 19, 244, 253; support for
　　Stukeley, 408; tiara, 271
Papal States, 9
Pardo, Pedron, 356
Pardo de Tavera, Juan, Cardinal-
　　Archbishop, 296
Park, Mungo, 35
Patras, capture, 253, 255, 288
Paul IV, Pope, 372
Pavia, battle of (1525), 245
Pecevi, Ibrahim, 265
Peele, George, 399
Peloponnese: invasion (1452), 79;
　　invasion (1460), 97
Penon de Velez de la Gomera, 53, 141,
　　163, 352
pepper, 187, 188, 400, 401, 402, 408
Perez de Pulgar, Hernan, 127
Persia (see also Iran): army, 179;
　　development of Shiite nation state of
　　Iran, 5, 267; Ismail's conquest, 175;
　　Ismail's successor, 266; Ottoman
　　invasion, 295; Ottoman relations, 4,
　　183, 225, 226, 254–5, 260, 262,
　　293, 316, 421; poetic culture, 174;
　　relationship with Portugal, 266; Shia
　　revolution, 196, 206; Shiite Empire,
　　4, 225; spice trade, 324
Persian Gulf, 58, 188, 198–9, 294, 321,
　　323
Peru, silver from, 319, 420

Pesaro, Jewish community, 372
Peter, King of Cyprus, 102
Peter (Dom Pedro), Prince Regent of
    Portugal, 17, 33–4, 36, 39, 42
Phanariotes, 377
Philip IV, King of France, 20, 101
Philip II, King of Spain: advice to
    Sebastian, 407–8, 420; character,
    329; crusade against North Africa,
    344; England expedition, 421;
    father's abdication, 324–5; father's
    advice, 324, 326–9; father's death,
    341; finances, 319; half-brother (Don
    John), 389–90, 396; Malta policy,
    354, 362–3; marriages, 329, 341,
    342; naval forces, 351–2, 387, 388;
    policies, 363–4; Protestant rebellion
    against, 395, 421; reception of
    Sebastian's body, 418; relationship
    with Sultan, 397; succession to
    Portuguese throne, 420; treatment of
    son (Don Carlos), 5, 329–30; troops
    for Sebastian's expedition, 410, 411,
    415
Philip the Good, Duke of Burgundy, 39,
    98, **231**
Philip the Handsome, Duke of
    Burgundy, 144, 145–6, 233
Philippa, Queen of Portugal, 16–17, 41
Phokaia, mines, 94
Phrantzes, historian, 85
Piale Pasha, Ottoman admiral:
    background, 3, 355; Corsica
    expedition, 320; Cyprus campaign,
    375, 382; Djerba victory, 346–7;
    Malta siege, 352, 354–5, 362;
    mutiny of janissaries, 371; Sicily raid,
    347; victory procession, 347
Pina, Ruy de, 47, 49
Pires, Ines, 22
Pires de Tavora, Alvaro, 410
Piri Reis, captain and cartographer, 14,
    262, 266, 321, **374**, **379**
Pius II, Pope (Aeneas Silvius
    Piccolomini), 138
Pius IV, Pope, 354, 362
Pius V, Pope, 387–8, 389, 390, 394
Pizarro, Francisco, 125, 258
Pizarro, Hernando, 258
Polo, Marco, 33
Ponzo, island, 319
Portugal: African wars, 321–2; borders,
    5, 120; coinage, 23, 34, 58; crusade
    against Morocco, 221; empire, 6,

27–8, 187, 400; expulsion of Jews,
    61, 62, 142, 401; Inquisition, 403;
    invasion of Morocco (1415), 10, 19,
    20–1; navy, 6, 10, 21, 196;
    relationship with Castile-Leon, 22,
    23; in 1360, 9
Prester John, 2, 38, 323, 421
Preveza, battle (1538), 1, 303–5, 306,
    308, 310, 391
Poland, elective monarchy, 9
Porto Farina, garrison, 395, 396
Postel, Guillaume, 334
Pragmatic Decree, 364
Principe, sugar growing, 401
Protestants: in Burgundy, 364, 395, 396,
    408; Charles V's policies, 253,
    308–9, 343; Dutch, 372, 395; in
    England, 421; in France, 395, 405;
    in Germany, 251, 294, 296; in
    Hungary, 308, 370; radical, 296–7;
    Reformation, 139, 296–7; St
    Bartholomew's Day Massacre (1572),
    395; soldiers, 408, 409; in Spain, 4,
    342–3
Proust, Marcel, 230
Pskov, Orthodox principality, 9

Qansuh, Mameluke Sultan, 180
Qassasa, Spanish fort, 141
Qeshm, sack, 321
Quassa, Spanish outpost, 163

Rabat, Hassan Tower, 15
Raidanya, battle (1517), 181
Ramadan, Cayto (Ramadan Bey),
    365–6, 407
Red Sea: Ottoman defence, 266;
    Ottoman fleet, 303, 305, 316, 321;
    Ottoman territory, 182, 321, 323;
    Portuguese position, 170, 201, 294
Regensburg, Diet of, 308
Reggio, raids on, 294, 319
Rhodes: base of Knights of St John, 2,
    28, 43, 99, 100, 113, 183, 261;
    Cem's visit, 166–7; conquest by
    Knights of St John, 101–2; conquest
    by Ottomans (1522), 243, 264–5,
    283; defences, 104–5, 263;
    evacuation of Knights of St John,
    255, 264–5; map, **262**; Ottoman
    attack (1476), 103; Ottoman attack
    (1480), 104–8; Ottoman attack
    (1522), 261–4, 267; Ottoman base,
    382; Ottoman governor-general, 157;

pilgrim route, 102; revenue from, 293; sea tower of St Nicholas, 104–7, 232; strategic importance, 261
Richard I, King of England, 376
Rincon, diplomat, 254
Rome: Charles V in, 301; Malta celebrations, 362; prostitutes, 388; sack (1527), 249–50, 283; Vatican, 301, 387; Venetian embassy (1570), 388
Romegas, Chevalier, 351
Ronda: fall (1484), 127; Moorish revolt, 140
Roxelana, wife of Suleyman, 330–3, 332, 336–7
Rumeli Hisari, castle, 78–9, 92
Rumi, Sufi poet, 173, 331
Rustem Pasha, 333–5, 337, 338, 350–1, 369
Ruti family, 207

Saadi, poet, 63, 88
Sadr al-Din, 173
Safavids: capital, 270; descent, 174; influence, 173; Ismail, 172, 174, 196; sheikhs, 172–3, 174; Ottoman relations, 254–5, 260, 293, 333, 337; Sufi brotherhood, 172
Safed, Kabbalistic studies, 372
Safi: abandoned by Portuguese, 221, 399; port, 56–7; Portuguese occupation, 193, 194, 201–2, 204, 215–16; siege (1534), 219
Safi al-Din Ishak, 173
Safiye, wife of Murat III, 398
Sagundino, Niccolo, 112
Sahaba Errahmania, 228, 406
Sahara: caravan trade, 14, 24, 29, 54, 130, 163, 206; gold trade, 26, 28, 34–5, 130; landscape, 30; Leo Africanus's travels, 202; Ottoman territories, 182; preachers in, 211; Sharifian position, 220; Spanish position, 189; trade routes, 206; trading cities, 35, 213; Zayyanid position, 278
St Bartholomew's Day Massacre (1572), 395, 405
Salah ibn Salah, Caid, 32
Salih Reis, 283, 284, 304, 314, 319
Salim al-Thumi, Sheikh, 276
saltpetre, 206–7, 212, 218, 409
Sammichele, Giovanni, 383

San Domingo, 257, 258
Sande, Alvaro de, 346, 348
Sandoval, chronicler, 278
Santa Cruz, fort, 193, 201, 213, 214–15, 218; fall (1541), 220, 222, 399
Santa Cruz, Portuguese nobleman, 217
Santa Hermandad, 123
Santiago the Moor-slayer, 131
Sao Gabriel, 61, 62
Sao Jorge da Mina, 53–4, 57, 193
Sao Miguel, 61, 62
Sao Rafael, 61, 62
Sao Tome, sugar growing, 401
Savonarola, Girolamo, 142
Savoragno, military engineer, 378–9
Savoy, naval forces, 388
Saxe, Marshal de, 18
Sayyaf, al- (ibn Suleyman), preacher, 211–12
Sebastian, Dom, King of Portugal, 421–2: army, 409–10, 411, 417; Battle of the Three Kings, 3, 414–18; body, 418; childhood, 403–4; crusading zeal, 404–5, 412; landing at Asilah, 410; legend of survival, 421–2; standard, 409; successor, 420; Tangier expedition (1574), 405
Selim I (the Grim), Ottoman Sultan: campaigns, 260, 281; campaigns against Ismail, 176, 178–9, 183, 260; campaigns against Mamelukes, 180–3, 260, 266; circumcision ceremony, 99; death, 183–4; deposition of father, 177–8, 183; father's accession, 166;
Selim I (the Grim), Ottoman Sultan – continued
massacre of Kizilbas, 350; murder of male relatives, 178, 183, 184, 264; policies, 368; relationship with Barbarossa, 281–2; successor, 184, 243; treatment of Jews, 207; treatment of last Abbasid, 182–3; writings, 165
Selim II (the Sot), Ottoman Sultan: accession, 371, 372–3; counsellors, 208; Cyprus conquest, 374–5, 377, 387; daughters, 355; death, 397; fear of army, 372–3, 387; lifestyle, 337–8, 367; mosque building, 387, 397; mother, 331; murder of brother, 350; relationship with Philip II, 397; rule, 373; struggle with brother Bayezid, 337, 344, 349–50, 373; Tunisian

expedition (1574), 396–7
Seljuks, 66
Semendria, battle of (1437), 96
Serbelloni, Gabrio, 397
Serbia, 9, 95, 97
Seven Cities, Island of the, 54–5
Seville: American trade, 257; Cardinal of, 328; the Giralda, 15; siege and fall, 126
Shabatz, fortress, 260
Shakespeare, William, 42, 289
Shams ad-Din Muhammad, 206
Sharif Al-Qaim, 3, 214–16
Sharifian dynasty: Battle of the Three Kings, 411–19; battles between brothers, 222; battles with Ottomans, 225–7, 404; battles with Portuguese, 220–1; battles with Wattasids, 132, 219, 222–3; descendants of the Prophet, 213–14; exiled princes, 228–9, 406–7; food distribution centres, 216; founder, 3, 214–16; invasion of Morocco by Abdul Malik, 407; invasion of Ottoman territories, 225; Leo Africanus, 202; murder of princes, 228; relationship with Wattasids, 214, 217–18, 220; rule, 224
shipping: caravels, 30, 31, 57, 138; cost of maintaining fleet of galleys, 397; galleases, 389, 391, 392–3, 394; galleons, 162, 191, 304; galleot, 159, 163; galleys, 30, 152, 160, 162–3, 304, 320, 391, 394, 397; ocean-going barges, 306; shipbuilding, 34, 307
Sicily: Charles V's arrival, 300; navy, 349, 359, 363, 388; Holy League fleet, 390–1; Ottoman fleet, 317; viceroy, 353, 359
Sidi Barakat, 213
Sidi Bel Abbes, 19
Sidon, Crusader port abandoned, 20
Sigismund, Holy Roman Emperor, 33, 71–2, 232
Sinan, architect, 69, 368–70, 387
Sinan ('The Jew of Smyrna'), corsair, 283
Sinan Pasha, Ottoman admiral, 317
Sivas, battle, 177, 183
Sixtus IV, Pope, 131, 135
Skanderbeg, Gjerj, 98
slaves: Abbasid palace guards, 70; African, 35, 257, 292, 401; Algiers slave markets, 313, 320; Christian captives of corsairs, 158; Christian slaves in Tunis, 299; Christian women, 292; galley slaves, 153–6, 154, 299, 394; Istanbul slave market, 100; janissaries, 69–70, 377; Lisbon slave markets, 402; Lisbon population, 403; Mameluke army, 70, 181; Muslim traditions, 69; Ottoman, 68–9; trade, 34–5, 95; white Christians, 95
Smolensk, Orthodox principality, 9
Smyrna (Izmir), 94, 98, 102, 103
Socotra: Christian Arabs, 199; fort, 170; Portuguese base, 266; Portuguese conquest, 198–9
Sofala, Portuguese base, 196
Sokullu Mehmet Pasha, grand vizier: background, 373; criticism of Lalla Mustapha Pasha, 386; Cyprus strategy, 375; influence, 373, 398; marriage, 355, 373; mosque, 369; Selim II's accession, 371; territorial policy, 396
Somali tribes, 321, 322
Songhai, empire of, 36, 211, 421
Sophianos, Ottoman ambassador, 103
Sorrento, Ottoman raid, 320
spahis, 70–1
Spain: borders, 5; crusading tax, 237; expulsion of Jews, 133–4, 156, 169; expulsion of Muslims, 140, 156; finances, 133, 319; Moorish rebellion (Alpujarras 1568), 228, 364, 365, 387, 390; naval forces, 303, 349, 388; orders of knightly chivalry, 122–3, 255; Pragmatic Decree, 364; rebellions and civil war, 242–3, 283; refugees, 156–7; refusal of crusading calls, 306; regency, 141, 237; Spanish forts on North African coast, 140–1; treatment of conversos, 242–3; Venetian embassy (1570), 388
Sperlonga, raid on, 295
spice trade, 188, 258, 324, 400, 401
Stenil, fall (1484), 127
Stukeley (Stucley), Sir Thomas, 408–9, 410
Suez, Egyptian base, 321
Sufis: Bayezid II's interest in, 176; Bektasi brotherhood, 64–5; brotherhoods, 3, 213; centres, 172–3; Halveti dervishes, 171; al-Jazuli, 211; Jazuli brotherhood, 215, 222; preacher burned in Istanbul, 350;

relationship with Sharifians, 217,
220; Safavid brotherhood, 172, 173;
status of sheikhs, 223, 226; Zarruq's
teachings, 210–11
Sufyan, mercenary, 222–3
sugar, 401–2
Suleyman Bey, 92
Suleyman the Magnificent, Ottoman
Sultan: accession, 184, 260; Aegean
campaign, 302; appearance, 184,
261, **336**; Corfu siege, 302; court,
208; crown, 271; death, 228, 371;
eastern European campaigns, 306,
308; emotional and family life, 272;
Hungarian campaigns, 243, 246–7,
269, 308–9, 370–1; Iraq campaign,
306; 'the law-maker', 368; Malta
siege, 370; meeting with Barbarossa,
288, 292–4; Moroccan policies, 226;
mosque building, 368–70, **369**;
mother, 330; murder of Ibrahim
Pasha, 271, 333; murder of sons and
grandsons, 334–5, 337, 350; naval
forces, 294; peace treaty with
Habsburgs, 225, 269, 270, 293;
peace treaty with Safavids, 293;
policies, 294; relationship with
corsairs, 157; relationship with
Francis I, 225, 296, 303; relationship
with Roxelana, 330–3; religious role,
270–1, 367–8; response to victory
procession (1560), 348; Rhodes
expedition, 261–5; sons, 5, 330,
331–6, 349–50; successor, 337; wars,
229, 243, 260
Suluc Mehmet Pasha, Ottoman admiral,
391
Suyuti, al-, scholar, 211
Swahili trading cities, 190
Szigetvar fortress, siege and capture,
370–1

Tabarka, free port, 274
Tabriz: capture (1534), 270; Ismail's
rule, 172, 175; sack (1514), 179, 183
Tafetna: fall, 215; harbour, 218
Tahmasp, Shah, son of Ismail, 350
Talavera, Hernando de, 135–6
Tangier: map, **14**; Portuguese capture
(1471), 49; Portuguese expedition
(1437), 31–3, 40; Portuguese
expeditions (1460–71), 48;
Portuguese position, 56, 163, 194,
205, 404; trade, 24

Tariq, military commander, 15, 40
Tarkuku, 218
Taroudant: arsenal, 218; control, 222
Tartar Khans, 94–5
Tavara, Francisco de, 417
taxation: crusading tax (*cruzada*), 133,
237, 352, 388; exemption from, 108,
223, 224, 268; in Granada, 132;
Islamic tithes, 97, 202, 213; *jihad*
funding, 223; Ottoman, 78, 97, 181;
poll tax on non-Muslims, 70, 97;
Portuguese, 36; in Rhodes, 264;
Sharifian system, 223, 224, 226; in
Spain, 133; tax holidays, 132, 264
Taza, city, 209, 227
Templar Order, *see* Knights Templars
Terrafina, island, 319
Testour, refugees in, 156
Tetouan: corsair base, 158–9, 223, 237;
evacuees in, 194; refugees in, 57, 156
Theophilus Palaeologus, 86
Thessaloniki, Jewish population, 137–8,
170
Thrace, 63, 65, 67, 71
Three Kings, Battle of the, 3, 414–19,
420, 421
Thucydides, historian, 2
Tibda, fortress, 310
Tiberias, Lordship of, 372
Timbuktu, 35, 202
Timoja, corsair, 197
Timur (Tamburlane): battles with
Mamelukes, 74, 180; capture of
Bayezid I, 74; conquests, 10, 103;
death, 200; defeat of Ottomans, 74,
98; descendants, 66, 75, 174; respect
for Safavids, 173; return to Central
Asia, 75
Titian, **325**, 326
Tlemcen: Abdul Malik in, 406;
Barbarossa's march on, 278; battle
(1517), 278; Boabadil in, 132;
control of port, 255; death of
Barbarossa, 281, 282; Ottoman
annexation, 226, 228; Sharif
Muhammad's death, 227; Sharifian
attack (1560), 228, 404; Sharifian
occupation, 225; Spanish attack,
280–1; Spanish expedition, 310;
Zayyanid rule, 163, 225, 226,
278
Toledo: Cardinal, 296, 327, 328; treaty
of (1480), 53, 120

Tordesillas: castle, 238; treaty of (1494), 53, 54
Toro, battle of, 51, 116
Torres, Diego de, 216
Toulon: corsair fleet, 4, 254; French fleet, 320; Ottoman fleet, 303, 313–14, 343
Transylvanian forces, 71–2, 75, 96, 246, 370
Trebizond: capture, 97; Christian presence, 174; Ottoman governorship, 176
Tripoli: corsair base, 349; Knights of St John, 296, 316, 317, 318; Ottoman capture, 318, 353; Spanish garrison, 141, 164, 255
Tristao da Cunha, 192
Troy, Mehmet's visit, 112–13
Tuat, oasis, 211
Tuman Bey, Mameluke ruler, 181
Tunis: abandoned by Hafsids, 295; corsair base, 237; culture, 7; defended by Barbarossa, 298; fall (1574), 397; Knights of St John, 317; lakes around, 297; sack (1573), 395; siege and sack (1535), 299–300, 316, 326, 365; Spanish garrison, 396; surrender to Uluj Ali, 365–6; trade, 396
Tunisia: battles for, 1; borders, 5; Hafsid rule, 10, 158, 161, 163, 295
Tursun Bey, 86
Tuscany, Duke of, 353, 408
Tver, Orthodox principality, 9
Tyndale, William, 139
Tyre: Crusader port abandoned, 20; siege, 106

Ulloa, Juan de, 343
Uluj Ali (Ali Pasha): background, 3, 7, 149, 365; career, 365; Dragut's death, 359; fleet, 394, 395; in Istanbul, 345; Lepanto battle, 391, 392–3, 395; Pasha of Algiers, 364; raids, 349; response to Alpujarras rebels, 364, 365; Tunis expedition (1569), 365–6; Tunisian expedition (1574), 396–7, 407
Urban, cannon founder, 79–80, 83, 124
Urbino, Duke of, 287
Uruj (Barbarossa, Khayr al-Din): appearance, 281; background, 149, 151–3; bases, 160, 161; Bejaia
campaign, 273–4; cloak, 282, 323; death, 281, 282; defence of Tlemcen, 280–1; ferrying refugees, 156–7; fleet, 163, 273; galley slave, 153; independent corsair captain, 159; Jijil rule, 275; languages, 160; leadership 277, 283; loss of arm, 274, 276; . name, 162; prizes, 161–2; relationship with Hafsid Sultan, 161, 163, 273, 274, 275; relationship with Ottomans, 275; siege of Spanish fort at Algiers, 276, 278; title from Ottoman Sultan, 163, 281; Tlemcen expedition, 278
Uzbeks, 267
Uzun Hassan, Turkic leader, 98, 174

Valencia: Aragonese court, 117; civil war, 242; expulsion of Moors, 140; trade, 15, 94
Valette, Jean de la, 314, 353, 357, 358, 359, 360–3
Valladolid: auto-da-fé, 342–3; entry of Charles V, 239
Valor, Hernandez de, 364
Varna, battle (1444), 65, 75, 77
Vasco da Gama, 31, 61–2, 187–9, 190, 322
Vaso, Marquis de, 298
Vatican, 301, 387
Veneziano, Agostino, **284**
Venezuela, 257, 258, 259
Venice: Arsenale, 34, 307, 387, 394; Cyprus rule, 375, 376–7, 382–3; empire, 170, 376, 382; fleet, 71, 303, 306, 388–9; merchants, 68; Ottoman demands for surrender of Cyprus, 377; Ottoman relations, 94, 98–9, 113, 170, 179, 183, 294, 306–7, 375; peace treaty with Ottomans (1540), 306–7, 308; peace treaty with Ottomans (1573), 395; response to Lepanto, 394; response to Malta defence, 363; rivalry with Genoa, 9; Senate, 306, 307, 376, 377; trading policies, 34; truce with Ottomans, 183
Vera, Don Diego de, 277, 278, 282
Vermeyen, Jan Cornelisz, 300
Viannello, Girolamo, 279
Vicente, Gil, 190
Vienna, Ottoman siege (1529), 251–2, 267–8, 269, 271, 286

Vijayanagar Empire, 195
Villiers de l'Isle Adam, Philip, 354
Viollet le Duc, Eugène, **380**
Viseu, Dom Dioga, Duke of, 52
Vital, courtier, 238
Vivaldi brothers, 29
Vladimir, Grand Duchy, 9
Voltaire, 273

Wallachia: forces, 71–2; religion, 9
Ward, William, 148
Wattasids: agents for, 202; battles with
    Portuguese, 193–4, 206; battles with
    Sharifians, 132, 219, 222–3; end of,
    223–4; relationship with Ottomans,
    320; relationship with Sharifians,
    214, 217–18, 220; rule, 211, 216;
    Sultans of Morocco, 193–4, 208–9,
    223; truce with Portuguese, 219
Welser family, 257–8
William (the Silent), Prince of Orange-
    Nassau, 208, 324, 372

Yacooub (or Mohammadi), father of
    Barbarossa, 149–51
Yahya-ibn-Tafuft, 202, 204, 215, 216
Yedikule Castle, 92, 111
Yemen, 306, 322, 373

Zahara, capture (1481), 121–2
Zapolya, John, Voivod of Transylvania,
    247–8, 267, 308
Zarruq, Sufi teacher, 210–11, 212
Zayyanids, 10, 163, 320
Zeno, Caterino, 172
Zheng He, 201
Ziyyani, chronicler, 213–14
Zoraya (Isabel de Solis), 126, 127
Zrinyi, Count, 370
Zuniga, Don Juan de, 328
Zurara, Gomes, 25